"In line with Pope Francis, Ormond Rush wants church leaders, theologians, and all the faithful to receive and live the whole vision of Vatican II. Rush remains faithful to his conviction that one can use the 'theo-logical' focus of *Dei Verbum* as a lens to interpret passages from other documents, but also grants a certain normativity to other documents of the mature Council (especially *Ad Gentes* and *Gaudium et Spes*). I was most impressed by Rush's ability to enrich his analysis of the different principles by combining sometimes unexpected references from different documents (intertextuality), such as using lines from *Sacrosanctum Concilium* to shed light on *Nostra Aetate*."

    —Peter De May
        Faculty of Theology and Religious Studies
        KU Leuven

"This is a highly important work. Ormond Rush models a symphonic and intertextual reading of the documents of the Second Vatican Council, placing them in their historical context, attending to both authors and receivers, and revealing the trajectory of vital insights that invite fresh theological thinking. Especially significant is Rush's contention that the council itself (and hence its interpretation) prioritizes the 'theo-logical' over the ecclesiological—encounter with the living God through Christ and the Spirit over its various mediations in the scriptures, the liturgy, and the life of the church. Grounded in the best of recent scholarship, this book will stand for years to come as point of reference for students of the council and its teaching."

    —Catherine E. Clifford
        Professor of Systematic and Historical Theology
        Saint Paul University, Ottawa, Canada

"*The Vision of Vatican II* expands and caps Ormond Rush's already-significant contribution to conciliar scholarship. In its detail, depth, and its affirmation of the ways in which the council can continue to enrich the church, *The Vision of Vatican II* is a truly magisterial work. For everyone committed to the thriving of the church's mission in the world, this book will be a wonderful source of hope and encouragement."

    —Richard Lennan
        Boston College School of Theology and Ministry

"Ormond Rush is one of the absolute top experts in the interpretation of Vatican II. His book is a long-awaited event in the debate on the council. *The Vision of Vatican II* is one of the major studies of Vatican II in the last quarter of a century and belongs to the canon of required texts."

    —Massimo Faggioli
        Professor of Historical Theology
        Villanova University

"Ormond Rush's *The Vision of Vatican II* develops an insightful and comprehensive matrix for understanding the council. The principles Rush proposes help readers to see Vatican II as a whole, while his careful attention to the council's history and documents aids exploration of conciliar themes. Rush's extensive scholarship and theological acumen makes *The Vision of Vatican II* a valuable and significant text for the ongoing interpretation and reception of Vatican II."

> —Amanda C. Osheim
> Endowed Professor of the Breitbach Catholic Thinkers and Leaders Program
> and Associate Professor of Practical Theology
> Loras College, Dubuque, Iowa

"*The Vision of Vatican II* opens a new way to communicate the message of the Council, its sixteen documents and their international theological interpretations during the last 50 years. Ormond Rush manages to bring hundreds and hundreds of quotations of the conciliar texts and the theological references into a brilliant and transparent convergence.

"Rush does not pretend a critical evaluation of the documents. Yet the positive presentation of the 'vision' guides the critical reader to discover the deficiencies in the actual reception of the Council and the discrepancies between the vision and the actual reality."

> —Peter Hünermann
> Professor Emeritus
> University Tübingen

"Well over five decades removed from Vatican II it can still be said that most Catholics, including many church leaders, are quite comfortable citing Vatican II while having little substantive comprehension of the council's most important contributions. For that reason, the entire church is in the debt of the Australian theologian Ormond Rush, who offers what is quite simply the most perceptive, accessible yet comprehensive articulation of why Vatican II still matters. His twenty-four principles synthesize the central and still quite compelling contributions of the council to the life of the church today. Moreover, Rush's brilliant articulation of the council's vision also illuminates the remarkable pontificate of Pope Francis who is, in so many ways, the preeminent 'Pope of the Council.'"

> —Richard R. Gaillardetz
> Joseph Professor of Catholic Systematic Theology
> Boston College

The Vision of Vatican II

Its Fundamental Principles

Ormond Rush

LITURGICAL PRESS
ACADEMIC

Collegeville, Minnesota
www.litpress.org

1	2	3	4	5	6	7	8	9

Library of Congress Cataloging-in-Publication Data

Names: Rush, Ormond, 1950– author.
Title: The vision of Vatican II : its fundamental principles / Ormond Rush.
Description: Collegeville, Minnesota : Liturgical Press, [2019] | Includes
    bibliographical references and index.
Identifiers: LCCN 2018058329 | ISBN 9780814680742 (hardcover) | ISBN
    9780814680995 (ebk.)
Subjects: LCSH: Vatican Council (2nd : 1962–1965 : Basilica di San Pietro in Vaticano)
    | Catholic Church—Doctrines.
Classification: LCC BX830 1962 .R873 2019 | DDC 262/.52—dc23
LC record available at https://lccn.loc.gov/2018058329

"It is the function of the church to render God the Father and his incarnate Son present and as it were visible, while ceaselessly renewing and purifying itself under the guidance of the Holy Spirit. This is brought about chiefly by the witness of a living and mature faith, one namely that is so well formed that it can see difficulties clearly and overcome them." (GS 21)

Contents

Acknowledgments

This book has benefitted from rich conversations with friends and colleagues. Many have kindly commented on particular chapters as the manuscript has progressed. I would like to acknowledge Gerald O'Collins, Richard Gaillardetz, James McEvoy, Paul Chandler, Tom Elich, Gerard Kelly, Myriam Wijlens, Massimo Faggioli, Peter De Mey, Cathy Clifford, and Gerard Hall. I am particularly grateful to Jared Wicks and Richard Lennan, who have read and commented on substantial sections of the manuscript. Thanks also to my colleagues at the Brisbane campus of Australian Catholic University, whose daily conversations have stimulated my thinking for this book more than they will ever know. I would like to express my gratitude to the staff of the Brisbane campus library, who have been unfailing in their kindness and willingness to assist me in my research. I am most grateful to Hans Christoffersen of Liturgical Press for his patience and gracious support throughout the writing of this book. Finally, a special thank you to my family for their love and encouragement.

I dedicate this book to Fr. Mick Mullins, the parish priest in my first parish after ordination. He radiated "the genuine face of God" (GS 19), through living those human virtues Vatican II called on every priest to exhibit (PO 3).

Abbreviations

Documents of the Second Vatican Council

AA   *Apostolicam Actuositatem:* Decree on the Apostolate of Lay People

AG   *Ad Gentes:* Decree on the Church's Missionary Activity

CD   *Christus Dominus:* Decree on the Pastoral Office of Bishops in the Church

DH   *Dignitatis Humanae:* Declaration on Religious Liberty

DV   *Dei Verbum:* Dogmatic Constitution on Divine Revelation

GE   *Gravissimum Educationis:* Declaration on Christian Education

GS   *Gaudium et Spes:* Pastoral Constitution on the Church in the Modern World

LG   *Lumen Gentium:* Dogmatic Constitution on the Church

NA   *Nostra Aetate:* Declaration on the Relation of the Church to Non-Christian Religions

OE   *Orientalium Ecclesiarum:* Decree on the Catholic Eastern Churches

OT   *Optatam Totius:* Decree on the Training of Priests

PC   *Perfectae Caritatis:* Decree on the Up-to-Date Renewal of Religious Life

PO   *Presbyterorum Ordinis:* Decree on the Ministry and Life of Priests

SC   *Sacrosanctum Concilium:* The Constitution on the Sacred Liturgy

UR   *Unitatis Redintegratio:* Decree on Ecumenism

Other Sources

AAS   *Acta Apostolicae Sedis*

DS   Heinrich Denzinger, *Compendium of Creeds, Definitions, and Declarations on Matters of Faith and Morals*

ES   Paul VI, *Ecclesiam Suam*

PG   J. P. Migne, *Patrologia Graeca*

PL   J. P. Migne, *Patrologia Latina*

Prologue

For an average of two months during autumn, over four years from 1962 to 1965, the Second Vatican Council of the Catholic Church met in St. Peter's Basilica in Rome.[1] Pope John XXIII had convened it in 1959, with the goal of renewing Catholic life and uniting all Christians. Over seventy schemas were prepared for the bishops' consideration. The council began on October 11, 1962, and concluded on December 8, 1965.

It was "quite possibly the biggest meeting in the history of the world."[2] More than three thousand bishops participated over the four sessions, although not all attended every session for various reasons.[3] On average, 2,200 bishops attended each session. They came from 116 countries, making Vatican II the most "ecumenical" council in the history of the church.[4] From opening to closing, it lasted thirty-eight months.[5] For only eight months of that time were the council members in session. The remaining thirty months were made up of the intersessions, those periods in between the sessions when much work was also done—informal and formal meetings of bishops and theological experts (*periti*) on the various commissions; reading of draft schemas by bishops and preparing written submissions; drafting by subcommissions. Over the four sessions, there were 168 general congregations

---

1. The dates of the four sessions were: Session 1: October 11–December 8, 1962; Session 2: September 29–December 4, 1963; Session 3: September 14–November 21, 1964; Session 4: September 14–December 8, 1965.

2. John W. O'Malley, *What Happened at Vatican II* (Cambridge, MA: Belknap Press of Harvard University Press, 2008), 18.

3. Not only bishops were voting participants. According to canon law, these also included, for example, representatives of the major religious orders. For simplicity, throughout this book I will refer to the voting participants of the council as "the bishops."

4. Details on the participants' names and attendance at the council can be found in Segreteria Generale del Concilio, "Tavole Riassuntive," in *I Padri Presenti al Concilio Ecumenico Vaticano II* (Roma: Segreteria Generale del Concilio, 1966).

5. On the statistics that follow, see Giuseppe Alberigo, "Luci e ombre nel rapporto tra dinamica assembleare e conclusioni conciliari," in *L'evento e le decisioni: Studi sulle dinamiche del Concilio Vaticano II*, ed. Maria Teresa Fattori and Alberto Melloni (Bologna: Il Mulino, 1997), 501–22, at 513; "Council Statistics," in *Council Daybook: Vatican II, Session 4*, ed. Floyd Anderson (Washington, DC: National Catholic Welfare Conference, 1966), 366.

(working days) and ten public sessions (when documents would be officially promulgated). The four sessions had thirty-six, forty-three, forty-eight, and forty-one general congregations, respectively. There were 2,212 speeches delivered and 4,361 written interventions submitted. Representatives from drafting commissions delivered a total of 147 reports (*relationes*) to the council, explaining the revision of drafts according to the bishops' wishes. On the various commissions, there were around 480 official *periti*. A total of 173 observers and guests, from forty-one different non-Catholic churches, ecclesial communities, and representative bodies, were also in attendance across the four years. The council's deliberations, with its debate, drafting, and intrigue, produced sixteen documents.

According to the historian John O'Malley: "Vatican II was an enormously complex event. It cannot be reduced to simplistic formulas. Nonetheless, we must never forget that the documents of Vatican II are not a grab bag of discreet elements. Unlike the documents of previous Councils, those of Vatican II form a coherent unit. That is, certain themes and orientations run through them as common threads. These themes and orientations transcend the individual documents, even though they are derived from them. The documents of Vatican II deliver messages bigger than those of the documents considered in isolation from one another."[6] Articulating what the council's vision was for the renewal and reform of the Catholic Church requires careful historical enquiry into the intricacies of the conciliar debate and drafting, and correlating that enquiry with a careful reading of the texts the council finally produced. This book proposes that, after such enquiry and correlation, the salient features of "the vision of Vatican II" can be synthesized in a set of interrelated principles.

The chapters that follow use the term "principle" in a broad sense, meaning: the succinct articulation of any authoritative judgment by an ecumenical council regarding an element of Christian faith and ecclesial life. The judgments made by the Second Vatican Council—reconstructed here as "principles"—were intended by the council to reevaluate, renew, and reform contemporary Catholic life, for the sake of the pastoral effectiveness of its mission in the second half of the twentieth century. These conciliar principles, in effect, are reconfigurations of the way the Catholic Church had previously articulated various dimensions of doctrine and church life, which Vatican II

---

6. John W. O'Malley, "Vatican II Revisited as Reconciliation: The Francis Factor," in *The Legacy of Vatican II*, ed. Massimo Faggioli and Andrea Vicini (New York: Paulist Press, 2015), 3–25, at 6.

judged to have become imbalanced. Accordingly, each principle proposes a proper balance between two aspects of doctrine or church life that the council wanted to realign. That the ecumenical council authoritatively promulgated these realignments to be normatively "constitutional," in the sense of "fundamental," for the Catholic Church is captured by the weight of the term "principle."

This book proposes that there are twenty-four such fundamental principles that together provide a comprehensive interpretation of Vatican II and its documents. First, it is proposed that interrelating the complex conciliar event with its final documents is best achieved through attention to six hermeneutical principles. Then, in the light of these *hermeneutical* principles, both *theo-logical* and *ecclesiological* elements of the conciliar vision are discussed. Even though the council intentionally focused on renewal and reform of the church, the book proposes that the comprehensive vision of Vatican II requires that priority be given to the theo-logical over the ecclesiological principles without setting them in opposition, with the theo-logical principles hovering, as it were, as meta-principles over each of the ecclesiological principles and qualifying each of them. There is a certain overlap in the issues at stake in the twofold principles, and focusing on one principle alone could give a narrow view of the conciliar vision. Each principle requires the other principles for mutual correction. The effect is symphonic; unless this symphonic character of the council's vision is recognized, the vision may be misreceived.

Each of the principles is formulated as two terms, groups, or roles set alongside each other. In each case, Vatican II wished to hold the two in dynamic relationship, often in an innovative way, given previous church teaching. The elements of each of the twofold principles are not to be seen in a dualistic way, one in opposition to the other—as if they were dichotomies, where one is understood to be more faithful to Vatican II and the other less faithful. They were seen by the council not as dichotomies but rather as Christian ecclesial realities to be included in any comprehensive vision of what the church should uphold and should itself be, as the twenty-first ecumenical council of the Catholic Church envisioned it. Both elements in each twofold principle, as the council saw it, encapsulates values to be safeguarded. Nevertheless, within the dynamic tension of each principle, Vatican II made explicit decisions regarding the proper balancing of the relationship between the two terms, groups, or roles. What that particular conciliar balance was, therefore, constitutes an important factor in all principles.

I am not claiming that the eighteen theo-logical and ecclesiological principles encompass all the issues that the council addressed. These are, however,
among the most important issues that caused the most heated debate—and
the council clearly wanted to clarify its stance on them. The scope of topics
addressed by the council was broad, and not all of those matters are treated
here in detail, highly important though these may be. Nevertheless, whatever
the issues addressed by the council, I propose the council's teaching on all
of them depends on, and can be explicated in terms of, these twenty-four
fundamental principles.

One advantage of such an approach, I believe, is that elements of continuity and of innovation are not set in opposition (even though innovation and
reform involve an element of discontinuity, as was clearly the understanding
of the majority of the council fathers). Each of the theo-logical and ecclesiological pairs named in the conciliar principles were explicitly or implicitly
addressed in some way during the sessions of Vatican II (although not necessarily in terms of the way a particular twofold principle is named here), and
the council, through its final promulgated documents, introduced elements
of innovation into all of them, at least in the way the values are meant to be
balanced. To what degree those elements of continuity and innovation have
been faithfully preserved and incorporated into the daily life of the Catholic
Church over the past five decades or so would be a significant aspect of assessing the council's reception, something that is beyond the scope of this
book. The book concludes, however, by proposing that all three sets of principles (hermeneutical, theo-logical, ecclesiological) can be employed as a
framework of criteria for assessing faithful or inadequate reception of the
vision of Vatican II over the last five decades—and for then setting the agenda
for ongoing reception of the council.

Part I begins with hermeneutical issues related to reconstructing the vision of Vatican II. The 1985 Extraordinary Synod of Bishops, meeting twenty
years after the close of Vatican II, proposed several hermeneutical principles
that remain valuable for guiding discussion more than fifty years after the
council.[7] Since that synod, reflection has continued as to the appropriate herme-

7. "The theological interpretation of the conciliar doctrine must show attention to all the
documents, in themselves and in their close inter-relationship, in such a way that the integral
meaning of the Council's affirmations—often very complex—might be understood and ex-

neutics for interpreting the council and its texts. Some one-dimensional approaches exaggerate exclusively either "continuity" or "discontinuity," or either "spirit" or "letter." Although with varying emphases, the more nuanced contributors to the hermeneutical debate give attention to all three elements of (1) the conciliar process, (2) the conciliar documents, and (3) the reception of the council and its documents. Some take more of a historical perspective, others more of a theological perspective.[8] The framework proposed here in Part I attempts to bring together many of the insights of these authors under six hermeneutical principles.

---

pressed. Special attention must be paid to the four major Constitutions of the Council, which contain the interpretative key for the other Decrees and Declarations. It is not licit to separate the pastoral character from the doctrinal vigor of the documents. In the same way, it is not legitimate to separate the spirit and the letter of the Council. Moreover, the Council must be understood in continuity with the great tradition of the Church, and at the same time we must receive light from the Council's own doctrine for today's Church and the men of our time. The Church is one and the same throughout all the councils" ("The Church, under the Word of God, Celebrates the Mysteries of Christ for the Salvation of the World," Final Report of the 1985 Extraordinary Synod [hereafter Final Report] I.5, http://www.saint-mike.org/library/synod_bishops/final_report1985.html).

8. The literature on the hermeneutics of Vatican II is extensive. For an examination of the different approaches to interpreting Vatican II, see Massimo Faggioli, *Vatican II: The Battle for Meaning* (New York: Paulist Press, 2012).

PART I

HERMENEUTICAL PRINCIPLES

Principle 1

The Council/The Documents

Principle 1: The documents of Vatican II must be interpreted in the light of the historical event (the council) that produced them, and the historical event must be interpreted in the light of the official documents that it promulgated.

Vatican II was an "event." I use the term "event" here, first, in a broad sense, referring simply to all the elements that made up "the council" from its being announced by Pope John XXIII on January 25, 1959, to the closing Mass, on December 8, 1965.[1] This includes not only the years of preparation but also the four sessions over four years, as well as the three intersessions of feverish activity between the sessions.[2] At the heart of this conciliar event was "the encounter of persons, the clashes of ideas, the conflicts of purpose, the coincidences of decisions."[3] To speak of "the council," then, is to speak inclusively of the motives and intentions of individual protagonists (as revealed in private diaries or minutes of conciliar commissions), informal meetings of bishops outside the formal meetings, the bishops' encounter with new theological frameworks from the council's theological experts, the bishops' speeches in the aula, written interventions by individual bishops or groups of bishops,

1. Later the more narrow sense of "event" will be discussed, i.e., Vatican II perceived retrospectively as a historic occurrence with great epochal significance in the broad sweep of church history. For explorations into the category of "event" to describe the council, see Maria Teresa Fattori and Alberto Melloni, eds., *L'Evento e le decisioni: Studi sulle dinamiche del Concilio Vaticano II* (Bologna: Il Mulino, 1997).

2. On the interrelationship between the sessions and the intersessions, see Evangelista Vilanova, "The Intersession (1963–1964)," in *History of Vatican II*, vol. 3: *The Mature Council; Second Period and Intersession, September 1963–September 1964*, ed. Giuseppe Alberigo and Joseph A. Komonchak (Maryknoll, NY: Orbis Books, 1998), 3:347–490, at 347n2.

3. Joseph A. Komonchak, "Is Christ Divided? Dealing with Diversity and Disagreement," *Origins* 33 (July 17, 2003): 140–47, at 140.

the work of drafting commissions and their *relationes* ("reports") back to the council assembly, and the bishops' voting on conciliar procedures, drafts, and final documents. A "hermeneutics of the authors" highlights the need to give attention to the complex interaction of all these factors.[4]

When referring to "Vatican II," a distinction can be made between "the council" as this multidimensional event and "the documents" it promulgated. A related distinction, used by the 1985 Synod of Bishops, is that between the "spirit" and the "letter" of the council. With both those distinctions, however, care must be taken not to set up the distinction as a dichotomy and pit one against the other. They are mutually interpretive, and each requires the careful interrelating of not only a hermeneutics of the authors but also a "hermeneutics of the texts."[5] The latter looks to the meaning of words, sentences, paragraphs, articles, and chapters within a document as a whole and that document's interrelationship with the other fifteen documents of the whole corpus. But interpreting the council and its documents takes place from shifting horizons, as the council is received within different contexts through time. Therefore, attention also needs to be given to a "hermeneutics of the receivers" (the ones who are interpreting and applying the council and its documents from forever changing perspectives).[6]

Several hermeneutical points can be selected as significant if an interpretation of "the council" and its "sixteen documents" is to be comprehensive and if it is to avoid setting the spirit and letter of the council in opposition.

First, the sixteen conciliar documents constitute a "fixed" criterion, a collection of documents that long outlives those who authored them. Without falling into a Romantic hermeneutic privileging "authorial intention,"[7] they could be legitimately termed expressions of "the mind of the council," in the qualified sense that, after much hard work and vigorous debate, they were

---

4. On a hermeneutics of the authors, see Ormond Rush, *Still Interpreting Vatican II: Some Hermeneutical Principles* (New York: Paulist Press, 2004), 1–34.

5. On a hermeneutics of the texts, see ibid., 35–51.

6. On a hermeneutics of the receivers, see ibid., 52–68.

7. "Any interpretation referring to 'the mind of the Council' . . . is problematic. It falls into the fallacy of a Romantic hermeneutic by reducing meaning to authorial intention and neglecting the complex compositional process behind the Council's texts. The final texts are agreed-upon statements that have meaning independently of any authorial intention and by their nature provide an openness to diverse receptions." Francis Schüssler Fiorenza, "Vatican II," in *The Routledge Companion to Modern Christian Thought*, ed. Chad Meister and James Beilby (New York: Routledge, 2013), 364–75, at 365.

voted on and promulgated by the overwhelming majority of the bishops of the world.

Second, while they constitute a "fixed" criterion once set in writing, the documents are nevertheless "finished in their unfinishedness."[8] They "overflow" the context of their original production and reception; there is a "surplus of meaning" that future generations might legitimately discover in the texts, meanings that might very well go beyond what the bishops explicitly intended.[9] Once set in writing the documents take on a life of their own. Readers, posing new questions to the texts from new contexts, take them in directions both legitimate and possibly illegitimate; interpretations of particular texts that go beyond authorial intention may well be faithful (or unfaithful) to the comprehensive vision of the council. Discerning the difference requires attention to all the interrelated principles that make up that vision.

Third, among the sixteen documents, the four constitutions function analogously like the four gospels within the New Testament. They provide "the interpretative key" for the other twelve documents.[10] Nevertheless, subtlety is needed when applying this hermeneutical key; there is a certain hierarchy or ordering within the constitutions, a hierarchy of importance not necessarily captured and determined by the wording of the titles, with words such as "dogmatic" and "pastoral." In this sense, the *theo*-logical focus of *Dei Verbum* can function as a lens for interpreting the more *ecclesio*logically focused constitutions *Sacrosanctum Concilium, Lumen Gentium*, and *Gaudium et Spes*.

Fourth, the development in the bishops' thinking regarding issues across the four sessions of conciliar debate must be taken into account in interpretation, especially when interrelating the four constitutions.[11] Over time, the

8. "In der Unfertigkeit fertig." The expression comes from Leo Popper, as quoted in Hans Robert Jauss, "Horizon Structure and Dialogicity," in *Question and Answer: Forms of Dialogic Understanding* (Minneapolis: University of Minnesota Press, 1989), 197–231, at 212.

9. See Paul Ricoeur, *Interpretation Theory: Discourse and the Surplus of Meaning* (Fort Worth: Texas Christian University Press, 1976).

10. Extraordinary Synod, Final Report I.5.

11. For example, Giuseppe Alberigo writes of the traces of development in the bishops' thinking that become evident in the final text and must be given hermeneutical priority: "A hermeneutic of Vatican II can and must find an indispensable point of reference in a critical reconstruction of *the historical and theological itinerary followed by the assembly*. In so far as a council is a peculiarly collective event, and in theological terms, highly ecclesial in the deepest sense of the word, this aspect cannot but be crucial in interpreting its decisions. An assembly which is aware of its historic role is not hegemonised by a leader or a group, but proceeds by way of wearisome and complicated dialectic, and its results are to be ascribed to *the matur-*

conciliar assembly "learned" to be a council. Along the way, it received into its thinking and its documents its own earlier documents. The bishops developed in their thinking, such that their later documents show development over the earlier ones and therefore are to be seen as qualifying the previous statements.[12]

Fifth, the conciliar documents themselves are complex texts. In places, they contain passages deliberately expressed either in an open-ended way or with juxtapositions of traditional and innovative formulations. Interpretation of such passages requires particular attention to *interrelating a hermeneutics of the text with a hermeneutics of the authors*. Within the debates, bishops with different perspectives argued for their view to be included in the final documents. The drafting commissions, faithful to their responsibility, genuinely attempted to incorporate the various perspectives, as their reports (*relationes*) to the assembly reveal. The result is often a juxtaposition of different theological approaches within the same treatment of a particular

---

ing of the consciousness of the assembly, rather than to the occasional roles played by this or that personality. This consciousness is therefore a fundamental point of reference for a deep understanding of the assembly's decisions. In the light of this, a dynamic reading of such decisions becomes possible, a reading capable of going beyond the banalisation which derives from a cold analysis of the official text isolated from its historical context, and therefore from the great currents of life and thought which have characterized that context. A critical emphasis on the lines which guided the drawing up of the text provides a unique key for understanding *those lines of development implicit in the text* which, in a consistent way, guarantee its continuing fecundity." Giuseppe Alberigo and Franca Magistretti, "Introduction," in *Constitutionis Dogmaticae Lumen Gentium: Synopsis Historica* (Bologna: Istituto per le Scienze Religiose, 1975), xvii–xxii, at xix. Emphasis added.

12. Elsewhere Alberigo remarks on the development in the conciliar thinking: "The conciliar assembly itself offered a model of a dynamic hermeneutic that takes into account the progressive expansion of its decisions. It is, in fact, perfectly clear that only the acquisition of an ecclesiology of communion, first in the constitution *Sacrosanctum concilium* and then in the constitution *Lumen gentium*, made further developments possible. The decree *Unitatis redintegratio* [*UR*] and the declaration *Dignitatis humanae*, but also the decree *Ad gentes* and finally the constitution *Dei verbum* contain propositions that presuppose the development already acquired by the council. This hermeneutical criterion, even if it was not always followed consistently, nevertheless constitutes a point of reference that cannot be ignored in postconciliar interpretation." Giuseppe Alberigo, "Transition to a New Age," in *History of Vatican II*, vol. 5: *The Council and the Transition; The Fourth Period and the End of the Council, September 1965–December 1965*, ed. Giuseppe Alberigo and Joseph A. Komonchak (Maryknoll, NY: Orbis Books, 2006), 5:573–644, at 604. For example, on the shifts in perspective among the Australian bishops at Vatican II, see Ormond Rush, "The Australian Bishops of Vatican II: Participation and Reception," in *Vatican II: The Reception and Implementation in the Australian Church*, ed. Neil Ormerod, Ormond Rush, et al. (Melbourne: John Garrett, 2012), 4–19.

subject. Some safeguard past formulations, generally couched in neoscholastic terms; others, appropriating more recent theologies, attempt to retrieve the tradition while embracing *ressourcement* approaches. Sometimes the juxtaposition is in terms of different streams of the Catholic tradition, for example, Augustinian or Thomist. Whatever the differentiating aspect, the juxtaposition in the final texts is not so much one of contradictory views but rather of differing perspectives on the same mystery. A "trajectory" toward a newer understanding of an issue is often evident, however, and this trajectory must be given a certain weight in the interpretation of the text.[13] As Hermann Pottmeyer proposes: "By being complemented the older thesis is relativized as one-sided and *bearings are given for further development* in understanding of the faith."[14] Generally it was the majority view that indicated a trajectory toward a new perspective. In these ways, either leaving open an issue or expressing it in terms of a juxtaposition of approaches, the council was able to come to a compromise and reach a "consensus," in a form of text that the vast majority of bishops, despite their theological differences, could vote on affirmatively.[15] Therefore, interpretation of the council and its docu-

13. On the importance of the "trajectory" implied behind the juxtaposition of classic and innovative theological frameworks within the documents, and the importance of giving a certain weight to that trajectory, see Gustave Thils, ". . . en pleine fidélité au Concile du Vatican II," *La foi et le temps* 10 (1980): 274–309. Thils proposes that fidelity to Vatican II requires application of two interrelated criteria: "In principle, fidelity to Vatican II would require that we (a) bring to bear on a question under discussion all the doctrines accepted and promulgated, each in its proper relation to the whole; and (b) point out the trajectory these doctrines traveled in the course of the debates, so that we may see which acquired increasing importance and which consistently lost in importance" (ibid., 278). This translation is taken from Hermann J. Pottmeyer, "A New Phase in the Reception of Vatican II: Twenty Years of Interpretation of the Council," in *The Reception of Vatican II*, ed. Giuseppe Alberigo, Jean Pierre Jossua, and Joseph A. Komonchak (Washington, DC: The Catholic University of America Press, 1987), 27–43, at 40–41. The image of a "trajectory" of the council's thinking is also used throughout Christoph Theobald, *La réception du concile Vatican II: I. Accéder à la source* (Paris: Cerf, 2009).

14. Pottmeyer, "A New Phase in the Reception of Vatican II," 38.

15. Alberigo speaks of "the recurring compromises in the development of the texts. Indeed, compromise was required for obtaining a broad consensus bordering on unanimity." Alberigo, "Transition to a New Age," 628. On the difficulty that such juxtapositions leave the interpreter, but also as a witness that juxtaposition and compromise were often the explicit method employed by a drafting commission, Edward Schillebeeckx recalls: "During the sometimes heated discussions about the final version of *Lumen Gentium*, I had an exchange with the theologian who played a crucial role in preparing that version and in the processing of the amendments, especially those concerning the principle of collegiality. He told me: 'We have intentionally formulated some texts in an ambivalent way, so that the minority can accept the principle of collegiality.' To my first reaction that in this way the council would become multi-interpretable

ments should attend to both sides of the juxtaposition, while at the same time attending to the trajectory toward a new approach indicated by the view of the majority, as Pottmeyer advises: "Fidelity to the Council requires that both juxtaposed theses be taken seriously and that an attempt be made through more penetrating theological reflection and a renewed ecclesial praxis to reconcile them in a synthesis that will allow further advances. Fidelity to the Council also requires that we pay heed to the stress that the Council itself laid on the one or the other thesis, according as a thesis was supported by the majority or the minority. The fact remains, however, that majority and minority alike agreed to both theses and in particular to their juxtaposition."[16] The bishops did not set out to present systematic treatises; they intended that theologians after the council should bring such open-ended formulations and juxtapositions into a new synthesis: "The Council did not claim to be expressing the final word on the subjects it treated, only to be pointing out *the direction* in which further reflection should develop."[17] It is the role of the interpreter to extrapolate these trajectories indicated in the council debates and final texts and bring them to synthesis.

Sixth, given the complexity of the texts' history and final composition, the interpreter should beware of speaking in simplistic terms of "authorial intention." The conflict of interpretations around Vatican II in the contemporary church often tends to center exclusively on how the bishops themselves interpreted what they were doing, what they set out to achieve, and the complex debates over the final wording of the documents they promulgated. While the spirit of the assembly is highly relevant and captured in their voting, the historical significance of the council and the meaning of

---

and in the end would be used in the opposite direction, he answered: 'In due course we will interpret the texts.' My response that I did not think this to be a fair procedure, and that moreover the fact that others—the official authorities rather than the theological redactors of the documents themselves—would interpret the constitution, and would do so in the direction of the minority position, was not taken into account in such a procedure, he brushed aside. His final comment on the whole matter was: 'Compromise is the only way to reach a degree of consensus.'" Edward Schillebeeckx, "Preface," in *The Concept of Church: A Methodological Inquiry into the Use of Metaphors in Ecclesiology*, ed. Herwi Rikhof (London: Sheed and Ward, 1981), xi–xiii, at xi–xii. Schillebeeckx goes on to highlight "a link between the ambivalences and lack of clarity created in this way and the quick change of mood in the period after the council—the change from an initial euphoria to a certain resignation and even indifference" (ibid., xii).

16. Pottmeyer, "A New Phase in the Reception of Vatican II," 39.

17. Joseph Doré, "Vatican II Today," in *Vatican II: A Forgotten Future?*, ed. Alberto Melloni and Christoph Theobald (London: SCM Press, 2005), 137–47, at 142. Emphasis added.

their texts are not to be restricted solely to what even they foresaw or intended. "History often tells what contemporaries did not know or consciously 'live.'"[18]

Seventh, "the council" is more than its final documents, and what the council communicates goes beyond the written word of those documents. The documents cannot capture the whole of what the council was and is.[19] In this sense, the spirit is more than the letter. For example, Joseph Ratzinger wrote after the third session regarding the change that was taking place in the bishops: "This spiritual awakening, which the bishops accomplished in full view of the Church, or, rather accomplished as the Church, was the great and irrevocable event of the Council. It was more important in many respects than the texts it passed, for these texts could only voice a part of the new life which had been awakened in this encounter of the Church with its inner self."[20]

As one example of how documents did not capture the council's fullness, John O'Malley notes how the reform of the Roman Curia is treated only once in the entire collection of documents.[21] The issue, however, was a cause of much heated discussion.[22] As O'Malley notes: "It is not the documents, therefore, that reveal how hot the issue was but the narrative of the battles for control of the council itself."[23] Furthermore, as the council would itself teach with regard to the nature of divine revelation occurring not only in words but also in deeds (DV 2), the council likewise taught and continues to teach not only in its words (its sixteen documents) but also in its deeds or actions. The council made some symbolic gestures through which it taught by example, beyond the words expressed in its documents. These symbolic moments and gestures include the practice of having the morning Eucharist according to different rites in the vernacular; the placement each morning of an open Book of the Gospels in front of the conciliar assembly, to symbolize Christ presiding over the council; the admission of non-Catholic observers and seeking out

18. Joseph A. Komonchak, "Vatican II as an 'Event,'" in *Vatican II: Did Anything Happen?*, ed. David G. Schultenover (New York: Continuum, 2007), 24–51, at 37.

19. An analogy with Scripture highlights the point. The revelatory event to which the scriptural writings witness surpasses the written witness.

20. Joseph Ratzinger, *Theological Highlights of Vatican II* (New York: Paulist Press, 2009), 194. Emphasis original.

21. Decree on the Pastoral Office of Bishops in the Church, *Christus Dominus* 9–10.

22. Cardinal Frings, in a speech to the assembly on November 7, 1963, allegedly written by his *peritus* Joseph Ratzinger, stated: "This reform of the Curia is necessary. Let us put it into effect." Quoted in Xavier Rynne, *Vatican Council II* (Maryknoll, NY: Orbis Books, 2002), 222.

23. O'Malley, *What Happened at Vatican II*, 304.

their observations; the admission of Catholic lay observers, first men, then extended to a few women.[24] Also papal gestures, although not strictly conciliar acts, did create a public perception as to what the council was doing—for example, Paul VI's renunciation of his papal tiara and his desire that it be sold and proceeds given to the poor (November 1963); his international visits to Israel (January 1964), India (December 1964), and the United Nations (October 1965); his meeting with Patriarch Athenagoras I of Constantinople on the Mount of Olives in Jerusalem (January 1964); and his ecumenical gesture of returning a reliquary of St. Andrew to the Greek Orthodox Church (September 1964).[25] A particularly poignant gesture on the second-to-last day of the council was the retraction by both parties of the 1054 mutual excommunication of Latins and Greeks. All these too are to be included in the historical event of Vatican II and were, and are still, significant in shaping the contemporary reception of what the council was intending to do and the kind of church it was attempting to fashion.

Eighth, the hermeneutical points above, on the significance of the council going beyond what even the participating bishops understood or imagined, as well as the council being more than its documents, can be further explored through the historical category of "event," in the narrow sense of an occur-

---

24. One of those was the Australian laywoman Rosemary Goldie, who was present for the third and fourth sessions, sitting right up front, as she records, "on the plush chairs of St Andrew's tribune, alongside the male auditors and the theologians." Rosemary Goldie, *From a Roman Window: Five Decades; The World, the Church and the Catholic Laity* (Blackburn, Vic.: HarperCollinsReligious, 1998), 71. For more on the contribution by women auditors at the council and Goldie's particular role, see Adriana Valerio, *Madri del Concilio: Ventitré donne al Vaticano II* (Rome: Carocci, 2012); Carmel Elizabeth McEnroy, *Guests in Their Own House: The Women of Vatican II* (New York: Crossroad, 1996); Regina Heyder and Gisela Muschiol, eds., *Katholikinnen und das Zweite Vatikanische Konzil: Petitionen–Berichte–Fotografien* (Münster: Aschendorff, 2018).

25. As the *peritus* Henri de Lubac later observed regarding the impact of the pope's visit to the Holy Land between the second and third sessions: "The third session is to be linked not to the last interventions of the second session, but to the new situation created by [the pope's intervening] pilgrimage [to the Holy Land]." Quoted in Charles Moeller, "Il fermento delle idee nella elaborazione della Costituzione," in *La Chiesa del Vaticano II: Studi e commenti intorno alla Costituzione dommatica 'Lumen Gentium'*, ed. Guilherme Baraúna (Firenze: Vallecchi Editore, 1965), 155–89, at 181. For example, on the discussion of the significance of the pope's visit to the Holy Land in January 1964, as encapsulating the christocentric focus of the council's debates, see ibid., 181. Moeller makes reference to the work of Bernard Lambert and the way he sees the pope's pilgrimage as summing up the second session of the council: Bernard Lambert, *De Rome à Jérusalem: Itinéraire spirituel de Vatican II* (Paris: Editions du Centurion, 1964), 250–60.

rence that marks a historic point in the church's life. The further in time we get from the council is not necessarily a disadvantage; a retrospective more than fifty years after an event in some ways enables a clearer judgment to be made regarding that event's historic significance.[26] On December 8, 1965, the council itself entered into history to be received through time. From the viewpoint of a fifty-year timeline, new perspectives on the historical significance of the council emerge.

In addition to these hermeneutical points concerning specifically the principle of interrelating the council and its documents, a further five hermeneutical principles can be singled out.

26. See Komonchak, "Vatican II as an 'Event.'"

Principle 2
Pastoral/Doctrinal

Principle 2: The council and its documents are to be interpreted in light of the council's primarily pastoral orientation; Vatican II's reformulation of doctrine aimed at teaching in words and actions that foster a more meaningful spiritual appropriation of God's revelation and salvation by the people of God.

While remembering the qualifications noted above regarding the interpretation and significance of "authorial intention," the intention of the pope who called and first oriented the council is an important element in interpreting the council and its documents. Pope John XXIII, in his opening speech to the first session of Vatican II, *Gaudet Mater Ecclesia*, expressed his desire that the council be primarily "pastoral" and that consideration of doctrine be expressed in a pastoral way.[1] Furthermore, the pope called for "a magisterium which is predominantly pastoral in character" and a pastoral leadership style in which "the medicine of mercy rather than that of severity" characterizes the church's way of governing and teaching.[2] The papal discourse had significant influence on the council fathers and is to be considered, according to Jared Wicks, as "the Council's first great text."[3] It became more than an opening address.

---

1. AS I/1, 166–75. Translated in Pope John XXIII, "Pope John's Opening Speech to the Council," in *The Documents of Vatican II*, ed. Walter M. Abbott (London: Geoffrey Chapman, 1966), 710–19.

2. Ibid., 715–16.

3. Jared Wicks, *Doing Theology* (New York: Paulist Press, 2009), 22. On John XXIII's opening address as a continuing guiding norm during the council debates, Wicks writes: "In the early weeks of the Council's deliberations, Council members began citing Pope John's address in their comments in St. Peter's as expressing the Council's purpose, namely, as assembled not to condemn errors, but to promote pastoral renewal and the cause of Christian unity. The address also served as a norm in some members' evaluation of draft texts prepared before the Council, for example, in positive assessments of the text on liturgical reform and in critical judgments on the text *The Sources of Revelation*, on scripture and tradition" (ibid., 141).

In many ways over its years of deliberation, the council enthusiastically adopted Pope John's pastoral focus, from the first session's debates on liturgy and revelation, to the last session's debates on the church in the world. The first line of the first document promulgated, *Sacrosanctum Concilium*, begins: "The sacred Council has set out to impart an ever-increasing vigor to the Christian lives of the faithful" (SC 1). In a footnote reference after the title of the document promulgated on the last working day of the council, *Gaudium et Spes*, states a principle that should guide interpretation of all the council's constitutions, decrees, and declarations: "The Constitution is called 'pastoral' because, while resting on doctrinal principles, it seeks to set forth the relation of the Church to the world and to the [people] of today. In Part I, therefore, the pastoral emphasis is not overlooked, nor is the doctrinal emphasis overlooked in Part II." In other words, *Gaudium et Spes* is both a pastoral and a doctrinal constitution. Similarly, *Lumen Gentium* is both dogmatic and pastoral, as are *Dei Verbum* and *Sacrosanctum Concilium*.

Christoph Theobald sees this "principle of pastorality" as *the* hermeneutical key for interpreting Vatican II.[4] According to him, the pastorality called for by John XXIII can be summed up in the axiom, "there can be no proclamation of the gospel without taking account of its recipients."[5] As the council would later teach, the primary receiver of God's revelation and salvation is the whole people of God; facilitating their reception of the gospel is of utmost importance for the effectiveness of the church's mission. The council's doctrinal statements regarding the church's life should be interpreted as directed to this pastoral aim. The ecclesiological reforms it proposed have as their ultimate purpose God's saving outreach to human beings—which implies deep spiritual appropriation by believers of God's offer of salvation if God's intention is to be realized. The church is a servant of that salvific goal. The opening article of *Dei Verbum* states this conciliar intention: "[This synod] wants the whole world to hear the summons to salvation." This pastoral/doctrinal principle is at play, in some way, in all the other principles that follow.

4. On the council's reception of John XXIII's "principle of pastorality" and its centrality for a hermeneutics of the council and its documents, see Theobald, *La réception du concile Vatican II: I. Accéder à la source*, 281–493.

5. Christoph Theobald, "The Theological Options of Vatican II: Seeking an 'Internal' Principle of Interpretation," in *Vatican II: A Forgotten Future?*, *Concilium* 2005/4, ed. Alberto Melloni and Christoph Theobald (London: SCM Press, 2005), 87–107, at 94.

Principle 3

Proclamation/Dialogue

Principle 3: The church's mission is to proclaim boldly and steadfastly God's loving offer of salvation to humanity in Jesus Christ through the Holy Spirit; proclamation of the Christian Gospel will be ineffective without dialogic openness to the perspectives and contexts of the intended receivers of the proclamation, whether they be believers or nonbelievers.

Related to the council's desire for pastoral effectiveness within the church was its desire for dialogic openness to the world and those "outside" the church. Once again John XXIII set the tone in his opening address, a tone adopted by his successor, Pope Paul VI, and the council as a whole. Vatican II deliberately avoids condemnation. The word *rapprochement*, while not used in the documents, nevertheless captures what was clearly perceived at the time, by both its opponents and its promoters in the assembly of bishops, as a clear shift in ecclesial policy, away from a church deliberately hostile to those around it to a church desiring engagement with those "others."[1] The council's intention was to rebuild broken relationships that had impeded God's effectiveness in the world. Furthermore, the council taught that the church should seek to know the perspective, language, and mind-set of the receivers of its message, in order that the "other" may see more clearly in the face of the Catholic Church "the genuine face of God" (GS 19).

Accordingly, the council sought a new start in relations with those "outside" it: with Eastern churches of the Great Schism of 1054; with the ecclesial

---

1. "*Rapprochement . . .* is not part of the corpus of Vatican II in a material way, but it belongs fully to the aims of Vatican II." Massimo Faggioli, "*Sacrosanctum Concilium* and the Meaning of Vatican II," *Theological Studies* 71 (2010): 437–52, at 452. Faggioli notes the frequency of the term *rapprochement* in the writings of Dom Lambert Beauduin (1873–1960), a pioneer in the liturgical and ecumenical movements prior to the council. O'Malley refers to Cardinal Léon-Joseph Suenens as "a disciple of Lambert Beauduin." O'Malley, *What Happened at Vatican II*, 117.

communities of the Reformation; with the Jewish people; with adherents of other religions; with those of no religious belief. The council extended this dialogic openness to "modernity," to "the world," to "culture," to "history." This openness manifests a clear desire to end the entrenchment mentality characteristic of the previous centuries of Catholicism, especially during "the long nineteenth century" since the French Revolution and its aftermath.[2] What is also clear, however, is that neither John XXIII and Paul VI nor the council as a body ever understood such *rapprochement* as a capitulation to the *Zeitgeist* of liberalism, relativism, or indifferentism. The ending of a hostile stance was for the sake of a more compelling and more effective proclamation of God's Good News for all humanity.

The council embedded throughout its documents this deliberate shift in tone, a shift away from hostile language toward "friendship words," such as brothers/sisters, cooperation, collaboration, partnership, freedom, and dialogue.[3] The last word, "dialogue" (translating both *dialogus* and *colloquium*), became a key leitmotif for capturing this element of the council's vision.[4] For O'Malley, the council was concerned not only about the "what" of the church but also and ultimately about "how" the church should be; John XXIII's call for pastoral reform and its adoption by the conciliar assembly expressed their desire to change the very style of being church.[5] Hermann Pottmeyer interprets the council's vision for ecclesial reform as a call above all to create "a culture of dialogue" *within* the Catholic Church itself.[6] It is significant that in its treatment of the four concentric circles of dialogue, *Gaudium et Spes* 92 begins with dialogue *within* the church before going on to speak of dialogue with other Christians, with adherents of other religions, and with nonbelievers.[7]

---

2. On "the long nineteenth century," see O'Malley, *What Happened at Vatican II*, 53–92.

3. Ibid., 306–7.

4. See James Gerard McEvoy, *Leaving Christendom for Good: Church-World Dialogue in a Secular Age* (Lanham, MD: Lexington Books, 2014); James Gerard McEvoy, "Church and World at the Second Vatican Council: The Significance of *Gaudium et Spes*," *Pacifica* 19 (2006): 37–57; James Gerard McEvoy, "Proclamation as Dialogue: Transition in the Church-World Relationship," *Theological Studies* 70 (2009): 875–903. See also Ann Michele Nolan, *A Privileged Moment: Dialogue in the Language of the Second Vatican Council, 1962–1965* (New York: Peter Lang, 2006).

5. For one formulation of this thesis, see O'Malley, *What Happened at Vatican II*, 305–7.

6. Hermann J. Pottmeyer, "Die Mitsprache der Gläubigen in Glaubenssachen. Eine alte Praxis und ihre Wiederentdeckung," *Internationale katholische Zeitschrift "Communio"* 25 (1996): 135–47, at 146–47.

7. The council reverses the order in which Paul VI had treated the same circles of dialogue in his encyclical on dialogue, *Ecclesiam Suam*, published on August 6, just five weeks before the start of the council's third session on September 14, 1964. See *Ecclesiam Suam* 96–117.

A stark example of the shift in attitude—from monologue to dialogue—toward those "outside" the church is evident in the heading and content of *Gaudium et Spes* 44: "What the Church Receives from the Modern World."

> Nowadays when things change so rapidly and thought patterns differ so widely, the Church needs to step up this exchange by calling upon the help of people who are living in the world, who are expert in its organizations and its forms of training, and who understand its mentality, in the case of believers and nonbelievers alike. With the help of the Holy Spirit, it is the task of the whole people of God, particularly of its pastors and theologians, to listen to and distinguish the many voices of our times and to interpret them in the light of the divine Word, in order that the revealed truth may be more deeply penetrated, better understood, and more suitably presented. (GS 44)[8]

This passage was inserted just a few days before the last working day of the council, December 7, 1965, almost as a final reminder by the council of what it saw as one of its most important principles.

---

8. Translation altered. Unless otherwise noted, translations of the documents of Vatican II come from *Vatican Council II: The Basic Sixteen Documents; Constitutions, Decrees, Declarations*, ed. Austin Flannery (Collegeville, MN: Liturgical Press, 2014).

Principle 4

Ressourcement/Aggiornamento

Principle 4: The need for constant renewal of the church demands re-receiving many of the past forms and practices of the tradition; interpretion of these past forms and practices for the present calls for critical adaptation for new times and contexts if genuine renewal is to take place.

With the two terms *ressourcement* ("return to the sources") and *aggiornamento* ("updating"), we come to the issues of "history" and "historical consciousness." Bruno Forte has called Vatican II "the Council of history."[1] It was the first council in the history of the church that explicitly worked out of a historical awareness.[2] The two leitmotifs in this *ressourcement/aggiornamento* principle capture necessarily interrelated dimensions of historical consciousness, which will be further explored later when discussing the faith/history principle.

The notion of *aggiornamento* had long been central to the vision of historian Angelo Roncalli.[3] As Pope John XXIII, his explicit use of and allusions to the notion, both before the council and during his opening address, are important factors to be considered in the continuing interpretation of Vatican II, because *aggiornamento* would enter into the imagination of the bishops in the council and shape their vision for renewal of the church. Pope John's suc-

---

1. Bruno Forte, "Le prospettive della ricerca teologica," in *Il Concilio Vaticano II: Recezione e attualità alla luce del Giubileo*, ed. Rino Fisichella (Milan: San Paolo, 2000), 419–29, at 420.

2. See Giuseppe Alberigo, "Cristianesimo e storia nel Vaticano II," *Cristianesimo nella Storia* 5 (1984): 577–92.

3. See Michael Bredeck, *Das Zweite Vatikanum als Konzil des Aggiornamento: Zur hermeneutischen Grundlegung einer theologischen Konzilsinterpretation* (Paderborn: Schöningh, 2007); Max Vodola, "John XXIII, Vatican II, and the Genesis of *Aggiornamento*: A Contextual Analysis of Angelo Roncalli's Works on San Carlo Borromeo in Relation to Late Twentieth Century Church Reform" (PhD thesis, School of Philosophical, Historical and International Studies, Monash University, Melbourne, 2010).

cessor, Paul VI, also embraced *aggiornamento*, considering it to be "the guiding criterion of the Ecumenical Council" and indeed adopting it as an expression of "the aim and object" of his own pontificate.[4] Although the Latin conciliar documents never explicitly use the Italian word *aggiornamento*, the opening paragraph of its very first promulgated text, *Sacrosanctum Concilium*, states: "The sacred council has set out . . . to adapt [*accommodare*] more closely to the needs of our age those institutions which are subject to change [*mutationibus*]." For both popes of the council, as for the conciliar assembly, this *aggiornamento* could be characterized as a fresh reception (through personal and institutional renewal and reform) of "the treasure of revelation entrusted to the church" (DV 26) from the beginning. The treasure to be received is always God's self-communication in Jesus Christ through the Holy Spirit, as it was witnessed to in Scripture and tradition and as it is experienced in history and made evident through certain contemporary signs of the times. Without *aggiornamento*, this treasure would not be meaningfully communicated to—and, in turn, appropriated by—new generations.

While its aim was an *aggiornamento* of the church's liturgy, the council's first promulgated document, *Sacrosanctum Concilium*, is at the same time a work grounded on *ressourcement* of the tradition. According to Massimo Faggioli: "The advocates of the anti-Vatican II 'new liturgical movement' are indeed right as they identify in *Sacrosanctum Concilium* the main target since this constitution is the most radical instance of *ressourcement* and the most obviously antitraditionalist document of the council. The principle of *ressourcement* affected *Sacrosanctum Concilium* like no other conciliar document; it is hard to find in the corpus of the documents passages more expressive of the very essence of the Church and driven by the idea of *ressourcement*."[5]

Similarly, in the early debates on the document that would become *Dei Verbum*, *ressourcement* of long-forgotten scriptural and patristic personalist notions of revelation and dynamic notions of tradition became important, as the bishops reflected on the nature of the divine revelatory event within history and its meaningful and effective transmission by the church throughout history. Likewise, toward the end of the council, when treating the church *ad extra* and the constant need for *aggiornamento*, the bishops' earlier theological discussions on revelation and living tradition were never far from the surface of debate:

---

4. *Ecclesiam Suam* 50, http://www.vatican.va/holy_father/paul_vi/encyclicals/documents/hf_p-vi_enc_06081964_ecclesiam_en.html.

5. Faggioli, "*Sacrosanctum Concilium* and the Meaning of Vatican II," 451.

The Church learned early in its history to express the Christian message in the concepts and languages of different peoples and tried to clarify it in the light of the wisdom of their philosophers: it was an attempt to adapt the Gospel to the understanding of all and the requirements of the learned, insofar as this could be done. Indeed, this kind of adaptation and preaching of the revealed word *must ever be the law of all evangelization*. In this way it is possible to create in every country the possibility of expressing the message of Christ in suitable terms and to foster vital contact and exchange between the Church and different cultures. (GS 44)[6]

For opening the minds of the bishops to a *ressourcement/aggiornamento* approach, the work of the so-called *ressourcement* theologians in the decades prior to the council was vital.[7] This biblical, patristic, liturgical, historical, ecumenical, and theological scholarship was directly mediated to the council members through the theological *periti* present, either as assistants to individual bishops and national groups of bishops or as theological advisers on various conciliar committees.[8] The magisterium/theologians principle below will highlight some of these theologians and their work during Vatican II.

With a new historical consciousness, and a retrieval of the notion that the ultimate "source" of the Christian faith throughout history is God's continuing self-communication in Christ through the Spirit, a greater appreciation emerged in the council assembly that all expressions of that source's reception

---

6. Emphasis added.

7. On the historical consciousness grounding the *ressourcement* scholarship by theologians of the so-called *nouvelle théologie*, see Gabriel Flynn and Paul D. Murray, eds., *Ressourcement: A Movement for Renewal in Twentieth-Century Catholic Theology* (Oxford: Oxford University Press, 2011); Hans Boersma, *Nouvelle Théologie and Sacramental Ontology: A Return to Mystery* (New York: Oxford University Press, 2009); Jürgen Mettepenningen, *Nouvelle Théologie— New Theology: Inheritor of Modernism, Precursor of Vatican II* (London: T & T Clark, 2010). Mettepenningen considers Vatican II's appropriation (and, effectively, approbation) of the work of these theologians as the fourth phase in his history of *la nouvelle théologie*.

8. On the effects of *ressourcement* theology within the final texts, see Gerald O'Collins, "*Ressourcement* and Vatican II," in *Ressourcement: A Movement for Renewal in Twentieth-Century Catholic Theology*, ed. Gabriel Flynn and Paul D. Murray (Oxford: Oxford University Press, 2011), 372–91. For a detailed study of the role before and during the council of theologians from the *ressourcement* Dominican "school" of Le Saulchoir (Marie-Dominique Chenu, Yves Congar, and Henri-Marie Féret), see Michael Quisinsky, *Geschichtlicher Glaube in einer geschichtlichen Welt. Der Beitrag von M.-D. Chenu, Y. Congar und H.-M. Féret zum II. Vaticanum* (Berlin: LIT Verlag, 2007). For assessments on the role of such theologians at Vatican II, see Alberigo, "Transition to a New Age," 602–4; Jared Wicks, "Theologians at Vatican Council II," in *Doing Theology* (New York: Paulist Press, 2009), 187–223.

by the church are historically conditioned, including Scripture itself. The council would teach that it was therefore appropriate for historical-critical methods to be applied to Scripture's interpretation, albeit within the historical process of ongoing interpretation and application in the church's living tradition. Similarly, the historical nature of doctrine was appreciated to a deeper degree; the American *peritus* John Courtney Murray believed "development of doctrine" was "*the* issue under the issues" at Vatican II.[9] Such "development" was an element of ongoing *aggiornamento*. A further consequence of this engagement with recent historical methods of scholarship, when applied to interpreting the whole sweep of church history, was a rediscovery by the council fathers of great diversity within the tradition and especially the rediscovery of a richly diverse Catholicism before the Counter-Reformation (or "Tridentine") Catholicism that still shaped the Catholic Church so pervasively up to the eve of the council.

Within the various streams of the tradition being resourced, the patristic period was especially privileged, particularly the writings of Augustine. The growing appreciation of the tradition's rich diversity led at times to significant differences in preferred elements for retrieval. For example, the early sessions of the council showed a united group wanting to reject the then-dominant "neoscholasticism" in favor of a more biblical and personalist theology from the patristic period. Nevertheless, there were those who, all the same, did not want to reject the deep Catholic insights of recent historical *ressourcement* of Thomas Aquinas before the scholasticism of the centuries following him, a scholasticism that dominated Catholic theology immediately before the council and shaped the initial schemas presented to the council. The differences between these conciliar groups would more and more mark the council's work and can be found woven throughout the later documents.[10] It can be broadly described as the Augustinian and Thomist threads within Catholicism. In the end, the council documents attempt to safeguard *both* the Augustinian and the Thomist approaches. Both incarnation and cross are highlighted: God's coming as a human being consecrates creation and human history as the *locus* where God is to be found ever new; however, within humanity's engagement with creation and history, evil and sin continue to impede God's reigning in the world.

---

9. John Courtney Murray, "This Matter of Religious Freedom," *America* 112 (January 9, 1965): 40–43, at 43.

10. See, for example, Joseph A. Komonchak, "Le valutazioni sulla *Gaudium et spes*: Chenu, Dossetti, Ratzinger," in *Volti di fine Concilio: Studi di storia e teologia sulla conclusione del Vaticano II*, ed. Joseph Doré and Alberto Melloni (Bologna: Il Mulino, 2000), 115–53.

The citations in the main text and footnotes of the documents reveal the council's desire to ground its positions in the rich tradition of Christianity highlighted by this *ressourcement*, going back to its first scriptural witness. Certainly there is an obvious concern to appeal to earlier popes, especially Pius XII (who is cited most among recent popes).[11] Showing the relationship with the previous council, Vatican I, was also seen to be important, as indeed was Vatican II's relationship with Trent. Even here, however, the appeal to Trent's authority, which had so dominated the period of "Tridentine Catholicism," is recontextualized, as Joseph Komonchak notes: at Vatican II, "the tradition was no longer read in the light of Trent; Trent was read in the light of the tradition."[12] That tradition was "the greater and wider tradition" of the church, a "living tradition" going back to the earliest church.[13] Footnote references in the documents to these early sources are, however, only surface indicators of the council's *ressourcement*. What lies under the surface is the council's reception of decades of preconciliar scholarship in biblical, patristic, liturgical, historical, ecumenical, and theological studies, now mediated to the council through its *periti*.

In adopting this principle of *ressourcement/aggiornamento*, Vatican II took on a historical consciousness and embraced a dynamic understanding of tradition: *ressourcement* is to *aggiornamento* as tradition is to reception. The history of tradition shows continuous adaptation; what is constant in that process is the need for reinterpretation for new times and contexts.

11. Ennio Innocenti, "Le citazioni pontifiche nei documenti conciliari," *Concretezza* 12 (July 16, 1966): 6–10. According to Innocenti, seven popes are cited more than ten times: Pius X (11 times), Benedict XV (21), Leo XIII (33), Paul VI (60), Pius XI (67), John XXIII (83), and Pius XII (162).

12. Joseph A. Komonchak, "The Council of Trent at the Second Vatican Council," in *From Trent to Vatican II: Historical and Theological Investigations*, ed. Raymond F. Bulman and Frederick J. Parrella (New York: Oxford University Press, 2006), 61–80, at 76.

13. On "the greater and wider tradition," see Walter Kasper, "The Continuing Challenge of the Second Vatican Council: The Hermeneutics of the Conciliar Statements," in *Theology and Church* (New York: Crossroad, 1989), 166–76, at 171. The council's retrieval of the notion of "living tradition" in *Dei Verbum* can be highlighted as one example of the council's appropriation of *ressourcement* scholarship (as indeed it can be highlighted as an example of how ongoing *aggiornamento* goes to the heart of the church's mission). See Yves Congar, *Tradition and Traditions: An Historical and a Theological Essay* (London: Burns & Oates, 1966), 189–221.

Principle 5
Continuity/Reform

Principle 5: The church is the one community of faith through time as a sacrament of God's offer of revelation and salvation; the form this sacrament takes in a particular time and place requires continual reform and must always be adapted to that context for the sake of the church's ongoing effectiveness and survival.

In the previous section, I indicated how *ressourcement* scholarship revealed rich diversity in the tradition and brought about the conciliar shift away from understanding Catholic identity in terms of a monolithic Tridentine Catholicism. In the latter, continuity had been understood as "uniformity through time"; continuity had meant the continuation of Tridentine Catholicism. In the early twentieth century, any theological attempts to go beyond that vision were severely resisted, as happened during the Modernist controversy.[1] Many of the bishops at Vatican II, who had been formed as seminarians between 1910 and 1940, would have had that anti-Modernist Catholicism deeply engrained in them. This section now extends discussion of the issues of *ressourcement* and *aggiornamento* but brings explicitly to the fore the tension that results in the interplay between them: the necessary tension between constancy and change, sameness and novelty, in effecting an *aggiornamento* of the tradition. "Although [the Italian *aggiornamento* and the French *ressourcement*] express almost diametrically opposed impulses—the first looking forward, the second backward—they are both geared to change."[2]

It should not be surprising that during the council and then during its aftermath we find being played out an ecclesiastical version of *la querelle des*

---

1. For an overview see Marvin R. O'Connell, *Critics on Trial: An Introduction to the Catholic Modernist Crisis* (Washington, DC: The Catholic University of America Press, 1994).

2. John O'Malley, "Vatican II: Did Anything Happen?," in Shultenover, *Vatican II: Did Anything Happen?*, 52–91, at 63.

anciens et des modernes, a seemingly eternal quarrel over the old and the new, tradition and innovation, the past and the present.[3] From the very first day of the council, in his opening speech, John XXIII raised this issue of continuity and adaptation. Of course, he said, the deposit of faith (divine revelation) is a nonnegotiable; what demands constant attention is the effective proclamation of this good news; the church, through this council, he urged, must look to anything in its life that is impeding this proclamation and remove it or reform it. The council did go on to embrace renewal (*renovatio*) and reform (*reformatio*) as part of its *aggiornamento* program.[4]

During the pontificate of Benedict XVI, debate over the proper hermeneutics of Vatican II at times narrowed to discussion of the issue of continuity versus discontinuity. The pope himself initially used this distinction to structure his own deliberate foray into the debate, nevertheless attempting thereafter to rename what he considered the proper terms of that debate—continuity/reform.[5] Joseph Komonchak, in his analysis of Benedict's 2005 speech to the Roman Curia, identifies Lefebvrites as the real target of the pope's criticism of a radical "hermeneutics of discontinuity." According to Komonchak, the pope's proposed "hermeneutic of reform" is much more subtle than its detractors would claim:

> The "reform" that Benedict sees as the heart of the council's achievement is itself a matter of "novelty in continuity," of "fidelity and dynamism"; indeed, in what is something like a definition, the pope says that "true reform" consists

3. The phrase comes from a seventeenth-century literary debate in France. See Hans Robert Jauss, "Ursprung und Bedeutung der Fortschrittsidee in der 'Querelle des Anciens et des Modernes,'" in *Die Philosophie und die Frage nach dem Fortschritt*, ed. H. Kuhn and R. Wiedmann (München: 1964), 51–72; Hans Robert Jauss, "Antiqui/moderni (Querelle des Anciens et des Modernes)," in *Historisches Wörterbuch der Philosophie*, ed. Joachim Ritter (Basel/Stuttgart: Schwabe & Co., 1971), 1:410–14.

4. The two nouns are used in a few places in the documents. *Lumen Gentium* 8 speaks of *renovatio* (renewal): "The church . . . , clasping sinners to its bosom, at once holy and always in need of purification, follows constantly the path of penance and renewal." *Unitatis Redintegratio*, in two articles, uses together both *renovatio* (renewal) and *reformatio* (reform or reformation): all Christian communions are required to undertake "the task of renewal and reform" (UR 4); "Christ summons the church, as she goes her pilgrim way, to that continual reformation [*perennem reformationem*] of which she always has need, insofar as she is a human institution here on earth" (UR 6). On the occurrence of the two terms, see Philippe Delhaye, Michel Guéret, and Paul Tombeur, *Concilium Vaticanum II: Concordance, index, listes de fréquence, tables comparatives* (Louvain: Publications du CETÉDOC, 1974), 553.

5. For the December 22, 2005, "Address of His Holiness Benedict XVI to the Roman Curia," see Benedict XVI, "Interpreting Vatican II," *Origins* 35, no. 32 (January 26, 2006): 534–39.

precisely in a "combination of continuity and discontinuity at different levels." It oversimplifies his position to see it as counterposing continuity and discontinuity, as is often done. It is no less an oversimplification to reduce the question of interpreting Vatican II to the same choice between continuity and discontinuity. Is there anyone who sees only continuity in the council, or anyone who sees only discontinuity? Pope Benedict's description of "true reform" invites an effort to discern where elements of continuity and elements of discontinuity may be found.[6]

The hermeneutics of the council proposed by Pope Francis also sees Vatican II encompassing elements of continuity and reform, but with a greater emphasis on the imbalances that the council wanted to correct. In his bull *Misericordiae Vultus* promulgating the Jubilee Year of Mercy, he spoke of his explicit intention to begin the Jubilee on the fiftieth anniversary of Vatican II's closure: "The Church feels a great need to keep this event alive. With the Council, the Church entered a new phase of her history. The Council Fathers strongly perceived, as a true breath of the Holy Spirit, a need to talk about God to men and women of their time in a more accessible way."[7] Francis then went on to speak of the elements of discontinuity and continuity that marked the council's work: "The walls which for too long had made the Church a kind of fortress were torn down and the time had come to proclaim the Gospel in a new way. It was a new phase of the same evangelization that had existed from the beginning. It was a fresh undertaking for all Christians to bear witness to their faith with greater enthusiasm and conviction. The Church sensed a responsibility to be a living sign of the Father's love in the world." Similar tones marked his homily when he opened the Holy Door on the council's fiftieth anniversary, seeing in the action an evocation of Vatican II's intention:

> Today, here in Rome and in all the dioceses of the world, as we pass through the Holy Door, we also want to remember another door, which fifty years ago the Fathers of the Second Vatican Council opened to the world. This anniversary cannot be remembered only for the legacy of the Council's documents, which testify to a great advance in faith. Before all else, the Council was an

---

6. Joseph A. Komonchak, "Benedict XVI and the Interpretation of Vatican II," in *The Crisis of Authority in Catholic Modernity*, ed. Michael James Lacey and Francis Oakley (New York: Oxford University Press, 2011), 93–110, at 105.

7. *Misericordiae Vultus*, 4. See https://w2.vatican.va/content/francesco/en/apost_letters /documents/papa-francesco_bolla_20150411_misericordiae-vultus.html.

encounter. A genuine encounter between the Church and the men and women of our time. An encounter marked by the power of the Spirit, who impelled the Church to emerge from the shoals which for years had kept her self-enclosed so as to set out once again, with enthusiasm, on her missionary journey. It was the resumption of a journey of encountering people where they live: in their cities and homes, in their workplaces. Wherever there are people, the Church is called to reach out to them and to bring the joy of the Gospel, and the mercy and forgiveness of God.[8]

What constitutes the precise elements of discontinuity introduced by Vatican II has been variously listed by the council's commentators. For example, Peter Hünermann notes that the council desired four major breaks with the past: a break with fifteen hundred years of Christendom, where church and state have common goals and work as one; a break with the thousand-year division between Eastern and Western Christianity; a break with the five-hundred-year separation between Catholics and Protestants; a break with the one hundred years of tense Catholic "lingering on the threshold of the modern."[9] Karl Rahner's thesis is well known: Vatican II marks an epochal change in the history of the church, from a Hellenistic model to a truly "catholic" world church.[10] I have already noted O'Malley's thesis regarding the deliberate and dramatic shift in the desired "style" of being church. Others could be noted.

What constitutes the elements of continuity that Vatican II perpetuated, albeit in a renewed way? Certain fundamental features are considered by Vatican II to be permanently enduring elements of the Catholic Church: evangelization; the Scriptures; the seven sacraments; service of neighbor, especially the poor; ordination and the threefold order of bishop, priest, and deacon; religious life; the papacy; conciliar government; authoritative teaching; prayer and the call to holiness; etc. Vatican II addressed all of these, and in its intention to bring about their renewal, it certainly saw itself and its vision to be in continuity with these elements of Catholicism.

8. Pope Francis, Homily for Opening of the Holy Door, December 8, 2015. See http://w2.vatican.va/content/francesco/en/homilies/2015/documents/papa-francesco_20151208_giubileo-omelia-apertura.html.

9. See Peter Hünermann, "Kriterien für die Rezeption des II. Vatikanischen Konzils," *Theologische Quartalschrift* 191 (2011): 126–47.

10. Karl Rahner, "Basic Theological Interpretation of the Second Vatican Council," in *Theological Investigations*, vol. 20 (London: Darton, Longman & Todd, 1981), 77–89.

I would argue, however, that Vatican II's fundamental enduring element, i.e., its deepest element of continuity, is more *theo*-logical than *ecclesio*logical. One of the most significant teachings of the council is its retrieval of the nature of divine revelation as first and foremost God's loving, personal self-communication to humanity in Christ through the Spirit and not simply a communication of divine truths. Ultimately, in the council's discussion of continuity, the *continuum* it primarily focused on, in the end, was not so much "the church" but more so "the treasure of revelation entrusted to the church" (DV 26): God's continuous revelatory and salvific presence and activity in human history in Jesus Christ, through the Holy Spirit (DV 2). It is this that never changes. Ecclesiologically, "continuity" relates to the church's ongoing reception of the divine *continuum*. In that reception, the church is *semper ipse sed nunquam idem* (always itself but never the same)—always itself as receiver of God's revelation yet constantly needing to reform itself so that it might be a more effective sacrament of that salvific revelation. Preservation of ecclesial continuity is maintained by always being effective in that mission. *Dei Verbum*'s notion of "living tradition" captures the ecclesial "mirror" of the divine *continuum* in history. In that sense *Dei Verbum* is as much about the church as are *Lumen Gentium* and *Gaudium et Spes*; the living tradition is the church living the Gospel in its daily life in whatever period in history.

Principle 6

Vision/Reception

Principle 6: The bishops of Vatican II proposed a vision for renewing and reforming the Catholic Church; that vision requires ongoing reception and implementation by the whole people of God for its realization.

Vatican II envisioned a renewed and reformed Catholic Church. In fashioning its vision, "the Council by no means claims encyclopedic completeness."[1] It did try, however, to address an extraordinarily broad range of issues:

> No subject escaped their attention: from Revelation to listening to the signs of the times, from marriage to international peace, from education and the communications media to ecumenical and interfaith dialogue, from the nature and mission of the Church to the redefinition of its various functions, ministries, and states of life, the bishops managed to depict a renewed vision of Christianity on a planet embarking on globalization, even to put forward a programme of reform that exceeds anything we might have dared to imagine earlier. None of the twenty preceding councils showed so much daring and ambition: allowing a consensus to emerge among those more than two thousand prelates from all continents and obtain their agreement on the responses to be made to virtually all the questions facing the Church at the dawn of a new age for humanity—such is the absolutely unheard-of legacy of these great twentieth-century assizes.[2]

While the final documents do not present systematic treatises on that wide range of issues, an examination of the debates and the documents clearly reveals trajectories toward a newly configured vision. As Yves Congar remarks:

---

1. Peter Hünermann, "The Ignored 'Text': On the Hermeneutics of the Second Vatican Council," in Melloni and Theobald, *Vatican II: A Forgotten Future?*, 118–36, at 126.
2. Theobald, "The Theological Options of Vatican II," 87.

A very serious attempt at integration was made at Vatican II. There was, for instance, no Scripture without Tradition and no Tradition without Scripture. There was no sacrament without the Word. There was no Christology without pneumatology and no pneumatology without Christology. There was no hierarchy without the people and no people without the hierarchy. There was no episcopate without the Pope and no Pope without the episcopate. There was no local Church that was not missionary and no mission that was not ecclesial. There was no Church which was not mindful of the whole Church and which did not provide universality within itself and so on.[3]

In hermeneutically reconstructing what the council envisaged and what it outlined in its documents, it is helpful to keep in mind "the hermeneutical function of distanciation."[4] An author of a text (in the world behind the text) commits a vision to writing by producing a text that imagines "a world" (the world of the text). The text projects and proposes this world to an implied reader and ultimately to a reader in the "real" world, inviting the reader to imagine that proposed world in his or her own context (the world in front of the text). In the reader's application to the real world, vision can become a reality, no matter how distant in time the receiver is from the production of the text.

Similarly, the bishops of Vatican II committed their vision to writing in sixteen texts. The increasing distance in time from the council does not leave us at a disadvantage; through the dynamic nature of writing, of texts, and of reading, we have access to the conciliar vision—through hermeneutical reception. The council documents project a world in front of the text, and that world is a proposed way of being church in the face of the rest of humanity and ultimately before God. This projected world is what could be called "the vision of Vatican II." The dominant features of how the council imagined the church need to be brought to synthesis; receivers in new contexts must, however, reimagine and apply that vision for their own time and place. The conciliar vision requires reception for its realization—contemporary receivers of those texts are invited to imagine that envisioned church now, more than half a century later, in a very different context from the one in which those texts were first produced, the 1960s. New questions may arise in the new

3. Yves Congar, "A Last Look at the Council," in *Vatican II: By Those Who Were There*, ed. Alberic Stacpoole (London: Geoffrey Chapman, 1986), 337–58, at 343–44.

4. For what follows, see Paul Ricoeur, "The Hermeneutical Function of Distanciation," in *From Text to Action: Essays in Hermeneutics, II* (Evanston, IL: Northwestern University Press, 1991), 75–88.

contexts and be posed to the conciliar texts for answers, questions that individual conciliar texts did not intend to answer or questions that the bishops could not have even envisaged at that time. Nevertheless, receivers may indeed find answers to those new questions, via a comprehensive interpretation of the council and all its documents, as they imagine the whole conciliar vision realized in their particular context.

This reception of Vatican II, however, necessarily encompasses more than just "Vatican II." First, *the documents* (themselves being read as a whole, both intratextually and intertextually) are to be interpreted intertextually within the whole textual tradition of the church, reaching right back to the Scriptures.[5] Second, *the council* too has to be read within a longer context—as a historical ecclesial "event" to be now situated, over fifty years later, in the context of a two-thousand-year living tradition. Third, Vatican II itself must be read in the light of "the signs of the times," in a globalized world so different from the world of the 1960s. Therefore, and fourth, since Vatican II ("the council" and "the documents") has now entered history, it must be interpreted within a comprehensive theological epistemology, interrelating Scripture and tradition (of which Vatican II is now an element), and, in the contemporary world church, dialogue between the ecclesial authorities of the *sensus fidelium*, theological scholarship, and the oversight of the episcopal magisterium. According to the council's own "principle of pastorality" (as formulated by Theobald, "there can be no proclamation of the gospel without taking account of its recipients"[6]), it is the intended recipients of the conciliar vision who are now part of the council's history, because it is they who will live it (or resist it). Those potential recipients make up the whole people of God, who the council emphasizes is the primary recipient of divine revelation. Therefore, there is a wide circle of voices and authorities within the contemporary church who are to participate in that comprehensive reception and assessment by the whole people of God (the *sensus fidelium*, theologians, and the episcopal magisterium), as taught by *Dei Verbum* 8.[7]

Alois Grillmeier has highlighted three dimensions of conciliar reception following councils in the early church: kerygmatic, theological, and spiritual

5. On the need to read the conciliar texts intratextually and intertextually, see Rush, *Still Interpreting Vatican II*, 40–48.

6. Theobald, "The Theological Options of Vatican II," 94.

7. For one proposal on that interrelation, see Ormond Rush, *The Eyes of Faith: The Sense of the Faithful and the Church's Reception of Revelation* (Washington, DC: The Catholic University of America Press, 2009).

reception.[8] They are helpful categories for examining the reception of the most recent council. *Kerygmatic reception* refers to the official interpretation, promulgation, and implementation through church law by church leadership once the council ends. *Theological reception* refers to the work of academic theologians attempting to synthesize the vision of the conciliar decisions and documents. *Spiritual reception* is the conversion of heart and mind by all the baptized to a greater fidelity to the Gospel, no matter what particular aspects of the Christian life and church life a council might be wishing to address. Since John XXIII's pastoral intention for Vatican II was for a more intense and meaningful proclamation and appropriation of the Gospel, spiritual reception, therefore, is the ultimate goal of Vatican II's reception; it is here that the pastoral intention of the council is realized. Renewing the church for the sake of a greater facilitation of that spiritual reception, however, was never intended by the council to be focused only on personal renewal of individuals; it saw renewal of ecclesial relationships and institutional reform as also key to its pastoral vision.[9]

"*Theological* reception" of Vatican II includes the task of synthesis. Theologians are charged with the task of bringing the elements of the conciliar vision into some form of comprehensive synthesis, keeping in mind the above hermeneutical principles. One particular aspect that emerges from the above hermeneutical considerations, and that such a theological synthesis would need to highlight, is the increasing emphasis given by the council to the saving activity of the tripersonal God's presence and actions in the movements of human history but with a new appreciation of "history." The chapters that follow propose such a theological synthesis, in an order, however, that attempts to be faithful to the increasing conciliar priority of God over church.

Soon after the council ended, the *peritus* Karl Rahner wrote: "The Second Vatican Council, we find if we carefully review all sixteen of its constitutions, decrees, and declarations, was concerned mainly with the Church."[10] Never-

---

8. See Alois Grillmeier, "The Reception of Chalcedon in the Roman Catholic Church," *Ecumenical Review* 22 (1970): 383–411; Alois Grillmeier, *Christ in Christian Tradition*, vol. 2: *From the Council of Chalcedon (451) to Gregory the Great (590-604); Part 1: Reception and Contradiction; The Development of the Discussion about Chalcedon from 451 to the Beginning of the Reign of Justinian* (Atlanta: John Knox Press, 1987), 7–10.

9. See Ormond Rush, "Ecclesial Conversion after Vatican II: Renewing 'the Face of the Church' to Reflect 'the Genuine Face of God,'" in *50 Years On: Probing the Riches of Vatican II*, ed. David G. Schultenover (Collegeville, MN: Liturgical Press, 2015), 155–74.

10. Karl Rahner, "The Church: A New Image," in *The Church after the Council* (New York: Herder and Herder, 1966), 35–73, at 37.

theless, Rahner then went on to highlight that, while Vatican II's explicit agenda was to propose a vision for ecclesial renewal and reform, the church gathered in council at Vatican II appropriately points beyond itself:

> The oldest and newest thing in the Church is what she herself says and mediates; but the Church does not say itself; rather she is the word which speaks of the Other, and she renders this Other present and effective for us. Ecclesiology is, therefore, to the other treatises of dogmatics what grammar, poetics, and semantics are to poetry. The Church understands herself best when she perfects herself: and this means, when she speaks of God and his grace, of Jesus Christ and his cross and resurrection, of everlasting life, when she allows herself to be seized by the grace of this word which she speaks.[11]

Similarly, Heinrich Fries calls for an interpretation of the council that is not ecclesio-centric: "The Second Vatican Council, though described as 'The Council of the Church on the Church,' did not by any means make the Church the focal point of Christian faith. Rather, by its comprehensive description of the Church it explained the latter's meaning and function and thus brought out the fact that *the Church is not the principal reality but is in the service of this.*"[12]

The council's four years of deliberation over ecclesial renewal and reform prompted greater and deeper attention to the *theo-logical* issues underlying such a project. By "*theo*-logical" I mean: specifically related to the Christian beliefs regarding the nature and mission of God. By "*ecclesio*logical" I mean: specifically related to Catholic beliefs regarding the nature and mission of the church. This distinction is not intended to set the two in opposition (for example, as if to make the church unnecessary in God's mission). The adjec-

---

11. Ibid., 70. Rahner goes on to note: "Or we might put it this way: the Church comprehends what she is as the institution of salvation only when she understands and perfects herself as the *fruit* of salvation. There is no doubt, moreover, that the *Constitution on the Church* has understood this fact, for it speaks at length (and why not?) about the Church as institution, about her offices and powers, about her hierarchical structure, about her didactic and pastoral offices, about the many apostolates in the Church's mission—that is, in sum, about the Church as institution and mediation of salvation. But behind all this is the much more basic understanding that the Church is the people of God gathered by the grace of God, and outgrowth of God's grace, the fruit of salvation." Ibid., 70–71.

12. Heinrich Fries, "Church and Churches," in *Problems and Perspectives of Fundamental Theology*, ed. René Latourelle and Gerald O'Collins (New York: Paulist Press, 1982), 309–26, at 315.

tive "theological" (without the hyphen) is used throughout this book in the general sense, referring to considered reflection on any matter of faith.

Therefore, in reconstructing the vision of Vatican II, there should be a methodological priority on the *theo-logical* over the *ecclesiological*. This priority can be highlighted here briefly by examining two assertions: (1) since the council's primarily *pastoral* aim was to awaken in the church a more lively and active *faith*, a synthesis of its attempts to do that should privilege the council's treatment of revelation and faith, as well as recognize the hermeneutical role of *Dei Verbum* within the corpus of sixteen documents; and (2) the council's principle of the "hierarchy of truths" (UR 11) can be applied retrospectively to the interpretation of the council itself.

First, over the council's four sessions, the bishops discussed a vast range of ecclesiological issues, but issues related to revelation and faith were always just below the surface of debate. Particularly toward the end of the council, as they drafted *Unitatis Redintegratio, Nostra Aetate, Dignitatis Humanae,* and *Gaudium et Spes*, the agenda of the council would also draw their attention back to the document that in the very first days of the council had caused such controversy, *De Fontibus Revelationis*. This was one of the seven schemas presented to the council fathers before they arrived in 1962, and it was the second to be brought to the floor of the council in the first session (November 14, 1962). This schema on revelation was famously rejected. After failing to reach the required two-thirds majority to send the schema back for total redrafting, John XXIII intervened to that effect. Consideration of three further drafts of the document remained on the agenda for all four sessions.[13] It would finally be promulgated (as *Dei Verbum*) on November 18, 1965, three weeks before the close of the council. Like the layers of an archeological dig, the stages in the history of *Dei Verbum* over four sessions trace the history of the conciliar assembly's theo-logical development. It was a development through which the bishops' Christocentric vision became more pneumatologically balanced, resulting in a more explicitly trinitarian vision of God's activity in the economy of salvation, a vision that pervades the sixteen documents taken as a whole. The council's desire to renew and reform the Catholic Church spiritually and institutionally was for the sake of making the church a more effective sacrament of *God's mission* in the world.

---

13. In the second session, the second draft was not actually debated on the floor of the council in any of the plenary meetings. Bishops were able to submit written submissions, however, and some were effective in reshaping this second draft considerably.

During the third session, the Doctrinal Commission stated that the document on revelation was "in a way the first of all the constitutions of this council, so that its Preface introduces them all to a certain extent."[14] *Dei Verbum* therefore has a central place among the four constitutions, as highlighted yet again in the fourth session by the *relator*, Cardinal Ermenegildo Florit from Florence, when introducing the near-final version of *Dei Verbum* to the council assembly on October 29, 1965. The constitution, he stated, "formed the very bond among all the questions dealt with by this Council. It sets us at the very heart of the mystery of the Church and at the epicentre of ecumenical considerations."[15]

It is also important, however, to see the development of *Dei Verbum* as taking place in parallel with all the other fifteen documents that the council produced. An internal conversation was taking place, as it were, among all the documents as they developed—despite the fact that, even as a collection, they do not present consistent, systematic treatises on individual themes. Over these four sessions, the ecclesiological elements of the council's emerging vision came to be presented in terms of a broader vista, that of the whole economy of salvation revealing how the tripersonal God is active within human history, now understood with a much keener historical consciousness. In turn, over these four sessions, this new appreciation of how God works in the economy of salvation began to bring forth an appreciation of how God works *within* the church throughout history. The council itself did not go on to make a synthesis of its own developing theo-logical vision "outside" and "inside" the church. A comprehensive interpretation of the council, more than five decades on, in the light of the hermeneutical principles outlined above, must therefore emphasize the significance of that

14. AS IV/1, 341. Translation here taken from Theobald, "The Theological Options of Vatican II," 91. On the centrality of *Dei Verbum* in the conciliar vision and on the significance of this statement by the Doctrinal Commission, Jared Wicks writes: "Vatican II stated revelation's evangelical content in [*Dei Verbum*'s] opening six paragraphs [i.e., Chapter 1, 'Divine Revelation Itself']. One can argue that *in the overall logic of the council documents, this passage stands first*, since the gospel that it states is the word by which the church is assembled as *congregatio fidelium* and priestly people for worship. This is the gospel that all church ministries and apostolates serve and promote. The same gospel creates the horizon of understanding within which Catholic Christians view the world and its structures for the unfolding of the human vocation. Because of this, Vatican II's Doctrinal Commission once said that the constitution on revelation is in a certain way (*quodammodo*) the first of all the council's constitutions." Jared Wicks, "Vatican II on Revelation—From behind the Scenes," *Theological Studies* 71 (2010): 637–50, at 640–41. The *relatio* referred to here accompanied the late 1964 revision of *Dei Verbum*.

15. AS IV/5, 741, quoted in Theobald, "The Theological Options of Vatican II," 91.

developing preoccupation with the ways of God in history and its articulation across the texts. Ongoing interpretation of the ecclesiological reforms of Vatican II should be informed by this rejuvenated theology of God's activity within history in the economy of salvation, to be discerned through carefully reading "the signs of the times" in the light of the Gospel.[16]

Second, the council's principle of the "order or 'hierarchy' of truths" calls for the methodological priority of the theo-logical over the ecclesiological in reconstructing the conciliar vision. The Decree on Ecumenism states: "When comparing doctrines with one another, [Catholic theologians] should remember that in Catholic doctrine there exists an order or 'hierarchy' of truths, since they vary in their relation [*nexus*] to the foundation of the Christian faith" (UR 11).[17] According to Vatican II's own teaching, "the foundation of the Christian faith" is perhaps best crystallized in *Dei Verbum*'s description of the event of divine self-revelation: "It pleased God, in his goodness and wisdom, to reveal himself and to make known the mystery of his will, which was that people can draw near to the Father, through Christ, the Word made flesh, in the Holy Spirit, and thus become sharers in the divine nature" (DV 2). Dimensions of the saving reality of the divine-human encounter come to be articulated in the church's history as "truths" through doctrinal formulation. Thus "the foundation of the Christian faith" is captured in the central doctrines of the incarnation, the Trinity, salvation, grace, and the human person. All other doctrines relate to and must be formulated and applied in a way that is consistent with these foundational truths.[18] This theological prin-

---

16. GS 4; see GS 11.

17. Vatican II is here advancing what Vatican I called the *nexus mysteriorum*, the relationship between the mysteries of faith, highlighting, however, the order or hierarchy in that *nexus*. DS 3016. See Norman P. Tanner, *Decrees of the Ecumenical Councils*, 2 vols. (Washington, DC: Georgetown University Press, 1990), 2:808. While Vatican I tended to speak of "the mysteries of faith" (focusing on revealed truths and faith as *fides quae creditur*), Vatican II (e.g., DV 2, 15, 17, and 24) gives to the singular "mystery" a particular nuance (focusing more on personal encounter and faith as *fides qua creditur*).

18. According to Wolfgang Beinert, "The principle of the hierarchy of truths . . . is not a reductionist model or a numerically based principle of selection. Rather, it is a principle of interpretation that is based on the fact that all elements of faith finally elucidate God's revelation as it took place through Jesus Christ in the Holy Spirit for the salvation of human beings. Therefore, faith in its essence is not a system of propositions, although it needs these. Rather it is the way in which the Christian comes to God in Christ through the work of the Spirit, thus a process that is directed to one singular goal. The core of the Christian faith is thus the trinitarian dogma together with the christological dogma in an anthropological orientation." Wolfgang Beinert, "Hierarchy of Truths," in *Handbook of Catholic Theology*, ed. Wolfgang Beinert and Francis Schüssler Fiorenza (New York: Crossroad, 1995), 334–36, at 336.

ciple orders dogmatic treatises in a hierarchy, from the fundamental truths to those deriving from those truths. Applying "the hierarchy of truths" means, for example, that one's notion of the nature and mission of the church should derive from how one understands the nature and mission of God.

Pope Paul VI, in his closing address for the second session, after having formally promulgated *Sacrosanctum Concilium*, referred to the appropriateness of having a document on the liturgy as the council's first document: "We may see in this an acknowledgement of *a right order of values and duties*: *God in the first place*; prayer our first duty; the liturgy the first school of spirituality."[19] According to that right order of theo-logical values and ecclesial duties, the next five principles will examine the council's vision regarding God and God's plan for human beings.

19. Pope Paul VI, "Closing Address: Second Session," in *Council Daybook: Vatican II, Sessions 1 and 2*, ed. Floyd Anderson (Washington, DC: National Catholic Welfare Conference, 1965), 331–35, at 333.

PART II

THEO-LOGICAL PRINCIPLES

Principle 7
Revelation/Faith

Principle 7: Revelation is the triune God's self-communication in love to human beings for the sake of their salvation, along with the communication of divine truths concerning that revelation and salvation; for such divine personal self-communication to be realized in the lives of the intended recipients, human faith is required—the personal and communal reception of God's self-gift in love, along with personal and communal assent to the divine truths communicated within that personal encounter.

At the heart of the *pastoral* vision of Vatican II is its teaching on the active, participatory role of *faith* in the divine-human encounter. Here the Dogmatic Constitution on Divine Revelation, *Dei Verbum*, is the key document, although other documents address the theme of revelation and faith and indeed develop the teaching beyond that of *Dei Verbum*.[1] For example, *Sacrosanctum Concilium*, *Lumen Gentium*, *Nostra Aetate*, *Ad Gentes*, and *Gaudium et Spes* all address the theme of revelation/faith in some way.[2] The council's teaching marks a shift from that of Vatican I's *Dei Filius* and the preparatory schema for Vatican II, *De Fontibus Revelationis*.[3] The shift is from a predominantly propositionalist notion of divine truth and revelation to a personalist notion

---

1. As Gerald O'Collins asserts: "For fundamental theology's central theme of revelation, *Dei Verbum* is beyond question *the* document. Nevertheless, it is at our peril that we neglect the other fifteen texts from the council. In differing ways they not only repeat and amplify the teaching from *Dei Verbum* on revelation, but at times they also add new and important points." Gerald O'Collins, *Retrieving Fundamental Theology: The Three Styles of Contemporary Theology* (New York: Paulist Press, 1993), 63.

2. See ibid., 63–78. For a detailed examination of the theme of revelation in *Gaudium et Spes*, see María del Carmen Aparicio Valls, *La plenitud del ser humano en Cristo: La revelación en la Gaudium et spes* (Roma: Pontificia Università Gregoriana, 1997).

3. For the Latin text and an English translation of *Dei Filius*, see Tanner, *Decrees of the Ecumenical Councils*, 2:804–11. For the Latin text of the draft schema *De Fontibus Revelationis*,

of divine truth and revelation. Christoph Theobald calls the shift "a change of paradigm."[4] When seen alongside the original schema *De Fontibus Revelationis*, according to Avery Dulles, "the view of revelation proposed by *Dei Verbum* may be characterized as concrete rather than abstract, historical rather than philosophical, biblical rather than scholastic, ecumenical rather than controversial, interpersonal rather than propositional."[5] Or, as René Latourelle summarizes the shift: "The transition to a personalist, historical, and christocentric conception of revelation amounts to a kind of Copernican revolution, compared with the extrinsicist, atemporal, and notional approach that prevailed until the 1950s."[6] This paradigm shift conditions all the other principles of the vision of Vatican II outlined below, functioning as a kind of megaprinciple.

Effecting this paradigm shift was, however, hard fought.[7] Beginning with the debate on the preparatory schema *De Fontibus Revelationis* in the first session, the council considered the theme throughout four of its sessions, until *Dei Verbum* was finally promulgated on November 18, 1965.[8] The story

---

see AS I/3, 14–26. An English translation can be found at https://jakomonchak.files.wordpress.com/2012/09/de-fontibus-1-5.pdf.

4. Christoph Theobald, "The Church under the Word of God," in *History of Vatican II*, vol. 5: *The Council and the Transition: The Fourth Period and the End of the Council, September 1965–December 1965*, ed. Giuseppe Alberigo and Joseph A. Komonchak (Maryknoll, NY: Orbis Books, 2006), 5:275–362, at 348n17.

5. Avery Dulles, *Revelation Theology: A History* (New York: Seabury Press, 1969), 157.

6. René Latourelle, "Dei Verbum: II. Commentary," in *Dictionary of Fundamental Theology*, ed. René Latourelle and Rino Fisichella (Middlegreen, Slough, UK: St Paul, 1994), 218–24, at 218.

7. See Giuseppe Ruggieri, "The First Doctrinal Clash," in *History of Vatican II*, vol. 2: *The Formation of the Council's Identity; First Period and Intercession, October 1962–September 1963*, ed. Giuseppe Alberigo and Joseph A. Komonchak (Maryknoll, NY: Orbis Books, 1997), 2:233–66; Hanjo Sauer, "The Doctrinal and the Pastoral: The Text on Divine Revelation," in *History of Vatican II*, vol. 4: *The Church as Communion: Third Period and Third Intersession, September 1964–September 1965*, ed. Giuseppe Alberigo and Joseph A. Komonchak (Maryknoll, NY: Orbis Books, 2004), 4:196–231; Theobald, "The Church under the Word of God."

8. There was no debate during the second session, but the bishops were given the opportunity to submit comments regarding a revised draft. For histories of the drafting, see Joseph Ratzinger, "Dogmatic Constitution on Divine Revelation: Origin and Background," in *Commentary on the Documents of Vatican II*, vol. 3, ed. Herbert Vorgrimler (New York: Herder, 1969), 155–66; Helmut Hoping, "Theologischer Kommentar zur Dogmatischen Konstitution über die göttliche Offenbarung," in *Herders theologischer Kommentar zum Zweiten Vatikanischen Konzil. Band 3*, ed. Peter Hünermann and Bernd Jochen Hilberath (Freiburg: Herder, 2005), 3:695–831; Ronald D. Witherup, *Scripture: Dei Verbum*, Rediscovering Vatican II (Mahwah, NJ: Paulist Press, 2006), 15–31; Massimo Epis, "Introduzione all costituzione dog-

over those four years is well described as a "clash" between two theological viewpoints.[9] Nevertheless, the conciliar debate was able to present, in its final text, a clear trajectory toward a new vision, above all regarding "the pivotal concept" of divine revelation.[10]

Revelation as a Loving Invitation to Relationship

In at least four major ways the council balances and enriches the exclusively propositional model of revelation presented in the draft schema by affirming: (1) revelation is primarily a dialogic divine-human encounter, not only a communication of truths; (2) divine revelation, as God's personal outreach embraced in faith, is therefore also a saving encounter for those who receive it; (3) revelation takes place through divine actions in history and not just through the communication of words; (4) revelation is not only something that happened in the past but a present reality and indeed will only be fulfilled at the end of time.

First, Vatican II emphasizes that revelation is not *primarily* instruction from the divine teacher and a communication of truths (information about God and God's vision for humanity—although it is certainly that); rather, at a deeply personal level it is the communication of God's very Self in love to human beings. Three Latin words recur in the council's documents and are used almost synonymously: *revelare, manifestare, communicare*. The first chapter of *Dei Verbum* (2–6) opens with the central affirmation: "It pleased God, in his goodness and wisdom, to reveal himself [*seipsum revelare*] and to make known [*notum facere*] the mystery [*sacramentum*] of his will, which was that people can draw near to the Father, through Christ, the Word made flesh, in the Holy Spirit, and thus become sharers in the divine nature" (DV 2).

The next article of *Dei Verbum* goes on to locate that divine self-revelation from the origins of humankind: "Wishing to open up the way to heavenly salvation, he manifested himself [*semetipsum manifestavit*] to our first parents from the very beginning" (DV 3). Three articles later: "By divine revelation God wished to manifest and communicate [*manifestare et communicare*] both himself [*seipsum*] and the eternal decrees of his will concerning the salvation of humankind" (DV 6). *Lumen Gentium* has a similar expression: "making both himself and his intentions known in the course of their history [*sese atque*

matica *Dei Verbum*," in *Dei Verbum: Commentario ai documenti del Vaticano II*, vol. 5, ed. Serena Noceti and Roberto Repole (Bologna: Edizioni Dehoniane, 2017), 13–89.

9. See Ruggieri, "The First Doctrinal Clash."

10. Theobald, "The Church under the Word of God," 346.

propositum voluntatis suae in eius historia manifestando]" (LG 9). The Pastoral Constitution on the Church in the Modern World reiterates the teaching: "In his self-revelation to this people, fully manifesting himself in his incarnate Son [*sese revelans usque ad plenam sui manifestationem in Filio incarnato*], God spoke in the context of the culture proper to each age" (GS 58).

When viewed across all documents, the council's teaching on God's self-manifestation is trinitarian. The formula "to the Father through the Son in the Holy Spirit" appears nine times.[11] For example, in *Unitatis Redintegratio*, when discussing the eucharistic ecclesiology of the Eastern churches, the trinitarian nature and goal of the church is highlighted: "In this [eucharistic] mystery the faithful, united with their bishops, have access to God the Father through the Son, the Word made flesh who suffered and was glorified, in the outpouring of the Holy Spirit. And so, made 'sharers of the divine nature' (2 Pt 1:4), they enter into communion [*communionem*] with the most Holy Trinity" (UR 15).

As stated in the opening sentence of chapter 1 of *Dei Verbum* quoted above, revelation involves the activity of God the Father in Christ through the Spirit in human history. This trinitarian vision is expressed in the key of love and friendship. Out of infinite love, God invites human beings into the very inner life of the Trinity, where a deep intimate loving knowledge beyond words will be revealed to the believer who responds: "By this revelation, then, the invisible God, from the fullness of his love, addresses [*alloquitur*] men and women as his friends, and lives among them [*cum eis conversatur*], in order to invite [*invitet*] and receive [*suscipiat*] them into his own company" (DV 2). These four Latin verbs evoke an intimate and dialogic relationship between God and human beings, in which the latter are invited to respond as friends.[12] Joseph Ratzinger notes that here is "an understanding of revelation that is seen basically *as dialogue*, as is indicated in the words *alloquitur* and *conversatur*."[13]

11. SC 6; LG 4, 28, 51; UR 15; DV 2; OT 8; PO 6; AG 7. See Yves Congar, "Die christologischen und pneumatologischen Implikationen der Ekklesiologie des II. Vatikanums," in *Kirche im Wandel: Eine kritische Zwischenbilanz nach dem Zweiten Vatikanum*, ed. Giuseppe Alberigo, Hermann J. Pottmeyer, and Yves Congar (Düsseldorf: Patmos, 1982), 111–23, at 122.

12. The verb *converso* can mean: "to live with, have intercourse with, keep company with." The verb *suscipio* can mean: "to take up [a new born child from the ground]; hence, to acknowledge, recognize, bring up as one's own." See Charlton T. Lewis and Charles Short, *A Latin Dictionary: Founded on Andrews' Edition of Freund's Latin Dictionary*, rev., enl., and in great part rewritten ed. (Oxford: Clarendon Press, 1951), 464, 1819.

13. Ratzinger, "Chapter I: Revelation Itself," 171. Emphasis added.

Further on in *Dei Verbum*, when treating the nature of tradition and the reality of revelation in the present, this dialogic nature of revelation is emphasized by use of the verb *colloquor* (to converse, to dialogue): "Thus God, who spoke in the past, continues to converse [*colloquitur*] with the spouse of his beloved Son. And the Holy Spirit, through whom the living voice of the Gospel rings out in the church—and through it in the world—leads believers to the full truth and makes the word of Christ dwell in them in all its richness" (DV 8). Later, in further developing the pastoral significance of divine revelation being a present reality, the cognate of *colloquor*, the noun *colloquium*, is used: "Prayer should accompany the reading of sacred scripture, so that it becomes a dialogue [*colloquium*] between God and the human reader" (DV 25). Ratzinger comments that the use of the word *colloquium* here "indicates the element of actuality that is contained in dialogue: *the dialogue of God is always carried on in the present.*"[14] Tellingly, this divine-human dialogue is spoken of as *between friends*. As George Tavard comments: "The God who manifests himself does not speak as a professor or a scholar, but as a person. He evokes not only intellectual acceptance of what he says,

---

14. Ibid., 171. Emphasis added. This dialogic depiction of revelation-faith, as the ground of a dialogic understanding of the church, was presented to the council fathers for consideration by Pope Paul VI in his first encyclical *Ecclesiam Suam* (hereafter, ES), on August 6, 1964, before the start of the council's third session. The pope speaks of dialogue as fundamental for understanding the church's mission and of the origins of that dialogue in the dialogic structure of Christian revelation—divine revelation requires faith if it is to be realized: "Here, then, Venerable Brethren, is the noble origin of this dialogue: in the mind of God Himself. Religion of its very nature is a certain relationship between God and man. It finds its expression in prayer; and prayer is a dialogue. Revelation, too, that supernatural link which God has established with man, can likewise be looked upon as a dialogue. In the Incarnation and in the Gospel it is God's Word that speaks to us. That fatherly, sacred dialogue between God and man, broken off at the time of Adam's unhappy fall, has since, in the course of history, been restored. Indeed, the whole history of man's salvation is one long, varied dialogue, which marvelously begins with God and which He prolongs with men in so many different ways. In Christ's 'conversation' (c.f. Bar 3:38) with men, God reveals something of Himself, of the mystery of His own life, of His own unique essence and trinity of persons. At the same time He tells us how He wishes to be known: as Love pure and simple; and how He wishes to be honored and served: His supreme commandment is love. Child and mystic, both are called to take part in this unfailing, trustful dialogue; and the mystic finds there the fullest scope for his spiritual powers" (ES 70). In the next article of the encyclical, Paul VI highlights the priority of the theo-logical over the ecclesiological: "This relationship, this dialogue, which God the Father initiated and established with us through Christ in the Holy Spirit, is a very real one, even though it is difficult to express in words. *We must examine it closely if we want to understand the relationship which we, the Church, should establish and foster with the human race*" (ES 71). Emphasis added.

but personal commitment to himself; he does not want only students and disciples, but friends attached to him through a personal relationship."[15]

This loving invitation to intimate friendship and dialogue is offered in Jesus Christ through the Holy Spirit: God's will is "that people can draw near to the Father, through Christ, the Word made flesh, in the Holy Spirit, and thus become sharers in the divine nature" (DV 2). Jesus Christ and the Holy Spirit are inseparably linked in this divine encounter with human beings. "The most intimate truth thus revealed about God and human salvation shines forth for us in Christ, who is himself both the mediator and the sum total of revelation" (DV 2); Christ is the one "in whom the entire revelation of the most high God is summed up" (DV 7). The Holy Spirit is required, however, to enable the believer to appropriate God's self-communication in Christ: it is "the Holy Spirit, who moves the heart and converts it to God, and opens the eyes of the mind and 'makes it easy for all to accept and believe the truth'" (DV 5).[16]

The second way in which Vatican II balances a propositional notion of revelation is the way the council documents, and particularly *Dei Verbum*, speak of "revelation" and "salvation" almost as synonyms. As George Tavard asserts: "The treatment of revelation by Vatican Council II is radically soteriological."[17] This overlap between the two terms was deliberately intended to avoid reducing revelation to a purely cognitive level; revelation also affects other levels of human being that the term "salvation" encompasses. Encounter with the triune God is a saving reality. Indeed, one could almost use the phrases "salvific revelation" and "revelatory salvation" to express the same reality of the divine-human encounter in history. According to Gerald O'Collins, "'Revelation' and 'salvation' merge so closely that the Second Vatican Council employed the terms almost interchangeably in *Dei Verbum*. . . . As far as the council was concerned, the history of revelation is the history of salvation and vice versa . . . . Together, revelation and salvation constitute the history of God's self-communication to human beings."[18] A clear example of this interchangeability of the terms can be seen

---

15. George H. Tavard, *De Divina Revelatione: The Dogmatic Constitution on Divine Revelation of Vatican Council II; Commentary and Translation* (Glen Rock, NJ: Paulist Press, 1966), 24–25.

16. *Dei Verbum* is here quoting the Council of Orange II, canon 7 (Denz. 180 [377]) and Vatican I, *Dei Filius*, chapter 3 (Denz. 1791 [3010]).

17. Tavard, *De Divina Revelatione*, 26.

18. Gerald O'Collins, *Rethinking Fundamental Theology* (Oxford: Oxford University Press, 2011), 71–72.

in the passage from *Dei Verbum* 2 in which "revelation" appears three times and "salvation" two times:

> The pattern of this *revelation* [*haec revelationis oeconomia*] unfolds through deeds and words which are intrinsically connected: the works performed by God in the history of *salvation* show forth and confirm the doctrine and realities signified by the words; the words, for their part, proclaim the works, and bring to light the mystery they contain. The most intimate truth thus *revealed* [*per hanc revelationem*] about God and human *salvation* shines forth for us in Christ, who is himself both the mediator and sum total of *revelation*. (DV 2)

In another key passage, the same pattern is evident: "By divine *revelation* God wished to manifest and communicate both himself and the eternal decrees of his will concerning the *salvation* of humankind" (DV 6).

Third, a propositional notion is balanced by the way the council teaches that revelation is not only disclosing information about God and human salvation through divine "words" but also bringing to realization God's salvation through divine "deeds" in history and in the lives of those who respond to God in faith. *Dei Verbum* states: "The pattern of this revelation unfolds through deeds and words which are intrinsically connected: the works performed by God in the history of salvation show forth and confirm the doctrine and realities signified by the words; the words, for their part, proclaim the works, and bring to light the mystery they contain" (DV 2). Later, when addressing the place of the Old Testament, it states: "[God] acquired a people for himself, and to them he revealed himself in words and deeds as the one, true, living God [*se tamquam unicum Deum verum et vivum verbis ac gestis revelavit*]" (DV 14). As Brian Daley observes: "*Dei Verbum* treats revelation as a verbal noun, an activity of the ever-mysterious and ever-present God in human history, rather than as a body of information to be studied."[19] Christoph Theobald calls it a "sacramental conception of revelation."[20]

The referent of the term "word of God" in *Dei Verbum* is primarily this event of divine revelation—God's personal "address" to humanity. Only secondarily does the term refer to God's "words," and so to Scripture, for which *Dei Verbum* generally uses phrases such as "the word of God . . . in its written form" (DV 10) or "the written word of God" (DV 24). In reference

---

19. Brian E. Daley, "Knowing God in History and in the Church: *Dei Verbum* and '*Nouvelle Théologie*,'" in *Ressourcement: A Movement for Renewal in Twentieth-Century Catholic Theology*, ed. Gabriel Flynn and Paul D. Murray (Oxford: Oxford University Press, 2011), 333–51, at 347.

20. Theobald, "The Church under the Word of God," 345.

to the opening words *"Dei Verbum"* ("The Word of God"), René Latourelle notes that the phrase refers primarily to the event of revelation and only secondarily to Scripture, or to Scripture and tradition, through which it is mediated throughout history: "The phrase, the *Word of God*, refers first of all to revelation, that first intervention by which God steps out of his mystery and speaks to humanity to disclose to it the secrets of divine life and to communicate to it his plan of salvation. This is the great fact which dominates the two Testaments and from which the Church draws her life. This word of God, spoken once and for all, endures throughout the ages, through Tradition and Scripture, always living and relevant."[21] *Dei Verbum* also uses the terms "the Gospel" (DV 7) or "the full and living Gospel" (DV 7) almost as synonyms for "the word of God," meaning not just words or a message about God, but indeed the very reality of God's outreach to humanity in history, above all in Jesus Christ, "the mediator and sum total of revelation" (DV 2); in him "the entire revelation of the most high God is summed up" (DV 7). Not just Christ's words but "everything to do with his presence and his manifestation of himself was involved in achieving this [revelation]: his words and works, signs and miracles, but above all his death and glorious resurrection from the dead, and finally his sending of the Spirit of truth. He revealed that God was with us, to deliver us from the darkness of sin and death, and to raise us up to eternal life" (DV 4).

Fourth, the council emphasizes throughout its documents that God's revelation has *past*, *present*, and *future* dimensions; it is not just some past reality to be preserved in a static way. Revelation is certainly a past event unsurpassably communicated in the Christ event through the Holy Spirit, but revelation is also a living encounter with God in Christ through the Spirit *in the present* (of whatever era). This can occur in manifold ways: in the church's liturgy, as a participation in Christ's paschal mystery; in the believer's spiritual life; in daily relational family, work, and social life; in outreach to neighbour and committed action for the sake of justice, peace, and reconciliation; in the events of history revealed in "the signs of the times" (GS 4). "Thus God, who spoke in the past, dialogues without interruption [*sine intermissione colloquitur*] with the spouse of his beloved Son. And the Holy Spirit, through whom the living voice of the Gospel rings out in the church— and through it in the world—leads believers to the full truth and makes the

---

21. René Latourelle, *Theology of Revelation* (Staten Island, NY: Alba House, 1966), 456.

word of Christ dwell in them in all its richness" (DV 8).[22] That God continues to converse with the church throughout history does not mean that new "content" is revealed beyond what has been revealed in Christ through the Spirit; rather, it means that the Holy Spirit actualizes in believers in every age the present salvific reality of revelation.

This desire to emphasize the present reality of saving revelation is a fundamental aspect of the council's pastoral concern: to stimulate a deeper faith response to God. Paul VI, in his opening address to the council's second session, referred to "the pastoral aim" as "the principal aim of the council" envisaged by John XXIII.[23] As we have seen, Christoph Theobald speaks of "the pastorality principle" guiding the council's agenda and vision.[24] The conciliar emphasis on revelation as a present reality is just one more dimension of the council's attempt to overcome the preparatory schema's propositional model of revelation. As Gerald O'Collins observes: "If one persists in thinking that revelation involves primarily the communication of hidden truths that have been disclosed, it becomes easier to relegate revelation to the past. As soon as the whole set of revealed doctrines was complete, revelation ended or was 'closed'. For this way of thinking, later believers cannot personally and directly experience revelation. All they can do is remember, interpret and apply truths revealed long ago to the Christians of the first century."[25]

This pastoral concern to emphasize the *present* reality of God's salvific and revelatory presence is evident in other documents. A few examples can be highlighted. In the first document it promulgated, the council teaches: "To accomplish so great a work [of salvation] Christ is always present in his church, especially in liturgical celebrations" (SC 7); "in the liturgy God speaks to his people, Christ is still proclaiming his gospel, and the people respond to God both in song and in prayer" (SC 33). Moreover, *Sacrosanctum Concilium*'s promotion of full, conscious, and active participation in the liturgy is an essential plank in the council's pastoral reform agenda. Participation in the liturgical rites mediates a participation in the paschal mystery. But, by extension—as Jeremy Driscoll asserts—when taking all of the council's documents together, this is

22. Translation corrected. On the temporal aspects of revelation, see Gerald O'Collins, "Revelation Past and Present," in *Vatican II: Assessment and Perspectives; Twenty-Five Years After (1962–1987)*, vol. 1, ed. René Latourelle (New York: Paulist Press, 1988), 1:125–37. See also O'Collins, *Retrieving Fundamental Theology*, 87–97.

23. Paul VI, "Opening Address: Second Session," 144.

24. See throughout Theobald, *La réception du concile Vatican II: I. Accéder à la source.*

25. Gerald O'Collins, "Vatican II's Constitution on Divine Revelation: *Dei Verbum*," *Pastoral Review* 9, no. 2 (2013): 12–18, at 15.

participation, "communion," with the tripersonal God: "Through participation in the liturgy we are made participators of the divine life. Participating in the divine life is the true, ultimate active participation."[26]

Moreover, in urging all to embrace a life of holiness (*Lumen Gentium*, chapter 5), the council presents holy people in the Christian community as mediators of God's revelatory presence: "In the lives of those companions of ours in the human condition who are more perfectly transformed into the image of Christ, God shows [*manifestat*], vividly, to humanity his presence and his face [*praesentiam vultumque suum*]. He speaks [*alloquitur*] to us in them and offers us a sign of his kingdom, to which we are powerfully attracted, so great a cloud of witnesses are we given and such an affirmation of the truth of the Gospel" (LG 50). The council's call to attend to God's present revelation in every age is a particularly dominant theme in *Gaudium et Spes*. According to Avery Dulles, "The Pastoral Constitution, with its positive orientation toward contemporary secular history, implicitly affirms that *revelation is a continuing process*, and that it must be newly expressed for every age in prophetic witness."[27]

The council was also intent, however, on emphasizing the future dimension of revelation and salvation. This eschatological perspective too pervades the council's vision, as we will examine more closely below when discussing another theo-logical principle: the protological/eschatological principle.

Faith as Loving God in Return

These four major shifts in Vatican II's teaching on divine revelation were paralleled by four major shifts, implicit and explicit, in the council's teaching on the human reception of revelation, i.e., faith. All four shifts regarding faith were central to the council's vision for the pastoral renewal of faith in the church, seen as *a community of faith*. This call for a renewal of the community of faith, with its understanding of "believing" now articulated in a deeper and broader way, is evident in themes such as the call for full, conscious, and active participation in the liturgy (through the primary rubric of participation in "the paschal mystery"); the universal call to holiness; and the vision of active participation by all believers in the three offices of Christ and, thereby, in the mission of the church.

---

26. Jeremy Driscoll, "Reviewing and Recovering *Sacrosanctum Concilium*'s Theological Vision," *Origins* 43, no. 29 (December 19, 2013): 479–87, at 486.

27. Dulles, *Revelation Theology*, 158. Emphasis added.

In the first shift, faith is presented as primarily a dialogical response to God's loving self-communication in Christ through the Spirit and secondarily as an assent to truths that have been communicated through that personal encounter. Faith is "our response to God who reveals" (DV 5). There is no dialogue without some response to the one who initiates it. Central, then, to the council's dialogic understanding of revelation is its dialogic understanding of faith. Divine saving revelation remains unrealized without a faith response; God's invitation to loving friendship and reciprocal dialogue finds its realization only when human beings respond.

> Human dignity rests above all on the fact that humanity is called to communion with God [*ad communionem cum Deo*]. The invitation to converse with God [*ad colloquium cum Deo*] is addressed to men and women as soon as they are born. For if people exist it is because God has created them through love, and through love continues to keep them in existence. They cannot live fully in the truth unless they freely acknowledge that love and entrust themselves to their creator. Many, however, of our contemporaries either do not at all perceive, or else explicitly reject, *this intimate and vital relationship* [*coniunctionem*] *with God*. (GS 19)

Such faith is a grace, a divine gift; God's Holy Spirit opens the minds and hearts of human believers to embrace and receive the triune God's invitation to loving friendship. Thus the Holy Spirit is the divine principle enabling faith's reception of revelation: "For this faith to be accorded we need the grace of God, anticipating and assisting it, as well as the interior help of the Holy Spirit, who moves the heart and converts it to God, and opens the eyes of the mind and 'makes it easy for all to accept and believe the truth.' The same Holy Spirit constantly perfects faith by his gifts, so that revelation may be more and more deeply understood" (DV 5).[28] *Gaudium et Spes* 15 strikingly extends reference to such human reception of the divine outreach beyond just Christians but also *to all human beings*, who likewise are enabled to do so by the Holy Spirit: "It is by the gift of the Holy Spirit that *humanity* [*homo*], through faith, comes to contemplate and savor the mystery of God's design" (GS 15). Similarly, we read in *Ad Gentes* of the universal attraction of the Holy Spirit: "When the Holy Spirit, *who calls all women and men* to Christ and arouses in their hearts the submission [*obsequium*] of faith by the seed

---

28. *Dei Verbum* is here quoting the Council of Orange II, canon 7: Denz. 180 (377), which in turn was quoted by Vatican Council I: Denz. 1791 (3010).

of the word and the preaching of the gospel, brings those who believe in Christ to a new life through the womb of the baptismal font, he gathers them into one people of God" (AG 15).[29]

While the Holy Spirit enables faith, faith nevertheless remains a free human act. The Declaration on Religious Liberty, *Dignitatis Humanae*, states "one of the key truths in Catholic teaching" as a basic principle: "that human beings should respond to the word of God freely, and that therefore nobody is to be forced to embrace the faith against their will. The act of faith of its very nature is a free act. The human person . . . can respond [*adhaerere*] to *God's self-revelation* [*Deo sese revelanti*] only through being drawn by the Father and through submitting to God with a faith that is reasonable and free" (DH 10).[30] Consequently, Vatican II promoted religious freedom for all believers, i.e., for all who respond to God's offer of friendship. According to "the principle of religious liberty," "in religious matters every form of human coercion should be excluded" (DH 10).

Parallel to its distinction regarding revelation (as a communication of God's very Self and as a communication of divine truths), the council distinguishes two dimensions of faith's response: faith as a loving relationship ("by faith one freely commits oneself entirely to God" [DV 5]) and faith as assent to the divine truths communicated ("willingly assenting to the revelation given by God" [DV 5]). Since the time of Augustine, these primary and secondary dimensions of faith have been distinguished as *fides qua creditur* and *fides quae creditur*.[31] As noted above, at Vatican I and in the preparatory schema for Vatican II, the human response of faith was understood primarily in terms of assent to "beliefs," propositions of faith; with Vatican II, faith is presented primarily as a personal response in love to God's loving outreach, without downplaying the dimension of faith as an assent to revealed truths expressed by the church in propositions.

There are three further shifts regarding faith that parallel the council's shifts regarding revelation: (2) the response of faith to the revealing God is also a *saving* encounter; (3) faith involves not only assent, interpretation, and application of God's *words* but also active discernment, interpretation, and response to God's presence and *actions* in history; and (4) faith has *past*,

---

29. Translation corrected. On the meaning of the Latin *obsequium*, see Ladislas Örsy, *The Church Learning and Teaching* (Dublin: Dominican Publications, 1987). See also Hermann J. Pottmeyer, "Reception and Submission," *The Jurist* 51 (1991): 269–92.

30. Translation corrected.

31. See this classic distinction in Augustine, *De Trinitate* 13.2.5.

present, and *future* aspects. These will be examined below as further principles are explored. Here, however, a brief treatment of the fourth shift is
needed. In the council's vision, faith is not only a response to God's past
saving revelation but also a graced and free response to God's present saving
revelation and a hopeful expectation of the fulfillment of God's saving and
revelatory purposes at the end of time. As Gerald O'Collins notes: "When
expressing the present reality of divine revelation, [*Dei Verbum*] recalls the
matching reality of human faith. 'The obedience of faith' must be given to
God in his self-disclosure (no. 5). The living reality of faith exists now, and
so too does the divine self-revelation to which faith responds. Revelation
aims at rousing faith and remains incomplete until it does so. *This mutual
relationship with faith means that the faith that happens now entails the revelation that happens now.*"[32]

One highly significant implication of this conciliar affirmation on the
present dimension of revelation-faith is to be found in Vatican II's teaching
in *Lumen Gentium* 12 regarding the "sense of the faith" (*sensus fidei*). This
sense of the faith is a capacity accompanying the gift of faith that the Holy
Spirit bestows on each baptized individual believer and on the whole community of baptized believers.

> The holy people of God shares also in Christ's prophetic office [*de munere
> prophetico Christi participat*]. . . . The whole body of the faithful [*universitas
> fidelium*] who have received an anointing which comes from the holy one (see
> 1 Jn 2:20 and 27) cannot be mistaken in believing [*in credendo falli nequit*]. It
> shows this characteristic through the entire people's supernatural sense of the
> faith [*mediante supernaturali sensu fidei totius populi*], when, "from the bishops
> to the last of the faithful," it manifests a universal consensus in matters of faith
> and morals. By this *sensus fidei*, aroused and sustained by the Spirit of truth,
> the people of God, guided by the magisterium which it faithfully obeys, re-
> ceives not the word of human beings, but truly the word of God, "the faith
> once delivered to the saints" (Jude 3). The people unfailingly adheres to this
> faith, penetrates it more deeply through right judgment, and applies it more
> fully in daily life.

This *sensus fidei*, both in the individual (as a *sensus fidei fidelis*) and in the
whole community (as a *sensus fidei fidelium*), is a capacity to interpret present
revelation within different contexts throughout different times in history.

---

32. O'Collins, "Vatican II's Constitution on Divine Revelation," 14. Emphasis added.

Lumen Gentium 12 gives this "sense of the faith of the faithful" a high epistemological value in the reception of revelation: this Spirit-enabled gift ensures an "infallibility in believing" (*infallibilitas in credendo*). Through it, the
ongoing dialogue between God and humanity throughout history is mediated
by means of the Holy Spirit, as noted above: "Thus God, who spoke in the
past, dialogues without interruption [*sine intermissione colloquitur*] with the
spouse of his beloved Son. And the Holy Spirit, through whom the living
voice of the Gospel rings out in the church—and through it in the world—
leads believers to the full truth and makes the word of Christ dwell in them
in all its richness" (DV 8). Attending to the *sensus fidei fidelium* therefore is
demanded by the revelation/faith principle and becomes a vital element in
realizing effectively the church's mission through time and place.

While the council gives significant treatment to the individual believer's
response of faith, such faith is not isolated in any individualistic sense. Certainly, *Dei Verbum* 5's treatment of faith focuses narrowly on the *individual's*
commitment to God and assent to the content revealed, all through the grace
of the Holy Spirit.[33] When the article is read intratextually in the light of the
whole of *Dei Verbum*, however, and intertextually in the light of the other
conciliar documents, "faith" in Vatican II is always explicitly or implicitly
related to a community of faith. For Christians, the church is primarily a
community of faith, a community of believers, a community of those who
have responded positively to God's loving outreach to them in Christ through
the Spirit. The church for Vatican II, if we take its *pastoral* aim seriously, is
primarily "a communion of the faithful [*communio fidelium*]": "It is the Holy
Spirit, dwelling in those who believe and pervading and ruling over the entire
church, who brings about that wonderful communion of the faithful and
joins them together so intimately in Christ that he [the Holy Spirit] is the
principle of the church's unity" (UR 2). The church is the community of

---

33. There were some bishops who called for *Dei Verbum* 5 to make more explicit this communal dimension of faith, for example, Archbishop Franjo Šeper. AS III/3, 499. The drafting
commission passed over his suggestion, however, on the ground that it would require too
lengthy an addition. On Šeper's intervention, see Joseph M. Gile, "*Dei Verbum*: Theological
Critiques from within Vatican II, 1964–1965; A Retrieval and Analysis of the Unaccepted
Theological Critiques Raised in Response to the Schema on Revelation during the Third and
Fourth Periods of the Second Vatican Council" (Unpublished Dissertation, Gregorian University, 2004), 100.

believers who have responded in faith to God's saving revelation offered in Jesus Christ through the Holy Spirit.[34]

But the council was not only concerned with Catholic Christians, or even simply with Christians (although that ecumenical concern is a significant focus). The council's ultimate focus, because it is God's ultimate focus, is *humanity*, as encapsulated in the church/world principle to be explored below. Whatever the *fides quae* of a human believer, their *fides qua* is not to be disrespected. God's Spirit dwells in the hearts of all human beings; any individual's loving response to God is to be respected in all its sanctity, as *Gaudium et Spes* 22 affirms: "All this holds true not only for Christians but also for all people of good will in whose hearts grace is active invisibly. For since Christ died for everyone, and since all are in fact called to one and the same destiny, which is divine, we must hold that the Holy Spirit offers to all the possibility of being made partners, in a way known to God, in the paschal mystery."[35]

These fundamental theo-logical themes regarding both the nature of divine revelation and of human faith resound throughout the conciliar documents and ground the ecclesiological principles below.

34. As Giuseppe Alberigo expresses it: "The Church can plausibly be described as the communion of those who 'receive' the gospel." Giuseppe Alberigo, "The Christian Situation after Vatican II," in *The Reception of Vatican II*, ed. Giuseppe Alberigo, Jean Pierre Jossua, and Joseph A. Komonchak (Washington, DC: The Catholic University of America Press, 1987), 1–24, at 3. See also John Zizioulas, "The Theological Problem of 'Reception,'" *Centro Pro Unione Bulletin* 26 (1984): 3–6.

35. This passage cites *Lumen Gentium* 16 and Rom 8:32.

Principle 8

Christological/Pneumatological

Principle 8: Jesus Christ is the incarnation in human history of God the Father's loving and saving self-communication to humanity through the Holy Spirit; this divine self-gift is only ever received and appropriated by human beings because of the presence and activity of the Holy Spirit throughout history in the church and in the world.

The centrality of this christological/pneumatological principle is confirmed by the trinitarian vision the council presents regarding the nature of revelation, the divine plan of salvation, and the church.[1] The word *trinitas* can be found six times throughout the whole corpus of Vatican II's documents. These references occur, however, in only two of those texts, each published on the same day toward the end of the third session—in *Lumen Gentium* (three times) and in *Unitatis Redintegratio* (three times).[2] The adjective *trinus* appears four times, likewise in these two documents—twice in the former, and twice in the latter.[3] As Bertrand de Margerie notes, these

---

1. On the theme of Trinity in the council documents, see, for example, Michel Philipon, "La Santissima Trinità e la Chiesa," in *La Chiesa del Vaticano II: Studi e commenti intorno alla Costituzione dommatica 'Lumen Gentium'*, ed. Guilherme Baraúna (Firenze: Vallecchi Editore, 1965), 329–50; Nereo Silanes, "Panorámica Trinitaria del Concilio," *Estudios Trinitarios* 1 (1967): 7–44; Nereo Silanes, "Trinidad y Revelación en la Constitución Dei Verbum," *Estudios Trinitarios* 17 (1983): 143–214; Anne Hunt, "The Trinitarian Depths of Vatican II," *Theological Studies* 74 (2013): 3–19.

2. LG 47, 51, 69; UR 2, 14, 15. See Delhaye, Guéret, and Tombeur, *Concilium Vaticanum II: Concordance*, 669. *Lumen Gentium* 47, in the chapter on religious, speaks of "the increase of the holiness of the church, to the greater glory of the one and undivided Trinity, which in Christ and through Christ is the source and origin of all holiness." Remarkably, there is no explicit reference here to the Holy Spirit.

3. LG 49, 50; UR 1, 12. See ibid., 669. In UR 12, once again, Christ is mentioned in relationship to the triune God, without concomitant reference to the Holy Spirit: "Before the whole

trinitarian emphases of Vatican II are "essentially economic. In contrast to Nicaea I, to Constantinople I and II, to Lyons and to Florence, Vatican II gave hardly any direct or explicit attention (rare allusions excepted!), to the mystery of the processions and of the intra-divine relations, but rather embraced it in implicit fashion by way of investigating the mysterious sending of the Son and of the Spirit, which presupposes these processions and is the foundation for all renewed ecclesiology."[4] One of those rare allusions to the immanent Trinity is found in *Ad Gentes* 2, with a remarkable formulation that follows the Eastern, rather than Western, theology of the immanent Trinity: God the Father is "the principle without principle from whom the Son is generated and from whom the Holy Spirit proceeds through the Son [*per Filium procedit*]."

This trinitarian focus is evident also structurally, in what have been called "the two fundamental texts of Vatican II about Trinitarian ecclesiology . . . [the council's] great Trinitarian and ecclesiological frescoes."[5] Articles 2, 3, and 4 of both *Lumen Gentium* and *Ad Gentes* parallel one another in their attention to God the Father (2), Jesus Christ (3), and the Holy Spirit (4), the latter document building on and supplementing the former theologically.[6] The very last word in the Latin text of *Lumen Gentium* is *Trinitatis*: "one people of God, for the glory of the most holy and undivided Trinity" (LG 69). *Ad Gentes* likewise ends with a trinitarian formulation: "that the glory of God, which shines in the face of Jesus Christ, might shed its light on all women and men through the Holy Spirit" (AG 42).

---

world let all Christians confess their faith in God, one and three, in the incarnate Son of God, our Redeemer and Lord."

4. Bertrand de Margerie, "The Trinitarian Doctrine of Vatican II," in *The Christian Trinity in History* (Still River, MA: St. Bede's Publications, 1982), 223–45, at 223. On the distinction between the "economic" and "immanent" Trinity, see Karl Rahner, *The Trinity* (New York: Herder and Herder, 1970).

5. De Margerie, "The Trinitarian Doctrine of Vatican II," 224–25.

6. As de Margerie notes, "It seems that the decree *Ad Gentes* on the Missions intended to complete, on the Trinitarian level, the fresco of *Lumen Gentium* [2–4]! A careful comparison of these two prologues would bring out many details which point in this direction; let us only note in passing a theology that is very conscious of the appropriation of the creative action to the Father, the supreme principle in the universe as in the divinity: 'This design (of God the Father) flows from the love-source (*ex fontali amore*) or charity of God the Father, who, being the Principle without Principle, from whom the Son is generated, from whom the Holy Spirit proceeds through the Son, has freely created us in his surpassingly great goodness and mercy' (AG 2)." Ibid., 226.

The origin of the church lies in the salvific plan of God the Father and the missions of the Son and Spirit. In language deliberately echoing the classical language regarding the divine processions, the church is said to proceed from the Father: "Proceeding [*procedens*] from the love of the eternal Father, the church was founded by Christ in time and gathered into one by the Holy Spirit" (GS 40). Furthermore, the church finds its outward thrust in the missions of the second and third Persons: "The church on earth is by its very nature missionary since, according to the plan of the Father, it has its origin in the mission of the Son and the Holy Spirit" (AG 2). In particular, the Holy Spirit has a special role: "For the church is driven by the Holy Spirit to play its part in bringing to completion the plan of God, who has constituted Christ as the source of salvation for the whole world" (LG 17).

The church is called to mirror the unity of the divine persons. *Lumen Gentium* 4 quotes St. Cyprian: "the universal church is seen to be 'a people made one by the unity of the Father, the Son and the Holy Spirit'" (LG 4).[7] According to Bernhard Nitsche, this trinitarian formulation in *Lumen Gentium* is later "received and deepened"[8] in *Unitatis Redintegratio* 2, where "the dynamic community of life in the triune God is now expressly presented as archetype of the church and the church as icon":[9] "This is the sacred mystery of the unity of the church, in Christ and through Christ, with the Holy Spirit energizing its various functions. The highest exemplar and source [*exemplar et principium*] of this mystery is the unity, in the Trinity of persons, of one God, the Father and the Son in the Holy Spirit" (UR 2).

Thus the church is presented as the People of God the Father, the Body of Christ the Son, and the Temple of the Holy Spirit. The very last sentence of *Lumen Gentium*'s second chapter implies that the chapter's particular focus on the "People of God (the Father)" motif is to be understood not in an exclusive but in a trinitarian way: "Thus the church both prays and works so that the fullness of the whole world may move into *the people of God, the body of Christ* and *the temple of the Holy Spirit*, and that in Christ, the head of all things, all honor and glory may be rendered to the Creator, the Father of the universe" (LG 17). This formulation is repeated in *Presbyterorum Ordinis* 1: "the People of God, the Body of Christ, and the Temple of the Holy

7. Quoting St. Cyprian, *De Orat. Dom.* 23: PL 4:553.
8. Bernhard Nitsche, "Geistvergessenheit und die Wiederentdeckung des Heiligen Geistes im Zweiten Vatikanischen Konzil," in *Atem des sprechenden Gottes: Einführung in die Lehre vom Heiligen Geist*, ed. Bernhard Nitsche (Regensburg: Pustet, 2003), 102–44, at 120.
9. Ibid., 120.

Spirit." Likewise, *Ad Gentes* 7 refers to "one People of God . . . one Body of Christ . . . one temple of the Holy Spirit."

Therefore, when viewed across all documents, the council's teaching on God's self-manifestation in history is trinitarian. As noted in the previous principle, the formula "to the Father through the Son in the Holy Spirit" echoes nine times.[10] For example, in *Unitatis Redintegratio*, when discussing the eucharistic ecclesiology of the Eastern churches, the trinitarian nature and goal of the church is highlighted: "In this [eucharistic] mystery the faithful, united with their bishops, have access to God the Father through the Son, the Word made flesh who suffered and was glorified, in the outpouring of the Holy Spirit. And so, made 'sharers of the divine nature' (2 Pt 1:4), they enter into communion [*communionem*] with the most Holy Trinity" (UR 15). As will be explored below, this *communio* of the church with the Trinity forms the foundation and model of the church as a *communio fidelium* (a communion of the faithful), a *communio ecclesiarum* (a communion of local churches), and *communio hierarchica* (communion among the bishops as a college, with and under the bishop of Rome).

But how consistent in all instances is the council in presenting a vision of the church that is faithful to the equality of all divine persons within the Trinity and in the economy of salvation?

Christocentrism—or Christomonism?

On September 29, 1963, a few months after his election as pope, Paul VI addressed the council at the opening of its second session; Yves Congar would later write, "I can still hear the enthusiastic tone and deep faith."[11] The new pope movingly addressed his predecessor, John XXIII, in the second person and embraced his primary pastoral aim in calling the council. After posing to the assembled bishops three rhetorical questions—regarding what should be the starting point, the path to follow, and the goal of the council—Paul VI proclaimed:

> These three very simple and at the same time very important questions have, as we well know, only one answer, namely that here and at this very hour we

---

10. SC 6; LG 4, 28, 51; UR 15; DV 2; OT 8; PO 6; AG 7. See Congar, "Die christologischen und pneumatologischen Implikationen," 122. The prepositions regarding Christ and the Spirit in the trinitarian formula vary: sometimes "through Christ in the Holy Spirit [*per Christum in Spiritu sancto*]," and others "in Christ through the Holy Spirit [*in Christo per Spiritum sanctum*]."

11. Ibid., 114.

should proclaim Christ to ourselves and to the world around us; Christ our beginning, Christ our life and our guide, Christ our hope and our end. . . . Let no other light be shed on this council, but Christ the light of the world! Let no other truth be of interest to our minds, but the words of the Lord, our only master! Let no other aspiration guide us, but the desire to be absolutely faithful to Him! Let no other hope sustain us, but the one that, through the mediation of His word, strengthens our pitiful weakness: "And behold I am with you all days, even unto the consummation of the world."[12]

"The main objectives of this council," the pope continued, presuppose this resolute focus on the church's founder. These objectives he outlined "in four points: (1) the knowledge, or—if you prefer—the awareness of the Church; (2) its reform; (3) the bringing together of all Christians in unity; (4) the dialogue of the Church with the contemporary world."[13] In other words, the council's attention to the renewal and reform of the church did not mean that the council was to be self-centered but rather *Christ*-centered—what Jacques Dupuis calls the council's desire for the "de-centration" of the Church—if any genuine renewal and reform was to be realized.[14] Between the second and third sessions, in January 1964, Pope Paul went on pilgrimage to Jordan and Israel. According to the Belgian *peritus* Charles Moeller, this trip was to be of vital importance for the direction of the council: "By means of his eyes, ears, hands and feet [Paul VI] concretized the 'decentering' of the Church on herself and her 'recentering' in Christ."[15] The bishops in council went on to embrace the pastoral and christological emphases of both popes. Not counting other allusions to and names for Jesus Christ, the word *Christus* itself appears 865 times in the documents.[16]

Throughout the council, this focus on Christ was symbolized every working day. After celebration of the Eucharist at nine o'clock in the morning,

12. Paul VI, "Opening Address: Second Session," 145.

13. Ibid., 146. Enumeration added.

14. "This '*de-centration*' of the Church is more fundamental for a true renewal than decentralization in the Church." Jacques Dupuis, "The Christocentrism of Vatican II," in *Jesus Christ and His Spirit: Theological Approaches* (Bangalore: Theological Publications in India, 1977), 33–58, at 35.

15. Charles Moeller, "History of *Lumen Gentium*'s Structure and Ideas," in *Vatican II: An Interfaith Appraisal*, ed. John H. Miller (Notre Dame, IN: University of Notre Dame Press, 1966), 123–52, at 140. Moeller goes on to note the title of the book by Bernard Lambert on the second session, as indicative of a major conciliar orientation: from Rome to Jerusalem. See Lambert, *De Rome à Jérusalem: Itinéraire spirituel de Vatican II*.

16. See Delhaye, Guéret, and Tombeur, *Concilium Vaticanum II: Concordance*, 93–102.

each session would begin with a ceremony: a Book of the Gospels was "enthroned" on an elaborate chair before the assembled bishops.[17] The *peritus* Henri de Lubac remarked on the meaning of the ceremony:

> When Paul VI was present, he did not leave to anyone else the responsibility for doing this. This ceremony has not always been fully understood. Many have seen in it simply the homage which the Church of Vatican II desired to pay to the Bible. While this view is not entirely erroneous, it is very incomplete. . . . It does not grasp the true meaning of the rite. After having been carried in procession, the book of the gospels was not placed on a lectern, but really installed on a throne. This was because it represented Christ himself.[18]

Despite orientating itself toward Christ, the council produced no separate conciliar document on Jesus Christ. Nevertheless, its whole pastoral orientation was deliberately focused on Jesus Christ and a more lively appropriation of him by the faithful, for the sake of a more effective proclamation of him by the church to the world.

The centrality of Christ for the church echoes throughout the sixteen final documents, from the first document on the liturgy ("Through Christ, the Mediator, [Christian believers] should be drawn day by day into ever more perfect union with God and each other, so that finally God may be all in all" [SC 48]) to the very last ("The Lord is the goal of human history, the focal point of the desires of history and civilization, the center of humanity, the joy of all hearts, and the fulfillment of all aspirations" [GS 45]). The Dogmatic Constitution on the Church begins with reference, not to the church, but to Christ, *lumen gentium*: "Christ is the light of the nations and consequently this holy synod, gathered together in the Holy Spirit, ardently desires to bring to all humanity that light of Christ which is resplendent on the face of the church, by proclaiming his Gospel to every creature" (LG 1). And then, in its other constitution on the church, the council asserts: "The church is not

---

17. For a history of this ritual at ecumenical councils, and photos of the codex used at Vatican II (the so-called "Urbinate Latin 10," from the time of Federico di Montefeltro, Duke of Urbino), as well as photos of the chair used at Vatican II, see Romeo De Maio, *The Book of the Gospels at the Oecumenical Councils* (Rome: Biblioteca Apostolica Vaticana, 1963). De Maio records: "At every General Congregation, after the celebration of Mass, each of the six Secretaries to the Council enthroned the Gospels after carrying them in procession through part of the Council hall, while the Fathers remained standing and sang liturgical antiphonies. After the first few days it was laid down that the ceremony of the enthronement should not be reserved to the Secretariat, but that the Bishops should also participate, as in fact they did." Ibid., 20.

18. Quoted in Theobald, "The Church under the Word of God," 354.

motivated by earthly ambition but is interested in one thing only—to carry on the work of Christ under the guidance of the Holy Spirit" (GS 3).

In his opening address in 1963, Paul VI seldom referred to the Holy Spirit. Nevertheless, he does state that "the council is striving . . . to enhance in the Church that beauty of perfection and holiness which imitation of Christ and mystical union with him in the Holy Spirit can alone offer."[19] Furthermore, he believed that throughout the rest of the council "we shall rejoice in the unfailing grace of the Holy Spirit, who is present, vivifying, teaching, strengthening."[20] The council, he continued, should therefore be marked "by docility to the interior illumination of the Holy Spirit"[21] (he himself had earlier that morning, after processing into St. Peter's, intoned before the main altar the *Veni Creator Spiritus*, alternating the verses with the bishops).[22] In the view of Joseph Ratzinger, the pope's christological emphasis in his opening address did not intend to deliberately downplay the Holy Spirit: "[Paul VI] saw the coming of the Spirit to Christ's disciples at Pentecost as an antetype of the Church. Thus the *christological* and *Holy Spirit-centered* elements were given preeminence by [Pope] Paul in the definition of the Church."[23] Certainly in his opening addresses for the third and fourth sessions, Pope Paul gave much more explicit attention to the Holy Spirit, indeed somewhat lyrically: "The Spirit is here, not yet to confirm with sacramental grace the work which all of us, united in the council, are bringing to completion, but rather to illuminate and guide our labors to the benefit of the Church and all mankind. The Spirit is here. We call upon Him, wait for Him, follow Him. The Spirit is here. Let us reflect on this doctrine and this present reality so that, above all, we may realize once more and in the fullest and most sublime degree possible our communion with the living Christ. It is the Spirit who joins us to Him."[24]

---

19. Paul VI, "Opening Address: Second Session," 147.

20. Ibid., 144.

21. Ibid., 146.

22. Yves Congar recalls: "Paul VI intoned the *Veni Creator*. The Church found its voice once more, a voice of great waters, to implore. When the Pope then alternated the verses with the choir of bishops, it was Peter who was praying with the Twelve. It was no longer the sixteenth century temporal prince." Yves Congar, *My Journal of the Council* (Collegeville, MN: Liturgical Press, 2012), 318.

23. Ratzinger, *Theological Highlights of Vatican II*, 68. Emphasis added.

24. Pope Paul VI, "Opening Address: Third Session," in *Council Daybook, Vatican II: Session 3*, ed. Floyd Anderson (Washington, DC: National Catholic Welfare Conference, 1965), 6–10, at 7. For Pope Paul VI's references to the Holy Spirit at the opening of the fourth session, see Pope Paul VI, "Opening Address: Fourth Session," in *Council Daybook: Vatican II, Session 4*, ed. Floyd Anderson (Washington, DC: National Catholic Welfare Conference, 1966), 4–7, at 4.

What, then, of the balance in the council's final vision between the centrality of Christ and the indispensability of the Holy Spirit? Jacques Dupuis believes that "the Church of Vatican II must in all humility admit its partial failure to do full justice to the function of the Spirit."[25] A proper elucidation, therefore, of the christological/pneumatological principle in the council's vision emerges only after, first, examining the concerns arising in the debates and drafting process over four years and then, second, viewing the final corpus of its documents (each intratextually and all together intertextually). In the end, the council does indeed give clear indicators (albeit unsystematically) that, when extrapolated, *point toward and evoke* greater christological and pneumatological balance in its vision of God, of church, and of human beings in community throughout history. A synthesis of the council's vision must bring those indicators to more systematic expression.

Much has been written on the lack of references to the indispensable role of the Holy Spirit in the draft schemas prepared by the preconciliar preparatory commissions and on the progressive sensitivity and consequent development in the bishops' pneumatological thinking throughout the drafting of the documents.[26] Adolf Laminski refers to "the discovery of the

---

25. Dupuis, "Western Christocentrism and Eastern Pneumatology," 25.

26. On the diachronic development over the four years evident in the drafting processes across several documents, see Henri Cazelles, "Le Saint-Esprit dans les textes de Vatican II," in *Le Mystère de l'Esprit Saint*, ed. Henri Cazelles, et al. (Tours: Mame, 1968), 161–86; Adolf Laminski, "Die Entdeckung der pneumatologischen Dimension der Kirche durch das Konzil und ihre Bedeutung," in *Sapienter ordinare: Festgabe für Erich Kleineidam*, ed. Fritz Hoffmann, Konrad Feiereis, and Leo Scheffczyk (Leipzig: St. Benno, 1969), 392–405; Congar, "Die christologischen und pneumatologischen Implikationen"; Nereo Silanes, "El Espiritu Santo y la Iglesia en el Concilio Vaticano II," in *Credo in Spiritum Sanctum: Atti del Congresso Teologico Internazionale di Pneumatologia* (Città del Vaticano: Libreria Editrice Vaticana, 1983), 2:1011–24; Yves Congar, "The Pneumatology of Vatican II," in *I Believe in the Holy Spirit*, vol. 1: *The Holy Spirit in the "Economy": Revelation and Experience of the Spirit* (New York: Crossroad, 1997), 167–73; Nitsche, "Geistvergessenheit und die Wiederentdeckung." On the developing pneumatological accents throughout the drafting of *Lumen Gentium*, see André Marie Charue, "Le Saint-Esprit dans *Lumen Gentium*," *Ephemerides Theologicae Lovanienses* 45 (1969): 359–79. On the development throughout the drafting of both *Lumen Gentium* and *Gaudium et Spes*, see Sally Vance-Trembath, *The Pneumatology of Vatican II: With Particular Reference to Lumen Gentium and Gaudium et Spes* (Saarbrücken: Lambert Academic Publishing, 2010). For a systematic presentation of the council's teaching on the Holy Spirit across all documents, see Heribert Schützeichel, "Die unbegrenzte Wirkkraft des Heiligen Geistes in der Sicht des II. Vatikanischen Konzils," *Theologische Zeitschrift* 108, no. 2 (1999): 108–22. For a summary in English of the latter, see Heribert Schützeichel, "The Holy Spirit according to Vatican II," *Theology Digest* 48, no. 2 (2001): 140–42. See also the more general comments of Mary Cecily

pneumatological dimension of the church by the council."[27] Highly significant in stimulating that development of the mind of the council was the presence and criticisms of official observers from other Christian churches, especially Eastern Orthodox, as well as the important interventions of bishops from Eastern churches within the Roman Catholic communion. A key issue for them was not so much any lack of affirmation by the council of the Holy Spirit's equality within the eternal inner life of God (the so-called immanent Trinity) but rather the lack of "a theology of [the Spirit's] role in the present stage of the economy of salvation"[28] (the so-called economic Trinity). Several commentators on the council's pneumatological development have acknowledged the assembly's initial Latin-Western approach to Christology and pneumatology. For example, Yves Congar notes: "During the Second Vatican Council . . . the Orthodox, Protestant and Anglican 'observers' frequently criticized the texts that were discussed for their lack of pneumatology. . . . It was certainly justified at the time."[29] Thus, as Walter Kasper observes, "the Council was reproached for Christomonism and a *one-sided*, Christocentric ecclesiology. It is true that the doctrine of the Council was Christocentric and remained within the framework of the Latin tradition of pneumatology. The council documents do, however, show that the council fathers endeavoured to break away from *a constricted and one-sided Christocentricism*, without sinking into the opposite extreme of *pure pneumatocentricism*, which is also to be excluded because, according to the scriptures, the Spirit is the Spirit of Christ."[30]

Over the four sessions, the council certainly endeavoured, to use Kasper's word, to make more explicit the role of the Holy Spirit in the Christian vision, but in the end, according to Jacques Dupuis, its development was incomplete:

> Everything seems to indicate that Vatican II has grown progressively, through its successive sessions, towards a fuller awareness of the function of the Spirit

---

Boulding, "The Doctrine of the Holy Spirit in the Documents of Vatican II," *Irish Theological Quarterly* 51 (1985): 253–67.

27. See the title of Laminski, "Die Entdeckung der pneumatologischen Dimension der Kirche durch das Konzil," 392.

28. Dupuis, "Western Christocentrism and Eastern Pneumatology," 24.

29. Congar, "The Pneumatology of Vatican II," 167.

30. Walter Kasper, "The Renewal of Pneumatology in Contemporary Catholic Life and Theology: Towards a Rapprochement between East and West," in *That They May All Be One: The Call to Unity* (New York: Burns & Oates, 2004), 96–121, at 100. Emphasis added.

in the creation and life of the Church; this awareness did not yet reach its perfect expression in the Council documents. However, while the Constitution on the Sacred Liturgy—the first fruits of the conciliar labour—remains in this regard the most defective, the last conciliar document, the Pastoral Constitution on the Church in the Modern World (*Gaudium et Spes*), appears vividly aware of the all-pervasive action of the Spirit in the Church's life and activity.[31]

Even a later document such as *Dei Verbum* (developed over the four sessions and finally promulgated just a few weeks before *Gaudium et Spes*) exhibits this pneumatological lack, as Gerald O'Collins observes:

> *Dei Verbum* refers twenty-three times to the Holy Spirit. Nevertheless, the document remains very christocentric. Despite the statistics, it illustrates a Latin [Western] tendency to subordinate the work of the Spirit to that of the Son. The chapter on the Old Testament (DV 14–16), for example, is oriented toward Christ but says nothing about the Holy Spirit. On October 5, 1964, during a debate on the revised text of *De Divina Revelatione* that was to become *Dei Verbum*, an eastern archbishop, Néophytos Edelby, in a remarkable speech indicated the need to recognize more fully the role of the Spirit in revelation and its transmission through scripture and tradition. . . . Unfortunately Edelby's intervention came too late and hardly affected the final shape of *Dei Verbum*.[32]

Likewise, as Adrian Hastings notes, early drafts of *Perfectae Caritatis*, the document on the renewal of religious life (promulgated on October 28, 1965), totally ignore the Spirit's role in the spiritual life of religious: "The draft of 1963, and for that matter the two drafts of 1964, have not between them one single reference to the Holy Spirit from beginning to end! The few references in the final text are all 1965 insertions. In fact the image of religious life presented by these first drafts was clearly one of law, rather than one of the spirit."[33]

Nevertheless, despite passages open to a Christomonist interpretation and although the synthesis of an adequately balanced Christology and Pneumatology cannot be found consistently across the final documents, there are, across the conciliar corpus, *markers of a conciliar direction toward a synthesis*

31. Dupuis, "Western Christocentrism and Eastern Pneumatology," 27.

32. O'Collins, *Retrieving Fundamental Theology*, 56. For the Latin text of the speech by Archbishop Edelby, see AS III/3, 306–8. For an English translation and commentary on Edelby's speech, see ibid., 174–77. Archbishop Edelby was an Eastern prelate of the Melchite Rite and the archbishop of Edessa.

33. Adrian Hastings, *A Concise Guide to the Documents of the Second Vatican Council*, vol. 2 (London: Darton Longman & Todd, 1969), 2:189–90.

evident in (1) the consensus emerging throughout the debates and (2) in the final council documents, when interpreted intertextually. To use once again the image of Gustave Thils, there was emerging in those debates a deliberate "trajectory" toward a more balanced Christology and Pneumatology, which a comprehensive interpretation of the whole conciliar corpus needs to highlight and realize.[34] Just as the trinitarian dimensions of the conciliar vision became more explicit over the four years, so too the council's christological focus was more and more balanced by a pneumatological focus.

Thus, there is a tension and a challenge in the council's christological/ pneumatological principle. In accord with its *pastoral* aim—"to impart an ever-increasing vigor to the Christian lives of the faithful" (SC 1)—the council's final vision could indeed be described as Christ-centred ("Christocentric"), without, however, being "Christomonist." Indeed, the fifth chapter of *Lumen Gentium* on the universal call to holiness has eight references to the Holy Spirit as the one who effects holiness in the lives of the faithful. And indeed it describes in trinitarian terms the one holiness to which all are called: "The forms and tasks of life are many but there is one holiness, which is cultivated by all who are led by God's Spirit and, obeying the Father's voice and adoring God the Father in spirit and in truth, follow Christ, poor and humble in carrying his cross, that they deserve to be sharers in his glory" (LG 41). Thus, throughout the documents we find statements affirming the centrality of Christ that are—at times—balanced by statements affirming the necessary mediating role of the Holy Spirit, if indeed Christ is to be appropriated into the lives of the faithful. For example: "The church believes that Christ, who died and was raised for the sake of all, can show people the way and strengthen them through the Spirit so that they become worthy of their destiny; nor is there given any other name under heaven by which they can be saved. The church likewise believes that the key, the center and the purpose of the whole of human history is to be found in its Lord and Master" (GS 10). Similarly, for example, it is stated: "Christ is now at work in human hearts *by the power of his Spirit*" (GS 38).

"Christocentrism" is a term that names "a systematic focusing of all theology and devotional life on the person and work of Jesus Christ."[35] "Christomonism" is a term that names the accusation regarding any christological

---

34. See Thils, ". . . en pleine fidélité au Concile du Vatican II," 278. This important hermeneutical principle regarding the "trajectory" of the council's thinking guides the proposals throughout Vance-Trembath, *The Pneumatology of Vatican II*, 204.

35. Gerald O'Collins and Edward G. Farrugia, *A Concise Dictionary of Theology*, 3rd ed. (New York: Paulist Press, 2013), 41.

assertion that purportedly subordinates the role of the Holy Spirit in the economy of salvation to that of the Son. Certainly, following Paul VI's injunction at the opening of the second session, the ecclesiological program embraced by the conciliar assembly was indeed Christocentric; the council centred its program not so much on the church itself but rather on its founder Jesus Christ and the church's mission to proclaim him as Savior of the world. Calls to renewal and reform in the church based on greater fidelity to Christ pervade the sixteen documents: "Without claiming that the whole Council—which is so rich in its doctrine that it defies any rapid synthesis—revolves round one single idea, Christocentrism is undoubtedly one of its characteristic features."[36]

The *peritus* Yves Congar concedes the usefulness of the term "christocentrism," if it is understood properly (as implying the concomitant mission of the Spirit), but rejects the term "pneumatocentricism" (if it is meant to refer to the mission of the Spirit disconnected from the mission of the Word). Accordingly, he states: "one cannot accuse *Lumen Gentium* of 'christomonism.' Christocentrism perhaps, if this term has any meaning. Vatican II is as christocentric as St Paul, nothing else."[37] Thus, Congar does not see in Vatican II a "christocentrism" in opposition to a "pneumatocentrism," or vice versa: "The Council preserved the Christological reference which is fundamentally biblical and the essential condition for the soundness of any pneumatology. The pneumatology of the Council is not [one-sidedly] pneumatocentric. It stresses that the Spirit is the Spirit of Christ; he carries out the work of Christ and builds up the Body of Christ. Again and again, the Holy Spirit is called the principle of the life of that Body, which is the Church."[38]

In other words, according to the trajectory apparent in the debates and drafting process, and evident in the final corpus, the elements of the tradition are reaffirmed: the missions of the Word and the Spirit in the economy of salvation are seen to presuppose each other and complement one another; the Spirit is the Spirit of Christ, and Christ's revealing and saving work is effective through the Holy Spirit. The ecclesiological implications of those elements of the tradition are realized in a deeper way, through the "rediscovery" by the council of the pneumatological dimension in the church, a discovery, however, that marked a beginning rather than an end point.[39] In this way, Vatican II is, yet again, "a building site" requiring further work, as

36. Dupuis, "The Christocentrism of Vatican II," 35.
37. Congar, "Die christologischen und pneumatologischen Implikationen," 112.
38. Congar, "The Pneumatology of Vatican II," 167–68.
39. See Nitsche, "Geistvergessenheit und die Wiederentdeckung."

Hermann Pottmeyer described the council.[40] The conciliar trajectory bequeaths to its receivers the task of synthesis.

Throughout this book, the christological and pneumatological accents of the council's vision, balanced or otherwise, will continue to be highlighted. At this stage, however, some prominent elements can be noted regarding Vatican II's teaching, first on Jesus Christ and then on the Holy Spirit. Regarding the role of Jesus Christ in the *present* life of the church, there is one particular conciliar rubric, which highlights the council's christocentric accent: the rubric of "the paschal mystery." It is linked in the documents to another key pastoral notion of the council, that of "participation."

Participating in the Paschal Mystery

The reception by the council of the "the paschal mystery" rubric is yet one more example of Vatican II's endorsement and appropriation of much preconciliar *ressourcement* scholarship. Particularly relevant here was the work of the liturgist Dom Odo Casel (1886–1948), a member of the "school" of Maria Laach, a Benedictine Abbey in Germany, which had been an important center of the liturgical reform movement.[41] Exploring the notion of *mysterion* (mystery) in St. Paul and early patristic writings and examining the dynamics of ancient mystery cults as a heuristic lens for understanding Christian liturgy,[42] Casel had "seized on the idea of mystery as key to how human participation in the liturgy works, even now,"[43] and applied it to Jesus' passion, death, and resurrection—just as Christ "passed over" from death to life in his death, resurrection, and glorification, so the Christian assembly is

---

40. "Here again, Vatican II has left us only with a building site." Hermann J. Pottmeyer, *Towards a Papacy in Communion: Perspectives from Vatican Councils I & II* (New York: Crossroad, 1998), 128.

41. For an analysis of Casel's key themes and their echo in chapter 1 of *Sacrosanctum Concilium*, see Burkhard Neunheuser, "Odo Casel in Retrospect and Prospect," *Worship* 50 (1976): 489–503. For an overview of Casel's theology of the paschal mystery, see Theresa F. Koernke, "Mystery Theology," in *The New Dictionary of Sacramental Worship*, ed. Peter E. Fink (Collegeville, MN: Liturgical Press, 1990), 883–91. For analysis and critique of Casel's theology of the paschal mystery, see also Irénée Henri Dalmais, "Theology of the Liturgical Celebration," in *The Church at Prayer: An Introduction to the Liturgy*, vol. 1: *Principles of the Liturgy*, ed. Aimé Georges Martimort, new ed. (Collegeville, MN: Liturgical Press, 1985), 227–80, at 266–72.

42. For a collection in English of some of his key writings on the theme, see Odo Casel, *The Mystery of Christian Worship, and Other Writings*, ed. Burkhard Neunheuser (Westminster, MD: Newman Press, 1962).

43. Rita Ferrone, *Liturgy: Sacrosanctum Concilium*, Rediscovering Vatican II (New York: Paulist Press, 2007), 23.

enabled in the liturgy to "pass over" from a life of sin to a life of grace and transformation.

The works of two other scholars also had made an impact in the decades before the council. In 1945, the French theologian Louis Bouyer published an examination of the ceremonies of the Easter Triduum, with the notion of the paschal mystery as the central theme.[44] Within biblical scholarship, a key related work was the 1954 study on the resurrection by the French biblical scholar François-Xavier Durrwell.[45] His book marked a deliberate shift away from the dominant soteriology of previous centuries, which focused exclusively on the passion and death of Jesus Christ as effecting human salvation. "The plain truth," Durrwell wrote in 1954, "is that the average theology of the Redemption is truncated and its intelligibility maimed. The basic reason is the omission of the Resurrection. The resurrection of Christ is essential in the mystery of salvation . . . a theology of redemption that pays exclusive attention to Christ's death is necessarily unbalanced and impoverished."[46] Durrwell regularly throughout the book refers to "the mystery of salvation" in terms of "the Paschal Mystery" and "the Easter Mystery" and of the resurrection as involving "the outpouring of the Holy Spirit."[47]

Therefore, the employment in *Sacrosanctum Concilium* of the rubric of "the paschal mystery" in a prominent way marked a major shift in the Catholic Church's official theology of salvation, as well as in the Catholic theology of the sacraments, particularly the Eucharist. As John O'Malley observes: "In chapter one [of *Sacrosanctum Concilium*] the 'mystery of Christ' [SC 2] was specified as 'the Paschal Mystery,' the mystery that began with Christ's passion *but went on to his resurrection and glorification*. With the Paschal Mystery expressed in this way as one of its themes, the text subtly shifted a mind-set among Catholics that since the Middle Ages had located the Redemption almost exclusively in Christ's suffering and death."[48] He further remarks that Vatican II "agreed with the Council of Trent that the Mass was rightly described as a sacrifice united with the sacrifice of Christ on the cross, but Vatican II went further by explicitly including the Resurrection in it, as the

---

44. Louis Bouyer, *The Paschal Mystery: Meditations on the Last Three Days of Holy Week* (Chicago: Regnery, 1950; French original 1945).

45. François-Xavier Durrwell, *The Resurrection: A Biblical Study* (New York: Sheed and Ward, 1960; French original 1954).

46. Ibid., xiii.

47. See chapter 3, "The Resurrection as Outpouring of the Holy Spirit," ibid., 78–107.

48. O'Malley, *What Happened at Vatican II*, 131. Emphasis added.

fullness of the 'Paschal Mystery'. It gave new emphasis to the Mass as a replication of the sacred banquet that was the Last Supper."[49]

During the preconciliar drafting meetings of the Preparatory Liturgy Commission in 1960, a French bishop, Henri Jenny—who before the council had himself written on the theme[50]—was the first to introduce the rubric into precouncil planning. Jenny proposed that the draft schema on the liturgy should use "the paschal mystery" as its foundation.[51] It went on to become so: "The paschal mystery is without a doubt the central theological concept of the liturgical renewal at Vatican II. . . . It is the interpretive key that unlocks the meaning of the whole reform."[52] In accord with the council's pastoral agenda, the primary purpose of the rubric is to emphasise the *present* reality of Christ's salvific work, as communicated especially through the liturgy. According to Annibale Bugnini, who was secretary to the Preparatory Liturgy Commission, the paschal mystery is "the heart of the entire liturgy. . . . Only by entering ever anew into this mystery (or, as Tertullian would say, 'immersing' itself in it) and drawing all the practical conclusions from this relationship will the world find salvation; only thus will Christian life be radically renewed."[53] Indeed, beyond its central importance in the liturgical constitution, "the paschal mystery" goes on to become, according to Angelus Häusling, a "heart-word" of the council,[54] employed beyond the liturgy constitution.

---

49. Ibid., 295.

50. Henri Jenny, *Le mystère pascal dans l'année chrétienne*, 4th rev. and augm. ed. (Paris: Equipes enseignantes, 1958). The work was published in English before the council as Henri Jenny, *The Paschal Mystery in the Christian Year*, trans. Allan Stehling and John Lundberg (Notre Dame, IN: Fides Publishers, 1962). On the tension within the subcommission on the "mystery of the liturgy" regarding the two rubrics of "incarnation" and "paschal mystery" and the eventual incorporation of both orientations within the final preparatory schema, see Joseph A. Komonchak, "The Struggle for the Council during the Preparation of Vatican II (1960–1962)," in *History of Vatican II*, vol. 1: *Announcing and Preparing Vatican Council II*, ed. Giuseppe Alberigo and Joseph A. Komonchak (Maryknoll, NY: Orbis Books, 1996), 167–356, at 206–11.

51. See Reiner Kaczynski, "Theologischer Kommentar zur Konstitution über die heilige Liturgie *Sacrosanctum Concilium*," in *Herders theologischer Kommentar zum Zweiten Vatikanischen Konzil*, ed. Peter Hünermann and Bernd Jochen Hilberath (Freiburg: Herder, 2004), 2:1–227, at 63.

52. Ferrone, *Liturgy: Sacrosanctum Concilium*, 23.

53. Annibale Bugnini, *The Reform of the Liturgy, 1948–1975* (Collegeville, MN: Liturgical Press, 1990), 40.

54. Angelus A. Häussling, "Pascha-Mysterium. Kritisches zu einem Beitrag in der dritten Auflage des Lexicon für Thelogie und Kirche," *Archiv für Liturgiewissenschaft* 41 (1999): 157–65, at 165. Quoted in Kaczynski, "Theologischer Kommentar zur Konstitution über die heilige Liturgie *Sacrosanctum Concilium*." See Massimo Faggioli, *True Reform: Liturgy and Ecclesiology in* Sacrosanctum Concilium (Collegeville, MN: Liturgical Press, 2012), 9.

As a working definition of the rubric, we can take that of the *peritus* Josef Jungmann, who understood it to be naming "the real kernel of the Christian order of salvation: the act with which Christ has redeemed us and which is continued in the activity of the Church. Like the *pascha* [Passover] of the Old Testament, it is a remembrance of God's redeeming acts of salvation, the presence of salvation and the promise of the consummating future. It underlies at the same time the basic triumphant Easter character, which is the essence of Christianity, of the work of the Church, its message and its sacraments."[55]

The precise phrase "the paschal mystery" (*mysterium paschale*) appears thirteen times, in five of the final documents: *Sacrosanctum Concilium* (eight times);[56] *Gaudium et Spes* (twice);[57] *Christus Dominus* (once);[58] *Optatam Totius* (once);[59] and *Ad Gentes* (once).[60] Moreover, it is alluded to in several other passages.[61] The second article of the liturgy constitution speaks of "the mystery of Christ" (alluding to, but not citing, Eph 3:4 and Col 4:3). "The paschal mystery" is then described as the liturgical immersion into the mystery of Christ in the present; it is above all through the liturgy that "the work of our redemption takes place" (SC 2). Article 5 goes on to state that the work of our redemption is achieved through the paschal mystery: "This work of human redemption and perfect glorification of God . . . Christ the Lord completed principally in the paschal mystery of his blessed passion, resurrection from the dead, and glorious ascension" (later, article 61 would refer to "the paschal mystery of the passion, death and resurrection of Christ"). Article 6 then states that it is through baptism that believers gain access to the salvific effects of that mystery: "Thus by baptism men and women are implanted in the paschal mystery of Christ; they die with him, are buried with him, and rise with him." Ever since the first Supper of the Lord and the day of Pentecost, the church continues to participate in the paschal mystery, especially through participation in the Eucharist: "From that time onward the church has never

---

55. Josef Andreas Jungmann, "Constitution on the Sacred Liturgy," in *Commentary on the Documents of Vatican II*, vol. 1, ed. Herbert Vorgrimler (London: Burns & Oates, 1967), 1:1–87, at 11–12.

56. SC 5, 6 (twice), 61, 104, 106, 107, and 109.

57. GS 22 (twice).

58. CD 15.

59. OT 8.

60. AG 14.

61. Examples of allusions to the phrase and Christ's redemptive work and its mediation through the sacraments, above all the Eucharist, are: SC 10, 47, 81, 102; LG 26; PO 2, 15; AG 13, 14.

failed to come together to celebrate the paschal mystery, reading those things 'which were in all the scriptures concerning him,' celebrating the Eucharist in which 'the victory and triumph of his death are again made present,' and at the same time 'giving thanks to God for his inexpressible gift' in Christ Jesus, 'in praise of his glory' through the power of the Holy Spirit" (SC 6).[62] This use of the rubric of "the paschal mystery" in the council's first document becomes programmatic for its use throughout later council documents.[63]

The role of the Holy Spirit in the council's use of "the paschal mystery" rubric is somewhat muted, but references can be found. If "the paschal mystery" and "the mystery of Christ" are overlapping terms, then *Sacrosanctum Concilium* 102 portrays a more pneumatological vision of "the work of salvation" (SC 5 and 6): "*the whole mystery of Christ* from the incarnation and nativity to the ascension, *to Pentecost and the expectation of the blessed hope of the coming of the Lord.*" This more expansive conception finds clearer expression two years later, in *Dei Verbum*, a document in which "revelation" and "salvation" are used almost synonymously, as we have seen. Here, the council presents a more comprehensive vision of the means through which Christ reveals and saves, although it does not use the precise phrase "the paschal mystery." Rather than focusing on just one element of Christ's earthly existence as achieving revelation and hence salvation—such as his passion and death and the events of Easter—*Dei Verbum* 4 delineates a vision that ties together the whole Christ event, including the sending of the Holy Spirit: "Everything to do with his presence and his manifestation of himself was involved in achieving this [revelation]: his words and works, signs and miracles, but *above all* [*praesertim*] his death and glorious resurrection from the dead, and finally his sending of the Spirit of truth. He revealed that God was with us, to deliver us from the darkness of sin and death, and to raise us up to eternal life."

When reading all these references and allusions to the paschal mystery across all documents, it is right to claim: "Clearly, the Second Vatican Council appreciated the widest parameters of meaning when referring to the Paschal Mystery. Allowing for the difference in topic and context, it is clear that the Council Fathers grew in their understanding of Paschal Mystery as the Council progressed. *Gaudium et Spes*, the last of the conciliar documents, clearly

---

62. The article is quoting four texts: Luke 24:27; Council of Trent, Session 13, October 11, 1551, Decree on the Holy Eucharist, chapter 5; 2 Cor 9:15; and Eph 1:12.

63. CD 15; OT 8; AG, allusions in 13 and 14; GS 22 (twice), 38 (in the Latin section title).

contains a much more developed theology of Paschal Mystery than does *Sacrosanctum Concilium*, which is the first of the Council documents."[64]

Related to the notion of the liturgy communicating to the faithful in the present the saving effects of Christ's redemptive work is the notion that Christ is continuously present in the church in various ways, but not without response from the faithful. Presence invites response.[65] "To accomplish so great a work [the paschal mystery] Christ is always present in his church, especially in liturgical celebrations" (SC 7). Five modes of Christ's presence in the liturgy are listed in *Sacrosanctum Concilium* 7: (1) in the person of the priest; (2) in the eucharistic species; (3) in the sacraments in general; (4) in the Word that is proclaimed; (5) in the whole assembly as it worships.[66] This work of redemption communicated in the liturgy is then described in terms of "the priestly office" (*munus sacerdotalis*) of Christ, i.e., "the sanctifying office" (*munus sanctificandi*) of Christ: "The liturgy, then, is rightly seen as an exercise of the priestly office of Jesus Christ. In the liturgy the sanctification of women and men is given expression in symbols perceptible by the senses and is carried out in ways appropriate to each of them" (SC 7). According to Piero Marini, "The foundation on which the entire conciliar Constitution [SC] rests is the understanding of the liturgy as the exercise of the priesthood of Christ and the making present of his paschal mystery through the action of the Church."[67] Christ the Priest performs the liturgy, but he does so through the action of the church, imaged here as Christ's Mystical Body: "In [the liturgy], complete and definitive public worship is performed by the mystical body of Jesus Christ, that is, by the Head and his members. From this it follows that every liturgical celebration, because it is

---

64. Jeffrey M. Kemper, "Liturgy Notes," *Liturgical Ministry* 8 (Winter 1999): 46–51, at 51.

65. This accent on the "presence" of Christ marks the work of Odo Casel.

66. On the preconciliar origins of the notion of the manifold presence of Christ in the liturgy, the development of the preparatory schema, and the history of the drafting of the constitution, see Franziskus Eisenbach, *Die Gegenwart Jesu Christi im Gottesdienst: Systematische Studien zur Liturgiekonstitution des II. Vatikanischen Konzils* (Mainz: Matthias-Grünewald-Verlag, 1982), 152–67. On article 7, see Gerald O'Collins, "Vatican II on the Liturgical Presence of Christ," in *The Second Vatican Council: Message and Meaning* (Collegeville, MN: Liturgical Press, 2014), 89–104. On the limited reception of the notion of Christ's "presence" in postconciliar theology up to the late 1990s, see Michael G. Witczak, "The Manifold Presence of Christ in the Liturgy," *Theological Studies* 59 (1998): 680–702; Gerald O'Collins, *Christology: A Biblical, Historical, and Systematic Study of Jesus* (Oxford: Oxford University Press, 1995), 306–23.

67. Piero Marini, *Serving the People of God: Remembering Sacrosanctum Concilium* (Ottawa: Novalis, 2006), 46.

an action of Christ the priest and of his body, which is the church, is a pre-eminently sacred action" (SC 7).

Also related to this notion in *Sacrosanctum Concilium*—of Christ's redemptive work in the paschal mystery becoming effective in the liturgy—is that of "participation." Before the council, the notion of participation had been a dominant motif in the calls for reform within the *ressourcement* liturgical movement and an increasing focus in papal teaching on the liturgy.[68] Therefore, already a notion familiar to many of the bishops, it was quickly appropriated into the constitution of the liturgy, where the motif resounds, like an antiphonal response, twenty-eight times throughout the final text.[69]

Since Christ "is present when the church prays and sings" (SC 7), central to the notion of participation is that the liturgy is the work of the whole assembly, not simply the priest: "every liturgical celebration [is] an action of Christ the priest and of his body, which is the church" (SC 7). Since the subject of the liturgy is Christ, present in his body the church, then all in the assembled faithful are called to be agents in the liturgical action: "It is very much the wish of the church that all the faithful should be led to take that full, conscious, and active [*plenam, consciam atque actuosam*] participation in liturgical celebrations which is demanded by the very nature of the liturgy, and to which the Christian people . . . have a right and to which they are bound by reason of their baptism" (SC 14).[70] If the subject of this participation is the liturgical assembly, then what they are participating in is "the liturgy" and, through the liturgy, "the paschal mystery" itself.

---

68. On the history of the notion within the liturgical movement and papal teaching, see Jozef Lamberts, "L'évolution de la notion de 'participation active' dans le mouvement liturgique du vingtième siècle," *La Maison-Dieu* 241 (2005): 77–120; Paul De Clerck, "La Participation Active: Perspectives Historico-Liturgiques, de Pie X à Vatican II," in *The Active Participation Revisited: La Participation Active 100 ans après Pie X et 40 ans après Vatican II* (2004), 13–31.

69. In *Sacrosanctum Concilium*, the verb *participare* appears thirteen times (SC 8, 10, 11, 17, 21, 33, 48, 53, 56, 85, 90, 106, 113); the noun *participatio* appears fifteen times (SC 12, 14 [twice in the article, and once in the section heading], 19, 26, 27, 30, 41, 50, 55, 79, 114, 121, 124). See Tom Elich, "Full, Conscious and Active Participation," in *Vatican Council II: Reforming Liturgy*, ed. Carmel Pilcher, David Orr, and Elizabeth Harrington (Hindmarsh, SA: ATF Theology, 2013), 25–42, at 25–26. For discussion of the key citations among these instances, see Armando Cuva, "La participation des fidèles à la liturgie selon la constitution *Sacrosanctum Concilium*," *La Maison-Dieu* 241 (2005): 137–49.

70. In *Sacrosanctum Concilium*, "the subject of the verb *participare* is always the liturgical assembly." Elich, "Full, Conscious and Active Participation," 26.

The words *actuosus* and *actuose* occur sixteen times in the liturgy constitution.[71] They connote "'full of activity,' 'very active or lively,' 'with zealous energy.'"[72] Throughout the constitution, a range of words accompany and amplify the meaning of *actuosus* and *actuose*; as summarized by Tom Elich: "participation is also to be full and complete (*plenus* and *plenarius*). People are to participate consciously, knowingly, intelligently, fully aware (*concius* and *scienter*). Liturgical participation is devout and conscientious (*pius*), fruitful and enriching (*fructose*), and communal (*comunitatis propria*)."[73] In other words, "Christian believers should not be there as strangers or silent spectators" (SC 48).

The constitution envisages two interrelated dimensions to active participation, "internal and external" (SC 19). The first refers to both an intelligent understanding of the rituals one is engaging in, as well as a deliberate attentiveness to and spiritual engagement with those rituals. Symbols require reception by the perceiver in order to communicate their meaning: "In order that the liturgy may be able to produce its full effects it is necessary that the faithful come to it with proper dispositions, that their minds be attuned to their voices, and that they cooperate with heavenly grace lest they receive it in vain . . . [and that they] participate fully aware of what they are doing, actively engaged in the rite and enriched by it" (SC 11).[74] *External* participation refers to any bodily activity called for by the rite: speaking, singing, listening, gesturing, moving, silently contemplating. "To develop active participation, the people should be encouraged to take part by means of acclamations, responses, psalms, antiphons, hymns, as well as by actions, gestures and bodily attitudes. And at the proper time a reverent silence should be observed" (SC 30). Of clear importance in facilitating this external participation is the council's permission for the use of vernacular language in the liturgy.[75]

Therefore, *internal participation* is more than interior dispositions, although it includes that; it refers to participation in the efficacious reality of God's loving and saving presence in the here and now, above all through the sacramental rituals of the liturgy. *External participation* is no mere exterior

71. SC 11, 14 (three times), 19, 21, 27, 30, 41, 48, 50, 79, 113, 114, 121, 124.
72. Elich, "Full, Conscious and Active Participation," 27. On what the constitution was *not* meaning to convey with the word *actuosus*, see ibid., 27.
73. Ibid.
74. Translation corrected.
75. SC 36.

performance of acts such as reciting, singing, processing, or gesturing, al-though it necessarily includes such rituals; the very rituals mediate and draw the worshiper into the divine realities they signify.

If the Eucharist, in being the action of Christ the Priest, is an action of his Body, the whole church, then the whole body of the faithful gathered in wor-ship are called to be active participants: "The church, therefore, spares no effort in trying to ensure that, when present at this mystery of faith, Christian believers should not be there as strangers or silent spectators. On the contrary, having a good grasp of it through the rites and prayers, they should take part in the sacred action, actively, fully aware, and devoutly [*sacram actionem conscie, pie et actuose participant*]. . . . Offering the immaculate victim, not only through the hands of the priest but also *together with him* [*sed etiam una cum ipso offerentes*], they should learn to offer themselves" (SC 48). As the council *peritus* Josef Jungmann notes regarding the drafting of this passage: "The faithful are called rather to active participation, indeed to offer the sac-rifice with the priest and not merely 'through him' as some had desired. *With-out using the word 'common priesthood', this was in fact what was stressed here with the greatest vigour.* . . . The participation called for in many other pas-sages of the Constitution has here been described more precisely. As many of the Council Fathers had strongly emphasized, it should above all be an interior participation, that is, a conscious participation elevating the heart and soul, which also expresses itself in—and is aided by—the exterior rite."[76]

There is no more important element in the council's vision for pastoral renewal and reform of the church than this notion of participation in the mystery of salvation, in a special way through the liturgy, the summit and source of the Christian life (SC 10; LG 11). *From its central place initially in the council's first document, the motif of "participation" then expands through-out the life of the council to become a key element in the council's whole vision*

76. Jungmann, "Constitution on the Sacred Liturgy," 34–35. Emphasis added. Jungmann goes on to highlight that "of far reaching importance" for assuring the integrated notion of internal and external "participation" in this passage was a proposal by Cardinal Augustin Bea: "The text of the schema had [originally] only required that the faithful should 'understand the rites and prayers well.' The Cardinal emphasized that this was not adequate and that the faith-ful should rather understand *the mystery itself* through the prayers and rites." Ibid., 35. Em-phasis added. This *participation in the very mystery itself and the consequent connatural knowledge of the mystery* will later be central to the council's teaching in *Lumen Gentium* 12 on the participation by all the faithful in the prophetic office of Christ, through the Spirit's gift to them of a supernatural *sensus fidei*. It also forms the background of the role of the faithful's *sensus fidei* in the "living tradition" (*Dei Verbum* 8).

of pastoral renewal and reform through involvement of all the faithful in the church's mission: liturgical participation in the mystery of faith both empowers and authorizes all believers to participate in the life and mission of the church at all levels. This trajectory begins with the liturgical constitution.

Participation through the Spirit

We have already seen how commentators, in a *diachronic* reading of the council debates (following a hermeneutics of the authors), trace a development in the mind of the council over the four years—toward a greater emphasis given to the role of the Holy Spirit in the economy of salvation. What of the council's teaching in the final documents regarding the Holy Spirit? A diachronic reading of the conciliar debates now needs to inform (and itself be complemented by) a *synchronic* reading of the whole corpus of final documents (following a hermeneutics of the texts), noting in particular the various articulations of the council's developing mind at its different stages, as embedded alongside each other in the final texts.

Heeding the advice of Yves Congar: "It would be tedious to go through every document and every conciliar discussion in search of references to the Holy Spirit. There are at least 258 of them in the conciliar texts! An enumeration of them would not, however, be sufficient as a basis for a pneumatology."[77] The conciliar documents were never intended as systematic presentations. Even so, as Congar states elsewhere, "The balance-sheets concerning Vatican II's pneumatology are still unsatisfactory."[78]

Nevertheless, in reviewing those 258 references, a number of scholars have attempted to systematize the council's teaching on the Holy Spirit. The following three commentators propose different but overlapping categorizations. Henri Cazelles gathers the references under six domains of the Spirit's activity: in the history of humanity; in the history of salvation; in the people of God, leading it to true communion; in the church, its religious, its hierarchy, its sacraments, and Mary; in divine revelation; and ("summarizing everything") in the Trinity.[79] Georges Chantraine attempts a similar systematization, but using different headings: the mystery of the church, the sacrament of the church, apostolicity and catholicity, holiness, Mary and the

77. Congar, "The Pneumatology of Vatican II," 167.

78. Yves Congar, "Renewed Actuality of the Holy Spirit," *Lumen Vitae: International Review of Religious Education* 28, no. 1 (1973): 13–30, at 20n17.

79. See the six sections of Cazelles, "Le Saint-Esprit dans les textes de Vatican II." For the quotation, see ibid., 163.

church.[80] He then goes on to explore some specific issues needing further development: the church and Mary, charisms and hierarchy, the spiritual sense of Scripture, and the liturgy.[81] Heribert Schützeichel summarizes the conciliar references under fourteen sections. The Holy Spirit, he sees stated in the documents, was sent at Pentecost, sanctifies the church, is the Spirit of Life, dwells in the church and in the hearts of believers, prays in the hearts of believers, bears witness to the adoption of the baptized as children of God, leads the church into all truth, unites the church in community (*communio*) and service, equips and guides the church with various hierarchical and charismatic gifts, graces the church with his fruits, rejuvenates the church by the Gospel, renews the church, leads the church to full unification with her bridegroom, and, finally, says with the church to Christ: Come![82] In his conclusion, Schützeichel argues that, with these affirmations, Vatican II was developing "a fourfold pneumatology": a pneumatology of revelation, an ecclesiological pneumatology, a liturgical pneumatology, and an anthropological pneumatology.[83] Unfortunately, he does not go on to explore these in any detail with reference to his previous analytical categories.

As well as these scholars exploring the pneumatology to be found across all the documents, other authors have focused specifically on the pneumatology of particular documents. For example, in summarizing the pneumatology to be found specifically in *Lumen Gentium*, the Belgian bishop André-Marie Charue—with the insight of having been a member of the conciliar Doctrinal Commission from the very first session—after examining the pneumatological development throughout the drafting of the text, gathers the constitution's teaching on the Holy Spirit under eight headings: its connection with the dogma of the Trinity, the plan of the economy of salvation, the analogy between the church and the incarnation, the Spirit's role in the church as a sacrament, the two periods in the history of salvation, the importance of Pentecost, eschatological perspectives, and, finally, Christ and the other Paraclete.[84]

---

80. Georges Chantraine, "L'Enseignement du Vatican II concernant l'Esprit Saint," in *Credo in Spiritum Sanctum: Atti del Congresso Teologico Internazionale di Pneumatologia* (Città del Vaticano: Libreria Editrice Vaticana, 1983), 2:993–1010, at 993–1004.

81. Ibid., 1004–10.

82. See the fourteen sections of Schützeichel, "Die unbegrenzte Wirkkraft des Heiligen Geistes." The English abstract of the German original reduces the headings to four: (the Holy Spirit) is present in prayer and in believers; unifies believers; renews the church; and effects unity between Christ and the church. See Schützeichel, "The Holy Spirit according to Vatican II."

83. See Schützeichel, "Die unbegrenzte Wirkkraft des Heiligen Geistes," 121–22.

84. Charue, "Le Saint-Esprit dans *Lumen Gentium*," 369–74.

Throughout the rest of this book, the council's teaching regarding the role of the Holy Spirit in many of these areas will be highlighted in greater detail. It is sufficient at this stage to present a brief and schematic synthesis of the council's pneumatology, using Heribert Schützeichel's reading of "a fourfold pneumatology" in the council's teaching. Schützeichel provides a useful, albeit undeveloped, heuristic framework for bringing together the perspectives of both a diachronic reading (from the perspective of a hermeneutics of the authors) and a synchronic reading (from the perspective of a hermeneutics of the texts).

First, the developing mind of the council and its articulation in the final documents together project a rejuvenated "pneumatology of revelation." "Christ is now at work in human hearts through the strength of his Spirit, not only instilling a desire for the world to come but also thereby animating, purifying and reinforcing the noble aspirations which drive the human family to make its life one that is more human and to direct the whole earth to this end" (GS 38).[85] As the previous section has shown, the Holy Spirit plays an indispensable role in the reception of divine revelation. By gifting human beings with faith, the Holy Spirit incites and enables through divine grace (in those open to the Spirit's promptings) personal response to God's self-communication (DV 5). Moreover, accompanying the gift of faith, the Spirit gifts "a sense of the faith" to individuals and to the church as a whole. This double gift from the Spirit—of *fides* and of a *sensus fidei*—enables faithful understanding, interpretation, and application to daily life of this personal relationship with God (LG 12), no matter at what time or place in history. *Synchronically*, within this diversity in the reception of revelation, across the diverse cultures and contexts of local churches, the Spirit maintains the community of faith in a unity of faith (LG 7, 13; UR 2). *Diachronically*, as this worldwide pilgrim people of God journeys through history toward the fulfillment of God's kingdom, the Spirit guides the church and leads it to the fullness of revealed truth, helping it to recognize what it has not yet understood of that fullness and helping it to recognize the new ways in which God is speaking to humanity (DV 8). In this way, "the Catholic Church [is] taught by the Holy Spirit" (LG 53). The Spirit teaches the church local and universal to recognize God's guiding presence in history and to read God's will for new times by enabling discernment of "the signs of the times" (GS 4, 11).

---

85. Tanner translation.

Second, in its rejuvenated "ecclesiological pneumatology," the council foregrounds in new ways the Spirit's necessary presence and activity within the church. According to Giuseppe Alberigo, "The call for a revival of pneumatology is inherent in the Council's conception of the Church. This conception, which moved beyond the Christo-monistic limitations typical of *Mystici corporis*, was based precisely on a rediscovery of the role of the Spirit."[86] The Dogmatic Constitution, in its first chapter on the trinitarian mystery of the church, devotes its fourth article to the Holy Spirit, and speaks of the church as the temple of the Holy Spirit: "The Spirit dwells in the church and in the hearts of the faithful, as in a temple" (LG 4). Then, in its second chapter on the people of God: "This [messianic] people possesses the dignity and freedom of the daughters and sons of God, in whose hearts the Holy Spirit dwells as in a temple" (LG 9). Yves Congar highlights three aspects in particular of the council's pneumatology that led to a rejuvenated vision of the life and mission of the church: its teaching on (1) charisms, (2) the local church, and (3) the need of the church local and universal to attend to the Spirit's teaching and guidance at different times throughout history and in different places and cultures.[87] One might add that in its treatment of the four marks or attributes of the church as one, holy, catholic, and apostolic, as stated in the Nicene-Constantinopolitan Creed, the council presents the Holy Spirit as the principle of the church's unity and the source of its holiness, diverse catholicity, and continuing apostolicity. These will be explored in later principles.

The remaining two areas of the council's pneumatology—its liturgical and anthropological pneumatology—especially will require of theology further work toward synthesis. The council's liturgical pneumatology is incomplete. It will require further enrichment through attention to the council's pneumatological shifts regarding other areas of church life. The judgement of Nereo Silanes echoes that of other commentators: of all the sixteen documents, *Sacrosanctum Concilium* is, "pneumatologically, the most unfortunate conciliar document."[88] It gives muted reference to the Holy Spirit at work in the liturgy: "The liturgy daily builds up those who are in the church, making of them a holy temple of the Lord, a dwelling-place for God in the Spirit, to the mature measure of the fullness of Christ" (SC 2). Two texts would later go beyond *Sacrosanctum Concilium* in this regard. *Lumen Gentium* 50 states: "in the liturgy, the power of the Holy Spirit acts on us through sacramental

86. Alberigo, "Transition to a New Age," 632.
87. See Congar, "The Pneumatology of Vatican II," 170–72.
88. Silanes, "El Espiritu Santo y la Iglesia en el Concilio Vaticano II," 1017.

signs" (LG 50). *Presbyterorum Ordinis* 5 speaks of priests as "participants in a special way in Christ's priesthood [who] act as ministers of him who *through his Spirit* continually exercises his priestly role for our benefit in the liturgy" (PO 5).[89] This latter text refers in a footnote to *Sacrosanctum Concilium* 7 (promulgated two years earlier) regarding the five modes of Christ's presence in the liturgy, including that of the priest. That article in *Sacrosanctum Concilium* had given no reference, however, to the role of the Holy Spirit in mediating the presence of Christ in those five modes.

The fourth area Schützeichel highlights is the council's pneumatological anthropology, a topic that the protological/eschatological principle will address.

In conclusion, the council's vision contains a call to a greater balance in applying the christological/pneumatological principle within the life of the church. It is a call for a more authentically trinitarian church. This is, as we have seen, an unfinished task bequeathed by the council to its receivers. With regard to the council's own pneumatological balance, Yves Congar states: "It is true that the pneumatological aspect at Vatican II is bound to the christological reality, but this is only the truth translated, which the inspired scriptures reveal to us. The Spirit is an independent *hypostasis*, the object of a distinct 'mission,' but he accomplishes no other work than the work of Christ. We admit that Vatican II in some respects is incomplete. Many of its statements are, if not compromises, then at least weak attempts which to some extend stop halfway."[90] For Silanes, likewise, the council marks an accomplishment, but only a beginning: "In the doctrine that the Council has not given about the Holy Spirit in the various fields of action in the life of the Church, it is necessary to see, rather than a systematic teaching, some formal principles of its mission in the Mystical Body. The pneumatology of Vatican II constitutes a point of arrival as much as a point of departure."[91]

In a general audience a few years after the council, Pope Paul VI indeed implied that a synthesis of the council's pneumatology was needed: "The Christology and especially the ecclesiology of the Second Vatican Council should be followed by a new study and a new cult of the Holy Spirit, as an

89. Translation corrected.
90. Congar, "Die christologischen und pneumatologischen Implikationen," 123.
91. Silanes, "El Espiritu Santo y la Iglesia en el Concilio Vaticano II," 1024.

indispensable complement of the conciliar teaching."[92] Vatican II's greater emphasis on the role and activity of the Holy Spirit in the economy of salvation is certainly among the most significant shifts taken at Vatican II; but it is perhaps among the least received into the life of the church over the last fifty years.

92. General Audience of June 6, 1973. *Doc. Cath.*, 1635 (July 1, 1973), 601. Quoted in Congar, "The Pneumatology of Vatican II," 172, 173n13. Congar goes on to quote Paul VI's Apostolic Exhortation *Marialis Cultus* (22 March 1974), art. 27, with its invitation to "think more deeply about the activity of the Spirit in the history of salvation."

Principle 9
Mystery/Sacrament

Principle 9: The transcendent and incomprehensible triune God of mystery can be truly encountered and known in creation and within human history, yet only in a sacramental way; the church, as a mystery that is best evoked in a variety of images and concepts, exists in the world in the nature of a sacrament mediating God's revelatory presence and saving grace, especially evident when the people of God celebrates the sacraments, particularly the Eucharist.

As with the other principles, the contribution of this principle in the conciliar vision becomes evident when one examines what particular emphases of previous teaching and theology the council deliberately set out to correct or balance.

On December 1, 1962—the last week of the first session—debate began on the schema *De Ecclesia* that had been distributed to the bishops the week before.[1] The major architect of the document was the Gregorian University theologian Sebastian Tromp, who had likewise been the main figure in the drafting of Pope Pius XII's 1943 encyclical *Mystici Corporis*, to which this draft schema had many similarities. Adrian Hastings likens the theology of the schema to that presented in one of the most influential neoscholastic manuals of theology before the council, that of Cardinal Louis Billot (1846–1931): "It was *apologetic* in approach. It defined the Church as a '*perfect society*,' understood in terms similar to those of a secular state. It was mostly concerned with the *visible* aspect of the Church. It spoke chiefly of the *governmental* side of the society. It explained that government in terms of

---

1. AS, I/4, 12–91. For an English translation by Joseph Komonchak of the draft schema *De Ecclesia*, see https://jakomonchak.files.wordpress.com/2013/07/draft-of-de-ecclesia-chs-1-11.pdf.

monarchy."[2] In a word, the draft schema exemplified the reigning ecclesiology of the time, which for over three hundred years, had been dominated by the post-Tridentine vision of the Jesuit Robert Bellarmine (1542–1621).[3] The council of Trent had reacted to the Protestant reformers' focus on the invisible church of the future *eschaton*. In their reception of Trent, Bellarmine and his later interpreters strongly emphasized the visibility of the church and, accordingly, the notion of the church as a "perfect society (*societas perfecta*)"; i.e., the church is just like any monarchical nation-state with all the requirements needed to exist independently in human society.[4] In terms of the nature of the church and its inner life, the weakness of Bellarmine's vision was its almost-exclusive emphasis on the juridical, hierarchical, and institutional dimensions of the church.

In the decades before Vatican II, this Bellarminian model had been challenged for its one-dimensionality by various renewal movements in Europe— the biblical, patristic, liturgical, ecumenical, social engagement, and lay movements. A key element of this reaction was the desire to bring some balance to the church's self understanding, by highlighting not only the visible aspects of the church but also its invisible, divine, spiritual aspects. To that end, the biblical and patristic testimonies to the church as a multidimensional "mystery" were highlighted in the writings of *ressourcement* theologians throughout these decades.[5] For example, Henri de Lubac was a trenchant critic of the reductionistic approach of the neoscholastic manuals of theology,[6] and his 1953 work *Méditation sur l'Église* had as its opening

2. Hastings, *A Concise Guide to the Documents*, 28–34, at 28–29. Original emphasis. For Billot's manual of theology, see Louis Billot, *Tractatus de ecclesia Christi: Sive continuatio theologiae de verbo incarnato*, 5th ed., 2 vols. (Romae: Universitatis Gregorianae, 1927).

3. For a history of ecclesiology after the Council of Trent and of a "Tridentinism" fashioned by Bellarmine's narrow interpretation of Trent, see Ormond Rush, "Roman Catholic Ecclesiology from the Council of Trent to Vatican II and Beyond," in *The Oxford Handbook of Ecclesiology*, ed. Paul Avis (Oxford: Oxford University Press, 2018), 263–92. On the ecclesiology of Bellarmine, see the (albeit favorable) summary in John A. Hardon, "Robert Bellarmine's Concept of the Church," in *Studies in Medieval Culture*, ed. John R. Sommerfeldt (Kalamazoo: Western Michigan University, 1966), 2:120–27.

4. See Patrick Granfield, "The Rise and Fall of *Societas Perfecta*," *Concilium* 157 (1982): 3–8; Patrick Granfield, "The Church as *Societas Perfecta* in the Schemata of Vatican I," *Church History* 48 (1979): 431–46.

5. Surveying Catholic theology in France in the decades before the council, James Connolly notes: "The mystery of the Church has become for many, if not for most of the contemporary theologians, the touchstone of their thought and work." James M. Connolly, *The Voices of France* (New York: Macmillan, 1961), 96.

6. In a 1930 article, de Lubac described the then-current neoscholastic theology as a "shabby" theology, a "separated" theology, that severed nature and supernature. Henri de Lubac, "Apol-

chapter "The Church as Mystery."[7] Similarly, as noted during discussion of the christological/pneumatological principle, Odo Casel had used the notion of "mystery" in his liturgical theology, and in particular, in highlighting the important notion of "the paschal mystery." Against this background of reaction by *ressourcement* theologians before the council to the reigning Bellarminian ecclesial model, when the draft schema of *De Ecclesia* was opened for debate, the response of most council fathers echoed the concerns of this theological scholarship in the previous decades.

Beyond Juridicism

When debate began on December 1, 1962, there were voices praising the draft schema, but several cardinals found little in the schema to recommend it.[8] On many points it reiterated the teaching of Pius XII in his encyclicals *Mystici Corporis* and *Humani Generis*.[9] The title of article 7 of the draft schema read "The Roman Catholic Church is [*est*] the Mystical Body of Christ," and the schema goes on: "The Roman Catholic Church is [*est*] the Mystical Body of Christ . . . and only the one that is Roman Catholic has the right to be called Church."[10] The first bishop to respond to Cardinal Alfredo Ottaviani's presentation of the schema was Cardinal Achille Liénart: "We must be very careful not to let formulas or ways of talking about the Church do an injustice to *the mystery*; for example, not to state the relationship and identity of the Roman Church with the Mystical Body as though the Mystical Body were to be found wholly within the confines of the Roman Church. For the Roman Church is the true Body of Christ but not coextensive with it. . . . Our Church, though it is the visible manifestation of the Mystical Body of Jesus Christ, cannot be absolutely and unqualifiedly identified

ogetics and Theology," in *Theological Fragments* (San Francisco: Ignatius Press, 1989), 91–104. For discussion of de Lubac's criticisms, see Joseph A. Komonchak, "Returning from Exile: Catholic Theology in the 1930s," in *The Twentieth Century: A Theological Overview*, ed. Gregory Baum (Maryknoll, NY: Orbis Books, 1999), 35–48, at 42–43.

7. Henri de Lubac, *The Splendor of the Church* (San Francisco: Ignatius Press, 1999), 15–50.

8. See Ruggieri, "Beyond an Ecclesiology of Polemics," 328–40.

9. See ibid., 281–98. For *Mystici Corporis*, see AAS 35 (1943), 221ff., translated in Pope Pius XII, "Mystici Corporis Christi," in *The Papal Encyclicals*, vol. 4: *1939–1958*, ed. Claudia Carlen (Wilmington, NC: McGrath Publishing Company, 1981), 37–63. For *Humani Generis*, see AAS 42 (1950), 571ff., translated in Pope Pius XII, "Humani Generis," in Carlen, *The Papal Encyclicals*, 4:175–84.

10. Translation from Francis A. Sullivan, "The Significance of the Vatican II Declaration That the Church of Christ 'Subsists In' the Roman Catholic Church," in *Vatican II Assessment and Perspectives: Twenty-Five Years After (1962–1987)*, vol. 2, ed. René Latourelle (New York: Paulist Press, 1989), 2:272–87, at 273.

with it."[11] The German cardinals Julius Döpfner and Joseph Frings likewise called for a document that would emphasize the mystery of the church and not give exclusive emphasis to the church's institutional and juridical aspects, as the schema had done.[12]

It was, however, Bishop Émile de Smedt from Belgium who delivered the speech that has been noted by most commentators as highly influential in ensuring the virtual dismissal of the schema.[13] He criticized the triumphalism of its tone, the clericalism of its sense of who is more important in the church, and the exclusive juridicism in its understanding of church life—all qualities that characterized the reigning Bellarminian ecclesiology.[14] Other bishops followed suit, with several likewise explicitly calling for a presentation of the church that highlighted the *mysterium* of the church and indeed the church as a *sacramentum*.[15] For these council participants, "the aim was to get away from the encrusted, narrow and one-sided elements of the traditional view held by scholastic theology. This fundamentally critical intention must be borne in mind if we want to understand properly what the council's statements really mean."[16]

While the schema was not officially rejected by the council, the Doctrinal Commission decided during the intersession period that a new draft was required. Several versions were proposed by *periti* and bishops; the commission decided on the version that the *peritus* Gérard Philips had authored. In the second session, a further revised version of Philips's text was presented to the bishops and discussed from September 20 until October 31, 1963.[17] The title of its first chapter was no longer—as in the preparatory schema—

11. AS I/4, 126–27. Translation from Bonaventure Kloppenburg, *The Ecclesiology of Vatican II* (Chicago: Franciscan Herald Press, 1974), 64–65. Emphasis added.

12. See Gérard Philips, "Dogmatic Constitution on the Church: History of the Constitution," in *Commentary on the Documents of Vatican II*, vol. 1, ed. Herbert Vorgrimler (London: Burns & Oates, 1967), 105–37, at 108.

13. AS I/4, 142–44.

14. For commentaries on de Smedt's intervention, see Philips, "Dogmatic Constitution on the Church: History of the Constitution," 109; Ruggieri, "Beyond an Ecclesiology of Polemics," 337.

15. Walter Kasper names among those bishops calling for an approach with these elements: Döpfner, Lercaro, Suenens, Volk, König, and Montini. Kasper, "The Church as a Universal Sacrament of Salvation," 113.

16. Ibid., 113.

17. On the intervening written submissions by bishops for consideration by the Doctrinal Commission, and the subsequent discussion in the aula, see Philips, "Dogmatic Constitution on the Church: History of the Constitution," 110–26.

"The Nature of the Church Militant" but now "The Mystery of the Church."[18] While this change was welcomed by the majority, there were some who objected, as the *peritus* Alois Grillmeier records:

> Various objections were raised at different stages to the title of Chapter 1, as for instance that the Church was not a mystery, since it was visible. Behind such objections there was a concept of mystery of very limited value, which restricted it to the secret or the abstruse. Many Fathers feared that the title might open up the way of abandoning the truth of the visible Church for the ideology of an invisible Church. The truth was that an effort was being made to arrive at a more adequate view of the complex reality of the Church than had hitherto been current. The biblical term "mystery" sought to indicate the true nature of the Church in all its contrasting facets, in an endeavour to compensate for the rather one-sided view of the Church which had been prevalent since Trent.[19]

An intervention on October 2, 1963 in favor of the notion, by the Italian bishop Emilio Guano, was later cited by the Doctrinal Commission as significant. Guano had urged: "This word [mystery] is taken from Sacred Scripture; it seems suitable for expressing the fact that the external visibility of Church, like the holy human nature of Christ, both conceals and reveals the inner divine reality of the Church, a reality which surpasses all knowledge."[20] Indeed, Pope Paul VI had a few days earlier, in his opening address for the second session, stated: "The Church is a mystery; she is a reality imbued with the divine presence."[21] Walter Kasper notes that, in its *relatio* to the council fathers in the third session regarding chapter 1 of *Lumen Gentium*, "the theological [i.e., doctrinal] commission found it necessary to explain expressly that 'mystery' does not mean something unknowable or abstruse, but is a fundamental biblical concept. It means a transcendent saving reality

---

18. A proposal by the German bishops, drafted in December 1962, was the first to have as the title of its first chapter "The Mystery of the Church." Other proposals, from the Chilean, Italian, and French bishops in January 1963, followed suit. For these proposed texts, see the appendices in Giuseppe Alberigo and Franca Magistretti, *Constitutionis Dogmaticae Lumen Gentium: Synopsis Historica* (Bologna: Istituto per le Scienze Religiose, 1975), 381–428.

19. Alois Grillmeier, "Chapter I: The Mystery of the Church," in *Commentary on the Documents of Vatican II*, vol. 1, ed. Herbert Vorgrimler (London: Burns & Oates, 1967), 1:138–52, at 138.

20. AS II/1, 455. Translation here is taken from Kloppenburg, *The Ecclesiology of Vatican II*, 14.

21. Paul VI, "Opening Address: Second Session," 146.

which is revealed and manifested in a visible way."[22] In the end, despite opposition to the notion, the desire of the majority prevailed: there would be a chapter on "the mystery of the church."

The council was explicitly alluding to the Pauline usage of the term, generally in reference to the nature and revelation of God's plan. Paul, for example, speaks of his own preaching in the language of mystery: "Now to God who is able to strengthen you according to my gospel and the proclamation of Jesus Christ, according to the revelation of the mystery that was kept secret for long ages" (Rom 16:25). Here, as elsewhere, the Greek word for mystery Paul uses is *mysterion*. In the West, the Latin *transliteration* for the Greek word was *mysterium*, and the Latin *translation* of the word was generally *sacramentum*. When Vatican II, however, wishes to speak of "mystery" in this general sense, it uses *mysterium*. It would use *sacramentum* in a more precise sense.

The council's attempt at "a more adequate view of the complex reality of the Church," as Grillmeier puts it,[23] is apparent in the final text of *Lumen Gentium* in (1) the very structure of the whole document and, more specifically, (2) the structure of its first chapter and the topics that each of its articles addresses.[24]

First, the significance for the council of emphasizing the "mystery" of the church (and not just its "visible" reality) is evident structurally, in the very titles given to its first and last chapters. The title of the first chapter is "The Mystery of the Church." The title of the eighth and last chapter is "The Blessed Virgin Mary, Mother of God, in the Mystery of Christ and of the Church." These two chapters bracket the intervening chapters on the people of God, the hierarchy, the laity, the universal call to holiness, the religious, and the eschatological character of the church. As George Tavard observes: "In this sequence the 'mystery' is at the beginning and at the end, the middle chapters finding their place in relation to the mystery of the Church. In other words, the essence of the Church, that which makes it what it is in God's eyes, is not the visible structure or even the members of it with their various and comple-

22. Kasper, "The Church as Communion," 151. For the Doctrinal Commission's *Relatio* regarding *Lumen Gentium* chapters 1 and 2, see AS III/1, 209–10. See also the text in Alberigo and Magistretti, *Constitutionis Dogmaticae Lumen Gentium*, 436f.

23. Grillmeier, "Chapter I: The Mystery of the Church," 138.

24. For an overview of the theme of "mystery" in *Lumen Gentium*, see Théodore Strotmann, "La Chiesa come mistero," in *La Chiesa del Vaticano II: Studi e commenti intorno alla Costituzione dommatica 'Lumen Gentium'*, ed. Guilherme Baraúna (Firenze: Vallecchi Editore, 1965), 314–28.

mentary functions, their human talents and achievements, their spiritual yearnings and experiences. It is mystery, a spiritual reality hidden within the structures."[25] The opening introductory article of the whole document had already spoken of the church as "a kind of sacrament" (*veluti sacramentum*) mediating God's offer of salvation to the world. The notion of the church as a "sacrament" would come to encapsulate in a paradigmatic way this understanding of the church as mystery, functioning as a leitmotif not only in *Lumen Gentium* but also in several of the subsequent documents.

Second, not only the structure of the whole document, but the structure of the first chapter and the topics each of its eight articles addresses begin to elucidate what the council means by the mystery of the church (the second chapter on the people of God would extend that). The first three articles of chapter 1 examine the essence of the mystery of the church as "the work of the Trinity":[26] the church's origins lie in the mystery of the plan of God the Father (LG 2), which is realized in the economy of salvation through the mission of the Son (LG 3) and the concomitant mission of the Holy Spirit (LG 4). It concludes this triad of articles with a voice from the ancient tradition, St. Cyprian of Carthage: "Hence the universal church is seen to be 'a people made one by the unity of the Father, the Son and the Holy Spirit.'"[27] The next article presents "the mystery of the holy church" (LG 5) in its relationship to "the kingdom of Christ" in history and to the eschatological fulfillment of "the kingdom of God" at the end of time. Then, article 6 notes that the church is a mystery that can only be captured in a wide variety of images, as it is in the biblical witness of the Old and New Testaments: the church is a sheepfold or a flock of sheep; a farm or a field; a building or a temple; a spouse.[28] Particular attention is then given in the next article (7) to a further biblical image of the church, the "body"

25. George H. Tavard, *The Church, Community of Salvation: An Ecumenical Ecclesiology* (Collegeville, MN: Liturgical Press, 1992), 79.

26. Francis A. Sullivan, *The Church We Believe In: One, Holy, Catholic, and Apostolic* (New York: Paulist Press, 1988), 11.

27. With references also to St. Augustine and St. John Damascene, the official footnote cites: St Cyprian, *De Orat. Dom.* 23: PL 4, 553. Hartel IIIA, p. 285; St Augustine, *Serm.* 71, 20, 33: PL 38, 463 f. St John Damascene, *Adv. Iconocl.* 12: PG 96 1358 D.

28. Some of these biblical images had been listed in the preparatory draft schema *De Ecclesia*, but not in any extended way: "In order more clearly and more definitely to reveal the character and nature of his Church, Christ, either by himself or through the Apostles, represented her in various images and called her by various names by which her social and mystical aspects are particularly described. Thus what is proclaimed to be God's kingdom, house, and temple is also declared to be a flock or a sheepfold, the Bride of Christ, the pillar and ground of truth." *De Ecclesia*, chap. 1, no. 3. Komonchak translation.

of Christ, an image that Pope Pius XII had brought to the fore in his 1943 encyclical *Mystici Corporis Christi* but that is here placed in a wider panorama alongside other biblical images. To be included also in the biblical images of the church the council presents is that of the church as "the people of God," to which it devotes the whole of the next chapter.[29]

Finally, in a concluding article (8), the council directly addresses the issue Bellarmine had made so problematic: the visibility of the church. Here we find a cluster of binaries that attempt to hold in tension the various dimensions of the church as a mystery of faith: the structural and the charismatic, the hierarchical and the mystical, the visible and the spiritual, the earthly and the heavenly, the sinful and the holy. The dimensions in each of these binaries, the council teaches, are "not to be thought of as two realities. On the contrary, they form one complex reality comprising a human and divine element" (LG 8). The analogy of the incarnation is presented as the paradigmatic key for understanding the way the church holds in tension its human and divine reality. And then, in a remarkable shift not only from the exclusivism and triumphalism of the original *De Ecclesia* schema but also from Roman Catholic assertions across several centuries, it states that this church, with all these dimensions of mystery, "subsists in" the Catholic Church (LG 8) rather than "is" the Catholic Church, as a previous draft had stated. Furthermore, it adds: "Nevertheless, many elements of sanctification and of truth are found outside its visible confines. Since these are gifts belonging to the church of Christ, they are forces impelling towards catholic unity" (LG 8). These carefully worded affirmations were deliberately intended to reconfigure the Roman Catholic imagination, by opening up not only a rejuvenated self-understanding but also significant ecumenical opportunities: "While continuing to identify mystical body and church, [Vatican II] no longer exclusively identifies the church with the Roman Catholic Church, thus

---

29. As the *relator* introducing chapter 2 on the people of God emphasized, the chapter is intrinsically related to the previous chapter 1 on the mystery of the church, implying that it is separated out as a separate chapter only for reasons of space and the desire for balance in size of the two chapters. Komonchak summarizes the *Relatio*: "Chapter 2, [the *Relatio*] said, was an intrinsic part of the consideration of the mystery of the church and must not be separated from its inner nature and purpose: the material had been divided into two chapters *simply because one chapter would have been too long*. The first chapter had considered the church in its great span from before creation in the plan of God until its fulfillment in heaven; Chapter 2 would discuss the same mystery in the time between the ascension and the Parousia, that time during which it lives by faith until it is perfected in the blessed vision." Joseph A. Komonchak, "The Ecclesiology of Vatican II," *Origins* 28 (April 22, 1999): 763–68, at 764. Emphasis added.

leaving open the possibility of our recognizing all baptized Christians, and not Catholics alone, as being really members of the body of Christ."[30]

Some further points need to be highlighted with regard to this concluding article of *Lumen Gentium*'s chapter on the mystery of the church. Its treatment of the binary dimensions of the church had already been anticipated in the previous year's constitution on the liturgy when it spoke about "the real nature of the true church": "the church is both human and divine, visible but endowed with invisible realities, zealous in action and dedicated to contemplation, present in the world, yet a migrant [*peregrinam*], so constituted that in it the human is directed toward and subordinated to the divine, the visible to the invisible, action to contemplation, and this present world to that city yet to come, the object of our quest" (SC 2). Furthermore, the liturgy constitution had likewise anticipated the use of the "mystery" motif, as we have seen in discussion of the previous principle, by the prominent place it gives to "the paschal mystery."

The council's use of the "analogy" of the incarnation to capture the mystery of the church represented a significant development toward greater balance in the church's understanding of the relationship of Christ to his church. In describing this relationship, "Vatican II did not take up the doctrine, disseminated in the first half of the twentieth century, of the Church as the continuation of the incarnation; rather it carefully differentiated and corrected this teaching."[31] *Lumen Gentium* 8 appeals to the incarnation in an *analogous* way, including—significantly—reference to the role of the Holy Spirit: "For this reason the church is compared, in no mean analogy [*non mediocrem analogiam*], to the mystery of the incarnate Word. As the assumed nature, inseparably united to him, serves the divine Word as *a living instrument of salvation*, so, *in somewhat similar fashion*, does the social structure of the church serve the Spirit of Christ who vivifies it, in the building up of the body" (LG 8). In this way, without using "mystery," the chapter ends by alluding back to the summary statement that introduced the chapter and related the church to *Christ*, the *lumen gentium* to whom the opening sentence of the constitution had referred: "the church, *in Christ*, is in the nature of a sacrament [*veluti sacramentum*]—a sign and instrument [*seu signum et instrumentum*], that is, of intimate union [*intimae unionis*] with God and of the unity of the entire human race" (LG 1).[32]

30. Sullivan, *The Church We Believe In*, 108.
31. Kasper, "The Renewal of Pneumatology," 100.
32. Translation corrected.

Lumen Gentium 8's third paragraph treats the poverty of the church. In a threefold parallelism, it calls for the church to imitate its master: (1) like the poor and persecuted Jesus, the church too is to follow the way of poverty, and it too will experience persecution; (2) like the humble and selfless Jesus, the church too must follow the way of humility and embrace self-denial; (3) like Jesus who sought out the poor and the moral failures, so too the church must serve the afflicted and itself undergo constant repentance and renewal. "The church encompasses with its love all those who are afflicted by human infirmity and it recognizes in those who are poor and who suffer, the likeness of its poor and suffering founder. It does all in its power to relieve their need and in them it endeavours to serve Christ" (LG 8). During the debate in the last week of the first session, among those who had criticized the original schema *De Ecclesia* for its triumphalist view of the church was Cardinal Giacomo Lercaro, who called for a church that evoked the mystery of Christ in the poor.[33] He quoted Pope John XXIII, who, in a radio speech a month before the first session began, had stated: "In dealing with the underdeveloped countries, the Church presents herself as she is and as she wants to be—as the Church of all men and especially *the Church of the poor*."[34] Lercaro went on: "We will not respond to the truest and deepest demands of our time nor to the hope of unity shared by all Christians if we treat the theme of the evangelization of the poor as one of the many themes of the Council. This is not a theme like others; in a way, it is *the* theme of our Council."[35]

According to Giuseppe Ruggieri, "Lercaro's vision, which was perhaps the most original and at the same time the most prophetic of this first period of the Council, was, as events would show, too advanced for the general consciousness of the fathers. In itself it was of a nature to make possible a real leap forward (to use Pope John's image) in the theological conception of the Church, but it proved to be only a stone thrown into a pond, causing merely a transient ripple of applause and agreement."[36] Nevertheless, throughout that first session of the council a study group had been meeting regularly at the Belgian College in Rome raising similar concerns and soon became

---

33. AS I/4, 291–94. For a summary and quotation of highlights in Lercaro's speech, see Ruggieri, "Beyond an Ecclesiology of Polemics," 345–46.

34. Pope John XXIII, "Radio Message of September 11, 1962," in *Discorsi Messagi Colloqui del S. Padre Giovanni XXIII* (Vatican City: Editrice Vaticana, 1960–1967), 4:524.

35. Translation from Gustavo Gutiérrez, *A Theology of Liberation: History, Politics, and Salvation*, rev. ed. (Maryknoll, NY: Orbis Books, 1988), 251n3.

36. Ruggieri, "Beyond an Ecclesiology of Polemics," 346.

known as "the group of the church of the poor."[37] Pope Paul VI kept in contact with them informally, supported their efforts, and attempted to highlight the same vision for the church, especially through the gesture of donating his papal tiara to the poor.[38]

The impact of "the group of the poor," like that of Lercaro's speech, turned out to be minimal in effecting a more substantial change in the conciliar documents. According to Giuseppe Alberigo, the passages in *Lumen Gentium* 8 evoking the mystery of "a church of the poor" are perhaps the most important legacy of the group, "but it was limited and marginal."[39] Likewise, for Gustavo Gutiérrez, while "the most important text is *Lumen Gentium* 8,"[40] "the final results of the Council, however, did not correspond to the expectations. The documents allude several times to poverty, but it is not one of the major thrusts."[41] And, within those documents, the issue is addressed "largely Christologically or in terms of mission."[42] Nevertheless, the meaning and impact of a council is not restricted to what the original authors intended or to the texts they produced; the receivers of those texts ask questions and bring to the fore elements that take on a new life. Indeed, over the last fifty years since the council, the minimal passages in the final documents would bring forth a

---

37. For an account of this group during the council, see Rohan Michael Curnow, *The Preferential Option for the Poor: A Short History and a Reading Based on the Thought of Bernard Lonergan* (Milwaukee, WI: Marquette University Press, 2012), 26–39; Rohan Curnow, "Stirrings of the Preferential Option for the Poor at Vatican II: The Work of the 'Group of the Church of the Poor,'" *The Australasian Catholic Record* 89 (2012): 420–32. See also Hilari Raguer, "An Initial Profile of the Assembly," in *History of Vatican II*, vol. 2: *The Formation of the Council's Identity; First Period and Intercession, October 1962–September 1963*, ed. Giuseppe Alberigo and Joseph A. Komonchak (Maryknoll, NY: Orbis Books, 1997), 2:167–232, at 200–203; Joseph Famerée, "Bishops and Dioceses and the Communications Media (November 5–25, 1963)," in *History of Vatican II*, vol. 3: *The Mature Council; Second Period and Intersession, September 1963–September 1964*, ed. Giuseppe Alberigo and Joseph A. Komonchak (Maryknoll, NY: Orbis Books, 1998), 3:117–88, at 164–66; Norman Tanner, "The Church in the World (*Ecclesia ad Extra*)," in *History of Vatican II*, vol. 4: *The Church as Communion; Third Period and Third Intersession, September 1964–September 1965*, ed. Giuseppe Alberigo and Joseph A. Komonchak (Maryknoll, NY: Orbis Books, 2004), 4:269–386, at 382–86.

38. On Paul VI's gift of his papal tiara, see Tanner, "The Church in the World," 372–76.

39. Giuseppe Alberigo, "Major Results, Shadows of Uncertainty," in *History of Vatican II*, 4:617–40, at 620.

40. Gutiérrez, *A Theology of Liberation*, 251n4.

41. Ibid., 162.

42. Curnow, *The Preferential Option for the Poor*, 36. Curnow lists: LG 23; GE 9; AA 8; GS 1, 15, 63, 69, 71, 81, 86, 88, 90; CD 13, 30; PO 6; OT 8, 9; AG 12; and, PC 13. He notes that three articles in *Gaudium et Spes* cohere with the vision of the Group for the Church of the Poor: GS 8, 76, and 90.

"surplus of meaning" in the history of their reception, especially in the light of other emphases in the council's vision, such as the role of the local church, the principles of social justice, the role of the church in promoting the kingdom of God in the present, and the consequent broader understanding of the "salvation" of which the church is called to be a "universal sacrament."[43]

Finally, in *Lumen Gentium* 8 the council begins its treatment of another aspect of the church's mystery, one that it will continue to address later in the constitution and in its decree on ecumenism—the tension between the holiness of the church and the reality of sinfulness in the church, and the consequent need for continual ecclesial repentance and renewal: "The church . . . clasping sinners to its bosom, at once holy and always in need of purification, follows constantly the path of penance and renewal" (LG 8). In a passage that, according to *Lumen Gentium*'s major drafter, Gérard Philips, "may well be the most important in the whole chapter,"[44] chapter 1 of *Lumen Gentium* concludes with a sentence stating that the church reveals in the world "faithfully, although with shadows, the mystery of its Lord until, in the end, it shall be manifested in full light" (LG 8). From a stance of triumphalism reflected in its first draft, the council here begins to acknowledge the dark side of the church's history and of its current reality. Addressing this aspect of the church's mystery will come to feature as one plank in the council's pastoral agenda for renewal and reform, for the sake of *aggiornamento*.

---

43. The reception of the council regarding these emphases was brought together in synthesis by liberation theologies, in the statements of international synods of bishops and the magisterium, and now with the priorities in the pontificate of Pope Francis. Making a distinction between "the council as a point of arrival" and "the council as a point of departure," Leonardo Boff sees these limited conciliar texts within other elements of the conciliar vision, such as its theology of local church and the emphasis on social justice: "[In Latin America, the council documents] were read in a sound box that made the spirit and main themes of the Council come alive with meaning. Vatican II was seen as granting universal endorsement to a regional church that had opened itself up to the world, the poor, and social justice. True, the mentality of the Council fell short of the critical social awareness that had been reached by our committed Christian groups. But the institutional support the Council lent to the efforts of these groups was priceless. The Council gave sanction to a church engaged in the social arena, a church involved in the lot of the abandoned of this world. It was as if the Council lived in Latin American practice first and then was embodied in verbal and written form in Rome. The council documents seemed to confirm, reinforce, make official, the stretch of the road that America had already traversed." Leonardo Boff, "Theology of Liberation: Creative Acceptance of Vatican II from the Viewpoint of the Poor," in *When Theology Listens to the Poor* (San Francisco: Harper & Row, 1988), 1–31, at 11.

44. Gérard Philips, "The Church: Mystery and Sacrament," in *Vatican II: An Interfaith Appraisal*, ed. John H. Miller (Notre Dame, IN: University of Notre Dame, 1966), 187–96, at 195.

"Sign and Instrument"

The key concept that the council uses to capture this multiplicity of dimensions of the *mysterium* of the church is the notion of the church as a *sacramentum*.[45] The notion is not so much some single overarching concept the bishops were using to integrate their whole vision of the nature and mission of the church. As this book argues throughout, no one metaphor or concept the council employs can bear the burden of functioning as such a single and comprehensive hermeneutical key. Nevertheless, the notion of the church as a sacrament is highly significant in the council's vision of *how the church functions in fulfillment of its mission.*[46]

Like the theme of the mystery of the church, the notion of the church as a sacrament was an important theme of *ressourcement* ecclesiologies in the decades before the council, emerging alongside other developments, such as Mystical Body ecclesiology. If the weakness of the latter is that it can tend to blur the distinction between Christ and the Church, then the strength of the former is that it holds the two in tension: a sacrament is a symbol of something other than itself, even while it makes the other truly present.[47] According to the analogy of the incarnation, the model of "church as sacrament" asserts that just as Christ is the sacrament of God, so the Church is a sacrament of Christ.[48] The reception of the nineteenth-century Tübingen

---

45. The most comprehensive study on this theme at Vatican II is Leonardo Boff, *Die Kirche als Sakrament im Horizont der Welterfahrung: Versuch einer Legitimation und einer struktur-funktionalistischen Grundlegung der Kirche im Anschluss an das II. Vatikanische Konzil* (Paderborn: Verlag Bonifacius-Druckerei, 1972), esp. 228–95. For other studies, see, for example, Peter Smulders, "La Chiesa sacramento della salvezza," in *La Chiesa del Vaticano II: Studi e commenti intorno alla Costituzione dommatica 'Lumen Gentium',* ed. Guilherme Baraúna (Firenze: Vallecchi Editore, 1965), 363–86; Kasper, "The Church as a Universal Sacrament of Salvation."

46. On this whole debate, see Herwi Rikhof, *The Concept of Church: A Methodological Inquiry into the Use of Metaphors in Ecclesiology* (London: Sheed and Ward, 1981).

47. See Susan Wood, "Continuity and Development in Roman Catholic Ecclesiology," *Ecclesiology* 7, no. 2 (2011): 147–72.

48. On the "model" of church as sacrament in Vatican II and in postconciliar theology, see Avery Dulles, *Models of the Church,* exp. ed. (New York: Image Books Doubleday, 2002), 55–67. In a more refined formulation, de Margerie sees in the council's vision an understanding of the church as a sacrament *of the Trinity*: "The mystery of a Church sent by the Father, by the Son and by the Spirit, by revealing to us the mysterious sending of the Son and the Spirit by the Father, renders 'visible' to us the incomprehensible salvific mystery of the Trinity which it bears within it: the Church is the sacrament of salvation only because it is *the sacrament of the Trinity*, the visible sign which bears in it the invisible and undivided Trinity so as to give it to the world. By receiving its unity from the unity of the Father, the Son and the Spirit, the Church is, so to speak, eternally generated with the Son and spirated with the Spirit who are

theologian Johann Adam Möhler in this development is evident.[49] In his 1938 work *Catholicisme*, Henri de Lubac wrote: "If Christ is the sacrament of God, the Church is for us the sacrament of Christ";[50] he would develop this further in his 1953 book *Méditation sur l'Église*.[51] Also in 1953, his fellow Jesuit Otto Semmelroth (1932–1979) published a book on the church as "the primordial sacrament," *Kirche als Ursakrament*.[52] The previous year the Le Saulchoir Domincan student Edward Schillebeeckx (1914–2009) had published the first part of his dissertation *De sacramentele Heilseconomie*, in which he delineated a notion of the seven sacraments in terms of the church itself as a sacrament of encounter with God; in 1960, he published a summary of his thesis in German and French, later translated in English as *Christ the Sacrament of the Encounter with God*.[53] In a similar vein, Karl Rahner in 1942 had written of the church as "the historico-sacramental permanent presence of the salvation reality of Christ."[54] In 1960 he took up the theme in terms of his 1959 work on the theology of symbol: "The Church is the abiding presence of that primal sacramental word of definitive grace, which Christ is in the world, effecting what is uttered by uttering it in sign. By the very fact of being in that way the enduring presence of Christ in the world, the Church is truly the fundamental sacrament, the well-spring of the sacraments in the strict sense."[55] De Lubac, Semmelroth, Schillebeeckx, and

---

sent to it and who, in it proceed from the Father. The Church is the sacrament of salvation by being a mystery which carries within it the fundamental mystery, the mystery of the redemptive Trinity." de Margerie, "The Trinitarian Doctrine of Vatican II," 226.

49. See Christopher O'Donnell, *Ecclesia: A Theological Encyclopedia of the Church* (Collegeville, MN: Liturgical Press, 1996), 414.

50. Henri de Lubac, *Catholicism: Christ and the Common Destiny of Man* (San Francisco: Ignatius Press, 1988), 76.

51. de Lubac, *The Splendor of the Church*, 202–35.

52. Otto Semmelroth, *Die Kirche als Ursakrament* (Frankfurt a.M.: Knecht, 1953). See Dennis M. Doyle, "Otto Semmelroth, SJ, and the Ecclesiology of the 'Church as Sacrament' at Vatican II," in *The Legacy of Vatican II*, ed. Massimo Faggioli and Andrea Vicini (New York: Paulist Press, 2015), 203–25.

53. Edward Schillebeeckx, *Christ the Sacrament of Encounter with God* (London: Sheed and Ward, 1963).

54. Karl Rahner, "Priestly Existence," in *Theological Investigations*, vol. 3: *The Theology of the Spiritual Life* (London: Darton, Longman and Todd, 1967), 3:239–62, at 248.

55. Karl Rahner, *The Church and the Sacraments* (Freiburg: Herder, 1963), 18. See also Karl Rahner, "The Theology of the Symbol," in *Theological Investigations*, vol. 4 (London: Darton, Longman & Todd, 1966), 4:221–52. See Richard Lennan, "'Narcissistic Aestheticism'? An Assessment of Karl Rahner's Sacramental Ecclesiology," *Philosophy and Theology* 25 (2013): 249–70.

Rahner played important roles at the council as official *periti* and theological advisers to bishops.

The council benefitted from these developments and, despite some initial opposition, quickly appropriated the notion of the church as a sacrament, applying it in several overlapping senses: the church is a sacrament of Christ; it is a sacrament of union with God; it is a sacrament of unity among human beings; it is a universal sacrament of salvation for the world. The Constitution on the Sacred Liturgy is the first to employ it, doing so in two passages, each of which appeals to different sources from the ancient tradition. *Sacrosanctum Concilium* 5 quotes St. Augustine, who speaks of "the wondrous sacrament of the whole church [*totius Ecclesiae mirabile sacramentum*]."[56] Article 26, quoting St. Cyprian, calls the church "the sacrament of unity [*unitatis sacramentum*]."[57]

The precise term *sacramentum* in reference to the church does not appear within *Lumen Gentium*'s chapter 1 on the *mysterium* of the church, except in reference to the seven sacraments. As Peter De Mey observes, however, naming the church as a sacrament "occurs at some of the most pivotal places in *Lumen Gentium*."[58] As noted above, it is given structural prominence in the very first article of the constitution, which functions as an introduction to chapter 1: "the church, in Christ, is like a sacrament [*veluti sacramentum*]— a sign and instrument [*seu signum et instrumentum*], that is, of intimate union [*intimae unionis*] with God and of the unity of the entire human race" (LG 1).[59] (The council will later quote this passage in its other constitution on the church, in *Gaudium et Spes* 42—in an example of reception history of a conciliar text within the duration of the council itself, an indication of the significance the council wanted to give to this key statement.)

56. The official footnote cites: Augustine, *Enarr. In Ps CXXXVIII (Exposition of Psalm 138)*, 2: CChr. 40, Turnhout, 1956, p. 1991. In addition, it mentions the prayer after the Second Lesson of Holy Saturday (Roman Missal, before the renewal of Holy Week).

57. The official footnote cites: St Cyprian, *De cath. eccl. unitate*, 7: ed. G. Hartel, in CSEL. t. III, 1, Vienna 1868, pp. 215–216; see Letter 66, n. 8,3: ed. G. Hartel, in CSEL. T. III, 2, Vienna 1871, pp 732–733.

58. Peter De Mey, "Church as Sacrament: A Conciliar Concept and Its Reception in Contemporary Theology," in *The Presence of Transcendence: Thinking "Sacrament" in a Postmodern Age*, ed. L. Boeve and J. Ries (Leuven: Peeters, 2001), 181–96, at 184.

59. Flannery translation, corrected. Flannery does not have any English word for *veluti*, having simply "a sacrament." The official Vatican website translation has "*like* a sacrament." Tanner has "*as* a sacrament." Francis Sullivan translates the phrase as "*a kind of* sacrament." Sullivan, *The Church We Believe In*, 8–11.

De Mey notes "the hesitation expressed by the word *veluti.*"[60] The word was first intended to address the initial disquiet on the part of some bishops, who claimed that the term caused unnecessary confusion with the seven sacraments. The council does not directly define the difference. As Congar notes: "The Council does not go any further in the clarification of this notion which, in the Council's mind, is related more to the economy of salvation than of [sacramental] theology."[61] The council also distances itself from any strict identification of the church with Christ, presenting the church rather as subordinate to but not separated from Christ.[62] The constitution begins, not with a reference to the church, but with reference to Christ, "light to the nations" (*lumen gentium*); the statement accordingly speaks of the church in reference to Christ: "the church, *in Christ*, is like a sacrament."[63] Later, in the last article of chapter 1, without using the term "sacrament," this subtle statement of the relationship between the church and Christ is reinforced in the discussion on the human and the divine in the church: "the church is compared, in no mean analogy [*non mediocrem analogiam*], to the mystery of the incarnate Word" (LG 8).

The notion of the church as a sacrament is used in other places in *Lumen Gentium*. In the opening article of its second chapter, "The People of God," it calls the church "the visible sacrament of this saving unity" (LG 9), citing St. Cyprian once again.[64] In the chapter on Our Lady, reference is made to "the sacrament of the salvation of the human race [*humanae salutis sacramentum*]" (LG 59).[65] *Ad Gentes* 5 speaks of the church as "the sacrament of salvation" (AG 5).

A particularly important use of the notion appears in the opening paragraph of chapter 7 on the "pilgrim church": "Christ . . . sent his life-giving Spirit upon his disciples and through him set up his body which is the church

60. De Mey, "Church as Sacrament," 183.

61. Yves Congar, "The People of God," in Miller, *Vatican II: An Interfaith Appraisal*, 197–207, at 205.

62. On this, see Christopher Ruddy, "'In My End Is My Beginning': *Lumen Gentium* and the Priority of Doxology," *Irish Theological Quarterly* 79 (2014): 144–64, at 149.

63. There is possible allusion here to Pauline usage. In the fourteen New Testament Pauline letters, the phrase "in Christ" can be found 144 times.

64. St Cyprian, *Epist.*, 69,6: PL 3, 1142 B; Hartel 3 B, p. 754: "the inseparable sacrament of unity."

65. Translation corrected. The Tanner, Flannery, and official Vatican translations all translate *sacramentum* here as "mystery." Peter De Mey believes it should be translated as "sacrament." De Mey, "Church as Sacrament."

as the universal sacrament of salvation [*universale salutis sacramentum*]" (LG 48). (The council will later quote this phrase twice, in documents published on its last working day, in *Ad Gentes* 1 and *Gaudium et Spes* 45.) It is particularly noteworthy that here the Holy Spirit is named as constituting the church as "the universal sacrament of salvation" in the world. As Adolf Laminski observes regarding the significance of this passage: "The description of the church as '*sacramentum*,' which is used in article 1 of the Constitution as a summary description of the nature of the church, *is here pneumatologically reinterpreted*. It is expressly said that the church is, *through the Holy Spirit sent by Christ*, the universal sign of salvation. The description of the church as '*sacramentum*' is therefore a concretization of the passage in article 7 of the first chapter [of *Lumen Gentium*] about the identity of the Spirit of Christ in the head and the members."[66] This passage in *Lumen Gentium* 7 (the article treating the image of the church as the Mystical Body of Christ) states: "for by communicating his Spirit, Christ mystically constitutes as his body his brothers and sisters who are called together from every nation."

In the crucial passage in *Lumen Gentium* 1, and in several other passages, the documents employ the words "sign" and "instrument" to explain its use of the word "sacrament," not as two separate aspects, but as interrelated. In other words, just like the seven sacraments, the church itself is an efficacious symbol. As a sign pointing to the reality of God's revealing and saving presence, the church is an instrument making present and effective that very reality. As a sign, the church manifests the reality to which it points; as an instrument, it brings that reality's efficacy to bear in human life.[67]

The first reference in Vatican II to the church as "a sign" had appeared in the second paragraph of its first document, where the theme of unity predominates: "[the liturgy] marvelously enhances [Christians'] power to preach

---

66. Laminski, "Die Entdeckung der pneumatologischen Dimension der Kirche durch das Konzil," 400. Emphasis added.

67. On this, see the commentary by the secretary of the commission that produced the draft that was eventually put to the bishops, with this explanation of "sacrament" as "sign and instrument": Gérard Philips, "L'Église, sacrement et mystère," *Ephemerides Theologicae Lovanienses* 42 (1968): 405–14, at 406. As Philips elsewhere notes: "Sign and instrument do not constitute *two* separate entities; it is through the symbol itself that divine action works. . . . Nor are sign and instrument separate *things*. Christ alone is the fundamental sacrament; the Church is a sacrament only by association with him. . . . The sign ensures a participation in a higher life. Hence it is quite rightly called an instrument, since it shows itself a bearer of divine efficiency. But let not the somewhat material resonance of the term 'instrument' deceive us. It is really a communion on the spiritual plane, even if it is established between men, therefore between bodies animated by spirit." Philips, "The Church: Mystery and Sacrament," 188. Original emphasis.

Christ and thus show the church to those who are outside as a sign lifted up among the nations, a sign under which the scattered children of God may be gathered together until there is one fold and one shepherd" (SC 2). In one of the last documents of the council, we read that "the Christian community will become a sign [*signum*] of God's presence in the world" (AG 15) and that the church is called to be "a bright sign [*lucidum signum*] of that salvation which comes to us in Christ" (AG 21).[68] Likewise: "By the power of the Holy Spirit the church is the faithful spouse of the Lord and will never fail to be a sign of salvation in the world" (GS 43). Similarly, the language of the church as an instrument appears. Just as the human nature of Christ serves the divine Word as the "living instrument of salvation [*vivum organum salutis*]" (LG 8), so too the church is the "instrument for the salvation of all [*instrumentum redemptionis omnium*]" (LG 9), a passage that finds an echo in the later passage regarding "the church as the universal sacrament of salvation [*universale salutis sacramentum*]" (LG 48).

Allusions to the church's nature as a sign and instrument can also be found in passages that focus on the church's presence in the world. The opening sentence of *Lumen Gentium* longs for a church where "the light of Christ . . . is resplendent on the face of the church" (LG 1). In the other constitution on the church, we find: "It is the function of the church to render God the Father and his incarnate Son present and as it were visible [*quasi visibilem*], while ceaselessly renewing and purifying itself under the guidance of the Holy Spirit" (GS 21). And: "What does most to show God's presence clearly is the familial love of the faithful [*caritas fraterna fidelium*] who, being all of one mind and spirit, work together for the faith of the Gospel and present themselves as a sign of unity" (GS 21).

It is striking that the late document, *Dei Verbum*, does not use the word *sacramentum* in reference to the church. Gerald O'Collins speaks, however, of *Dei Verbum*'s "'sacramental' way of presenting God's saving and revealing self-communication."[69] In considering the vision of the council in a comprehensive way, the notion of sacrament conditions several elements of that vision. God's self-revelation occurs through words and deeds. God can be encountered in human history, which is guided by divine Providence through the Holy Spirit enlightening human beings to read the signs of God's presence. God is encountered in the church's liturgy, as the Christian community celebrates the living presence of Christ through the Spirit. *Lumen Gentium* 11

68. Translation corrected.
69. O'Collins, *Retrieving Fundamental Theology*, 54.

treats each of the seven sacraments of the church, in the context of the priestly office of the whole people of God and the universal call to holiness.

While this notion of the church as a *sacramentum* encapsulates for the council the *mysterium* of the church in a special way, Walter Kasper warns against choosing any one of the conciliar motifs as an exclusive hermeneutical key:

> The definition of the church as a universal sacrament of salvation is one definition among others. The council uses a whole series of other descriptions in addition. The phrase "people of God" is especially important. But there are other terms or images as well: sheepfold, flock, cultivated field, tillage, building, temple, family of God, bride of Christ and—not least—body of Christ. It would therefore be completely wrong if we were to try to tie down post-conciliar Catholic ecclesiology exclusively to the term sacrament. The council describes the church rather as a mystery which cannot be exhausted by any single concept. If we are to approach the mystery of the church, *we need a multiplicity of complementary images and terms which mutually interpret and also correct one another.*[70]

As this book argues, no one metaphor or concept or aspect of ecclesiology can bear the burden of functioning as a single and comprehensive hermeneutical key for interpreting Vatican II's vision of the church.

Already the notion of the church as the "universal sacrament of salvation" has introduced the notion of salvation, which requires investigation in its own right and indeed should be foregrounded as a separate principle. Accordingly, the next conciliar principle brings to the fore the mission of the church as a sacrament *of salvation.*

---

70. Kasper, "The Church as a Universal Sacrament of Salvation," 115. Emphasis added.

Principle 10

Soteriological/Ecclesiological

Principle 10: God's plan in creating the world and engaging in history is for the salvation of human beings; the church is called to mediate this salvation, which consists not only in human beings' communion with the triune God in this life and eternally but also in the unity, peace, and justice of all human beings living a fully human life on earth.

The council does not set out to provide a comprehensive presentation of all elements of the Christian tradition regarding "salvation." A trajectory toward a synthesis is, however, evident.

Just as the terms "revelation" and "salvation" are employed throughout the council documents almost synonymously, so too are the terms "salvation" and "redemption." "Salvation," however, is the preferred conciliar term: the word *salus* is used 159 times, and *redemptio* thirty-one times. Occasionally, both are used together, emphasizing their semantic overlap; for example, we find: "[Christ] brought his revelation [*revelationem*] to perfection when he accomplished on the cross the work of redemption [*redemptionis*] by which he achieved salvation and true freedom [*salutem et veram libertatem*] for the human race" (DH 11).

Regarding "salvation," Vatican II is emphatic on several assertions of the Christian tradition, albeit with fresh perspectives. First, God's salvific will extends to all of humanity. "In his great love God intended the salvation of the entire human race" (DV 14); "This universal plan [*propositum*] of God [is] for the salvation [*salutis*] of humanity" (AG 3). The classic biblical text regarding the divine salvific will is 1 Timothy 2:4: "God our Savior . . . desires everyone to be saved and to come to the knowledge of the truth."[1]

---

1. NRSV translation. The fuller passage states: "This is right and is acceptable in the sight of God our Savior, who desires everyone to be saved and to come to the knowledge of the

This passage is quoted in the council texts four times and paraphrased and cited another three times.[2] Generally, each passage refers to the biblical text in terms of the divine plan of salvation. For example, *Dignitatis Humanae* 11 speaks of "the plan [*propositum*] of God the Saviour, 'who desires that everybody be saved and come to the knowledge of the truth" (DH 11). Thus, "all of humankind [are] called by God's grace to salvation" (LG 13). The council affirms how non-Christian religions "all share a common destiny, namely God. His providence, evident goodness, and saving designs extend to all humankind" (NA 1).

Second, in classic trinitarian theology, the work of salvation by the triune God is "appropriated" to Jesus Christ. He is "the source [*principium*] of salvation for the whole world" (LG 17),[3] "the author of salvation and the source of unity and peace" (LG 9), "the author of salvation" (AG 9). The Holy Spirit enables reception of the salvation Christ offers: "Christ sent the Holy Spirit from the Father to exercise inwardly his saving influence" (AG 4). The council quotes the classic biblical texts that affirm Christ as the unique source of divine salvation. For example, we read: "The reason for [the church's] missionary activity lies in the will of God, 'who wishes everyone to be saved and to come to the knowledge of the truth. For there is one God and one Mediator between God and humanity, himself a man, Jesus Christ, who gave himself as a ransom for all,' 'neither is there salvation in any other'" (AG 7, quoting 1 Tim 2:4-5 and Acts 4:12).

Third, Christ brings about salvation in the past, in the present, and its fulfillment in the future, not just through his saving passion and death, or just through his death and resurrection, but through his whole existence, including the sending of his Spirit and his continuing presence as risen Lord. We have already seen how an intertextual reading of the documents shows the council's expanded understanding of the means by which salvation is brought about. *Sacrosanctum Concilium* 102 speaks of "the whole mystery of Christ from the incarnation and nativity to the ascension, to Pentecost and the expectation of the blessed hope of the coming of the Lord." As we

---

truth. For there is one God; there is also one mediator between God and humankind, Christ Jesus, himself human, who gave himself a ransom for all" (1 Tim 2:4–6).

2. The quotations are found in SC 5; DH 11 and 14; AG 7. Biblical citations are given in texts where there is a paraphrase of the biblical passage in the main text of the conciliar document: LG 16; NA 1; AG 42. For example, citing 1 Timothy 2:4, the opening article of *Nostra Aetate* states that all human beings "share a common destiny, namely God. His providence, evident goodness, and saving designs [*consilia salutis*] extend to all humankind."

3. Tanner translates *principium* as "principle."

have seen, *Dei Verbum* presents a more comprehensive vision of the means through which Christ reveals and saves, including the sending of the Holy Spirit: "Everything to do with his presence and his manifestation of himself was involved in achieving this [revelation]: his words and works, signs and miracles, but above all his death and glorious resurrection from the dead, and finally his sending of the Spirit of truth. He revealed that God was with us, to deliver us from the darkness of sin and death, and to raise us up to eternal life" (DV 4).

Fourth, the church has a unique and indispensable role in mediating Christ's salvation to all humanity throughout history. Indeed, the church is necessary for salvation. *Lumen Gentium* 14 (albeit in a section addressed specifically to the Catholic faithful) teaches: "this pilgrim church is required for salvation. Present to us in his body which is the church, Christ alone is mediator and the way of salvation. He expressly asserted the necessity of faith and baptism and thereby affirmed the necessity of the church, which people enter through baptism as through a door. Therefore, those could not be saved who refuse either to enter the church, or to remain in it, while knowing that it was founded by God through Christ as required for salvation" (LG 14). The council consistently describes the mission of the church, and the roles within the church, in terms of the salvation not only of those within the church but also of all human beings. Here, as in other elements of the conciliar vision, *Lumen Gentium* provides a foundation. Exploration of the previous principle has noted several passages across the conciliar corpus where the notion of the church as a sacrament is linked to salvation: the church is a sacrament of salvation for all humanity (LG 1, 9, 48; AG 5). "This messianic people [is] a most certain seed of unity, hope and salvation [*salutis*] for the whole human race. Established by Christ as a communion of life, love and truth, it is taken up by him also as the instrument for the salvation [*redemptionis*] of all" (LG 9). Thus, "the church is driven by the Holy Spirit to play its part in bringing to completion the plan of God [*propositum Dei*], who has constituted Christ as the source of salvation [*principium salutis*] for the whole world" (LG 17).

Other conciliar texts reiterate yet expand on the church's soteriological function. Christ "founded his church as the sacrament of salvation [*sacramentum salutis*]" (AG 5). "The church was founded so that by spreading Christ's kingdom throughout the world to the glory of God the Father, every man and woman may share in the saving work of redemption [*omnes homines salutaris redemptionis participes efficiat*], and so that through them the entire world may be truly directed towards Christ" (AA 2). "The church's mission is concerned with people's salvation" (AA 6). The pastoral constitution begins with reference to the human condition, salvation, and the church's mission:

> The joys and hopes, the grief and anguish of the people of our time, especially of those who are poor or afflicted, are the joys and hopes, the grief and anguish of the disciples [*discipulorum*] of Christ as well. Nothing that is genuinely human fails to find an echo in their hearts. For theirs is *a community of people united in Christ and guided by the Holy Spirit in their pilgrimage towards the Father's kingdom, bearers of a message of salvation* [salutis] *for all humanity.* That is why they cherish a feeling of deep solidarity [*intime coniunctam*] with the human race and its history (GS 1).[4]

Throughout the remainder of the pastoral constitution we find echoes of the same theme: "Proceeding from the love of the eternal Father, the church was founded by Christ in time and gathered into one by the Holy Spirit. It has a saving and eschatological purpose [*finem salutarem et eschatologicum*], which can be fully attained only in the next life. But it is now present here on earth and is composed of women and men; they, the members of the earthly city, are called to form the family of the one children of God even in this present history of humankind and to increase it continually until the Lord comes" (GS 40). Thus, "the church has but one sole purpose—that the kingdom of God may come and the salvation of the human race may be accomplished" (GS 45).

Since the whole church is called to be a mediator of divine salvation and all baptized in the church are called to participate in that mission, the council speaks of those with specific ministries and apostolates in the church in terms of salvation. "[Christ] constantly makes available in his body, which is the church, gifts of ministries through which, by his power, we provide each other with the helps needed for salvation so that, doing the truth in love, we may in all things grow into him who is our head" (LG 7). Accordingly: "The apostolate of the laity is a participation [*participatio*] in the church's salvific mission. . . . All the laity, then, have the exalted duty of working for the ever greater extension of the divine plan of salvation to all people of every time and every place. Every opportunity should therefore be given them to participate [*participent*] zealously in the salvific work of the church according to their ability and the needs of the times" (LG 33).[5] Those dedicated to religious life too play a role in this salvific work: "Those [religious] who make

---

4. Translation corrected.
5. Translation corrected.

profession of the evangelical counsels should seek and love above all else God who has first loved us. In all circumstances they should take care to foster a life hidden with Christ in God, which is the source and stimulus of love of the neighbor, for the salvation of the world and the building-up of the church" (PC 6). The ordained, too, are called to mediate God's saving presence: "Ministers, invested with a sacred power [*sacra potestas*], are at the service of [*inserviunt*] their brothers and sisters, so that all who belong to the people of God and therefore enjoy true Christian dignity may attain to salvation through their free, combined and well-ordered efforts in pursuit of a common goal" (LG 18). "The spiritual gift which priests have received at ordination does not prepare them merely for a limited and circumscribed mission, but for the fullest, in fact the universal mission of salvation 'to the ends of the earth'" (PO 10). "The bishops [have received] the mission of teaching all peoples, and of preaching the Gospel to every creature, so that all may attain salvation through faith, baptism and the observance of the commandments" (LG 24).

The ecclesial norm of Scripture is likewise spoken of in terms of salvation and its mediation. When treating, for example, themes such as the inerrancy of Scripture, the council comes up with a formulation that develops the church's teaching: "the books of scripture . . . teach that truth which God, *for the sake of our salvation*, wished to see confided to the sacred scriptures" (DV 11). Here the council is applying to the topic of truth its renewed understanding of revelation, beyond a propositional notion of truth: revelation and salvation are primarily a saving encounter with the triune God. Hence, the primary witness to that historical encounter—the written Word of God—mediates, through its prayerful reading and hearing, that divine offer of salvation, revealing on a personal level the truth of God. "The word of God, which to everyone who has faith contains God's saving power, is set forth and marvelously displays its power in the writings of the New Testament" (DV 17).

So too, when speaking of the sacraments in the life of the church, the council does so in the key of salvation: "The sacraments of salvation [*sacramenta salutis*]" (PO 4)[6] play a central role in mediating the salvific effects of the work of Christ through the Spirit in the past into the present, opening the hearts of believers to a future and final salvation. *Lumen Gentium* 11, after treating each of the seven sacraments in turn, states: "Strengthened by so many and such great means of salvation, all the faithful, whatever their

---

6. Translation corrected.

condition or state are called by the Lord—each in his or her own way—to that perfect holiness by which the Father himself is perfect." Moreover, the section above on the christological/pneumatological principle has already raised the important rubric of "the paschal mystery" in the council's vision regarding the source of human salvation. This saving reality is available to believers in the present through their immersion in the paschal mystery—by participation in the sacraments, above all, in the Eucharist.

But what does Vatican II mean by "salvation"? Does it concern only individuals, or communities, or the whole of humanity, or the whole of creation? Is it related only to future life after death or to present existence during earthly life? Does it concern only forgiveness of sins or, more broadly, freedom from anything that, through no fault of one's own, diminishes one's full humanity—as God would desire it? Does divine salvation concern only human beings or also flora, fauna, and the natural environment? In fact, all of these elements can be found in the documents, either explicitly or implicitly, the latter only in a tangential way (as we will see in the next section on the protological/eschatological principle). Within the council's explicit or implicit treatment of all these issues, however, there is a trajectory apparent, with signposts pointing toward a synthesis of these elements.

Such a synthesis has been brought to the fore in the postconciliar reception of the council, and Francis Sullivan proposes that the notion of "integral salvation" names such a synthesis. He demonstrates cogently how the notion of integral salvation is "at least implicitly contained in the teaching of Vatican II."[7] A brief examination of that postconciliar reception will enable us to understand better the conciliar vision itself. The phrase "integral salvation" is used for the first time in official pronouncements in a final brief declaration of the fourth synod of bishops in 1974, on evangelization: "Among the many matters treated at the Synod we paid particular attention to the problem of the inter-relation between evangelization and *integral salvation*, or the full liberation of man and peoples. It is a matter of considerable importance and we were profoundly at one in reaffirming the close link between evangelization and liberation."[8] This synod was building on the previous synod in 1971 on "Justice in the World," which, in its own reception of Vatican II's social justice teaching, had stated starkly: "Action on behalf of justice and participation in the transformation of the world fully appear to us as *a constitutive dimension* of the preaching of the Gospel, or, in other words, *of the*

7. Sullivan, *The Church We Believe In*, 133.
8. Quoted in ibid., 141. Emphasis added.

Church's mission for the redemption of the human race and its liberation from every oppressive situation."[9] In its synthesis of the council and review of twenty years of reception, the 1985 Extraordinary Synod of Bishops in its Final Report affirms in the council's vision "a missionary openness for *the integral salvation of the world.* Through this, all truly human values not only are accepted but energetically defended: the dignity of the human person, fundamental human rights, peace, freedom from oppression, poverty and injustice. But *integral salvation* is obtained only if these human realities are purified and further elevated through grace and familiarity with God, through Jesus Christ, in the Holy Spirit."[10]

A key grounding in the Vatican II documents of its implicit notion of "integral salvation" is the council's cluster of teachings on the church as a sacrament, above all, in that paradigmatic statement of *Lumen Gentium* 1: "The church, in Christ, is in the nature of a sacrament—a sign and instrument, that is, of (1) *intimate union with God* and of (2) *the unity of the entire human race.*"[11] Two premises of Sullivan's interpretation are that "the major cause of the *disunity* of the human race at the present time is the objectively unjust situation in which relatively few people enjoy the advantages of prosperity while the great majority of the people of the world suffer all the disadvantages of poverty; [and that] the unity of the whole human race can only be achieved by the establishment of a just global society."[12] As Francis Schüssler Fiorenza observes regarding *Lumen Gentium* 1: "This statement underscores that the sacramental nature of the church is the basis of its mission precisely insofar as the church is a sacrament of unity. The church is a sacrament not merely of the unity with God, nor simply of the unity of humankind, but rather of *the double unity* that exists between the unity with God and the unity of the whole human race."[13] Therefore "the 'unity of the whole human race' that can come about only through the achieving of a truly just global society is correctly understood to be a component of the 'salvation'

---

9. Quoted in ibid., 140. Emphasis added.

10. Final Report, II, D, 3. Translation from Extraordinary Synod of Bishops, "Final Report," in *Documents of the Extraordinary Synod of Bishops November 28–December 8, 1985* (Homebush, Australia: St Paul Publications, 1986), 17–51, at 45. Emphasis added.

11. Numbering added.

12. Sullivan, *The Church We Believe In*, 133.

13. Francis Schüssler Fiorenza, "Church, Social Mission of," in *The New Dictionary of Catholic Social Thought*, ed. Judith A. Dwyer and Elizabeth L. Montgomery (Collegeville, MN: Liturgical Press, 1994), 151–71, at 161. Emphasis added.

of which the church is a sacrament."[14] Thus, Vatican II, in Sullivan's interpretation, imagines the church as a "sacrament of *integral* salvation."[15]

Gaudium et Spes has a clear statement implying this belief: "The council . . . can find no more eloquent expression of this people's solidarity, respect and love for the whole human family, of which it forms part, than to enter into dialogue with it about all these various problems, throwing the light of the Gospel on them and supplying humanity with the saving resources which the church has received from its founder under the promptings of the Holy Spirit. It is the human person that is to be saved, human society which must be renewed" (GS 3). As Francis Sullivan comments on this passage: "One could hardly have put more strongly the conviction that the church's saving mission is not limited to the eternal salvation of 'souls.' "[16] And, one might add, one could hardly have put more strongly the conviction that it is not only one's personal sinfulness that one needs to be saved from; there are forces outside of individuals' human control that diminish human beings' dignity and full humanity and from which God desires their liberation.

The bishops at Vatican II, in discerning the signs of the times, chose to focus on the positive and negative aspects of five areas of human existence: family life, culture, economic and social life, politics, and the international order. In analyzing the negative aspects, they implicitly asked: what in these five areas needs redemption? In examining political life, for example, the document speaks of people's "inability to achieve a truly human life [*vitam plene humanam*]" (GS 74). Perhaps this phrase is the closest Vatican II comes to defining "integral salvation" in our earthly sojourn—living "a fully human life [*vita plene humana*]." God offers salvation from human beings' inability to achieve a truly human life. Such a potential life would experience the earthly kingdom of God as "the kingdom of truth and life, the kingdom of holiness and grace, the kingdom of justice, love and peace" (LG 36).[17]

As a sacrament of a fully human life, "the church is called upon to be a sign to the world of what a truly just society would be, and to work, with all the resources proper to it, to overcome the causes of injustice and to promote justice in the world."[18] As both a *sign* and an *instrument*, it both *prefigures*

14. Sullivan, *The Church We Believe In*, 133.

15. This phrase is the title of the relevant chapter in Sullivan's book.

16. Sullivan, *The Church We Believe In*, 135.

17. A footnote refers to the Preface of the Feast of Christ the King in the then-current Roman Missal.

18. Sullivan, *The Church We Believe In*, 133.

and *promotes* "integral salvation": "All are called to this catholic unity of the people of God which prefigures and promotes [*praesignat et promovet*] universal peace" (LG 13). The council's vision has no hint of Pelagianism; it is all the work of Christ and his Spirit within responding human hearts: "Christ is now at work in human hearts by the power of his Spirit; not only does he arouse in them a desire for the world to come but he quickens, purifies, and strengthens the generous aspirations of humanity to make life more human [*humaniorem*] and conquer the earth for this purpose" (GS 38). Thus the salvation of which the church is a sign and instrument, and therefore of its saving mission, is to work toward making the world more human: "The church, then, believes that through each of its members and its community as a whole it can help to make the human family and its history still more human [*humaniorem*]" (GS 40). And, as the protological/eschatological principle will stress, the supreme model of "a fully human life" is Jesus Christ, but only the Spirit enables living the Christ life, as the christological/pneumatological principle has emphasized.

The soteriological/ecclesiological principle can be summed up in a passage with which the pastoral constitution ends its first part: "Whether it aids the world or whether it benefits from it, the church has but one sole purpose—that the kingdom of God may come and the salvation of the human race may be accomplished. Every benefit the People of God can confer on humanity during its earthly pilgrimage is rooted in the church's being 'the universal sacrament of salvation,' at once manifesting and actualizing the mystery of God's love for humanity" (GS 45, quoting LG 48).

Principle 11

Protological/Eschatological

Principle 11: God creates the world in love and creates human persons in the image of the triune God, revealing their true destiny in Jesus Christ, the incarnate image of the invisible God, who, through the Holy Spirit, comes to reveal their Creator to them and to save them; this divine plan of revelation and salvation—and the church's role in that plan—is realized within the conditions of creation and the particular contexts of human history, yet it will only be fulfilled at the end of human time.

While the Vatican II documents do not use the word "protology," the word captures a dominant theme in the conciliar vision: "creation" and "history" together constitute the *locus* for God's plan of revelation and salvation. Protology, following the word's Greek etymology, is "the study of first things"; that is, it looks to the beginning of creation and the origin of human existence. In systematic theology, its correlate is eschatology, "the study of the last things," the end and goal of creation and human existence. Both terms imply the reality of "time," of "history," and are therefore interrelated. Protology concerns God's creation of the cosmos and of human beings within time and history; eschatology concerns the fulfillment of God's purposes at the end of human time and history.

Vatican II directly addressed both of these dimensions of the Christian vision, a dual focus that is here formulated in terms of the protological/eschatological principle. This eleventh principle captures several overlapping themes in the conciliar vision: its theology of the divine plan and of divine providence; its theology of creation; its "theological anthropology" (its understanding of the human person, especially his or her dignity and freedom); its theology of sin; its linking of the components of "the divine mystery of creation and redemption" (AA 29); its vision of the place of the church in God's plan. An eschatological tone colors the council's presentation of all these themes. For example, the protological/eschatological principle is captured in the opening paragraph of the council's document on the church's relation to non-Christian religions: "Humanity forms but one community. This is so because all stem from one stock which God created to people the entire earth, and also because all share a common destiny, namely God. His providence, evident goodness, and saving designs [*consilia salutis*] extend to all humankind, against the day when the elect are gathered together in the holy city which is illumined by the glory of God, and in whose splendor all peoples shall walk" (NA 1).

Perhaps most striking of all, it is the council's growing awareness of the historicity of human existence that is a particularly innovative characteristic of the council's protological/eschatological principle. The council will come to present an evolutionary understanding of "creation" and a more historically conscious understanding of "history." In this shift, the council embraces as its own certain contemporary perceptions about the world and history: "The accelerated pace of history is such that one can scarcely keep abreast of it. The destiny of the human race is viewed as a complete whole, no longer, as it were, in the particular histories of various peoples: now it merges into a complete whole. And so humankind substitutes a dynamic and more evolutionary concept of nature [*ordinis rerum*] for a static one, and the result is an immense series of new problems calling for a new endeavor of analysis and synthesis" (GS 5).

God's Plan

The council's protological/eschatological principle affirms that, from the beginning, God has a plan for humanity, that God has revealed that plan (ultimately in Jesus Christ), and that God's continuing providence (above all, through the activity of the Holy Spirit) will ensure its fulfillment at the end of time. The church has a special role in the realization of God's plan; because that plan is a mystery, which will only be fully realized and revealed at the end of time, the church must be in "dialogue" with God in order to discern God's will in the ever-new contexts in which the church finds itself in history.

The council documents give regular reference to this "plan," "purpose," or "design" of God, using the words *propositum* and *consilium* almost interchangeably. The texts also speak of God's "will" (*voluntas*), of the "economy (plan) of salvation" (*oeconomia salutis*), and of the "history of salvation" (*historia salutis*). Once again, following the paradigm of the liturgy constitution (SC 14), the notion of "participation" is to the fore also here. The divine plan is depicted as involving *a double participation*: participation in the divine life and participation in helping bring to fulfillment God's plan. "The eternal Father, in accordance with the utterly free and mysterious design [*arcano consilio*] of his wisdom and goodness, created the entire world [*mundum*]. He chose to raise up men and women to participate [*participandam*] in his own divine life; and when they had fallen in Adam, he did not abandon them, but at all times offered them the means of salvation [*salutem*], bestowed in consideration of Christ, the Redeemer [*redemptoris*]" (LG 2).[1] *Dei Verbum* likewise speaks of God's plan for human participation in the divine life: "It pleased God, in his goodness and wisdom, to reveal himself and to make known the mystery of his will [*sacramentum voluntatis suae*], which was that people can draw near to the Father, through Christ, the Word made flesh, in the Holy Spirit, and thus become sharers in the divine nature" (DV 2). This divine plan God made known to human beings: "From the beginning [*ab initio*] of the history of salvation, God chose certain people as members of a given community, not as individuals, and revealed his plan [*consilium*] to them" (GS 32).

While the sending of Christ and the Spirit is the high point of the divine plan in history, the church is called to collaborate with God in bringing it to fulfillment. *Ad Gentes* 9 brings many of these themes together: "[The church's] missionary activity is nothing else, and nothing less, than the manifestation of God's plan [*propositi Dei*], its epiphany and realization in the world and in history [*in mundo et in eius historia*]; that by which God, through mission, clearly brings to its conclusion the history of salvation [*historiam salutis*]" (AG 9). Thus, while God's plan is most clearly revealed in Jesus Christ, the plan nevertheless remains a "mystery" until its fulfillment. As the revelation/faith principle asserts regarding the nature of divine revelation, God's self-revelation (and therefore, the revelation of God's "plan") has *past, present,* and *future* dimensions.

Some preliminary points can be noted here regarding particular elements the council brings to the fore in its presentation of God's plan: (1) the goodness of creation; (2) the divisive reality of sin as a thwarting of God's plan; (3) God's preeminent concern for unity among human beings; (4) the active participation of human beings, particularly the church, in the realization of God's plan; (5) the role of the Holy Spirit in effecting God's purposes, especially through the Spirit's empowerment of human beings in helping to facilitate the ongoing realization of God's plan; and (6) the eschatological character of the divine plan.

---

1. Translation corrected.

First, the council, in accord with ancient tradition, affirms the goodness of the created world within the divine plan and rejects any notion of gnostic dualism. Appropriating the creation of the world to God the Father, the council states: "The eternal Father, in accordance with the utterly free and mysterious plan [*consilium*] of his wisdom and goodness, created the entire world [*mundum universum*]" (LG 2).[2] Consequently, the created world is essentially good and can, moreover, mediate God's saving presence. The emphasis on the goodness of creation flows through the council's texts, from its first document ("There is scarcely any proper use of material things which cannot thus be directed towards people's sanctification and the praise of God" [SC 61]) to its last ("So God, as we read again in the Bible, saw 'all the things that he had made, and they were very good' [Genesis 1:31]" [GS 12]). In its sacramental view of revelation, *Dei Verbum* affirms that the created world is revelatory of God: "God, who creates and conserves all things by his Word, provides constant testimony to himself [*perenne sui testimonium*] in created realities" (DV 3).[3]

Second, human beings, however, have sinned against God and are in need of redemption. Sin has caused division among human beings, a division that is contrary to God's plan. As will be seen below when discussing the church/world principle, the debate on *Gaudium et Spes* surfaced strong differences among the bishops regarding how best to give proper emphasis to both the human propensity to sin and the effectiveness of divine grace. These debates resulted in a final document that attempts to balance out both a pessimistic and an optimistic view of humanity, each broadly in line with Augustinian and Thomistic perceptions of the Catholic tradition.

Third, and consequently, there is a recurring emphasis throughout the documents on God's desire for the *unity* of all human beings, becoming a central feature of the council's articulation of the church's mission: "All women and men are called to belong to the new People of God. This people, therefore, whilst remaining one and unique, is to be spread throughout the whole world and to all ages in order that the plan [*propositum*] of God's will [*voluntatis*] may be fulfilled: he made human nature one in the beginning and has decreed that all his children who were scattered should be finally gathered together as one" (LG 13). Alois Grillmeier remarks on this passage: "The presuppositions of this unity [among all peoples] are the unity of the human race by virtue of creation, and the decree of God to heal the divisions

---

2. Translation corrected.
3. Translation corrected.

of sin and its consequent alienations, by gathering men once more into one in Christ and giving them life from the one Spirit."[4]

Fourth, God does not bring the divine plan to realization without the free participation of human beings, and especially their free participation in the mission of the church. Through their activity in the world—for example, in their workplace—human beings are called in freedom to collaborate with God: "They can rightly look upon their work as a prolongation of the work of the creator, a service to other men and women, and their personal contribution to the fulfilment in history of the divine plan [*consilium*]" (GS 34). "By the work of our hands or with the help of technology, we till the earth to produce fruit and to make it a dwelling place fit for all humanity; we also play our part in the life of social groups. In so doing we are realizing God's plan, revealed at the beginning of time [*consilium Dei, initio temporum patefactum*], to subdue the earth and perfect the work of creation; at the same time we are perfecting ourselves and observing the command of Christ to devote ourselves to the service of our sisters and brothers" (GS 57).

Fifth, it is only through divine grace that human beings are able both to know God and collaborate with God. This divine enlightenment and empowerment are the work of the Holy Spirit. Once again, the council attempts to give a certain balance between its intense focus on Jesus Christ as savior for sinful humanity and the role of the Holy Spirit in realizing the grace of Christ.

Sixth, while God's plan has been initiated "from the beginning" (GS 32) and finds its salvific and revelatory high point in Jesus Christ, the divine plan is still a mystery awaiting its eschatological fulfillment. The church is guaranteed the assistance of the Holy Spirit to discern the meaning of God's plan for the present, leading the church ever toward a fuller understanding in the future, until the eschaton: "As the centuries go by, the church is always advancing towards the plenitude of divine truth, until eventually the words of God are fulfilled in it. . . . The Holy Spirit, through whom the living voice of the Gospel rings out in the church—and through it in the world—leads believers to the full truth and makes the word of Christ dwell in them in all its richness" (DV 8). Therefore, God's plan requires constant discernment and interpretation by the church throughout history: "The people of God believes that it is led by the Spirit of the Lord who fills the whole world. Impelled by that faith, they try to discern the true signs of God's presence and plan [*consilii*] in the events, the needs and the desires, which it shares

---

4. Grillmeier, "Chapter II: The People of God," 167.

with the rest of humanity today. For faith casts a new light on everything and manifests the plan [*propositum*] which God has for the integral vocation of humanity, thus guiding the mind towards solutions that are fully human" (GS 11).[5] Therefore, the mystery of God's plan is a constant provocation for the church, because it will only be realized and revealed in its fullness at the end of time. As a collaborator in God's plan while imperfectly fulfilling its mission, the church lives in the shadow of the mystery of God's will until the eschaton. The first chapter of *Lumen Gentium*, titled "The Mystery of the Church," ends with the eschatological note: "so that [the church] may reveal in the world, faithfully, although with shadows [*sub umbris, fideliter tamen*], the mystery of its Lord until, in the end, it shall be manifested in light" (LG 8). What was given "in the beginning" will only be realized "at the end." As the christological/pneumatological principle has highlighted, over the council's four years the Holy Spirit assumes a greater significance in the council's vision regarding how the church in history can be guided on its journey to that unknown future.

These six affirmations outline fundamental elements of what is here called the council's protological/eschatological principle. Other conciliar rubrics such as "history" and "world" will further explore these affirmations, as developed below, especially in the faith/history principle and the church/world principle.

Human Beings and the Perfect Human Being

On to this vast canvas portraying God's plan of revelation and salvation from beginning to fulfillment, the council paints its picture of the individual human person living in community within this drama of history. One of the key documents here is *Gaudium et Spes*, which constitutes "the first time that a council has consciously endeavored to set forth a systematic account of Christian anthropology in an independent thematic context."[6] Especially in its introduction (4–10) and the four chapters of part 1 (11–45), the pastoral constitution presents its vision of the origin, vocation, concrete reality, and destiny of the human person in community, from creation to the eschaton.

Three issues of tension in particular plagued the debates and drafting and remain evident in the final text: (1) the issue of the document's proper methodological starting point and central focus (anthropology or Christology?);

---

5. Translation corrected.
6. Walter Kasper, "The Theological Anthropology of *Gaudium et Spes*," *Communio* 23 (1996): 129–40, at 129.

(2) the issue of whether to approach "human nature" and "salvation" from an abstract, ahistorical viewpoint or in a concrete, historical way; and (3) the further related issue, dependent on how the previous two issues are addressed, of how to integrate "the order of creation" and "the order of redemption."[7] In addressing each of these issues, the council presents in the final texts a mosaic of juxtaposed elements, albeit only indicating the dominant features for a more harmonious and more finely articulated synthesis.

As the text that was eventually promulgated as *Gaudium et Spes* went through different numberings and versions, the methodological starting point and central focus kept shifting.[8] Each of these separate drafts had its own strengths and weaknesses, as does the final text. As Walter Kasper remarks:

> Text 3 [the version presented to the bishops for discussion in the third session], after setting forth the *status quaestionis* on the basis of a reading of the situation of today's world, makes Christology the starting-point for its statement on anthropology. This move was also intended to bring out the methodological point that Christology is the presupposition and measure of anthropology. However, the subsequent texts [Texts 4–6] take the opposite path: their method is to ascend from anthropology to Christology and to attempt a solution to the problem of the exact relation between the two in terms of a "Christology from below."[9]

7. *Apostolicam Actuositatem* 29 alludes to this classic distinction: "[Laypeople] should learn to accomplish the mission of Christ and the church, living by faith in *the divine mystery of creation and redemption*, moved by the Holy Spirit who gives life to the People of God and urging everyone to love God the Father, and in him to love the world of men and women" (AA 29). Emphasis added. On the classic distinction between "the order of creation" and "the order of redemption," see, for example, Gabriel Daly, *Creation and Redemption* (Wilmington, DE: M. Glazier, 1989).

8. A detailed examination of the history of *Gaudium et Spes*'s drafting will be presented in the chapter below on the church/world principle. A fundamental text for that history is Giovanni Turbanti, *Un Concilio per il Mondo Moderno: La Redazione della Costituzione Pastorale "Gaudium et Spes" del Vaticano II* (Bologna: Il Mulino, 2000).

9. Kasper, "The Theological Anthropology of *Gaudium et Spes*," 136. In referring to "Text 3" and subsequent versions, Kasper is following the numbering of the various Latin versions, as outlined in the appendices of Thomas Gertler, *Jesus Christus: Die Antwort der Kirche auf die Frage nach dem Menschsein. Eine Untersuchung zu Funktion und Inhalt der Christologie im ersten Teil der Pastoralkonstitution "Gaudium et Spes" des Zweiten Vatikanischen Konzils* (Leipzig: St. Benno, 1986), 397–426. This numeration differs from that presented throughout Francisco Gil Hellín, ed., *Constitutionis pastoralis de ecclesia in mundo huius temporis Gaudium et spes: Concilii Vaticani II synopsis in ordinem redigens schemata cum relationibus necnon patrum orationes atque animadversiones* (Città del Vaticano: Libreria Editrice Vaticana, 2003). For Hellín's explanation of his numbering, see ibid., xxviii–xxix. Other commentaries refer variously to different versions according to: its place of initial drafting, e.g., Rome, Malines

The final document attempts to combine both approaches; it aims to be both anthropocentric and Christocentric. As we will see, the argument of *Gaudium et Spes* proceeds in an elliptical movement around two focal points: the human person as the "image of God" and Jesus Christ as "the image of the invisible God."

Thus, from one perspective, the vision of *Gaudium et Spes* is emphatically anthropocentric. At the end of its preface, it states: "It is the human person [*persona humana*] that is to be saved, human society which must be renewed. It is the human person [*homo*], therefore, which the key [*cardo*] to this discussion, each individual human person in her or his totality, body and soul, heart and conscience, mind and will" (GS 3). Moreover, the document places human beings at the center of its theology of creation. The opening sentence of chapter 1 affirms: "Believers and unbelievers agree almost unanimously that all things on earth should be ordained to humanity [*hominem*] as to their center and summit" (GS 12). Human beings have been "set by [God] over all earthly creatures that they might rule them, and make use of them, while glorifying God" (GS 12). Accordingly, technological progress and social, economic and political activity must have the good of human persons as their goal; for example, "economic production is meant to be at the service of humanity in its totality" (GS 64).

While intended to showcase the dignity of the human being as central to all moral concerns, aspects of the council's anthropocentrism were to become problematic in the years following the council, particularly in the light of the ecological crisis, of which the bishops of Vatican II were unaware.[10] Nonetheless, *Gaudium et Spes* is somewhat nuanced in its anthropocentrism: "Often refusing to acknowledge God as their source [*principium*], men and women have also upset the relationship which should link them to their final destiny; and at the same time they have broken the right order that should exist within themselves as well as between them and other people and all created reality [*omnes res creatas*]" (GS 13).[11] Thus, the document explicitly rejects humanity as "the absolute measure of all things" (GS 12). The measure of all things is Christ, "the perfect human being [*perfectus homo*)]" (GS 38). Consequently, *Gaudium et Spes* is strongly Christocentric, while being emphatically anthropocentric.

(also referred to as Louvain), Zürich, Ariccia; its number on the official list of documents yet to be discussed on the council floor (Schema XVII, Schema XIII); or its various iterations after discussion began in the aula (*textus receptus, textus recognitus, textus denuo recognitus,* etc.).

10. This will be explored below in the chapter on the church/world principle.

11. Translation corrected.

There are five key articles referring to Christ as the criterion of true humanity. Intratextually, they constitute important structural points in the document, being placed at the end of the introduction (GS 10) and at the end of each of the four chapters making up part 1, "The Church and the Human Vocation" (GS 22, 32, 38–39, 45):

> [Jesus Christ is] the key, the center, and the purpose [*clavem, centrum et finem*] of the whole of human history. (GS 10)[12]

> In reality it is only in the mystery of the Word made flesh that the mystery of humanity truly becomes clear. (GS 22)

> From the beginning of the history of salvation, God chose certain people as members of a given community, not as individuals, and revealed his plan to them, calling them "his people" and making a covenant on Mount Sinai with them. This communitarian character is perfected and fulfilled in the work of Jesus Christ, for the Word made flesh willed to take his place in human society. (GS 32)

> The Word of God, through whom all things were made, became man and dwelt among us; a perfect man, he entered world history, taking that history into himself and recapitulating it. He reveals to us that "God is love" and at the same time teaches that the fundamental law of human perfection, and consequently of the transformation of the world, is the new commandment of love. (GS 38)[13]

> The Word of God, through whom all things were made, was made flesh, so that as a perfect man he could save all women and men and sum up all things in himself. The Lord is the goal of human history, the focal point of the desires of history and civilization, the center of humanity, the joy of all hearts, and the fulfillment of all aspirations. (GS 45)[14]

The theological anthropology of Vatican II, therefore, is grounded on Christ as the exemplar of "being human" according to the plan of God.[15]

---

12. Thomas Gertler calls this "the Christological credo" of the whole constitution. Gertler, *Jesus Christus*, 94.

13. The text is quoting 1 John 4:8.

14. Each of these christological articles is discussed in detail in Gertler, *Jesus Christus*, 93–324.

15. George Karakunnel summarizes the elliptical movement and balance of the final text: "The anthropology of the Council cannot be isolated from its christology. Nor can its christology be understood independently of its anthropology. The full truth of man is understood only in Christ, the perfect man. Therefore, anthropology is carried over into christology illuminating the mystery of man in the mystery of Christ, the God-man." George Karakunnel,

Central to the council's efforts to achieve a balance between its anthropo-logical and Christological affirmations was its appeal in *Gaudium et Spes* to two biblical passages: Genesis 1:26-27, regarding the first human being cre-ated according to "the image of God" (*imago Dei*),[16] and Colossians 1:15, regarding Jesus Christ as "the image of the invisible God."[17]

In order to capture human persons' "dignity and vocation" (GS 12), *Gaud-ium et Spes*, citing Genesis 1:26, employs the rubric of "the image of God" (*imago Dei*)—"the nucleus of the Council's anthropology."[18] "Sacred scripture teaches that women and men were created in the image of God" (GS 12). According to Walter Kasper:

> The systematic clasp holding together anthropology and Christology [in *Gaudium et Spes*] is the concept of the "image of God." The theology of the image of God is the connecting link with whose aid the Council Fathers at-tempt to bring man's personality, his social constitution, as well as his creative organization of the world, into relation with the mystery of Christ. For as the image of God, man finds his ultimate and definitive fulfillment and completion only in that intimate communion with God which has appeared in a unique and unsurpassable way in Jesus Christ the God-man.[19]

The Christian Vision of Man: A Study of the Theological Anthropology in "Gaudium et Spes" of Vatican II (Bangalore: Asian Trading Corp., 1984), 3.

16. "Then God said, 'Let us make humankind in our image, according to our likeness; and let them have dominion over the fish of the sea, and over the birds of the air, and over the cattle, and over all the wild animals of the earth, and over every creeping thing that creeps upon the earth.' So God created humankind in his image, in *the image of God* he created them; male and female he created them." NRSV translation. Emphasis added. *Gaudium et Spes* 12 also refers to the use of the rubric in Wisdom 2:23: "God created us for incorruption, and made us in the image of his own eternity."

17. "He is *the image of the invisible God*, the firstborn of all creation; for in him all things in heaven and on earth were created, things visible and invisible, whether thrones or dominions or rulers or powers—all things have been created through him and for him." NRSV translation. Emphasis added. The footnote reference in *Gaudium et Spes* 22 to Col 1:15 also gives reference to 2 Cor 4:4: "In their case the god of this world has blinded the minds of the unbelievers, to keep them from seeing the light of the gospel of the glory of *Christ, who is the image of God.*" NRSV translation. Emphasis added.

18. Karakunnel, *The Christian Vision of Man*, 4. For detailed examination of the motif throughout *Gaudium et Spes*, see Anthony O. Erhueh, *Vatican II: Image of God in Man; An Inquiry into the Theological Foundations and Significance of Human Dignity in the Pastoral Constitution on the Church in the Modern World, "Gaudium et spes"* (Rome: Urbaniana Uni-versity Press, 1987); Gertler, *Jesus Christus*, 358–75.

19. Kasper, "The Theological Anthropology of *Gaudium et Spes*," 137.

Moreover, the *imago Dei* motif therefore grounds an eschatological notion of the baptized human person as called to a life of holiness, as *Lumen Gentium* highlights in its fifth chapter, "The Universal Call to Holiness" (LG 39–42). Entering into an intimate relationship with God by virtue of their creation, the baptized believer is called to a deeper faith relationship with their Creator: "The followers of Christ . . . have been made sons and daughters of God by the Baptism of faith and partakers of the divine nature, and so are truly sanctified. They must therefore hold on to and perfect in their lives that holiness which they have received from God" (LG 40).

As *imago Dei*, the human person is intrinsically relational, in the present life and in the life to come. As Barnabas Ahern comments: "There is no place for atomistic individualism in the economy of God's plan. Christian life and Christian fulfillment at the endtime have an essentially *social* character."[20] Their social character is brought out in at least two ways. First, the ground of that relationality is the nature of the Creator God as triune, of whom the human creature is an image: "There is a certain similarity between the union existing among the divine persons and the union of God's children in truth and love. It follows, then, that if human beings are the only creatures on earth that God has wanted for their own sake, they can fully discover their true selves only in sincere self-giving" (GS 24). Second, by virtue of God's creating human persons as either male or female, interrelationality is part of the human condition. "God did not create men and women as solitary beings. From the beginning 'male and female God created them.' This partnership [*consociatio*] of man and woman constitutes the first form of communion of persons [*communionis personarum*]. For by their innermost nature men and women are social beings; and if they do not enter into relationships with others they can neither live nor develop their gifts" (GS 12).[21] In a special way, marriage and family life constitutes a "community of love" (GS 47). While affirming that "marriage and married love are ordered to the procreation and education of the offspring" (GS 48), the council equally affirms: "But marriage was not instituted solely for the procreation of children: its nature as an indissoluble covenant between two people and the good of the children demand that the mutual love of the partners be properly expressed, that it should grow and mature" (GS 50).

20. Barnabas Ahern, "The Eschatological Dimensions of the Church," in *Vatican II: An Interfaith Appraisal*, ed. John H. Miller (Notre Dame, IN: University of Notre Dame, 1966), 293–300, at 295. Original emphasis.

21. The passage quoted is Gen 1:27.

The *imago Dei* in humanity has, however, been disfigured by sin. There is an eschatological tension in the experience of individuals and societies. Despite their "dignity and vocation" (GS 12), human beings have "abused their freedom" (GS 13) and sinned: "they have broken the right order that should exist within themselves as well as between them and other people and all creatures" (GS 13). Only Christ, the perfect man and divine Savior, can restore human beings:

> They are therefore divided interiorly. As a result, the entire life of women and men, both individual and social, shows itself to be a struggle, and a dramatic one, between good and evil, between light and darkness. People find that they are unable of themselves to overcome the assaults of evil successfully, so that everyone feels as if in chains. But the Lord himself came to free and strengthen humanity, renewing it inwardly and casting out the "prince of this world," who held it in the bondage of sin. For sin diminished humanity, preventing it from attaining its fulfillment. (GS 13)

Throughout the debates and drafting, it was particularly the German bishops and *periti*, including Karl Rahner and Joseph Ratzinger, who were concerned that the reality of sin was being downplayed in some of the earlier drafts and that an overly optimistic notion of human beings was being presented.[22] The final text attempts to balance optimism and pessimism when portraying "the high calling and the deep misery [*simul sublimis vocatio et profunda miseria*]" (GS 13) that human beings experience.

Parallel to the motif of the human being as *imago Dei* is the motif of Christ as "the 'image of the invisible God'" (GS 10, 22).[23] "He who is the 'image of the invisible God' is himself the perfect man who has restored in the children of Adam that likeness to God which had been disfigured ever since the first sin" (GS 22). The council's key anthropological affirmations—regarding the dignity of the human person, the social nature of the human person, the dignity of marriage, the common good, human rights, religious liberty, and the significance of culture—are thus grounded in this perfect human being, Jesus Christ, who, while fully divine, is fully human: "Human nature, by the very fact that it was assumed, not absorbed, in him, has been raised in us also to a dignity beyond compare. For, by his incarnation, he, the Son of God,

---

22. These issues will be treated in greater detail below in the chapter on the church/world principle.

23. Quoting Col 1:15.

has in a certain way united himself with each individual. He worked with human hands, he thought with a human mind. He acted with a human will, and with a human heart he loved. Born of the Virgin Mary, he has truly been made one of us, like to us in all things except sin" (GS 22). This theological interrelating of the anthropological and the Christological conditions the spiral methodology between Christology and anthropology followed throughout the document: "in the light of *the Gospel* and of *human experience* [*sub luce evangelii et humanae experientiae*]" (GS 46).[24]

Historical Consciousness and Theological Tensions

A related issue to that of the relationship between anthropology and Christology was that of how theological anthropology itself was to be approached in the document. The dominant neoscholastic theology leading up to the council approached anthropology with an abstract, ahistorical understanding of "human nature"; likewise, the "salvation" that Jesus Christ brings was understood in an abstract, ahistorical way. These approaches were apparent in various drafts. Many bishops, however, proposed a more concrete and historical approach to the nature of the human person and the salvation Jesus Christ brings. The council ends up juxtaposing both approaches. Although at times employing doctrinal formulations in the mode of neoscholasticism, *Gaudium et Spes* attempts also to consider the human person within the specific context of—to cite the title of the pastoral constitution—"the world of this time [*in mundo huius temporis*]," or, as it later expresses it, "the world of today [*in mundo hodierno*]" (GS 2). Then, before turning to its more theological considerations, the constitution lays out an introduction (GS 4–10) titled "The Condition of Humanity in the World Today" (*De hominis condicione in mundo hodierno*), which examines various elements of the contemporary situation, with its opportunities and crises.[25]

A particularly pertinent example of the council's historical consciousness is its more nuanced appeal to the traditional notion of "natural law." The bishops began to perceive more acutely the concrete and varied "condition" of human existence. While the traditional essentialist notion is reiterated, a more historical approach is apparent. As Josef Fuchs observes:

24. Emphasis added.

25. Such section titles were reading aids that were part of the distributed texts, and still included in most editions, but they were not officially part of the text voted on by the bishops.

> The traditional teaching on natural law is explicitly defended many times in the texts of the Second Vatican Council, as well as the twofold distinction of the natural law [*secundum naturam* and *secundum rationem*], yet it is possible to show that *a tendency to change this teaching* also exists. The council tends to refer human behaviour less to set, formulated laws and norms than to the God-given task of more fully humanizing the human person and the world. This is a different perspective, one that issues quite different challenges. It displays a better and deeper understanding of the natural law.[26]

While we have here another case of juxtaposition in the final text, hermeneutical weight must be given to evidence of the council's "tendency to change this teaching," as Fuchs here proposes, in the way that Hermann Pottmeyer, following Gustave Thils, gives hermeneutical weight to the trajectory toward a desire for change in certain teachings.[27] Charles Curran too sees in the council's approach to natural law a shift away from a classicist approach to one that is historically conscious.[28]

Likewise, the *salvation* that Christ effects is considered in the light of the specific anxieties, needs, and crises of human persons in their historical context: the concrete issues of marital, cultural, societal, economic, and political life, as well as relations between groups and nations. Christ is presented as offering salvation to human beings with specific salvific needs, at a specific

26. Josef Fuchs, "Natural Law," in *The New Dictionary of Catholic Social Thought*, ed. Judith A. Dwyer and Elizabeth L. Montgomery (Collegeville, MN: Liturgical Press, 1994), 669–75, at 673. Emphasis added.

27. On this hermeneutical issue, see the discussion above in the council/the documents principle.

28. Curran believes the council is proposing that "a historically conscious approach should replace the classicism of the accepted natural law theory. . . . Classicism begins with an unchanging element named human nature. Then one works methodically from the abstract and universal toward the more concrete and particular. In doing so, one is involved in the casuistry of applying universals to concrete reality. One begins with the definition of a human being that applies to every human being with properties verified in every person. One thus knows the human being as such, which is unchangeable. On the other hand, the historically conscious approach begins from people where they are performing intentional acts that give meaning and significance to human living. Just as meaningful performance is constitutive of human living, so common meaning is constitutive of community. This understanding sees humankind as a concrete aggregate developing over time and not something totally fixed and immutable. Human nature itself is historically developing and changing." Charles E. Curran, "Strand Three: Natural Law," in *The Development of Moral Theology: Five Strands* (Washington, DC: Georgetown University Press, 2013), 73–147, at 99. For the distinction, Curran is drawing on Bernard J. F. Lonergan, "The Transition from a Classicist Worldview to Historical-Mindedness," in *A Second Collection*, ed. William F. J. Ryan and Bernard J. Tyrrell (London: Darton, Longman and Todd, 1974), 1–9.

time and place. While the divine source and eternal goal of salvation history is reaffirmed by Vatican II, the freshness of its vision lies in its attention to human salvation as context-specific—salvation in Jesus Christ as experienced in the concrete, particular problems of the present. As noted earlier, the council attempts to give equal attention to the *past, present,* and *future* dimensions of revelation and salvation. What is distinctive about *Gaudium et Spes* is an approach to "humanity" that is grounded in a perception of the existential reality of human beings as concretely situated in the 1960s. Consequently, the document manifests a decisive movement by the official magisterium away from an understanding of the human person as possessing an eternally-the-same "nature," as presupposed in the neoscholastic manuals and papal declarations before the council, as well as in the schemata of the Preparatory Commission. This is key for understanding the council's protological/eschatological principle.

In addition to its distinctive methodology and movements toward a historically conscious approach, the council attempts to interrelate, without separating, the order of creation and the order of redemption. This issue was closely related to the debate concerning the relationship between nature and grace, an important theme in the work of those *ressourcement* theologians calling for a renewal in Catholic theology in the decades before the council, criticizing in particular the notion of "pure nature" that had become an important tenet of the preconciliar neoscholastic theology of grace.[29] As Kasper observes: "The background of *Gaudium et Spes* is a theological conception which assumes the unity of the orders of creation and redemption in salvation history. Although the document [*Gaudium et Spes*] makes anthropology its starting-point, Christology is nevertheless the criterion of all its statements about anthropology and remains the horizon in which they are to be understood."[30] The desire to emphasize this interrelationship

---

29. For a history and analysis of these debates among the key theologians in the decades leading up to Vatican II, see throughout Hans Boersma, *Nouvelle Théologie and Sacramental Ontology: A Return to Mystery* (New York: Oxford University Press, 2009); Gabriel Flynn and Paul D. Murray, eds., *Ressourcement: A Movement for Renewal in Twentieth-Century Catholic Theology* (Oxford: Oxford University Press, 2011). Specifically on the criticism by Henri De Lubac of neoscholasticism as a "separated theology," see Joseph A. Komonchak, "Theology and Culture at Mid-Century: The Example of Henri de Lubac," *Theological Studies* 51 (1990): 579–602, at 582–84. As an example of another theologian's critique of the scholastic notion of "pure nature," see Richard Lennan, "The Theology of Karl Rahner: An Alternative to the *Ressourcement*?," in Flynn and Murray, *Ressourcement*, 405–22.

30. Kasper, "The Theological Anthropology of *Gaudium et Spes*," 137.

between the order of creation and of redemption was starkly stated by the *relator*, when presenting the schema to the council for debate in the final session. He noted the concern of the drafting committee meeting earlier that year at Ariccia, February 1–6, 1965: that "the document proceed from facts and truths accepted by most people, even non-believers, but in such a way as to arrive gradually at the presentation of the whole truth . . . natural truths have to be seen with the eyes of the Gospel—without *that reprehensible separation* between what belongs to the 'purely natural' order and what belongs to the 'order of redemption,' *since even the creation itself is embedded in the order of redemption.*"[31] *Gaudium et Spes* presents the orders of creation and redemption as intersecting axes: on the one hand, a horizontal (*anthropological*) axis and a vertical (*Christological*) axis, without ever disconnecting the junction of both axes.

In these debates over Christology and different aspects of the mystery of Jesus Christ, two tensions in particular came to the fore: tension between an incarnational and a cross-centered Christology, and tension between an incarnational and an eschatological Christology. Both of these two issues relate, once again, to the council's desire not to separate "the order of creation" from "the order of redemption."

Regarding the first tension, emphases on either the *incarnation* or the *cross* were each defended by different bishops and *periti* for a variety of theological purposes. Those foregrounding the incarnation highlighted the consequent sanctity of the created world and of the human person, along with the optimism that one should have in graced human beings, despite their sinfulness. The incarnation has sanctified the human and indeed saved human beings from the consequences of sin. On the other hand, there were those who, sensing a "naïve optimism" in the former position, emphasized how the cross in the paschal mystery of Christ is a central affirmation of the Christian tradition.[32] Sin continues to exert its power on individuals and on the course of human history, a power that only the Crucified One can defeat; suffering and hardship continue to mark the lives of human beings in history, and only the cross of Christ gives them hope in a God who is with them in their "griefs and anxieties" (GS 1).

---

31. AS IV/1, 523. Translation from ibid., 136–37. Emphasis added.

32. For the phrase "naïve optimism," see Joseph Cardinal Ratzinger, "Review of the Postconciliar Era—Failures, Tasks, Hopes," in *Principles of Catholic Theology: Building Stones for a Fundamental Theology* (San Francisco: Ignatius Press, 1987), 367–78, at 372.

Regarding the second tension, there were differing concerns among some bishops to give greater accent to either the *incarnational* or the *eschatological* aspects of "the mystery of Christ." Once again, those emphasizing the incarnation wanted to give theological value to the "present" time and the active presence of Christ through the Spirit within history. Within the context of this particular debate,[33] those who emphasized the eschatological dimensions of the mystery of Christ wanted to highlight not only the unfinished nature of God's plan but also the element of divine judgment at the end of time. Two years before the council, John Courtney Murray—later a *peritus* to the US bishops—had written of a tension in the Catholic tradition, making a distinction between "incarnational humanism" and "eschatological humanism" and outlining the extreme versions that both positions can assume.[34] In a similar way, Zachary Hayes retrospectively perceives a debate taking place at Vatican II between "Incarnationalists" and "Eschatologists," two schools of thought that had characterized Catholic theology in the decades before the council.[35] The former position highlights the value of the human contribution to history through cultural, social, economic, and political engagement for the sake of a fuller humanity; the latter highlights that God's transcendent future will be a gift beyond human imagining, a future that God will bring about as pure gift, regardless of the positive contribution human beings may have made throughout history.

Both positions can be found within the council texts, at times dialectically juxtaposed. In some instances, both perspectives are woven more tightly together. For example, *Gaudium et Spes* 39 affirms:

> Far from diminishing our concern to develop this earth, the expectation of a new earth should spur us on, for it is here that the body of a new human family grows, foreshadowing in some way the age which is to come. That is why, although we must be careful to distinguish earthly progress [*progressus*] clearly from the increase of the kingdom of Christ, such progress is of vital concern

---

33. In conciliar debates on other issues, the eschatological dimension was appealed to in order to highlight the conditioned nature of present understandings of "God's plan" and "God's will" and interpretations of past doctrinal formulations of the faith according to time-conditioned frameworks.

34. John Courtney Murray, "Is It Basket Weaving? The Question of Christianity and Human Values," in *We Hold These Truths: Catholic Reflections on the American Proposition* (New York: Sheed and Ward, 1960), 175–96, esp. 184–96.

35. See Zachary Hayes, *Visions of a Future: A Study of Christian Eschatology* (Collegeville, MN: Liturgical Press, 1990), 126–34.

to the kingdom of God, insofar as it can contribute to the better ordering of human society. . . . Here on earth the kingdom is mysteriously present; when the Lord comes it will enter into its perfection. (GS 39)

Echoing the sensibilities of these two schools of thought, the two major contributors to both of these conciliar debates—relating to the incarnation/cross and the incarnation/eschaton—were generally the French and the German bishops along with their *periti*, who were concerned to uphold the important truths related to aspects of the Christian tradition at stake within each of these issues.[36] Regarding these two positions throughout the drafting of *Gaudium et Spes*, Anthony Erhueh notes: "The optimistic view, sponsored largely by French theologians, had a positive attitude to the world; creation already initiated the incarnation and redemption; the pessimistic view stresses the presence of sin (as a result of the Fall) in the world, and therefore suspicion of the truly human; it regards eschatology as the predominant factor in man's history. This view was largely supported by the Germans. The two views, optimistic and pessimistic, represent the Incarnational and the Eschatological aspects of *Gaudium et Spes*. They balance the entire Pastoral Constitution."[37] Any synthesis of the vision of Vatican II must hold together both aspects of the tradition, although Vatican II shows a trajectory toward a greater appreciation of incarnational humanism, in order to bring to the foreground an element the Catholic Church had somewhat backgrounded in the centuries before the council.[38] The chapter below on the church/world principle will explore further aspects of these tensions.

On Pilgrimage to God's Future

The protological/eschatological principle of Vatican II articulates not only the council's vision of the individual person and of human persons in community in the world but also its vision of the community of those persons

36. Often the French bishops were aligned in these matters with the Belgian and Dutch bishops and *periti*.

37. Erhueh, *Vatican II: Image of God in Man*, 107n9. Erhueh is here summarizing the postconciliar insights of the Belgian *peritus* Charles Moeller, "Église dans le Monde d'aujourd'hui," *Documentation Catholique* 63 (September 1966): 1485–507, esp. cols 504–505.

38. On this debate throughout the history of Catholic theology, and the necessity of both perspectives for a coherent Christian theology, Hayes notes: "The tension between these two schools of thought is not just of historical interest. On the contrary, the polarities that are here drawn out into two conflicting styles of theology are present as dialectically related poles within the heart of the Christian faith." Hayes, *Visions of a Future: A Study of Christian Eschatology*, 130.

who freely choose to become disciples of Jesus Christ in the world throughout history until the end of time.[39] Related specifically to the church, the proto-logical/eschatological principle highlights "the mystery of the Church in its beginning and in its final goal."[40] The principle further articulates the deep hope that vibrates through the first of the council's theo-logical principles, that of revelation/faith: the hope aroused by the Good News that the revelatory and saving desire of God is to draw humanity and all of creation into the very life of the triune God. The word *spes* is repeated sixty-five times in the conciliar documents, with twenty references in *Gaudium et Spes* alone, including the constitution's *incipit*.[41]

While an eschatological tension characterizes many of the sixteen documents, there are two documents in particular that give the theme sustained attention: *Lumen Gentium* and *Gaudium et Spes*. Remarkably, *Lumen Gentium*'s whole chapter 7 on the eschatological character of the church was a late addition to the document. In the preparatory draft *De Ecclesia*, the eschatological theme was not even addressed. When the bishops debated the schema at the end of the first session, the eschatological lack was tellingly noted.[42] Pope John XXIII himself was particularly concerned that the topic of veneration of the

---

39. For a comprehensive study of the council's eschatology with an *ecclesiological* focus, see Christof Müller, *Die Eschatologie des Zweiten Vatikanischen Konzils: Die Kirche als Zeichen und Werkzeug der Vollendung*, Würzburger Studien zur Fundamentaltheologie, Bd. 28 (Frankfurt am Main: Peter Lang, 2002). Müller explores the eschatological dimension of the church in terms of the inner life of the church (*ad intra*) and its place in the world (*ad extra*). See also Paolo Molinari, "L'indole escatologica della Chiesa peregrinante and i suoi rapporti con la Chiesa celeste," in *La Chiesa del Vaticano II: Studi e commenti intorno alla Costituzione dommatica 'Lumen Gentium'*, ed. Guilherme Baraúna (Firenze: Vallecchi Editore, 1965), 1113–33; Ahern, "The Eschatological Dimensions of the Church."

40. Grillmeier, "Chapter I: The Mystery of the Church," 142–43.

41. An *incipit* is the first few Latin words of a document, often used to refer to the whole document, e.g., "*Gaudium et Spes*."

42. The theologically astute bishop from Mainz, Hermann Volk, was on this point of theology—as on others throughout the council—an important voice, as the *peritus* Barnabas Ahern remembers: "When [Volk] first read the schema, he instantly asked the pertinent question 'Wohin denn gehen wir? [But then, where are we going to?].' To him the schema seemed to be so concerned with the life of the Church on earth that it had almost nothing to say about the Church's destiny. God's pilgrims were furiously on the march; but the schema had them marching a treadmill. Happily, Bishop Volk acted promptly; two days later on the Council floor he expressed his consternation and, with charged voice, uttered the heartfelt request of many of the bishops that a chapter be added to the schema under the title 'The Eschatological Nature of the Pilgrim Church and Her Union with the Heavenly Church.'" Ahern, "The Eschatological Dimensions of the Church," 294.

saints had not been addressed, a view that Paul VI likewise later endorsed.[43] Accordingly, Cardinal Arcadio Larraona, prefect of the Congregation of Rites, was given the task of setting up a commission to prepare a text on the veneration of the saints for inclusion in the document on the church. It became an important conciliar moment. As the *peritus* Otto Semmelroth observes, the theme of veneration of the saints raised broader issues:

> Of course, without going into the veneration of the saints in the life of the Church, one can establish that a doctrine of the Church is possible which does not mention that veneration. Nevertheless the introduction of this theme proved to be of major service to the Church in her self-presentation. For it called attention to the fact that an essential feature of the church, without which she cannot be properly described, had not indeed been forgotten but had not been explored: her eschatological dynamism. Not only can and must it be discussed along with her institutional aspect; if it is not, then the Church will be incorrectly represented even as an institution.[44]

The new chapter 7 rapidly went through four drafts throughout 1964, the year of the constitution's official promulgation.[45]

Not only that chapter but indeed the corpus of Vatican II documents, when taken as a whole, is markedly eschatological in its orientation when referring to the church. From one perspective, many of the affirmations are simply reiterations of themes from the Catholic tradition concerning the purpose of human existence and the fulfillment of God's plan at the end times: death, judgment, praying for the dead, the second coming of Christ, the communion of saints, resurrection of the dead, and the consummation of God's plan.[46]

---

43. Ahern remarks that "Pope John XXIII recognized the merit of Bishop Volk's intervention and he himself warmly seconded his words." Ibid.

44. Otto Semmelroth, "The Eschatological Nature of the Pilgrim Church and Her Union with the Heavenly Church," in *Commentary on the Documents of Vatican II*, vol. 1, ed. Herbert Vorgrimler (London: Burns & Oates, 1967), 280–84, at 280.

45. For the dates of the four drafts, see the first page of the synopses in Alberigo and Magistretti, *Constitutionis Dogmaticae Lumen Gentium*, 227.

46. Barnabas Ahern notes regarding the eschatology of chapter 7 of *Lumen Gentium*: "Because every thread of the texture is drawn from Scripture, the chapter simply affirms the truths of revelation as the Church has always understood them. In substance it presents the Church as always moving forward to a heavenly home and as already sharing on the march some of the joy and fulfillment of the endtime. Any Catholic child who has studied the catechism will recognize in this chapter a familiar medley of the truths he has learned: the end of the world, resurrection and heaven, purgatory, the communion of saints, prayer for the dead and prayer to those who are already with God. Even the most unlettered Catholic will find nothing new

This traditional view could well be described as a balance between a "this-worldly" eschatology and an "other-worldly" eschatology.[47] Here in the seventh chapter of *Lumen Gentium*, however, the eschatological significance of "this world" is somewhat undervalued; it would seem that any human action aiding God's purposes in the world would not contribute to "the new heavens and the new earth" (LG 48) that God will bring about at the end of time. Attention is mainly given to *the goal* of the church's earthly journey rather than to the journey through history itself. Parallel to this is the accent given to the passing nature of the present world and a downplaying of its importance in bringing God's plan toward fulfillment. In this sense, as Monika Hellwig remarks— perhaps too strongly—"one would look in vain to Vatican II for an explicit account of a *renewed* understanding of eschatology."[48]

From another perspective, however, the council makes some significant shifts with regard to previous teaching, particularly in its "this-worldly" eschatology.[49] The opening paragraph of *Lumen Gentium*'s seventh chapter begins with a paradigmatic statement regarding its eschatological vision of the church: "The church, to which we are all called in Christ Jesus, and in which by the grace of God we attain holiness, will receive its perfection only in the glory of heaven, when the time for the renewal [*restitutionis*] of all things will have come. At that time, together with the human race, *the world itself* [*universus mundus*], *which is closely related to humanity and which through it attains its destiny*, will be perfectly established in Christ" (LG 48).[50]

Shortly after the council, the biblical *peritus* Barnabas Ahern commented critically on the importance of this passage and of its undeveloped impact on the rest of the seventh chapter:

---

here. At the same time, however, the Council Fathers have presented the age-old familiar doctrines with special attention to perspective and proportion." Ahern, "The Eschatological Dimensions of the Church," 294.

47. For the terminology "other-worldly eschatology" and "this-worldly eschatology" to describe the eschatology of *Lumen Gentium*, see Bernard P. Prusak, *The Church Unfinished: Ecclesiology through the Centuries* (New York: Paulist Press, 2004), 295–96.

48. Monika Hellwig, "Eschatology," in *Systematic Theology: Roman Catholic Perspectives*, ed. Francis Schüssler Fiorenza and John P. Galvin (Minneapolis: Fortress Press, 1991), 2:349–72, at 359n10. Emphasis added.

49. For a discussion of the church's teaching on eschatology prior to the council, in the preconciliar suggestions by bishops around the world and in the draft schemas prepared before the council, see Müller, *Die Eschatologie des Zweiten Vatikanischen Konzils*, 14–21.

50. Emphasis added.

Unfortunately . . . only half of the theme enunciated in this opening sentence is developed in the ensuing chapter. The treatment in chapter 7 envisages only man, his future destiny and his present spiritual participation in it: this chapter describes only the *height and depth* of the Church's eschatological dimensions. The vast expanse of *length and breadth* must be painted into the picture with the deft strokes of the Constitution on the Church in the Modern World. The thought of the Council Fathers on eschatology, therefore, comes to us as a composite picture; *their full teaching must be gleaned from several parts of the Conciliar corpus.* . . . Too many people will read only one Constitution and overlook another; and even those who do read the whole Conciliar documentary may fail to synthesize its complementary teaching.[51]

For Ahern, the "height and depth" of the council's eschatological vision refers to the "vertical" relationship between God and creation/humanity; the "length and breadth" refers to the "horizontal" *length*-dimension of that vertical relationship through time and to the "horizontal" *breadth*-dimension that includes the wider created world within which humanity dwells. Using Bernard Prusak's terminology, the "height and depth" captures one particular understanding of the "other-worldly"/"this-worldly" binary, with "length and breadth" offering a renewed understanding of the "this-worldly" dimension—from a historically conscious perspective and a more inclusive understanding of the consummation of all God's creation, including the nonhuman world—as *Gaudium et Spes* would go on to hint, albeit tentatively.

Therefore, despite its more expansive opening programmatic statement, most of chapter 7 of *Lumen Gentium* presents, along with its "other-worldly" eschatology, a "this-worldly" eschatology in which the church is depicted as "a pilgrim [*peregrinus*]." "Pilgrim" language colors several of the conciliar texts.[52] But the notion has a range of meanings across the documents, taking on a different nuance as the council assumes a greater historically conscious understanding and embraces a greater appreciation of the eschatological

51. Ahern, "The Eschatological Dimensions of the Church," 293–94. Emphasis added. By the phrase "eschatological dimensions" and the terms "height," "depth," "length," and "breadth," Ahern means "the Church charged with momentum impelling it upwards and, at the same time, rich to its very depths with heavenly life; the Church reaching out to the length and breadth of all creation so that one day, when the end comes, God may be all in all." Ibid., 293.

52. The noun "pilgrimage" (*peregrinatio*) occurs six times (LG 21, 58; GS 1, 45; AA 4; UR 3); the verb "to journey" (*peregrinor*) eighteen times (LG 6, 7, 8, 9, 14, 48, 49, 62, 68; UR 2, 6; DV 7; AA 4; DH 12; AG 2; GS 45, 57); the adjective "pilgrim" (*peregrinus*) once (SC 2); and the noun "pilgrim" (*peregrinus*) twice (SC 8; CD 16). See Delhaye, Guéret, and Tombeur, *Concilium Vaticanum II: Concordance*, 484–85.

value of the earthly phase of its existence. Here in chapter 7 there is a sense in which the term *peregrinus* can tend to undervalue earthly life: the earthly church is an alien (*peregrinus*) travelling in a land that is not its true home. Earlier, at the end of its chapter on the mystery of the church, *Lumen Gentium* had quoted St. Augustine, considering the church to be "like a stranger in a foreign land [*peregrinando*]" (LG 8).[53] The people of God journey through history toward its goal beyond history.[54] Indeed, when the church reaches its goal, its pilgrim nature will come to an end; even the sacraments and structures that give it life along its earthly journey will pass away:

> Already the final age of the world is with us and the renewal of the world is irrevocably under way; it is even now anticipated in a certain real way, for the church on earth is endowed already with a sanctity that is true though imperfect. However, until the arrival of the new heavens and the new earth in which justice dwells *the pilgrim church [*ecclesia peregrinans], *in its sacraments and institutions, which belong to this present age, carries the mark of this world which will pass*, and it takes its place among the creatures which groan and until now suffer the pains of childbirth and await the revelation of the children of God. (LG 48)[55]

Such texts express the great hope that sustains the Christian vision: beyond death and existence in the world, the eternal bliss of life with God awaits us.

One needs to look to the second constitution on the church, *Gaudium et Spes*, promulgated a year later, to find a fuller exposition of the council's eschatology. While there is a similar balance in this constitution between the "other-worldly" and the "this-worldly," it conceives the pilgrimage with a renewed sense of length and breadth. Certainly, the church continues to be conceived as "the *pilgrim* church [*ecclesia peregrinans*]" (GS 48). *Gaudium et Spes*, however, presents a more positive evaluation of the contribution made by human activity toward the new world God will bring about at the end times: "In their pilgrimage [*peregrinantes*] to the heavenly city Christians are to seek and value the things that are above; this involves not less, but

---

53. Quoting St. Augustine, *De Civitate Dei*, XVIII, 51, 2: PL 41, 614. The above translation of *peregrinando* is the Flannery translation. The Vatican website translation too has "like a stranger in a foreign land." Tanner has "on its pilgrim way."

54. This notion of the church as a pilgrim people was first retrieved into modern Catholic ecclesiology with the publication of Robert Grosche, *Pilgernde Kirche* (Freiburg im Breisgau: Herder, 1938). It became an emerging theme in writings up to its official reception by Vatican II.

55. Emphasis added.

greater commitment to working with everyone for the establishment of a more human world" (GS 57). What happens in history matters.

The whole document highlights the significance of the church's engagement with the world during its earthly journey, even while its fulfillment will be realized only at the end of time: "Proceeding from the love of the eternal Father, the church was founded by Christ in time and gathered into one by the Holy Spirit. It has a saving and eschatological purpose [*finem*] which can be fully attained only in the next life. But it is now present here on earth and is composed of women and men; they, the members of the earthly city, are called to form the family of the one children of God even in this present history of humankind and to increase it continually until the Lord comes" (GS 40). Thus: "Animated and drawn together in his Spirit we press onwards on our journey [*peregrinamur*] towards the consummation of history which fully corresponds to the plan of his love: 'to unite all things in him, things in heaven and things on earth'" (GS 45).[56] *Unitatis Redintegratio* similarly highlights the eschatological character of the church: "During its pilgrimage [*peregrinatione*] on earth, this people [of God], though still in its members liable to sin, is growing in Christ and is guided by God's gentle wisdom, according to God's hidden designs, until it shall happily arrive at the fullness of eternal glory in the heavenly Jerusalem" (UR 3).

Paralleling yet amplifying this conciliar discussion regarding the pilgrim church and its fulfillment at the end of time is the council's treatment of the relationship between the kingdom of God and the church. In the decades before the council, biblical scholarship on the topic had been presenting a spectrum of interpretations of the New Testament materials. This spectrum ranged between two extreme views: from one that saw Jesus as exclusively focused on a future culmination of God's purposes at the end of time (imminent eschatology) to one that saw Jesus exclusively concerned about effecting change in the present (realized eschatology).[57] The council deliberately does not enter into the debate in an explicit way. As George Tavard observes, the conciliar texts show "no allusion to the widely advertised controversy over 'future' or 'realized' eschatology.'"[58] One could say, however, that the council's vision, while appealing simply to Catholic tradition rather than to

---

56. The passage is here quoting Eph 1:10.

57. The literature on this issue is immense. For an overview of the debate, see Wendell Willis, ed., *The Kingdom of God in 20th-Century Interpretation* (Peabody, MA: Hendrickson Publishers, 1987).

58. George H. Tavard, *The Pilgrim Church* (New York: Herder and Herder, 1967), 117.

contemporary biblical interpretation, does align with one of the contemporary positions among scholars, that of a "now-but-not-yet" eschatology.[59]

The council documents bring to the fore the significance of the kingdom of God motif in Jesus' ministry (e.g., LG 3, 5; DV 17). As Avery Dulles remarks: "Vatican II is indeed remarkable for its emphasis on the kingdom of God."[60] At times, the documents employ the motif to capture the notion of God's plan, as Bonaventure Kloppenburg notes: "To understand what this kingdom is [for the council], we may turn to what the Council says of the eternal Father's plan. The kingdom of God is the final goal of this plan, the 'consummation' that will be effected when all things are made new."[61] Similarly, when summarizing *Lumen Gentium*'s discussion of God's plan in its first chapter on the mystery of the church, John Fuellenbach asserts: "The most comprehensive symbol for God's plan with creation is the biblical phrase kingdom of God."[62] Nevertheless, although the final kingdom is presented as the goal of God's plan, the council makes a distinction between the kingdom of God in history and the fulfillment of the kingdom of God at the end of human time. And, moreover, it carefully distinguishes the church's relationship with both phases of the kingdom.

The kingdom has been inaugurated in history by Jesus Christ: "Christ established on earth the kingdom of God" (DV 17); "principally the kingdom is revealed in the person of Christ himself" (LG 5), manifest in Jesus' words, deeds, and behavior. This kingdom will, however, be fully realized only "when Christ presents to his Father an eternal and universal kingdom" at the end

59. Tavard summarizes the council's position: "For Catholic thought, future and realized eschatologies are neither contradictory nor exclusive. Far from it, they are mutually correlative, for the *eschaton* is future in so far as it is not yet entirely upon us; yet it would not be the *eschaton* for us unless it was already somehow upon us. The wave of the future for which the Church waits in eager expectation has already left the trace of its shape upon the visible realities of the Church. . . . Thus the Kingdom of God is both present and yet not totally so in the Church; the second coming is taking place, yet not finalized, in the sacraments; the vision is anticipated, yet not exhausted, in faith; the glory is dimly discerned in grace. An exaggeration of the presence of glory leads to a theology of glory without a corresponding theology of the cross; and the sense of the triumphant Church without the corresponding sense of the suffering Church leads to the 'triumphalism' that was so often denounced in the debates of the Ecumenical Council. In this spirit, the Council emphasizes the two aspects of eschatological dialectics." Ibid., 118–19.

60. Avery Dulles, "Vatican II and the Church's Purpose," *Theology Digest* 32 (1985): 341–52, at 343.

61. Kloppenburg, *The Ecclesiology of Vatican II*, 36.

62. John Fuellenbach, *Church: Community for the Kingdom* (Maryknoll, NY: Orbis Books, 2002), 75.

of time (GS 39). Thus: "Here on earth the kingdom is mysteriously present; when the Lord comes it will enter into its perfection" (GS 39). For the council, the notion of God coming to reign within human history creates an arc between the coming of Christ inaugurating the kingdom of God in history and his Second Coming bringing the fulfillment of the kingdom and the realization of God's plan at the end of earthly time.

Regarding the pilgrim church's relationship with this kingdom in history, "Vatican II handled the question very cautiously."[63] Before the council, the church was sometimes identified as itself the kingdom of God.[64] Other commentators contrasted the church and the kingdom.[65] Certainly, for Vatican II, "the church [is] the kingdom of Christ already present in mystery" (LG 3). Nonetheless, the council states that the church is not identical with the kingdom of God in history; it is related rather to its inauguration by Jesus Christ and works toward its realization at the end of time. The church "receives the mission of proclaiming and establishing among all peoples the kingdom of Christ and of God, and is, on earth, *the seed and the beginning of that kingdom*" (LG 5).[66] Moreover, "while it slowly grows to maturity, the church longs for the completed kingdom and, with all its strength, hopes and desires to be united in glory with its king" (LG 5). "[The church's] destiny

63. Avery Dulles, "The Church and the Kingdom," in *A Church for All Peoples: Missionary Issues in a World Church*, ed. Eugene LaVerdiere (Collegeville, MN: Liturgical Press, 1993), 13–30, at 21.

64. For a survey of approaches to the depiction of this identification reaching back to Augustine, see Peter Hünermann, "Reign of God," in *Sacramentum Mundi: An Encyclopedia of Theology*, ed. Karl Rahner (New York: Herder and Herder, 1970), 5:233–40. For a survey of such approaches in both Catholicism and Protestantism, see Howard A. Snyder, *Models of the Kingdom* (Nashville: Abingdon Press, 1991), 67–76. For an identification of the kingdom of God with the church, see the draft document prepared for the First Vatican Council (although never debated), which stated that the church is "this perfect city which holy writ calls the Kingdom of God"; quoted in Christopher Butler, *The Theology of Vatican II* (London: Darton Longman & Todd, 1967), 144. Butler likewise observes that "a similar identification was made in the draft on the Church presented to the fathers of Vatican II in 1962" (ibid.). The identification of church and kingdom was not, however, pervasive in preconciliar papal teaching; Pius XI, for example, did not restrict the reign of Christ to the Church. See Dulles, "The Church and the Kingdom," 21.

65. See Dulles, *Models of the Church*, 96. Dulles is criticizing such approaches.

66. Emphasis added. It is unclear from the texts whether the council wishes to distinguish "the kingdom of Christ" and "the kingdom of God." It may be that, in employing the distinction, Vatican II is taking it over from the highly influential 1959 work by the German Catholic exegete Rudolf Schnackenburg, *God's Rule and Kingdom* (New York: Herder and Herder, 1963). Here the phrase "kingdom of Christ" appears to refer to the kingdom in history, and the phrase "kingdom of God" to the final realization at the end of time.

[*finis*] is the kingdom of God which has been begun by God himself on earth and which must be further extended until it is brought to perfection by him at the end of time" (LG 9). It is above all, however, the passage in *Gaudium et Spes* 45 that highlights the importance of the church within the kingdom in history, as well as affirming its nonidentification with that kingdom: "Whether it aids the world or whether it benefits from it, the church has but one sole purpose—that the kingdom of God may come and the salvation of the human race may be accomplished. Every benefit the People of God can confer on humanity during its earthly pilgrimage is rooted in the church's being 'the universal sacrament of salvation,' at once manifesting and actualizing the mystery of God's love for humanity" (GS 45).[67]

In conclusion, the council's vision of the relationship between the church and the kingdom in history can be stated negatively: the council does not *identify* the church with the kingdom in history; the council does not *subordinate* the church to the kingdom of God in history; and the council does not *separate* the church from the kingdom of God in history. The life and activity of the church do not coincide with the kingdom active in the world, because the council presents the church and the kingdom as distinct, even though Vatican II moves toward an attitude of appreciative, albeit critical, dialogue with the world. While the kingdom of God in history is broader than the church, the church has a central role as sacramental sign and instrument of the kingdom in those domains "in the world" beyond the church.[68]

But what of the relationship between the church at the end of time (after the passing of the pilgrim church when history ends) and the kingdom of God in its full realization? Here again, one could say—as Dulles does regarding the council's approach to the pilgrim church's relationship with the kingdom in history—"Vatican II handled the question very cautiously."[69] The

67. The council is here quoting LG 48.

68. Karl Rahner presents a succinct summary of the relationship between the church and the kingdom of God: "The Church is not identical with the kingdom of God. It is the sacrament of the kingdom of God in the eschatological phase of sacred history that began with Christ, the phase that brings about the kingdom of God. As long as history lasts, the Church will not be identical with the kingdom of God, for the latter is only definitively present when history ends with the coming of Christ and the last judgment. Yet the kingdom of God is not simply something due to come later, which later will replace the world, its history and the outcome of its history. The kingdom of God itself is coming to be in the history of the world (not only in that of the church)." Karl Rahner, "Church and World," in *Sacramentum Mundi: An Encyclopedia of Theology*, ed. Karl Rahner (New York: Herder and Herder, 1968), 1:346–57, at 348.

69. Dulles, "The Church and the Kingdom," 21. Dulles does believe, however, that the council went close to saying that the church in glory is the kingdom in its fullness. Neverthe-

church does not come to an end with the passing of the pilgrim church in history. As the *peritus* Otto Semmelroth observes in his commentary on chapter 7 of *Lumen Gentium*, "The Church does not fully possess her sacramental form in this world, which is destined to be done away with at the last day, to merge into the heavenly consummation where the Church no longer exists except in an analogical sense, as the Church triumphant."[70]

As it held regarding the church in history and the kingdom in history, the council does not clearly *identify, subordinate,* or *separate* the eschatological church in relationship with the kingdom in its fullness. Certainly the pilgrim church will pass away, including its sacraments and institutions (LG 48), but the heavenly church continues; the church does not come to an end but rather comes to its fulfillment. Even though the fulfillment of God's plan at the end of time will be of God's doing, it will not be through a cancellation of the contribution of human beings throughout history: "Men and women were created in God's image. . . . When men and women provide for themselves and their families in such a way as to be of service to the community as well, they can rightly look upon their work as a prolongation of the work of the creator, a service to other men and women, and *their personal contribution to the fulfilment in history of the divine plan [consilium divinum in historia]*" (GS 34).[71] This personal contribution is itself a dimension of the mystery of the kingdom: "Far from diminishing our concern to develop this earth, the expectation of a new earth should spur us on, for it is here that the body of a new human family grows, foreshadowing in some way the age which is to come. That is why, although we must be careful to distinguish earthly progress clearly from the increase of the kingdom of Christ, such progress is of vital concern to the kingdom of God, insofar as it can contribute to the better ordering of human society" (GS 39).

Moreover, the church does not completely coincide with the kingdom in its fullness, since the kingdom in its fullness includes the created world, the cosmos, which too will be transformed. The *mundus universus*, along with

---

less, Dulles fails to note the passages where the council speaks not only of the transformation of humanity but also of the transformation of the created world. For example, "[The church's] destiny [*finis*] is the kingdom of God which has been begun by God himself on earth and which must be further extended until it is brought to perfection by him at the end of time when Christ our life will appear and '*creation itself also will be delivered from its slavery to corruption* into the freedom of the glory of the sons and daughters of God' (Rom 8:21)" (LG 9). Emphasis added.

70. Semmelroth, "The Eschatological Nature of the Pilgrim Church," 281.

71. Emphasis added.

the earthly church, will be transformed. In a more nuanced formulation, Dulles concludes: "Perhaps one should say that the heavenly church will be at the heart and center of the ultimate kingdom. The new heavens and the new earth, while they may include more than the transfigured Church, will serve to mediate and express the blessed life of the redeemed."[72]

Ultimately, the council is apophatic in its assertions about the ultimate kingdom: "We do not know the moment of the consummation of the earth and of humanity nor the way the universe will be transformed" (GS 39). The *peritus* Ahern strikingly captures this apophatic vision:

> What will be the finishing touch that God himself will provide, the Council wisely leaves unsaid. . . . But the day and the hour and the manner of the final consummation are really of little importance. What really matters is the tremendous truth affirmed by the Council that all worthwhile human activity is part of the creative plan of God and of the redemptive ministry of Christ who dies that he might re-establish all things and might transform them into the perfect eschatological kingdom of his Father. The whole world—the heavens and the earth, the vast oceans and the verdant fields, the tangled bush of Africa and the trampled streets of New York, men of all colors and of all backgrounds—all that God has made is alive with an *élan* [impulse] to God.[73]

72. Dulles, "The Church and the Kingdom," 18.
73. Ahern, "The Eschatological Dimensions of the Church," 299.

PART III
ECCLESIOLOGICAL PRINCIPLES

Principle 12

Scripture/Tradition

Principle 12: Since the source of revelation and salvation is the living God reaching out to humanity in Jesus Christ through the Holy Spirit, tradition is not just a patrimony of authoritative teachings and practices from the past but also, in its deepest sense, the active, living process of transmission by communities of faith who respond to the Gospel and put it into practice throughout history; Scripture is itself such a historically conditioned product of the early church's transmission of divine revelation but also an ecclesial norm that must be continually actualized within the shifting contexts of the church's ongoing living tradition.

The theo-logical principles outlined in the previous chapters—especially concerning the conciliar shifts in understanding revelation and faith and the importance of maintaining a christological and pneumatological balance in all matters of faith—are concretized in the council's renewed teaching concerning the transmission of faith through Scripture and tradition. These two faith-witnesses to revelation are interrelated, according to the council's vision, because of the particular relationship each has to the church itself, the community of faith responding to divine revelation. A corollary of their common origin in the church is that the church, in turn, finds its own DNA in Scripture interpreted within the tradition; together they constitute the genome, as it were, that fashions the church's ongoing life and identity when interpreted in different times and contexts. Therefore, their interrelationship is formulated here as specifically an *ecclesiological* principle. The dynamic of their interrelationship is central to the council's pastoral aim and to its agenda for *aggiornamento*.

The four shifts taken by Vatican II regarding *revelation and faith* have already been examined. This chapter now examines the implications of those shifts for the council's articulation of the relationship between *revelation and tradition*, the relationship between *revelation and Scripture*, and the relationship between

Scripture and tradition. First, according to the vision of Vatican II, tradition is primarily the church handing on God's offer of saving revelation through its doctrine, its worship, and indeed its whole life. Second, Scripture, while it witnesses to and plays a preeminent role in mediating God's revelation, is not to be equated with the living divine-human encounter that revelation is. Third, tradition gives rise to Christian Scripture, which then rules the church's life and mediates ongoing encounter with the revealing God, but Scripture is to be interpreted within the ongoing tradition.

A Contentious Issue from New Perspectives

The council's articulation of these dynamic relationships emerged out of many of the bishops' engagement, both before and during the council, with *ressourcement* scholarship regarding the methods and themes of the biblical and patristic renewal movements. This scholarship revealed that the length, breadth, and depth of the Catholic tradition are richer than the reductionist notion that had developed in recent centuries, equating "tradition" with the doctrinal teaching of the magisterium. Furthermore, this expansion of the bishops' understanding of "the great tradition" led to the consequent development in the council fathers of a historical consciousness regarding the faith/history relationship.[1]

As with all the other principles, this one too needs to be understood in terms of the shifts the council took *away from* certain positions proposed in the preparatory schemata, in this case particularly the one on revelation, *De Fontibus Revelationis.* Thus, a clearer understanding of the council's teaching in the final version of *Dei Verbum* is aided, in part, by understanding what it was implicitly arguing against. And it was an argument. The council debates on Scripture, tradition, and their interrelationship were among the most heated in the council's four years, lasting the whole length of the council and involving much political intrigue on the part of a minority and a majority among the bishops. Regarding the specific chapter of *Dei Verbum* on the transmission of revelation where the Scripture/tradition relationship is treated, Joseph Ratzinger writes: "Chapter II of the Constitution still bears the marks of the bitter struggle from which the final version of the text emerged."[2] The preparatory schema on the "sources" of revelation, *De Fontibus Revelationis,* was the second major item on the agenda during the first

---

1. The phrase "the great tradition" is used in the document of the Extraordinary Synod of Bishops, "Final Report," 22.
2. Ratzinger, "Chapter II: The Transmission of Divine Revelation," 181.

session. Discussion began on November 14, 1962; a final version called *Dei Verbum* would be promulgated in the fourth session on November 18, 1965, three weeks before the close of the council. What John O'Malley asserts regarding all the council's documents is particularly true of *Dei Verbum*: "The sixteen final documents of the council give no sense of before and after; nor do they indicate, except occasionally in a soft way, that what they are saying changes anything that earlier seemed normative."[3]

Pope John, in his opening address, had invited the council to go beyond the divisive debates of the past and to move into a new ecclesial space, that of ecumenism—of openness to other Christians through dialogue. Four weeks later, when debate on *De Fontibus Revelationis* began, the bishops were asked to give consideration to a schema that set out to continue the divisive debates regarding issues at the very heart of the Reformation, especially that of Scripture and tradition and their interrelationship. The bishops' response would test the seriousness of the council's ecumenical intent. They had received the schema *De Fontibus Revelationis* even before arriving in Rome for this first session and had time to give it consideration, as well as to get advice from their *periti*.[4] Even before discussion began, alternative schemas of the revelation document were being proposed and distributed among the bishops.[5]

The schema's content and tone would have been no surprise. The text resembled a treatise on the subject in any manual of theology of the time. It was condemnatory in tone regarding positions held by Protestants; its approach was apologetic and framed in the terminology of scholastic theology; it made no attempt to appropriate in a positive way contemporary historical-critical biblical and patristic scholarship of the previous decades. Just as Vatican I had predominantly approached the matter of revelation and faith in terms of a communication of divine truths formulated as doctrines, so too the *De Fontibus* schema saw revelation, faith, Scripture, and tradition (by the magisterium) similarly in propositionalist terms. Furthermore, the schema was couched in the language of the so-called two-source theory of

3. O'Malley, *What Happened at Vatican II*, 9.

4. The schema was one of seven sent out to the bishops in July 1962. For the Latin text, see AS I/3, 14–26. For an English translation, see the website of Joseph Komonchak (http://jakomonchak .files.wordpress.com/2012/09/de-fontibus-1-5.pdf). For a history of the preparatory schema's drafting, see Karim Schelkens, *Catholic Theology of Revelation on the Eve of Vatican II: A Redaction History of the Schema De fontibus revelationis (1960–1962)* (Boston: Brill, 2010), esp. 157–219. Also among the seven was the schema *De Deposito Fidei Pure Custodiendo*, dealing with a topic closely related to *De Fontibus Revelationis*.

5. For a summary of some of these texts, see Wicks, "Vatican II on Revelation."

revelation: Scripture and tradition were presented as two sources of God's revelation (understood as the communication of truths or beliefs). The Council of Trent had indeed used the term "source" (*fons*) in its document on Scripture and tradition, but only in the singular, and then in reference to "the Gospel."[6] Catholic theologies of tradition in the centuries following Trent had not been so subtle, however, formulating a two-source theory of revelation, which was dominant in the manuals of theology on the eve of Vatican II.[7] Accordingly, the schema not only spoke of Scripture and tradition as two "sources" of revelation but conceived of them as separate and distinct channels: the truths of revelation were said to be contained *partly* in Scripture and *partly* in tradition.[8]

When debate began on November 14, 1962, speaker after speaker criticized the schema.[9] Eventually, on November 20, a vote was taken on the question: "Should the discussion be interrupted?" The number of yes votes required to reject the schema fell short of the required two-thirds majority by just 105 votes, "a trifling percent of the total number of votes cast."[10] A group of cardinals, including Augustin Bea and the Canadian Paul-Émile Léger, quickly communicated their concerns to the pope. The day after the vote, Pope John XXIII announced that the clear wish of the majority was to be respected, despite the council regulations, and that the schema would be withdrawn from discussion and rewritten. Also, a special commission, a "mixed" com-

---

6. DS 1501. Tanner, *Decrees of the Ecumenical Councils*, 2:663.

7. As Gerald O'Collins notes: "Despite Trent's language about the gospel being 'the source' (in the singular), there emerged in Catholic theology the so-called 'two-source' theory of revelation, according to which scripture and tradition are two distinct sources for revealed truths. Tradition could and does supply some truths that were not to be found in scripture. In other words, scripture is not merely 'formally insufficient' (=needing to be interpreted and actualized) but also 'materially insufficient' (=not containing all revealed truth). This view obviously privileged a propositional view of revelation: namely, the model of revelation as the communication of truths which would otherwise remain hidden in God." O'Collins, *Retrieving Fundamental Theology*, 49. For a discussion of the Council of Trent on Scripture and tradition, the development of the two-source theory in later centuries, and the trend to equate tradition with the teaching of the magisterium, see Congar, *Tradition and Traditions*, 156–221. On developments after Trent, see also James P. Mackey, *The Modern Theology of Tradition* (New York: Herder and Herder, 1963).

8. See Joseph Ratzinger, "On the Interpretation of the Tridentine Decree on Tradition," in *Revelation and Tradition*, ed. Karl Rahner and Joseph Ratzinger (New York: Herder and Herder, 1966), 50–66.

9. For an account of these dramatic days, see Ruggieri, "The First Doctrinal Clash," 249–66. See also Riccardo Burigana, *La Bibbia nel concilio: La redazione della costituzione "Dei verbum" del Vaticano II* (Bologna: Il Mulino, 1998), 132–69.

10. Ruggieri, "The First Doctrinal Clash," 263.

mission, was to be created, consisting of cardinals and *periti* both from the precouncil Preparatory Theological Commission (which had drafted the original schema) and from the ecumenically sensitive Secretariat for Promoting Christian Unity, under the presidency of the former rector of the Biblical Institute, Cardinal Bea, a known ecumenist. The Secretariat had been created by Pope John in 1960, when he set up the structure of the council's overseeing commissions, perhaps deliberately giving this body the vague title of "secretariat" to enable it to be free of the strictures of the council's rules.[11] The Secretariat had earlier been critical of the preparatory schema on ecumenical grounds, even producing its own alternative text. Including the Secretariat now in this mixed commission was a highly significant ecumenical gesture on Pope John's part, particularly given the negative comments of the Protestant observers regarding the draft schema.

On the historical significance of the debate and the November 20 vote regarding *De Fontibus Revelationis*, as well as Pope John's decision to intervene, Joseph Ratzinger wrote:

> The real question behind the discussion could be put this way: Was the intellectual position of "anti-Modernism"—the old policy of exclusiveness, condemnation and defense leading to an almost neurotic denial of all that was new—to be continued? Or would the Church, after it had taken all the necessary precautions to protect the faith, turn over a new leaf and move on into a new and positive encounter with its own origins, with its brothers and with the world of today? Since a clear majority of the fathers opted for the second alternative, *we may even speak of the Council as a new beginning.* We may also say that with this decision there was a major advance over Vatican Council I. Both Trent and Vatican Council I set up bulwarks for the faith to assure it and to protect it; Vatican Council II turned itself to a new task, building on the work of the two previous Councils.[12]

The vote and its immediate aftermath were, according to Ratzinger, decisive for the direction of the council: "With the majority vote of November 20 and its authoritative reinforcement the next day, the basic decision of the first session was made. Compared to this, everything else in the first session appears derivative and supplementary."[13] Yves Congar cites favorably the

---

11. See Komonchak, "The Struggle for the Council during the Preparation of Vatican II (1960–1962)," 263–71.

12. Ratzinger, *Theological Highlights of Vatican II*, 44. Emphasis added.

13. Ibid., 49.

dramatic interpretation of Robert Rouquette: "that 20 November 1962, the date when the Fathers voted to reject the schema on the two sources, Scripture and Tradition, marked the end of the Counter-Reformation."[14] Giuseppe Ruggieri's judgment is even more dramatic: "Without its yet being put in writing, the Council had perhaps made one of the most important changes in the doctrinal development of the Catholic Church: the choice of a teaching that was 'pastoral.' . . . [A]n entirely new era was beginning."[15]

The Protestant Reformation was not the only background against which the bishops were reading critically the preparatory schema on revelation. Also at issue was the church's attitude to Modernity and to those children of the Enlightenment, the natural and the human sciences. Hovering over the debates was the role that disciplines such as history, philology, and literary criticism might play in understanding the nature of Scripture and tradition and, consequently, their appropriate interpretation in the present. A crucial question was: what is the role of a historical consciousness for understanding the nature and interpretation of Scripture and tradition? Furthermore, how does it inform their interrelationship? The bishops at Vatican II were only too aware of the decades of biblical, patristic, and liturgical renewal movements that were reaching back to the sources of the tradition, in a *ressourcement* that highlighted the historically conditioned nature of that tradition. And they were only too aware that, despite his tentative openings to historical-critical scholarship in his 1943 encyclical *Divino Afflante Spiritu*, Pius XII's encyclical *Humani Generis* in 1950 had directly cautioned against the methods and conclusions of such *nouvelle théologie* scholarship.[16] Eventually the majority at the council came to embrace such scholarship. During the council there would be other official moves to do so; several months before the council's third session, on April 21, 1964, the Pontifical Biblical Commission published its instruction *Sancta mater ecclesia* on the historical truth of the gospels.[17] The final text of *Dei Verbum* would go on to approve such historical-

---

14. See Congar, "A Last Look at the Council," 343. Congar is referring to Robert Rouquette, "Bilan du concile," *Études* (January 1963): 94–111, at 104.

15. Ruggieri, "The First Doctrinal Clash," 266.

16. Pius XII, *Divino Afflante Spiritu*; Pius XII, *Humani Generis*. See also Joseph A. Komonchak, "*Humani Generis* and *Nouvelle Théologie*," in *Ressourcement: A Movement for Renewal in Twentieth-Century Catholic Theology*, ed. Gabriel Flynn and Paul D. Murray (Oxford: Oxford University Press, 2011), 138–56.

17. AAS 56 (1964): 713–16. See translated excerpts in Heinrich Denzinger, *Compendium of Creeds, Definitions, and Declarations on Matters of Faith and Morals*, ed. Peter Hünermann, et al., 43rd, rev. and enl. ed. (San Francisco: Ignatius Press, 2012), nos. 4402–7.

critical methods for the interpretation of the biblical writings and for viewing the whole tradition process (DV 12).

The method and fruits of historical-critical scholarship were mediated to the council fathers through the *periti*, either as assistants to individual bishops or episcopal conferences or as papal appointees to drafting commissions or subcommissions. Many of these *periti* had been significant scholars in the various biblical, patristic, historical, philosophical, theological, ecumenical, and lay apostolate renewal movements in the decades before the council was called. France in particular saw rich *ressourcement* scholarship. Appointed to the drafting commissions for the document on revelation across the years of the council were several well-known biblical scholars using historical-critical methods in their own writings, e.g., Barnabas Ahern, Pierre Benoit, Lucien Cerfaux, and Béda Rigaux. Also, other *periti* were historians and theologians open to the perspectives and methods of *ressourcement* scholarship, e.g., Marie-Dominique Chenu, Yves Congar, Damien Van den Eynde, and Henri de Lubac.

The drafting of what came to be called *Dei Verbum* lasted most of the council.[18] The "mixed commission" set up by Pope John on November 21, 1962, produced a new draft before the second session the following year. It was never discussed in the aula during that second session; however, the bishops had the opportunity to provide written submissions to the drafting commission. In the light of those comments, a new "mixed" subcommission was set up, which included theologians and biblical scholars of a *ressourcement* mind-set. The completely revised version they produced "largely reflected the *nouvelle théologie* perspective."[19] Much of this third draft formed

---

18. For the various drafts, analyses on the debates, and a history of the drafting process, see Francisco Gil Hellín, ed. *Constitutio dogmatica de divina revelatione, Dei verbum: Concilii Vaticani II synopsis in ordinem redigens schemata cum rclationibus necnon patrum orationes atque animadversiones* (Città del Vaticano: Libreria Editrice Vaticana, 1993); "Dogmatic Constitution on Divine Revelation," in *Commentary on the Documents of Vatican II*, vol. 3, ed. Herbert Vorgrimler (New York: Herder, 1969), 155–272; Hanjo Sauer, *Erfahrung und Glaube: Die Begründung des pastoralen Prinzips durch die Offenbarungskonstitution des II. Vatikanischen Konzils* (Frankfurt am Main: P. Lang, 1993); Burigana, *La Bibbia nel concilio: La redazione della costituzione "Dei verbum" del Vaticano II*; Umberto Betti, *La dottrina del concilio Vaticano II sulla trasmissione della rivelazione: Il capitolo II della costituzione dommatica Dei Verbum* (Roma: Spicilegium Pontificii Athenaei Antoniani, 1985); Hoping, "Theologischer Kommentar zur Dogmatischen Konstitution über die göttliche Offenbarung"; Serena Noceti and Roberto Repole, eds., *Dei Verbum: Commentario ai documenti del Vaticano II*, vol. 5 (Bologna: Edizioni Dehoniane, 2017). For a brief summary of the document's drafting, see Witherup, *Scripture: Dei Verbum*, 1–31.

19. Daley, "Knowing God in History and in the Church," 346.

the basis of the *Dei Verbum* we have today. "Most of the best passages in the constitution date from this revision."[20] When put to the bishops for discussion in the third session, it was mainly the issue of Scripture and tradition, as well the issue of the historical nature and inerrancy of the gospels, that aroused acrimonious debate, leading to further changes. Now with a new title, *Dei Verbum*, a final version was approved and promulgated by Paul VI on November 18, 1965.

"Living Tradition"

Dei Verbum's renewed teaching on the nature of revelation in its first chapter (outlined above in the revelation/faith principle) finds its correlate in its second chapter, which examines the nature of tradition. As Gerald O'Collins observes:

> A propositional view of revelation lay behind the typical Catholic version of the tradition/Scripture issue. Once the shift came to an interpersonal model of revelation (Chapter 1), the whole discussion was reshaped. Whether in the foundational or in the dependent stage, revelation primarily means a gracious call to enter by faith into a relationship with the tripersonal God. Revelation is something which happens and is not, properly speaking, "contained' in a book (the Bible) or in traditions that Christians inherit from previous generations of believers. Since revelation is the living reality of a personal encounter with God, it cannot be happily described as "contained" in anything, whether it be Scripture or tradition.[21]

Just as revelation is given to the whole church, so too, by implication, tradition as the transmission of revelation involves the whole church; *Dei Verbum* teaches that the word of God (revelation) "is entrusted to the church" (DV 10), not just to the magisterium. Furthermore, what was said in the previous chapter of *Dei Verbum* regarding revelation *as a present reality* in every age is affirmed through the council's shift in chapter 2 toward a richer notion of tradition as not only a criterion from the past but also a *present* task for the church. The historical consciousness being embraced by the council fathers affected their understanding of "tradition" in two ways. First, they became

---

20. Adrian Hastings, *A Concise Guide to the Documents of the Second Vatican Council*, 2 vols. (London: Darton Longman & Todd, 1968–1969), 1:151.

21. Gerald O'Collins, *Revelation: Towards a Christian Interpretation of God's Self-Revelation in Jesus Christ* (Oxford: Oxford University Press, 2016), 137.

more aware of "the great tradition,"[22] "the whole tradition,"[23] beyond the Tridentine Catholicism of the previous four hundred years, with its increasing focus on doctrine alone, transmitted by the teaching of the magisterium alone. Second, this historical *ressourcement* brought to the fore a more dynamic notion of tradition, that of "the living tradition."

To understand *Dei Verbum*'s final teaching with regard to "tradition" in chapter 2 (art. 7–10), three classical distinctions of scholastic theology need to be kept in mind, because they are presumed throughout the conciliar debates: tradition is (1) the content to be transmitted (*traditio objectiva* or *traditum*); (2) the process of transmission and receiving (*traditio activa* or *actus tradendi et recipiendi*); (3) the subjects or bearers of the tradition (*traditio subjectiva* or *tradentes*).[24] For the schema *De Fontibus Revelationis*, tradition was understood primarily in the first sense, as the deposit of beliefs formulated by popes and councils up to the eve of Vatican II; the process of tradition and receiving, accordingly, was seen to be one of teaching by the magisterium and obedient assent by the faithful; the subject or bearer of the tradition, understood as the bearer of divine truths, was seen to be the magisterium alone. By the end of Vatican II's four years of debates on these issues, *Dei Verbum* would end up presenting (1) *traditio objectiva* as not simply revealed truths but as God's personal self-communication in Christ through the Spirit, "the full and living Gospel" (DV 7). (2) *Traditio activa* comes to be formulated as much more than a passing on of these truths expressed in doctrinal propositions, in a circle of teaching and assenting to orthodox doctrine; rather, *traditio activa* is understood primarily as the church's daily, ongoing reception of the living Gospel in diverse contexts, where the church actualizes the Gospel from one generation to another. This is how the living faith is handed on. Therefore, (3) the subject or bearer of the tradition process (*traditio subjectiva*) is understood to be the entire body of the faithful, not simply the magisterium.

The notion of "living tradition" had been a key notion for *ressourcement* theologians such as Jean Daniélou, Marie-Dominique Chenu, Henri de Lubac, and especially Yves Congar.[25] One of the *periti* on the drafting commission for the document on revelation, Congar had already written on the

---

22. Extraordinary Synod of Bishops, "Final Report," 22.

23. Kasper, "The Continuing Challenge of the Second Vatican Council," 172.

24. See Hermann J. Pottmeyer, "Tradition," in *Dictionary of Fundamental Theology*, ed. René Latourelle and Rino Fisichella (Middlegreen, Slough, UK: St Paul, 1994), 1119–26, at 1119.

25. See Boersma, *Nouvelle Théologie and Sacramental Ontology*, 190–241.

pervasiveness of the notion and reality of living tradition throughout the church's history, even though the precise term was not used until the nineteenth century.[26] He was crucial in bringing these historical facts to the notice of the bishops. The notion of "living tradition" pervades the whole of *Dei Verbum* 8, though the precise phrase *traditio viva* is not used in that article. Nevertheless, regarding the drafting of this article, Ratzinger notes: "It is not difficult . . . to recognize the pen of Y. Congar."[27] Phrases can be found such as "the enlivening [*vivifica*] presence of this tradition" and "the living voice [*viva vox*] of the Gospel (ringing out) in the church." The phrase is later used explicitly in *Dei Verbum* 12, in reference to "the living tradition [*traditio viva*] of the whole church."[28] The explicit phrase is also found in *Unitatis Redintegratio* 17, which speaks of "the living tradition of the apostles [*viva apostolica traditione*]."

The whole of chapter 2 of *Dei Verbum* (7–10) outlines a dynamic notion of tradition within the apostolic age (7), the history of the church (8), and in the Scripture/tradition relationship (9–10). *Dei Verbum* 7 describes the formation of the New Testament writings in terms of an active process of tradition in the apostolic church. Jesus Christ commands the apostles to proclaim "the Gospel" they have received as "the source of all saving truth and moral law." Like the document's previous teaching on God's self-communication as revelation being realized in "deeds" and "words," the document here too speaks of the apostles, aided by "the promptings of the Holy Spirit," handing on the Gospel through the same media: "by oral preaching, by their example, by their dispositions." This tradition involves not just "words" but "communicating God's gifts" (*dona divina communicantes*), a passage that parallels the use of *communicare* in the previous chapter regarding God's self-communication. This is "the full and living Gospel [*evangelium integrum et vivum*]." Furthermore, once again under the inspiration of the same Holy Spirit, the "apostles and others associated with them . . . com-

---

26. Congar published in French in 1960 and 1963 two volumes on the topic, which would have been known to the bishops at the council. See the one-volume English translation Congar, *Tradition and Traditions*. Congar notes the particular role of the "Tübingen School" of the nineteenth century, especially Johann Adam Möhler. See ibid., 189–96. Congar, in tracing the emergence of the notion of "living tradition," highlights "the birth of *the sense of history*" as crucial for that emergence. See ibid., 191. Walter Kasper notes how later in the century "the Roman School" appropriates this notion. See Walter Kasper, *Die Lehre von der Tradition in der römischen Schule: Giovanni Perrone, Carlo Passaglia, Clemens Schrader* (Freiburg: Herder, 1962).

27. Ratzinger, "Chapter II: The Transmission of Divine Revelation," 184.

28. Flannery translation corrected. Strangely, Flannery here omits the word "living."

mitted the news [*nuntium*] of salvation to writing."[29] (The following article 8 will go on to state that, in these biblical writings, "the apostolic preaching . . . is expressed *in a special way* [*speciali modo*]," a passage that implicitly notes the privileged function of Scripture over the tradition that produced it.) Here, in *Dei Verbum* 7, the document states that the apostles also hand on the role of preserving the Gospel to bishops of future generations: "In order that the full and living Gospel might always be preserved [*servaretur*] in the church the apostles left bishops as their successors . . . [giving them] 'their own teaching authority.'"[30] The chapter finishes by describing this whole process as "this sacred tradition."

The same dynamic tradition by which the apostles transmit the full and living Gospel, and that gave rise to the New Testament writings, is then attributed in *Dei Verbum* 8 to the way the church, beyond the apostolic times, continues to transmit the full and living Gospel: "What was handed on by the apostles comprises everything that serves to make the people of God live their lives in holiness and increase their faith. In this way the church, in its doctrine, life and worship, perpetuates and transmits to every generation all that it itself is, all that it believes." In this critical passage, the scholastic notion of tradition as a body of beliefs and practices is redefined. Therefore, with regard to the issue of the *traditum* (the reality handed on), it is the saving reality of revelation that is being handed on in the present: the communication and reception of God's gifts. With regard to the *traditio activa*, all dimensions of the church's life and mission constitute the tradition process: preaching, evangelization, catechesis, public liturgy (especially the sacraments of initiation), private prayer, personal reading and study of Scripture, sacramental gestures such as genuflection, social engagement for the sake of justice and peace, etc. With regards to the issue of *traditio subjectiva* (i.e., the *tradentes*, those who pass on this living faith), *Dei Verbum* states that it is not just the magisterium that is the bearer of the tradition but rather "the church" (DV 8): "the word of God . . . is entrusted to the church . . . the entire holy people" (DV 10).

Moreover, just as the Spirit assists the apostles in interpreting Jesus (as affirmed in the previous article, 7), so too article 8 affirms that the same Holy Spirit guides the church of future generations in the same way: "The tradition that comes from the apostles makes progress in the church, with the help of the Holy Spirit." Just as "the promptings of the Holy Spirit" (DV 7) enabled

---

29. Translation corrected.
30. The document is here citing St Irenaeus, *Adv. Haer.*, III, 3,1: PG 7, 848.

the apostles to come to a deeper understanding of the words, way of life, person, and works of Christ, so too, under the influence of the Holy Spirit in the tradition, "there is a growth in insight into the realities and words that are being passed on." Such guidance by the Spirit, giving growth in insight, is effected through the three means of (1) theological scholarship, (2) the *sensus fidelium*, and (3) the magisterium: "This comes about through (1) the contemplation and study of believers who ponder these things in their heart. It comes from (2) the intimate sense of spiritual realities which they experience. And it comes from (3) the preaching of those who, on succeeding to the office of bishop, have received the sure charism of truth."[31] Thus, on the cognitive level of understanding and insight into revelation, the Holy Spirit's guidance goes beyond just the activity and judgment of the magisterium. According to Walter Kasper, the order of these three ecclesial realities is deliberate: "It is no accident that the magisterium is only mentioned in third place. The ecclesiality of faith is not exhausted by an attitude of obedience to the Church's teaching authority. That authority is situated within the community of believers and under the authority of the word of revelation. It is not a super-criterion ruling over the Church and its common search for truth in lonely Olympian majesty and issuing condemnations."[32]

The eschatological dimension of this vision is then emphasized: "Thus, as the centuries go by, the church is always advancing towards the plenitude of divine truth, until eventually the words of God are fulfilled in it. . . . Thus God, who spoke in the past, continues to dialogue [*colloquitur*] with the spouse of his beloved Son. And the Holy Spirit, through whom the living voice of the Gospel rings out in the church—and through it in the world— leads believers to the full truth and makes the word of Christ dwell in them in all its richness." Thus, it is through the living tradition that Scripture is actualized as a saving truth: "By means of the same tradition . . . the holy scriptures themselves are more thoroughly understood and constantly made effective in the church" (DV 8). Scripture, the result of the living tradition, is passed on by tradition and becomes revelatory only when read within the tradition. Just as the production of the New Testament Scriptures emerged originally out of the living tradition during apostolic times, so too the Christian Scriptures (Old and New Testament) receive their authentic interpretation and application from within the faith community, within the living

31. Numbering added.
32. Walter Kasper, *An Introduction to Christian Faith* (London: Burns & Oates, 1980), 146–47.

tradition. Through this dynamic transmission, revelation-salvation is actualized as a reality in the present.

In summary, regarding tradition, *Dei Verbum* teaches: if revelation is not just about communication of truths (and faith is not primarily about assent to those truths), then tradition is not just handing on truths; if revelation is God's self-giving to human beings (and faith is human beings' embracing in love God's loving outreach), then tradition is a process through which the church enables human beings to respond in faith to God's loving offer of salvific revelation, which is ultimately understood as participating in the very life of the triune God. Correlatively, the mission of the church is to hand on (*tradere*) God's offer of salvific revelation. Tradition, therefore, goes to the very heart of the identity and mission of the church.

A Mutual Relationship

It is only after its explication of the formation of Scripture through tradition and of Scripture's ongoing actualization by means of the living tradition that *Dei Verbum* goes on to treat the relationship between tradition and Scripture. Whereas the exposition of living tradition in article 8 paralleled and was grounded in the sacramental notion of revelation from chapter 1, the conciliar debate over how best to formulate the Scripture/tradition relationship nevertheless failed to fully appropriate that foundational shift from an exclusively propositional model to one that is sacramental, historical, and dialogic. The debate was plagued by clashing models of revelation presupposed by the members of the drafting commission, especially within the Doctrinal Commission during its deliberation throughout the fourth session of the council. Different notions regarding the nature of Scripture and of tradition emerged from the two different models of revelation being presupposed. Still working primarily from a propositionalist notion of revelation, the minority saw Scripture as containing truths about God and humanity and tradition as the static process of handing down divine truths intact, some in addition to those contained in Scripture.

Therefore, a key concern for this minority of bishops during these debates was that a formulation be included in the constitution, which stated clearly that tradition handed on additional truths not found in Scripture. A sleeper issue behind all this discussion was the authority of papal teaching. The Marian dogmas—the dogma of the Immaculate Conception promulgated by Pius IX in 1854 and the dogma of the Assumption of the Blessed Virgin Mary promulgated by Pius XII in 1950—were the classic examples, for both Catholics and Protestants, of "traditions" that have no explicit grounding in

Scripture. For the minority, Scripture and tradition, as "sources" of revelation, were separate and independent channels of divine truths. The majority, on the other hand, did not want to make a ruling on the matter, but wanted rather to keep the issue open for further theological discussion. At the heart of the debate, then, was an implicit question regarding the nature of revelation itself: was it just a communication of divine truths? The answer to that question would determine how one sees tradition and Scripture (and indeed, how one understands the nature and mission of the church). If revelation was primarily divine truths revealed by God, then tradition was the passing on of those truths faithfully throughout history; Scripture was the recording of truths about God. If revelation, however, was primarily God's self-communication in saving love, then the relationship between tradition and Scripture was to be understood in a much more dynamic way.

In the end, after several proposals had been considered,[33] a compromise formula was found and eventually inserted into the final text (albeit containing an unecumenical-sounding reference to Luther's phrase *sola scriptura*): "Thus it is that the church does not draw its certainty about all revealed truths from the holy scriptures alone [*non per solam sacram scripturam*]" (DV 9). But, as the cardinal who presented the text to the assembly on behalf of the drafting commission explained: "Sacred Tradition is not presented as a quantitative supplement to Sacred Scripture, nor is Sacred Scripture presented as a codification of all revelation."[34] By its compromise formulation, the council left the controversial issue open. As Gerald O'Collins remarks: "Although *Dei Verbum* did not rule out the 'two-source' theory, that theory is certainly much more difficult to maintain in the face of the council's understanding of divine revelation (as being primarily God's self-revelation) and its stress on the unity between scripture and tradition."[35]

Despite its juxtaposition at times of theological theses from the minority alongside those from the majority, *Dei Verbum* highlights the inseparability of Scripture and tradition. Brian Daley summarizes the vision the council eventually came up with: "What is distinctive here [in *Dei Verbum*] is that scripture and the tradition not explicitly contained in scripture are both seen as part of a larger, ongoing process of proclamation, reception, and interpre-

---

33. For the history of the tortuous debate in the Doctrinal Commission throughout 1965, and Pope Paul VI's intervention on the addition of a formula to DV 9, see Theobald, "The Church under the Word of God."

34. AS IV/5, 741. Translation from O'Malley, *What Happened at Vatican II*, 279.

35. O'Collins, *Retrieving Fundamental Theology*, 49.

tation located within the church, as the structured, divinely guided body of believers."[36] Vatican II's vision of the Scripture/tradition relationship is one in which neither ecclesial element can be fully understood or seen to function in the church without the other: "Scripture simply cannot be conceived separately from tradition, nor tradition separately from the Church, nor the latter separately from either of the two others."[37]

With regard to one of the key sticking points, *Dei Verbum* ended up providing no alternative term to "sources" (*fontes*), except perhaps the word "witness." In the promulgated version, the term "source" is not used explicitly of Scripture. It is, however, used of "the Gospel . . . the source [*fons*] of all saving truth and moral law, communicating God gifts" (DV 9). Rather than constituting a separate source of revelation, Scripture is described at times as a "witness" to the event of God's self-communication in Christ through the Spirit within human history. For example: "The writings of the New Testament stand as a perpetual and divine witness [*testimonium*] to these realities" (DV 17). And, in the very next sentence, concerning the Gospels: "Among all the inspired writings, including those of the New Testament, the Gospels have a special place, rightly so, because they are our principal witness [*testimonium*] for the life and teaching of the incarnate Word, our Saviour" (DV 18). While not using the word "witness" with regard to tradition itself, in the context of its discussion of the process of tradition, we find in *Dei Verbum* 8: "The sayings of the church Fathers are a witness to [*testificantur*] the life-giving presence of this tradition, showing how its riches are poured out in the practice and life of the believing and praying church."

Deliberately eschewing, therefore, any language of "sources" of revelation, *Dei Verbum* refers to the single, originating event of revelation as "the divine well-spring": "Sacred tradition and sacred scripture, then, are bound closely together, and communicate one with the other. Flowing from the same divine well-spring [*scaturigine*], both of them merge, in a sense, and move towards the same goal. . . . Scripture and tradition must be accepted and honored with equal devotion and reverence" (DV 9). What flows from this divine wellspring is not a series of statements on divine truths; rather, God's very self is poured forth—given in Jesus Christ through the Holy Spirit. Together, Scripture and tradition help facilitate that saving encounter.

The statement that "scripture and tradition must be accepted and honored with equal devotion and reverence" (DV 9) is later qualified in chapter 6 by

36. Daley, "Knowing God in History and in the Church," 349.
37. Ratzinger, "Chapter II: The Transmission of Divine Revelation," 197–98.

what Christoph Theobald calls "the most important statement in this 'ecclesiological' chapter":[38] "The church has always venerated the divine scriptures as it has venerated the Body of the Lord, in that it never ceases, above all in the sacred liturgy, to partake of the bread of life and to offer it to the faithful from the one table of the word of God and the Body of Christ" (DV 21). "This," according to Theobald, "is the final manifestation in the constitution of *the sacramental conception of revelation* that is at the center of the first chapter [of *Dei Verbum*]."[39]

Both "tradition and scripture make up a single sacred deposit of *the word of God*, which is entrusted to the church" (DV 10). The phrase "the word of God" here, as elsewhere in *Dei Verbum*—including those very first words of the document—is to be understood as a synonym for divine revelation itself: God's self-communication to human beings in Christ through the Spirit. God's personal address ("word") to humanity goes beyond "words" and includes deeds, gestures, acts in history (DV 2). *Dei Verbum* does not refer to Scripture by itself as simply "the word of God." Scripture, rather, is spoken of as "the word of God . . . in its written form" (DV 10) or "the written word of God" (DV 24). Scripture is not divine revelation itself, nor is the living tradition itself divine revelation, because neither is itself or together the living, personal, dialogic encounter between the triune God and human beings who respond in faith. They both, together, facilitate that encounter.

The order of naming the pair is not consistent throughout the document, although the difference in ordering often relates to context. Generally, the order "tradition and Scripture" is used in chapter 2, "The Transmission of Divine Revelation" (art. 7–10), when speaking of the two in relationship to revelation ("the divine well-spring"). Thus, article 9 begins "Sacred tradition and sacred scripture" when discussing their common origins in "the same divine well-spring." Article 10 likewise begins with "Tradition and scripture" when treating their relationship to "the word of God, which is entrusted to the church." This ordering highlights that tradition constitutes revelation being actively received as a present reality and that Scripture has itself emerged from this tradition process within the early church (DV 17–20). Nevertheless, we do find in chapter 2 the reverse ordering: "both scripture and tradition must be accepted and honored with equal devotion and reverence" (DV 9). The order Scripture/tradition is used when the context relates specifically to the need for Scripture to be interpreted ecclesially as well as when the emphasis

---

38. Theobald, "The Church under the Word of God," 345.
39. Ibid. Emphasis added.

is on the normative nature of Scripture and tradition in the church: "[The church] has always regarded and continues to regard the scriptures, taken together with sacred tradition, as *the supreme rule of its faith*" (DV 21). That *Lumen Gentium* would make a similar statement regarding "the Gospel" as the primary regulating principle for the church suggests an intertextual interpretation: that "the Gospel" and "Scripture and tradition" are being used synonymously—"[T]he Gospel which [the apostles] were obliged to hand on [*ab eis tradendum*] is the principle of all the Church's life for all time" (LG 20).

Critically, just as it emphasizes the eschatological dimension of the living tradition (DV 8), *Dei Verbum* depicts the interrelationship between Scripture and tradition in an eschatological perspective. Together, tradition and Scripture "are a mirror, in which the church, during its pilgrim journey here on earth, contemplates God . . . until such time as it is brought to see him face to face as he really is" (DV 7). With its use of the "mirror" metaphor, the council is alluding to St. Paul's statement in 1 Corinthians 13:12: "For now we see in a mirror, dimly, but then we will see face to face. Now I know only in part; then I will know fully, even as I have been fully known."[40] The protological/eschatological principle above has already highlighted the eschatological dimension of the pilgrim church's journey through history. The last sentence of chapter 1 in *Lumen Gentium,* on the mystery of the church, states: "that it may reveal in the world, *faithfully, although with shadows,* the mystery of its Lord until, in the end, it shall be manifested in full light" (8).

The agent for bringing the church to fuller understanding of revelation is the Holy Spirit: "the Holy Spirit . . . leads believers to the full truth and makes the word of Christ dwell in them in all its richness" (DV 8). *Dei Verbum* 5 had earlier taught that the Holy Spirit enables reception of revelation through the gift of faith. The role of the Holy Spirit is likewise emphasized in the production and reception of Scripture and tradition. The apostles interpret Jesus "through the promptings of the Holy Spirit" (DV 7). "The tradition that comes from the apostles makes progress in the church, with the help of the Holy Spirit" (DV 8). Scripture is written "under the inspiration of the same Holy Spirit" (DV 7). And the same Holy Spirit enables the actualization of Scripture through time: "[The scriptures] make the voice of the Holy Spirit sound again and again in the words of the prophets and apostles" (DV 21). "Taught by the Holy Spirit, the spouse of the incarnate Word, which is the church, strives to reach an increasingly more profound understanding

---

40. NRSV translation. On the allusion to 1 Cor 13:12, see Ratzinger, "Chapter II: The Transmission of Divine Revelation," 183.

of the sacred scriptures" (DV 23). Accordingly, "sacred scripture must be read and interpreted with the same Spirit in which it was written" (DV 12). In their oversight of Scripture's faithful interpretation, the bishops are "enlightened by the Spirit of truth" (DV 9).

Dei Verbum's discussion of the magisterium's relationship to the Word of God (revelation) begins by grounding the Scripture/tradition interrelationship in the church itself. *Dei Verbum* 10 sets out the interrelationship between revelation, its reception by the whole church, the transmission of revelation through Scripture and tradition, and the particular role within the church of the magisterium for ensuring proper interpretation of Scripture and tradition. The article begins by proclaiming that the primary recipient of revelation is the whole church. "Tradition and scripture make up a single sacred deposit of the word of God, which is *entrusted to the church*." The very next sentence, structurally, refers to "the church" as "the entire holy people [*tota plebs sancta*]." It only then goes on to speak of the relationship between Scripture, tradition, and the magisterium, within the life of "the entire holy people": "in maintaining, practicing and professing the faith that has been handed on there is a unique interplay [*conspiratio*] between the bishops and the faithful."[41] The Latin word *conspiratio* is here an intertextual clue to the work of the Holy Spirit in the lives of human beings open to Spirit's promptings.[42] The document also stresses, however, that the task of "authoritatively" (*authentice*) interpreting the word of God ("whether in its written form or in the form of tradition") has been entrusted to the magisterium.[43] The text then refers to the magisterium's need for receptiveness before God and openness to the Spirit's guidance: "This magisterium is not superior to the word of God [i.e., God's revelation in Christ through the Spirit—witnessed to in Scripture and handed on through the living tradition] but is rather its servant. It teaches only what has been handed on to it. At the divine command and with the help of the Holy Spirit, it listens [*audit*] to this devoutly, guards [*custodit*] it reverently and expounds [*exponit*] it faithfully." Thus scholasticism's notion of the magisterium as the proximate rule of faith is implicitly done away with.

René Latourelle highlights the importance of this article in the Dogmatic Constitution: "[DV 10] is made up of two parts. The first discusses the rela-

---

41. See the references to this *conspiratio* throughout John Henry Newman, *On Consulting the Faithful in Matters of Doctrine* (New York,: Sheed and Ward, 1962).

42. Throughout the conciliar corpus, *conspiratio* appears six times and *conspirare* ten times.

43. On translating the adverb *authentice* here as "authoritatively," see Francis A. Sullivan, *Magisterium: Teaching Authority in the Catholic Church* (New York: Paulist Press, 1983), 26–28.

tionship of Tradition and Scripture to *the entire Church*: faithful and hierarchy. The second treats the relationship of Tradition and Scripture to the Church's *Magisterium*. . . . Although not a doctrinal innovation, the statement of this first part of the paragraph does, however, represent progress over the earlier documents, primarily those of Vatican I and the encyclical *Humani Generis*, which were content to consider the relationship of Scripture and Tradition only to the Magisterium of the Church."[44] Joseph Ratzinger comments on the significance of this affirmation, over against the position of the initial draft schema:

> [DV10] first makes the point that the preservation and active realization of the word is the business of the whole people of God, not merely of the hierarchy. The ecclesial nature of the word, on which this idea is based, is therefore not simply a question which concerns the teaching office, but embraces the whole community of the faithful. If one compares the text with the corresponding section of the encyclical *Humani Generis* (*DS* 3886), the progress that has been made is clear. . . . This idea of *solo magisterio* is taken up here in the next paragraph, but the context makes it clear that the function of authentic interpretation which is restricted to the teaching office is a specific service that does not embrace the whole of the way in which the word is present, and in which it performs an irreplaceable function precisely for the whole Church, the bishops and laity together.[45]

A Church Inspired and Nourished by Scripture

Chapter 3 of *Dei Verbum* (11–13) addresses the divine inspiration and interpretation of Scripture. There, article 12 states that interpreters should give attention to historical factors that conditioned the communication of the biblical authors: "the customary and characteristic patterns of perception, speech and narrative which prevailed in their time, and to the conventions which people then observed in their dealings with one another" (DV 12). The same article goes on to affirm, however, that such historical and literary approaches that acknowledge the original context in which the writings were created must not ignore either the context of faith in which they were written or the context of faith in which these writings are interpreted in different times throughout history and in the present day. It therefore affirms the need for an ecclesial interpretation of Scripture, alongside historical and literary approaches.

44. Latourelle, *Theology of Revelation*, 481–82.
45. Ratzinger, "Chapter II: The Transmission of Divine Revelation," 196.

Undergirding this ecclesial reading is the belief that the same Holy Spirit who inspired the writings in their production and their being chosen as part of the church's canon of writings likewise is at work in the present-day reading of the texts by interpreters open to the Spirit: "Sacred scripture must be read and interpreted in the same Spirit through whom it was written [*eodem Spiritu quo scripta est*]" (DV 12).[46] Once again, the document returns to the theme of Scripture needing to be read in faith within the context of the living tradition. Moreover, this affirmation of the Spirit at work in the reception of Scripture aligns with the document's previous affirmation of the Spirit impelling the church's active tradition process. *Dei Verbum* 8 states: "The tradition which comes from the apostles makes progress [*proficit*] in the church, with the help of the Holy Spirit" (DV 8). The document then showcases three rules that ensure an ecclesial reading of Scripture. Thus, the interpretation of particular passages must keep in mind "(1) the content and coherence of scripture as a whole, taking into account (2) the whole church's living tradition [*vivae traditionis*] and (3) the sense of perspective given by faith [*analogiae fidei*]" (DV 12).[47]

This emphasis on an ecclesial reading of Scripture goes to the heart of the council's pastoral vision. A highly significant issue in that vision concerned the use of Scripture by the faithful, which the sixth chapter of *Dei Verbum* sets out to address. The vision of Vatican II calls for a biblical church, in which renewal of faith is necessarily grounded in an encounter with God through Scripture. "All the preaching of the church, as indeed the entire Christian religion, should be nourished and ruled by sacred scripture" (DV 21). Therefore, "access to sacred scripture ought to be widely available to the Christian faithful" (DV 22) through suitable translations. On this matter, Vatican II in *Dei Verbum* 22 once again represents a significant shift from the past, as Joseph Ratzinger remarks:

46. Corrected translation. See Ignace de la Potterie, "Interpretation of Holy Scripture in the Spirit in Which It Was Written (*Dei Verbum* 12c)," in *Vatican II: Assessment and Perspectives; Twenty-Five Years After (1962–1987)*, vol. 1, ed. René Latourelle (New York: Paulist Press, 1988), 1:220–66.

47. Tanner translation. Numeration added. Strangely, the Flannery translation has only "tradition" for "*vivae traditionis.*" The analogy of faith "is nothing but the consciousness of the unity of the revelation of God in its whole history and in its development in the Church." Alois Grillmeier, "Dogmatic Constitution on Divine Revelation: Chapter III," in *Commentary on the Documents of Vatican II*, vol. 3, ed. H. Vorgrimler (New York: Herder, 1969), 3:199–246, at 226.

The barriers that had been erected from the 13th, and especially from the 15th, century against the Bible in the vernacular and the reading of it by those who were not theologians, are here firmly removed. Our text represents the final and definitive overcoming of the restrictions set up in the various forms of the index of Paul IV, and from Pius IV, Sixtus V, Clement VIII down to Gregory XVI, and proves itself here to be a revision of the Tridentine decisions: the *inhaerens vestigiis* (DV 1) again proves to be an advance. If at that time the fight against the Reformation had led to a sequestration of Scripture, now the concern for dialogue led to a return to it in the most intensive way.[48]

The council's desire for a church more deeply nourished by Scripture resounds through all of its documents. The preaching of the Gospel is presented as the first responsibility of all the faithful. The rubric the council uses for this responsibility is that of the prophetic office of Christ, in which "the whole body of the faithful" participates—bishops, priests, deacons, religious, and laity (LG 12). Reiterating the injunction of the Council of Trent,[49] Vatican II teaches: "Among the principal offices [*munera*] of bishops, that of preaching the Gospel is pre-eminent" (LG 25).[50] Likewise for priests, "it is the first task of priests as co-workers of the bishops to preach the Gospel of God to all" (PO 4). Deacons are called to "service of the liturgy, of the word and of charity" (DV 29). So too: "Let religious see to it that through them the church may truly and ever more clearly show forth Christ to believers and unbelievers alike—Christ . . . proclaiming the kingdom of God to the crowds" (LG 46). The laity too participate in the preaching office of Christ, the prophetic office:

> Christ is the great prophet who proclaimed the kingdom of the Father both by the testimony of his life and by the power of his word. Until the full manifestation of his glory, he fulfills this prophetic office, not only through the hierarchy who teach in his name and by his power, but also through the laity. He accordingly establishes them as witnesses and provides them with a sense of the faith [*sensus fidei*] and the grace of the word so that the power of the Gospel may shine out in daily family and social life. . . . This evangelization—that is, the proclamation of Christ by word and the witness of their

---

48. Ratzinger, "Sacred Scripture in the Life of the Church," 264. The phrase *inhaerens vestigiis* refers to the claim in *Dei Verbum* 1 that the dogmatic constitution is "*following in the steps of* the councils of Trent and Vatican I."

49. *Lumen Gentium* cites in a footnote: *Decree. de reform.*, session 5, ch. 2; n. 9, and session 24, canon 4.

50. Translation corrected.

lives—acquires a special character and a particular effectiveness because it is accomplished in the ordinary circumstances of the world. (LG 35)

The council teaches that the training of priests should foster the study and spiritual appropriation of Scripture: "Students are to be trained most diligently in the study of scripture, which ought to be the very soul of all theology. After a suitable introduction, let them be carefully initiated into exegetical method, study closely the main themes of divine revelation and find inspiration and nourishment in daily reading of the sacred books and meditation on them" (*Optatam Totius* 16). A similar injunction to theologians regarding Scripture is made in *Dei Verbum*: "Sacred theology relies on the written word of God, taken together with sacred tradition, as its permanent foundation. . . . [T]he study of the sacred page should be the very soul of sacred theology" (DV 24).

The council, through its own procedures and priorities, models its own injunction in the very opening sentence of *Dei Verbum*: "Hearing the Word of God reverently and proclaiming it confidently, this synod . . ." (DV 1). Apart from its formal teaching in *Dei Verbum* regarding the nature of Scripture and its place in the life of the church, this receptiveness to the Word of God and acknowledgment of its importance is evident in a number of ways through the council's methodology and procedures. First, the Book of the Gospels was ceremoniously placed each morning before the council assembly began its deliberations. Second, the council called on biblical scholars to help them with the drafting of the documents. In doing so, the council was receiving the fruits of the biblical movement in Catholic *ressourcement* scholarship in the previous decades. Third, the council took a biblical approach to many issues, moving away from static neoscholastic, juridical categories, employing biblical motifs such as "people of God," "charisms," "*imago Dei*," "service," and "witness." Fourth, regularly throughout its documents, the Scriptures are either quoted or cited.[51] For example, in *Dei Verbum* itself, there are three

---

51. See O'Collins, "Was the Teaching of Vatican II Nourished and Ruled by the Word of God?" See also Charles Henry Miller, *"As It is Written": The Use of Old Testament References in the Documents of Vatican Council II* (St. Louis: Marianist Communications Center, 1973). Two helpful tools for researching Vatican II's appeal to biblical passages are the indices provided in Tanner, *Decrees of the Ecumenical Councils*, 2:1173–88; Peter Hünermann and Bernd Jochen Hilberath, "Verzeichnis der Bibelstellen," in *Herders theologischer Kommentar zum Zweiten Vatikanischen Konzil. Band 1. Die Documente des Zweiten Vatikanishen Konzils: Konstitutionen, Dekrete, Erklärungen* (Freiburg: Herder, 2004), 751–60.

quotations and seventy-three citations of Scripture.[52] The council's first document, on the liturgy, shows that, from the very start, the council was intent on spiritual renewal of the church through the promotion of Scripture. *Sacrosanctum Concilium* 24 states: "Sacred scripture is of the greatest importance in the celebration of the liturgy. . . . Hence, in order to achieve the restoration, progress, and adaptation of the sacred liturgy it is essential to promote that warm and lively appreciation [*affectus*] of sacred scripture to which the venerable tradition of eastern and western rites gives testimony" (SC 24).

Dei Verbum's teaching on the Scripture/tradition relationship, however, leaves receivers of the council with work to do. Synthesis of its teaching is needed. This certainly applies to this reconstruction of the council's scripture/tradition principle. We have seen how certain passages within the final documents of Vatican II were arrived at through a need to find consensus, because of conflict at times among the bishops' personal positions. Often such conflict was "skirted with the help of a 'compromise.'"[53] Such consensus through compromise was arrived at either through the juxtaposition of statements, which presume different theological frameworks, or through formulations, which leave an issue open-ended for further theological discussion rather than closing it through a ruling on the issue. For example, two such interrelated issues in *Dei Verbum* are the role that the Scriptures should play in critiquing tradition for the sake of ecclesial renewal and the implications of a historical-critical approach to Scripture on the issue of the foundation of the church and its structures. This latter issue had arisen in the drafting of the third chapter of *Lumen Gentium* on the hierarchy, and several bishops requested that it be addressed, but to no avail. Several bishops then raised the same matter in the context of the *Dei Verbum* debates, but it was never discussed. Christoph Theobald sees here yet another open issue that requires synthesis by the contemporary interpreter, for which the council does give a deliberate trajectory:

> The overall image that Neo-Scholasticism had formed of the foundation of the Church was a kind of ahistorical and even ideological retrojection of the present-day hierarchical structure and doctrinal architecture of the Church into an immemorial past; this had suddenly become uncertain. Strictly speaking, we cannot speak here of a doctrinal compromise, because the shared

---

52. On the biblical orientation of *Dei Verbum*, see O'Collins, *Retrieving Fundamental Theology*, 51–52.

53. Theobald, "The Church under the Word of God," 349.

ground of *Dei Verbum* and *Lumen Gentium* had never been discussed, either in the commission or in the Council hall. *But the tacit elimination of a problem is also a way of leaving areas of shadow in a text and of making an appointment with the future.*[54]

This brings us to our next principle and a more explicit formulation of Vatican II's new awareness regarding the dynamic relationship between the reception of revelation by the community of faith and the community of faith's continual situatedness in history.

54. Ibid., 350. Emphasis added.

Principle 13

Faith/History

Principle 13: God's offer of revelation and salvation to human beings in Christ through the Spirit is not just a past event but a continual encounter with human beings in all epochs throughout history; human reception of that encounter in faith is always conditioned by the multiple facets of human existence at a particular time and place.

"The appearance of historical self-consciousness is very likely the most important revolution among those we have undergone since the beginning of the modern epoch. Its spiritual magnitude probably surpasses what we recognize in the applications of natural science, applications which have so visibly transformed the surface of our planet. The historical consciousness which characterizes contemporary man is a privilege, perhaps even a burden, the likes of which has never been imposed on any previous generation."[1] Hans-Georg Gadamer here neatly captures the privilege and burden facing the bishops of Vatican II in 1962 as they set about addressing the pastoral challenges of their generation. By the time it had concluded in 1965, the Second Vatican Council had become the first council in the history of the church to operate out of a "historical consciousness," in the specifically modern sense of the term that has emerged since the European Enlightenment.[2]

1. Hans-Georg Gadamer, "The Problem of Historical Consciousness," *Graduate Faculty Philosophy Journal* 5, no. 1. "H.-G. Gadamer," Special Issue (1975): 8–52, at 8.

2. On the origins of historical thought in premodern times and the emergence of a modern historical consciousness, see the summary of John Langan, "Christian Doctrine in a Historically Conscious World," in *Faithful Witness: Foundations of Theology for Today's Church*, ed. Leo J. O'Donovan and T. Howland Sanks (New York: Crossroad, 1989), 132–50, at 135–40.

"History" at the Council

Throughout the life of the church, the term "historical" has been understood in different senses, both premodern and modern, all of them operating in some way at Vatican II, either explicitly or implicitly. The first sense of "historical" is that of facticity.[3] Here "historical" is distinguished from "fictional." The church has always seen itself and the Christian narrative as founded on "facts," events that really happened in time and space. In other words, Christianity is not based on fantasy or legend but rather is a historical religion. The church has long believed in the historical nature of Christianity in this sense, and it is a given for the bishops of Vatican II. A second sense distinguishes the "historical" from the "eternal." It differentiates events and beliefs in human time from those beyond human time, in the eternal realm; thus, while some realities and dimensions of existence are timeless and understood to float above and beyond human time and space (for example, abstract concepts and eternal truths), such eternal realities and dimensions impinge in some way and need expression within human time, in "history." The two realms are, however, sometimes understood to be seemingly like oil and water. This sense is likewise operative during the council, particularly in those presupposing the theological frameworks of neoscholasticism. A third sense of the word "historical" is sometimes used of events, people, and actions in the sense of "historic"; that is, they attain a significance over time as paradigmatic for Christian believers and shape their thinking into the future.[4]

The fourth and fifth senses of the term "historical" name aspects of "historical consciousness" in the specifically modern sense. They both reflect a hermeneutical approach to human understanding and interpretation as historically conditioned.[5] The fourth sense concerns the awareness that human existence is conditioned by a person's situatedness in a specific time,

---

3. In what follows, I am drawing on the categorizations in Will Herberg, "Five Meanings of the Word 'Historical,'" *The Christian Scholar* 47, no. 4 (1964): 327–30.

4. On the difference between the merely "historical" and "the historic" captured by the German words *historisch* and *geschichtlich*, see ibid., 328–29. This distinction is used in the 1956 classic work of Martin Kähler, *The So-Called Historical Jesus and the Historic Biblical Christ* (Philadelphia: Fortress Press, 1988). The German title is *Der sogenannte historische Jesus und der geschichtliche, biblische Christus*. Further on the nuance within the German use of the word "historical," see John O'Donnell, "Historie/Geschichte," in *Dictionary of Fundamental Theology*, ed. René Latourelle and Rino Fisichella (Middlegreen, Slough, UK: St Paul, 1994), 432–33.

5. The classical exposition of hermeneutical consciousness in this sense, and of "the elevation of the historicity of understanding to the status of a hermeneutic principle," is Hans-Georg Gadamer, *Truth and Method*, 2nd rev. ed. (New York: Crossroad, 1989), esp. 265–379. This work in German was first published in 1960, two years before the start of Vatican II.

culture, and context. Eschewing any notion of a static and unchanging "human nature" over time, this sense affirms rather that both individuals and communities, and indeed the natural world, are constituted by their prior history; we are who we are because of our past, and nature too has its history. In the nineteenth century, Charles Darwin changed thinking regarding the origins of the species, as did Sigmund Freud regarding the origins of an individual's personality.

The fifth sense extends this notion of the historicity of human beings to their capacity, and indeed responsibility, to participate in shaping their own future, i.e., to shape history. Aware that they have emerged from a historically conditioned past, human beings become aware of their freedom to choose what they will become. In this fifth sense of "historical," "[the self's] historicity consists not only, and perhaps not primarily, in its being constituted by its history, but in its existential self-constituting in the face of future possibility. Man's 'nature,' insofar as he has one, is, so to speak, radically open-ended; it is forever being made and remade by choice, decision, and action, which is what constitutes man's historicity."[6]

While each of these five senses in some way were operative in the council debates and are found embedded in the final documents, it is the last two senses together that especially characterize the move toward a greater historical consciousness at Vatican II and constitute what could be called a hermeneutical turn in the self-understanding of the Catholic Church.

"Historical consciousness," according to John O'Malley, is "the realization of man's radical historicity."[7] For Brian Gerrish, it is "the awareness, which we all have, in greater or lesser degree, that our entire existence is given under the categories of space and time";[8] "historicity," then, is "the existence of human beings as historical beings."[9] Bruno Forte speaks of "the three dimensions of historical consciousness": the past, the present, and the future.[10] Thus, more expansively, historical consciousness can be defined as the recognition "that all humans live within structures of culture, language,

6. Herberg, "Five Meanings of the Word 'Historical,'" 329.

7. John W. O'Malley, "Reform, Historical Consciousness, and Vatican II's *Aggiornamento*," in *Tradition and Transition: Historical Perspectives on Vatican II* (Wilmington, DE: Michael Glazier, 1989), 44–81, at 77.

8. Brian A. Gerrish, "Theology and the Historical Consciousness," in *Revisioning the Past: Prospects in Historical Theology*, ed. Mary Potter Engel and Walter E. Wyman (Minneapolis: Fortress Press, 1992), 281–97, at 282.

9. Ibid., 283.

10. Forte, "Le prospettive della ricerca teologica," 420.

imagination, etc., that frame, and to some extent limit, the capacity to ask questions, to see responses and certain challenging disjunctions, and so forth."[11] Some commentators see historical consciousness functioning at Vatican II in the manner of a "threshold concept."[12] A threshold concept is a new way of thinking about a particular subject matter that opens up deeper knowledge of that matter.[13] Without using the term "threshold concept," Giuseppe Ruggieri observes a similar dynamic, with a new way of knowing emerging during the council, albeit inchoately:

> The main novelty of Vatican II was rather its consideration of history as related to the gospel and the Christian truth. Whereas for the most part in the past there had been an awareness that history as experienced by human beings was ultimately of no importance for the understanding of the gospel (I use the term "awareness," although "in reality" it was never such a thing), the major question of the Second Vatican Council was precisely this, even if the words used (pastoral nature, *aggiornamento*, signs of the time [*sic*]) were not immediately understood clearly by all.[14]

To appreciate that Vatican II was indeed "the council of history,"[15] however, it is necessary to recall the *ahistorical* perspective that had dominated Catholic theology before the council. Throughout "the long nineteenth century" before

11. See Michael G. Lawler, Todd A. Salzman, and Eileen Burke-Sullivan, *The Church in the Modern World:* Gaudium et Spes *Then and Now* (Collegeville, MN: Liturgical Press, 2014), 42.

12. Ibid., 42–47.

13. For Jan Meyer and Ray Land: "A threshold concept can be considered as akin to a portal, opening up a new and previously inaccessible way of thinking about something. It represents a transformed way of understanding, or interpreting, or viewing something without which the learner cannot progress. As a consequence of comprehending a threshold concept there may thus be a transformed internal view of subject matter, subject landscape, or even world view. This transformation may be sudden or it may be protracted over a considerable period of time, with the transition to understanding proving troublesome. Such a transformed view or landscape may represent how people 'think' in a particular discipline, or how they perceive, apprehend, or experience particular phenomena with that discipline (or more generally)." Jan H. F. Meyer and Ray Land, "Threshold Concepts and Troublesome Knowledge: Linkages to Ways of Thinking and Practising within the Disciplines," in *Improving Student Learning: Theory and Practice, 10 Years on*, ed. Chris Rust, *Proceedings of the 2002 10th International Symposium Improving Student Learning* (Oxford: Oxford Centre for Staff & Learning Development, 2003), 412–24, at 412.

14. Giuseppe Ruggieri, "Towards a Hermeneutic of Vatican II," *Concilium* 1 (1999): 1–13, at 3.

15. Forte, "Le prospettive della ricerca teologica," 420.

Vatican II,[16] there was a clear suspicion of historical approaches to Scripture, doctrine, and the church's self-understanding, evidenced especially in promulgations of Pius IX and in particular the *Syllabus of Errors* of 1864.[17] The Modernist crisis brought the issue of historical consciousness to a head, with an official response encapsulated in two documents of the magisterium. In 1907, both the Holy Office decree *Lamentabili*[18] and the papal encyclical *Pascendi Dominici Gregis*[19] artificially grouped together and condemned positions that could not be attributed to any one scholar. A core issue in the whole affair was the historicity of human knowing: "Here, it seems, in clashing theories of knowledge, lay the central quarrel of the Modernist crisis."[20] For Giuseppe Ruggieri, "a calm assessment" would reveal that "the real issue in the so-called Modernist crisis [was] on the one hand, the recognition of the historical character of Christianity and, on the other, a religious anthropology that would do greater justice to the findings of historical consciousness."[21] *Pascendi*, in response, firmly reasserted "a metaphysical realism" and "a realist epistemology."[22] Then, in 1910, the *motu proprio* of Pius X, *Sacrorum Antistitum*, prescribed that all church officeholders take an Oath against the Errors of Modernism.[23] A period of vigilantism followed throughout the Catholic world. The "sinister" procedures of the Roman Curia monsignor Umberto

16. This is the chapter title of O'Malley's discussion of the context in which Vatican II met; O'Malley, *What Happened at Vatican II*, 53–92. See also Joseph A. Komonchak, "The Enlightenment and the Construction of Roman Catholicism," *Annual of the Catholic Commission on Intellectual and Cultural Affairs* (1985): 31–59; Joseph A. Komonchak, "Vatican II and the Encounter between Catholicism and Liberalism," in *Catholicism and Liberalism: Contributions to American Public Philosophy*, ed. R. Bruce Douglass and David Hollenbach (Cambridge: Cambridge University Press, 1994), 76–99; Joseph A. Komonchak, "Modernity and the Construction of Roman Catholicism," *Cristianesimo nella Storia* 18 (1997): 353–85.
17. See the selection of documents in Denzinger, *Compendium of Creeds, Definitions, and Declarations*, nos. 2775–999. For the *Syllabus of Errors* in particular, see ibid., nos. 2901–80.
18. Ibid., nos. 3401–66.
19. Pope Pius X, "Pascendi Dominici Gregis," in *The Papal Encyclicals*, vol. 3: *1903–1939*, ed. Claudia Carlen (Wilmington, NC: McGrath Publishing Company, 1981), 71–98.
20. O'Connell, *Critics on Trial*, 344.
21. Giuseppe Ruggieri, "Faith and History," in *The Reception of Vatican II*, ed. Giuseppe Alberigo, Jean Pierre Jossua, and Joseph A. Komonchak (Washington, DC: The Catholic University of America Press, 1987), 91–114, at 95.
22. O'Connell, *Critics on Trial*, 344.
23. Denzinger, *Compendium of Creeds, Definitions, and Declarations*, nos. 3537–50. For another English translation of the Oath, see Gabriel Daly, *Transcendence and Immanence: A Study in Catholic Modernism and Integralism* (Oxford: Oxford University Press, 1980), 235–36. The requirement to take this oath was finally suspended in 1967.

Benigni (1862–1934) set the tone,[24] especially with his *Sodalitium Pianum*—
"the chilling parody of a secret service."[25] Despite a tentative openness to
historical-critical methods in his 1943 *Divino Afflante Spiritu*, Pius XII's 1950
encyclical *Humani Generis* nevertheless perpetuated the climate of suspicion
regarding use of historical methods by scholars following the line of the so-
called *nouvelle théologie*.[26]

All the bishops attending Vatican II twelve years later would have undertaken their seminary training within these post-Modernism years and would
have lived their ministry in an atmosphere demanding anti-Modernist vigi-
lance. Nevertheless, despite this atmosphere, during the four decades after
World War I and up to the calling of Vatican II, Roman Catholic theology
had seen a flowering of biblical, patristic, liturgical, lay, social action, and
ecumenical renewal movements. Many of these scholars were now taking a
historical perspective of the past, precisely in order to better address the new
challenges of the present.[27] All of the bishops at Vatican II would have been
aware of such developments before the council began, and many would have
welcomed them. The event of their gathering as an ecumenical council
brought this scholarship to the forefront of their attention and led to sometimes acrimonious debate, as the previous section has shown regarding the
historicity of Scripture and tradition.

On the very opening day of Vatican II, the church historian Pope John
XXIII reminded the assembled bishops: "History . . . is the teacher of life."[28]
He set a striking tone: "Authentic doctrine . . . should be studied and ex-

24. See O'Connell, *Critics on Trial*, 361–65.

25. Daly, *Transcendence and Immanence*, 218.

26. Pius XII, "Humani Generis." See also Komonchak, "*Humani Generis* and *Nouvelle Théologie*."

27. Giuseppe Ruggieri sums up this shift: "It is chiefly the generation after the Modernist crisis that must be credited with preparing the ground for a calmer and more productive vision. A number of factors combined to give rise to a new and different appreciation of history: the rediscovery of patristic thought and the resultant breakdown of the claims made by the neo-scholastic approach; the consciousness of an irreversible crisis in relationships between church and society, which could be re-established only on a new foundation; the impact of the ecu-menical and liturgical movements; the crisis in Western civilization itself, which imposed a serious examination of conscience on all; and so on." Ruggieri, "Faith and History," 95. See also Leo Scheffczyk, "Main Lines of the Development of Theology between the First World War and the Second Vatican Council," in *The Church in the Modern Age*, ed. Hubert Jedin, Konrad Repgen, and John Dolan, History of the Church (New York: Crossroad, 1981), 10:260–98. For a history of these movements, see also Rush, "Roman Catholic Ecclesiology," 272–79.

28. John XXIII, "Pope John's Opening Speech," 712.

pounded through the methods of research and through the literary forms of modern thought. The substance of the ancient doctrine of the deposit of faith is one thing, and the way in which it is presented is another. And it is the latter that must be taken into great consideration with patience if necessary, everything being measured in the forms and proportions of a magisterium which is predominantly pastoral in character."[29] The pope's opening address became decisive in encouraging historical approaches to the issues under debate. The council would go on to appropriate to some degree "the three dimensions of historical consciousness": the past, the present, and the future.[30] From initially endorsing the use of the historical methods for interpreting the *past* (employed by the *ressourcement* theologians who were now *periti* at the council), the historical consciousness of the council members developed in a greater appreciation of the historicity of the *present* receivers of revelation in changing contexts throughout the world, as they face an unknown *future*.[31]

John O'Malley observes that "Vatican II takes more explicit notice of history than any council before it."[32] This is not only apparent in the dynamic approach the council took to several major issues, as we have begun to see, but also in its language. The Latin noun *historia* (history) appears sixty-three times throughout the conciliar documents; the adjective *historicus* (historical), fourteen times. Moreover, as Giuseppe Alberigo has shown, a whole new vocabulary of "history words" appears regularly throughout the documents, for the first time in any council.[33] But the council's changed language is indicative of a deeper shift. Accordingly, Ruggieri proposes a helpful distinction:

29. Ibid., 715.

30. Forte, "Le prospettive della ricerca teologica," 420.

31. One of those *ressourcement* theologians who were acting as a personal *peritus* for a bishop and influencing wider groups of bishops was the Le Saulchoir theologian Marie-Dominique Chenu. In a sense, the development of the council's historical consciousness over four years could be said to have followed that same development within Chenu himself. Christophe Potworowski remarks: "There is a development in Chenu's thought from *an extrinsic use of the historical method applied to the study of primary sources*, to the progressive realization of *historicity as an intrinsic dimension of the Word of God*, by virtue of the concrete character of the Christ event." Christophe F. Potworowski, *Contemplation and Incarnation: The Theology of Marie-Dominique Chenu* (Montreal: McGill-Queen's University Press, 2001), 102–3. Emphasis added.

32. O'Malley, "Reform, Historical Consciousness, and Vatican II's *Aggiornamento*," 59.

33. Alberigo lists as "history words": aetas, aevum, adaptatio, aptare, condicio, crescere, dies, discernere, dynamicus, eventus, evolutio, fieri, frequens, historia, hodie, hodiernus, hora, innovatio, modernus, mutabilis, mutare, mutatio, novus, novitas, nunc, peregrinare, progredior, progressus, recens, reformare, renovatio, saeculum, signum, tempus, testimonium, ultimatum, urgens, urgeo. Alberigo, "Cristianesimo e storia nel Vaticano II," 577n1.

"We need to pay attention not only to (1) *the explicit consideration of history* present in the Council, but also to (2) *the presence of a historical awareness* which is implicit and operative in other assertions of the Council."[34]

The council's debates and final texts concerning a more dynamic understanding of Scripture, of living tradition, and of their interrelationship (as discussed in the previous section regarding the Scripture/tradition principle) can now be considered as a paradigmatic example of the council's "explicit consideration of history" and "the presence of a historical awareness"[35] in their treatment of particular themes. In other words, the dynamism at the heart of the Scripture/tradition principle needs to be brought to articulation in a separate conciliar principle, the faith/history principle. We have already examined the historically conscious approach apparent in *Dei Verbum's* treatment of the origins of the gospels and the consequent need to include historical-critical methods in their interpretation. Regarding "tradition," a sense of the length and theological diversity of "the great tradition" seen from a historical perspective (beyond that of a monolithic Tridentine Catholicism) was evident in the dramatic speech of Cardinal Joseph Frings during the first session, when he criticized the schema *De Ecclesia* for not being Catholic enough, i.e., limiting its vision to only the form of Catholicism of the previous few centuries.[36] As O'Malley remarks: "Frings here put his finger on *the major methodological effort of Vatican II*—to rise above 'the nineteenth century,' and to a large extent the sixteenth century, in order to place the council in an older and larger tradition."[37]

Aligned with this historically conscious view of the length and theological diversity of the Catholic past was a historically conscious *philosophical* reas-

---

34. Ruggieri, "Towards a Hermeneutic of Vatican II," 13n23. Numeration and emphasis added.

35. Ibid., 13n23.

36. *AS*, I/4, 218–19. A section of Frings's speech deserves lengthy quotation, because it brought to the surface what was to become one of the fundamental concerns of the council: "The schema prepared by commissions still under the control of the Roman Curia does not take account of the entire Catholic tradition in its presentation of the Church's teaching, but only of a small segment, the tradition of the last hundred years. Almost nothing is said of the Greek tradition and very little of the ancient Latin tradition, although both are extremely rich. This limitation is clear from the notes accompanying the schema and from the sources cited in them. In Chapter IV, for example, there are six pages of notes, but in the six pages there are only two brief citations from a Greek father. And the references to the Latin fathers and the Middle Ages are not that much more numerous; the six pages are almost entirely filled with references to the last hundred years. . . . The same pattern is to be found in all the chapters of the constitution. Is such a procedure to be called right, universal, ecumenical, and catholic— in Greek: *katholon*, that is, embracing everything and keeping everything in view?" Translation from Ruggieri, "Faith and History," 99.

37. O'Malley, *What Happened at Vatican II*, 156. Emphasis added.

sessment of Catholic theology. Greek philosophy had long been dominant as *the* background theory for Catholic theology, indeed its "perennial philosophy," as exemplified in Pope Leo XIII's assessment of St. Thomas Aquinas.[38] A significant number of the bishops at the council understood the prevailing ahistorical framework of neoscholasticism as a nonnegotiable element of the Catholic tradition. Nevertheless, *ressourcement* scholarship in Thomistic studies in the decades before the council had revealed, not a monolithic Thomism, but a diversity of interpretations regarding Thomas's philosophy and theology within the very scholastic tradition itself.[39] Attending all four council sessions as the abbot of Downside, Christopher Butler perceived throughout that time a significant shift in the "thought-scheme" of the council, away from ahistorical thinking:

> Theologically, the council may be said to bear witness to a shift of emphasis from a static model of the Christian reality, and in particular of the Church, to a dynamic model. Such a change of emphasis does not entail a rejection of the truths enunciated at an earlier stage of theological development. The second council of the Vatican, like all previous ecumenical councils since the first, was conscious of an inheritance from the Church's dogmatic past which it was commissioned to preserve and to carry forward. The change of emphasis, however, was real, and implicit in it was the adoption of a framework of thought other than that which had given birth to the static model. The great fathers of the [early] church, and after them the medieval schoolmen, utilised in the service of Christian truth the thought-scheme that lay to hand in Greek philosophy. Christianity has been well served by that thought-scheme. . . . It was almost as though the fathers [of the early church] were constructing a Mercator's Projection of Christian truth, a plane-surface map of a reality that was three-dimensional. I venture to think that it is the modern science of historical interpretation and criticism that has made it possible for our generation to realise better than its predecessors that the gospel yields more of its mystery to those who think in terms of history and eschatology—incarnational

---

38. Pope Leo XIII, "Aeterni Patris," in *The Papal Encyclicals*, vol. 2: *1878–1903*, ed. Claudia Carlen (Wilmington, NC: McGrath Publishing Company, 1981), 17–27.

39. See, for example, Gerald A. McCool, *From Unity to Pluralism: The Internal Evolution of Thomism* (New York: Fordham University Press, 1989); Joseph A. Komonchak, "Thomism and the Second Vatican Council," in *Continuity and Plurality in Catholic Theology: Essays in Honor of Gerald A. McCool*, ed. Anthony J. Cernera (Fairfield, CT: Sacred Heart University Press, 1998), 53–73; Fergus Kerr, *After Aquinas: Versions of Thomism* (Malden, MA: Blackwell Publishers, 2002). For a historical approach to the *Rezeptionsgeschichte* of Aquinas' *Summa Theologiae*, see Bernard McGinn, *Thomas Aquinas's Summa Theologiae: A Biography* (Princeton, NJ: Princeton University Press, 2014).

eschatology—than to those who think in terms of Aristotle. The council's shift of emphasis was perhaps more instinctive then reflective.[40]

The tensions between these ahistorical and historical approaches accounts for much of the heat evident in conciliar debates.[41] Moreover, Butler sees both worldviews still apparent in the final texts, which therefore, by implication, demand of the postconciliar interpreter a new synthesis: "This tension [between a historical and an essentialist view] is latent—some would say unresolved—in the *juxtaposition* of the hierarchical view of the Church, of her unchanging basic structure, with that of the Church as energized, rendered dynamic, by the charisms or grace-gifts of the Holy Ghost who is no respecter of persons or of office. This charismatic aspect of the Church is what makes her, while unchanging in her essence, unpredictable in her history. *Les portes de l'avenir sont toujours grand-ouvertes* (Bergson) [The doors of the future are always wide-open]."[42]

Extrapolating from the trajectory evident in these shifts within the council and its documents, we can speak of a faith/history principle characterizing the vision of Vatican II. This principle asserts that faith has always been and is historically conditioned, whether it be faith in the sense of *fides qua* (God's relationship with human beings) or *fides quae* (the Scripture, doctrines, and practices formulated throughout the history regarding that relationship between God and the community of faith). Human beings' loving response to the revealing and saving God always takes place within the constraints of historical situatedness. Likewise, formulation of expressions of "the faith" (in Scripture, doctrine, practices) are necessarily and inevitably conditioned by the particularities of time and place.

Seeing God *in* History

Several themes of the council can be selected as illustrations of the faith/history principle at work: the signs of the times, the human condition, culture

---

40. Butler, *The Theology of Vatican II*, 156–57. Butler was attending the council in his capacity as president of the English Benedictine Congregation.

41. "Among the many dynamic tensions of the second Vatican Council, the tension between [an] historical, or as some would say existentialist, view of the Church and her doctrines, and the 'essentialist' view of 'non-historical orthodoxy', was something which was liable to crop up at any moment. It could affect decisions even when the spokesmen in debate were not fully aware of their own motives." Ibid., 150.

42. Ibid., 151.

and other aspects of society, engagement with the sciences, and Scripture and doctrine.

Perhaps the key leitmotif revealing the council's emerging historical consciousness is that of "the signs of the times."[43] John XXIII had used the term when he officially called the council on December 25, 1961, with the papal bull *Humanae Salutis*: "While distrustful souls see nothing but darkness falling upon the face of the earth, we prefer to restate our confidence in our Savior, who has not left the world he redeemed. Indeed, making our own Jesus' recommendation that we learn to discern 'the signs of the times' (Mt 16:4), it seems to us that we can make out, in the midst of so much darkness, more than a few indications that enable us to have hope for the fate of the Church and of humanity."[44] During the intersession period between the first and second sessions, the phrase appeared in a section heading of Pope John's encyclical *Pacem in Terris* (April 11, 1963).[45] And, while he does not use the expression directly in his opening address to the council on October 11, 1962, he clearly evoked the ideas behind the phrase. What did John XXIII mean by the term? It seems that, while he was intending to take up Jesus' usage of the term, he wanted to extend the term beyond its original biblical apocalyptic meaning. Thus commentators make a distinction between this narrow biblical sense of the term and the broader understanding intended by Pope John.[46]

43. From the extensive literature on this theme at the council and in its documents, the following are basic: Peter Hünermann, ed. *Das Zweite Vatikanische Konzil und die Zeichen der Zeit heute* (Freiburg im Breisgau: Verlag Herder, 2006); Hans-Joachim Sander, "Das singulare Geschichtshandeln Gottes: Eine Frage der pluralen Topologie der Zeichen der Zeit," in *Herders theologischer Kommentar zum Zweiten Vatikanischen Konzil. Band 5. Die Documente des Zweiten Vatikanishen Konzils: Theologische Zusammenschau und Perspektiven*, ed. Peter Hünermann and Bernd Jochen Hilberath (Freiburg: Herder, 2006), 5:134–47; Fernando Berríos, Jorge Costadoat, and Diego García, eds., *Signos de estos tiempos. Interpretación teológica de nuestra época* (Santiago de Chile: Ediciones Universidad Alberto Hurtado, 2008); J. Verstraeten, ed. *Scrutinizing the Signs of the Times in the Light of the Gospel*, Proceedings of the Expert Seminar Leuven-Louvain-la-Neuve, 9–11 September 2004 (Leuven: Peeters Press, 2007).

44. This English translation is taken from https://jakomonchak.files.wordpress.com/2011/12/humanae-salutis.pdf.

45. For the section, "the signs of the times" (art. 126–29), see Pope John XXIII, "Pacem in Terris," in *The Papal Encyclicals*, vol. 5: *1958–1981*, ed. Claudia Carlen (Wilmington, NC: McGrath Publishing Company, 1981), 107–29, at 121.

46. See Dennis P. McCann, "Signs of the Times," in *The New Dictionary of Catholic Social Thought*, ed. Judith A. Dwyer and Elizabeth L. Montgomery (Collegeville, MN: Liturgical Press, 1994), 881–83, at 881. On the theology of John XXIII, see Giuseppe Ruggieri, "Esiste una teologia di papa Giovanni?," in *Un cristiano sul trono di Pietro: Studi storici su Giovanni XXIII*, ed. Enzo Bianchi (Gorle, Bologna: Servitium, 2003), 253–74.

It is in the development of Schema XIII on the church *ad extra* that the term *signa temporum* begins to be deliberately employed as a theological rubric.[47] During the second session (November 1963), a mixed commission made up of members of the Theological Commission and the Commission on the Apostolate of the Laity was created with the responsibility of drafting a new schema. The following year, in September 1964, during the third session but before debate had started on the latest schema, a special subcommission (with the title *De Condicione Hodierna*) was formed. With Bishop Mark Gregory McGrath, CSC (bishop of Santiago de Veraguas, Panama), as its president, it had the task of drafting a chapter on the human condition, what was eventually to become the introduction to *Gaudium et Spes* (art. 4–10). This subcommission gave particular consideration to the meaning and deliberate use of the term *signa temporum*.[48] To guide its early work, the subcommission proposed the following as a working definition of the term *signa temporum*: "The phenomena which occur so frequently and so pervasively that they characterize a given epoch and seem to express the needs and aspirations of contemporary humanity."[49]

Yves Congar, with regard to the council's use of the motif, says understanding "the intention implicit in the language used" is key: "The aim is a full recognition of the *historicity* of the world and of the Church itself [*reconnâitre pleinement l'historicité du monde et de l'Eglise elle-meme*] which, though distinct from the world, is nonetheless bound up with it. Movements in the world must have their echo in the Church, at least to the extent that they raise problems."[50]

47. On June 26, 1964, the Coordinating Commission changed the numbering of Schema XVII to Schema XIII.

48. Turbanti lists as members: (bishops) McGrath, Fernández Conde, Fernández A., Nagae, Zoa, Anastasio del S. Rosario; (*periti*) Medina (secretary), Houtart, Dubarle, Sugranyes de Franch, Vasquez. See Turbanti, *Un Concilio per il Mondo Moderno*, 632. According to the minutes of a meeting the following year (September 23, 1965), at that stage the bishops on the special subcommission were McGrath, Nagae, D'Souza, Fernandes, Wright, and Câmara. The *periti* were Ligutti, Martelet, Medina, Galilea, Gregory, Chenu, Houtart, Caramuru, Sugranyes de Franch and Habicht. See Gilles Routhier, "Finishing the Work Begun: The Trying Experience of the Fourth Period," in *History of Vatican II*, vol. 5: *The Council and the Transition; The Fourth Period and the End of the Council, September 1965–December 1965*, ed. Giuseppe Alberigo and Joseph A. Komonchak (Maryknoll, NY: Orbis Books, 2006), 5:49–184, at 143n378.

49. Secretarial Report by Philippe Delhaye and François Houtart, November 17, 1964. Quoted in Marie-Dominique Chenu, "The Signs of the Times," in *The Church Today: Commentaries on the Pastoral Constitution on the Church in the Modern World*, ed. Group 2000 (New York: Newman Press, 1967), 43–59, at 48n4.

50. Yves Congar, "Bloc-Notes sur le Concile," *Information Catholique Internationale* (15 November 1964): 14–16, at 14. Original emphasis. Quoted in Ruggieri, "Faith and History," 97. The French from the original has been added here.

History can be revelatory of God's presence and purposes, if perceived with the eyes of faith and evaluated through the lens of the Gospel.

The actual phrase (*signa temporum* or *signa temporis*) appears five times, in documents promulgated in the second half of the council.[51] The key occurrence appears in the structurally significant opening paragraph of the introduction to *Gaudium et Spes*:

> In every age, the church carries the responsibility of reading the signs of the times [*signa temporum perscrutandi*] and of interpreting them in the light of the Gospel [*sub Evangelii luce interpretandi*], if it is to carry out its task. In language intelligible to every generation, it should be able to answer the ever recurring questions which people ask about the meaning of this present life and of the life to come, and how one is related to the other. We must be aware of and understand the aspirations, the yearnings, and the often dramatic features of the world in which we live. . . . Ours is a new age in history with profound and rapid changes spreading gradually to all corners of the earth. (GS 4)

Similarly, the placement of *Gaudium et Spes* 11 is structurally significant. Just as *Gaudium et Spes* 4 is the opening article of the introduction to the whole constitution, *Gaudium et Spes* 11 is the opening article to the constitution's first major section, part 1. The article is given the heading "Responding to the Promptings of the Spirit." While the actual phrase "signs of the times" is not used in the article itself, the phrase "signs of God's presence" is seen by commentators to be synonymous with, and indeed to be amplifying the meaning of, the phrase in article 4: "The people of God believes that it is led by the Spirit of the Lord who fills the whole world. Impelled by that faith, they try to discern the true signs of God's presence and purpose [*vera signa praesentiae vel consilii Dei discernere*] in the events, the needs and the desires which it shares with the rest of humanity today. For faith [*fides*] casts a new light on everything and makes known the full ideal which God has set for humanity, thus guiding the mind towards solutions that are fully human" (GS 11).

Later, while not using but implying the phrase "signs of the times," the pastoral constitution goes on to state: "With the help of the Holy Spirit, it is the task of the whole people of God, particularly of its pastors and theologians, to listen to and distinguish *the many voices of our times* [*varias loquelas nostri temporis*] and to *interpret* them in the light of the divine word [*sub lumine verbi divini*], in order that the revealed truth may be more deeply

---

51. *Unitatis Redintegratio*, 4 (November 21, 1964); *Apostolicam Actuositatem*, 14 (November 18, 1965); *Dignitatis Humanae*, 15 (December 7, 1965); *Presbyterorum Ordinis*, 9 (December 7, 1965); *Gaudium et Spes*, 4 (December 7, 1965).

penetrated, better *understood,* and more suitably *presented*" (GS 44).[52] The verbs in this sentence have strong echoes of those in the summary sentence in *Lumen Gentium* 12, after its statements earlier in the paragraph on the *sensus fidelium*: "The people unfailingly *adheres to* this faith, *penetrates* it more deeply through right judgment, and *applies* it more fully in daily life" (LG 12). By implication, it is the *sensus fidelium* that is the key means through which the whole people of God discern the signs of the times.

Three theological points are significant in these three key passages. First, they variously, but synonymously, name the criterion to be used in discerning the signs of the times: "the Gospel" (GS 4), "faith" (GS 11), "the divine word" (GS 44). Second, the subject who is discerning is not a group within the church but "the church" (GS 4), "the People of God" (GS 11), and "the whole People of God" (GS 44). Third, the divine assistance given to the whole people of God in carrying out this discernment is the Holy Spirit and the Spirit's gift for discerning the faith, the "sense of the faith."

The council's revelation/faith principle portrays God and humanity as being in dialogue, in conversation. Likewise, it understands the encounter between God and the church in history as an ongoing dialogue, facilitated by the Holy Spirit. "Thus God, who spoke in the past, continues to converse [*colloquitur*] with the spouse of his beloved Son. And the Holy Spirit, through whom the living voice of the Gospel rings out in the church—and through it to the world—leads believers to the full truth and makes the word of Christ dwell in them in all its richness" (DV 8). While God's unsurpassable revelation has taken place in Jesus Christ through the Holy Spirit, the signs of the times can be indicators for what God is doing and saying anew (always in Christ through the Spirit) *in the present.* These signs reveal the meaning of the Christian Gospel in these new contexts. In this dialogic model, God and humanity are not in opposition to one another but rather in a cooperative partnership.[53] God calls the church to be an engaged and dialogic collaborator and to play its part in the unfolding of God's plan. Human participation and discernment is required.

Through engaging in a discernment of the signs of the times, the council understood itself to be encountering God in a new way, because, in the ongo-

---

52. Translation corrected. Emphasis added.

53. Richard Gaillardetz neatly captures this aspect of the conciliar vision with his phrase "non-competitive relationship" to describe the God/humanity relationship as paradigmatic for relationships within the church. See Richard R. Gaillardetz, *An Unfinished Council: Vatican II, Pope Francis, and the Renewal of Catholicism* (Collegeville, MN: Liturgical Press, 2015), 91–113.

ing newness of history and its changing conditions, God is unfolding his plan afresh. Vatican II wanted to be attentive to both the revelation of God's will within new contexts of history and the resistances to God and any impediments to God's will in contemporary life. Such discernment is forever incumbent on the church, the council taught. Vatican II understood this attention to history and discernment of the signs of the times as not just *a pedagogical principle*; i.e., the church must learn to address the "events, needs and desires" (GS 4) and speak to the language, symbols, and customs of the addressees of the Gospel (GS 44). The council's concentration on the signs of the times presents also *a theological principle*: the God who has spoken within history *in the past* speaks in a new way *in the present*, because the historical conditions of the present are different from the conditions of the past. Through these historical dimensions of human existence, God is teaching the church new things about the meaning of the Gospel *for this time and place*. To discern what God is saying, the church needs to understand "the world of today": "the world as the theatre of human history, bearing the marks [*signatum*] of its travail, its triumphs and failures" (GS 2); that is, "the world in which we live, together with its expectations, its desires and its frequently dramatic character" (GS 4). The council elsewhere will speak of this world as characterizing "the human condition."

Thus, parallel with the council's dialogic understanding of the God-humanity encounter within and throughout history is its dynamic notion of the human person, as already explored in the protological/eschatological principle. Once again, the language of the council is important. "Even in its vocabulary, the Council speaks rather of the human *condition* than of human *nature* as such, by contrast with Vatican I. Without setting aside an essentialist philosophy, one can readily have recourse to existential analyses."[54] The word "condition" (*condicio*) in relationship to the historical context of human beings appears 195 times in the conciliar corpus and forty-five times in *Gaudium et Spes*.

And then, related to its more historical understanding of human "nature" is the council's attention to the various dimensions that comprise the human

---

54. Marie-Dominique Chenu, "The History of Salvation and the Historicity of Man in the Renewal of Theology," in *Theology of Renewal*, vol. 1: *Renewal of Religious Thought*, ed. L. K. Shook (New York: Herder and Herder, 1968), 153–66, at 164. On the significance in the thought of Marie-Dominique Chenu of the distinction between the static notion of "human nature" and the more historical notion of "the human condition," see Potworowski, *Contemplation and Incarnation*, 92–96, esp. 94.

"condition": culture, society, economic life, and political life. "Culture" can be selected here as one example of the council's historically consciousness approach. In the reception of the council, the term "inculturation" has come to be used of its vision regarding the need to engage with the context in which the church proclaims the faith and in which believers appropriate the Gospel into their lives. The council does not use the term "inculturation," but it can be legitimately invoked to describe this aspect of the council's vision.

The noun *cultura* appears ninety-one times; the adjective *culturalis*, thirty-four times. This attention to the significance of culture is evident in an arc that stretches from the very first document (*Sacrosanctum Concilium*) to two of the last documents of the council (*Ad Gentes* and *Gaudium et Spes*).[55] The council here arrives at a deeper understanding of "catholicity"—no one culture is to be normative, since the Gospel must be universally proclaimed and experienced as salvific in all cultures (GS 58). The council's historical consciousness affects its view of the nature of the church *through time* as well as its sense of what it means for the church to receive and pass on divine revelation and salvation across different cultures and peoples *at any one time* throughout history. Consequently, not only does the council become more historically conscious of the church through time (*diachronic* historical consciousness), but it also becomes more globally conscious of itself as a truly catholic church (*synchronic* historical consciousness).

The council's attention to God's continuing self-communication throughout history is the theological foundation of its discussion of inculturation and adaptation, especially in missionary work: "In his *self-revelation* to his people, fully *manifesting himself* in his incarnate Son [*sese revelans usque ad plenam sui manifestationem in Filio incarnato*], God spoke in the context of the culture proper to each age. Similarly the church has existed through the centuries in varying circumstances and has utilized the resources of different cultures to spread and explain the message of Christ in its preaching, to examine and understand it more deeply, and to express it more perfectly in the liturgy and in the life of the multiform community of the faithful" (GS 58). In the opening part of this quotation (in italics above) we find an example of reception in a later document of the council's teaching in an earlier one, *Dei Verbum* (albeit promulgated only nineteen days before). Moreover, it shows a significant development of that previous teaching by applying it to culture. Thus, the council is here neatly summarizing the theology of

---

55. See, for example, SC 37–40; LG 13, 17, 23; AG 9–11, 21–22; GS 53–62.

revelation and faith in *Dei Verbum, and yet developing its theology of faith* in a way that highlights the historicity of the human receiver.

To capture the dynamic interplay between Gospel and culture, the council uses the language of "adaptation" (*aptatio*) and employs the theological analogy of the incarnation. *Ad Gentes* 22 states: "*Just as happened in the economy of the incarnation*, the young churches [in 'mission' countries] . . . borrow from the customs, traditions, wisdom, teaching, arts and sciences of their people everything which could be used to praise the glory of the Creator, manifest the grace of the saviour, or contribute to the right ordering of Christian life." The passage then refers in a footnote to *Lumen Gentium* 13, on catholicity and legitimate diversity among local churches.

This interplay between Gospel and culture is not one way; the church can indeed learn from the cultures in which it evangelizes:

> Just as it is in the world's interest to acknowledge the church as a social reality and a driving force in history, so too the church is not unaware of how much it has profited from the history and development of humankind. It profits from the experience of past ages, from the progress of the sciences, and from the riches hidden in various cultures, through which greater light is thrown on human nature and new avenues of truth are opened up. The church learned early in its history to express the Christian message in the concepts and languages of different peoples and tried to clarify it in the light of the wisdom of their philosophers: it was an attempt to adapt the Gospel to the understanding of all and the requirements of the learned, insofar as this could be done. Indeed, *this kind of adaptation and preaching of the revealed word must ever be the law of all evangelization.* (GS 44)[56]

Thus, one consequence of historical thinking is a recognition of the limited nature of one's own perspective and the possibility of learning from others with different perspectives. Here, *Gaudium et Spes* 44 marks a paradigmatic shift away from the official teaching of the Catholic Church during the centuries leading up to Vatican II. It states that the church is not the sole bearer of knowledge, human and divine, but can indeed "learn" from the world, culture, and society around it—in matters human and divine.

One particularly striking aspect of this openness to learn is the council's desire to break away from preconciliar attitudes and to seek *rapprochement* with the scientific worldview of Modernity. Interpreting reality from a scientific

---

56. Emphasis added.

perspective is also a form of historical thinking, because it recognizes the shifting perspectives of human understanding through time. The council acknowledged that the natural and human sciences can indeed help the church to understand better the human condition of the receivers of the Gospel.

> Therefore, the faithful ought to work closely with their contemporaries and ought to try to understand their ways of thinking and feeling, as these find expression in current culture. Let the faithful incorporate the findings of new sciences and teaching and the understanding of the most recent discoveries into Christian morality and thought, so that their practice of religion and their moral behaviour may keep abreast of their acquaintance with science and of the relentless progress of technology: in this way they will succeed in evaluating and interpreting everything with an authentically Christian sense [*integro christiano sensu*]. (GS 62)[57]

Engagement with the *human* sciences (psychology, sociology, philosophy, history, literary studies, etc.) underlay the council's shift toward a more historically conscious understanding *of the human receiver* of revelation in community throughout history. Engagement with *natural* sciences (geology, biology, physics, astronomy, etc.) underlay the council's shift to an evolutionary view *of the created world*—nature too has a history, across the ages since creation. Now, the council stated, "humankind substitutes a dynamic and more evolutionary concept of nature for a static one" (GS 5). Here, the thought of Pierre Teilhard de Chardin was the "subterranean influence."[58] According to Stephen Schloesser, "Teilhard de Chardin's embrace of temporality was adopted by the council."[59]

---

57. Translation corrected. This "authentic Christian sense" evokes the "sense of the faith" (*sensus fidei*) bestowed by the Holy Spirit, about which the council teaches elsewhere (e.g., LG 12, 35).

58. Nicholas Boyle, "On Earth, As In Heaven," *The Tablet*, July 9, 2005, 12–15, at 12. Quoted in Stephen Schloesser, "Against Forgetting: Memory, History, Vatican II," in *Vatican II: Did Anything Happen?*, ed. David G. Schultenover (New York: Continuum, 2007), 92–152, at 123. On the perception by some of the bishops that Teilhard's thought was adversely affecting some aspects of the council documents, see O'Malley, *What Happened at Vatican II*, 111, 258–59.

59. Schloesser, "Against Forgetting," 123. Schloesser remarks that, although it was Teilhard's explanation of the doctrine of original sin that brought him into conflict with the Vatican, "this particular doctrinal question, important as it might be, obscured the deeper impact of Teilhard's thought, namely, an embrace of temporality—the fact of *change* in human history—and, as a corollary, of the importance of terrestrial existence in salvation history. The shift from a cyclical or static view of human existence to a notion of an always accelerating linear history had taken place gradually between 1500 and 1800. Reinhart Koselleck identifies this shift as

Science is now seen as a potential dialogue partner for the Christian community. "In pastoral care sufficient use should be made, not only of theological principles, but also of the findings of secular sciences, especially psychology and sociology: in this way the faithful will be brought to a purer and more mature living of the faith" (GS 62). Science can present positive challenges not previously recognized: "In fact, recent research and discoveries in the sciences, in history and philosophy bring up new questions [*novas questiones*] which have an important bearing on life itself and demand new scrutiny by theologians" (GS 62).[60] Often, these new questions raise issues that Scripture and prior generations within the tradition had not addressed or could not even have envisaged. Historical consciousness is both an awareness of a sameness and an awareness of a continual *novum* in the human condition through time.

One important implication of this openness to the human sciences was the impact of literary studies on Catholic biblical scholarship. As already explored in the Scripture/tradition principle, the council recognizes the historically conditioned origins of the scriptural writings and, accordingly, recognizes that methods of historical criticism are appropriate for their interpretation (DV 12). An extension of this awareness can be seen in the council's openness to the development of doctrine. As we have seen, Pope John set the scene in his address at the opening of the first session: "Authentic doctrine . . . should be studied and expounded through the methods of research and through the literary forms of modern thought. The substance of the ancient doctrine of the deposit of faith is one thing, and the way in which it is presented is another."[61] The Declaration on Christian Education, *Gravissimum Educationis*, in speaking of "the faculties of the sacred sciences [promoting] research in the different fields of sacred learning," alludes to the development of doctrine. It highlights four objectives that the faculties should promote: "that an ever-growing understanding of sacred revelation be achieved, that the inheritances of Christian wisdom handed down by former generations be more fully appreciated, that dialogue with our separated brothers and sisters and with non-Christians be promoted, and that questions

---

the 'temporalization (*Verzeitlichung*) of history' that characterizes 'modernity' (*Neuzeit*)." Ibid., 125. Schloesser is quoting Reinhart Koselleck, *Futures Past: On the Semantics of Historical Time* (Cambridge, MA: MIT Press, 1985), 3–20.

60. Translation corrected.

61. John XXIII, "Pope John's Opening Speech," 715.

arising from the development of doctrine may be addressed [*questionibus a doctrinarum progressu exortis respondeatur*]" (GE 11).[62]

As the famous statement of John Courtney Murray notes, development of doctrine was "*the* issue under the issues" at Vatican II—and it remains embedded in its vision for the church.[63] In his introduction to the Abbott translation of *Dignitatis Humanae*, John Courtney Murray remarks:

> It can hardly be maintained that the Declaration [on Religious Freedom] is a milestone in human history—moral, political, or intellectual. The principle of religious freedom has long been recognized in constitutional law, to the point where even Marxist-Leninist political ideology is obliged to pay lip-service to it. In all honesty it must be admitted that the Church is late in acknowledging the validity of the principle. In any event, the document is a significant event in the history of the Church. *It was, of course, the most controversial document of the whole Council, largely because it raised with sharp emphasis the issue that lay continually below the surface of all the conciliar debates—the issue of the development of doctrine. The notion of development, not the notion of religious freedom, was the real sticking-point for many of those who opposed the Declaration even to the end.* The course of the development between the *Syllabus of Errors* (1864) and *Dignitatis Humanae Personae* (1965) still remains to be explained by theologians. *But the Council formally sanctioned the validity of the development itself; and this was a doctrinal event of high importance for theological thought in many other areas.*[64]

Another topic where "the issue under all the issues" was evident was the collegiality debate, particularly when the *Nota Explicativa Praevia* was appended to *Lumen Gentium*, just as it was about to be promulgated. The *Nota* was not a text formulated with the authority of the council. At the time, the *peritus* Joseph Ratzinger wrote of how its forced appendage to the conciliar document without the approval of the council "injected something of bitterness into the closing days of the [third] session, otherwise so full of valiant hopes."[65] What was being challenged, against its adoption by the majority of council fathers, was the issue of "historical thinking" emerging in *Lumen Gentium*. Concerning the "conservative" view of the primacy/collegiality relationship that was behind the note, Ratzinger writes:

62. Translation corrected.
63. Murray, "This Matter of Religious Freedom," 43.
64. John Courtney Murray, "Religious Freedom," in *The Documents of Vatican II*, ed. Walter M. Abbott (London: Geoffrey Chapman, 1966), 672–74, at 673. Emphasis added.
65. Ratzinger, *Theological Highlights of Vatican II*, 170.

The conservatism of this view is based on its aloofness from history and so it basically suffers from a lack of tradition—i.e., of openness to the totality of Christian history. It is important that we see this because it gives us an insight into the inner pattern of *the opposing alignments of thought in the Council*, often mistakenly described as an opposition between progressives and conservatives. It would be more correct to speak of a contrast between *historical thinking* and formally juridical thinking. The "progressives" (at least the large majority of them) were in fact concerned precisely with "tradition," with *a new awareness of both the breadth and depth of what had been handed down in Christian tradition*. This was where they found the norms for renewal which permitted them to be fearless and broad in their outlook. It was an outlook which came from the intrinsic catholicity of the church.[66]

Vatican II, in its approach to faith and history, constitutes *an opening up* to a model of renewal and reform, beyond what is captured either individually or collectively by the three key terms *"ressourcement," "development,"* and *"aggiornamento."*[67] *There is something new happening here*; the whole is greater than the sum of the parts. Yves Congar, writing in 1972, hints at such a different and indeed new model of reform, which is present at Vatican II, albeit in an inchoate way. "Our epoch of rapid change and cultural transformation (philosophical ferments and sociological conditions different from those which the Church has accustomed itself to until now) calls for a revision of 'traditional' forms which goes beyond the level of adaptation or *aggiornamento*, and which would be instead a new creation. *It is no longer sufficient to maintain, by adapting it, what has already been; it is necessary to reconstruct it.*"[68] Likewise, Avery Dulles, writing in 1974, notes the implications of the new type of reform beginning to emerge at Vatican II, a type of reform he calls "creative transformation":

> I would hold that, although the Church cannot accept what is simply alien, it can discern the presence of Christ in the signs of the times. *In dialogue with the contemporary world, the Church can make innovations that do not simply grow out of its own previous tradition.* Reform by development and assimilation may have seemed an adequate model when the Church was the

66. Ibid., 171–72. Emphasis added.

67. See this triad in O'Malley, *What Happened at Vatican II*, 299–302; John O'Malley, " 'The Hermeneutic of Reform': A Historical Analysis," *Theological Studies* 73 (2012): 517–46, at 536–42.

68. Yves Congar, "Renewal of the Spirit and Reform of the Institution," in *Readings in Church Authority: Gifts and Challenges for Contemporary Catholicism*, ed. Gerard Mannion, et al. (Burlington, VT: Ashgate, 2003), 512–17, at 516. Emphasis added.

controlling influence in Western culture. But today [1974] a proper respect for the autonomy of human culture demands a less possessive and a more dialogic relationship. The Church must creatively respond to the initiatives of others.[69]

Such a shift constitutes nothing less than a conversion of the Catholic imagination regarding God and humanity, faith and history. One could well call it something of a hermeneutical turn in the history of the Catholic Church's self-understanding regarding its life, doctrine, and worship. As the church moves into ever-new historical contexts, new questions arise and are addressed to the tradition that the church has never asked before, nor even envisaged—because it was inconceivable to have even thought of them, due to the worldviews at the time. *The authoritative past here needs the present receiver to find answers.* Vatican II marks a significant recalibration of the Catholic imagination concerning a truth always held but now newly perceived: *the present* too, not just the past, is revelatory and authoritative. As the Holy Spirit leads the church in history through conversion to the fullness of truth, God is challenging the church to discern the new things that God is doing in Christ through the Spirit—by scrutinizing the signs of the times in the light of the Gospel.

The next four principles continue to articulate the council's ecclesiological vision. The elements of that vision are to be found not only in the two constitutions explicitly devoted to the church (*Lumen Gentium* and *Gaudium et Spes*) but also throughout all the other documents, especially in *Sacrosanctum Concilium* on the worshiping church, in *Unitatis Redintegratio* on healing the church's disunity, and in *Ad Gentes* on the missionary church, especially the first chapter with its rich trinitarian emphasis.[70]

---

69. Avery Dulles, "The Church Always in Need of Reform: *Ecclesia Semper Reformanda*," in *The Church Inside and Out* (Washington, DC: United States Catholic Conference, 1974), 37–50, at 42–43.

70. Ecclesiological themes developed in *Lumen Gentium*, promulgated on November 21, 1964, were further explored in documents specifically devoted to those particular themes, e.g., chapter 3 of *Lumen Gentium* on bishops, in *Christus Dominus* (promulgated October 28, 1965); *Lumen Gentium* 28 on priests, in *Optatam Totius* (October 28, 1965) and *Presbyterorum Ordinis* (December 7, 1965); chapter 4 of *Lumen Gentium* on the laity (as well as chapter 2, articles 9–14), in *Apostolicam Actuositatem* (November 18, 1965); *Lumen Gentium*'s chapter 6 on religious women and men in the church, in *Perfectae Caritatis* (October 28, 1965); *Lumen*

The first of the previous two chapters examined the ecclesial witnesses to the apostolic faith, Scripture, and tradition; these remain for the church, as a twofold criterion, the basis for all Christian life, doctrine, and practice. From the council's renewed understanding of the dynamic relationship between Scripture and living tradition emerged a normative pattern of interpretation, which became for the council another ecclesiological principle, the faith/history principle: the Gospel must be continually reinterpreted from within new contexts. These two principles, together, had important implications for how the council envisaged contemporary renewal and reform of Catholic self-understanding. The following chapters now examine four such implications: the relationship between particular and universal dimensions of ecclesial life; between the *communio* nature of the church and its *missio* nature; between unity and diversity in the faith in a world church; and between the church *ad intra* and *ad extra*.

If the two principles in the previous two chapters have highlighted the *diachronic* reception of revelation by the church across the ages, the four principles in these chapters highlight the *synchronic* reception of revelation in the church, i.e., the church's "nature and universal mission" (LG 1) in different contexts at the one time. The principles capture the various aspects of the reception of revelation as a matrix of various polarities and tensions at one time throughout the world church (albeit within the ongoing flow of history). Each principle was frequently at issue, explicitly or implicitly, in so much of the debate throughout the council. Each touches on the notion of "catholicity." As with all principles in the council's final vision, these four principles overlap and inform each other; moreover, just as the terms within each principle stand in a tensive relationship with each other, so do the four principles with each other.

Gentium 15 on other Christian churches and ecclesial communities, in *Unitatis Redintegratio*; *Lumen Gentium* 16 on other religions, in *Nostra Aetate* (October 28, 1965); *Lumen Gentium* 17 on the church's missionary activity, in *Ad Gentes* (December 7, 1965).

Principle 14

Particular/Universal

Principle 14: A local church, pastored by its bishop—in communion with all other local churches—is truly the catholic church in that place; the universal catholic church is the whole people of God as a single community of faith consisting of a communion of all local churches in communion with the local church of Rome and its bishop.

This chapter examines the particular/universal principle. A later chapter will examine the same issue from another angle, by means of the college of bishops/bishop of Rome principle. In order to be faithful to the whole vision of Vatican II, it is important methodologically to examine the former before the latter, i.e., to address the community of faith before addressing the issue of those entrusted to oversee it. This order helps to avoid several misconceptions that the vision of Vatican II clearly excludes and that some one-dimensional interpretations of the council continue to affirm.

First, the council clearly does not equate the universal church with the local church of Rome. Nor does the council, second, portray the local church of Rome as being "outside of" or "over against" the communion that exists between and among "the rest" of the local churches. Furthermore, and third, discussion of the administrative role of the Roman Curia, and its relationship to the bishop of Rome and to the whole college of bishops, is likewise more appropriately considered *after* discussion of the particular/universal principle and addressed when considering the council's teaching regarding the college of bishops and the bishop of Rome. Such an ordering for examining these principles precludes a misconception: that the Roman Curia is to be understood as the official voice and central governing body of the universal church. The Roman Curia is the administrative arm of the pope, the bishop of Rome, in his capacity as the Roman pontiff, the visible sign of unity of the universal church as the head of, and in communion with, the college of bishops. The dicasteries of the Roman Curia, in their own right, do not have authority over the local churches.

Where does the council begin its exploration of this principle, with the local or with the universal? As Angel Antón points out: "It is clear that both *Lumen Gentium* and *Christus Dominus* take as their *methodological* point of departure the notion and reality of the universal church."[1] Similarly, Joseph Komonchak stresses "the ambiguity or, if you prefer, the transitional character, of the council's doctrine of the Church. . . . Not only did the council begin its work within the perspectives of the universalist ecclesiology long dominant in the West, but its recovery of an ecclesiology of communion that underlies a theology of the local church was hesitant and unsystematic."[2] Despite this ambiguity, however, interpretation of this principle in tensive relationship with other principles will lead us to a comprehensive interpretation of the council and its documents on this theme.

The conciliar documents are not consistent in the vocabulary used for the two dimensions of "locality" and "universality."[3] When speaking of individual instances of the church, the council documents use both *particularis* (particular) and *localis* (local). Similarly, while the two terms can be taken as synonyms, they are used at times to refer to different manifestations, e.g., a diocese, a patriarchal church, an assembly of the faithful in a certain place. In reference to assemblies at the local level, the phrase *congregatio fidelium* is also used.

---

1. Angel Antón, "Local Church/Regional Church: Systematic Reflections," *The Jurist* 52 (1992): 553–76, at 568. Emphasis added.

2. Joseph A. Komonchak, "The Local Church and the Church Catholic: The Contemporary Theological Problematic," *The Jurist* 52 (1992): 416–47, at 427. Yves Congar notes with regard to this universalist ecclesiology: "More dominant, above all, after the Gregorian Reform and the appearance of the mendicant orders, was what has been called the ecclesiology of the universal church. That is taken to be a view in which the church is seen as a homogenous whole of which the dioceses are considered to be quantitative parts. In the end, the universal church would be only an extension of the Church of Rome." Yves Congar, *Diversity and Communion* (London: SCM Press, 1984), 42.

3. On the diverse terminology used in the conciliar documents, see Komonchak, "The Local Church and the Church Catholic," 416–17; Winfried Aymans, "Die Communio Ecclesiarum als Gestaltgesetz der einen Kirche," *Archiv für katholisches Kirchenrecht* 39 (1970): 70–75; Gianfranco Ghirlanda, "Universal Church, Particular Church, and Local Church at the Second Vatican Council and in the New Code of Canon Law," in *Vatican II Assessment and Perspectives: Twenty-Five Years After (1962–1987)*, vol. 2, ed. René Latourelle (New York: Paulist Press, 1989), 2:233–71.

When speaking of the dimension of universality, the council speaks of "the church" (in the singular) in several ways: *ecclesia universa* (the entire church, e.g., LG 23); *ecclesia universalis* (the universal church, e.g., LG 23); *ecclesia catholica* (the Catholic Church, e.g., LG 8); *ecclesia tota* (the whole church, e.g., UR 2); *ecclesia una* (the one church, e.g., LG 23). While these five terms can be taken as synonyms, each nonetheless can bring to the fore a different aspect of the dimension. In addition, the council uses other all-encompassing terms, such as "the communion of the faithful [*communio fidelium*]" (e.g., UR 2); "the whole body of the faithful [*universitas fidelium*]" (e.g., LG 12); "the whole company of the faithful [*multitudo fidelium*]" (e.g., LG 23); "the Lord's flock" and "the church of God" (e.g., LG 28; UR 15); "the church of Christ" (e.g., LG 9; 26). Furthermore, since "the entire church [*ecclesia universa*] is seen to be 'a people made one by the unity of the Father, the Son and the Holy Spirit'" (LG 4),[4] the council also employs (together and individually) the trinitarian images of "the People of God, the Body of the Lord, and the Temple of the Holy Spirit" (LG 17) to refer to "the church" in the singular. Among all of these references to the universal church, however, it is, above all, the church as "the People of God" that is "the principal paradigm of the Church in the documents of Vatican II."[5]

Alongside the council's trinitarian focus is its eucharistic perspective for conceiving the interrelationship between local and universal. The church universal is only ever fully realized at the local level, because it is here that a community of faith, a "congregation of the faithful [*congregatio fidelium*]" (LG 26), responding in the here and now to God's salvific revelation, celebrates Eucharist and is thereby nourished to live the Gospel. It is at the local level, at Eucharist above all, that the church is realized. Implicit in the eucharistic ecclesiology of Vatican II is the affirmation that, while it is one and the same Eucharist that all local communities celebrate, there cannot be realistically a universal liturgy of the Eucharist, involving every single member of the whole people of God throughout the world around the one altar.[6] There can only ever be local eucharistic realizations of the church; it is the *congregationes fidelium* that constitute the universal church.

4. Translation corrected. Quoting St. Cyprian (*De Orat. Dom.* 23 PL 4, 553; Martel III A, p. 285; St. Augustine (*Serm.* 71, 20, 33: PL 38, 463 f.); and St. John Damascene (*Adv. Iconocl.* 12: PG 96 1358 D). As cited in Flannery, 11n4.

5. Dulles, *Models of the Church*, 45.

6. Francis Sullivan notes: "It is the very nature of the Eucharist that it can only be celebrated locally: in a particular place with a particular congregation. This fact gives a unique importance to the local church as 'the church of God in this place.'" Sullivan, *The Church We Believe In*, 49.

The first document promulgated by the council, *Sacrosanctum Concilium*, sets forth the foundation of what would develop into the council's eucharistic-focused ecclesiology: "For the liturgy, through which 'the work of our redemption takes place,' especially in the divine sacrifice of the Eucharist, is supremely effective in enabling the faithful to express in their lives and portray to others the mystery of Christ and *the real nature of the true church*" (SC 2).[7] Likewise, it states: "*The principal manifestation of the church* consists in the full, active participation of all God's holy people in the same liturgical celebrations, especially in the same Eucharist, in one prayer, at one altar, at which the bishop presides, surrounded by his college of priests and by his ministers" (SC 41).[8] Parishes too "in some way [*quodammodo*] represent the visible church established throughout the world" (SC 42). *Lumen Gentium* would later teach: the celebration of the Eucharist is "the source and summit of the Christian life" (LG 11). Therefore, the paradigmatic conciliar image of a eucharistically centered church is that of the local bishop presiding at Eucharist surrounded by priests and congregation and, at the parish level, of the priest gathering the congregation for Eucharist.[9]

The key formulation of the particular/universal principle is found in *Lumen Gentium* 23. In the context of discussion regarding collegiality and a bishop's relationship with the church local and universal, the council states: "Individual bishops are the visible source and foundation of unity in their own particular churches, which are formed in the image of the universal church; it is in and from these that the one and unique catholic church exists [*in suis Ecclesiis particularibus, ad imaginem Ecclesiae universalis formatis in quibus et ex quibus una et unica Ecclesia catholica exsistit*]" (LG 23). This

7. Emphasis added. The passage is quoting the then-current Roman Missal's prayer over the gifts for the Ninth Sunday after Pentecost.

8. Emphasis added.

9. Massimo Faggioli highlights the significance of *Sacrosanctum Concilium*'s *ressourcement* of patristic ecclesiologies for interpreting the later ecclesiology of *Lumen Gentium*: "Long before the hard-reached balance between the ecclesiology of the universal and local Church could be set in *Lumen Gentium*'s watchful wording, the liturgical constitution put forward the role of the local bishop, underlining the episcopal character of liturgy and the unity of the local Church with its bishop and the clergy. . . . The ecclesiology of the local Church thus emerges, in the first constitution of Vatican II, not as a political, ideological, or institutional option to reverse the trend of the second millennium of Church history, but as the natural outcome of the new centrality of the Eucharist in Church life. Ecclesiological *ressourcement* owes much more to the final outcomes of the liturgical renewal and its 'conservative' aim (restoring the liturgical life in secularized Western society) than to the allegedly radical or liberal ecclesiologists active at Vatican II." Faggioli, *True Reform*, 78.

formulation, *in quibus et ex quibus*, is, according to the canonist Eugenio Corecco, "the most important ecclesiological formula of the Council, according to which the universal Church comes into being *in* and *from* the particular churches."[10] Joseph Komonchak points out that while this formulation, in the light of the council's overall vision, does indeed have great significance, it did not originate from within the council itself: "Authors who attribute axial significance to this phrase in LG 23 might note that it was already found in the first draft *De Ecclesia*, presented to the council in 1962. . . . The statements do not seem to have been the object of controversy or even of much discussion during the elaboration of the text."[11] *Christus Dominus* would later reiterate this central conciliar teaching from *Lumen Gentium* 23: "A diocese is a section [*portio*] of God's people entrusted to a bishop to be guided by him with the assistance of his clergy so that, loyal to its pastor and formed by him into one community in the Holy Spirit through the Gospel and the Eucharist, it constitutes one particular church in which the one, holy, catholic and apostolic church of Christ is truly present and active" (CD 11).

Lumen Gentium 23 goes on to speak of "the whole church," "the universal church," and "the whole mystical body" as "a body of churches [*corpus ecclesiarum*]."[12] The article later states: "This multiplicity of local churches [*ecclesiarum localium varietas*], unified in a common effort, shows all the more resplendently the catholicity of the undivided church" (LG 23). Although the phrase *communio ecclesiarum* appears only twice in the documents of Vatican II (AG 19, 38), in the reception of its vision the latter phrase has come to serve as *the* formula for capturing the various aspects of the council's particular/universal principle. For example, according to Angel

10. Eugenio Corecco, "Aspects of the Reception of Vatican II in the Code of Canon Law," in *The Reception of Vatican II*, ed. Giuseppe Alberigo, Jean Pierre Jossua, and Joseph A. Komonchak (Washington, DC: Catholic University of America Press, 1987), 249–96, at 274.

11. Komonchak, "The Local Church and the Church Catholic," 420n5. Komonchak quotes the 1962 schema: "Quoniam Episcopi singuli centrum et fundamentum et principium unitatis sunt in suis Ecclesiis particularibus, prout in illis et ex illis, ad imaginem Ecclesiae universalis formatis, una et unica Ecclesia Catholica existit, cuius centrum et fundamentum et principium unitatis est successor Petri." Komonchak goes on to suggest *Mystici Corporis* as a possible source of the formula, with its sentence "de particularibus . . . Christianorum communitatibus, cum Orientalibus tum Latinis, *ex quibus una constat ac componitur Catholica Ecclesia*." AAS 35 (1943) 211, quoted in ibid.

12. A footnote reference to this phrase cites: (1) St. Hilary of Poitiers, *In Ps.* 14, 3; PL 9, 206; CSEL 22, p. 86; (2) St. Gregory the Great, *Moral.* IV, 7, 12: PL 75, 643 C; (3) Pseudo Basil, *In Is.* 15, 296: PG 30, 637 C.

Antón, although the actual phrase *communio ecclesiarum* is used only those two times, what is evident is the "model" of the church as a communion of churches. We have seen how Antón observes the council methodologically starting from a "universalist ecclesiology." Nevertheless, he says, "although the council did not accept the model of the Church as a communion of churches as a point of departure, this model was not totally absent from the conciliar debates and was employed in very significant contexts in the formulation of the conciliar decrees. In a series of passages Vatican II left us several pronouncements on the Church as a communion of churches (*communio Ecclesiarum*) which, within its universalist focus, offer very rich ecclesiological data on which to sketch a theology of the local/regional church."[13] Twenty-five years after the council, the Extraordinary Synod of Bishops concluded: "The ecclesiology of communion is the central and fundamental idea of the Council's documents."[14] The chapter below, on the *communio/ missio* principle, will examine that claim and explore other interrelated dimensions of the notion of *communio*.

Lumen Gentium 26 further elucidates the particular/universal principle and, by implication, the "communion of churches" model. Two particular hermeneutical issues are relevant here: (1) the development in theological thinking of the conciliar assembly over the four years and the consequent *relocating*, in the light of this development, of passages formulated previously in an earlier draft of a document, as well as (2) the *insertion* of new passages (based on newly developed thinking) into paragraphs already voted on but that had been formulated according to a previous ecclesiological mind-set. A classic example of this is the later insertion of the following passage into an earlier draft of *Lumen Gentium* 26:

> This church of Christ is really present in all legitimately organized local groups of the faithful [*fidelium congregationibus localibus*] which, united with their pastors, are also called churches in the New Testament. For these are in fact, in their own localities, the new people called by God, in the Holy Spirit and with full conviction. In them the faithful are gathered together by the preaching of the Gospel of Christ, and the mystery of the Lord's Supper is celebrated "so that, by means of the flesh and blood of the Lord the whole brotherhood and sisterhood of the body may be welded together." (LG 26)[15]

13. Antón, "Local Church/Regional Church," 572.
14. *Final Report*, II. C. 1.
15. The document is here quoting an ancient (Spanish) Mozarabic prayer. PL 96, 759B.

Karl Rahner notes that this inserted passage does seem "out of place, out of context, almost awkwardly pasted in."[16] He goes on: "It can be easily seen that it was inserted into the main text at a relatively late date, into a text which, on the whole, had been based on Catholic Scholastic theology and canonistics [canon law studies], into a text whose general orientation was to see the Church as the universal Church, into a text whose citations of the New Testament can all be considered *a priori*."[17] Consequently, the interpretation of such juxtaposed theologies requires a comprehensive hermeneutic, as outlined earlier; the council is urging a new perspective that it believes is not rejecting but refocusing the earlier perspective.

Other passages can be cited that convey the conciliar vision of the church local and universal always implying each other. The above passage from *Lumen Gentium* 26 goes on to speak of each of these "legitimate local assemblies of the faithful" as an "altar community" (*altaris communitas*). It states: "In these communities, though they may often be small and poor, or dispersed, Christ is present through whose power and influence the one, holy, catholic and apostolic church is constituted" (LG 26). Two articles later the same point is reiterated: "[Priests] should preside over and serve their local community in such a way that it may deserve to be called by the name which is given to the one people of God in its entirety, that is to say, the church of God" (LG 28).[18] The article then goes on to state: "Priests who, under the authority of the bishop, sanctify and govern that portion of the Lord's flock assigned to them render the universal church visible in their locality and contribute effectively towards building up the whole body of Christ" (LG 28). The decree on bishops gives the succinct formulation: "A diocese is a section [*portio*] of God's people entrusted to a bishop [which] constitutes one particular church in which the one, holy, catholic and apostolic church of Christ is truly present and active" (CD 11).

The council urges that local churches maintain a sense of responsibility for other local churches. At the local level, priests are called to cultivate a lively awareness of being part of a worldwide Christian community on mission: "The pastor's task is not limited to individual care of the faithful. It extends by right also to the formation of a genuine Christian community. But a properly cultivated community spirit must embrace not only the local [*localem*] church but the universal church" (PO 6). This extends to common ecclesial effort at an international level: "Taking into account the immensity

16. Karl Rahner, *The Church after the Council* (New York: Herder and Herder, 1966), 45.
17. Ibid., 46.
18. Citing 1 Cor 1:2; 2 Cor 1:1; and passim.

of the hardships which still afflict a large part of humanity, and with a view to fostering everywhere the justice and love of Christ for the poor, the council suggests that it would be most opportune to create some organization of the universal church whose task it would be to encourage the catholic community to promote the progress in areas which are in want and foster social justice between nations" (GS 90). Indeed, such effort works toward the realization of God's desire for all humanity—unity: "The universality which adorns the people of God is a gift from the Lord himself whereby the catholic church ceaselessly and effectively strives to recapitulate the whole of humanity and all its riches under Christ the Head in the unity of his Spirit" (LG 13).

In the end, the two elements forming the council's particular/universal principle stand in tension throughout the final texts, requiring of the interpreter a coherent synthesis of the principle. According to Richard Gaillardetz,

> Unfortunately the emerging theology of the local church was not maintained consistently in the conciliar documents. The exploration of a eucharistic theology of the local church did not sufficiently inform a second topic, namely, the college of bishops' relationship to the pope, sharing in pastoral authority over the universal church. The teaching on episcopal collegiality emerged as a reaction to the papo-centrism of the last century. This teaching was not developed, however, in tandem with the theology of the local church, which saw the universal church as a communion of local churches. Consequently, we can discern in the conciliar documents two ecclesiological approaches that stand in some tension: one begins with the local church and sees the universal church as a communion of local churches, and the other maintains a preconciliar universalist ecclesiality that privileges the universal church.[19]

Consequently, in the postconciliar period, interpretation of the particular/universal principle has been contentious, as was classically captured in the debate between the then-Cardinal Joseph Ratzinger and Cardinal Walter Kasper.[20] The literature on this issue shows how much the council stimulated

---

19. Richard R. Gaillardetz, *Ecclesiology for a Global Church: A People Called and Sent* (Maryknoll, NY: Orbis Books, 2008), 109.

20. Walter Kasper, "On the Church: A Friendly Reply to Cardinal Ratzinger," *America* 184 (April 23–30, 2001): 8–14; Joseph Ratzinger, "The Local Church and the Universal Church: A Response to Walter Kasper," *America* 185 (November 19, 2001): 7–11. For an analysis of the debate, see Kilian McDonnell, "The Ratzinger/Kasper Debate: The Universal Church and Local Churches," *Theological Studies* 63 (2002): 227–50. See also Solange Lefebvre, "Conflicting Interpretations of the Council: The Ratzinger–Kasper Debate," in *The New Pontificate: A Time for Change? Concilium 2006/1*, ed. Erik Borgmann, Maureen Junker-Kenny, and Janet Martin Soskice (London: SCM, 2006), 95–105.

a renewed theology of the local church.[21] One question is sometimes raised in this discussion: which dimension has "priority," universal or local?[22] According to Komonchak, the question is "ill-posed."[23] For him, the council teaches that there exists a relationship of "reciprocal or mutual inclusion" between the local and the universal.[24] Angel Antón speaks of "the principle of the reciprocal interpenetration and inclusion of the universal Church and the local church";[25] Richard Gaillardetz writes similarly of "interpenetration" and "mutual interiority";[26] or, as Susan Wood formulates it: "The local church, although wholly church, is not the whole church."[27] Komonchak summarizes the interrelationship with the axiomatic formulation: "The council's teaching is finely balanced: The church is not *catholic* if it is not particular, that is, *local*; but the particular or local is not the church unless it is *catholic* at every level, that is, redemptively integrated. . . . The many churches are not churches except in the one church; the one church does not exist except in and out of the many churches."[28]

In the articulation of this particular/universal principle, and in its insistence on mutual inclusion of the two dimensions, the council was making a significant ecclesiological shift, when seen against preconciliar teaching. The shift was a recognition of "the local" and a consequent focus on "location" and "particularity": the church in a particular culture, geographical place, and time, with specific problems and hopes.

Besides treating the particular/universal principle concerning the issue of "the church and the churches" *within* the Catholic communion, however, Vatican II simultaneously addressed the issue in its ecumenical sense, i.e., concerning "the church" and "the churches" *outside* Catholic communion.

21. See, for example, Wolfgang Beinert, "Die Una Catholica und die Partikularkirchen," *Theologie und Philosophie* 42 (1967): 8–10; Antón, "Local Church/Regional Church"; Patrick Granfield, "The Church Local and Universal: Realization of Communion," *The Jurist* 49 (1989): 449–71; Jean-Marie Tillard, *L'église locale: Ecclésiologie de communion et catholicité* (Paris: Cerf, 1995); Joseph A. Komonchak, "The Local Church," *Chicago Studies* (1989): 320–34; Komonchak, "The Local Church and the Church Catholic."

22. For a survey of positions, see Patrick Granfield, "The Priority-Debate: Universal or Local Church?," in *Ecclesia Tertii Millennii Advenientis: Omaggio al P. Angel Antón*, ed. Fernando Chica Arellano, Sandro Panizzolo, and Harald Wagner (Casale Monferrato: Piemme, 1997), 152–61.

23. Komonchak, "The Ecclesiology of Vatican II," 768.

24. Ibid., 765.

25. Antón, "Local Church/Regional Church," 569.

26. Richard R. Gaillardetz, *The Church in the Making: Lumen Gentium, Christus Dominus, Orientalium Ecclesiarum*, Rediscovering Vatican II (New York: Paulist Press, 2006), 63, 65.

27. Wood, "Continuity and Development in Roman Catholic Ecclesiology," 165.

28. Komonchak, "The Ecclesiology of Vatican II," 765. Original italics.

Its vision regarding one had implications for the other, and vice versa. Ecumenically, three interrelated questions were raised. (1) From a Catholic perspective, are other Christian bodies to be included in "the universal church"? (2) From a Catholic perspective, are other Christian bodies to be considered particular churches? And, (3) from a Catholic perspective, how is the relationship between "the Church of Christ" (the universal church) and the Catholic Church itself to be understood? Having explicitly adopted ecumenism as one of the key items on its agenda, the council felt an urgency to find answers to these three questions. Those answers would constitute one of the most remarkable shifts of Vatican II, away from an exclusive identification of the universal church of Christ with the Catholic Church, with implications for viewing the ecclesial status of non-Catholic communities. Later, discussion of the Catholic/ecumenical principle will explore these issues in greater detail, but an initial treatment is required here.

In the draft schema *De Ecclesia* presented to the bishops before they arrived at the council in 1962, the answer to the third question was quite explicit, with the answer to the other two questions implied. The heading of article 7 of the schema stated, "The Roman Catholic Church is the Mystical Body of Christ," and the article went on to affirm that "only the one that is Roman Catholic has the right to be called Church."[29] A new schema presented the following year, in article 8, stated: "This church, true mother and teacher of all, constituted and organized as a society in the present world, is [*est*] the Catholic Church." It was only in the third session, when the council was debating a further revised draft, that the Doctrinal Commission had substituted the word *est* in the relevant sentence of article 8 with *subsistit in*.[30] And so began the history of what Richard Gaillardetz has called "perhaps the most significant single word change in the history of all the council documents."[31] The report to the assembly by the Doctrinal Commission gave as its reason for the change: "so that the expression might better accord with the affirmation of ecclesial elements that *are present* elsewhere."[32] Johannes

29. Translation here taken from Sullivan, "The Significance of the Vatican II Declaration," 273.

30. For the various draft schemas of the relevant passage set alongside one another, see Francisco Gil Hellín, ed. *Constitutio dogmatica de ecclesia, Lumen Gentium: Concilii Vaticani II synopsis in ordinem redigens schemata cum relationibus necnon patrum orationes atque animadversiones* (Città del Vaticano: Libreria Editrice Vaticana, 1995).

31. Gaillardetz, *The Church in the Making*, 22.

32. Translation from Joseph A. Komonchak, "Toward an Ecclesiology of Communion," in *History of Vatican II*, vol. 4: *The Church as Communion; Third Period and Third Intersession, September 1964–September 1965*, ed. Giuseppe Alberigo and Joseph A. Komonchak (Maryknoll, NY: Orbis Books, 2004), 1–93, at 42. Komonchak's emphasis.

Willebrands remarks that "close study of the speeches in the aula and of remarks sent in in writing shows that the change from *est* to *subsistit in* did not arouse a 'wave of reactions' announced by one journalist."[33]

In the final version, the key passage states: "This church [the unique church of Christ], constituted and organized as a society in the present world, *subsists in* the Catholic Church, which is governed by the successor of Peter and by the bishops in communion with him. Nevertheless, many elements of sanctification and of truth [*elementa plura sanctificationis et veritatis*] are found [*inveniantur*] outside its visible confines. Since these are gifts belonging to the church of Christ [*dona ecclesiae Christi propria*], they are forces impelling towards catholic unity" (LG 8).[34] Generally English translations simply transliterate the Latin verb *subsistere*. Most commentators believe the verb is to be taken in its ordinary-language sense rather than according to some philosophical framework.[35] Accordingly, the *peritus* Gérard Philips, who played a central role in the drafting of *Lumen Gentium*, translates the key sentence in his commentary: "The Church of Christ *is found in* the Catholic Church."[36] The mind of the council with regard to the replacement

33. Johannes Willebrands, "Vatican II's Ecclesiology of Communion," *One in Christ* 23 (1987): 179–91, at 179.

34. The verb *subsistere* is also used ecclesiologically in three passages (UR 4 and DH 1, which mirror the affirmation of LG 8, and UR 13, which refers to the Anglican church). The latter passage, in referring to those separated churches of the Reformation, states: "Among those in which Catholic traditions and institutions in part continue to exist [*ex parte subsistere pergunt*], the Anglican communion occupies a special place." *Unitatis Redintegratio* 4 states: "This unity [of the one and only church], we believe, subsists in the Catholic Church [*in ecclesia catholica subsistere*] as something she can never lose, and we hope that it will continue to increase until the end of time" (UR 4). *Dignitatis Humanae* 1 affirms: "We believe that this one true religion exists in [*subsistit in*] the Catholic and Apostolic church."

35. For example, Marie-Joseph le Guillou asserts: "It would be a false interpretation of the expression *subsistit in* to read into it some sort of ecclesial Platonism, as if the Church had a kind of super-self which pre-exists its tangible manifestation, and as if this manifestation was never adequate to its original archetype. Certainly the Church is never fully itself, and of its very nature there is in it a movement towards its full realization that we must accept and will, so that we can work for its fulfillment. But the starting point for any true conception of the Church is of necessity the risen Christ himself in the historical growth of his Body. There is no place for a kind of universal essence of the Church, of which the real world contains only vestiges or drafts, even if one goes on to say that there is one particular and privileged place, namely the Catholic Church, where this mystery, although never completely realized, really does 'subsist.'" Marie-Joseph le Guillou, "Church: II. Ecclesiology," in *Sacramentum Mundi: An Encyclopedia of Theology*, ed. Karl Rahner (New York: Herder and Herder, 1968), 1:317–27, at 324.

36. "L'Église du Christ se trouve dans la Catholica." Gérard Philips, *L'Église et son mystère au II Concile du Vatican: Histoire, texte et commentaire de la Constitution Lumen Gentium*

is deliberate, according to Kilian McDonnell; it was meant to be vague, in contrast to the unambiguous word, *est*, it replaces:

> When a conciliar document moves from a clear, unambiguous text to an unclear ambiguous text this has meaning in terms of the theological intent of the council. It is undoubted that the word *subsistit* was carefully chosen for its ambiguity. . . . In setting aside the word *est* of the second draft and substituting the word *subsistit* the council was able to express the identification between the church which Christ founded and the Roman Catholic Church, without making the absolute claim of being the only manifestation of that church. The move from *est* to *subsistit* is clearly a move to loosen up the exclusive claim of the Roman Church to be the one and only manifestation of Christ's church.[37]

As Heinrich Fries formulates it: "*Est* is exclusive; *subsistit* is positive and open."[38] The implication for understanding Vatican II's particular/universal principle is that, while the church of Christ can be found in the Catholic Church, the council does not exclusively identify the universal church with the Catholic Church. This raises the further question whether, and, if so, in what way, the separated communities of faith arising from the various Reformations can be called "particular churches." These issues will be explored below in the council's Catholic/ecumenical principle.

(Paris: Desclée, 1967), 1:119. Quoted in Karim Schelkens, "*Lumen Gentium*'s 'Subsistit in' Revisited: The Catholic Church and Christian Unity after Vatican II," *Theological Studies* 69 (2008): 875–93, at 893.

37. Kilian McDonnell, "The Concept of 'Church' in the Documents of Vatican II as Applied to Protestant Denominations," *Worship* 44 (1970): 332–49, at 336. As to the meaning of the word, George Tavard writes: "'Subsistence in' implies that the Church, which is the body of Christ in mystery, now lives in a hidden state. It is invisible to the eyes of the flesh, and therefore its existence and nature as the Church are empirically unverifiable. Yet being constituted and organized as a society, it also is an organic body, the members of which relate to one another according to some effective norms. By confessing that this Church subsists in the Roman Catholic institution, the council indicates that it knows where the Church is. Yet it also teaches that the Church of Christ is invisible, lying where it is in a hidden state that may not be recognizable to all Christian believers. And the council says nothing for or against the possibility of its also invisibly subsisting in other ecclesial institutions and other visible churches. Logic would seem to make this contention acceptable in the problematic of Vatican II." Tavard, *The Church, Community of Salvation*, 86.

38. Fries, "Church and Churches," 317.

Principle 15
Communio/Missio

Principle 15: Relationships across humanity and within the church should be characterized by communion, mirroring the church's own relationship with the triune God from whom the church originates; the mission of the church in the world involves the whole people of God, which is sent as a sacrament of divine salvation to all humanity, with whom God desires communion.

In the assessment of Adrian Hastings: "It is perhaps these two words [communion and mission] which better than any other can together express the nature of the Church as the Council sees her to be."[1] During the council's reception over the last fifty years, the incipient trajectory of its *communio* ecclesiology and the incipient trajectory of its *missio* ecclesiology have often been developed along divergent paths. A comprehensive interpretation of the conciliar vision needs to integrate an ecclesiology both of communion and of mission. Not that the ecclesiology of Vatican II can be confined to these two dimensions, let alone one of them. It is necessary not only to bring *communio* and *missio* into one tensive principle but also to put this principle in tensive relationship with other principles. No one principle—or the two terms it incorporates—can capture the mystery of the church as envisioned by Vatican II. All the principles together, however, can lead toward a more comprehensive vision. As Richard McBrien remarks: "Even if there is no single synthesis within the documents themselves, there is a singleness of intention from which a synthesis can be constructed."[2]

A major catalyst for the predominance of *communio* as *the* interpretive key for the council's ecclesiology came twenty years after the conclusion of Vatican

---

1. Hastings, *A Concise Guide to the Documents*, 2:225–26.
2. Richard P. McBrien, *The Church: The Evolution of Catholicism* (New York: HarperOne, 2008), 164.

II. In 1985, Pope John Paul II convoked an extraordinary meeting of the international Synod of Bishops to assess the reception of the council. In its final report, the synod asserted: "The ecclesiology of communion is the central and fundamental idea of the Council's documents."[3] As Richard Lennan remarks: "The contemporary emphasis on communion ecclesiology suggests a particular reception of the Council. Even if Vatican II did not invoke 'the church as communion' to cover all the matters to which we now apply the term, it is appropriate to argue that today's applications attempt to receive faithfully both the intent and specific understanding of the Council fathers. . . . The ecclesiology of communion came to be regarded as crystallising the major emphases of Vatican II."[4] Indeed, as Lennan (writing in 2007) goes on to observe, "In the last two decades, this theology has become the dominant framework in Roman Catholic theology, and beyond, for reflecting on the church."[5]

The selection of *communio* as the primary hermeneutical lens has a certain appeal and legitimacy. Like Walter Kasper, Dennis Doyle is among those who see in *communio* an integrating category for the council's ecclesiological vision. He also acknowledges, however, the problem with this restricted hermeneutic:

> I have come to agree that [communion ecclesiology] is indeed *the key to the Council*, as well as the key to a better understanding of the Church today, one that can support continued renewal and reform. But I have also become aware that differences in interpretation do not simply go away once communion ecclesiology arrives on the scene. For there are different versions of it, and even those with virtually identical versions might still encounter some differences in applying communion ecclesiology to the Council documents.[6]

---

3. Extraordinary Synod of Bishops, "Final Report." page 35, C.1. The role of the theological secretary of the synod, Walter Kasper, in the emergence of *communio* as the integrating key was not insignificant, as he intimates regarding his own theological development: "The actual breakthrough [of *communio* as the guiding principle for Kasper's own ecclesiology] came when Pope John Paul II made me the theological secretary of the Extraordinary Synod of Bishops in 1985. . . . While studying the council documents in preparation for my work, I came to the conclusion that *communio*-ecclesiology was the central concern and the main motif of the conciliar ecclesiology. Together with the relator of the Synod, Cardinal Godfried Daneels von Meecheln, I was able to contribute this aspect to the Synod. It has become fundamental for me ever since." Walter Kasper, *The Catholic Church: Nature, Reality and Mission* (London: Bloomsbury, 2014), 21.

4. Richard Lennan, "Communion Ecclesiology: Foundations, Critiques, and Affirmations," *Pacifica* 20 (2007): 24–39.

5. Ibid., 26–27.

6. Dennis M. Doyle, *Communion Ecclesiology: Vision and Versions* (Maryknoll, NY: Orbis Books, 2000), 73.

I propose that the council does not so much privilege any one model (e.g., *communio*) such that it can be the single hermeneutical lens for integrating its whole vision; other perspectives on the church's mystery are presented, requiring a more comprehensive hermeneutic.

Before the council, *ressourcement* studies—such as the work of Yves Congar,[7] Henri de Lubac,[8] Ludwig Hertling,[9] and Jérôme Hamer[10]—had progressively brought the notion of *communio* to the fore.[11] Once the council began, a *communio* ecclesiology emerged as one way to go beyond the overly juridical and exclusively hierarchical ecclesiology of the draft *De Ecclesia*. Two commentaries in particular are important here, those of Antonio Acerbi and Oskar Saier. Acerbi's historical study of the drafting of *Lumen Gentium* traces in detail what he calls two "tendencies" or "trends" throughout the conciliar debates: the juridical-hierarchical approach and the emerging *communio* approach.[12] Acerbi shows how the first had long dominated Catholic ecclesiology for most of the second millennium, and in a particular way from Vatican I to the eve of Vatican II, and how this ecclesiological vision clearly shaped the preparatory schemas. The second ecclesiology Acerbi highlights was the result of preconciliar *ressourcement* theologies, which began impacting the council debates, either through the bishops' own awareness of these theological trends or through the *periti* at the council. As Acerbi narrates, in the council's second and third sessions, and in the redrafting of the schema *De Ecclesia*, these two approaches came head to head—"two ecclesiologies" in "confrontation" with each other.[13] In the final text of *Lumen Gentium*, Acerbi proposes, these two ecclesiologies can still be found juxtaposed. The more

---

7. Published originally in French in 1937, see Yves Congar, *Divided Christendom: A Catholic Study of the Problem of Reunion* (London: Geoffrey Bles, 1939).

8. In 1944 and 1953, de Lubac published in French the following: Henri de Lubac, *Corpus Mysticum: The Eucharist and the Church in the Middle Ages; Historical Survey*, ed. Laurence Paul Hemming and Susan Frank Parsons (London: SCM, 2006); de Lubac, *The Splendor of the Church*.

9. In 1943, Hertling published in German: Ludwig Hertling, *Communio: Church and Papacy in Early Christianity* (Chicago: Loyola University Press, 1972).

10. In 1962, on the eve of the council, Hamer published in French: Jérôme Hamer, *The Church Is a Communion* (London: Geoffrey Chapman, 1964).

11. For a survey, see Joseph A. Komonchak, "Concepts of Communion: Past and Present," *Cristianesimo nella Storia* 16 (1995): 321–40.

12. Antonio Acerbi, *Due ecclesiologie: Ecclesiologia giuridica ed ecclesiologia di comunione nella "Lumen Gentium"* (Bologna: Edizioni Dehoniane, 1975).

13. Ibid., esp. 239–483. Acerbi consistently uses the Italian word *confronto* throughout the text.

systematic-theological work by Oskar Saier likewise highlights the focus on *communio* at the council and complements that of Acerbi.[14]

The word *communio* appears 111 times across all the documents (the word *missio* appears 141 times)—thirty-three times in *Lumen Gentium* and thirty-six times in *Unitatis Redintegratio*. Not only does the word have different dimensions and applications, however, but the "concept" is conveyed through other words, as Walter Kasper notes:

> Although the *concept* of communion is central to the council's texts, the word used to express this concept is by no means strictly fixed. Apart from the word *communio*, we meet a whole series of similar terms—*communitas, societas,* and so forth. Moreover the term *communio* itself has various levels of meaning in the texts. So in the conciliar documents we have to do with *a concept which is only in the process of development.* This linguistic finding is an indication that the council found itself up against a substantial problem *which it was unable to follow through completely,* and which it in fact passed on to us.[15]

In that "whole series of similar terms," there is one especially important cluster of words, that of "union" (*unio*, forty-six times), "unity" (*unitas*, 156 times), and "to unite" (*unire*, forty-seven times). These are often used synonymously for aspects for which the word *communio* is elsewhere applied. For example, "The highest exemplar of this mystery [of the unity of the church] is the unity [*unitas*], in the Trinity of Persons, of one God, the Father and the Son in the Holy Spirit." "Union" is such an important word in the council's vision that the next principle will examine the notion of unity/diversity more closely, albeit focusing more narrowly on unity *within* the church. But "union," like "communion," has a much broader application.

Broadly speaking, there are two dimensions to the council's use of *communio*, a vertical dimension and a horizontal dimension. Each of these dimensions, in turn, has a twofold aspect: relating to all of humanity and relating to the church in particular. The vertical dimension is used of the divine-human relationship—communion between God and humanity and communion between God and the church (including the communion between God and individual baptized believers). The horizontal dimension is used of the human-human relationship—communion among all human

---

14. Oskar Saier, *"Communio" in der Lehre des Zweiten Vatikanischen Konzils: Eine rechtsbegriffliche Untersuchung* (Munich: EOS Verlag, 1973), esp. 1–181.

15. Kasper, "The Church as Communion," 151. Original emphasis, with other emphases added.

beings and communion within the church. The latter is called by God to be a sign and instrument bringing about the former; the church's mission is thus to be an agent of communion among humanity.

The "source" of communion on the human level is God, and the "exemplar" of communion on the human level is the communion among the three persons of the triune God. While it is not always explicit, the presupposition is that the call to *communio* is based on the *communio* between the divine persons in the Trinity. The Trinity is "the mystery" in which all else finds its origin and meaning. As Kasper notes: "The term *communio* does not initially have anything to do with questions about the church's structure. The word points rather to 'the real thing' (*res*) from which the church comes and for which it lives. *Communio* is not a description of the church's structure. It describes its nature or, as the council puts it, its 'mystery.' "[16]

The *vertical* dimension of *communio* concerns God's ultimate plan for *communio* between God and humanity:

> Human dignity rests above all on the fact that humanity is called to communion with God [*ad communionem cum Deo*]. The invitation to dialogue with God [*ad colloquium cum Deo*] is addressed to men and women as soon as they are born. For if people exist it is because God has created them through love, and through love continues to keep them in existence. They cannot live fully in the truth unless they freely acknowledge that love and entrust themselves to their creator. Many, however, of our contemporaries either do not all perceive, or else explicitly reject, *this intimate and vital relationship with God.* (GS 19)[17]

The chapter above on the protological/eschatological principle has already discussed the trinitarian "shape" of "God's plan" in the economy of salvation. God "chose to raise up men and women to participate in his own divine life [*ad participandam vitam divinam*]" (LG 2). "The mystery of his will" was "that people can draw near to the Father, through Christ, the Word made flesh, in the Holy Spirit, and thus become sharers in the divine nature . . . [that is,] to invite and receive them into his own company [*ad societatem Secum invitet in eamque suscipiat*]" (DV 2). Thus, according to God's plan, "the mission [*missio*] of the Son and the Spirit" (AG 2) is to bring humanity into *communio* with, i.e., into the *communio* of, the triune God.

---

16. Ibid., 151.
17. Translation corrected. Emphasis added.

More specifically, the vertical dimension concerns the relationship between God and the church. Just as there is *communio* within the triune God, and just as the triune God creates the world and sends the Son and the Spirit on mission in order to enter into *communio* with humanity, so too God "invites and receives" the church into a *communio* relationship with God to be a sign of the triune God in the world and to be an instrument for effecting God's plan. It is in Eucharist, above all, that this *communio* is realized.

The *horizontal* dimension of *communio* first of all concerns God's desire for communion among all human beings. Kasper has noted the council's use of other words to convey the meaning intended by the actual word *communio*. For example, the council often uses *communio* and *unio* synonymously. Regarding the immanent Trinity as the exemplar of *communio* in the horizontal dimension, we read: "There is a certain similarity between the union existing among the divine persons and the union of God's children [*unionem personarum divinarum et unionem filiorum Dei*] in truth and love. It follows, then, that if human beings are the only creatures on earth that God has wanted for their own sake, they can fully discover their true selves only in sincere self-giving" (GS 24). Likewise, we find: "The union [*unio*] of the human family is greatly consolidated and perfected by the unity which Christ established among the sons and daughters of God" (GS 42).

The horizontal dimension also relates to the mission of the church: "Established by Christ as a *communio* of life, love and truth, [the messianic People of God] is taken up by him also as the instrument for the salvation of all" (LG 9). Here the programmatic statement at the beginning of *Lumen Gentium* deserves repetition: "Since the church, in Christ, is like [*veluti*] a sacrament—a sign and instrument, that is, of intimate union [*intimae cum Deo unionis*] with God and of the unity of the entire human race—it here proposes . . . to describe more clearly . . . its own nature and universal mission" (LG 1).[18] Thus the church is meant to be a sacrament of *communio*. As Francis Schüssler Fiorenza notes: "This statement underscores that the sacramental nature of the church is the basis of its mission precisely insofar as the church is a sacrament of unity. The church is a sacrament not merely of the unity with God, nor simply of the unity of humankind, but rather of the double unity that exists between the unity with God and the unity of the whole human race."[19]

---

18. Translation corrected.
19. Schüssler Fiorenza, "Church, Social Mission of," 161.

Three Dimensions of Horizontal Ecclesial *Communio*

As the sign and instrument of communion with God, the church itself (*ad intra* and *ad extra*) is called to model the *communio* within the Trinity. Here the council uses three terms that capture three aspects of the church's mystery: as a *communio* of believers (*communio fidelium*), as a *communio* of churches (*communio ecclesiarum*), and as a *communio* among the bishops, with and under the pope (*communio hierarchica*). We will now examine each of these aspects, but in the reverse order.

One of the great achievements of Vatican II is its teaching on collegiality as articulated below in the college of bishops/bishop of Rome principle. The doctrine attempts to complete the unfinished work of Vatican I, with its teaching on the jurisdictional "primacy" of the pope. Vatican II goes on to affirm that the bishops, in succession with the "college" of the apostles, likewise constitute a college. The college of bishops relates in a *communio hierarchica*, with and under the bishop of Rome. This new notion of *communio hierarchica* enabled the council to avoid to some extent the traditional, juridical distinction between *ordo* and *iurisdictio* in the original *De Ecclesia*, and to reformulate it in the language of *communio*.[20] In addressing the issue of collegiality and the question whether a bishop receives his episcopacy from the pope or "from God," *Lumen Gentium* 21 teaches that "the fullness of the sacrament of Orders is conferred by episcopal consecration. . . . Episcopal consecration confers, together with the office of sanctifying, the offices also of teaching and ruling, which, however, of their very nature can be exercised only in hierarchical communion [*hierarchica communione*] with the head and members of the college" (LG 21). The article that follows reiterates the teaching: "A person is made a member of the episcopal body in virtue of the sacramental consecration and by hierarchical communion with the head and members of the college" (LG 22). The constitution later highlights the consequence of this teaching: "Nor are they to be regarded as vicars of the Roman Pontiff; for *they exercise a power which they possess in their own right* and are most truly said to be at the head of the people whom they govern" (LG 27).[21]

---

20. For a canonical interpretation that sees *communio hierarchica* "constituting" *communio catholica* and privileges the notion over other dimensions of *communio*, see Gianfranco Ghirlanda, *"Hierarchica communio": Significato della formula nella "Lumen Gentium"* (Roma: Università Gregoriana Editrice, 1980). Ghirlanda's approach can be found summarized in Ghirlanda, "Universal Church, Particular Church, and Local Church."

21. Emphasis added.

Despite the gains made with the notion, the problematic nature of the phrase *communio hierarchica* was dramatically highlighted in the last week of the third session—*la settimana nera* ("the black week")—when *Lumen Gentium* was all but ready to be promulgated, as it would be at the end of the week. Coming from a "higher authority" (presumably Pope Paul VI, at the urging of the minority among the bishops), the nonconciliar *Nota Explicativa Praevia* was presented to the council as an instruction on how the doctrine of collegiality was to be interpreted, almost reinforcing the preconciliar understanding of the pope's authority over the college of bishops.[22] Tellingly, the document employs the phrase *communio hierarchica* several times in defense of its argument, bringing to the fore its problematic character.

The phrase thus has both strengths and weaknesses, as demonstrated by the *Nota Explicativa Praevia*: while certainly employing the notion of *communio*, it nevertheless can be used to advance a weakened interpretation of the doctrine of collegiality. Walter Kasper acknowledges the advance the phrase achieves but highlights the problems it raises:

> *Communio hierarchica* is . . . a typical compromise formulation, which points to a juxtaposition of a sacramental *communio* ecclesiology and juristic unity ecclesiology. It has consequently been said that the Vatican II texts contain two ecclesiologies. The compromise proved useful at the council, since it made it possible for the minority to agree to the Constitution on the Church. But just to say this is not entirely satisfactory. The compromise indicates a deeper problem. For the Catholic principle about living tradition makes it impossible simply to eliminate the tradition of the second millennium. The continuity of tradition demands a creative synthesis of the traditions of the first millennium and the second. The synthesis brought about by the last council was highly superficial, and in no way satisfactory. But then it is not the function of councils to draw up theological treatises. A council presents the indispensable "frame of reference." The synthesis is then a matter for the theology that comes afterwards.[23]

The notion of *communio hierarchica* is a compromise formula that attempts to broaden the juridical vision of the preparatory *De Ecclesia*, which saw the

---

22. On "*la settimana nera*" and the *Nota Explicative Praevia*, see Luis Antonio Tagle, "The 'Black Week' of Vatican II (November 14–21 1964)," in *History of Vatican II*, vol. 4: *The Church as Communion; Third Period and Third Intersession, September 1964–September 1965*, ed. Giuseppe Alberigo and Joseph A. Komonchak (Maryknoll, NY: Orbis Books, 2004), 4:387–452.

23. Kasper, "The Church as Communion," 158. In referring to the thesis that *Lumen Gentium* is juxtaposing two ecclesiologies, Kasper cites Acerbi, *Due ecclesiologie*.

church primarily in terms of a pyramid—with the pope as the primary juridical authority and the bishops then as his juridical delegates.[24] Taken alone, however, the formula would present a one-dimensional view of the church. Because of its weaknesses, the notion of *communio hierarchica* remains problematic and needs to be interpreted intratextually and intertextually, in the light of other notions of *communio* (and other conciliar principles). In the vision of Vatican II, there are two other dimensions of the church's mystery as a *communio* that must balance that of *communio hierarchica*.

The first is the notion of the church as a *communio ecclesiarum* (a communion of churches), which the previous chapter began to explore. *Sacrosanctum Concilium* laid the foundations for a *communio* ecclesiology in general and, more specifically, for a theology of *communio ecclesiarum*: it is in Eucharist in local churches above all that the church universal is manifest. While *Lumen Gentium* unfortunately fails to bring out the implications of, and develop, this "eucharistic ecclesiology,"[25] the later developments in *Lumen Gentium*, and then *Gaudium et Spes* and *Ad Gentes*, regarding a theology of local churches do build on, or at least presume, the eucharistic ecclesiology of *Sacrosanctum Concilium*. As with several themes in the council, here Vatican II—even over its four years of development—in some ways still marks a transition. But the trajectory toward the comprehensive vision is apparent: "In the council documents we have an undeveloped but nevertheless significant shift toward an ancient vision of the universal church as a *communio ecclesiarum*, a communion of churches."[26] The fundamental direction is given.

Lumen Gentium does not use the precise term *communio ecclesiarum*. Nevertheless, in article 13—addressing the catholicity of the church and the Eastern Catholic churches—it states: "There are, legitimately, in ecclesiastical communion, particular churches [*in ecclesiastica communione legitime adsunt ecclesiae particulares*] which retain their own traditions, without prejudice to the Chair of Peter which presides over the entire assembly of charity" (LG 13). Moreover, "Between all the diverse parts of the church there are bonds of intimate communion [*vincula intimae communionis*] whereby spiritual riches, apostolic workers and temporal resources are shared. For the members

---

24. For a graphical representation of this conception, see Richard R. Gaillardetz, *Teaching with Authority: A Theology of the Magisterium in the Church* (Collegeville, MN: Liturgical Press, 1997), 242.

25. This is the thesis throughout Faggioli, *True Reform*.

26. Gaillardetz, *The Church in the Making*, 64.

of the people of God are called upon to share their goods, and the words of the apostle apply also to each of the churches, 'according to the gift that each has received, administer it to one another as good stewards of the manifold grace of God' (1 Peter 4:10)" (LG 13).[27] Article 23 speaks of the church as a *corpus ecclesiarum* ("a body of churches"). Departing in significant ways from Pius XII's *Mystici Corporis, Lumen Gentium*'s renewed "mystical body" ecclesiology is to be understood here in terms of a trinitarian *communio* ecclesiology.[28] Thus the phrase *corpus ecclesiarum* in the following sentence can be taken as a synonym for *communio ecclesiarum*: "The whole mystical body [is] also a body of churches [*corpus ecclesiarum*]" (LG 23). It would seem that the richer notion of *communio ecclesiarum* grew from the seeds of these notions of the church as a *corpus ecclesiarum* and of the particular churches existing in *communio ecclesiastica*.

To illustrate the newness of the notion of *communio ecclesiarum*, and the remarkable fact of its eventual acceptance on the council floor, the *peritus* Yves Congar's journal entry for June 6, 1964, is illuminating. That day he had been given an audience with Pope Paul VI. It was a few months before the start of the council's third session.

> I said to him that the ecumenical openness and the gestures he had made towards the Patriarchs call for (just as the renewal of the liturgy calls for) an ecclesiology that has not yet been worked out, an ecclesiology of Communion, in which the Church would be seen as a Communion of Churches. The Holy Father said he did not see quite what I meant. I explained a little further. But the Pope said: there is only one church. Our Lord wanted only one. Certainly it admits of a variety of rites, usages and customs. But it must be *one* single church.[29]

Nevertheless, the third and fourth sessions would show a development in the mind of the council toward a deeper understanding of the church as a communion of churches.

The actual phrase *communio ecclesiarum* appears only twice in all the documents, both times in *Ad Gentes*, a document written over a short span of time in the last year of the council and yet one of the richest ecclesiological documents in the whole conciliar corpus. *Ad Gentes* was promulgated a year

27. Translation corrected.

28. On the decline of "Mystical Body of Christ" ecclesiology before the council, and its realignment at Vatican II, see Timothy R. Gabrielli, *One in Christ: Virgil Michel, Louis-Marie Chauvet, and Mystical Body Theology* (Collegeville, MN: Liturgical Press, 2017), 91–103.

29. Congar, *My Journal of the Council*, 556. Original emphasis.

after *Lumen Gentium*, on the second-to-last working day of the council. It thus had the advantage of drawing on the riches of the other documents, including the ones still being drafted and discussed, especially *Gaudium et Spes*. But *Ad Gentes* was not only able to draw on the developments of other documents; it went on to develop them further, in a new synthesis that these other documents did not quite accomplish.

The first instance of the term *communio ecclesiarum* is *Ad Gentes* 19. Significantly, the passage contains allusions to other conciliar themes: *communio hierarchica, sensus fidei, sensus Christi,* and the ancient advocation of *sentire cum ecclesia*:

> Bishops and their priests must think and live with the universal church, becoming more and more imbued with a sense of Christ and the church [*cum universali ecclesia sentiant atque vivant*]. The communion of the young churches with the whole church [*ecclesiarum novellarum communio cum tota ecclesia*] should remain intimate, they should graft elements of its tradition on to their own culture and thus, by a mutual outpouring of energy, increase the life of the mystical body. To this end, those theological, psychological and human elements which would contribute to this sense of communion with the whole church [*sensum communionis cum ecclesia universali*] should be fostered. (AG 19)

The second instance of *communio ecclesiarum*, once again also implying *communio hierarchica*, is to be found in *Ad Gentes* 38:

> All bishops, as members of the body of bishops which succeeds the college of the apostles, are consecrated not for one diocese alone, but for the salvation of the whole world. The command of Christ to preach the gospel to every creature applies primarily and immediately to them—with Peter, and subject to Peter [*cum Petro et sub Petro*]. From this arises that communion and cooperation of the churches [*communio et cooperatio ecclesiarum*] which is so necessary today for the work of evangelization. Because of this communion [*communionis*], each church cares for all the others, they make known their needs to each other, they share their possessions, because the spread of the body of Christ is the responsibility of the whole college of bishops. (AG 38)

In addition, article 22 of the missionary decree, without using the actual phrase, states: "So new particular churches, each with its own traditions, have their place in the communion of the church [*ecclesiastica communio*], the primacy of Peter which presides over this universal assembly of charity all the while remaining intact" (AG 22).

In these passages we can see that, despite the recurring appeals to the authority of the bishops and the authority of the pope, the particular strength of the notion of *communio ecclesiarum* is the way it balances the sole focus of *communio hierarchica* on the local bishop with an attention to the local church of which he is the bishop.[30] The notion of *communio ecclesiarum* thus brings to the fore the people of God in that place, to whom the local bishop is called in service. Moreover, with this notion, the *communio/missio* principle is brought into tensive relationship with two other principles. First, regarding the particular/universal principle, in understanding the church as a communion of local churches, the question is raised: how are the local and the universal held in balance? As Richard Lennan remarks: "The relationship between the 'local' and 'universal' church [is] perhaps the most controverted aspect of today's focus on *koinonia*."[31] Second, and similarly, understanding the church as a communion of local churches raises a question related to the next principle we will examine, the unity/diversity principle: how in the communion of the churches are both the unity and legitimate diversity of faith and practice maintained?

Despite its strengths in balancing the notion of *communio hierarchica*, the notion of the church as a *communio ecclesiarum* needs to be understood alongside a third dimension of the church's nature as a *communio*: the notion of the church as a *communio fidelium* (communion of the faithful). Here the focus is on the church as all those who profess faith in Jesus Christ and who, dispersed throughout the world in diverse places and cultures, are constituted as the one community of faith by the Holy Spirit, who binds them together with all their diversity.

The *communio fidelium* is the primary bond fashioning a common identity and unity between all who call Jesus Christ "Lord" in the Holy Spirit.[32] As the fundamental revelation/faith principle affirms, the church is, *in the first instance*, a community *of faith*, a community of flesh-and-blood believers

30. On this imbalance in the documents, see Hervé Legrand, "Les évêques, les églises locales et l'église entière: Évolutions institutionnelles depuis Vatican II et chantiers actuels de recherche," *Revue des Sciences Philosophiques et Théologiques* 85, no. 1 (2001): 461–509, at 462–72.

31. Lennan, "Communion Ecclesiology," 26.

32. The notion of *communio fidelium* has certain similarities to the model of church Avery Dulles calls "the community of disciples" model. Dulles, *Models of the Church*, 198. For Dulles: "This concept can be seen as a variant of the communion model. It precludes the impression that ecclesial communion exists merely for the sake of mutual gratification and support. It calls attention to the ongoing relationship of the Church to Christ, its Lord, who continues to direct it through his Spirit." Ibid., 198.

who respond to God's offer of revelation and salvation in Christ through the Spirit. As well as *communio fidelium*, the council speaks similarly of the universal church as "the whole body of the faithful [*universitas fidelium*]" (e.g., LG 12); "the whole company of the faithful [*multitudo fidelium*]" (e.g., LG 23); and, of course, "the People of God." This emphasis on all believers is not a false dichotomizing of the "universal" over the "local" but rather illustrates a concern to highlight the church as a community of *fides*, which is always found manifested in the concrete Christian life and "where two or three are gathered in my name" (Matt 18:20).[33]

The precise phrase *communio fidelium* appears only once in the documents, in a passage evoking the image of the church as the temple of the Holy Spirit: "It is the Holy Spirit, dwelling in those who believe [*credentes*] and pervading and ruling over the entire church [*totam ecclesiam*], who brings about that wonderful communion of the faithful [*communionem fidelium*] and joins them together so intimately in Christ that he is the principle of the church's unity" (UR 2). A few sentences earlier this article had spoken of the Holy Spirit gathering the church "into a unity of faith, hope and charity" (UR 2). While not exactly using the precise phrase *communio fidelium*, *Lumen Gentium* 13 states: "All the faithful [*fideles*] scattered throughout the world are in communion [*communicant*] with each other in the Holy Spirit" (LG 13). Similarly, we read of "Christ's faithful, gathered together in the church from all the nations [*Christifideles ex gentibus cunctis in ecclesia congregati*]" (AG 15).

In addition to "the faithful" or "the Christian faithful" (*fideles* or *Christifideles*), there are other collectives used in the documents to name those who constitute the group of Jesus' followers at any one time throughout the world and throughout history. *Sacrosanctum Concilium* 1 speaks of promoting "the union of all who believe in Christ [*ad unionem omnium in Christum credentium*]." *Lumen Gentium* 2 speaks of "those who believe in Christ [*credentes in Christum*]" (LG 2). Similarly, the church is "*all those, who in faith look towards Jesus*, the author of salvation and the source of unity and peace, [and whom] God has gathered together and established as the church, that it may be for each and everyone the visible sacrament of this saving unity" (LG 9).[34] The word "disciples" (*discipuli*) is another synonym for *fideles* and *credentes*. Avery Dulles observes: "The term 'community of disciples' does not appear

33. NRSV translation. The documents cite or quote this passage four times: SC 7; PC 15; UR 8; AA 18.
34. Emphasis added.

as such in the documents of Vatican II, but these documents more than twenty times refer to church members as disciples. From this it is but a short step to calling the Church the community of disciples."[35] Significantly, the document that uses the phrase *communio fidelium*, *Unitatis Redintegratio*, refers in its opening article to the common identity of Catholics and non-Catholics as disciples of Christ when it speaks of the council's "desire for the restoration of unity among all the disciples of Christ [*omnes Christi discipulos*]." Likewise, the opening article of *Gaudium et Spes* refers to the church in terms of discipleship: "The joys and hopes, the grief and anguish of the people of our time, especially of those who are poor or afflicted, are the joys and hopes, the grief and anguish of the disciples of Christ as well [*etiam Christi discipulorum*]."[36]

Other passages capture the sense of the church as a *communio fidelium*. *Ad Gentes* speaks of how on the day of Pentecost "was foreshadowed the union of all peoples in the catholicity of the faith [*unio populorum in fidei catholicitate*] by means of the church of the New Covenant, a church which speaks every language, understands and embraces all tongues in charity, and thus overcomes the dispersion of Babel" (AG 4). *Apostolicam Actuositatem* 18 captures several of these collectives: "The faithful [*Christifideles*] are called as individuals to exercise an apostolate in their various situations. They must, however, remember that people are social by nature and that it has been God's pleasure to assemble those who believe in Christ [*credentes in Christum*] and make of them the people of God [*populum Dei*], a single body [*unum corpus*]. . . . The group apostolate . . . offers a sign of the communion and unity of the church in Christ [*communionis et unitatis ecclesiae in Christo*]" (AA 18). The pastoral constitution on the church presents what could be a definition of the church as a *communio fidelium*: "As the firstborn of many, and by the gift of his Spirit, [Christ] established, after his death and resurrection, a new communion of sisters and brothers [*novam fraternam communionem*] among all who received him in faith and love [*inter omnes qui Eum fide ac caritate recipiunt*]; this is the communion of his own body, the church, in which all as members one of the other would render mutual service in the measure of the different gifts [*dona diversa*] bestowed on each" (GS 32).

A further parallel notion is that of "eucharistic communion": "Really sharing in the body of the Lord in the breaking of the Eucharistic bread, we are taken up into communion with him and with one another [*ad*

35. Dulles, *Models of the Church*, 198.
36. Translation corrected.

communionem cum eo ac inter nos elevamur]" (LG 7). Eucharist is both personal spiritual sustenance and spiritual communion with all other Christians: "Christ left to his followers a pledge of this hope and food for the journey in the sacrament of faith, in which natural elements, cultivated by human beings, are changed into his glorified Body and Blood, as a supper of brotherly and sisterly communion [*communionis*] and the fore-taste of the heavenly banquet" (GS 38).[37]

We have examined three dimensions: the *communio hierarchica*, the *communio ecclesiarum*, the *communio fidelium*. What is the proper way in which these three dimensions of *communio* are to be ordered, given the vision of Vatican II, when interpreted in a hermeneutically comprehensive way? Examination of the debates at the council and of its final documents shows that Vatican II, in wanting to complete Vatican I, started off with its focus clearly set on the first dimension (*communio hierarchica*), discovered the second dimension (*communio ecclesiarum*), and ended up placing a primary and pervasive emphasis on the third dimension (*communio fidelium*), albeit in a way that inextricably links all three dimensions. Walter Kasper calls the concept of *communio fidelium* "Vatican II's great idea."[38] He believes that the fundamental nature of this ecclesial notion requires a reordering in importance of the three dimensions of *communio*: "the communion of the churches and the collegiality of the bishops is based on the more fundamental communion which is the church, the people of God itself."[39] A comprehensive account of the *communio* ecclesiology of Vatican II, therefore, conceives the church in its basic sense as a *communio fidelium*, a communion of the faithful who, with various charisms and ministries, live out their mission in local churches united throughout the world as a *communio ecclesiarum*, each of which is a church led in humble service by a bishop who is bound in a *communio hierarchica* with all other local bishops, with and under the Bishop of Rome. While this may seem to be an affirmation of the universal over the particular, and in contradiction of a balanced understanding of the particular/universal principle, the theo-logical revelation/faith principle requires it, without contradiction. The revelation/faith principle shows how faith begins with the particular individual disciple responding to the call of Jesus. Of course, this call to the individual is mediated through the preaching of other disciples and includes a call to join the group of Jesus' disciples. An

37. Translation corrected.
38. Kasper, "The Church as Communion," 163.
39. Ibid., 161. Emphasis added.

important corollary to the notion of *communio fidelium* that will be examined below is that of *sensus fidelium*—the sense that all of Christ's disciples make of him and of the Gospel in the multiple contexts in which they live their faith. This was first explored in the revelation/faith principle above; it will be raised again when we look to the unity/diversity of the faith, as well as in the chapter on the *fideles/fidelis* principle.

For capturing the trinitarian mystery of the church, and overcoming an exclusively juridical and hierarchical conception of the church, Vatican II found in *communio* ecclesiology a valuable insight, as Acerbi and Saier have demonstrated.[40] Can the council's whole vision of the church, however, be interpreted through this single hermeneutical lens? Joseph Komonchak offers a more hermeneutically nuanced view:

> Some interpreters claim that there is no single ecclesiology in the council but only a variety of images or models of the church. The council does, no doubt, employ many images. . . . This variety has led some people to speak of several distinct conciliar ecclesiologies and others to identify a single underlying notion that would capture the essence of Vatican II's view of the Church, some opting for "People of God," others for "*communio*," and so forth. . . . The council sought to set out the elements of the Church's life but it left it to theologians to construct a synthesis of them. The elements are many, but the council's ecclesiology includes them all and is, therefore, single in intention. Most unfortunate is the claim sometimes made, implicitly or explicitly, that one must choose among the conciliar notions.[41]

A single notion such as *communio* alone cannot bear the weight of capturing the renewed ecclesiology of Vatican II. Other conciliar notions balance out and give further nuance to the mystery of the church beyond that of *communio*. One such notion is that of *missio*.

Missionary by Nature

The council's treatment of *missio* was fundamental for realizing its pastoral aim: since the very *raison d'être* of the whole church is to proclaim the Gospel, the council calls for a renewal of this missionary fervor in all the faithful. Moving away from (but not ignoring) a more narrow preconciliar focus on

---

40. Acerbi, *Due ecclesiologie*; Saier, *"Communio" in der Lehre des Zweiten Vatikanischen Konzils*.

41. Joseph A. Komonchak, "The Significance of Vatican Council II for Ecclesiology," in *The Gift of the Church: A Textbook on Ecclesiology in Honor of Patrick Granfield, O.S.B*, ed. Peter C. Phan (Collegeville, MN: Liturgical Press, 2000), 69–92, at 76.

the "saving of souls," on "missions," and on "missionaries" sent to lands where the Gospel had not been preached, the council expands its vision to a broader perspective on the world and its problems and the church's place in that world as a sacrament of God's salvation.

The opening article of *Lumen Gentium* proclaims the council's keen hope: "Christ is the light of the nations and consequently this holy synod, gathered together in the Holy Spirit, ardently desires to bring to all humanity that light of Christ which is resplendent on the face of the church, by proclaiming his Gospel to every creature" (LG 1). Then, after speaking of the church in terms that evoke *communio* ("a sacrament . . . of intimate union with God and of the unity of the entire human race"), the council goes on to state the more specific intention of the Dogmatic Constitution, explicitly mentioning *missio*: "to describe more clearly, and in the tradition laid down by earlier councils, its own *nature and universal mission*" (LG 1).[42] Indeed, in the council's later reception of this teaching the following year, *Ad Gentes* would go on to present the church's *natura* and *missio* as inextricably linked: "The pilgrim church [*ecclesia peregrinans*] is by its very nature missionary [*natura sua missionaria*]" (AG 2).[43] As Suso Brechter asserts: "No Council has ever so consciously emphasized and so insistently expounded the Church's pastoral work of salvation and its worldwide missionary function as Vatican II."[44]

As with other conciliar teachings, that of Vatican II on "mission" did not emerge out of a vacuum. First, in the four decades leading up to Vatican II, four popes had written encyclicals on the theme, albeit with a fundamental focus on "the missions" and of "missionary activity" as the responsibility of the Holy See.[45] Here, there were openings that Vatican II would take up and develop. For example, Pius XII's *Evangelii Praecones* showed an appreciation for local cultures, a theme Pope John XXIII reaffirmed in his *Princeps Pastorum* on November 28, 1959, ten months after he announced his intention to convene the council.[46] Second, as with other theological developments that Vatican II went on to embrace, here too preconciliar *ressourcement*

---

42. Emphasis added.

43. Translation corrected.

44. Suso Brechter, "Decree on the Church's Missionary Activity," in *Commentary on the Documents of Vatican II*, vol. 4, ed. Herbert Vorgrimler (New York: Herder and Herder, 1969), 4:87–181, at 87.

45. A convenient collection of these encyclicals can be found in Thomas Burke, ed., *Catholic Missions: Four Great Missionary Encyclicals* (New York: Fordham University Press, 1957).

46. For relevant passages and a discussion of these shifts, see Gaillardetz, *Ecclesiology for a Global Church*, 48–49.

scholarship was important. The so-called missionary movement in the first half of the twentieth century saw developments in missiology, particularly in the so-called Münster School and the Louvain School.[47] Stephen Bevans observes that while interpreters have rightly highlighted the significance of the *ressourcement* scholarship of other renewal movements before the council (biblical, liturgical, patristic, ecumenical, etc.) the significance of the missionary renewal movement has been neglected as a factor at Vatican II.[48]

Ad Gentes is "the centerpiece of the council's explicit reflections on mission."[49] Although the final text was basically drafted only in the last year of the council, discussed in the aula for only a total of a few days, and promulgated on the last day of the council, the council was deliberating on the theme of "mission" throughout its entire course. Before the council met, the Preparatory Commission on the Missions had drafted seven schemas on the missions.[50] These were rejected, as were further drafts in the second and third sessions.[51] The main objectors were bishops from "missionary countries." Toward the end of the third session, a new subcommittee was set up and entrusted with presenting a whole new document. It was to be chaired by Johannes Schütte, the

---

47. Surveying the missiological studies of the first half of the twentieth century, the distinctive features of and differences between the two dominant Münster and Louvain schools of thought are summarized by William McConville: "[The Münster school] is identified with the work of J. Schmidlin. Its approach is christocentric and personal, emphasizing proclamation of the gospel, conversion, and the salvation of souls . . . An alternative model, associated with Louvain and missiologists P. Charles and A. Seumois, has been characterized as 'curial-canonical.' It gives priority to the implantation of the church. The establishment of the hierarchy and indigenous churches is stressed. Although its emphasis is ecclesiocentric and territorial, the Louvain school tends to be less 'European-centred' and more sensitive to cultural differences." William McConville, "Mission," in *The New Dictionary of Theology*, ed. Joseph A. Komonchak, Mary Collins, and Dermot A. Lane (Dublin: Gill and Macmillan, 1987), 664–68, at 665.

48. See Stephen B. Bevans, "Revisiting Mission at Vatican II: Theology and Practice for Today's Missionary Church," *Theological Studies* 74 (2013): 261–83, at 261.

49. Ibid., 269.

50. On the drafting history of the missionary document, see Brechter, "Decree on the Church's Missionary Activity," 87–111; Peter Hünermann, "Theologischer Kommentar zum Dekret über die Missionstätigkeit der Kirche: *Ad gentes*," in *Herders theologischer Kommentar zum Zweiten Vatikanischen Konzil. Band 4*, ed. Peter Hünermann and Bernd Jochen Hilberath (Freiburg: Herder, 2005), 4:219–336, at 243–52; Stephen B. Bevans, "Decree on the Church's Missionary Activity," in *Evangelization and Religious Freedom: Ad Gentes, Dignitatis Humanae*, ed. Stephen B. Bevans and Jeffrey Gros (New York: Paulist Press, 2009), 3–148, at 9–29.

51. Adrian Hastings summarizes the criticisms of the previous drafts: "too juridical, too remote, the repetition of well-worn platitudes." Adrian Hastings, *A Concise Guide to the Documents of the Second Vatican Council*, vol. 1 (London: Darton Longman & Todd, 1968), 1:209.

superior general of the missionary order, the Society of the Divine Word.[52] Included among its *periti* were Yves Congar and Joseph Ratzinger.[53] In January 1965, the subcommittee met for several weeks of intense drafting. A draft document was ready by May to be sent out to the bishops for responses and then further revision, before being presented to the bishops at the fourth session. Brief discussion in the council hall from October 7–11 called for further revisions of what was generally a welcomed text. Officially promulgated on December 7, 1965, *Ad Gentes* is the third-longest conciliar document and among the least discussed during the council, yet the most overwhelmingly approved. With 2,394 in favor and only five against, "it received the highest number of votes of all the decrees of Vatican II."[54]

The broad acceptance by the council of *Ad Gentes* is in large part due to its being written in the council's maturity. It builds on the theology of mission explicit and implicit in already promulgated documents and in others still being drafted in the fourth session. Joseph Ratzinger has shown how these other documents illuminate the theme of mission in various ways, especially *Lumen Gentium* (November 21, 1964), *Nostra Aetate* (October 28, 1965), *Apostolicam Actuositatem* (November 18, 1965), *Presbyterorum Ordinis* (December 7, 1965), and *Dignitatis Humanae* (December 7, 1965).[55] And, as Stephen Bevans has remarked concerning *Gaudium et Spes*: "The whole document is a mission document *par excellence*."[56] *Ad Gentes* brings together many of these insights, at times developing them, and weaves them into a synthesis, adding its own distinctive features.

Across the documents, the most striking feature of Vatican II's theology of mission is its trinitarian breadth. Deliberately paralleling the separate articles on the Father, the Son, and the Holy Spirit in *Lumen Gentium* 2, 3, and 4, *Ad Gentes* 2, 3, and 4 begin the first chapter on the doctrinal principles of mission with articles on the Trinity and the trinitarian missions in the economy of salvation. Article 2 begins with the programmatic statement: "The pilgrim church is by its very nature missionary since, according to the

52. Fr. Schütte had been appointed to the Commission on Mission in the second session. See Vilanova, "The Intersession (1963–1964)," 390n132.

53. On the chair Cardinal Agagianian's opposition to Congar's inclusion, and Congar's own account, see Congar, *My Journal of the Council*, 693.

54. Brechter, "Decree on the Church's Missionary Activity," 111.

55. See the detailed discussion of "mission" in each of these documents in Joseph Ratzinger, "La mission d'après les autres textes conciliaires," in *L'activité missionnaire de l'Eglise: Décret "Ad gentes,"* ed. Louis-Marie Dewailly, et al. (Paris: Cerf, 1967), 121–47.

56. Bevans, "Revisiting Mission at Vatican II," 266.

plan of the Father, it has its origin in the mission of the Son and the Holy Spirit" (AG 2).[57] Trinitarian formulations echo throughout the whole chapter (art. 2–9). Not only does the church's mission originate in the Trinity, but the ecclesial goal of that mission has a trinitarian "shape": God's plan is "that the whole human race might become one people of God [the Father], form one Body of Christ, and be built up into one Temple of the Holy Spirit" (AG 7). "Thus missionary activity tends towards eschatological fullness; by it the People of God is expanded. . . . [T]he Mystical Body is enlarged; . . . the spiritual Temple where God is adored in spirit and in truth grows and is built up" (AG 9).[58] *Dei Verbum*, promulgated a few weeks before, had likewise stated God's plan in trinitarian form: "that people can draw near to the Father, through Christ, the Word made flesh, in the Holy Spirit, and thus become sharers in the divine nature . . . [when God will] receive them into his own company" (DV 2).

Just as the Son and the Spirit are sent, so too the church: "Just as Christ was sent by the Father, so also he sent the apostles, filled with the Holy Spirit" (SC 6). Just as Christ in the Spirit was sent to inaugurate the kingdom of God, so too the church "receives the mission of proclaiming and establishing among all peoples the kingdom of Christ and of God" (LG 5). It is the Holy Spirit who enables the church to be missionary: The Holy Spirit "[inspires] in the hearts of the faithful [*in cordibus fidelium*] that same spirit of mission which impelled Christ himself" (AG 4).

The mission is entrusted to the whole church, not just to a few within it. "The whole church is missionary, and the work of evangelization [is] the fundamental task of the People of God" (AG 35). "All disciples of Christ are obliged to spread the faith to the best of their ability" (LG 17). "Each and every one of the Christian faithful" (AG 36) is sent out on mission, each in their own way playing their part according to their state of life and individual charisms. Participation of all the faithful in the church's mission is described in terms of the "three offices of Christ" (preaching, sanctifying, and govern-ing): "In the church, there is diversity of ministry but unity of mission. To the apostles and their successors, Christ has entrusted the office of teaching, sanctifying and governing in his name and by his power. Lay people too, sharing in the priestly, prophetical and kingly office of Christ, play their part in the mission of the whole people of God in the church and in the world" (AA 2). This passage cites in a footnote *Lumen Gentium*, where it affirms:

57. Translation corrected.
58. Translation corrected.

"The apostolate of the laity is a participation [*participatio*] in the church's saving mission. Through baptism and confirmation all are appointed to this apostolate by the Lord himself. . . . Thus, all lay people, through the gifts which they have received, are at once the witnesses and the living instruments of the mission of the church itself" (LG 33). As Richard McBrien notes, it is significant here that the role of the laity is no longer conceived as a "delegated participation"; they are sent out on mission not by delegation from their bishop but by virtue of their baptism and confirmation.[59]

The church's singular mission is described in multiple ways across the documents, but not always using the word *missio*: the church is to proclaim the Gospel, to proclaim the kingdom of Christ and of God, to spread the faith and salvation of Christ, to reveal the mystery of Christ, etc.[60] But the primary conciliar rubric for naming the church's mission is to be a "sacrament" in the world: the church is sent to be "a kind of sacrament—a sign and instrument, that is, of intimate union with God and of the unity of the entire human race" (LG 1), i.e., to be "the universal sacrament of salvation" (LG 48; GS 45). Indeed, "the encouragement of unity is in harmony with *the deepest nature of the church's mission*, for it is 'a sacrament' [quoting LG 1]" (GS 42).[61]

This mission includes within it the so-called social mission of the church. Discussion of the soteriological/ecclesiological principle above has already highlighted how the notion of "integral salvation" "is at least implicitly contained in the teaching of Vatican II."[62] While not expressing it as explicitly as the 1971 international Synod of Bishops in its appropriation of Vatican II's vision—"the mission of the people of God [is] to further justice in the world"[63]—trajectories within the council debates and in its documents certainly point toward that synthetic definition. Already in its "Message to the World" on October 20, 1962, the council had stated: "So, in our labors we shall give an important place to all world problems which concern the dignity of man and a genuine community of peoples. . . . For such indeed is the plan of God that through charity the kingdom of God may in some way

---

59. McBrien, *The Church*, 166.

60. For a list of references to diverse descriptions of the mission of the church, see Kloppenburg, *The Ecclesiology of Vatican II*, 99–100.

61. Emphasis added.

62. Sullivan, *The Church We Believe In*, 133.

63. On the history of the term "integral salvation," see ibid., 139–51.

emerge upon earth as a faint sketch of his eternal kingdom."[64] *Lumen Gentium* went on to state: "Christ was sent by the Father 'to bring good news to the poor . . . to heal the broken hearted,' 'to seek and to save what was lost.' Similarly, the church encompasses with its love all those who are afflicted by human infirmity and it recognizes in those who are poor and who suffer, the likeness of its poor and suffering founder. It does all in its power to relieve their need and in them it endeavours to serve Christ" (LG 8). At the end of the council, Pope Paul VI strikingly highlighted this aspect of the council's work: "The old story of the Good Samaritan has been the model of the spirituality of the council. A feeling of boundless sympathy has permeated the whole of it. The attention of our council has been absorbed by the discovery of human needs."[65]

Gaudium et Spes is the *magna carta* of the church's social mission and begins with its programmatic profession of Christian faith and of solidarity with a suffering humanity:

> The joys and hopes, the grief and anguish of the people of our time, especially of those who are poor or afflicted, are the joys and hopes, the grief and anguish of the disciples of Christ as well. Nothing that is genuinely human fails to find an echo in their hearts. For theirs is a community of people united in Christ and guided by the Holy Spirit in their pilgrimage towards the Father's kingdom, bearers of a message of salvation for all of humanity. That is why they cherish a feeling of deep solidarity with the human race and its history. (GS 1)[66]

A parallel and equally emphatic passage is found in *Ad Gentes* 12:

> As Christ went about all the towns and villages healing every sickness and infirmity, as a sign that the kingdom of God had come, so the church, through its children, joins itself with people of every condition, but especially with the poor and afflicted, and willingly spends itself for them. It shares their joys and sorrows, it is familiar with the hopes and problems of life, it suffers with them in the anguish of death. It wishes to enter into fraternal dialogue with those who are working for peace, and to bring them the peace and light of the gospel.

Along with *Dignitatis Humanae*, *Gaudium et Spes* presents a vision of the church's mission that promotes human dignity, full human flourishing, a world

64. As quoted in Yves Congar, "The Church: Seed of Unity and Hope for the Whole Human Race," *Chicago Studies* 5 (1966): 25–39, at 25–26.
65. Paul VI, "Closing Address: Fourth Session," 360.
66. Translation corrected.

community of peace, "the welfare of society as a whole" (GS 63), and what it calls "economic development [*progressione*]" (GS 64–66). Moreover, in political life, the church through its members works actively to promote the rights and duties of the individual and to advance the common good, so that all may achieve "a fully human life [*vitam plene humanum*]" (GS 72).[67] By elucidating in this way "the social mission of the church as an expression of the church's salvific mission, [Vatican II] makes a decisive shift insofar as it incorporates into its vision of modern society three traditions that many in the church had previously contested: the tradition of human and civil rights, the tradition of a constitutional state, and the tradition of modern democracy."[68] The church is called to be an agent of change in social, economic, cultural, and political life: "Even in the secular history of humanity the gospel has acted as a leaven in the interests of liberty and progress, and it always offers itself as a leaven with regard to fellowship, unity and peace" (AG 8). Thus: "Whether it aids the world or whether it benefits from it, the church has but one sole purpose—that the kingdom of God may come and the salvation of the human race may be accomplished. Every benefit the people of God can confer on humanity during its earthly pilgrimage is rooted in the church's being 'the universal sacrament of salvation,' at once manifesting and actualizing the mystery of God's love for humanity" (GS 45, quoting LG 48).

The particular place of the social dimension in the church's mission was a problematic issue throughout the drafting of *Gaudium et Spes*. In its final form, the constitution proposes the compromise formulation that, while the church's mission is a religious one, it does not exclude the social, economic, cultural, and political implications of its religious mission. Despite—remarkably—having devoted *whole chapters* each to the *political, economic,* and *social* dimensions of the church's presence in the world, the pastoral constitution asserts, in a classic compromise statement: "Christ did not bequeath to the church a mission in the political, economic, or social order: the purpose [*finis*] he assigned to it was religious. But this religious mission can be the source of commitment, direction, and vigor to establish and consolidate the human community according to the law of God" (GS 42).

Joseph Komonchak notes this "oscillation" in *Gaudium et Spes* regarding the religious and the political-economic-social dimensions of the church's mission and the juxtaposition of both dimensions in the final document:

---

67. Translation corrected.
68. Schüssler Fiorenza, "Church, Social Mission of," 161–62.

Perhaps it cannot be said that the council was completely successful in integrating what it called the church's proper religious mission and its participation in the common human project on earth. Disagreements on this matter within the so-called progressive majority were in fact particularly sharp, with French theologians such as Yves Congar and M.-D. Chenu urging a generally optimistic incarnational approach and German theologians such as Karl Rahner and Joseph Ratzinger, along with the Italian theologian Giuseppe Dossetti, insisting on what Rahner called the "Christian pessimism" that is required by the important role of the cross in the Christian vision. The final text of *Gaudium et Spes* reflects the, at times, uneasy compromises that were necessary for the constitution to gain a consensus.[69]

The *peritus* Bonaventure Kloppenburg, in language echoing that of the Council of Chalcedon on the two natures of Christ, sums up the tensive conciliar vision regarding the social dimension of the church's mission:

> Thus the growth of the kingdom of Christ and the progress of the temporal order are not to be identified or confused, but neither are they to be separated or opposed. They are part of a single divine plan and are ordered to a single goal which is the perfected kingdom of God. In a similar way, we must distinguish—without identification and confusion; without separation, dualism, dichotomy, antinomy, and opposition; but requiring harmony, collaboration, co-existence, and even interpenetration—between *evangelization* and *humanization*. Both of these are part of a single plan and both must lead to the same final kingdom of God.[70]

Reception of *Gaudium et Spes*'s vision, therefore, needs to hold these inner tensions in balance.

Since "the church's mission is concerned with people's salvation" (AA 6), another issue that emerges in discussion of the church's social mission is that of the very meaning of salvation, something the soteriological/ecclesiological principle addresses. Does salvation concern only redemption from personal sin, a theology that grounded the urgency of missions as "saving souls"? *Gaudium et Spes*'s broader and richer understanding of the human condition

---

69. Komonchak, "The Ecclesiology of Vatican II," 767. See also Joseph A. Komonchak, "Augustine, Aquinas or the Gospel *sine glossa*? Divisions over *Gaudium et spes*," in *Unfinished Journey: The Church 40 Years after Vatican II; Essays for John Wilkins*, ed. Austen Ivereigh (London: Continuum, 2003), 102–18. For a more developed argument, see Komonchak, "Le valutazioni sulla *Gaudium et spes*: Chenu, Dossetti, Ratzinger."

70. Kloppenburg, *The Ecclesiology of Vatican II*, 104. Emphasis added.

and its multiple aspects brings to the fore the notion of salvation as encompassing the social, cultural, political, and economic dimensions of human flourishing, of "a fully human life" (GS 72). In the end, a broader notion of *missio* went hand in hand with a broader notion of salvation and the church as a sacrament of that salvation. Walter Kasper has referred to this broader perspective: "The Church's mission, which is rooted in the absolute claim of Christianity, is not so much to save the individual—who in principle can be saved outside the visible communion—as *to represent and proclaim the love of God, to give testimony to hope, and so to be a sign among the nations.*"[71]

Vatican II's recurring preoccupation with promoting "unity" among the peoples of the world—as fundamental to its mission—relates to another striking feature of the council's vision: the emphasis on *the way* the church is to be missionary and *how* it can best achieve its goal. We will see below how the *ad intra/ad extra* principle and the church/world principle—regarding *rapprochement* with the world, with Modernity, with "the other"—illuminate further this aspect of the *communio/missio* principle. Eschewing aggressive approaches seen in the church's past, Vatican II presents *a sacramental view of mission.* As a "sign and instrument," the *tone* and *demeanor* of ecclesial presence to the other is of the essence for effectively mediating God's saving presence. The church's mode of carrying out its mission imitates that of God's mission of self-revelation in Christ through the Spirit: "The pattern of this revelation unfolds through deeds and words which are intrinsically connected: *the works* performed by God in the history of salvation show forth and confirm the doctrine and realities signified by the words; *the words*, for their part, proclaim the works, and bring to light the mystery they contain" (DV 2). In other words, the way the church works must illuminate the words it speaks, and vice versa.

Vatican II calls for purification, renewal, and reform in the style or manner in which the church is a sacrament of salvation—the sign cannot be an effective instrument if it does not authentically point to the one whom it is meant to signify. Proclamation includes not only the *what* of the message but *how* it is proclaimed. The church/world principle will highlight the council's desire for the church to radiate "the genuine face of God" (GS 19),[72] so that "the light of Christ" might be "resplendent on the face of the church" (LG 1), as it manifests sacramentally God's saving presence. As Jesus Christ was a *lumen gentium*, so too the church is called to be a light to the nations. Accordingly, the council's whole program of purification, renewal, and reform

---

71. Quoted (without reference) in McConville, "Mission," 667. Emphasis added.
72. Translation corrected.

is fundamental to its desire for the church to be more missionary: "Since the whole church is missionary, and the work of evangelization the fundamental task of the People of God, this sacred synod invites all to undertake a profound interior renewal [*renovationem*] so that being vividly conscious of their personal responsibility for the spread of the gospel they might play their part in missionary work among the nations" (AG 35).[73]

The council's theology of mission is a theology of ecclesial presence in the world. The words "presence" and "present" are peppered throughout the texts of Vatican II, especially *Ad Gentes*, where the very reiteration of the theme is telling. Since speaking is not enough, Christians are to "bear witness to the love and kindness of Christ and thus prepare a way for the Lord, and in some way *make him present* [*praesentem reddere*]" (AG 6). "The mission of the church is carried out by means of that activity through which, in obedience to Christ's command and moved by the grace and love of the Holy Spirit, the church makes itself fully present [*praesens*] to all individuals and peoples in order to lead them to the faith, freedom and peace of Christ by the example of its life and teaching, by the sacraments and other means of grace. Its aim is to open up for all men and women a free and sure path to full participation in the mystery of Christ" (AG 5). "Missionary activity makes Christ present [*praesentem reddit*]" (AG 9). Article 11 begins: "The church must be present [*praesens*] to these groups through those of its members who live among them or have been sent to them" (AG 11). Likewise, article 12 begins: "The presence of Christians [*praesentia christifidelium*] among these human groups should be one that is animated by that love with which we are loved by God" (AG 12). "By the example of the lives of the faithful and of the whole community [the local church must be] a sign indicating Christ" (AG 20).

A spirit of *dialogue* must characterize this ecclesial presence, precisely because it characterized the spirit of Christ's own mission: "Just as Christ penetrated to people's hearts and by a truly human dialogue [*colloquio*] led them to the divine light, so too his disciples, profoundly pervaded by the Spirit of Christ, should know and converse with those among whom they live, that through sincere and patient dialogue [*dialogo*] they themselves might learn of the riches which a generous God has distributed among the nations. They must at the same time endeavour to illuminate these riches with the light of the gospel, set them free, and bring them once more under the dominion of God the saviour" (AG 11). All of *Gaudium et Spes* is an extended commentary on this theology of dialogical presence. In its penultimate article it concludes:

---

73. Translation corrected.

"In virtue of its mission to enlighten the whole world with the message of the Gospel and to gather together in one spirit all women and men of every nation, race and culture, the church shows itself as a sign of that amity which renders possible sincere dialogue [*dialogum*] and strengthens it" (GS 92).

Dialogical openness should characterize the manner of the church's mission in several ways, for example, through respectful openness to local cultures, to the followers of other religions, to benign and even belligerent atheists. Here the important shift the council makes with regard to culture is particularly relevant. Openness to local cultures and customs was apparent in the council's very first constitution on the liturgy: "Even in the liturgy the church does not wish to impose a rigid uniformity in matters which do not affect the faith or the well-being of the entire community. Rather does it cultivate and foster the qualities and talents of the various races and nations" (SC 37). *Lumen Gentium* 17 (the embryonic statement on the mission of the church that *Ad Gentes* would go on to expand and develop) already affirms the fundamental value of "whatever good is found sown in people's hearts and minds, or in the rites and customs of peoples" (LG 17). *Gaudium et Spes* speaks of all that the church receives from the world (GS 44) and of the significance of culture (GS 53–62). The pastoral constitution provides two fundamental axioms. First, "It is a feature of the human person that it can achieve true and full humanity only by means of culture" (GS 53); and, second, "By its nature and mission the church is universal in that it is not committed to any one culture or to any political, economic or social system" (GS 42). These two axioms, it could be said, provide the foundation of what the council calls "the law of evangelization":

> The church profits from . . . the riches hidden in various cultures, through which greater light is thrown on human nature and new avenues to truth are opened up. The church learned early in its history to express the Christian message in the concepts and languages of different peoples. . . . Indeed, this kind of adaptation in preaching [*accommodata praedicatio*] the revealed word must ever be the law of all evangelization. In this way it is possible to create in every country the possibility of expressing the message of Christ in suitable terms and to foster vital contact and exchange between the church and different cultures. (GS 44)

But this "adaptation in preaching" (as Stephen Bevans notes: "we might [today] say 'inculturated' or 'contextual' preaching"[74]) is more than a mere

---

74. Bevans, "Revisiting Mission at Vatican II," 279.

pedagogical principle, concerned with speaking and celebrating the Gospel in the language, thought-forms, and symbols of a culture. It is much more a deeply *theological* principle. God is at work revealing and saving already within local cultures, and the church is here being called to discern God's presence and to learn from it.

Gaudium et Spes's two axioms and its law of evangelization are also presupposed in the theology of mission in *Ad Gentes*, which too speaks positively of "those elements of truth and grace which are found among peoples, and which are, as it were a secret presence of God" (AG 9). This positive evaluation of cultures reflecting "a secret presence of God" is grounded in the council's theology of the Holy Spirit, as outlined in article 4: "without a doubt, the Holy Spirit was at work in the world *before Christ was glorified*" (AG 4).[75] Indeed, the Holy Spirit "even at times visibly anticipates apostolic action, just as in various ways he unceasingly accompanies and directs it" (AG 4). Likewise, the mission of the Word can precede explicit proclamation of the Gospel. In an allusion—without citation—to Justin Martyr's *logos spermatikos*, Christian missionaries are encouraged to "be familiar with [locals'] national and religious traditions and uncover with gladness and respect those *seeds of the word* which lie hidden among them" (AG 11);[76] Christians must "learn of the riches which a generous God has distributed among the nations" (AG 11).

The corollary of this positive evaluation of culture and local context is the council's theology of the local church, already explored in the particular/universal principle above. Building on the theology of the local church enunciated in *Lumen Gentium*, particularly articles 13 and 23, *Ad Gentes* presents a rich theology of the local churches and their *communio* with one another. The word *communio* appears eleven times in *Ad Gentes*. It is significant that the only two occurrences of the phrase *communio ecclesiarum* appear here in a missionary document that provides a strong theology of the local churches.

As we have seen above, the council presents several vertical and horizontal dimensions of *communio*, and they can be found explicitly or implicitly in *Ad Gentes*: *communio* between God and humanity; between human beings themselves; within the church, between local bishops in the college of bishops (*communio hierarchica*); within the church, between a local church and other local churches (*communio ecclesiarum*); within the church, between one individual believer and all other believers among the worldwide community of disciples professing faith in the God of Jesus Christ (*communio fidelium*). Some of the *communio* passages in *Ad Gentes* refer to either or both the

---

75. Emphasis added.
76. Emphasis added. See Justin Martyr, *Second Apology*, 8, 10, 13.

communion between God and humanity or the communion among human beings themselves: God sent his Son "in order to establish a relationship of peace and communion [*communionem*] with himself, and in order to establish communion among people [*fraternamque societatem inter homines*]" (AG 3); by seeing the witness of Christians, non-Christians might "more fully perceive . . . the universal bond of the communion of humankind [*communionis hominum universale vinculum*]" (AG 11).[77]

There are two passages in *Ad Gentes* where both *communio* and *missio* appear. The first speaks of the Holy Spirit as the source of *communio* in the church: "Throughout the ages the Holy Spirit 'unites' the entire church 'in communion and ministry [*in communione et ministratione unificat*]' and provides her with different hierarchical and charismatic gifts, giving life to ecclesiastical structures, being as it were their soul, and inspiring in the hearts of the faithful that same spirit of mission [*missionis animum*] which impelled Christ himself" (AG 4; quoting here LG 4).[78] The other text relates to the role of missionary priests: "Priests represent Christ and are the collaborators of the order of bishops in that threefold sacred office which, of its nature, pertains to the mission of the church. They must be profoundly aware of the fact that their very life is consecrated to the service of the missions. Since by their own ministry—which consists mainly in the Eucharist, which gives the church its perfection—they are in communion with [*communicent*] with Christ the head, and are leading others to this communion [*communionem*]" (AG 39).

The first use of *communio ecclesiarum* appears in a sentence in which both *communio hierarchica* and *communio fidelium* are also evoked: "Bishops and their priests must think and live with the universal church, becoming more and more imbued with a sense of Christ and the church [*cum universali ecclesia sentiant atque vivant*]. The communion of the young churches with the whole church [*ecclesiarum novellarum communio cum tota ecclesia*] should remain intimate, they should graft elements of its tradition on to their own culture and thus, by a mutual outpouring of energy, increase the life of the mystical body. To this end, those theological, psychological and human elements which would contribute to this sense of communion with the whole church [*sensum communionis cum ecclesia universali*] should be fostered" (AG 19).

The second instance of *communio ecclesiarum* also implies *communio hierarchica*: "All bishops, as members of the body of bishops which succeeds the college of the apostles, are consecrated not for one diocese alone, but for

77. Translation corrected.
78. Translation corrected.

the salvation of the whole world. The command of Christ to preach the gospel to every creature applies primarily and immediately to them—with Peter, and subject to Peter [*cum Petro et sub Petro*]. From this arises that communion and cooperation of the churches [*communio et cooperatio ecclesiarum*] which is so necessary today for the work of evangelization. Because of this communion [*communionis*], each church cares for all the others, they make known their needs to each other, they share their possessions, because the spread of the body of Christ is the responsibility of the whole college of bishops" (AG 38).

One passage evokes the sense of *communio ecclesiarum* when it speaks of the young churches' "communion with the universal church [*communio cum ecclesia universali*]" (AG 20). Another also evokes *communio ecclesiarum*: "So new particular churches, each with its own traditions, have their place in the ecclesiastical communion [*in ecclesiastica communione*], the primacy of Peter which presides over this universal assembly of charity all the while remaining intact" (AG 22) We also find a passage which, although it uses the synonym *unio*, clearly implies *communio fidelium*: on the day of Pentecost "was foreshadowed the union of all peoples in the catholicity of the faith [*unio populorum in fidei catholicitate*] by means of the church of the New Covenant, a church which speaks every language, understands and embraces all tongues in charity, and thus overcomes the dispersion of Babel" (AG 4).

Therefore, while in the fifty years since the council there has been a certain divide between *communio* ecclesiologies and *missio* ecclesiologies, this cannot be substantiated in the council and its documents when read intratextually and intertextually. Moreover, even if the documents do not present the *communio/missio* principle in a systematic way, conciliar trajectories point the way toward such a synthesis. To that end, Stephen Bevans aptly captures the council's trinitarian theology of both *communio* and *missio* with a mutually inclusive formula "*communio*-in-*missio*": "Sharing [God's] mission is indeed constitutive of the church, which, like the Trinity, is a communion-in-*mission*."[79]

---

79. Bevans, "Revisiting Mission at Vatican II," 276. Original emphasis.

Principle 16
Unity/Diversity

Principle 16: In its inner life, the church is called to preserve the unity of faith; however, the appropriation of the one faith from manifold contexts necessarily finds diverse expression.

The unity/diversity principle names the conciliar concern for preserving the unity of faith within the Christian church, while at the same time acknowledging and promoting legitimate diversity, precisely in order to preserve that unity of faith. The principle captures an important element of the council's vision regarding the catholicity of the church.

The recognition and promotion of "legitimate diversity" both *outside* (UR 17) and *within* (GS 92) the Catholic Church emerges as a renewed awareness at Vatican II because of at least four developments. First, the council's understanding of revelation as primarily God's self-giving in love required a more differentiated understanding of the reception of that revelation through faith; this, in turn, required a more subtle Catholic understanding of the "deposit of faith" (UR 6) and "the faith once delivered to all the saints" (Jude 3; quoted in LG 12). Second, the use of the plural word "churches" (*communio ecclesiarum*) to capture the mystery of the one church immediately raised the issues of plurality and, consequently, of diversity. Third, historical consciousness had highlighted the diversity of ecclesial forms before monolithic Tridentine Catholicism within the Latin Catholic Church[1] and the diversity of traditions in Eastern churches both in communion with it and separated from it. Fourth, the council's ecumenical fervor for unity with the separated ecclesial communities of the Reformations raised the issue of legitimacy

---

1. "From the late Middle Ages until Vatican II the characteristic emphasis of Catholicism had been on the universal church, commonly depicted as an almost monolithic society." Avery Dulles, "Vatican II Reform: The Basic Principles," in *The Catholic Faith: A Reader*, ed. Lawrence Cunningham (New York: Paulist Press, 1988), 47–63, at 57.

concerning the diverse doctrines and traditions that had emerged within those communities since separation.

God's Will for Unity

Before exploring the council's teachings on unity-*in-diversity*, it is important to examine the abiding preoccupation the council fathers had with "unity" in a broader sense; while our focus in this principle is the inner life of the church, these wider conciliar concerns for unity redound upon that *ad intra* discussion. Like the notion of *communio* on the "horizontal" level discussed above, the conciliar concern for unity addresses several aspects: (1) the unity in faith, life, and worship among Catholics; (2) unity among separated Christians; and (3) unity among all humanity in a pluralistic and fragmented world. Desire for the latter shaped its concern for inner-ecclesial reform; if the church was to be a "sign and instrument" of that unity (LG 1), then unity within its own life would be highly significant for its credibility and effectiveness in achieving unity among humanity. By the end of the council, "unity" within the church would be understood in the sense of a unity-in-diversity.

Unity in the church, of course, had been a matter of major concern for Pope John XXIII when he called the council, as he later reiterated in his opening address on October 11, 1962.[2] The scandal of disunity among Christians, he said, was an urgent matter that the council should address for the sake of the church's pastoral effectiveness. Furthermore, the divisions among humanity, in the wake of World War II and in the midst of the Cold War, made peace and unity among nations a particularly urgent task for the council meeting in the early 1960s.[3] But in that opening address the pope

---

2. "Indeed, if one considers well this same unity which Christ implored for His Church, it seems to shine, as it were, with a triple ray of beneficent supernal light: namely, the unity of Catholics among themselves, which must always be kept exemplary and most firm; the unity of prayers and ardent desires with which those Christians separated from this Apostolic See aspire to be united with us; and the unity in esteem and respect for the Catholic Church which animates those who follow non-Christian religions." John XXIII, "Pope John's Opening Speech," 717.

3. Stephen Schloesser notes the council's preoccupation with global unity was expressive more of hope than of the reality of the world at the time of the council's meeting: "In 1962, when the council posed the question 'What is the church?', this was the context: a Cold War division of the world into two mutually exclusive superpower ideologies; the bitter and bloody fragmentation of colonial possessions into multiple smaller nation-states, in conflict both within themselves as well as with other states; and a need to move beyond an Orientalist perspective. . . . Contrary to the claims of the council, the idea of human unity was not a reflection of fact. It was instead a representation of deep hope for a world that seemed impossible in 1962–1965.

raised the issue of diversity within the church when he said: "The substance of the ancient doctrine of the deposit of faith is one thing, and the way in which it is presented is another. And it is the latter that must be taken into great consideration with patience if necessary, everything being measured in the forms and proportions of a magisterium which is predominantly pastoral in character."[4]

The actual Latin word *unitas* appears 156 times throughout the documents; in addition, there are multiple occurrences of related words such as *unio, unus,* and *communio.* Therefore, the desire for unity rings like a clarion call throughout the documents, from the first document to the last. For example, the very first paragraph of *Sacrosanctum Concilium* includes ecumenical unity as one of the four aims of the council: "to encourage whatever can promote the union of all who believe in Christ" (SC 1). The fact that the very first paragraph of *Lumen Gentium* also highlights the theme of unity shows its significance for the council fathers. In just one sentence of that opening paragraph, it speaks of the unity of humanity with God, the unity of all humanity among themselves, and the church's mission in God's plan to effect that unity: "Since the church, in Christ, is like [*veluti*] a sacrament—a sign and instrument, that is, of intimate union with God and of the unity of the entire human race—it here proposes . . . to describe more clearly . . . its own nature and universal mission" (LG 1).[5] And then in the very last sentence of *Lumen Gentium,* deliberately employing the literary device of "inclusion," the council proclaims the church's hope: that "all families of people, whether they are honored with the title of Christian or whether they still do not know the Saviour, may be happily gathered together in peace and harmony into one people of God, for the glory of the most holy and undivided Trinity" (LG 69).[6] Thus, this vision of what *Lumen Gentium* earlier

---

This hope for unity in turn led to a magnanimous answer in reply to a very big question: 'What is the church?'" Schloesser, "Against Forgetting," 103. Also on the historical context within which the council was meeting, see Giacomo Martina, "The Historical Context in Which the Idea of a New Ecumenical Council Was Born," in *Vatican II Assessment and Perspectives: Twenty-Five Years After (1962–1987),* ed. René Latourelle (New York: Paulist Press, 1988), 1:3–73.

4. John XXIII, "Pope John's Opening Speech," 715.

5. Translation corrected.

6. On the deliberate use of "inclusion" here, Yves Congar writes: "Those familiar with the Bible will recognize here an instance of 'inclusion,' well-known in the Old Testament and frequently found in the Johannine writings, in which at the end of a passage is repeated the formula with which it began and which generally contains the dominant theme of the passage. In this case it is the notion of the universal unity of the people of God insofar as it is a seed and a hope of unity for the human race in its totality. The Constitution on the Church opens

calls "catholic unity" is truly universal in scope, embracing of all humanity: "All are called to this catholic unity [*catholicam unitatem*] of the people of God which prefigures and promotes universal peace. And to it belong, or are related in different ways: the catholic faithful, others who believe in Christ, and finally all humankind, called by God's grace to salvation" (LG 13).

In treating the three aspects of unity on the horizontal level, the documents employ a series of phrases: the "exemplar and source" of unity; the "principle of unity"; the "sacrament" of unity; the "visible source and foundation" of unity; etc. The unity of humanity is central to "the design [*propositum*] of God's will" (LG 13), which is effected through the mission of the Word and the mission of the Spirit: "he made human nature one in the beginning and has decreed that all his children who were scattered should be finally gathered together as one. It was for this purpose that God sent his Son. . . . This, too, is why God sent the Spirit of his Son . . . who is for the church and for each and every believer the principle of their union and unity" (LG 13). The triune God is the exemplar and source of ecclesial unity: "This is the sacred mystery of the unity of the church, in Christ and through Christ, with the Holy Spirit energizing its various functions. The highest exemplar and source of this mystery is the unity, in the Trinity of Persons, of one God, the Father and the Son in the Holy Spirit" (UR 2).[7] While Jesus Christ is "the author of salvation and the source of unity and peace" (LG 9), the Holy Spirit is "the principle of unity" (LG 7) in the church. Thus, among the persons of the Trinity, the council underscores the special role in the economy of salvation of the Holy Spirit, "who for the church and for each and every believer is the principle of their union and unity" (LG 13). "It is the Holy Spirit, dwelling in those who believe and pervading and ruling over the entire church, who brings about that wonderful communion of the faithful [*communionem fidelium*] and joins them together so intimately in Christ that he is the principle of the church's unity . . . a unity of faith, hope and charity" (UR 2). "All the faithful scattered throughout the world are in communion [*communicant*] with each other in the Holy Spirit" (LG 13). As we will see, the same Holy Spirit arouses diversity in the reception of the one faith.

---

and closes on this note; it is one of its dominant themes, and in fact the same idea is repeated in the documents on the missions and on the Church in the world." Congar, "The Church: Seed of Unity and Hope for the Whole Human Race," 27.

7. On the council's trinitarian approach to unity/diversity, see particularly Elias Zoghby, "Unità e diversità della Chiesa," in *La Chiesa del Vaticano II: Studi e commenti intorno alla Costituzione dommatica 'Lumen Gentium'*, ed. Guilherme Baraúna (Firenze: Vallecchi Editore, 1965), 522–40.

234 Ecclesiological Principles

Among the seven sacraments of the church, the Eucharist especially is the sacrament of unity. "In the sacrament of the Eucharistic bread, the unity of believers, who form one body in Christ, is both expressed and achieved. All are called to this union with Christ" (LG 3). "Strengthened by the body of Christ in the Eucharistic communion, [the faithful] manifest in a concrete way that unity of the people of God which this most holy sacrament aptly signifies and admirably realizes" (LG 11). Similarly, the Decree on Ecumenism speaks of "the Eucharist, by which the unity of the church is both signified and brought about" (UR 2). Moreover, the church possesses certain visible elements that together manifest the unity of the church. For example, the pope is "the perpetual and visible source and foundation of the unity both of the bishops and of the whole company of the faithful [*fidelium multitudinis*]" (LG 23). Similarly, "individual bishops are the visible source and foundation of unity in their own particular churches" (LG 23).

"Legitimate Diversity"

For the council, disunity among the separated churches and ecclesial communities is a scandal that has impeded the proclamation of the Gospel and must therefore be urgently addressed. Vatican II realized that a renewed self-understanding on the part of the Catholic Church was needed if indeed it was to reach out to the separated churches and ecclesial communities. Significant for such a renewed self-understanding was a renewed appreciation of the importance of diversity in ecclesial unity. In its vision for unity in the Catholic Church and in Christianity, the council eschews any sense of unity as sameness or uniformity. Its final vision fosters "legitimate diversity" (UR 17; GS 92), "legitimate variety" (SC 38; LG 13).

According to Adrian Hastings, "a repeated stress upon the benefits brought by diversity is a recurrent theme of the Council documents."[8] There are twenty-six instances of "diversity" (*diversitas*) and 105 of "diverse" (*diversus*). Often used synonymously with these are the words "variety" and "various"; there are sixteen occurrences of *varietas* and 166 of *varius*. Another similar word-set, "pluralism" and "plurality," is also used, but not in reference directly to the inner life of the church. The word "pluralism" (*pluralismus*) appears twice across the documents, in *Gravissimum Educationis* 6 and 7, in both instances being used in a neutral sense to describe the current reality of multiplicity and difference in contemporary societies. The word "pluralistic"

8. Adrian Hastings, "The Key Texts," in *Modern Catholicism: Vatican II and After*, ed. Adrian Hastings (London: SPCK, 1991), 56–67, at 59.

(*pluralisticus*), found only in *Gaudium et Spes* 76, is likewise used to describe the given reality of diverse societies. The word "plurality" (*pluralitas*) occurs only once, in *Gaudium et Spes* 53, in reference to "the plurality of cultures" throughout the world. Thus, the words "diversity," "variety," and "plurality" are used in their commonsense meaning to describe multiplicity and difference without necessarily implying a lack of unity.

There are two theo-logical groundings of the unity/diversity principle, the first following on from the revelation/faith principle, and the second from the christological/pneumatological principle. The first grounding of the unity/diversity principle is best expressed in *Unitatis Redintegratio* where, in discussing the diverse traditions of Western and Eastern Christianity, it states: "The heritage handed down by the apostles was *received differently* and in different forms, so that from the very beginnings of the church its development varied from region to region and also because of differing [*diversitatem*] mentalities and ways of life" (UR 14).⁹ This stark and dramatic statement recalls the fundamental dynamic of the revelation/faith principle discussed above: the human reception of divine revelation, by means of the Spirit's gift of faith, necessarily occurs from within the vastly diverse contexts of each individual believing receiver and his or her community of faith. Thus, "from the beginning of its history [*ab initio suae historiae*] the church learned to express the Christian message in the concepts and languages of different peoples and tried to clarify it in the light of the wisdom of their philosophers: it was an attempt to adapt the Gospel to the understanding of all and the requirements of the learned, insofar as this could be done. Indeed, this kind of adaptation in preaching [*accommodata praedicatio*] of the revealed word must ever be the law of evangelization" (GS 44).¹⁰ Vatican II sought to embrace this law and make it its own, with what Theobald calls its "pastorality principle": "There can be no proclamation of the gospel without taking account of its recipients."¹¹ As the medieval axiom states: *Quidquid recipitur ad modum recipientis recipitur* (that which is received is received in the mode of the receiver).

The Dogmatic Constitution on Revelation implies that this axiom is at the heart of the early church's reception of divine revelation. It teaches that the *fourfold* Gospel is the authoritative norm for ensuring preservation of the one faith; the apostles and others of the apostolic age "handed on to us in writing the same message they had preached, the foundation of our faith:

---

9. Emphasis added.
10. Translation corrected.
11. Theobald, "The Theological Options of Vatican II," 94.

the fourfold Gospel, according to Matthew, Mark, Luke and John" (DV 18).
Yet, these four diverse gospels, while they give us "the authentic truth about
Jesus," are nevertheless told differently by each, "with an eye to the situation
of the churches" (DV 19). *Lumen Gentium* 12 alludes to this dynamic process
as the activity of the Holy Spirit, who bestows on the baptized and the church
as a whole a *sensus fidei*, a sense for the faith. Through this gift, the people
"receive . . . the word of God. . . . The people unfailingly adheres to this
faith, penetrates it more deeply through right judgment, and applies it more
fully in daily life" (LG 12). It is thus the Holy Spirit, through this *sensus fidei*,
who brings about "legitimate diversity" in the reception of the faith throughout history.

The second grounding of the unity/diversity principle follows on from
the christological/pneumatological principle above. *Lumen Gentium* 7, evoking the ecclesial vision of St. Paul in 1 Corinthians, presents a christological/
pneumatological vision of unity and diversity within the church:

> As all the members of the human body, though they are many, form one body,
> so also do the faithful in Christ. A diversity [*diversitas*] of members and func-
> tions is engaged in the building up of Christ's body too. There is only one Spirit
> who, out of his own richness and the needs of the ministries, gives his various
> gifts for the welfare of the church. Among these gifts the primacy belongs to
> the grace of the apostles to whose authority the Spirit subjects even those who
> are endowed with charisms. The same Spirit who of himself is the principle
> of unity in the body, by his own power and by the interior cohesion of the
> members produces and stimulates love among the faithful.

The constitution goes on to state: "The distinction which the Lord has made
between the sacred ministers and the rest of the people of God implies
union. . . . [A]mid their variety [*varietate*] all bear witness to the wonderful
unity [*unitate*] of the body of Christ: this very diversity [*diversitas*] of graces,
of ministries and of works gathers the children of God into one, for 'all these
things are the work of the one and the same Spirit'" (LG 32).[12] As the Decree
on the Apostolate of Lay People succinctly formulates it: "In the church, there
is *diversity of ministry* but *unity of mission*" (AA 2).[13] Thus, unity and diversity
in the church is grounded in the nature of the church as both the Body of
Christ and the temple of the Holy Spirit.

---

12. Quoting 1 Cor 12:11.
13. Emphasis added.

One of several key factors leading to Vatican II's rediscovery of the unity/ diversity principle was its explicit recognition of the *de facto* multiplicity of postapostolic traditions and rites within the Catholic Church itself, rites that exist alongside the dominant Latin tradition. Across the 450 or so years since the Council of Trent, a monolithic Tridentine Catholicism was the uniform norm in matters of liturgy, theology, spirituality, and discipline throughout the (Latin) Catholic world.[14] At Vatican II, the nearly two-thousand-year-old diversity of the Catholic Church would have been apparent to any observers as they watched the procession of bishops filing into the council hall for one of its sessions, with diversely vested bishops and prelates from the Eastern Catholic churches (in communion with Rome) visually asserting their presence.[15] This diversity was a simple historical fact of the Catholic Church, as *Lumen Gentium*—albeit with some irony—acknowledges: "There are, legitimately, in the ecclesial communion particular churches which retain their own traditions, without prejudice to the Chair of Peter which presides over the entire assembly of charity, and protects [*invigilat*] their legitimate variety [*legitimas varietates*] while at the same time taking care that these differences [*particularia*] do not diminish unity, but rather contribute to it" (LG 13). These churches, "while safeguarding the unity of the faith [*fidei unitate*] and the unique divine structure of the universal church, have their own discipline, enjoy their own liturgical usage and inherit a theological and spiritual patrimony. . . . This variety [*varietas*] of local churches, unified in common effort, shows all the more resplendently the *catholicity* of the undivided church" (LG 23).[16]

Across the council's four years, the small group of participating bishops and prelates from these Eastern Catholic churches, numbering a mere 130, made

14. On the "Tridentine paradigm," see Paolo Prodi, *Il paradigma tridentino: Un'epoca della storia della Chiesa* (Brescia: Morcelliana, 2010). On the emergence of "Tridentinism," see John W. O'Malley, *Trent: What Happened at the Council* (Cambridge, MA: Belknap Press of Harvard University Press, 2013), 260–75. See also Rush, "Roman Catholic Ecclesiology," 264–68.

15. Photos of the entrance procession can be seen in Alberto Melloni, "Eastern Rite Catholics," in *Vatican II: The Complete History*, ed. Alberto Melloni, Federico Ruozzi, and Enrico Galvotti (New York: Paulist Press, 2015), 186–87. Regarding these Catholic churches of the Eastern rites, Richard Gaillardetz remarks: "The four centuries prior to Vatican II were characterized by an almost inexorable movement toward greater uniformity in church discipline, liturgy, and theology. Nevertheless, along the ecclesial periphery of Roman Catholicism stood a number of Eastern Catholic churches, each with its own unique history and all of which had retained, more or less successfully, distinct canonical, liturgical, and theological traditions that distinguished them from the Latin church." Gaillardetz, *The Church in the Making*, 38.

16. Translation corrected. Emphasis added.

up 4.6 percent of the total number of participants. These included Melkites, Ukrainians, Maronites, Chaldeans, Armenians, Syrians, Malabars, Copts, Ethiopians, Romanians, Italo-Albanians, Syro-Malankars, Russians, Hungarians, Yugoslavians, Ruthenians, Bulgarians, and Greeks.[17] From the second session on, the six Eastern Catholic Patriarchs (after their insistence) were prominently seated at the front of the council hall, opposite the Latin Cardinals. Each public and general session began with a liturgy celebrated according to the rites of all the Catholic churches, not only the Latin Rite.[18] Moreover, when any of the Eastern bishops or prelates spoke throughout the council sessions, they refused to speak in Latin. Thus the council was reminded daily of the already-existing— but little acknowledged—diversity within the one communion of the Catholic churches. "The liturgical heritage and discipline of these Churches (the use of living languages, concelebration, communion under both kinds, married clergy) played a role in opening the eyes of many bishops who had considered the East remote; and it allowed them to have an experience of collegiality, which was part of their tradition, but which revealed a way of exercising *communio ecclesiarum* that had been forgotten in the Latin Church."[19]

Sacrosanctum Concilium in its introduction recognizes this diversity in the Catholic Church's liturgical heritage: "In faithful obedience to tradition, the sacred council declares that the church holds all lawfully recognized rites to be of equal legal force and dignity; that it wishes to preserve them in the future and to foster them in every way" (SC 4). The following year, on November 21, 1964 (the same day as *Lumen Gentium* and *Unitatis Redintegratio*), the council promulgated the Decree on the Catholic Eastern Churches (*Orientalium Ecclesiarum*).[20] This is the first time that an ecumenical council had produced a document on the Eastern Catholic churches. In a condensed

---

17. See the list in Melloni, "Eastern Rite Catholics," 187. For helpful examples of the diversity in theological, liturgical, and disciplinary traditions of the twenty-two Eastern Catholic churches, see Ronald Roberson, *The Eastern Christian Churches: A Brief Survey*, 6th rev. ed. (Roma: Orientalia Christiana, 1999); Edward Faulk, *101 Questions and Answers on Eastern Catholic Churches* (Mahwah, NJ: Paulist Press, 2007).

18. For a list of these diverse rites for daily Eucharist throughout the four sessions of the council, see the third column ("Liturgical Rite") of the calendar chart in Alberto Melloni, "Calendar of the Congregations," in *Vatican II: The Complete History*, ed. Alberto Melloni, Federico Ruozzi, and Enrico Galvotti (New York: Paulist Press, 2015), 240–57. On the reactions at the time to these liturgies and their impact on the conciliar liturgical reform, see Peter De Mey, "The Daily Eucharist at the Council as Stimulus and Test Case for Liturgical Reform," *Questions Liturgiques/Studies in Liturgy* 95 (2014): 28–51.

19. Melloni, "Eastern Rite Catholics," 186.

20. The date of 1965 given in the Table of Contents of Flannery is incorrect.

passage alluding to various conciliar motifs (the church as a *communio fide-lium*, the three offices of Christ, the church as a *communio ecclesiarum*, and as a *communio hierarchica*), article 2 of *Orientalium Ecclesiarum* presents the diversity of the Eastern Catholic churches (and their rites) as something of an exemplar of the unity/diversity principle:

> The holy Catholic Church, which is the Mystical Body of Christ, is made up of the faithful who are organically united in the Holy Spirit by the same faith, the same sacraments and the same government, and who, coming together in various hierarchically linked different groups, thus form particular churches or rites. Between those churches there is such a wonderful communion [*communio*] that this variety [*varietas*], so far from diminishing the Church's unity [*unitati*], rather serves to emphasize it. For the Catholic Church wishes the traditions of each particular church or rite to remain whole and entire, *and it likewise wishes to adapt its own way of life to the various needs of time and place*. (OE 2)[21]

As the last sentence implies, the council sees the diversity of the Eastern Catholic traditions as something the Latin church(es) should emulate. The following article then goes on to reaffirm *Lumen Gentium* 13's statement regarding the role of the pope to protect (*invigilare*) legitimate diversity: "These individual churches, both Eastern and Western [Latin], while they differ somewhat among themselves in what is called 'rite,' namely in liturgy, in ecclesiastical discipline and in spiritual tradition, are none the less all equally entrusted to the pastoral guidance of Roman Pontiff, who by God's appointment is successor to Blessed Peter in primacy over the universal church. Therefore these churches are of equal rank, so that none of them is superior to the others because of its rite" (OE 3). Adrian Hastings remarks on the significance of this acknowledgment: "In the past we have often spoken of all the non-Eastern part of the Church as forming one Western, 'Latin' Church. Clearly this was theologically mistaken. Today we see the world Church as a vast communion of local churches—Rome, Antioch, Zambia, England, etc. In this development out of the old uniform Latin rite of numerous genuine particular churches, the already existent example of the Eastern churches can be of very special helpfulness."[22]

The unity/diversity principle also comes to the fore in the council's treatment of the Eastern churches *separated from* the Catholic Church. The Decree

21. Emphasis added.
22. Hastings, *A Concise Guide to the Documents*, 2:179.

on Ecumenism defines such churches as those resulting from "divisions which occurred in the East, either because of the dispute over the dogmatic formulae of the Councils of Ephesus and Chalcedon, or later by the dissolving of ecclesiastical communion between the Eastern Patriarchates and the Roman See" (UR 13). Some of these churches responded to the invitation to send representatives to Vatican II. These and other official observers were seated at the front of St. Peter's during council sessions—already an indication of *rapprochement* and openness to diversity.[23] The newly elected Pope Paul VI, in his opening address at the second session, tellingly turned to the observers from other churches and ecclesial communities and said: "Our voice is trembling and our heart is moved, because your presence is an unspeakable consolation to us and a source of joyous hope."[24] The multilingual conclusion of the pope's address seemed to Joseph Ratzinger at the time to be of symbolic importance for the future of the council: "The concluding words, spoken in Greek and Russian, seemed to me of great significance, in that here the framework of Latin had unmistakably been discarded. A Church which spoke in all languages had affirmed its hope for the unity of Pentecost."[25]

The Decree on Ecumenism, in a gesture of openness and desire for dialogue and full communion, went on to acknowledge the "legitimate diversity" (UR 17) of these separated churches. Their diversity of "disciplines," "customs," and "observances," it acknowledges, contributes to "the fullness of Christian tradition" (UR 15). Moreover: "Far from being an obstacle to the church's unity [*unitati ecclesiae*], such diversity [*diversitas*] of customs and observances only adds to the beauty of the church and contributes greatly to carrying out her mission" (UR 16). Importantly, a fundamental pastoral reason is given as justification for preserving these diverse traditions: "*since these are better suited to the character of their faithful and better adapted to foster the good of souls*" (UR 16).[26] The council acknowledges that this pastoral principle, while not always upheld throughout the church's history, should nevertheless be fostered now for the very sake of ecclesial *unity*: "The perfect observance of

23. For a list of Eastern Orthodox observers and a discussion of those invited who did not attend, see Alberto Melloni, "Observers and Guests," in *Vatican II: The Complete History*, ed. Alberto Melloni, Federico Ruozzi, and Enrico Galvotti (New York: Paulist Press, 2015), 192–99, at 94–97. See also John R. H. Moorman, "Observers and Guests of the Council," in *Vatican II: By Those Who Were There*, ed. Alberic Stacpoole (London: Geoffrey Chapman, 1986), 155–69.
24. See translation in Ratzinger, *Theological Highlights of Vatican II*, 70.
25. Ibid., 70.
26. Emphasis added.

this traditional principle—which however has not always been observed—is a prerequisite for any restoration of union" (UR 16).

Then, in a remarkable ecumenical statement, *Unitatis Redintegratio* goes on to acknowledge, in reference to differences and divisions that in some cases reach back to the early centuries of the church, the possibility of including within "legitimate diversity" the very doctrinal formulations of the separated churches that had in fact caused such divisions in the first place:

> What has already been said about legitimate diversity [*legitima diversitate*] we are pleased to apply to differences in theological expression of doctrine [*diversa theologica doctrinarum enuntiatione*]. In the study of revealed truth East and West have used different methods and approaches in understanding and confessing divine things. It is hardly surprising, then, if sometimes one tradition has come nearer to a full appreciation of some aspects of a mystery of revelation than the other, or has expressed them better. In such cases, these various theological formulations are often to be considered *complementary rather than conflicting* [*compleri . . . quam opponi*]. (UR 17)[27]

These acknowledgments had important implications for opening the minds of the conciliar participants to the importance of diversity within the Latin (Roman) church itself (as a *communio ecclesiarum* of Latin Catholic local churches), within the fullness of the Catholic Church (as a broader *communio ecclesiarum* of many churches of diverse rites and traditions).

The conciliar journey to an explicit articulation of the unity/diversity principle—specifically applied to the Latin (Roman) Rite—began with the drafting of the council's very first document, *Sacrosanctum Concilium*. After acknowledging diverse liturgical rites in the Catholic Church's historical past and present (in regard to the Eastern Catholic rites), the liturgical constitution's final text then acknowledges the importance of fostering liturgical diversity within the Latin Rite. "Even in the liturgy the church does not wish to impose a rigid uniformity [*rigidam unius tenoris formam*] in matters which do not affect the faith or the well-being of the entire community. Rather does it cultivate and foster the qualities and talents of the various races and nations. Anything in people's way of life which is not indissolubly bound up with superstition and error the church studies with sympathy, and, if possible, preserves intact. It sometimes even admits such things into the liturgy itself, provided they harmonize with its true and authentic spirit" (SC 37). The liturgical constitution

---

27. Translation corrected. Emphasis added.

goes on then to present as a principle: "Provided that the substantial unity [*substantiali unitate*] of the Roman rite is preserved, provision shall be made, when revising the liturgical books, for legitimate variations and adaptations [*legitimis varietatibus et aptationibus*] to different [*diversos*] groups, regions and peoples, especially in mission countries" (SC 38).[28]

In the reform of the liturgy envisaged by *Sacrosanctum Concilium*, the competent authority for overseeing such "legitimate variations and adaptations" is set out in article 22, with numbering referring to a twofold authority (particular/universal): "(1) Regulation of the sacred liturgy depends solely on the authority of the church, that is, on the apostolic see, and, in accordance with law, on the [local] bishop. (2) In virtue of the power conferred on them by law, the regulation of the liturgy within certain defined limits belongs also to various kinds of groupings of bishops, legitimately established, with competence in given territories" (SC 22). Throughout the rest of the document, reference is made to "the competent territorial ecclesiastical authority mentioned in article 22.2" (SC 36.3), regarding use of the vernacular in the liturgy, or, regarding the liturgical books setting out "adaptations, especially as regards the administration of the sacraments, sacramentals, processions, liturgical language, sacred music and the arts," it is for "the competent territorial ecclesiastical authority mentioned in article 22.2" to decide (SC 39). These references to local authority continue to be repeated (e.g., SC 40, 44), albeit with reference to the need for final approbation by the Holy See.

Sacrosanctum Concilium, in affirming the diversity of local churches and their cultures, clearly intended to shift the approval of liturgical matters away from exclusive authority residing with the Holy See (as affirmed at the Council of Trent) toward more authority being granted to local churches. Coincidentally, on December 3, 1963, the council assembly held a solemn commemoration of the four hundredth anniversary of the close of the Council of Trent. The next day (the last day of the second session), the council formally voted on the final text of *Sacrosanctum Concilium*; it was passed with an overwhelming majority of 2,147, with only four bishops rejecting the document. Pope Paul VI then officially promulgated the constitution.

On return to his Australian archdiocese of Hobart later that December, the liturgist Archbishop Guilford Young commented that "400 years to the very day separated the decision of the Council of Trent to hand over to the

---

28. On uniformity and pluralism in the liturgy from Trent to Vatican II, see Giuseppe Alberigo, "Dalla uniformità liturgica del concilio di Trento al pluralismo del Vaticano II," *Rivista Liturgica* 69, no. 5 (1982): 604–19.

Pope all power in liturgical matters and the 1963 [Vatican II] decision which gave bishops definite powers to work out a liturgy suitable for their people."[29] One of the key drafters of the original schema on the liturgy, Fr. Annibale Bugnini, later recalled the significance of the pope's promulgation:

> It was an emotional moment, a historical moment. The date was exactly four centuries from the day, December 4, 1563, when the Council of Trent, anxious to conclude its work, left to the Holy See the task of effecting a liturgical reform. Such a reform had been called for in many quarters; in the overall plan of the Council of Trent, however, it was regarded as of secondary interest and so ended up as one of the problems the Council left untouched. Four centuries had passed. What seemed a marginal problem at Trent had become the number one problem at Vatican II and was the first to be dealt with there.[30]

With its devolved model of authority in matters liturgical and its recognition of local cultural symbols and vernacular languages in the liturgy, the liturgy constitution had brought the issue of *culture* to the fore. The implications of such a recognition for understanding unity and diversity was then further developed over the next two years, especially in *Gaudium et Spes* (53–62) and *Ad Gentes* (22). The pattern of the incarnation is presented as the pattern of effective proclamation: "If the church is to be in a position to offer all women and men the mystery of salvation and the life brought by God, then it must implant itself [*sese inserere debet*] among all these groups in the same way that Christ by his incarnation committed himself to the particular social and cultural circumstances of the women and men among whom he lived" (AG 10). The same document later affirms: "So too indeed, just as happened in the economy of the incarnation, the young churches . . . borrow from the customs, traditions, wisdom, teaching, arts and sciences of their people everything which could be used to praise the glory of the Creator, manifest the grace of the Saviour, or contribute to the right ordering of Christian life" (AG 22). The Brazilian commentator on Vatican II, Bonaventure Kloppenburg, succinctly summarizes this element of the conciliar vision: "To the extent that the Church does not in fact become Brazilian, the Brazilian will not be of the Church."[31]

---

29. Quoted in W. T. Southerwood, *The Wisdom of Guilford Young* (George Town, Tas.: Stella Maris Books, 1989), 276.

30. Bugnini, *The Reform of the Liturgy*, 37.

31. Kloppenburg, *The Ecclesiology of Vatican II*, 153.

The term "inculturation" does not appear in the conciliar texts, emerging only in the first decade of the council's reception.[32] The council speaks rather of "adaptation" (*aptatio*) and "accommodation" (*accommodatio*), terms that, in the council's reception, would come to be seen as too "extrinsic."[33] Nevertheless, when viewing the overall vision of the council, the reality named by the term "inculturation" (as later understood) is clearly present in the council's overall dynamic sense of the necessary interaction between Gospel and culture.[34] This dynamic sense constitutes a crucial element in Vatican II's unity/diversity principle with regard to the reception of faith from multiple cultures and contexts.[35]

Another aspect of the council's appreciation of diversity within the Catholic Church once again relates to the council's ecumenical intent. In discussing the ecumenical importance of the Catholic Church making "a careful and honest appraisal of whatever needs to be renewed and done *in the Catholic household itself*" (UR 4), the Decree on Ecumenism goes on to affirm the unity/diversity principle as one area of relevance in this Catholic self-appraisal: "While preserving unity in essentials, let all in the church,

32. Christopher O'Donnell briefly summarizes the history of the term: "The neologism 'inculturation' came into Catholic theology in the mid-1970s, especially in the writings of the Jesuit General, P. Arrupe. It appears in a Roman document for the first time in the message of the fifth Synod of Bishops (1977). But from two years earlier we have what has been called the 'Charter of Inculturation,' viz., the exhortation on evangelization, *Evangelii Nuntiandi* (1976) of Pope Paul VI. The term 'inculturation' has been frequently used by Pope John Paul II." Christopher O'Donnell, "Inculturation," in *Ecclesia: A Theological Encyclopedia of the Church* (Collegeville, MN: Liturgical Press, 1996), 210–11, at 210. Also on the reception of the council's teaching, and the options of other possible terms available for capturing the whole conciliar vision regarding Gospel and culture (adaptation, accommodation, contextualization, indigenization, acculturation), see Roest Crollius, "What Is So New about Inculturation?," *Gregorianum* 59 (1978): 721–38, at 722–25.

33. Crollius, "What Is So New about Inculturation?," 723.

34. Crollius describes this dynamic interaction: "the inculturation of the Church is the integration of the Christian experience of a local Church into the culture of its people, in such a way that this experience not only expresses itself in elements of this culture, but becomes a force that animates, orients and innovates this culture so as to create a new unity and communion, not only within the culture in question but also as an enrichment of the Church universal." Ibid., 735.

35. Marcello Azevedo sees two complementary theological positions on "inculturation" in the conciliar texts. The first position, centered in *Lumen Gentium* and related documents, he calls "a church-in-relation" position. The second, centered on *Gaudium et Spes*, focuses on the relationship between church and world. See Marcello de C. Azevedo, "Inculturation: I. The Problem," in *Dictionary of Fundamental Theology*, ed. René Latourelle and Rino Fisichella (Middlegreen, Slough, UK: St Paul, 1994), 500–510, at 504–5.

according to the office entrusted to them, preserve a proper freedom in the various forms of spiritual life and discipline, in the diversity [*diversitate*] of liturgical rites, and *even in the theological elaborating of revealed truth*. In all things let charity prevail. If they are true to this course of action, they will be giving ever richer expression to the authentic *catholicity* and *apostolicity* of the church" (UR 4).[36] This passage alludes to an ancient axiom that Pope John XXIII had already appealed to in an encyclical before the council: *in necessariis unitas, in dubiis libertas, in omnibus caritas* (unity in essentials, freedom in doubtful issues, love in all things).[37]

The axiom is quoted in the second-to-last paragraph of the council's very last document promulgated, as a rule for finding communion among the diversity not only *outside* the visible communion of the Catholic Church but also *within* it. The document begins its four concentric circles of dialogue by addressing dialogue within the Catholic Church: "[The church's] mission requires us first of all to create *in the church itself* mutual esteem, reverence and harmony, and to acknowledge all legitimate diversity [*legitima diversitate*]; in this way all who constitute the one People of God will be able to engage in ever more fruitful dialogue [*colloquium*], whether they are pastors or other members of the faithful. For the ties which unite the faithful together are stronger than those which separate them: let there be unity in what is necessary, freedom in what is doubtful, and charity in everything" (GS 92).[38] After promoting dialogue and legitimate diversity within the Catholic Church as the first step to ensuring credible witness in the next three circles of dialogue, this article then goes on to promote dialogue with other Christians, with other believers in God, and with nonbelievers.

Of significance in the council's call for a more dialogic Catholic Church is the statement above from *Unitatis Redintegratio* 4 regarding legitimate diversity "*even in the theological elaborating of revealed truth*" within the Catholic Church. This is a significant shift away from the preconciliar demand for neoscholastic uniformity in theological expression. One element of this openness to theological diversity is the recognition that past doctrinal formulations might have been deficient: "Every renewal of the church

36. Emphases added.

37. AAS 51 (1959): 513. See also John XXIII, "Ad Petri Cathedram." For bibliographical references to works that present a history of the axiom, see Yves M.-J. Congar, "Unité, diversité et divisions," in *Sainte Église: Études et approches ecclésiologiques* (Paris: Cerf, 1963), 105–30, at 118n3.

38. A footnote reference here cites the encyclical *Ad Petri Cathedram*, AAS 51 (1959): 513.

essentially consists in an increase of fidelity to her own calling. . . . Christ summons the church, as she goes her pilgrim way, to that continual reformation of which she always has need, insofar as she is a human institution here on earth. Consequently, if, in various times and circumstances, there have been deficiencies in moral conduct or in church discipline, *or even in the way that church teaching has been formulated*—to be carefully distinguished from the deposit of faith itself—these should be set right at the opportune moment and in the proper way" (UR 6).[39]

We have already seen the council acknowledge legitimate diversity in the different theological formulations of Eastern churches, both outside and within communion, as well as acknowledge the "proper freedom" that should be accorded to Catholic theologians in the Latin church (UR 4). By extension, in a synthesis of the council's vision, the ecumenical acknowledgment of complementary but not conflicting theological diversity regarding non-Catholic Eastern churches can be seen to apply *within* the Latin Catholic Church:

> What has already been said about legitimate diversity [*legitima diversitate*] we are pleased to apply to differences in theological expression of doctrine [*diversa theologica doctrinarum enuntiatione*]. In the study of revealed truth East and West have used different methods and approaches in understanding and confessing divine things. It is hardly surprising, then, if sometimes one tradition has come nearer to a full appreciation of some aspects of a mystery of revelation than the other, or has expressed them better. In such cases, these various theological formulations are often to be considered *complementary rather than conflicting* [*compleri . . . quam opponi*]. (UR 17)[40]

What Adrian Hastings observes with regard to this passage in its original context applies as much to its application for theological enquiry within the Latin Catholic Church: "It would be quite impossible to find a comparable commendation of theological, or indeed ecclesiastical, pluralism coming from pre-conciliar Rome. It should be linked with the equally remarkable assertion that there exists within doctrine 'a hierarchy of truths' (UR 11)."[41]

Later, the magisterium/theologians principle will highlight how the council's greater appreciation of culture (AG 22) brought to the foreground the

---

39. Emphasis added.

40. Translation corrected. Emphasis added. Jacques Dupuis sees such statements as not only conciliar acknowledgment of theological diversity but indeed of "dogmatic pluralism." See Dupuis, "Unity of Faith and Dogmatic Pluralism."

41. Hastings, "The Key Texts," 59–60.

indispensable role of local theologians. But, beyond the letter of its final texts, an equally compelling *symbolic* teaching Vatican II gives with regard to unity/diversity in theological expression is the creative dynamic at work in the conciliar process itself. We have already seen that the history of the debates and the conciliar documents themselves attest to a diversity of theological views within the conciliar assembly. This diversity is paralleled in the theological approaches of the *periti* advising the bishops, both as personal advisors and as official consultants on the various drafting committees. Those *periti* with a historical consciousness helped the bishops become more aware of a diachronic diversity in Catholic liturgical, canonical, and theological traditions. In the end, both by means of this conciliar dynamic and through the references to diversity in the final documents, the council affirms unity/diversity in theological expression, as the *peritus* Bonaventure Kloppenburg remarks:

> The Council rejects the idea of a single theology that is ready made, already formulated, definitive, and perennial. It is not enough to repeat what was said and to use the formulations of even the most eminent and distinguished theologians or Doctors of the Church or even of the ordinary and extraordinary Magisterium. The theologian who is satisfied to be a simple repeater or passer-on of traditional theses and doctrines, in their traditional formulation, does not deserve his title or fulfill his duty. With all desirable clarity the Council affirms that within the unity of the Church a theological pluralism ("different methods and ways of understanding and expressing the divine mysteries") is not only possible but legitimate and necessary in view of the catholicity and apostolicity proper to the Church.[42]

The issue of unity/diversity came to the fore in a particular way in the conciliar debate on collegiality. After the council, the *peritus* Karl Rahner, in writing "on the divine right of the episcopacy," highlighted the implications for asserting what he calls the divine right of diversity in the faith.[43] Ladislas Örsy summarizes Rahner's argument: "that by divine right there ought to be unity and diversity in the church, and that while the papacy is the principle of unity, the episcopal college is the representative and guardian of diversity. . . . By divine law, the Christian community must have its unity; by

---

42. Kloppenburg, *The Ecclesiology of Vatican II*, 145–46. Kloppenburg refers here to UR 17.
43. Karl Rahner, "On the Divine Right of the Episcopate," in *The Episcopate and the Primacy*, ed. Karl Rahner and Joseph Ratzinger (London: Burns & Oates, 1962), 64–135.

the same divine law, it must have diversity."[44] As *Lumen Gentium* affirms: "[The college of bishops], in so far as it is composed of many members, is the expression of the variety [*varietatem*] and universality [*universalitatem*] of the people of God; and of the unity of the flock of Christ, in so far as it is assembled under one head" (LG 22). The *peritus* Joseph Ratzinger, configuring the issue in terms of unity and plurality, characterized the very essence of the church as embracing both. Concerning "the central idea in the Council's doctrine of collegiality," Ratzinger wrote during the council of "the problem of centralism": "The unifying papal office remains in principle undiminished [by the teaching on collegiality], although it is seen now more clearly in its proper context. The function of the office is not monarchic rule, but rather coordination of the *plurality* which belongs to the Church's essence."[45] Moreover, he continues, "the *plurality* of the various bishops' Churches belongs essentially to the unity of the Church. This plurality constitutes the inner structure of the one Church."[46]

Each of the three principles enunciated in these last three chapters (particular/universal, *communio/missio*, unity/diversity) complements the other two and yet stands in tension with them, as do the two terms that make up each of the principles. While the two terms of each principle are to be understood as balancing one another, the council did make significant shifts toward retrieving a Catholic balance: toward a greater appreciation of the local churches, toward a more evangelical understanding of its mission, toward a greater sense of Catholic diversity.

It was precisely in these conciliar shifts that Karl Rahner came to recognize the basic historical-theological innovation the council was deliberately embracing: "The Second Vatican Council is the beginning of a tentative approach by the Church to the discovery and official realization of itself as *world-Church*."[47] This marks an epochal change, whose historic importance

44. Ladislas Örsy, "Episcopal Conferences: *Communio* among the Bishops," in *Receiving the Council: Theological and Canonical Insights and Debates* (Collegeville, MN: Liturgical Press, 2009), 16–34, at 32.

45. Ratzinger, *Theological Highlights of Vatican II*, 138.

46. Ibid.

47. Rahner, "Basic Theological Interpretation," 78.

can be compared only to the transition from a Palestinian Christianity to a Hellenistic Christianity, which endured until the eve of the council.

As Rahner also observed, however, "it cannot be denied that the actualization of the Church's nature as world-Church was manifested at the Council only in a very rudimentary way and hesitatingly. Nor can it be concealed that there are movements in the opposite direction."[48] Certainly postconciliar reception of these three principles has been partial and has seen "movements in the opposite direction." Twenty years after the council, the 1985 International Synod of Bishops met to review the reception of the council over that time. Attending the synod in his capacity as the president of the episcopal conference in Australia, Archbishop Francis Rush, who had been a participant throughout Vatican II's four sessions, addressed the synod on what he saw as the inadequate reception of the council's teachings concerning collegiality, local churches, subsidiarity, and diversity:

> The question of collegiality and the relationship of the local church to the universal church are major internal questions, which are causing sufficient anxiety and wasting enough energy to distract the church from what should be its major concerns. . . . Diversity among the local churches and the principle of subsidiarity argue that local solutions should be found for local problems, as long as these solutions do not jeopardise the unity of the local churches with and under the Holy Father. Bishops and theologians sometimes get the impression that their orthodoxy is questioned lightly and that their difficulties and industry are not appreciated. This leads to a loss of trust, which only damages the church. . . . We see the need for an even more refined theology, and more effective use, of episcopal conferences.[49]

The next principle, the *ad intra/ad extra* principle, captures the desire of the council for reform of relationships within its internal life, so that its proclamation of the Gospel to those outside the church will be credible.

48. Ibid., 79.
49. Francis Rush, "Speech at the 1985 Extraordinary Synod of Bishops, Rome, 27 November 1985," in *Life to Me Is Christ: Selected Talks and Homilies of Archbishop Francis Rush*, ed. Ormond Rush and Mary Coman (Strathfield, NSW: St Pauls Publications, 2010), 92–94, at 92–93.

Principle 17

Ad Intra/Ad Extra

Principle 17: Pastoral renewal of the church's inner life is to be undertaken for the sake of a more effective witness by the church in the world; the church must renew the way it is present in the world so that it might more faithfully reflect the face of God.

The phrase *ecclesia ad intra* (literally, "the church within") refers to "the internal life of the church"; the phrase *ecclesia ad extra* (literally, "the church beyond") refers to "the relationship of the church to the religious and secular worlds beyond it," as well as to the created world of "the environment," the "cosmos."[1] The *ad intra/ad extra* principle encapsulates two interrelated aspects of the renewal and reform agenda of the council: inner pastoral renewal and reform is to be undertaken for the sake of a more effective witness *ad extra* by the church; conversely, a new understanding of how the church should conduct itself in the world must lead to a renewed understanding of how its inner life should be conducted, if its witness *ad extra* is to be credible. The *ad intra/ad extra* principle, while overlapping in certain ways with the *communio/missio* principle, requires separate articulation. The former relates to the tenor of relationships within the church and the church's relationships to the world "around" it; the latter relates to the church's "nature and universal mission" (LG 1).

The distinction between the church *ad intra* and the church *ad extra* was suggested during Vatican II in a plan proposed by Cardinal Léon-Joseph Suenens, first to Pope John XXIII and then in a speech to the council assembly, as a way of guiding and integrating the council's further work.[2] By

---

1. For these translations and definitions, see McBrien, *The Church*, 164.

2. For Suenens's own reflections on the plan, see Léon-Joseph Cardinal Suenens, "A Plan for the Whole Council," in *Vatican II: By Those Who Were There*, ed. Alberic Stacpoole (London: Geoffrey Chapman, 1986), 88–105. For a detailed study of the stages of Suenens's contri-

the end of the first session, the bishops had become aware not only of the inadequacy of the preparatory *De Ecclesia* schema but also of the fact that no document had yet been promulgated in the first session—and there were still more than seventy schemas to be discussed, many of which seemed disconnected from each other. On December 4, 1962, a few days before the session was due to end, Suenens proposed his plan in a speech to the assembly.[3] The council, he said, should indeed be a council on the church, but should divide its work, focusing first on the church's inner life (the church *ad intra*), and then on the church in relation to the world in which it lives out its mission (the church *ad extra*).

Seeing their value for realistically structuring the council's further work, the council adopted both the distinction and Suenens's plan (though not all elements of the plan would be incorporated into the council's agenda). When in late December 1962 a new Coordinating Commission was set up to give the council's work more precise direction, the influence of Cardinal Suenens among the bishops led to acceptance of his *ad intra/ad extra* distinction. The commission decided that these two dimensions of the church should be addressed in two separate documents. These eventually became a much-revised *De Ecclesia* (finally *Lumen Gentium*) and Schema XVII (later Schema XIII, and finally *Gaudium et Spes*). Accordingly, the *ad intra/ad extra* principle highlights the importance of keeping the two constitutions in intertextual dialogue, if the council's full vision for the church is to be appreciated. The mystery of the church includes both dimensions. In many respects, the focus of *Lumen Gentium* is indeed *ad intra*, although it does have its *ad extra* elements; likewise, the focus of *Gaudium et Spes* is indeed *ad extra*, although it does have its *ad intra* elements. Therefore, both constitutions must be taken as precisely that: "constitutive" for understanding the nature and mission of the church. Moreover, given the council's overall pastoral orientation, *Lumen Gentium* too is to be interpreted in a pastoral way, just as *Gaudium et Spes* has doctrinal-dogmatic elements, as the council's footnote to the title indicates.[4]

---

bution to refining the agenda of the council, see Mathijs Lamberigts and Leo Declerck, "The Role of Cardinal Léon-Joseph Suenens at Vatican II," in *The Belgian Contribution to the Second Vatican Council*, ed. Doris Donnelly, et al. (Leuven: Peeters, 2008), 61–217, at 66–89.

3. AS I/4, 222–227. On the significance of Suenens's speech, see Ruggieri, "Beyond an Ecclesiology of Polemics," 343–44; O'Malley, *What Happened at Vatican II*, 157–58.

4. As was noted above, that *Gaudium et Spes* is promulgated one year after *Lumen Gentium* means that it is a later product of a conciliar assembly that was growing in its understanding of itself and its vision. Furthermore, that *Gaudium et Spes* is a "pastoral" constitution is not to

By the end of the council, the major contribution of the *ad intra/ad extra* distinction would be that it refashioned the church's imagination with regard to the world around it and those who were previously deemed to be the church's opponents. Certainly, in retrospect, a disadvantage of the distinction was that it was "not very rigorous theologically."[5] For example, the distinction could lead to a dichotomizing of what are two "movements" of the one ecclesial reality—the church's inwardly directed and outwardly directed energies: being drawn together by God as a community of faith to be nourished by word and sacrament, and being sent out by God into the world "outside" to proclaim the God of Jesus Christ. A similar danger was that of separating the action of God within the church from the activity of God in the world. Moreover, the distinction could be interpreted as fostering a dichotomy between "the doctrinal" and "the pastoral."[6] Such weaknesses in the distinction did lead to tensions in the later council debates, opening up problems in the postconciliar reception.[7] Nevertheless, the distinction did have its value, and, because it names an important structuring principle for the council's work, it is necessary to formulate it as a separate principle in the council's final vision.

The word *rapprochement* (reconciliation) has been used to name the shift in attitude the council made with regard to its self-understanding of the church in its *ad intra* and *ad extra* relationships. For Massimo Faggioli, "*The basic motion* of Vatican II [is] *rapprochement* inside and outside the Church. *Rapprochement*—a term used many times by the pioneer of ecumenism and liturgist Dom Lambert Beauduin—is not part of the corpus of Vatican II in

---

be used to downgrade its authority; the principle of "pastorality," according to Theobald, is the primary key for interpreting the whole council.

5. Ruggieri, "Beyond an Ecclesiology of Polemics," 344.

6. According to Christoph Theobald, in reference to the acceptance of Suenens's distinction: "With hindsight, there is no denying that the planning of the work of the Council and the span of reception of the 'pastorality' principle became separated from that moment." Theobald, "The Theological Options of Vatican II," 90.

7. Christopher Ruddy, for example, remarks: "Despite *Lumen Gentium*'s clear statement in its first paragraph that it seeks to set forth teaching on 'the nature of the Church and its universal mission,' it must be admitted that it did so insufficiently. One sees here the limits of the distinction drawn by Cardinal Suenens of Belgium and adopted by the Council, between the Church *ad intra* and the church *ad extra*. *Lumen Gentium*, however unwittingly, became the *ad intra* document and *Gaudium et Spes* the *ad extra* one—a bifurcation that has had harmful theological and pastoral effect, not least when some Catholics call themselves '*Lumen Gentium* Catholics' or '*Gaudium et Spes* Catholics.' This kind of polarization or ecclesial schizophrenia needs to be overcome." Ruddy, "'In my end is my beginning': *Lumen Gentium* and the Priority of Doxology," 150.

a material way, but it belongs fully to the aims of Vatican II."[8] Others have interpreted this *rapprochement* as more a naïve capitulation to relativism and the principles of Modernity.[9] A comprehensive interpretation of the conciliar debates and of its final documents (despite their tensions) does not support such an interpretation. For the council, the ultimate standard to be held was always—clearly—the Gospel of Jesus Christ, as *Gaudium et Spes* strongly proclaims. What the council deliberately wanted to change was the adversarial stance that had for centuries characterized the church's efforts to uphold the truth of the Gospel. Faggioli's application of the word *rapprochement* to renewal in both *ad intra* and *ad extra* relationships is helpful: according to Vatican II, this confrontational approach must be abandoned, both in relationships within the church as well as with those outside.

A key catalyst, of course, for this remarkable change of tone was the pope who called the council, John XXIII, as tellingly expressed in his opening address of October 11, 1962:

> Nowadays, however, the Spouse of Christ prefers to make use of the medicine of mercy rather than that of severity. She considers that she meets the needs of the present day by demonstrating the validity of her teaching rather than by condemnations. . . . That being so, the Catholic Church, raising the torch of religious truth by means of this Ecumenical Council, desires to show herself to be the loving mother of all, benign, patient, full of mercy and goodness toward the brethren who are separated from her. To mankind, oppressed by so many difficulties, the Church says, as Peter said to the poor who begged alms from him: "I have neither gold nor silver, but what I have I give to you; in the name of Jesus Christ of Nazareth, rise and walk" (Acts 3:6).[10]

John O'Malley's well-known thesis asserts that the fundamental aim of Vatican II was to change "the style" of the church, in both its inner life and its outer life. He sees this as a fundamental shift, from the style of Tridentine Catholicism and of "the long nineteenth century" leading up to the council, to a new way of being church.[11] His litany of shifts captures the envisioned change of style *ad intra* and *ad extra*: "from commands to invitations, from

---

8. Faggioli, *True Reform*, 17. Emphasis added.

9. See, for example, the discussion of Joseph Ratzinger's approach in McEvoy, *Leaving Christendom for Good*, 143–61.

10. John XXIII, "Pope John's Opening Speech," 716.

11. On the style of Catholicism in the 150 years leading up to Vatican II, see O'Malley, *What Happened at Vatican II*, 53–92.

laws to ideals, from definition to mystery, from threats to persuasion, from coercion to conscience, from monologue to dialogue, from ruling to serving, from withdrawn to integrated, from vertical to horizontal, from exclusion to inclusion, from hostility to friendship, from rivalry to partnership, from suspicion to trust, from static to ongoing, from passive acceptance to active engagement, from fault-finding to appreciation, from prescriptive to principled, from behavior modification to inner appropriation."[12]

A key word in O'Malley's list is "dialogue." It became an important leitmotif during the council for enunciating the *ad intra/ad extra* principle.[13] Cardinal Suenens had spoken of dialogue in his programmatic speech at the end of the first session. Pope Paul VI gave it great prominence in his encyclical *Ecclesiam Suam*.[14] One of the key *periti* who helped incorporate the notion into *Gaudium et Spes* was Marie-Dominique Chenu. He believed in giving dialogue "its whole wealth of meaning: recognition of the other as other, loving others as they are and not as people to be won over, accepting that they are different from me, without trying to encroach on their consciences and on their searching, without asserting my reservations before I give my trust."[15]

---

12. Ibid., 307.

13. Regarding the emergence of the two motifs "signs of the times" and "dialogue" in the various drafts of *Gaudium et Spes*, McEvoy notes: "The period from the preparation for the third session of the council in December 1963 until the end of the fourth session in December 1965 was the most significant for the development of *Gaudium et Spes*. During this time two concepts emerged which are fundamental to the final document's articulation of the church-world relationship. The relationship was conceived of in terms of both dialogue and of the church reading the 'signs of the times.' . . . Both concepts are found in the Zürich schema written from January 1964 and the Ariccia schema written from February 1965. Yet the theme of the signs of the times plays a larger role in the later draft, while the theme of dialogue has a stronger place in the earlier. Although these concepts have the capacity to elicit quite different images of the church's action in the world . . . they neatly cohere in *Gaudium et Spes* to form a single model of the church's relationship with the world." McEvoy, *Leaving Christendom for Good*, 72.

14. Pope Paul VI, "Ecclesiam Suam," in *The Papal Encyclicals*, vol. 5: *1958–1981*, ed. Claudia Carlen (Wilmington, NC: McGrath Publishing Company, 1981), 135–60. On the impact of *Ecclesiam Suam* on the council, see Vilanova, "The Intersession (1963–1964)," 448–57. According to Giuseppe Alberigo, "the importance and relevance of an attitude of dialogue was to be a main focus of Montini's pontificate. . . . But while Paul VI's appraisal of the contemporary world was sympathetic, it was primarily critical. Consequently, the dialogue represented an attitude of openness but not necessarily of agreement or brotherliness." Alberigo, "Transition to a New Age," 589–90.

15. Quoted in Alberigo, "Transition to a New Age," 589n37.

Across the documents, the council uses two Latin words, *colloquium* and *dialogus*.[16] The first instances of these words occur in *Unitatis Redintegratio*, promulgated at the end of the third session. All documents promulgated after that have at least one dialogue word. Strikingly, then, *Lumen Gentium* nowhere uses the precise words *colloquium* or *dialogus* to speak of a new kind of relating within the church, a point that highlights the importance of reading both church constitutions intertextually when understanding the *ad intra/ad extra* principle. The most references to dialogue appear in three documents: the ecumenism decree and the two documents published on the last day of the council, *Ad Gentes* and *Gaudium et Spes* (which has the most of all).[17]

For James McEvoy, "dialogue is [*Gaudium et Spes*'s] fundamental metaphor in interpreting the church-world relationship."[18] *Gaudium et Spes* 92 can be taken as representative of the spirit of *rapprochement* envisaged by the council's use of the dialogue metaphor. The article ends the constitution with a programmatic vision, employing both terms *dialogus* and *colloquium* synonymously. After stating that the church is to be "a sign of that amity which renders possible sincere dialogue [*dialogum*] and strengthens it," the article reverses the order in which *Ecclesiam Suam* had addressed the same "series of concentric circles" of dialogue.[19] Rather, the pastoral constitution states that dialogue begins at home; the first circle of dialogue must be dialogue *ad intra*: "[The church's] mission requires us first of all to create in the church itself mutual esteem, reverence and harmony, and to acknowledge all legitimate diversity; in this way all who constitute the one People of God will be able to engage in ever more fruitful dialogue [*colloquium*] whether they are pastors or other members of the faithful. For the ties which unite the faithful together are stronger than those which separate them: let there be unity in what is necessary, freedom in what is doubtful, and charity in everything" (GS 92).[20] Then the dialogue turns *ad extra*. Dialogue with the church's "others" radiates out like concentric circles of engagement with a divided world: dialogue with other Christian churches and ecclesial communities; dialogue with followers

---

16. For an analysis of the notion and the words for "dialogue" in the documents, see Nolan, *A Privileged Moment: Dialogue in the Language of the Second Vatican Council, 1962–1965*, 177–223.

17. See ibid., 180–81.

18. McEvoy, *Leaving Christendom for Good*, 74.

19. *Ecclesiam Suam* 96. On the four circles, see ibid., 96–117.

20. The constitution is here quoting John XXIII, Encyclical *Ad Petri Cathedram*, June 29, 1959. AAS 55 (1959): 513.

of other religions; and dialogue with all humanity, "leading to truth by way of love alone" (GS 92).

In this desire to distance itself from a previous ecclesial style both *ad intra* and *ad extra*, it could be said that the council was wanting the church itself to embrace and to manifest—as *ecclesial virtues*—the "human virtues" it would seek, for example, from its priests:

> Priests will be helped to achieve this [i.e., a more effective proclamation of the Gospel] by cultivating those qualities which are rightly held in high esteem in human relations, qualities such as goodness of heart, sincerity, strength and constancy of mind, careful attention to justice, courtesy [*urbanitas*] and others which the apostle Paul recommends when he says: "Whatever is true, whatever is honorable, whatever is just, whatever is pure, whatever is lovely, whatever is gracious, if there is any excellence, if there is anything worthy of praise, think about these things." (*Presbyterorum Ordinis* 3)[21]

In colloquial terms, it seems that Vatican II wanted to remove the scowl from the face of the church of centuries past and present a smile to the world, and even shed a tear in solidarity with the "griefs and anxieties" of all humanity (GS 1). The ideal was that "the face of the church" should reflect "the light of Christ" (LG 1) to the world. In other words, Vatican II wanted to change the church's tone of voice, remove the harshness of previous centuries, and speak and relate in a gentler, more pastoral, indeed more Christlike manner.

Richard Gaillardetz has summarized the conciliar vision in this regard as the church embracing a "noncompetitive" understanding of its relationships *ad intra* and *ad extra*.[22] Principles 18, 19, 20, and 21 below will explore the *ad intra* implications of the council's trajectory toward a noncompetitive vision. Principles 22, 23, and 24 then will further explore the hints that Gaillardetz gives as to the application of the notion of noncompetitiveness to the church's *ad extra* relationships.[23] In these *ad extra* relationships, the council above all wanted to seek *rapprochement* with those long perceived as adversaries—the Jewish people; the separated churches of the East; the separated ecclesial communities of the sixteenth-century Reformations in the West;

---

21. The council is here quoting Phil 4:8. See also the reference to the "human virtues" in *Optatam Totius* 11, which alludes to the human virtues, and lists them as "sincerity of spirit, constant concern for justice, fidelity to one's promises, courtesy in behaviour, and modesty and charity in speech."

22. Gaillardetz, *An Unfinished Council*, 91–113.

23. Ibid., 113.

"Modernity," modern science, or many of the movements included in Pope Pius IX's *Syllabus of Errors*.[24] As Joseph Ratzinger observes, which the church/world principle below will treat in greater detail, Vatican II proposes nothing less than "a revision of the Syllabus of Pius IX, a kind of countersyllabus."[25] In the striking image of John O'Malley: "Liberty, equality, and fraternity as well as other formerly unwelcome guests knocked at the door [of Vatican II] and gained entrance to the feast."[26]

One decisive shift the council made in its self-understanding *ad extra* was the new way Vatican II conceived the relationship between church and state. Here the shift was one more of critical distance than of *rapprochement*. The complex history of the church-state relationship reached back to the era of Emperor Constantine in the fourth century. With Vatican II, no longer did the council see that the church should marry the state or that the desired outcome was the baptism of every person on the planet. Regarding this dramatic shift after at least a millennium, James McEvoy writes of the council's desire for "leaving Christendom for good,"[27] recognizing that the Gospel demands a critical distance between church and state and that witness and persuasion rather than edict and force must now characterize proclamation of the Gospel. Moving away from the church's intransigent position of "error has no rights," the council's *Dignitatis Humanae*, along with *Gaudium et Spes*, proclaim the right of all to religious freedom, based on the human dignity and conscience of all. Moreover, after centuries of resisting the reality of a changed world and persistent clinging to a medieval worldview, "the church came to accept the practices and institutions of modernity."[28] In this way, *Gaudium et Spes* sounds the death-knell of "the project of Christendom."[29]

In terms of *rapprochement* rather than an adversarial stance in relationships *ad extra*, Vatican II envisages two clusters of relationships. The first is *rapprochement* between church and *world*, between church and *Modernity*, between church and *culture*, which the faith/history principle has already begun to explore. The second cluster of relationships concerns *rapprochement* between the church and particular groups in society: between the church and the Jewish people, between the church and other Christian churches and

24. See Denzinger, *Compendium of Creeds, Definitions, and Declarations*, nos. 2901–80.
25. Ratzinger, "Church and World," 381.
26. O'Malley, *What Happened at Vatican II*, 306.
27. See the title of, and throughout, McEvoy, *Leaving Christendom for Good*.
28. Ibid., 170.
29. Ibid., xii.

communities, between the church and other religions, between the church and nonbelievers, between the church and those hostile to it, and indeed between the church and the world. The council's vision regarding both clusters of relationship will be further articulated in principles 22, 23, and 24.

In terms of *rapprochement* rather than an adversarial stance in relationships *ad intra*, principles 18–21 will explore the relationships between the whole community of faith of the Catholic Church and the individual believer; between the entire people of God within the Catholic Church and the hierarchy within it which serves it; between the college of bishops and the Bishop of Rome; and between the magisterium and theologians. In all of these relationships Vatican II envisioned a new style of relating, so the church would be a more credible sign in the world. It is to these intra-ecclesial relationships that we now turn.

Principle 18
Fideles/Fidelis

Principle 18: Through faith and baptism, a Christian is incorporated into the *communio fidelium* and called to participate fully in the mission of the church by participating in the threefold office of Christ; all the faithful have an equal dignity and a common call to holiness, each contributing to the life of the community *ad intra* and its mission *ad extra* through their holiness, their sense of the faith, their charisms, and their specific ministry.

The *fideles/fidelis* principle is a corollary of the primary principle of the vision of Vatican II, the revelation/faith principle: the primary identity of the Christian is one who believes in God and responds in faith to God's loving outreach to humanity in Jesus Christ through the Holy Spirit. This *fideles/fidelis* principle thus brings to the fore the fundamental identity of the church as a community of the *fideles* and, consequently, the proper ordering of the three dimensions of ecclesial *communio* highlighted in the *communio/missio* principle: the church is, before all else, a *communio fidelium*—a communion of those who believe in Jesus Christ through the Holy Spirit. The *fideles/fidelis* principle is also to be understood in tandem with the one that follows, the people of God/hierarchy principle. If this current principle names the common identity of everyone in the church (as outlined in chapter 2 of *Lumen Gentium*, as well as in chapter 5 regarding their common call to holiness), then the next principle—accordingly—brings to synthesis chapters 2 and 3 of *Lumen Gentium*, a synthesis that, for various reasons, remains undeveloped in the final text of the Dogmatic Constitution.

There are two aspects to the *fideles/fidelis* principle: the significance that all believers have a shared dignity as disciples of Jesus Christ, as *Christifideles*, and the importance of the single believer within the community of all believers.

A Copernican Revolution

The first aspect of this principle is the council's affirmation of the shared dignity and consequent equality of all the baptized in the church, regardless of charisms and ministries. In deliberately moving away from the vision of church depicted in the preparatory schema *De Ecclesia*, one of the most consequential decisions of Vatican II was *not* to view the church primarily from the perspective of the pope and the bishops, the so-called pyramidal vision of the church.[1]

After the assembly's virtual rejection of the preparatory schema on the church at the end of the first session, the Coordinating Commission organized the drafting of a new version. From several unofficial texts already in circulation, the commission selected, and then refined, a text largely penned by the Belgian *peritus* Gérard Philips.[2] This version would become the basic text to be submitted to the council and consisted of only four chapters: (1) the mystery of the church; (2) the hierarchical constitution of the church, in particular the episcopate; (3) the people of God, especially the laity; (4) the universal vocation to holiness and the religious. At the Coordinating Commission's third meeting on July 4 and 5, 1963, Cardinal Suenens presented a report on the current state of the drafting process of the constitution on the church. He then suggested a change to the text that was being tabled: that the then-third chapter in this draft be split into two separate chapters, one on the people of God and one on the laity; moreover, he suggested that the resulting new chapter on the people of God as a whole should precede that on the hierarchy. His reason: what is common to all should be treated before what differentiates. "This change was accepted at once almost unanimously."[3] According to Mathijs Lamberigts and Leo Declerck, it was Suenens's assis-

---

1. This image of the pyramid has become common for describing preconciliar ecclesiology. As Bonaventure Kloppenburg summarizes the notion: "We have been used to thinking of the Church as a pyramid: at the top, the pope, bishops, and priests, who preside, teach, sanctify, and govern, possessed of authority and power; at the base, the Christian people, passive recipients who seem to occupy a clearly inferior and secondary place." Kloppenburg, *The Ecclesiology of Vatican II*, 311.

2. Philips's draft had been chosen from several others which had been in circulation after the clear desire to not accept the original preparatory *De Ecclesia* in December 1962. For some of the alternative texts proposed in turn over December 1962 and January 1963 (by the German, Chilean, Italian, and French bishops and *periti*), see Alberigo and Magistretti, *Constitutionis Dogmaticae Lumen Gentium*, 381–428.

3. Philips, "Dogmatic Constitution on the Church: History of the Constitution," 110.

tant, the Belgian *peritus* and rector of the Belgian College in Rome, Albert Prignon, who had earlier made these suggestions to Suenens.[4]

When the council opened for its second session a few months later in 1963, this basic text was put to the bishops for approval and was adopted as the *textus receptus* (the base text) for ongoing discussion. The council deliberated on the document for the next four weeks. At this stage, Suenens's suggestion regarding a new chapter and its placement had yet to be officially endorsed. Among the speakers when debate opened on September 30, 1963, was the bishop of Bolzano-Bressanone, Giuseppe Gargitter. He proposed that the chapter on "the People of God and especially the laity" be divided up, with the general material on the people of God in a new chapter to be located before that on the hierarchy; then, after the hierarchy chapter, there should be a chapter specifically on the laity. This was more or less the same restructure that Suenens had suggested earlier in July to the Coordinating Commission.[5] After two weeks of intense debate on the chapter on the hierarchy, the next two weeks were then devoted to the chapter on "the People of God and especially the laity" (still, at this stage, chapter 3). Other bishops requested that in the next version of the document, a chapter on the people of God as a whole be placed before that on the hierarchy. There was "fairly general agreement" among the assembly that the change should take place.[6] The revised version, presented to the council for debate the following session in 1964, had the chapters in the new ordering. When the content of this

4. It seems that the idea of a chapter on the whole church before one on the hierarchy had also been raised in other quarters, as Lamberigts and Declerck acknowledge: "This idea had indeed been suggested in the circles of the Secretariat for the Unity (cf. e.g. the letter from Thijssen to Thils and the letter from Bea to Döpfner on January 23, 1963: 'In Sectio II [of the text Philips, by Bea indicated as the text De Smedt] wäre m.E. nicht an erster Stelle die Hierarchie zu setzen, sondern die "Fideles," und zwar nicht nur die "laici," sondern das ganze Kirchenvolk.') Still the credit for suggesting this at a crucial moment must go to Prignon." Lamberigts and Declerck, "The Role of Cardinal Léon-Joseph Suenens at Vatican II," 103n210. The sentence in German reads: "In Section II . . . it would be better in my opinion not to put the hierarchy in the first place, but the 'Fideles', namely, not only the 'laici', but the whole church people."

5. Alberto Melloni notes that, although Suenens had already made the proposal back in July of that year, Gargitter's intervention was significant: "But it was only *after* the Bishop of Bolzano (who always maintained that he had not spoken with others) made his intervention in St Peter's that this proposal, rich in systematic value and doctrinal importance, was put on the agenda again and became a reality." Alberto Melloni, "The Beginning of the Second Period: The Great Debate on the Church," in *History of Vatican II*, vol. 3: *The Mature Council; Second Period and Intersession, September 1963–September 1964*, ed. Giuseppe Alberigo and Joseph A. Komonchak (Maryknoll, NY: Orbis Books, 1998), 3:1–115, at 44. Original emphasis.

6. Philips, "Dogmatic Constitution on the Church: History of the Constitution," 119.

chapter 2 on the people of God was then debated, it was more or less accepted without major controversy.

This change in chapter order arguably constitutes one of the most significant shifts in the history of Vatican II. When compared with the dominant self-understanding characterizing the church across the whole of the second millennium, the change constitutes nothing less than a reconfiguration of the Catholic imagination regarding the nature of the church. As Jan Grootaers remarks: "The restructuring meant a fundamental reorientation of ecclesiology that would put an end to the pyramidal vision of the Church. It showed that bishops, laity, and religious were all part of the people of God, the description of which took precedence over the chapter on the episcopate. The first two chapters laid the foundations for membership in the Church in a spiritual dimension in which all members are equal by reason of their baptism, prior to any differentiation by the functions described in the next two chapters."[7] Yves Congar saw the structural change as highly significant: "We believe that this decision was one of the most important made, and that chapter 2 on the People of God, as it was finally drawn up and voted by the assembly, has the greatest promise for the theological, pastoral and ecumenical future of ecclesiology."[8] Likewise, for the *peritus* Charles Moeller, the change "was a stroke of genius; this produced the first of the Copernican revolutions which marked the elaboration of the Constitution."[9] Consequently, in the intratextual and intertextual interpretation of *Lumen Gentium* and of the documents derived from it, overall hermeneutical priority is to be given to the fundamental revisioning of the church conveyed by this radical structural change.

Lumen Gentium's chapter 2 on the people of God (art. 9–17) lays out the fundamental identity and mission of all in the church, no matter what their charism or ministry. Yves Congar highlights the significance of the chapter's placement: "Indeed *what is common to all* is nothing less than Christian existence. Under these conditions, the Council committed itself not only to giving at least a quick look at what a Christian man is, but to recognizing the priority and even the primacy of the ontology of grace, which makes a man

---

7. Jan Grootaers, "The Drama Continues between the Acts: The 'Second Preparation' and Its Opponents," in *History of Vatican II*, vol. 2: *The Formation of the Council's Identity; First Period and Intercession, October 1962–September 1963*, ed. Giuseppe Alberigo and Joseph A. Komonchak (Maryknoll, NY: Orbis Books, 1997), 2:359–514, at 411.

8. Congar, "The People of God," 197.

9. Moeller, "History of *Lumen Gentium*'s Structure and Ideas," 127–28.

Christian, over organizational structures and hierarchical positions."[10] Throughout Christian history, the term "the people" had often been used to name "the laity," "the faithful" other than the pope, bishops, priests, and religious. The bishops at Vatican II, however, use the terms "people" and "the faithful" in chapter 2, and in all its documents, to refer to all the baptized in the church, "from the bishops to the last of the lay faithful [*ab episcopis usque ad extremos laicos fideles*]" (LG 12).[11]

Tellingly, the chapter does not name that common status of all the faithful as the "lay" state. The terms "layperson" (*laicus*) or "laity" (*laicatus*) do not appear at all in *Lumen Gentium* chapter 2 in reference to this common status of the *fideles* making up the people of God. There is the one instance of *laicus*, but only in the direct quote from St. Augustine referring to laypeople among the entire church: "from the bishops to the last of the lay faithful" (LG 12).[12] Chapter 4 of *Lumen Gentium* will go on to focus on laypersons (*laici*) in particular (as chapter 3 does of bishops, priests, and deacons in particular). But—equally as telling—the chapter on the laity describes the apostolate of the *laici* simply in terms of what has already been laid out in chapter 2 regarding *all individuals* in the church and, indeed, of *the church as a whole*.

> The term "layman," as understood in chapter 4 of *Lumen Gentium*, is *a further specification of a wider and more general term*: "Christian," "believer," "member of the people of God." Before someone is looked upon as either layman or deacon or priest or bishop or even pope, he should be considered first of all as a Christian or member of God's people. These terms express the *basic condition*, the *primal state*, the *common element*, the *most important aspect*, indeed the very reason why there exists a divine plan for the human creature. It is in this *common foundation* on which all else rests, that the greatness, dignity, and newness brought by Christ properly reside. Without it we would be nothing, whether we happened to be pope, bishop, priest, deacon, or layman.[13]

What Kloppenburg here calls "the basic condition," "the primal state," "the common element," "the most important aspect," or the "common foundation," and what Congar calls "what is common to all,"[14] Kenan Osborne calls "the

10. Congar, "The People of God," 198.
11. Translation corrected. The council is here quoting St. Augustine, *De Praed. Sanct.* 14, 27: PL 44, 980. Tanner has "faithful laity."
12. Translation corrected.
13. Kloppenburg, *The Ecclesiology of Vatican II*, 309–10. Emphasis added.
14. Congar, "The People of God," 198.

common matrix for all Christians."[15] The chapter following that on the people of God will go on to speak of the role of the hierarchy *within* the people of God in terms of *service* to the people of God.

Lumen Gentium and the other documents use several overlapping terms to refer to all baptized members of the church: *populus* (the people), *fideles* (the faithful), *Christifideles* (the Christian faithful), *Christiani* (Christians), *credentes* (believers), *discipuli* (disciples), *baptizati* (the baptized). Of those synonyms used to name the individuals within the people of God, that of *fidelis* is the most used, the singular and plural noun being found 249 times across all the documents.[16] The title of *Lumen Gentium*'s second chapter uses the term *populus Dei*.[17] The word *populus* appears 282 times throughout the conciliar documents and is Vatican II's most used term for the church; the terms are interchangeable: "the church or the People of God" (LG 13). The people of God are "those who believe in Christ" (LG 9), "all those, who in faith look towards Jesus" (LG 9), "the baptized" (LG 10), "all the disciples of Christ" (LG 10), "the whole body of the faithful [*universitas fidelium*]" (LG 12). *Lumen Gentium* 23 later speaks of "the whole company of the faithful [*multitudo fidelium*]." Thus the church as the people of God is a *communio fidelium* (UR 2), a communion of the *fideles*. And, in the midst of the faithful, as she did at Pentecost, stands the first among the faithful, the Virgin Mary, the church's "exemplar and outstanding model in faith and charity" (LG 53).[18]

Baptism incorporates those with faith into the people of God.[19] Baptism calls the faithful to holiness as followers of Jesus Christ in the Holy Spirit and calls them to participate in the mission of the church through participation in the three offices of Christ as priest, prophet, and king. As chapter

15. Kenan B. Osborne, *Ministry: Lay Ministry in the Roman Catholic Church, Its History and Theology* (New York: Paulist Press, 1993), 530.

16. The other nouns are less regularly used: *Christianus* (seventy-nine times); *Christifidelis* (seventy-seven times); *credens* (forty-two); *discipulus* (twenty-one times in reference to individuals in the contemporary church); *baptizati* (three times).

17. See Yves Congar, "The Church: The People of God," *Concilium* 1, no. 1 (1965): 7–19; Otto Semmelroth, "La Chiesa, nuovo populo di Dio," in *La Chiesa del Vaticano II: Studi e commenti intorno alla Costituzione dommatica 'Lumen Gentium'*, ed. Guilherme Baraúna (Firenze: Vallecchi Editore, 1965), 439–52.

18. See Jean Galot, "Maria, tipo and modello della Chiesa," in *La Chiesa del Vaticano II: Studi e commenti intorno alla Costituzione dommatica 'Lumen Gentium'*, ed. Guilherme Baraúna (Firenze: Vallecchi Editore, 1965), 1156–71.

19. On the council's theology of baptism, see Karl J. Becker, "The Teaching of Vatican II on Baptism: A Stimulus for Theology," in *Vatican II Assessment and Perspectives: Twenty-Five Years After (1962–1987)*, vol. 2, ed. René Latourelle (New York: Paulist Press, 1989), 2:47–99.

4 describes it: "All the faithful, that is, who by Baptism are incorporated into Christ, are constituted the people of God, who have been made sharers in their own way [*suo modo*] in the priestly, prophetic and kingly office of Christ and play their part in carrying out the mission of the whole Christian people in the church and in the world" (LG 31). The next chapter in this book on the people of God/hierarchy principle will examine in greater detail the council's use of the rubric of the three offices of Christ. The rubric provides a loose structure for the organization of *Lumen Gentium* chapter 2. All the faithful participate in these offices: articles 10–11 treat the priestly office; article 12 examines the prophetic office; and article 13 alludes to the kingly office and the kingdom of God.

In treating the participation of all in the priestly office, *Lumen Gentium* 10 refers to the common matrix of the people of God (including the ordained) in terms of its being a priestly people. The article makes a distinction between the "common" and "ministerial or hierarchical" priesthood: "Though they differ essentially and not only in degree [*essentia et non gradu tantum*], the *common* priesthood of the faithful and the *ministerial or hierarchical* priesthood are none the less interrelated [*ad invicem ordinantur*]; each in its own way shares in the one priesthood of Christ" (LG 10).[20] Some commentators presume that the use of the word "essence" in this passage refers to a superiority of the *ordained* over the *nonordained*.[21] As Peter De Mey notes, however, "*Lumen Gentium* 10 does not speak about the essential difference between the laity and the ordained but rather about the essential difference between *all believers* on the one hand and the *ordained believers* on the other."[22] In article 10, the referent of "the common priesthood of the faithful [*fidelium*]" is variously named as "the baptized" or "all the disciples of Christ." In other words, the participation of the whole people of God in the priestly office and

20. Emphasis added. For a detailed study of the conciliar debates surrounding the language used in this distinction, see Melvin Michalski, *The Relationship between the Universal Priesthood of the Baptized and the Ministerial Priesthood of the Ordained in Vatican II and in Subsequent Theology: Understanding "essentia et non gradu tantum," Lumen gentium no. 10* (Lewiston, NY: Mellen University Press, 1996), 11–65. See also the analysis in Jean-Pierre Torrell, *A Priestly People: Baptismal Priesthood and Priestly Ministry* (Mahwah, New Jersey: Paulist Press, 2013), 128–52.

21. Against this interpretation, Jean-Pierre Torrell remarks: "*Essentia* does not mean an essential superiority of the ministerial priesthood, but rather the opposite. It is only by a true inversion of values that certain theologians used to be able to think otherwise." Torrell, *A Priestly People*, 139.

22. Peter De Mey, "Recent Views of *Lumen Gentium*, Fifty Years after Vatican II," *Horizons* 39, no. 2 (2012): 252–81, at 262n39. Emphasis added.

the participation of the hierarchy in that office are to be "interrelated [*ad invicem ordinantur*]" (LG 10), but in a way that starts from the common matrix (as called for by the change in chapter order). Regarding the translation of the phrase *ad invicem ordinantur*, Jean-Pierre Torrell asserts: "If we translate it as 'coordinated to one another,' we readily see how the ministerial priesthood is related to the royal priesthood: It is at its service."[23]

Similarly, with regard to the other offices of Christ, "the holy People of God . . . the whole body of the faithful [*universitas fidelium*]" (LG 12) participates in the prophetic office and thereby is infallible in believing. And likewise, "all the faithful" participate in the kingly office (LG 13).[24] The words *laicus* or *laicatus* do not appear in any of these passages (except that one instance in the Augustine quote). Therefore, as Osborne observes:

> It is abundantly clear that in this entire second chapter the word "people" (Greek: *laos*) does not mean a group of people *over and against a hierarchical or clerical leadership*. . . . Clearly, the bishops at Vatican II did not have such a view of *laos*/people in mind. For them, people, *laos*, meant everyone in the church, as yet undifferentiated by such terms as cleric/non-cleric. The bishops were focusing on the common matrix, the fundamental equality and dignity of each and every follower of Jesus, not on a sector of such followers who were the "people," as distinct from a different sector of followers who were the leaders.[25]

Article 13, when addressing the catholicity of the church and alluding to the governing (kingly) office, does go on to address the unity and diversity of "duties" among the people of God:

> In virtue of this catholicity, each part contributes its own gifts to other parts and to the entire church, so that the whole and each of the parts are strengthened by the mutual communication of all [*ex omnibus invicem communicantibus*] and by the common effort to achieve fullness in unity. Hence, it is that the People of God is not only an assembly of different peoples, but in itself is made up of various ranks [*ordinibus*]. This diversity [*diversitas*] among its members is either by reason of their duties [*officia*]—some exercise the sacred ministry for the good of their brothers and sisters; or it is due to their condi-

---

23. Torrell, *A Priestly People*, 140.

24. This section of *Lumen Gentium* 13 alludes to the relation of the people of God to the kingdom of God, without direct reference to the rubric "kingly office." Later passages in the conciliar corpus, however, as we will see in the next chapter, do make the rubric explicit, and can be presumed here.

25. Osborne, *Ministry*, 531. Original emphasis.

tion and manner of life, since many enter the religious state and, in tending to sanctity by the narrower way, stimulate their brothers and sisters by their example. (LG 13)[26]

These "various ranks" and "duties" find their primary ecclesial significance in each of the faithful's participation in the common matrix. This is true not only for laypersons. Joseph Ratzinger, in discussing the council's teaching on bishops and collegiality, articulates a prior ecclesial principle that undergirds the ecclesial identity of bishops and priests:

> [The] immediate meaning [of collegiality] was that the episcopal ministry is a ministry with others. It is not that a particular bishop succeeds a particular apostle, but rather that the college of bishops is the continuation of the college of apostles. Thus one is not alone as bishop but essentially with others. That is true also of the priest. One is not alone as a priest; to become a priest means to enter into the priestly community that is united to the bishop. *Ultimately, a basic principle of Christianity itself is evident here: it is only in the community of all the brothers and sisters of Jesus Christ that one is a Christian, not otherwise.* The Council tried to convert this basic principle into a practical reality by forming organizations by means of which *the insertion of the individual into the whole became the basic rule of all ecclesial action.*[27]

This principle, here articulated as the *fideles/fidelis* principle, has consequences for the way the role of those in the hierarchy (bishops, priests, deacons) is conceived; their place in the church is not *over-against* the rest of the church but *within* the people of God, of which they are a part and which they serve, as the next chapter on the people of God/hierarchy principle will explore.

Two Approaches Juxtaposed

When it came to debating and formulating in the texts the specific identity of the layperson, in *Lumen Gentium* chapter 4 and *Apostolicam Actuositatem*, the council did not arrive at a systematic presentation of its vision. In the final texts, there are fundamentally two approaches juxtaposed, albeit with a dominant trajectory emerging from the texts: one, the remnant of a theology that would want to place the chapter on the hierarchy before that on the whole body of the faithful, and another that would want to reverse that order and forge a fresh vision of the layperson, the religious, and the hierarchy

---

26. Translation corrected.
27. Ratzinger, "Review of the Post-conciliar Era," 375. Emphasis added.

within the church as a whole. One reason for this final juxtaposition is that the text of some passages that had already been debated and voted on by the council did not then change after the change of chapter order. These remain embedded in the document, alongside passages written after the decision to restructure and insert a new chapter. Another reason for the remaining juxtaposition of views is that a minority of bishops who had rejected the order change continued to demand inclusion of their dichotomizing theology of ordained and laity.

Giovanni Magnani has named these two positions as a "contrasting" approach and an "intensifying" approach.[28] Richard Gaillardetz summarizes them as "contrastive" and "intensive": "The contrastive view of the laity is so named because it seeks to *contrast* the identity of the laity with that of the clergy, treating each as complementary categories in the church. . . . By 'intensive' [Magnani] means an approach that presents the laity, not as radically distinct from the clergy (or professed religious), but as *a more intensive realization of the situation of all the Christian faithful,* including those who are ordained and who belong to professed religious life."[29] This intensive understanding is similar to what we have seen Kloppenburg observe: "The term 'layman,' as understood in chapter 4 of *Lumen Gentium,* is *a further specification of a wider and more general term:* 'Christian,' 'believer,' 'member of the people of God.' "[30] It is this latter intensive view that emerges as the dominant trajectory of the two. Despite the remaining inconsistencies in the documents, "*the dynamism of the Council's thought* moved toward the identification of 'Christian' and 'layperson' and thus toward assuming as the task of the entire Church that which was held to be distinctive of the laity."[31] As Bernard Cooke observes regarding the problematic nature of the clergy/laity contrast: "Without overdramatizing the elements of opposition in this division, for a great deal of loving concern of each group for the other has been the more prominent characteristic of this relationship, it does stand as one of the major barriers to formation of a Christian community in which all have basic equality and dignity as brothers and sisters of Christ."[32] In the end,

28. Giovanni Magnani, "Does the So-Called Theology of the Laity Possess a Theological Status?," in *Vatican II Assessment and Perspectives: Twenty-Five Years After (1962–1987),* vol. 1, ed. René Latourelle (New York: Paulist Press, 1988), 1:568–633, at 611.

29. Gaillardetz, *The Church in the Making,* 54. Emphasis added.

30. Kloppenburg, *The Ecclesiology of Vatican II,* 309. Emphasis added.

31. Magnani, "Does the So-Called Theology of the Laity," 600.

32. Bernard J. Cooke, *Ministry to Word and Sacraments: History and Theology* (Philadelphia: Fortress Press, 1976), 397–98.

the council takes a fresh path. Magnani speaks of "'the novelty' of the Council as regards the laity," a novelty characterized by "the consistent manner in which the Council as a whole spoke of the laity in entirely positive terms, with clear admonitions in the text to eliminate all categorizing positions of contrast."[33] Such negative categorizing of one group in terms of another (cleric/noncleric, religious/nonreligious, or lay/nonlay) had marked the pyramidal understanding the council wanted to eschew. Yet these can still be found in places within the conciliar texts.

A classic example of the contrastive, and, by implication, negative, description of the laity as "over-against" the clergy and religious is the description early in chapter 4: "The term laity is here understood to mean all the faithful *except those* in holy Orders and those who belong to a religious state approved by the church" (LG 31). Also able to be read from a contrastive view are those passages that affirm a secular vocation exclusive to the laity alone: "To be secular is the special characteristic of the laity" (LG 31). When read from a contrastive point of view, this distinguishes the laity from the ordained who are "principally and expressly" focused on a "sacred" ministry, as well as religious who are likewise engaged (LG 31).[34]

Alongside the preconciliar contrasting view is an "intensifying" approach: what is affirmed of the *laicus* in chapter 4 of *Lumen Gentium* is merely an *identification with* but yet an *intensification of* what is affirmed of the *fidelis* in chapter 2. Rather than negative descriptions, these passages "are *all* clearly *positive*";[35] that is, they don't portray the role of the layperson only in terms "over against" that of the supposedly more exalted role of the ordained and the religious. In such positive depictions, laypeople are Christians who are more intensively engaged in their baptismal commitment within their particular life context. In such "intensifying" passages, "there can be no doubt that the theological basis and the details of the tasks of the laity given in the conciliar texts *add nothing specific to the status and the tasks that are common to all Christians*, even when they attempt to give more precise indications of the application of the schema on the threefold *munus*, or of the evangelizing and apostolic or missionary task of lay people."[36] This intensifying approach

33. Magnani, "Does the So-Called Theology of the Laity," 593.

34. On the Doctrinal Commission's *relatio* concerning the "typological" description of the laity's role as "secular," rather than an ontological description, see Komonchak, "The Ecclesiology of Vatican II," 766.

35. Magnani, "Does the So-Called Theology of the Laity," 597. Original emphasis.

36. Ibid., 598. Original emphasis.

is clearly formulated at the start of chapter 4 on the laity, as a basic herme-neutical principle for interpreting the chapter that is to follow: "*Everything that has been said of the people of God [in chapter 2] is addressed equally to laity, religious and clergy*" (LG 30).[37]

An example of this intensifying approach can be found juxtaposed along-side the negative description of the laity cited above: "The term laity is here understood to mean all the faithful *except those* in holy Orders and those who belong to a religious state approved by the church" (LG 31). But then, in the very next sentence, the article returns to the common matrix of the laity, ordained, and religious, almost as a caveat to the previous sentence: "All the faithful, that is, who by Baptism are incorporated into Christ, are constituted the people of God, who have been made sharers in their own way [*suo modo*] in the priestly, prophetic and kingly office of Christ and play their part in carrying out the mission of the whole Christian people in the church and in the world" (LG 31).

While the juxtaposition of the contrastive and intensive views are to be found in the first constitution on the church and the decree on the laity, Magnani sees the more dominant trajectory of the intensive view becoming much more clearly delineated in the second constitution on the church, *Gaudium et Spes*. He notes "the drastic reduction to *only six instances* of the term 'layman' in the text, which—what is more—does not figure at all until number 43."[38] He continues:

> This goes against the current of thought found in *Lumen Gentium* and *Apostolicam Actuositatem*, which would have emphasized the reference to the laity precisely in the Constitution that spoke of the relationship between the Church and the world, and thus dealt more closely with the area that had formerly been designated as the "distinctive" sphere of the laity. Instead of this, however, *Gaudium et Spes* drastically cuts down on its use. It is as if the Fathers had realized that the task of ordering temporal things toward God, of taking them up to transform them in Christ, and of the recapitulation that involves the whole of the created order is now seen to be distinctive of the whole Church and not only of lay people, or not to be attributed to them exclusively or to an excessive degree. This may be why the Constitution prefers to use the more

37. Emphasis added.
38. Magnani, "Does the So-Called Theology of the Laity," 600. Original emphasis.

general terminology of "Christian," "member of the Christian faithful," or, indeed, the term "Church."[39]

To understand this conciliar dynamic toward "intensification" in the council's new theology of the layperson, it is helpful to note a similar "intensification" theology to be found in the council's new theology of "the missionary." There the council moved from a view that a few of the faithful are called to be missionaries to a view that the whole church is "by its nature missionary" (AG 2); what was formerly affirmed of a few in the church shifts to being affirmed of the whole church. Accordingly, in the light of this shift, there arises in the council a revised understanding of those with "a missionary vocation" (AG 23): they "take on the duty of evangelization, which is the responsibility of the whole church, and make it as it were their own special task [*proprium officium*]" (AG 23).

This is precisely the kind of shift the council makes regarding the "special vocation" (*vocatione propria*) of the laity in the world: the lay vocation is an intensification of the mission in the world of the whole church. What was previously affirmed of a special group within the church is affirmed of the church as a whole, and, accordingly, in this new view, the laity are no longer seen as having a responsibility that others in the church don't have.[40] But a *laicus* is a *fidelis* who has consciously embraced in a more intensive way in their life situation that element of the church's mission whereby it engages with the secular world. The layperson is a Christian who, in their single or married life, in their personal, social, or work life, consciously embraces their baptismal identity and commits themselves to being a more engaged disciple of Jesus Christ in the world. "It is the special vocation of the laity to seek the kingdom of God by engaging in temporal affairs and directing them according to God's will. They live in the world, in each and every one of the world's occupations and callings in the ordinary circumstances of social and family

---

39. Ibid., 600–601.

40. As Bruno Forte remarks: "The relationship with temporal realities is proper to all the baptized, though in a variety of forms, joined more to personal charisms than to static contrasts between laity, hierarchy and religious state. . . . No one is neutral toward the historical circumstances in which he or she is living, and an alleged neutrality can easily become a voluntary or involuntary mask for ideologies and special interests. . . . It is the entire community that has to confront the secular world, being marked by that world in its being and in its action. The entire People of God must be characterized by a positive relationship with the secular dimension." Bruno Forte, *The Church: Icon of the Trinity; A Brief Study* (Boston, MA: St Paul Books and Media, 1991), 54–55.

life which, as it were, form the context of their existence. There they are called by God to contribute to the sanctification of the world from within, *like leaven*" (LG 31).[41] "The characteristic of the lay state being a life led in the midst of the world and of secular affairs, lay people are called by God to make of their apostolate, through the vigor of the Christian spirit, a leaven in the world" (AA 2). There is nothing that is affirmed here of the laity in particular that is not affirmed of the church as a whole, either in chapter 2 of *Lumen Gentium* or in the first part of the pastoral constitution on the church in the world of today (GS 1–45). *Gaudium et Spes*, in opening its fourth chapter—on "the role of the church in the world of today"—similarly states that the church "is to be *a leaven* and, as it were, the soul of human society in its renewal by Christ and transformation into the family of God" (GS 40).[42]

Another shift that made way for this reconception of lay identity is the reconception of the church/world relationship, noted above in the *ad intra/ad extra* principle and to be explored further in the church/world principle. There is no doubt that there are still operating in the final texts two diverse approaches to the relationship between the two spheres of "sacred" and "secular." Both can be found juxtaposed in the texts, with the familiar pattern: there is a dominant trajectory that points in a particular direction, in this case, toward a view of the world as not devoid of God's presence but consecrated by virtue of the incarnation—church and world are both spheres of God's activity.

Thus, the council eschews any notion that the hierarchy and religious alone are concerned with some exclusively "sacred" realm that is the church *ad intra* and not concerned with the church in some exclusively "nonsacred" world *ad extra*. The texts state that, while the hierarchy and religious may have a predominant concern in one realm, there is to be no clear-cut division between those concerned with the church *ad intra* and those concerned with the church *ad extra*. It is stated that "all the faithful . . . play their part in carrying out the mission of the whole Christian people *in the church* and *in the world [in ecclesia et in mundo]*" (LG 31). Regarding the ordained and professed religious, there is no clear-cut restriction of their lives to some exclusively sacred realm: "Although people in holy Orders *may sometimes be engaged in secular activities, or even practice a secular profession,* yet by reason of their particular vocation they are principally and expressly ordained to the sacred ministry, while religious bear outstanding and striking witness

---

41. Emphasis added.
42. Emphasis added.

that the world cannot be transfigured and offered to God without the spirit of the beatitudes" (LG 31).

Nor for the laity is there intended a clear-cut isolation to some exclusively secular realm, which the clergy and religious do not inhabit. While it is affirmed that "to be secular is the special characteristic of the laity" (LG 31), the council also makes a qualification: "It is to the laity, *though not exclusively to them*, that secular duties and activity properly belong" (GS 43). Moreover, laypeople are not exclusively involved "in the world"; they too are called to participate fully and actively in the inner life of the church. This is a major feature of the conciliar vision, beginning with the reform proposals in *Sacrosanctum Concilium* for full and active participation of all in the liturgy. While laypeople predominantly work in the "secular" world, they also should participate fully in the inner life of the church. "The laity are called to participate actively in the entire life of the church; not only are they to animate the world with the spirit of Christianity, they are to be witnesses to Christ in all circumstances and at the very heart of the human community" (GS 43). Separate articles in chapter 4 of *Lumen Gentium* are each devoted to the ways in which the laity participate in the priestly (art. 34), prophetic (art. 35), and kingly (art. 36) offices of Christ *in the church*, for the sake of the church's more effective witness *in the world*: "In this way the field of the world is better prepared for the seed of the divine word and the doors of the church are opened more widely to allow the message of peace to enter the world" (LG 36).

Thus there is nothing that Vatican II affirms of the *laicus* that it does not affirm of the mission of the church as a whole, as the people of God. If it is the special characteristic of the whole church to be a sign and instrument of universal salvation in the secular world, the *laicus* participates in that special characteristic by his or her daily life within family, work, and society. The council did not present a synthesis of this view of laypeople simply being church in the world, but its fundamental features are evident structurally, intratextually, and intertextually in the documents, despite the juxtaposition of preconciliar frameworks alongside this new trajectory.

Within this vision, "hierarchy" and the sacrament of "orders" can no longer be conceived in terms of grades in holiness but rather in terms of service to the whole. The fourth chapter specifically on the laity reads not only like an extension of the second chapter on the whole people of God but also like a prelude introducing all the motifs to be further explicated in the fifth chapter referring to the call of all to holiness: "In the church not everyone walks along the same path, yet all are called to holiness and have obtained an equal privilege of faith through the justice of God" (LG 32). This is further emphasized and expanded in chapter 5, on "the universal call to holiness": "All in the church, whether they belong to the hierarchy or are cared for by it, are called to holiness" (LG 39); "It is therefore quite clear that all Christians in whatever state or walk of life are called to the fullness of Christian life and to the perfection of charity, and this holiness is conducive to a more human way of living even in society here on earth" (LG 40); "The forms and tasks of life are many but there is one holiness, which is cultivated by all who are led by God's Spirit and, obeying the Father's voice and adoring God the Father in spirit and in truth, follow Christ, poor and humble in carrying his cross, that they may deserve to be sharers in his glory" (LG 41).

This universal call to holiness highlights that renewal of the church begins with the personal renewal of each of its members. "Each individual lay person [*unusquisque laicus*] must be a witness before the world to the resurrection and life of the Lord Jesus, and *a sign of the living God*. All together, and each one to the best of his or her ability, must nourish the world with spiritual fruits" (LG 38).[43] "Let everyone be aware that the primary and most important contribution they can make to the spread of the faith is to lead a profound Christian life" (AG 36).

The Ecclesial Importance of the Individual Believer

Through all these conciliar shifts, "the *Christifidelis* [is] restored to his role as human protagonist in the church."[44] The vision of Vatican II brings into the foreground of its ecclesial self-understanding the individual baptized believer and his or her singular importance in the mission of the church, without downplaying the communal and social nature of Christian faith. It is here where faith begins, in the heart of the individual; from his or her creation, each is called into a saving, revelatory relationship with the Creator. These are themes that resound through the documents of Vatican II. They affirm the particularity of the individual single disciple and the particularity of their faith. Although faith is a gift from the Holy Spirit that is called forth from and finds its home in the community of faith, faith itself begins in the heart and mind of an individual. " 'The obedience of faith' must be our response to God who reveals. By faith one freely commits oneself entirely to

---

43. Emphasis added.

44. Piero Antonio Bonnet, "The *Christifidelis* Restored to His Role as Human Protagonist in the Church," in *Vatican II Assessment and Perspectives: Twenty-Five Years After (1962–1987)*, vol. 1, ed. René Latourelle (New York: Paulist Press, 1988), 1:540–67.

God, making 'the full submission of intellect and will to God who reveals,' and willingly assenting to the revelation given by God" (DV 5).

The protological/eschatological principle above has already highlighted the social nature of the human person. It is God's plan to save human beings, "not as individuals without any bond between them, but rather to make them into a people who might acknowledge him and serve him in holiness" (LG 9). As Richard Gaillardetz, highlighting the communal nature of faith, points out regarding the Pauline ecclesiology the council was retrieving in *Lumen Gentium* 7: "For Paul, life in Christ meant life in the body of Christ, the church. The church was no mere aggregate of individuals. Rather by baptism into the Christian community one participated in a new reality; one was a new creation. As Yves de Montcheuil put it, 'It is not Christians who, in coming together, constitute the Church; it is the Church that makes Christians.' "[45]

Nevertheless, while never forgetting faith's communal dimension, Vatican II forcefully brings to the fore the significance of the individual human being, whether located within or outside the church: "It is the human person [*persona hominis*] that is to be saved, human society [*societas humana*] which must be renewed. It is the human person [*homo*] therefore, which is the key to this discussion, each individual human person in her or his totality, body and soul, heart and conscience, mind and will" (GS 3). This "new humanism" (GS 55), in which the individual in his or her unique dignity is always seen in their social, relational context, is applied ecclesiologically: the role of the individual disciple is heightened, while never losing sight of their ecclesial identity.

There are several conciliar teachings that bring out of the ecclesial shadows the single follower of Jesus and put the spotlight on his or her significance for the church as a whole: each human being created in the image of God; the consequent human dignity of each single person, baptized or not; the Spirit-given charisms that baptized individuals bring to their community; the importance of the Spirit's gift of an individual believer's sense of the faith (*sensus fidei*) for the community's sense of the faith; the integrity of an individual's conscience before God. Some of these have already been treated above in some way. Three of them—conscience, *sensus fidei,* and charism— need to be examined more closely here within the specific context of the *fideles/fidelis* principle. The classic treatment of the council's teaching on conscience is found in *Gaudium et Spes*'s chapter on the dignity of the human person (GS 16); the classic treatment of both *sensus fidei* and charism is

45. Gaillardetz, *The Church in the Making*, 45. Gaillardetz is here quoting Yves de Montcheuil, *Aspects de l'Église*, Unam Sanctam, 18 (Paris: Les Éditions du Cerf, 1949), 51.

located in *Lumen Gentium* 12's discussion of the participation of all the faithful in the prophetic office of Christ, theoretically preparing the way for a revised treatment of the participation by the hierarchy in the prophetic office (a revision that the council did not go on to complete).

The council teaches about conscience in both *Gaudium et Spes* and *Dignitatis Humanae*.[46] "Deep within their consciences men and women discover a law which they have not laid upon themselves and which they must obey. Its voice, ever calling them to love and to do what is good and to avoid evil, tells them inwardly at the right moment: do this, shun that. For they have in their hearts a law inscribed by God. Their dignity rests in observing this law, and by it they will be judged" (GS 16). As a consequence of the dignity of each human person as an image of God, the Decree on Religious Liberty affirms the freedom of enquiry that comes with both the individual and communal search for truth: "Everybody has the duty and consequently the right to seek the truth in religious matters so that, through the use of appropriate means, they may form prudent judgments of conscience which are sincere and true" (DH 3). It goes on to link this freedom with the communal search for truth: "The search for truth, however, must be carried out in the manner that is appropriate to the dignity and social nature of the human person: that is, by free enquiry with the help of teaching or instruction, communication and dialogue. It is by these means that people share with each other the truth they have discovered, or think they have discovered, in such a way that they help one another in the search for truth. Moreover, it is by personal assent that they must adhere to the truth they have discovered" (DH 3). Without explicitly naming the relationship to faith of conscience and the search for truth, the council's teaching evokes the revelation/faith principle, especially its focus on the act of believing (*fides qua creditur*): "Their conscience is people's most secret core, and their sanctuary. There they are alone with God, whose voice echoes in their depths. By conscience, in a wonderful way, that law is made known which is fulfilled in the love of God and of one's neighbour" (GS 16). In exercising their conscience, believers intimately relate and communicate with the revealing God. In an intertextual

46. On the two "competing accounts" (conscience as obedience and conscience as discernment) in *Dignitatis Humanae* and *Gaudium et Spes*, see Linda Hogan, "Conscience in the Documents of Vatican II," in *Conscience*, ed. Charles E. Curran, Readings in Moral Theology 14 (New York: Paulist Press, 2004), 82–88, at 83. For a more expansive presentation, see Linda Hogan, *Confronting the Truth: Conscience in the Catholic Tradition* (New York: Paulist Press, 2000).

reading, the council's notion of an individual's "conscience" is, therefore, coupled with the notion of their "sense of the faith [*sensus fidei*]."

In the chapter on the revelation/faith principle, we examined how the council teaches that along with the Spirit's gift to the individual of *fides* comes the Spirit's gift of a sense of the faith, or, perhaps better, a sense *for* the faith (*sensus fidei*). With this interpretive sense, each individual believer (and ultimately the church, as a whole), "receives" the Word of God, "unfailingly adheres" to it, "penetrates it more deeply through right judgment, and applies it more fully in daily life" (LG 12). This same gift is given to all, but with it all interpret the faith from their own perspective. This fundamental sense for the faith continues to be operative throughout the life of any individual *fidelis*, be they a layperson, religious, deacon, priest, bishop, or pope. For example, regarding laypersons, Christ "fulfils [his] prophetic office, not only through the hierarchy who teach in his name and by his power, but also through the laity. He accordingly both establishes them as witnesses and provides them with a sense of the faith (*sensu fidei*) and the grace of the word so that the power of the Gospel may shine out in daily family and social life" (LG 35).[47] That it is through this gift to all individuals (and therefore to the church as a whole) that the church continues to be infallible in believing (LG 12) "requires us first of all to create in the church itself mutual esteem, reverence and harmony, and to acknowledge all legitimate diversity; in this way all who constitute the one People of God will be able to engage in ever more fruitful dialogue, whether they are pastors or other members of the faithful" (GS 92). Through such dialogue among the faithful, the whole church can arrive at "a universal consensus in matters of faith and morals" (LG 12). This common quest for truth is similarly affirmed in the council's teaching on conscience: "Through loyalty to conscience, Christians are joined to others in the search for truth and for the right solution to so many moral problems which arise both in the life of individuals and from social relationships" (GS 16). For Vatican II, therefore, the *sensus fidei* of each individual *fidelis* has an indispensable ecclesial importance.

Throughout the church's history, and despite the predominance in Pauline ecclesiology of charisms in the early church, there has been a suspicion of charisms, particularly since the strengthening of the institutional aspects of Catholicism in the second millennium. Vatican II—eventually—overcame these long-held suspicions, despite the opposition to the very use of the term

---

47. Translation corrected.

from Cardinal Ernesto Ruffini.[48] Not surprisingly, two approaches were evident in the council debates, and each finds its place in the final texts: on the one hand, charisms are only rare and exceptional in the church's life; on the other hand, charisms are to be found in the everyday life of the church.[49] "In the end," as Albert Vanhoye remarks, "the second position eventually prevailed."[50] Despite the ongoing presence of both views in the documents, a clear trajectory is apparent, especially when such passages are interpreted in the light of the christological/pneumatological principle. Charisms came to be highlighted as an essential element in a church now imaged in a non-pyramidal way as "the People of God, the Body of the Lord, and the Temple of the Holy Spirit" (LG 17).

The council brought forth a renewed appreciation of the so-called "charismatic structure of the church."[51] During the second session, on October 22, 1963, an emphatic speech by Cardinal Léon-Joseph Suenens on charisms was received positively by the assembly, which substantially incorporated it into its teaching on charisms, above all in *Lumen Gentium* 12, but also throughout other documents.[52] Early in *Lumen Gentium*, it is stated that the Holy Spirit "bestows upon [the church] different hierarchic and charismatic gifts" (LG 4). *Lumen Gentium* 12 goes on to treat the charismatic gifts. While the Spirit gifts all believers with a *sensus fidei*, the Spirit nevertheless gifts different individuals with different charisms; the former (*sensus fidei*) is given to all

48. In a speech to the council, Ruffini said: "We cannot stably and firmly rely on charismatic lay persons for the advancement of the Church and the apostolate, for charisms—contrary to the opinion of many separated brethren who freely speak of the ministry of charismatics in the Church—are today very rare and entirely singular." Quoted in John C. Haughey, "Charisms: An Ecclesiological Exploration," in *Retrieving Charisms for the Twenty-first Century*, ed. Doris Donnelly (Collegeville, MN: Liturgical Press, 1999), 1–16, at 4.

49. On these two approaches in the council debates, see Albert Vanhoye, "The Biblical Question of 'Charisms' After Vatican II," in *Vatican II Assessment and Perspectives: Twenty-Five Years After (1962–1987)*, vol. 1, ed. René Latourelle (New York: Paulist Press, 1988), 1:439–68, at 442–46.

50. Ibid., 443.

51. See the commentary on the debate regarding *Lumen Gentium* 12 in Hans Küng, "The Charismatic Structure of the Church," *Concilium* 4 (1965): 23–33, esp. 23–25.

52. AS II/3, 175–78. For an English translation, see Léon-Joseph Cardinal Suenens, "The Charismatic Dimension of the Church," in *Council Speeches of Vatican II*, ed. Hans Küng, Yves Congar, and Daniel O'Hanlon (Glen Rock, NJ: Paulist Press, 1964), 25–34. Adolf Laminski notes: "The first part of the section of the Constitution on charisms [LG 12b] is taken from this speech of Cardinal Suenens and contributes not insignificantly to highlight the charismatic dimension of the church as a fruit of the efficacy of the Holy Spirit." Laminski, "Die Entdeckung der pneumatologischen Dimension der Kirche durch das Konzil," 399.

baptized believers and to the church as a whole; the latter (charisms) are given to believers in diverse and complementary ways, for the sake of the whole church. Both of these effects of the Spirit's presence and activity in the church manifest and bring to realization the nature of the church as the temple of the Holy Spirit. By foregrounding in this way the charismatic dimension of the church, the council made a remarkable shift away from the almost-exclusively Christomonist and juridical ecclesiology characterizing the original schema on the church, *De Ecclesia*.

Lumen Gentium 12, in the paragraph immediately after treatment of the *sensus fidei*, underscores the unique role of individual charisms while also noting that these gifts are given for the whole community: "Allotting his gifts [*dona*] 'at will to each individual' (1 Cor 12:11), he also distributes special graces [*gratias*] among the faithful of every rank. By these gifts, he makes them fit and ready to undertake various tasks [*opera*] and offices [*officia*] for the renewal and building up of the church, as it is written, 'the manifestation of the Spirit is given to everyone for profit' (1 Cor 12:7)" (LG 12b).

In the very next sentence, the need for those in authority to welcome these gifts is also emphasized, precisely because they are gifts intended for and needed by the whole: "Whether these charisms [*charismata*] be very remarkable or more simple and widely diffused, they are to be received with thanksgiving and consolation since they are primarily suited to and useful for the needs of the church" (LG 12). Discernment, of course, is needed and judgments made, as noted at the end of article 12: "Those who have charge over the church should judge the genuineness and orderly use of these gifts, and it is especially their office not indeed to extinguish the Spirit, but to test all things and hold fast to what is good (see 1 Thess 5:12 and 19–21)" (LG 12). Two passages in other documents underscore this need to respect and utilize charisms, particularly of laypeople. "[Priests] should be willing to listen to lay people, give brotherly consideration of their wishes, and recognize their experience and competence in the different fields of human activity. In this way they will be able to recognize along with them the signs of the times. While testing the spirits to discover if they be of God, they must discover with a sense of the faith [*cum sensu fide*], recognize with joy, and foster diligently the many and varied charismatic gifts [*charismata multiformia*] of the laity, whether these be of a humble or more exalted kind" (PO 9). Likewise, the Decree on the Laity states:

> [F]or the exercise of the apostolate, [the Holy Spirit] gives the faithful special gifts. . . . From the reception [*acceptione*] of these charisms, even the most

ordinary ones, there follow for all Christian believers [*unoquoque credentium*] the right and duty to use them *in the church* and *in the world* [*in ecclesia et in mundo*] for the good of humanity and the development of the church, to use them in the freedom of the Holy Spirit who "chooses where to blow," and at the same time in communion with the sisters and brothers in Christ, and with the pastors especially. It is for the pastors to pass judgment on the authenticity and good use of these gifts, not certainly with a view to quenching the Spirit but to testing everything and keeping what is good. (AA 3)[53]

The other constitution on the church, *Gaudium et Spes*, likewise emphasizes the importance of "gifts" bestowed by the Spirit on each individual for the sake of the community, in a passage already noted that could well be a description of the church as a *communio fidelium*: "As the firstborn of many, and by the gift of his Spirit, [Christ] established, after his death and resurrection, a new communion of sisters and brothers among all who received him in faith and love; this is the communion of his own body, the church, in which all as members one of the other would render mutual service in the measure of the different gifts [*dona diversa*] bestowed on each" (GS 32). For laypeople, these charisms, far from being exceptional or rare, characterize their very lives as Christians living in the secular world: "This lay spirituality [*laicorum spiritualis vitae ratio*] will take its particular character from the circumstances of one's state in life—married and family life, celibacy, widowhood—from one's state of health and from one's professional and social activity. Whatever their circumstances, all have received qualities and gifts [*qualitates et dotes*] and these should be cultivated, as should the personal gifts [*donis*] they have from the Holy Spirit" (AA 4).[54] In these ways, Vatican II brings to the foreground the vital role of each individual believer in the life of the church and its mission in the world.

Just as the *fideles* are gifted diversely with different charisms, so too are they called to diverse ministries. Here the implications of reversing the chapter order of *Lumen Gentium* are significant. The preconciliar view of the hierarchy had reduced the laity's role to one of cooperation in the apostolate of the hierarchy. Now, in beginning with the common participation of all in the mission of the church, the role of the hierarchy, laity, and religious are seen in terms of a diversity of ministries, all in service of the one mission. Thus, as Bruno Forte observes, the council's vision is an attempt to surmount

---

53. Quoting 1 Cor 12:7. Alluding to 1 Thess 5:12, 19, 21. Emphasis added.
54. Translation corrected.

"the double duality of 'hierarchy-laity' and 'religious-nonreligious' with the dual term '*community-charisms and ministries*.'"[55]

In its vision of "a wonderful diversity [*mira varietate*]" (LG 32) in the church, the council brings to the fore St. Paul's image of the church community as a body with diverse parts that work together for the good of the whole. Earlier in article 7 on the church as the Mystical Body of Christ, *Lumen Gentium* had stated: "As all the members of the human body, though they are many, form one body, so also do the faithful in Christ (1 Cor 12:12). A diversity of members and functions is engaged in the building up of Christ's body too. There is only one Spirit who, out of his own richness and the needs of the ministries, gives his various gifts for the welfare of the church (1 Cor 12:1-11)" (LG 7). In chapter 4, the constitution also quotes Romans 12:4-5 (LG 32) and Ephesians 4:15-16 (LG 30) on the image of the body. In effect, the council reconfigures the preconciliar ecclesiology of the Mystical Body: instead of the hierarchy (bishops, priests, deacons) representing Christ the Head, here all are united to Christ the Head, and from that common identity, diversity throughout the body follows.

> The sacred pastors, indeed, know well how much the laity contribute to the well-being of the whole church. For they know that they were not established by Christ to undertake by themselves the entire saving mission of the church to the world. They appreciate, rather, that it is their exalted task to shepherd the faithful and at the same time acknowledge their ministries and charisms [*ministrationes et charismata*] so that all in their separate ways [*suo modo*], but of one mind, may cooperate in the common task [*commune opus*]. For it is necessary that all "doing the truth in love, must grow up in all things in him who is the head, Christ, from whom the whole body, joined and knit together by every ligament with which it is supplied, as each part is working properly, promotes the body's growth in building itself up in love." (LG 30, quoting Eph 4:15-16)

Article 32—like much of chapter 4, reiterating and developing themes from chapter 2—emphasizes the ecclesial significance of the equality of all, before any call to particular ministry:

> The chosen people of God is, therefore, one: "one Lord, one faith, one Baptism" (Eph 4:5); there is *a common dignity* of members deriving from their re-birth in Christ, *a common grace* as sons and daughters, *a common vocation* to perfection, *one salvation, one hope and undivided charity*. In Christ and in the

---

55. Forte, *The Church*, 54.

church there is, then, no inequality arising from race or nationality, social condition or sex, for "there is neither Jew nor Greek; there is neither slave nor freeman; there is neither male nor female. For you are all one in Christ Jesus" (Gal 3:28 Greek; see Col 3:11). (LG 32)[56]

The same article goes on to address the distinctions within the common matrix in terms of the unity/diversity principle and the work of the Holy Spirit. Once again, it is not without significance that the passage, although located within chapter 4 on the laity, does not use the terms "the laity" or "laypersons" as the counterpoint to the ordained but rather uses the phrases "the rest of the People of God" and "the other faithful."

Although by Christ's will some are appointed teachers, dispensers of the mysteries and pastors for the others, yet all the faithful enjoy a true equality with regard to the dignity and the activity which they share in the building up of the body of Christ. The distinction [*distinctio*] which the Lord made between the sacred ministers and the rest of the people of God [*reliquum populum Dei*] implies union, for the pastors and the other faithful [*alii fideles*] are joined together by a close relationship. The pastors of the church, following the example of the Lord, should minister to each other and to the other faithful [*alliisque fidelibus*]; the latter should eagerly collaborate with the pastors and teachers. And, amid their variety [*varietate*] all bear witness to the wonderful unity of the body of Christ: this very diversity [*diversitas*] of graces, of ministries and of works gathers the children of God into one, for "all things are the work of the one and the same Spirit" (1 Cor 12:11). (LG 32)[57]

The Decree on the Apostolate of Lay Persons expands on this diversity within the church: "In the church, there is *diversity of ministry but unity of mission.* To the apostles and their successors, Christ has entrusted the office of teaching, sanctifying and governing in his name and by his power. Lay people too, sharing in the priestly, prophetical and kingly office of Christ, play their part in the mission of the whole People of God in the church and in the world" (AA 2).

Ultimately, the documents of Vatican II do not present a systematic outline of what this new direction in ecclesial self-understanding will mean. Some texts continue to imply the dichotomous binaries such as cleric/noncleric, religious/nonreligious, and lay/nonlay. But what is clear is that the council is wanting to eschew any negative categorization of lay identity. In its positive

---

56. Emphasis added.
57. Translation corrected.

vision of the laity, the council's fundamental and nondichotomous distinction, as Bruno Forte proposes, is "community-charisms and ministries."[58] Certainly, a juxtaposition remains. The texts in a few passages continue to use the clergy/lay distinction in a dichotomizing way but also, in most passages, in a way that realigns both groups to a position, not of subservience of one group to another, but of both groups together in service to the mission of the church as a whole. Therefore, despite the juxtapositioning, there is a dominant trajectory that can be extrapolated toward a synthesis. That synthesis demands a reconfiguration of the Catholic imagination whenever the terms "clergy," "religious," and "laity" are used to speak of groups of individuals in the church. While there continue to be distinctions between these three groups, each of these is to be considered a subset of the fundamental distinction between the *fideles* and their particular charisms and ministries of service to the whole.

The next chapter will explore one major implication of this *fideles/fidelis* principle, the council's people of God/hierarchy principle.

---

58. Forte, *The Church*, 54.

Principle 19

People of God/Hierarchy

Principle 19: The image of the church as the people of God encompasses all the *fideles*: lay people, religious, and the hierarchy (bishops, priests, deacons); the hierarchy are ordained to service of the people of God.

The previous chapter on the *fideles/fidelis* principle underscored the structural placement of chapters 2 and 4 of *Lumen Gentium* for understanding the church primarily as a *communio fidelium*. The people of God/hierarchy principle here extends that discussion and examines the tensive relationship that remains between chapters 2 and 3 in the final text of *Lumen Gentium*. This chapter synthesizes into a principle the council's implicit vision regarding the relationship between these two ecclesial dimensions. In terms of the council's *communio* ecclesiology, the principle outlines the interdependent relationship between the *communio fidelium* and the *communio hierarchica*.

By "hierarchy," Vatican II means the descending "orders" of bishop, priest, and deacon: "The divinely instituted ecclesiastical ministry is exercised in different degrees by those who even from ancient times have been called bishops, priests and deacons" (LG 28).[1] Often, however, the discussion focuses just on the pope and the bishops, as indicated in the title of chapter 3: "On the Hierarchical Constitution of the Church, *and in Particular the Episcopate*." Context determines which sense is intended.

Overcoming "Hierarchology"

As already noted, the significance of Vatican II as a historic "event" emerges only against the backdrop of the church's two-thousand-year history.

---

1. See also, for example, *Lumen Gentium* 29, which speaks of deacons as being "at the lower level of the hierarchy" and of the diaconate as "a proper and permanent rank (*gradus*) of the hierarchy."

This is also true for evaluating the significance of all principles in the vision of Vatican II and is especially true for this current principle. The prehistory of the issues it addresses stretches back to the early church, but with a decisive turning point at the beginning of the second millennium with "the invasion of legalism."[2] Against that background, the people of God/hierarchy principle at Vatican II stands out itself as an equally decisive turning point in the Catholic Church's self-understanding.

Yves Congar sees a sharp divide in the history of ecclesiology between the first millennium, which operated out of a "*communio* ecclesiology," and the second millennium up to Vatican II, which operated out of an almost exclusively hierarchical ecclesiology—"a wholly pyramidal conception of the Church as a mass totally determined by its summit."[3] This vision saw the church as a top-down system of power and authority coming directly from God, through the pope, to the bishops, and eventually to the laity, in a structured hierarchy of divine mediation that came to be systematized and codified in laws and obligations requiring passive obedience from those below. The beginnings of this juridical view can be found, to a great extent, in the Gregorian reform of the eleventh century, with its legitimate desire to renew the church and ensure its independence from secular authorities.[4] This juridical conception became absolutized, however, and then further entrenched with apologetical elements after the Reformation, in a Catholic reaction to its Protestant critics. It reached its height in nineteenth-century papal responses to Enlightenment and revolutionary threats to church and papal power. The end result was "the papalization of Catholicism."[5]

2. See the section heading of Yves Congar, "Titles and Honours in the Church: A Short Historical Study," in *Power and Poverty in the Church* (Baltimore: Helicon, 1964), 101–31, at 103–10.

3. Yves Congar, "Reception as an Ecclesiological Reality," *Concilium* 77 (1972): 43–68, at 60.

4. Congar, "Titles and Honours in the Church," 103. See also Klaus Schatz, "The Gregorian Reform and the Beginning of a Universal Ecclesiology," in *Reception and Communion Among Churches*, ed. Hervé Legrand, Julio Manzanares, and Antonio García y García (Washington, DC: The Catholic University of America Press, 1997), 123–36. On "the Gregorian form of the church" in the second millennium, see Ghislain Lafont, *Imagining the Catholic Church: Structured Communion in the Spirit* (Collegeville, MN: Liturgical Press, 2000), 37–64. On the agenda of "the Gregorian reform," see John W. O'Malley, *Four Cultures of the West* (Cambridge, MA: Belknap Press of Harvard University Press, 2004), 50–56.

5. John W. O'Malley, "The Millennium and the Papalization of Catholicism," in *Catholic History for Today's Church: How Our Past Illuminates Our Present* (Lanham, MD: Rowman & Littlefield, 2015), 7–13. O'Malley contrasts the second millennium with the first: "In the first millennium popes did not 'run the church,' nor did they claim to. They defined no doctrines;

Congar uses the term "hierarchology" to describe this vision. On the eve of the council it could be found neatly formulated in any manualist treatise on the church that would have shaped the seminary education of the bishops at the council: "The *de Ecclesia* [treatise] was principally, sometimes almost exclusively, a defence and affirmation of the reality of the Church as machinery of hierarchical mediation, of the powers and primacy of the Roman see, in a word, a 'hierarchology.' On the other hand, the two terms between which that mediation comes, the Holy Spirit on the one side, the faithful people or the religious subject on the other, were as it were kept out of ecclesiological consideration."[6] It was precisely these two terms—the Holy Spirit and the faithful people—which Vatican II wanted to bring to the fore once again in Catholic ecclesial self-understanding, without jettisoning the essential elements of the church's hierarchical constitution.

"Hierarchology" certainly characterized the preparatory draft schema *De Ecclesia* that evoked such negative reactions from the majority of bishops.

---

they wrote no encyclicals; they called no bishops *ad limina*. They did not convoke ecumenical councils, and they did not preside at them. In fact, their roles in the first eight councils were generally insignificant. In the early Middle Ages (and well beyond) the popes' principal duty, many believed, was to guard the tombs of the apostles and officiate at the solemn liturgies at the great basilicas. In that period, although some of the popes of course had a broad vision of their responsibilities and dealt about weighty matters with the leaders of society, for the most part they behaved as essentially local figures, intent on local issues." Ibid., 11.

6. Yves Congar, *Lay People in the Church: A Study for a Theology of Laity*, trans. Donald Attwater, 2nd rev. ed. (Westminster, MD: Newman Press, 1965), 45. Elsewhere, with a slightly different spelling in the English translation ("hierarchiology"), Congar writes: "Ecclesiology, as far as the instruction of clerics and of the faithful is concerned, became fixed in a set pattern in which the question of authority is so predominant that the whole treatise is more like a hierarchiology or a treatise on public law. In this assertion of authority, the papacy receives the lion's share. The idea of authority, the exercise of authority in contemporary Catholicism, are first and foremost the idea and the exercise of papal authority. The pope is really *episcopus universalis* [universal bishop]. Each individual Catholic has a much more immediate relationship with him than with his own bishop, as far as the general pattern of his Christian life is concerned. The encyclicals tell him what he ought to think, the liturgy is regulated by Roman documents, as are also fasting, canonical preparation for marriage, the *ratio studiorum* of seminaries and the canonically erected faculties. The saints we venerate are those canonized by Rome; religious congregations ask Rome for the authorization of their rule and it is from Rome that the secular Institutes have received theirs. Rome intervenes directly in the question of adapting apostolic methods to the needs of the times (worker priests, *Mission de France*). She keeps a sharp eye on publications, books, reviews, even catechisms, and, on occasion, orders their suppression. In short, the exercise of authority in the modern Catholic Church is largely that of its central and supreme seat in Rome." Yves Congar, "The Hierarchy as Service: Scriptural and Historical Development," in *Power and Poverty in the Church* (Baltimore: Helicon, 1964), 15–100, at 70.

On the first day of discussion on the schema, Bishop Émile-Joseph de Smedt, in that famous speech denouncing "triumphalism," "clericalism," and "juridicism," said: "We must bear in mind that hierarchic power is a transitory thing, limited to this time of pilgrimage. In the life to come, our final state, such power will have no place, for the elect will have reached perfect unity in Christ. The people of God abides forever, the ministry of the hierarchy passes away. We must be careful not to fall into a 'hierarchism' when we speak of the Church; we must avoid every appearance of clericalism or bishopolatry or papolatry [*episcopolatriam vel papolatriam*]. *The important thing is the people of God*."[7]

The notion of the church as "the people of God" had been emerging as a major theme in Catholic *ressourcement* studies on the church since the 1940s. By the time Vatican II met, this depiction of the church would have been familiar to many of the bishops. Its reception by the council illustrates yet again the significant role *ressourcement* studies played in helping the council realize its renewal agenda, either through bishops' knowledge of the works of *ressourcement* scholarship or through their mediation to the council by *periti* schooled in the *ressourcement* mentality.

This scholarship examined the biblical roots of the notion of the church as the people of God as well as its importance as a theme in patristic writings on the church. As Werner Löser summarizes: "In the early church, 'people of God' was a common designation for the church (it is central in Augustine), but from the Middle Ages on it yielded place to the concept of Body of Christ."[8] The spiritual notion of the church as the mystical Body of Christ also faded, however, until, in an attempt to move away from a juridical ecclesiology, its retrieval into ecclesiology by the nineteenth-century Tübingen theologian Johann Adam Möhler and then by the Roman School theologians of the late nineteenth century. This "Mystical Body ecclesiology" was brought to further prominence with the 1936 biblical and patristic study of Émile Mersch.[9] Pius XII's 1943 encyclical *Mystici Corporis* incorporated the, by

7. AS I/4, 142–44, at 143. Translated in Kloppenburg, *The Ecclesiology of Vatican II*, 311. Emphasis added.

8. Werner Löser, "People of God," in *Handbook of Catholic Theology*, ed. Wolfgang Beinert and Francis Schüssler Fiorenza (New York: Crossroad, 1995), 527.

9. Émile Mersch, *The Whole Christ: The Historical Development of the Doctrine of the Mystical Body in Scripture and Tradition*, trans. John R. Kelly (Milwaukee: The Bruce Publishing Company, 1938). On the dominance of "mystical body" ecclesiology leading up to *Mystici Corporis*, see Gabrielli, *One in Christ*, 1–49. For an extensive bibliography of works on the theme throughout the half century before the encyclical, see J. J. Bluett, "The Mystical Body of Christ: 1890–1940," *Theological Studies* 3 (1942): 261–89.

now, maturing theological work on the topic, nevertheless still conceiving the biblical notion predominantly in juridical terms.[10]

The encyclical was written partly in reaction to a 1940 book by Mannes Dominikus Koster that proposed the notion of the church as the Body of Christ was inadequate as an integrating category for ecclesiology. Koster suggested that such a role was best taken by the biblical notion of the people of God.[11] One of the first to bring the theme to greater prominence in the twentieth century had been the Benedictine Anscar Vonier (1875–1938), abbot of Buckfast Abbey, with his 1937 theological study, *The People of God*.[12] In 1947, the Belgian biblical scholar Lucien Cerfaux (later a *peritus* at the council) published *La théologie de l'Église suivant saint Paul* in which he outlined how "the Jewish idea of 'God's people' is basic to Paul's theology of the church."[13] Cerfaux's work therefore showed "that the concept of the (Mystical) Body was not, for St Paul, the *fundamental* concept to be used in *defining* the church."[14] Likewise, liturgical studies were highlighting the frequency of "people of God" language in liturgical texts,[15] while patristic scholars were showing the importance of the theme in the ecclesiology of writers such as Ambrose of Milan.[16] Furthermore, studies on the notion of the people of God as a *pilgrim* people brought to the fore the eschatological dimension of the church in history.[17] Parallel to this focus was greater attention to "salvation history" and the journey of God's people through time. The Lutheran biblical scholar Oscar Cullmann's 1946 work *Christus und die Zeit* was very influential on Catholic ecclesiologists in this regard.[18] In fact, Cullmann was sitting up front among the official observers and guests for all four sessions of Vatican II and had regular contact with the council bishops and *periti*.

The *fideles/fidelis* principle has already highlighted that, after a new version of *De Ecclesia* was presented to the bishops at the start of the second

10. Pius XII, *Mystici Corporis Christi*.

11. Mannes Dominikus Koster, *Ekklesiologie im Werden* (Paderborn: Bonifacius-Druckerei, 1940).

12. Anscar Vonier, *The People of God* (London: Burns, Oates & Washburn, 1937).

13. Lucien Cerfaux, *The Church in the Theology of St Paul*, 2nd ed. (Edinburgh: Thomas Nelson, 1959), 7.

14. Congar, "The Church: The People of God," 9. Original emphasis.

15. A. Schaut, "Die Kirche als Volk Gottes: Selbstaussagen der Kirche im römischen Messbuch," *Benediktinische Monatsschrift* 25 (1949): 187–95.

16. J. Eger, *Salus gentium* (University of Munich: Unpublished dissertation, 1947).

17. Grosche, *Pilgernde Kirche*.

18. Oscar Cullmann, *Christ and Time: The Primitive Christian Conception of Time and History*, rev. ed. (Philadelphia: Westminster Press, 1964).

session, the chapter on the hierarchy was extensively discussed for two weeks in early October 1963. It was then revised further in the following intersession period in the light of that discussion and, in a new draft, was resituated as chapter 3, without, however, any major revision in the light of the radical rethinking required because of its placement after the chapter on the people of God. Therefore, traces of a "hierarchology" can be detected in this third chapter of the final text. Karl Rahner remarks that, apart from new elements such as its teaching on episcopal collegiality and the relationship of local churches to the universal church, the rest of chapter 3 describes the place of the hierarchy in the church "without any notable advances by comparison with the First Vatican Council," apart from "sporadic attempts" to overcome the Vatican I model of hierarchical authority, attempts that "remained precisely at the level of initiatives and no more."[19] While chapter 3 advances Catholic teaching regarding the *communio hierarchica* and *communio ecclesiarum*, it leaves undeveloped the new vision of the interrelationship between the *communio hierarchica* and the *communio fidelium* opened up in chapter 2. Placing the people of God chapter before that on the hierarchy had not brought about a more integrated vision regarding the relationship between the two. Such a synthesis has been left to the receivers of the document. There are, however, elements of chapter 3 that indicate a trajectory toward such a synthesis. This is discernible especially in two matters: (1) the biblical theme of service and (2) a reconceived application of the rubric of the threefold office of Christ.

Facilitating Full Participation in the Three Offices of Christ

Viewing the hierarchy through the lens of "service" is one of the most significant ways in which Vatican II moves away from a predominantly juridical view of the church.[20] From this new perspective, the hermeneutical lens for understanding the church is no longer who has power and authority but rather what Jesus requires of all the *fideles*: "For who is greater, the one who is at the table or the one who serves? Is it not the one at the table? But

19. Karl Rahner, "The Teaching Office of the Church in the Present-Day Crisis of Authority," in *Theological Investigations*, vol. 12 (London: Darton, Longman & Todd, 1974), 12:3–30, at 4 and 5.

20. See Magnus Löhrer, "La gerarchia al servizio del populo christiano," in *La Chiesa del Vaticano II: Studi e commenti intorno alla Costituzione dommatica 'Lumen Gentium'*, ed. Guilherme Baraúna (Firenze: Vallecchi Editore, 1965), 699–712. On Vatican II's vision, see also Myriam Wijlens, "The Doctrine of the People of God and Hierarchical Authority as Service in Latin Church Legislation on the Local Church," *The Jurist* 68 (2008): 328–49, at 336–43.

I am among you as one who serves" (Luke 22:27).[21] Thus, in a move similar to the depiction of the laity's vocation *ad extra* in the secular realm being presented as an intensification of what is required of all the *fideles*, the hierarchy's place in the church *ad intra* is depicted as an intensification of the call to all the *fideles* of service to one another and to the world. Service becomes the defining feature of Vatican II's renewed vision of the relationship of the hierarchy to the people of God (of which they are members). The hierarchy are called to serve the whole people of God by actively promoting and facilitating the participation of all in the mission of the church, particularly through their participation in the three offices of Christ. Once again, this change in perspective comes as a consequence of the insertion of the chapter on the people of God, as Congar notes:

> This meant that the most profound value is not what makes the Church a society, "*societas inequalis, hierarchica*," but what makes it a community through the participation of a great number of people in the same goods of divine life. Hence, the first value is not organization, mediatorial functions, or authority, but the Christian life itself and being a disciple. All this was evident to one who reads Holy Scripture, the Fathers of the Church, even the medieval and great scholastic theologians. The Council went back to this tradition. That is also why it often presented the greatness of the hierarchy as one of service: a service of the sovereign action of God, of his word, a service to men and the world for their salvation, a service of the lasting greatness of holiness. The sublimity of hierarchical functions consists in *their ordination to service*. What nobler thing can one do than to make men disciples of the gospel?[22]

---

21. This Lukan passage is cited in the main text of *Lumen Gentium* 27 and in a footnote reference of *Christus Dominus* 16. On appeal to this whole group of passages in Luke 22, see Peter De Mey, "Authority in the Church: The Appeal to Lk 22:21–34 in Roman Catholic Ecclesiology and in the Ecumenical Movement," in *Luke and His Readers: Festschrift A. Denaux*, ed. R. Bieringer, Gilbert van Belle, and Jozef Verheyden (Dudley, MA: Leuven University Press, 2005), 307–23. Luke resituates the sayings within the context of the Last Supper; according to De Mey, "the verses which correspond to the other synoptic gospels have the character of a last will and testament. . . . Luke certainly had the leaders of the early church in mind." Ibid., 308.

22. Congar, "The People of God," 200. Bonaventure Kloppenburg makes a similar point with regard to the foregrounding of service from this changed perspective: "It is very important to grasp this basic point [regarding the common foundation of all the *fideles*] if we are to be able to see the Church and its varied membership as Vatican II does. This basic fact about the Church explains why the chapter on the hierarchy comes only in third place; it is also why those who make up the hierarchy (pope, bishops priest, deacons) are deliberately and consistently presented as 'servants of the people of God,' nothing more. They are not the owners of the Church, the diocese, the parish, the community; they are not masters to be served and

The very first paragraph of chapter 3 opens with the theme of service, as a bridge from the previous chapter on the people of God: "In order to ensure that the People of God would have pastors and would enjoy continual growth, Christ the Lord set up in his church a variety of ministries [*ministeria*] whose aim is the good of the whole body. Ministers, invested with a sacred power [*sacra potestas*], are at the service of [*inserviunt*] their brothers and sisters, so that all who belong to the People of God and therefore enjoy true Christian dignity may attain to salvation through their free, combined and well-ordered efforts in pursuit of a common goal" (LG 18). Notable here is the juxtaposition of the juridical notion of *sacra potestas* with the biblical notion of service. As has been often noted, such juxtapositions were a favorite conciliar approach for gaining acceptance from the minority of bishops wanting to preserve in some way the preconciliar, juridical ecclesiology and the majority wanting to emphasize the mystery of the church.

The theme of service continues to be highlighted throughout chapter 3, with the words *ministerium* and *servitium* being used synonymously and with the model of "shepherd" always in the background. Article 20 states: "The bishops, therefore, with priests and deacons as helpers, took on the service of the community [*communitatis ministerium*], presiding in God's place over the flock of which they are the pastors, as teachers of doctrine, priests for sacred worship and ministers of government" (LG 20).[23] The bishops are "shepherds [*pastores*] of the church" (LG 20).[24] Through them, Christ himself cares for his flock: "Indeed, it is primarily through their signal service [*servitium*] that [Christ] preaches the words of God to all peoples and administers unceasingly to believers the sacraments of faith. . . . Chosen to shepherd the Lord's flock, these pastors are servants of Christ [*ministri Christi*]" (LG 21).

The second way in which the council moved away from "hierarchology" was through a broader application of the rubric of the "threefold office" (*triplex munus*) of Christ in the church, i.e., "the three offices [*tria munera*] of Christ," as prophet, priest, and king. Historically, this rubric had been used to refer to three major areas of the church's life and mission: (1) preaching,

---

glorified. The frequency and insistency with which the Constitution on the Church uses the words 'service,' 'ministry,' 'diakonia' in speaking of the action of the members of the hierarchy, indicates that the Council is here attempting to correct an outlook which is not quite evangelical but to which we had nonetheless become accustomed due to an unfortunate tradition dating back for centuries." Kloppenburg, *The Ecclesiology of Vatican II*, 310–11.

23. Translation corrected.
24. Translation corrected.

teaching, and witness—the prophetic office (*munus propheticum* or *munus docendi*); (2) prayer and worship—the priestly office (*munus sacerdotalis* or *munus sanctificandi*); and (3) leadership and governance—the kingly office (*munus regalis* or *munus regendi*). The rubric had been used in papal teaching before the council and was in fact employed in the draft schema on the church presented to the bishops at the end of the first session. But its use in these instances referred exclusively to the ministry of the bishops, in which the laity were seen to participate derivatively and not in their own right.

Use of the threefold rubric to apply not just to the hierarchy but to the whole people of God initially emerged during the discussion on *Lumen Gentium*. The liturgical constitution had already spoken of Christ's priestly office: "The liturgy, then, is rightly seen as an exercise of the priestly office of Jesus Christ" (SC 7). And, early in the drafting of *Lumen Gentium*, the council had employed the single rubric of the priestly office of Christ as a way of promoting participation by all the faithful in the life and mission of the church: all the faithful, not just the bishops and the priests, participate in the priesthood of Christ by virtue of baptism (also already affirmed in SC 14), with the distinction here being introduced between "common" and "ministerial" priesthood.[25] *Lumen Gentium* 10 and 11 capture that early, single focus on participation of the whole people of God in the priestly office of Christ: "Though they differ essentially and not only in degree, the common priesthood of the faithful and the ministerial or hierarchical priesthood are none the less interrelated; each in its own way participates [*participant*] in the one priesthood of Christ" (LG 10).[26] Employment of this narrower rubric of "a priestly people" to capture the participation of all the faithful in the life

---

25. Melvin Michalski summarizes the council's vision: "The distinction '*non gradu tantum, sed essentia*' between common and ministerial priesthoods refers to a sacramental difference: the Church is sacrament as *communio*, as a priestly people called to the fullness of priesthood in the heavenly temple; ordained priesthood is sacrament as official ministry *in persona Christi capitis*—it is sacrament 'within a sacrament' for the life of the Church." Michalski, *The Relationship between the Universal Priesthood of the Baptized and the Ministerial Priesthood of the Ordained*, 239. On the common priesthood, see Émile-Joseph de Smedt, "Il sacerdozio dei fedeli," in *La Chiesa del Vaticano II: Studi e commenti intorno alla Costituzione dommatica 'Lumen Gentium'*, ed. Guilherme Baraúna (Firenze: Vallecchi Editore, 1965), 453–64. Bishop de Smedt had, before the council, written on the theme; see Émile-Joseph de Smedt, *The Priesthood of the Faithful* (New York: Paulist Press, 1962). On the distinction, see Peter J. Drilling, "Common and Ministerial Priesthood: *Lumen Gentium*, Article Ten," *Irish Theological Quarterly* 53 (1987): 81–99.

26. Translation corrected.

and mission of the church was, however, soon subsumed into the expansive threefold rubric.[27]

Discussion of the *fideles/fidelis* principle has already noted how, in the drafting of *Lumen Gentium*, after the decision to place a chapter on the whole People of God before the chapters on the hierarchy, the laity, and the religious, this more expansive rubric eventually became something of a structuring principle for chapter 2 of *Lumen Gentium* on the People of God. In the final texts, after being used in chapter 2 to name what was common to all the faithful, it is then used regularly throughout the rest of the constitution regarding specific participation, in chapter 3 of the hierarchy, and in chapter 4 of the laity.[28] And then in later documents, it is similarly used to capture what specifies the ministry of bishops, of priests, and of the laity.[29]

Concerning the bishops, the rubric is used to describe, and then to structure discussion of, the ministry of bishops: "The bishops, therefore, with priests

---

27. For the history of the conciliar debates and drafting regarding the incorporation of the *triplex munus* (or *tria munera*) rubric into *Lumen Gentium*, including reference to the more important secondary literature, see Ormond Rush, "The Offices of Christ, *Lumen Gentium* and the People's Sense of the Faith," *Pacifica* 16 (2003): 137–52, at 143–48. Throughout the drafting, the rubric is initially applied only to the ministry of bishops but is later extended to apply to all the faithful. Particularly important is a schema submitted to the drafting subcommission in January 1963 by the bishops of Chile, in which the people of God are described as a *priestly* people, an *apostolic* people, and a *royal* people. For the Chilean schema, see Alberigo and Magistretti, *Constitutionis Dogmaticae Lumen Gentium*, 403–4. When the second session of the council began later in the year of 1963, the archbishop of Santiago, Chile, Raúl Silva Henríquez once again proposed to the assembly the traditional *tria munera* rubric for describing the participation of all in the mission of the church, both laity and hierarchy, but this time naming the threefold rubric as "priestly, *prophetic* (rather than apostolic), and royal." See AS II/1, 366. Other bishops later made similar calls. Especially important was the October 18 intervention by Émile de Smedt (Bruges, Belgium), during which he made reference to the use of the threefold rubric by John Henry Newman. De Smedt claimed sixty subscribers to his intervention. See AS II/3, 103.

28. *Lumen Gentium* 31 later summarizes the teaching of chapter 2: "all the faithful, that is, who by Baptism are incorporated into Christ, are constituted the people of God, who have been made sharers [*participes*] in their own way in the priestly, prophetic and kingly office of Christ and play their part in carrying out the mission of the whole Christian people in the church and in the world."

29. In the order of promulgation: UR 4; CD 12–21; AA 2, 10; AG, 15; PO 1–6. Echoing *Lumen Gentium* 31, the Decree on the Apostolate of the Laity states: "Lay people too, participating in [*participes*] the priestly, prophetical and kingly office of Christ, play their part in the mission of the whole people of God in the church and in the world" (AA 2). The same document later repeats: "Participating in [*participes*] the office of Christ, priest, prophet and king, the laity have an active [*activas*] part of their own in the life and activity of the church" (AA 10). Translations corrected.

and deacons as helpers, took on the ministry to the community, presiding in God's place over the flock of which they are the pastors, as *teachers of doctrine, priests for sacred worship* and *ministers of government*" (LG 20).[30] Moreover, this responsibility comes, not from a "jurisdiction" bestowed by the pope, but rather through a bishop's sacramental ordination by other bishops (albeit in communion with the Bishop of Rome): "Episcopal consecration confers, together with the office of sanctifying, the offices also of teaching and ruling" (LG 21). A separate article then treats each of the offices in turn: preaching and teaching (LG 25), sanctifying (LG 26), and governing (LG 27). The parallel discussion in *Christus Dominus* follows the same order (12–14, 15, 16).[31]

Each of the three offices is presented in terms of a particular service that bishops perform for the people of God: facilitating the full participation of all the faithful in those offices. According to this reconfiguration, the preaching and teaching office of the hierarchy must serve to facilitate the participation by all the faithful in the preaching and teaching of "the faith once delivered to *all the saints*" (Jude 3; quoted in LG 12).[32] The sanctifying office of the hierarchy must serve to facilitate the participation by all the faithful in the church's mission to be a sacrament of Christ's sanctifying presence in the world. The kingly office of the hierarchy must serve to facilitate the participation by all the faithful in the reign of Christ who came to serve and not be served.

Not only the bishops, but also priests and deacons participate in the three offices by serving the people of God. "The priests, prudent cooperators of the episcopal college and its support and instrument, [are] called to the service [*inserviendum*] of the People of God" (LG 28). They too participate in the threefold office: "Priests who, under the authority of the bishop, sanctify and govern that portion of the Lord's flock assigned to them render the universal church visible in their locality and contribute effectively towards building up the whole Body of Christ" (LG 28). Likewise, "deacons serve [*inserviunt*] the People of God . . . in the service [*diakonia*] of the liturgy, of the word and of charity" (LG 29).

---

30. Emphasis added. A footnote in the document here cites as sources of the three offices notion related to the bishop: St. Clement of Rome, St. Ignatius of Antioch, St. Justin, and St. Cyprian.

31. On the bishops' participation in the threefold office of Christ in the Vatican II documents, see Joseph Lécuyer, "Il triplice ufficio del Vescovo," in *La Chiesa del Vaticano II: Studi e commenti intorno alla Costituzione dommatica 'Lumen Gentium'*, ed. Guilherme Baraúna (Firenze: Vallecchi Editore, 1965), 851–71; Peter de Mey, "The Bishop's Participation in the Threefold *Munera*: Comparing the Appeal to the Pattern of the *Tria Munera* at Vatican II and in the Ecumenical Dialogues," *The Jurist* 69 (2009): 31–58.

32. Emphasis added.

That the bishops are called to service comes above all to the fore in Vatican II's depiction of their participation in the *munus regalis*, the *munus regendi*, i.e., the office of governance. The predominantly juridical, and indeed monarchical, vision of governance in the church had seen those at the base of the ecclesial pyramid as subjects over whom the hierarchy were authorized to rule. While much of the language of power and authority is still to be found in the documents regarding governance, it is tempered with descriptions of the bishop in terms of the biblical image of a shepherd safeguarding the flock. This was one of the very images from the Bible used in the first chapter of *Lumen Gentium* precisely to evoke the mystery of the church, over against an exclusively juridical view: "The church is . . . a sheepfold, the sole and necessary entrance to which is Christ. It is also a flock, of which God foretold that he would himself be the shepherd, and whose sheep, although watched over by human shepherds, are nevertheless at all times led and brought to pasture by Christ himself, the Good Shepherd and prince of shepherds, who gave his life for his sheep" (LG 6). This theme of service constitutes a radical re-conception of relationships in the governance by the hierarchy of the people of God. Seen in terms of service, the hierarchy are seen to be *fideles* among the people of God, not rulers over it.

The council generally refers to the "kingly" office in terms rather of a "pastor" or "shepherd," evoking the fact that King David was originally a shepherd but also evoking the way Jesus himself exercised his authority: "[A] bishop should keep before his eyes the example of the Good Shepherd, who came not to be served but to serve and to lay down his life for his sheep. Taken from among human beings and subject to weakness himself, he can sympathize with those who are ignorant and erring. He should not refuse to listen to his subjects whose welfare he promotes as of his very own children and whom he urges to collaborate readily with him" (LG 27).

But the juridical view remains alongside the pastoral. When taken together, the bishops' participation in the *munus regalis* is described in ways that attempt to bridge the pastoral and the juridical: "The bishops, as vicars and legates of Christ *govern by their counsels, persuasion and example* the particular churches assigned to them, and also by the *authority and sacred power* which they exercise exclusively for the spiritual development of their flock in truth and holiness, keeping in mind that *the greater must become like the lesser*, and the leader [*praecessor*] as the servant [*ministrator*]" (LG 27).[33] Here we see, almost as an attempt to satisfy two camps in the conciliar

---

33. Emphasis added. The document here cites Luke 22:26-27.

assembly, a pendulum swing from a nonjuridical, to a juridical, back to a nonjuridical notion of authority exercised through persuasion and humble service. In another example of the juxtaposition of the juridical and the pastoral in one sentence, *Christus Dominus* states regarding the *munus regalis* of the bishop: "In exercising their office of fathers and pastors, bishops should be with their people as those who serve, as good shepherds who know their sheep and whose sheep know them, as true fathers who excel in their love and solicitude for all, to whose divinely conferred authority all readily submit" (CD 16).

Parallel with the theme of service, the documents use two other motifs to capture the new way of governing envisaged, that of participation and of dialogue. These have already been touched on and need only to be noted here. The council envisaged institutional structures that would allow for a more participatory and dialogic form of ecclesial governance, such as diocesan and parish pastoral councils. But more than structural change was envisaged. Both participation and dialogue at the deepest level relate to the change of "style" in the church that the council was desiring overall.[34] The laity will know if their participation in the three offices is genuinely welcomed by their bishop and priests and whether their advice will be listened to. Richard Gaillardetz has neatly captured this style of leadership with the word "noncompetitive."[35] The spirit of the council's vision is captured in *Gaudium et Spes*, when it addresses the mutual dialogue between laity and priests:

> For guidance and spiritual strength let them turn to the clergy; but let them realise that their pastors will not always be so expert as to have a ready answer to every problem, even every grave problem, that arises; this is not the role of the clergy: it is rather the task of lay people to shoulder their responsibilities under the guidance of Christian wisdom and with careful attention to the teaching authority of the church. Very often their Christian vision will suggest a certain solution in some given situation. Yet it happens rather frequently, and legitimately so, that some of the faithful, with no less sincerity, will see the problem quite differently. Now if one or other of the proposed solutions is readily perceived by many to be closely connected with the message of the Gospel, they ought to remember that in those cases no one is permitted to identify the authority of the church exclusively with his or her own opinion. Let them, then, try to guide each other by sincere dialogue [*colloquium*] in a

---

34. See John O'Malley's basic interpretation of Vatican II, for example in O'Malley, *What Happened at Vatican II*, 43–52, 305–8.

35. See Gaillardetz, *An Unfinished Council*, 91–113.

spirit of mutual charity and with a genuine concern for the common good above all. The laity are called to participate actively in the entire life of the church. (GS 43).

All of *Lumen Gentium* 37 likewise captures "this familiar relationship between the laity and the pastors" (LG 37), which should ensue from reimagining the governance of the church in this participatory, dialogic, and "noncompetitive" way.

Although not as explicit as in the treatment of the governing office, the theme of service characterizes the council's vision of the hierarchy's participation in the priestly office. Once again, this marks a shift away from the preconciliar vision.[36] The key element in that shift concerns the role of the priest in the liturgy.

The priest is a *fidelis* among the *fideles* in service of the church and is not over and above the other *fideles* in honor or holiness. That there is an essential difference between the common priesthood of the whole people of God and the hierarchical or ministerial priesthood of the ordained (LG 10) does not negate the essential equality that the second chapter of *Lumen Gentium* affirms of all the *fideles*: "There is a common dignity of members deriving from their re-birth in Christ, a common grace as sons and daughters, a common vocation to perfection, one salvation, one hope and undivided charity" (LG 32). The "common" and the "hierarchical" priesthood are "interrelated [because] each in its own way shares in the one priesthood of Christ" (LG 10).

The preconciliar framework had depicted the role of the priest in the liturgy as *alter Christus*.[37] While the priest is still spoken of as acting "in the person of Christ" (LG 10), *Sacrosanctum Concilium* marks a different tone, through its teaching that it is Christ present in the whole congregation, his Body, who performs the liturgy; the liturgy is an action of the church and not just of the

---

36. "The manual theology of the nineteenth and twentieth centuries reinforced, almost unanimously, the scholastic approach to priesthood which defined the priest in terms of his relationship to the eucharist. This was the 'traditional' doctrine, or scholastic doctrine, which was standard in the Catholic Church at the onset of the council. This eucharistic approach was not only the basis for a *theology* of the priesthood, but it was also the basis for the *spirituality* of priesthood and for the ordination ritual. It was precisely this definition which was set aside, changed, or modified by Vatican II. This does not mean that the scholastic understanding of priesthood was rejected as wrong; rather, it was deemed too narrow and needed to be enriched and enlarged." Kenan B. Osborne, *Priesthood: A History of Ordained Ministry in the Roman Catholic Church* (New York: Paulist Press, 1989), 315. Original emphasis.

37. See throughout ibid. See also Torrell, *A Priestly People*, 142–52.

priest alone.[38] Article 7 begins by listing the different ways in which Christ is present in the liturgy: in the person of the minister, in the eucharistic species, in the proclamation of the word, and in the gathering of the church.[39] This is the only time that the role of the priest or bishop in the liturgy is mentioned in chapter 1's first section, "The Nature of the Sacred Liturgy and Its Importance in the Life of the Church" (SC 5–13). An exclusive focus on the priest is avoided; this section on first principles speaks constantly of "the church." Article 7 intimates a vision that *Lumen Gentium* would later crystallize through its symbolic insertion of a chapter on the people of God before that on the ordained: "The liturgy, then, is rightly seen as an exercise of the priestly office [*sacerdotalis muneris*] of Jesus Christ. . . . In it, complete and definitive public worship is *performed by the mystical Body of Jesus Christ*, that is, by the Head and his members. From this it follows that every liturgical celebration, because it is *an action of Christ the priest and of his body*, which is the church, is a preeminently sacred action. No other *action of the church* equals its effectiveness by the same title nor to the same degree" (SC 7).[40] *Sacrosanctum Concilium* highlights that the Eucharist, in being the action of Christ the Priest, is an action of the whole church, his Body: "The church, therefore, spares no effort in trying to ensure that, when present at this mystery of faith, Christian believers should not be there as strangers or silent spectators. On the contrary, having a good grasp of it through the rites and prayers, they should take part in the sacred action, actively, fully aware, and devoutly. . . . Offering the immaculate victim, not only through the hands of the priest but also *together with him*, they should learn to offer themselves" (SC 48).[41]

The hierarchy, in their participation in the priestly office, serve both the people of God and the world in which the church gives witness to Christ. "The liturgy daily builds up those who are in the church. . . . At the same time it marvelously enhances their power to preach Christ and thus show the church to those who are outside as a sign lifted up among the nations" (SC 2). The *ad intra* liturgical life of the church is thus orientated toward the mission of the church *ad extra*. To this end, the ordained serve the participation of the laity in the mission of the church in the world:

---

38. See James F. Puglisi, "Presider as *Alter Christus*, Head of the Body?," *Liturgical Ministry* 10 (Summer 2001): 153–58.

39. See throughout O'Collins, "Vatican II on the Liturgical Presence of Christ." O'Collins lists a fifth, more general way Christ is present: in the sacraments.

40. Emphasis added.

41. Emphasis added.

> To them [the laity], whom he intimately joins to his life and mission, he also
> gives a share in his priestly office of offering spiritual worship for the glory of
> the Father and the salvation of humanity. Hence the laity, dedicated as they
> are to Christ and anointed by the Holy Spirit, are marvelously called and
> prepared so that ever richer fruits of the Spirit may be produced in them. For
> all their works, if accomplished in the Spirit, become spiritual sacrifices ac-
> ceptable to God through Jesus Christ: their prayers and apostolic undertakings,
> family and married life, daily work, relaxation of mind and body, even the
> hardships of life if patiently borne. In the celebration of the Eucharist, these
> are offered to the Father in all piety along with the body of the Lord. And so,
> worshipping everywhere by their holy actions, *the laity consecrate the world
> itself to God*. (LG 34)[42]

The priestly office (the sanctifying office) of the people of God names one
aspect of the nature and mission of the church as the sacrament of universal
salvation in the world. In the life of the church *ad intra*, the liturgy is "the
source from which all its power flows" (SC 10), enabling the church to be a
priestly people in the world. Liturgy serves the mission of the church. Yves
Congar notes for Vatican II the relationship between its naming the church
as the "sacrament of salvation" and as "the people of God": the designation
of the church as the sacrament of salvation "means that the Church is the
historic and visible form which God's will for the salvation of men takes. What
is interesting here is that the theme is applied to the Church insofar as it is
the People of God. It is not, therefore, solely a question of the institution, of
the ensemble of objective means of grace. It is the People of God that transmits
through the world the offer of grace and of the Covenant."[43] The laity, above
all, transmit that offer; the ordained in the liturgy serve the laity, whose role,
in turn, is to work primarily in the secular world, consecrating it to God.

The *munus propheticum* relates to both preaching and teaching in the
church. In preconciliar ecclesiology, this function had been reduced in Catholic
understanding to the activity of teaching the official doctrine of the church.
Moreover, it was a function that was *de facto* seen to be the preserve of the
hierarchy alone, as captured in the distinction between the *ecclesia docens* (the
teaching church) and the *ecclesia discens* (the learning church).[44] This conception viewed revelation almost solely according to a propositionalist model of
revelation and of truth; in such a view, revelation is a communication by God

---

42. Emphasis added.
43. Congar, "The People of God," 205.
44. See Örsy, *The Church Learning and Teaching*.

of statements in human words about God and humanity. Correlatively, the magisterium was understood as the protector of this doctrinal "deposit of the faith," which the laity must receive passively and obediently. At Vatican II, a personalist notion of revelation is retrieved, along with an active conception of the reception of revelation by all the faithful (as the revelation/faith principle has outlined).

The first task of the church is to proclaim the Gospel: "The church . . . receives the mission of proclaiming and establishing among all peoples the kingdom of Christ and of God, and is, on earth, the seed and the beginning of that kingdom" (LG 5). This is the task of all the *fideles*, lay, religious, or ordained: "All disciples of Christ are obliged to spread the faith to the best of their ability" (LG 17). Consequently, among the offices of Christ in the church, it is the prophetic office that is primary, and so too for bishops: "Among the principal *munera* of bishops, that of preaching the Gospel is pre-eminent [*eminet*]" (LG 25).[45] Just as the treatment of the kingly office retrieves the biblical image of the shepherd, so the council's treatment of the prophetic office retrieves the biblical image of the prophet. Preaching the word is now given prominence alongside teaching doctrine. Rahner, in commenting on *Lumen Gentium* 25, remarks: "It is noteworthy (and important for an ecumenical theology) that the more doctrinal concept of teaching attributed to the bishops as *doctores* is subordinated to the biblical and more comprehensive or existential conception of preaching."[46] Likewise, "it is the first task [*officium*] of priests as co-workers of the bishops to preach the Gospel of God to all" (PO 4).

Despite this emphasis on preaching by Vatican II (in line with the Council of Trent), however, the council nevertheless reiterates the doctrinal emphasis of Vatican I and the teaching authority of the pope and bishops. But these statements are now situated within a broader ecclesial vision resulting from the reordering of chapters 2 and 3. Juxtaposed alongside repetitions of Vatican I statements regarding teaching authority is a conception of the participation of the hierarchy in the prophetic office in terms of service.

First, the hierarchy's participation is a service to the people of God: "That office [*munus*] [that is, the mission of teaching all peoples and of preaching the Gospel to every creature], which the Lord committed to the pastors of

45. Translation corrected.

46. Karl Rahner, "The Hierarchical Structure of the Church, with Special Reference to the Episcopate. Articles 18–27," in *Commentary on the Documents of Vatican II*, vol. 1, ed. Herbert Vorgrimler (London: Burns & Oates, 1967), 186–218, at 208.

his people, truly is a service [*servitium*], which is called very expressively in sacred scripture a *diakonia* or ministry [*ministerium*]" (LG 24).[47] Second, the hierarchy's participation is a service in aid of safeguarding "the treasure of divine revelation entrusted to the church" (DV 26). In their capacity as the *magisterium*—the church's formal preaching and teaching authority—the pope and the bishops are servants of that divine self-gift to the whole church. *Lumen Gentium* 25 teaches: "When the Roman Pontiff, or the body of bishops together with him, define a doctrine, they do so in conformity with revelation itself, by which all are bound to abide and to which they are obliged to conform." This subservience to God's self-revelation as witnessed to in Scripture and tradition is later formulated more starkly in *Dei Verbum*: "This magisterium is not superior to the word of God but rather serves it [*ministrat*]. It teaches only what has been handed on to it. At the divine command and with the help of the Holy Spirit, it listens to this devoutly [*pie audit*], guards it reverently and expounds it faithfully" (DV 10). In the sentence before that passage, the phrase "the word of God" is described as "whether in its written form or in the form of tradition" (DV 10). This "single sacred deposit of the word of God . . . is entrusted to the church . . . the entire holy people" (DV 10), not just to the magisterium. Nevertheless, "the task of authoritatively [*authentice*] interpreting the word of God, whether in its written form or in the form of tradition, has been entrusted to the living magisterium of the church alone" (DV 10).[48] However, as the very opening line of the Dogmatic Constitution asserts, the word of God (*Dei Verbum*) demands a "listening reverently [*religiose audiens*]."[49] Therefore, the magisterium's service to the word of God includes also "listening reverently" to the entire holy people's reception of the word of God.

This relationship between the magisterium's participation in the prophetic office and the participation in that office by "the entire holy people" is largely implied in the documents of Vatican II. The two participations are generally

47. The council cites Acts 1:17 and 25; Rom 11:13; 1 Tim 1:12.

48. Translation corrected. On translating *authentice* as "authoritatively," see Sullivan, *Magisterium*, 26–28. "If this meaning of *authentice* is not kept in mind, one could think that the Council was making the absurd claim that only bishops could give a genuine interpretation of the Word of God, or that they were the only ones who would interpret Scripture or Tradition with any kind of authority at all. The Council surely did not intend to deny that theologians and exegetes speak with the authority which their expertise confers on them. What the Council attributes exclusively to the 'living magisterium' is authority to speak as pastors of the Church, endowed with the mandate to teach the Gospel in the name of Jesus Christ." Ibid., 28.

49. Translation corrected.

allowed to stand in tension without explicit discussion of the implications. This is true especially of two interrelated dimensions of the prophetic office: the *infallibilitas in credendo* (infallibility in believing) of the people of God affirmed in chapter 2 (LG 12) and the *infallibilitas in docendo* (infallibility in teaching) of the hierarchy affirmed in chapter 3 (LG 25). As Rahner observes: "Here [in *Lumen Gentium* 12] an infallibility of faith is attributed to the people of God as a whole, as also to the people of the Church as the recipients of teaching in particular. The Council itself has not attempted to carry this further by relating what it says in these chapters to the statements in chapter III, where it is the hierarchical structure of the Church which is dealt with."[50] Alois Grillmeier similarly notes the implicit interrelationship between the two:

> All members of the people of God share in this transmission of the reality of revelation and salvation *in credendo*. This article [LG 12], in fact, like the whole of Chapter II, is concerned with basing the infallibility of the Church, like that of the magisterium, on the people of God as a whole. In the mind of the faithful, as in that of the magisterium, the gift of infallibility has been too one-sidedly concentrated on the office [of the episcopate], and even on a papal primacy which was considered in isolation from the episcopate as a whole. This could only lead to passivity and indifference with regard to responsibility for the word of God. According to Vatican II, watch and ward is truly kept over the reality of revelation and salvation by the people of Christ as a whole, though in various degrees of active service. The people of Christ as a whole, including the holders of office, is infallible *in credendo*, which, however, is not to be taken in a passive sense. It is something active, by which the faith is vigorously preserved and attested, penetrated ever more profoundly and made the formative element in life. The holders of office are infallible, not merely *in credendo* along with the whole people of God, but also *in docendo*, by virtue of the charism given to them, which embraces their teaching. *The instinct of faith [sensus fidei] in the people as a whole and the infallible magisterium of the Church stand in the same relation to each other as the common priesthood of all the faithful to the consecrated priesthood, into which is absorbed the priesthood of all the baptized.*[51]

This interrelationship between the *sensus fidelium* and the magisterium within the prophetic office is left unexplored in any extensive way in the council

---

50. Rahner, "The Teaching Office of the Church," 5n4.
51. Grillmeier, "Chapter II: The People of God," 164–65. Emphasis added.

documents, leaving the interpreter the task of synthesis. But, yet again, like many of Vatican II's juxtapositions between preconciliar frameworks and new approaches, a trajectory toward a synthesis is given. In this particular case, attention to the council's overall Pneumatology provides the key.

The Dynamism of the Spirit of Truth

The documents emphasize the Spirit's role in both the participation by all the faithful in the prophetic office and the participation by the hierarchy. The relevant passages for each must be read intratextually and intertextually, so that they are interpreted in the light of the council's overall Pneumatology. Regarding the Spirit enabling the participation of the *universitas fidelium*, *Lumen Gentium* 12—on how "the holy People of God participates [*participat*] also in Christ's prophetic office"[52]—mentions the Holy Spirit twice in the first paragraph ("the Holy One" and "the Spirit of truth"), with allusions to the Spirit in every sentence of the second paragraph on charisms in the church. Because the Spirit anoints all the faithful, they "cannot be mistaken in believing [*in credendo falli nequit*]." This anointing bestows "a supernatural sense of the faith of the entire people [*supernaturali sensu fidei totius populi*], which is aroused and sustained by the Spirit of truth."

Regarding the participation of the bishops in particular, *Lumen Gentium* 25 mentions the Spirit four times. "*Under the light of the Holy Spirit* [bishops] cause that faith to radiate, drawing from the storehouse of revelation new things and old." The pope's "definitions [regarding faith and morals] are rightly said to be irreformable by their very nature and not by reason of the consent of the church, in as much as they were *made with the assistance of the Holy Spirit* promised to him in blessed Peter; and as a consequence they are not in need of the approval of others, and do not admit of appeal to any other tribunal." Likewise, concerning "the supreme teaching office" of the body of the bishops together with the pope: "The assent of the church can never be lacking to such definitions *on account of the same Holy Spirit's influence*, through which Christ's whole flock is maintained in the unity of the faith and makes progress in it." Finally, "*through the light of the Spirit of truth* [revelation] is scrupulously preserved in the church and unerringly explained. The Roman Pontiff and the bishops, in virtue of their office [*officio*] and because of the seriousness of the matter, are assiduous in examining this revelation by every suitable means and in expressing it properly."

---

52. Translation corrected.

In these passages, the Spirit's assistance to the magisterium can be conceived in either an "extrinsicist" or an "immanentist" way.[53] According to a juridical mind-set, the light and influence of the Holy Spirit comes directly without mediation and requires passive reception. A comprehensive view of the council's Pneumatology, however, requires a more dynamic and "immanentist" interpretation, especially when all references to the Spirit and revelation are read intratextually (e.g., across chapters 2 and 3 of *Lumen Gentium*) and intertextually (e.g., across *Lumen Gentium* and *Dei Verbum*). With regard to the latter, key to a comprehensive pneumatological view of the prophetic office is a passage on the living tradition, *Dei Verbum* 8: "The [living] tradition that comes from the apostles makes progress in the church, with the help of the Holy Spirit. There is a growth in insight into the realities and words that are being passed on. This comes about through . . ." And then three means through which the Spirit works in generating the living tradition are listed: "the contemplation and study of believers" (i.e., the work of theologians); believers' "intimate sense of spiritual realities which they experience" (the *sensus fidei fidelium*); and the preaching of the bishops who have received "the sure charism of truth."[54] The paragraph concludes: "Thus, as the centuries go by, the church is always advancing towards the plenitude of divine truth, until eventually the words of God are fulfilled in it" (DV 8). This last sentence of the middle paragraph alludes to the Johannine passage: "When the Spirit of truth comes, he will guide you into all the truth" (John 16:13). And then the third and concluding sentence of the whole article ends with a parallel affirmation of the Spirit's role in actualizing the living tradition, alluding again to the same Johannine passage: "Thus God, who spoke in the past, continues to dialogue [*colloquitur*] with the spouse of his beloved Son. And the Holy Spirit, through whom the living voice of the Gospel rings out in the church— and through it in the world—leads believers to the full truth and makes the word of Christ dwell in them in all its richness" (DV 8).[55]

This dynamic sense of the Spirit generating the living tradition throughout history envisages an interactive relationship between three groups within the church: theological scholars, all the faithful and their *sensus fidei*, and

53. On this distinction as a way of depicting preconciliar and conciliar theology from the perspective of Maurice Blondel's philosophy, see Gregory Baum, *Man Becoming: God in Secular Language* (New York: Herder and Herder, 1970), esp. 3–36.

54. The chapter below on the magisterium/theologians principle will examine in greater detail this reference to "the contemplation and study of believers" as a reference to the work of theologians.

55. Translation corrected.

the bishops. In the prophetic office, these three groups constitute three ecclesial authorities in the transmission of revelation throughout history, by means of the guidance of the one Holy Spirit. Therefore, the four passages in *Lumen Gentium* 25 referring to the Spirit's guidance to the episcopate must be read in the light of this more comprehensive Pneumatology.

The chapter below on the magisterium/theologians principle will address the participation in the prophetic (teaching) office of the episcopate and of theologians and the consequent conception of their interrelationship. Here brief consideration is needed regarding the mutual participation of the episcopate and all the faithful in the prophetic office and the consequent relationship between them that is implied.

The council states that the receptive attitude of the people of God to certain teaching of the pope and bishops should be characterized by "adhering [*adhaerere*]" with "a religious docility of spirit [*religioso animi obsequio*]" (LG 25). In response to certain teaching of the pope, a "religious docility of the will and intellect [*religiosum voluntatis et intellectus obsequium*]" (LG 25) is required. The language here accords with that of the preconciliar juridical model, with the proper response of subjects to their superiors being one of passive obedience. What is not clearly specified is the concomitant responsibility of the hierarchy to the people of God and their lived "sense of the faith." This dialogic relationship is implied in the text of *Lumen Gentium* 12, as well as in the symbolic placement of the chapter on the people of God before that on the hierarchy.

The magisterium teaches the faith of the church, and its infallibility *in teaching* is a consequence of the infallibility *in believing* of the whole people of God. When it comes to the infallibility attributed to the teaching by the pope and the bishops, *Lumen Gentium* 25, following Vatican I, is careful to affirm that it is the faith of the whole church that the magisterium teaches. For example: "The Roman Pontiff does not deliver a pronouncement as a private person, but rather does he expound and defend the teaching of the catholic faith as the supreme teacher of the universal church, in whom, as an individual [*singulariter*], *the charism of infallibility of the church itself* is present. The infallibility *promised to the church* is also present in the body of bishops when, together with Peter's successor, they exercise the supreme teaching office" (LG 25).[56] The passages in article 25 on the Roman Pontiff are accompanied by four footnote references to the careful clarifications by

56. Emphasis added.

Bishop Vincent Gasser in his *Relatio* to the First Vatican Council regarding the infallibility of the whole church and the relationship of the pope and bishops to that infallibility.[57]

Lumen Gentium 12 aligns the faith of the people of God with "the entire people's supernatural sense of the faith." This supernatural gift is given to the whole church and to all the *fideles*, "from the bishops to the last of the faithful" (LG 12). Within the *fideles*, however, the overwhelming majority of the faithful are the laity. The *sensus laicorum* (the sense of the laity), therefore, while it does not encompass totally the *sensus fidelium*, is a vital source for the magisterium in discerning the lived faith of the church in different contexts throughout history: "[Christ] fulfils this prophetic office, not only through the hierarchy who teach in his name and by his power, but also through the laity. He accordingly both establishes them as witnesses and provides them with a sense of the faith [*sensu fidei*] and the grace of the word [*gratia verbi*] so that the power of the Gospel may shine out in daily family and social life" (LG 35). This description of the active and lived faith of the people of God in the context of their daily lives evokes the verbs of *Lumen Gentium* 12 affirmed of all the *fideles*: "By this sense of the faith [*sensu fidei*], aroused and sustained by the Spirit of truth, the People of God, guided by the magisterium which it faithfully obeys, receives not the word of human beings, but truly the word of God, 'the faith once for all delivered to the saints' (Jude 3). The people unfailingly adheres to this faith, penetrates it more deeply through right judgment, and applies it more fully in daily life" (LG 12). Once again, what is affirmed of the laity is an intensification of what is affirmed of all the *fideles*.

The key, therefore, to arriving at a new synthesis of Vatican II's teaching on the prophetic office is a dynamic conception of the relationship between the People of God and the hierarchy. This dynamic conception will be thoroughly pneumatological and dialogic. The council already provides the beginnings of dialogic structures in which the *sensus fidelium* can play a part in the formulation and reformulation of the church's teaching on faith and morals, beginning from the local parish level to an ecumenical council: parish and diocesan councils, local and regional synods, national and regional

---

57. For the full text of Gasser's *Relatio*, see Vinzenz Gasser, *The Gift of Infallibility: The Official Relatio on Infallibility of Bishop Vincent Gasser at Vatican Council I*, ed. James T. O'Connor, 2nd updated ed. (San Francisco: Ignatius Press, 2008). On Gasser's presentation, see John W. O'Malley, *Vatican I: The Council and the Making of the Ultramontane Church* (Cambridge, MA: The Belknap Press of Harvard University Press, 2018), 216–19.

episcopal conferences, the international synod of bishops (including prior consultation of the laity).

Gaudium et Spes 92 states the tone in which such dialogue within the church should proceed: "mutual esteem, reverence and harmony, and to acknowledge all legitimate diversity; in this way *all who constitute the one people of God* will be able to engage in ever more fruitful dialogue, whether they are pastors or other members of the faithful. For the ties which unite the faithful together are stronger than those which separate them: let there be unity in what is necessary, freedom in what is doubtful, and charity in everything" (GS 92).[58] The term "noncompetitive," Richard Gaillardetz believes, "aptly describes the way the council overcame the hierocratic church's tendency to pit key ecclesial elements in competitive, oppositional relationships."[59] It certainly captures the essence of the people of God/hierarchy principle (as it does for the next two principles).[60]

There is, in one sense, continuity between what was said of the hierarchy in preconciliar theology and what Vatican II affirms; the latter continues to speak at times of the authority and power of the hierarchy in juridical terms. But the place of that important juridical aspect of the church's nature is radically reoriented and realigned within a whole new nonpyramidal framework. As Rahner remarks:

> [T]he Church comprehends what she is as the institution of salvation only when she understands and perfects herself as the *fruit* of salvation. There is no doubt, moreover, that the *Constitution on the Church* has understood this fact, for it speaks at length (and why not?) about the Church as institution, about her offices and powers, about her hierarchical structure, about her didactic and pastoral offices, about the many apostolates in the Church's mission—that is, in sum, about the Church as institution and mediation of salvation. But behind all this is the much more basic understanding that the Church is the people of God gathered by the grace of God, and outgrowth of God's grace, the fruit of salvation.[61]

58. Emphasis added.
59. Gaillardetz, *An Unfinished Council*, 91.
60. Regarding a noncompetitive relationship between the teaching magisterium and the whole Christian faithful, see ibid., 98–101. In the next chapter, we will see how Gaillardetz also interprets the council's trajectory as leading to "a non-competitive theology of the relationship between pope and bishops." See ibid., 93–98.
61. Rahner, *The Church after the Council*, 70–71. Original emphasis.

Thus, "the image of 'the People of God' provides an inclusive and catholic understanding of Church that places the institutional and bureaucratic elements of the Church in a larger perspective, and places the whole Church in a wider communal and universal context."[62] Now, as the *fideles/fidelis* principle asserts, and as Kasper remarks, "the common existence of the people of God precedes all differences of functions, charismata and ministries."[63] Nevertheless, as Antonio Acerbi's study shows, the juridical aspects of the hierarchy's position in the church and the broader *communio* ecclesiology grounded in the church as the people of God remain in tension.[64] Christopher Butler sees this tension in terms of two lines of thought, what he calls a "historical" view and an "essentialist" view: "This tension is latent—some would say unresolved—in the *juxtaposition* of the hierarchical view of the Church, of her unchanging basic structure, with that of the Church as energized, rendered dynamic, by the charisms or grace-gifts of the Holy Ghost who is no respecter of persons or of office. This charismatic aspect of the Church is what makes her, while unchanging in her essence, unpredictable in her history. *Les portes de l'avenir sont toujours grand-ouvertes* (Bergson) [The doors of the future are always wide-open]."[65] But now Vatican I has been balanced by Vatican II, which, in effect, affirms "that the Church is a community with a hierarchical structure rather than a hierarchical body with spiritual subjects."[66]

---

62. John J. Markey, *Creating Communion: The Theology of the Constitutions of the Church* (Hyde Park, NY: New City Press, 2003), 96, see also 99n25.

63. Kasper, "The Church as Communion," 162.

64. See Acerbi, *Due ecclesiologie.*

65. Butler, *The Theology of Vatican II*, 151. Emphasis added.

66. Richard P. McBrien, "People of God," in *The HarperCollins Encyclopedia of Catholicism*, ed. Richard P. McBrien (New York: HarperCollins, 1995), 984–85, at 985.

Principle 20
College of Bishops/Bishop of Rome

Principle 20: In their service to the people of God, the bishops constitute a college in succession to the college of apostles, with the bishop of Rome as a member of the college and its head; the Bishop of Rome serves the college of bishops as the principle of its unity.

The previous principle envisions the place of the hierarchy in the church in its relationship of service to the whole people of God; this next principle formulates the appropriate relationship, *within* the hierarchy, between the college of bishops and the Bishop of Rome. The ordering of terms in this conciliar principle is significant; the first term is the college of bishops, with the second term referring to one who is a member of the college but also its head. The principle thus articulates Vatican II's vision of episcopal collegiality and papal primacy. While the main text is *Lumen Gentium* 22, the other articles in chapter 3 present significant teachings that impinge on the principle. Moreover, other documents touch on the topic, especially *Sacrosanctum Concilium*, *Christus Dominus*, and *Ad Gentes*.

Re-Receiving Vatican I into a New Framework
This principle emerges from Vatican II's re-reception of the teaching of the First Vatican Council regarding the primacy of the pope (the following principle will examine its re-reception regarding the infallibility of the pope). The ecclesiology of Vatican I crystallizes what the historian John O'Malley calls "the papalization of Catholicism," a process that began with the Gregorian reforms of the eleventh century and, increasing with ever greater force across the centuries, reached its high point a millennium later with the declarations of Vatican I.[1] Western Catholic ecclesiology by that time was

1. See O'Malley, "The Papalization of Catholicism." As Hermann Pottmeyer stresses, it is important to remember the historical context for some of this development: "It would be a

predominantly juridical and papal, with an "ultramontane" emphasis on relationships of power and authority.[2] Accordingly, in its "first dogmatic constitution on the church of Christ," *Pastor Aeternus*, Vatican I confirmed the majority of bishops' ultramontane view of the pope's juridical primacy, i.e., his primacy of jurisdiction over the bishops.[3] A minority of bishops at the council, however, were able to temper a potentially maximalist portrayal of papal primacy in the final document, a portrayal that would envisage the pope as *de facto* the single bishop of the whole world, and of bishops as virtually his parish priests under his authority. Nevertheless, despite its balance, the postconciliar reception of Vatican I's teaching saw the predominance of this maximalist attitude—an "inflated ultramontanism, so different from the vastly more prudent and sober tone of *Pastor Aeternus*."[4]

Vatican I had certainly intended to address the collegial nature of the episcopate in a larger project, a second constitution on the church, *De Ecclesia*, although the decision to focus first on papal primacy and papal infallibility meant these doctrines were presented without the context of a fuller notion of the church.[5] The original preparatory document (*Supremi Pasto-*

---

mistake to regard the Roman attempt to make bishops dependent on the pope as merely Rome's will to power. Rather, behind this attempt were also Rome's efforts to remove the bishops from their dependence on the political powers under which they found themselves in many countries. It is no exaggeration to speak of a centuries-long 'Babylonian Captivity' of the episcopacy which became the pawns of the interests of nobles, princes, and national governments." Hermann J. Pottmeyer, "The Episcopacy," in *The Gift of the Church: A Textbook on Ecclesiology in Honor of Patrick Granfield, O.S.B*, ed. Peter C. Phan (Collegeville, MN: Liturgical Press, 2000), 337–53, at 345. For a brief account of the bishops/pope relationship throughout church history, see William Henn, *The Honor of My Brothers: A Short History of the Relation between the Pope and the Bishops* (New York: Crossroad, 2000).

2. On the rise of "ultramontanism" till the eve of Vatican I, see O'Malley, *Vatican I*, 55–132.

3. See Tanner, *Decrees of the Ecumenical Councils*, 2:811–16. On the background, debates and definition at Vatican I regarding the papal primacy of jurisdiction, see Pottmeyer, *Towards a Papacy in Communion*, 51–75. For a fuller treatment, see Hermann J. Pottmeyer, *Unfehlbarkeit und Souveränität: Die päpstliche Unfehlbarkeit im System der ultramontanen Ekklesiologie des 19. Jahrhunderts* (Mainz: Matthias-Grünewald-Verlag, 1975), esp. 346–428. For a summary of Vatican I's teaching on papal primacy, see Kloppenburg, *The Ecclesiology of Vatican II*, 169–204. On the dynamics of the conciliar debates, see O'Malley, *Vatican I*, 180–224.

4. J. M. R. Tillard, *The Bishop of Rome* (Wilmington, DE: Michael Glazier, 1983), 32. For a similar interpretation, proposing "that the issue of papal primacy at Vatican I may be more open than often thought," see Margaret O'Gara, "Three Successive Steps toward Understanding Papal Primacy in Vatican I," *The Jurist* 64, no. 1 (2004): 208–23, at 223.

5. Regarding the surprising decision by the presidents of the council on April 29, 1870, to focus only on papal primacy and papal infallibility, John O'Malley observes: "The decision had an extremely significant theological implication: primacy and infallibility were now to be considered in isolation from the larger context of the church, or, in the words of the minority,

ris) had failed to receive a positive reception from the council (although its eleventh chapter would be taken over into *Pastor Aeternus*).[6] The Roman theologian Joseph Kleutgen was then entrusted with drafting a second version of the document on the church, now with the title *Tametsi Deus*.[7] It addressed the matter of collegiality, acknowledging that the bishops participate in governing the church. Therefore, in the wings of Vatican I was a potential doctrine of collegiality.[8] Due to the start of the Franco-Prussian war on July 19, 1870, and the premature pause of the council, the bishops never debated this larger project. Time permitted discussion of mainly two ecclesiological themes, papal primacy and papal infallibility, resulting in chapters 3 and 4, respectively, of *Pastor Aeternus*. "Thus the First Vatican Council slipped into an adjournment that within a few decades seemed destined to be everlasting—the soft but definitive end of ecumenical councils. After all, *Pastor Aeternus* had rendered such gatherings obsolete."[9]

Vatican I was never officially concluded. Popes in the twentieth century did consider recalling it. When John XXIII convened a council, he clearly wanted his council to be a different one. He deliberately named it the *Second Vatican Council*.[10] Despite his desire for a new openness, it would clearly need to address unfinished business from Vatican I. So, when it came to discussion

---

as a head severed from the body. In retrospect we know, moreover, that had this change in the order of business not been made, the definition [of infallibility] would not have happened. The issue would not have come to the council before the seizure of Rome on September 20 and the resulting indefinite adjournment of Vatican I." O'Malley, *Vatican I*, 185.

6. On the drafting, structure, and content of *Supremi Pastoris*, particularly its concretization of the prevailing notion of the church as a *societas perfecta*, see Granfield, "The Church as 'Societas Perfecta,'" 432–41. Also on *Supremi Pastoris*, see O'Malley, *Vatican I*, 162–63, 181–85.

7. Giovanni Domenico Mansi, *Sacrorum conciliorum, nova et amplissima collectio*, 54 vols. (Graz: Akademische Druck-u. Verlagsanstalt, 1960), 53:308–17. On the ecclesiology of *Tametsi Deus*, see Granfield, "The Church as 'Societas Perfecta,'" 441–46.

8. In his report from the council's "doctrinal commission" (called the "Deputation of the Faith") on *Pastor Aeternus* chapter 3 on papal primacy, Bishop Federico Zinelli stated, in an attempt to placate the minority: "We willingly agree that full and total ecclesiastical sovereignty over all the faithful resides also in ourselves as gathered in ecumenical Council, in ourselves, the bishops united to their head. Yes, this perfectly fits the Church united to the head. Gathered with their leader in ecumenical Council, in which case they represent the whole Church, or dispersed, yet in union with their leader, in which case they are the Church herself, the bishops therefore have supreme authority." Mansi, *Sacrorum conciliorum, nova et amplissima collectio*, 52:1109. Quoted in Tavard, *The Pilgrim Church*, 94.

9. O'Malley, *Vatican I*, 224.

10. See Giuseppe Alberigo, "The Announcement of the Council: From the Security of the Fortress to the Lure of the Quest," in *History of Vatican II*, vol. 1: *Announcing and Preparing Vatican Council II*, ed. Giuseppe Alberigo and Joseph A. Komonchak (Maryknoll, NY: Orbis Books, 1996), 1:1–54, at 50–52.

of the doctrine of collegiality, Vatican II saw itself to be "following in the steps of the First Vatican Council" (LG 18). Vatican II's preparatory schema on the church (*Aeternus Unigeniti Pater*) deliberately wanted to complete the agenda of Vatican I. Its fourth chapter treated the college of bishops. As Adrian Hastings points out, however, this did not necessarily ensure a new vision of papal primacy: "In Vatican II, [the preparatory draft] already had a lot to say about the episcopate, but of course to balance the papacy with the episcopate was not as such to get away from a governmental and juridical view of ecclesiology, and this is just what [the preparatory draft] failed to do."[11]

It was not only Vatican I's juridical emphasis on papal primacy that the council should set out to address but also "false interpretations which distorted its meaning," as called for by the Melkite Patriarch Maximos in his speech during the second session debates on the church at Vatican II.[12] He went on to request: "It seems to us that the Council should not be satisfied to repeat what the First Vatican Council had to say on this point since this is already an accepted part of the Church's patrimony. What this Council should do is clarify and complete the words of Vatican I in the light of the teaching about the divine institution and the inalienable rights of the episcopacy."[13] In its final formulation, Vatican II's doctrine of collegiality "simply brings out into the open what was understood at the First Vatican Council [regarding collegiality], and incorporates into the official texts what had been said, and admitted by all, during the debates in 1870. The collegiality endorsed by Vatican II is therefore not meant to correct the doctrine of Vatican I, but to eschew the exaggerations that had misinterpreted Vatican I."[14]

To achieve that, Vatican II would need a less juridical, less "Western," theology of the church, one more open to the ecclesiology of the Eastern churches. Catholic *ressourcement* studies before the council had already been bringing these Eastern sensibilities to bear on Catholic theology.[15] The crucial new framework for reenvisioning the doctrines of Vatican I regarding the bishops and the pope is that outlined in the two mutually interpretive principles of Vatican II: the *fideles/fidelis* principle and the People of God/hierarchy principle.

11. Hastings, *A Concise Guide to the Documents*, 1:42–43.

12. Patriarch Maximos IV, "Servant of the Servants of God," in *Council Speeches of Vatican II*, ed. Hans Küng, Yves Congar, and Daniel O'Hanlon (Glen Rock, NJ: Paulist Press, 1964), 72–75, at 72.

13. Ibid., 72–73.

14. Tavard, *The Pilgrim Church*, 95.

15. See the comments in ibid., 85–87.

Vatican II's college of bishops/bishop of Rome principle emerges for the most part from three major affirmations of *Lumen Gentium*'s third chapter: (1) the college of bishops, within which the pope is member and head, continues the functions of the college of apostles; (2) a *fidelis* enters into the episcopal college through the sacrament of episcopal consecration celebrated by other bishops; and (3) episcopal consecration, through an intensification of the elect's baptismal participation in the three offices of Christ, confers those offices on the bishop in a distinctive way, that of service to the whole body of the faithful. Despite the statement of these three themes in some way in the preparatory constitution, they ended up being the ones that caused the most heated debate.[16] In the preparatory draft of *De Ecclesia*, says Rahner, "we find substantially the same doctrine as in the final version of the Constitution, which does not, therefore, go beyond the first draft except in some minor modifications."[17]

The reason for the fierce opposition by the minority at Vatican II to finishing the agenda of Vatican I on the matter of the episcopate was precisely the broader ecclesiology into which the doctrine of collegiality would be developed, one that would preclude any "inflated ultramontanism" regarding the primacy of the pope and "the centring of everything on Rome."[18] According to Rahner:

> The explanation [for the fierce opposition by the minority] lies in the circumstances. An ancient truth was re-appearing *in a new situation* of the spiritual and historical development of the Church and giving a completely novel impulse to the life and practice of the Church. . . . The content of the affirmation is not new, and it does not mark any notable progress in dogmatic development compared to the previous stage, all the more so since so many individual questions are left open. But the fact that the affirmation was expressly made is now the consequence (and in future no doubt will be the cause) of *a changed*

---

16. For the drafting history of *Lumen Gentium*, chapter 3, the classic text is Umberto Betti, *La dottrina sull'episcopato del Concilio vaticano II: Il capitolo III della Costituzione dommatica Lumen Gentium* (Roma: Spicilegium Pontificii Athenaei Antoniani, 1984), 81–329. For Betti's commentary on each of articles 18–27, see ibid., 342–440.

17. Rahner, "The Hierarchical Structure of the Church," 186. For example, regarding *Lumen Gentium* 22 (the article that specifically focuses on what is here formulated as the college of bishops/bishop of Rome principle), Rahner remarks: "The text propounds a doctrine which had never been proposed so explicitly before by the extraordinary magisterium but which does not, in effect, really go beyond the traditional teaching, as proposed for instance at Vatican I by the official reporters Gasser and Zinelli or Kleutgen." Ibid., 195.

18. Tillard, *The Bishop of Rome*, 35.

mentality which takes a critical attitude towards a certain type of Roman centralization and curial administration earlier in vogue, which are by no means identical with the primacy and its exercise. This is what makes the chapter so important in the pastoral life and in the history of the Church.[19]

With regard to this "changed mentality," as we have seen, a major cause of the minority's angst was the restructuring of *Lumen Gentium* in the revised draft presented to the bishops for discussion in the third session, with the former second chapter on the hierarchy now coming after that on the people of God. The minority at Vatican II recognized the implications of this shift for not only reconceiving the church but also tempering a maximalist view of papal primacy: the pope is not "above" the church or "above" the episcopate but to be situated *within the church* and *within the college of bishops*.

The proper ordering of the terms of this principle has already been noted. It derives from the progression of argument throughout *Lumen Gentium* 18, which opens the chapter on the hierarchy. Otto Hermann Pesch observes in this article "two noteworthy accents" that are highly relevant for interpreting Vatican II's reception of Vatican I's teaching on episcopal collegiality and papal primacy.[20] The first is negative: remarkably, it does not appeal straight off to the famous biblical text regarding papal primacy, Matthew 16:18 (although it will appropriately go on to do so later in articles 19 and 22).[21] The second is positive: in *Lumen Gentium* 18, the whole group of apostles are spoken of first, before Peter as their head. The same order holds for its discussion of the college of bishops, which continues analogously the function of the apostolic college. Thus collegiality and primacy, and their proper ordering, are placed within the context of *apostolicity*. This order reverses that of Vatican I, as Jean-Marie Tillard notes:

> Where Vatican I sees the Church in its earthly form starting from its "head," the bishop of Rome, Vatican II sees it starting from the bishops as "successors of the apostles," and who taken together as a whole, comprise the foundation of the universal Church. . . . Vatican II is thus entirely clear: the fullness of that ministry which builds, guides and leads the whole Church belongs to the body of bishops as such, following in the wake of the mission entrusted to the

---

19. Rahner, "The Hierarchical Structure of the Church," 187. Emphasis added.

20. See Otto Hermann Pesch, *The Second Vatican Council: Prehistory—Event—Results—Posthistory* (Milwaukee: Marquette University Press, 2014), 226.

21. "And I tell you, you are Peter, and on this rock I will build my church, and the gates of Hades will not prevail against it." NRSV translation.

apostles as a group. *Lumen Gentium* sets the *officium* of what it still calls "the Roman Pontiff" firmly within this shared mission, treating it indeed as a function of that mission.[22]

It is this college, including the pope, which governs the whole church (albeit *in service* of the whole church, which participates in the governing office). "Continuing with this same undertaking [i.e., Vatican I's teaching regarding papal primacy and infallibility], [Vatican II] intends to profess before all and to declare the teaching on bishops, successors of the apostles, who together with Peter's successor the Vicar of Christ and the visible head of the whole church, *govern the house of the living God*" (LG 18). That the bishops are not mere functionaries of the pope is later even more explicitly stated: "The pastoral office [*munus pastorale*], that is, the permanent and daily care of their sheep, is entrusted to [the bishops] fully; nor are they to be regarded as vicars of the Roman Pontiff; for they exercise a power which they possess in their own right and are most truly said to be at the head of the people whom they govern" (LG 27). Indeed, the bishops themselves, in their own right, are, like the pope, "vicars and legates of Christ" (LG 27). The pope is first and foremost a member of this college. Tillard notes the simple implication: "The scheme no longer has the shape of a pyramid. The line no longer travels from the pope to the bishops, with the weight on the former at the expense of the latter; but from the bishops to the pope."[23] Thus papal primacy is now set within the context of episcopal collegiality, and not vice versa. For the canonist Hervé Legrand, this changed mentality regarding episcopal collegiality constitutes "the central plank of Vatican II's institutional reform,"[24] and he quotes others, for whom it is "the dorsal fin of the whole Council," "the centre of gravity of Vatican II."[25]

22. Tillard, *The Bishop of Rome*, 36. Patrick Granfield similarly observes: "Vatican II, unlike Vatican I, began its description of the hierarchical structure not with the Pope but with the College of Bishops as successor of the college of the Apostles under the leadership of the Pope, successor of Peter. . . . The Pope, then, is placed within the College of Bishops; he himself is a fellow bishop and head of the college." Patrick Granfield, *The Limits of the Papacy: Authority and Autonomy in the Church* (London: Darton, Longman and Todd, 1987), 43.

23. Tillard, *The Bishop of Rome*, 36.

24. Hervé Legrand, "Forty Years Later: What Has Become of the Ecclesiological Reforms Envisaged by Vatican II?," in *Vatican II: A Forgotten Future?*, ed. Alberto Melloni and Christoph Theobald (London: SCM Press, 2005), 57–72, at 58.

25. Ibid., 58. Legrand is here quoting Cardinal Eyt who attributes the first expression to Umberto Betti (without citing the source) and the second to A. Wenger. See A. Wegner, "La collégialité épiscopale," in *Le deuxième concile du Vatican* (Rome: 1989), 54.

This proper ordering of terms within the principle finds its theological grounding in the council's teaching on episcopal consecration.[26] In wanting to balance Vatican I's juridically formulated doctrine of papal primacy, the council gives emphasis, not to a juridical delegation by the pope for becoming a member of the episcopate, but rather to the conferring of the fullness of the sacrament of orders through episcopal consecration. Significantly, the imposition of hands by other bishops in the sacrament is depicted as a passing on of the gift of the Spirit and the special character of the sacrament. "The holy synod teaches . . . that the fullness of the sacrament of Orders is conferred by episcopal consecration" (LG 21). Ancient tradition is cited as the basis for this belief: "in the liturgical rites and in the customs of both the eastern and western church" (LG 21).

Moreover, the sacrament of consecration confers the three offices of Christ as prophet, priest, and king. This assertion is a significant break with a long-held belief that only the priestly office ("the power of orders") is conveyed in a bishop's consecration and that the bishop's teaching and governing offices related to "the power of jurisdiction" are granted to them only by the pope.[27] Vatican II shifts away from this jurisdictional framework to a new sacramental concept regarding the *teaching* and *governing* aspects of the bishop's ministry, with authorization coming, not through the pope, but *through the Holy Spirit*, albeit with the minority's *de rigueur* qualification of papal approval: "Episcopal consecration confers, *together with* the office of sanctifying, the offices *also* of teaching and ruling, which, however, of their very nature can be *exercised* only in hierarchical communion [*hierarchica communione*] with the head and members of the college. . . . [T]hrough the imposition of hands and the words of consecration, the grace of the Holy Spirit is given, and a sacred character is impressed in such a way that bishops, eminently

---

26. For the notion of the sacramentality of the episcopate in preconciliar theology and the history of its treatment across the various drafts of *Lumen Gentium*, see the detailed study of G. Nicolussi, "La sacramentalità dell'episcopato nella 'Lumen Gentium,' Cap. III: Brevi cenni sulla penetrazione dell'idea nel testo conciliare," *Ephemerides Theologicae Lovanienses* 47 (1971): 7–63.

27. As Hermann Pottmeyer remarks: "The tasks which the council attributes to the bishop emerge likewise out of the concept of the sacramental representation of Christ. Jesus Christ is present in the Church in three ways: in his word, in the sacraments, and in the unity and communion of his Mystical Body which is the Church. Hence, there are three classical tasks of the bishop by which he represents Christ as teacher, priest, and shepherd in the Church: the ministry of preaching, the ministry of the sacraments, and the ministry of leadership. . . . [For the medieval theologians] only the priestly office of the bishop was grounded in his consecration." Pottmeyer, "The Episcopacy," 348–49.

and visibly, take the place of Christ himself, *teacher, shepherd and priest*, and act in his person" (LG 21).[28]

The council is here making a distinction between the *conferral* through sacramental consecration of the three offices and the *power* (*potestas*) *to exercise* these offices, which only the pope can delegate. A juridical mind-set has once again been reinserted into the text. Here we have yet another case of juxtaposition in order to placate a seriously concerned minority. The key mediating category here is "hierarchical communion" (*communio hierarchica*); through it, "the old distinction between *ordo* and *iurisdictio* is preserved in a new way. *Communio hierarchica* is therefore a typical compromise formulation, which points to a juxtaposition of sacramental *communio* ecclesiology and juristic unity ecclesiology. . . . The compromise proved useful at the council, since it made it possible for the minority to agree to the Constitution on the Church."[29] The notion of *communio hierarchica*, therefore, as we saw when examining the *communio/missio* principle, has its weaknesses and strengths. Hermann Pottmeyer believes that the notion was attempting to address a tension within the assembly of bishops: "On the basis of this concept the council seeks to solve one of the most difficult problems of ecclesiology and church order: how to bind together the responsibility of each bishop for his church, his insertion into the episcopal college, and his subordination to the pope, *without jeopardizing any one of them*."[30] The concept of "hierarchical communion" at least is an attempt to hold together a *sacramental* and *juridical* understanding of the episcopate. Within all this debate on the conferral of the three offices of Christ on the ordained through episcopal consecration, however, there is, regrettably, no attempt to relate the bishops' participation in the three offices of Christ with the affirmation of the previous chapter in *Lumen Gentium* on the participation by all the *fideles* in those same three offices.

It is noteworthy here that the pope is not depicted as the one who directly admits a person to the episcopal college, but rather it is "for [the ordaining] bishops to admit newly elected members into the episcopal body by means of the sacrament of Orders" (LG 21). That the conferral of sacramental character enables a bishop to sacramentally represent Christ and his three offices "represents a significant advancement in the theology of orders by the council, whereby the three offices are conferred by sacramental consecration itself

28. Emphasis added.
29. Kasper, "The Church as Communion," 158.
30. Pottmeyer, "The Episcopacy," 349. Emphasis added.

rather than being the result of a *missio canonica* from the pope."[31] There is certainly reference to "hierarchical communion with the head and members of the college," which is repeated in the following article of *Lumen Gentium*: "A person is made a member of the episcopal body in virtue of the sacramental consecration and by hierarchal communion [*communio hierarchica*] with the head and members of the college" (LG 22). Regarding this juxtaposition of "sacramental consecration" and "hierarchical communion," Tillard observes: "A Christian becomes a member of the episcopal college by virtue of sacramental consecration (*vi consecrationis*) and taking into account hierarchical communion (*communione*) with the head of the college (the pope). The meaning of the passage is clear. *Hierarchical communion is not a cause but simply a condition*."[32] By implication, this grounding of the episcopate in sacramental consecration calls for the identity of the Bishop of Rome himself to be conceived primarily as a member of the episcopal college, as Tillard observes:

> The full weight of this assertion from *Lumen Gentium* [regarding episcopal ordination] needs to be brought to bear on the theology of the papacy. For it is clear that whatever is founded upon a sacrament must have priority within the Church of God: the Church comes about by faith and sacraments and all its essential marks are to be found within the osmosis of faith and sacraments. . . . For the election of a pope has never been reckoned a sacrament.

---

31. Susan Wood, "The Sacramentality of Episcopal Consecration," *Theological Studies* 51 (1990): 479–96, at 485. Pottmeyer sketches the historical background: "A fateful development in the theology of the episcopacy occurred in the scholastic understanding which placed the bishop's shepherding tasks of *teaching* [*magisterium*] and *leadership* [*regimen*] outside the sacrament of orders. His pastoral ministry, detached from his sacramental power, became a mere power of jurisdiction. Consequently, ministry became a juridical rule. This juridical concept is often connected with the canonical theory according to which the bishop's jurisdiction is not bound with his episcopal office conferred sacramentally, but is a concession from the pope. This theory is at the heart of Roman centralism, which treats bishops as mere vicars of the pope." Pottmeyer, "The Episcopacy," 345.

32. Tillard, *The Bishop of Rome*, 47. Emphasis added. Tillard goes on to discuss the maximalist interpretation of Journet who sees episcopal ordination as only an initial entry into the college of bishops, with full membership being authorized by a canonical approval from the pope. Tillard quotes the rejection of that interpretation by the *peritus* Gustave Thils: "This analysis . . . reduces to an *initium* that which Christ brings about sacramentally, and raises to a fullness that which is added at a juridical level by hierarchical authority. A ruling of this kind respects neither the text nor the spirit of Vatican II. The analysis betrays the sense of the document." Quoted in ibid.

What is more, neither the election nor the enthronement of a pope conveys any "indelible character"; when a pope resigns he simply ceases to be pope.[33]

Pottmeyer highlights two ways in which collegiality is approached in the conciliar texts, what he calls "collegiality from above and collegiality from below."[34] Both were seen as ways to overcome the centralization of ecclesial governance in Rome. One approach starts with the universal church and emphasizes the role of the bishops and the pope as responsible for the universal church. In this sense, collegiality is seen in terms of a *communio hierarchica* among the bishops with and under the pope. As Pottmeyer summarizes this approach: "*The bishops are not members of the college insofar as they are the shepherds of particular churches; rather, they are shepherds of particular churches because they are members of the college of bishops.*"[35]

The other approach starts with the local (particular) church, for which the local bishop is primarily responsible. In this sense, collegiality is seen in terms of the church as a *communio ecclesiarum*. One could well formulate this approach, paralleling Pottmeyer's summary of the universalist approach: *The bishops are not shepherds of particular churches because they are members of the college of bishops; rather, they are members of the college of bishops insofar as they are shepherds of particular churches.* Here it is the *communio ecclesiarum* that is the ground of collegiality, not the *communio hierarchica.* This model would conceive the primacy of the pope also in terms of his local church, as Pottmeyer observes: "Insofar as a bishop heads an individual church as a successor of the apostles, he is also a member of the college consisting of the other successors of the apostles. The pope does not simply happen to be also the bishop of Rome; on the contrary, it is precisely because he is bishop of the church of Rome, which preserves the heritage of Peter and whose bishop is the successor of Peter, that he is a member and head of the college of bishops and visible head of the church."[36] Both of these approaches to collegiality, and by implication primacy, can be found within the

---

33. Ibid., 38–39.

34. See Pottmeyer, *Towards a Papacy in Communion*, 117–25. Pottmeyer refers to the discussion in Joseph Ratzinger, "La collegialità episcopale: Spiegazione teologica del testo conciliare," in *La Chiesa del Vaticano II: Studi e commenti intorno alla Costituzione dommatica 'Lumen Gentium'*, ed. Guilherme Baraúna (Firenze: Vallecchi Editore, 1965), 733–60, at 745–47. This early analysis by Ratzinger stands somewhat in contrast with his position in the later debate with Walter Kasper. For an overview, see McDonnell, "The Ratzinger/Kasper Debate."

35. Pottmeyer, *Towards a Papacy in Communion*, 118. Emphasis added.

36. Ibid.

texts of Vatican II; while they stand in positive tension with each other, the latter approach is underdeveloped throughout the texts and requires greater foregrounding in the light of the council's full teaching on other related matters.[37] "Both forms of the concept of collegiality are important for the development of a primacy in communion; both are present in the texts of the council, and both are concerned with moving beyond centralization."[38]

Another tension—less positive—marks the council's attempts to articulate its teaching on episcopal collegiality and papal primacy. This tension emerges from the juxtaposition of attempts by the minority to maintain an ultramontanist interpretation of the Vatican I teachings and attempts by the majority to "re-receive" those teachings within a new ecclesial framework. Antonio Acerbi has captured the essence of this tension between "two ecclesiologies" within the conciliar debates.[39] An important element of the tension lies in the unrelenting resistance by the minority to "the changed mentality." In the debate of the chapter on the hierarchy in the 1963 schema, their main objection to a doctrine of collegiality was the belief that any acknowledgment of the authority of the college of bishops would automatically threaten the jurisdictional primacy of the pope affirmed by Vatican I.

Their tactics were effective. The *peritus* Gérard Philips, entrusted with incorporating their requests into the text, refers to "the repeated and almost sickly insistence on the papal prerogatives" by the minority.[40] "The text of the draft itself came back again and again on the point with repeated warnings and assurances, so that no misunderstandings could arise."[41] From the perspective of a majority of bishops, the 1963 draft had already (seemingly) excluded any misunderstanding of the college as capable of acting independently of the pope; but it did this by situating the pope *within* the college, yet as head of the college. In response to objections by the minority, a further revised draft presented to the bishops the following year (1964) reintroduced elements of an "over-against" mentality: pope versus bishops. "A perusal of the text shows that it is full of additions designed to block at the start every attack on the primacy of the Pope. The overloading of the text with all these soothing precautions makes it somewhat prolix and hinders the flow of the

---

37. On the council's failure to properly balance these two approaches, see Hervé Legrand, "Collégialité des évêques et communion des églises dans la réception de Vatican II," *Revue des Sciences Philosophiques et Théologiques* 75 (1991): 545–68.

38. Pottmeyer, *Towards a Papacy in Communion*, 121.

39. Acerbi, *Due ecclesiologie*.

40. Philips, "Dogmatic Constitution on the Church: History of the Constitution," 115.

41. Ibid., 115.

style—as can easily be seen if one puts the reassuring clauses in brackets."[42] Rahner speaks of "repetitions inspired by over-anxiety, even in contexts where it was not called for by the subject matter."[43] As Klaus Schatz points out: "What was new in the version of 1964 was an additional description of a 'supra-collegial' position of the pope as vicar of Christ. While it appeared in the 1963 draft that the college of bishops, of course in union with the pope, was the proper agency of the highest authority in the Church, there now appears once more to be a twofold authority: on the one hand the college of bishops in union with its head, but on the other hand the head by itself."[44] This tension between a twofold ultimate authority remains unresolved in the final text, albeit within the new context opened up by the very structure and overall vision of *Lumen Gentium*, and indeed the whole conciliar vision, as George Tavard observes: "The conciliar text redundantly affirms the Pope's independent right of action, so that the Pope appears to be both part of the episcopal college and above it. . . . That [papal primacy] had to be repeated over and over again is, however, another matter, which would be disconcerting *if we did not keep the perspective of Vatican II in mind.*"[45]

Council and Pope

For the assembled bishops, this tension inherent in the council's attempt to articulate the college of bishops/bishop of Rome principle was being played out before their eyes, in terms of the council/pope relationship. Both popes of the council initially attempted to maintain a certain distance from the conciliar assembly. "The decision of John XXIII not to take part personally in the conciliar session was continued by Paul VI. But both popes had roles of extensive and decisive importance in the life of Vatican II. During the preparation and the four periods of activity, the Pope gradually became the decisive point of reference for the assembly."[46] Each pope, however, had different approaches to their role of maintaining unity. Whereas John would intervene for the sake of the majority within the assembly, Paul would generally intervene for the sake of the minority; whereas John was content with a majority in the voting, Paul deliberately worked for unanimous consensus.

---

42. Ibid., 129.

43. Rahner, "The Hierarchical Structure of the Church," 196.

44. Klaus Schatz, *Papal Primacy: From Its Origins to the Present* (Collegeville, MN: Liturgical Press, 1996), 169–70.

45. Tavard, *The Pilgrim Church*, 96–97. Emphasis added.

46. Alberigo, "Transition to a New Age," 597.

John never attended a General Congregation of the council. But he would watch the proceedings on close-circuit television. In terms of his operational relationship with the council and its deliberation on issues and documents, however, John was certainly not averse to direct intervention. For example, when the vote to reject *De Fontibus Revelationis* didn't quite meet the two-thirds vote requirement, he wanted the majority's wishes to be respected; he therefore intervened, sending the schema back for revision by a new Mixed Commission. As Alberigo remarks: "From the rejection of the elections of commission members to the crucial confirmation of the vote of November 1962 [to reject the preparatory draft schema *De Fontibus Revelationis*], and on to the creation of the Coordinating Commission, Pope John intervened repeatedly in the life of the Council."[47]

Paul VI was even more active, however, in the deliberations of the council. According to Alberigo, "Paul's chosen method was a constant trickle of interventions in the texts, perhaps under the naïve belief that such interventions could be taken as simply the corrections of any Council father. In reality, on each occasion there was an 'incident' and a resulting trauma. The interventions were so many occasions for the minority to voice again its own points of view and to slip them into the cracks thus opened up."[48] Paul VI gradually felt a greater need to assert his own papal authority over the assembled bishops, given the emerging affirmation of the episcopate's collegial authority. This reticence to allow the council its freedom seems to have been due to constant pressure from the Curia, with whom he had had a delicate relationship, as well as his own cautious disposition. For example, not at ease with allowing the world episcopate assembled in council to decide on delicate issues that they were raising in their speeches, Paul reserved to himself the final decision on a range of matters (e.g., mandatory celibacy, artificial birth control, an ongoing synod of bishops, reform of the Curia).[49]

One intervention by the pope turned out to be particularly embarrassing. On November 6, 1964, the day before debate on the missionary document *Ad Gentes*, Paul VI decided to attend the session. Up until that visit, according to John O'Malley, "no pope had attended a working session of a council

47. Ibid.

48. Ibid., 598–99.

49. See Alberto Melloni, "Controversies: Subjects Taken on by the Pope," in *Vatican II: The Complete History*, ed. Alberto Melloni, Federico Ruozzi, and Enrico Galvotti (New York: Paulist Press, 2015), 232–35. Seven issues are discussed: the reform of the Curia; the synod of bishops; clerical celibacy; the bomb; birth control; condemnation of communism; the relationship between Judaism and the church.

since the Fifth Lateran in the early sixteenth century."[50] The document coming up for debate was seen by many to be theologically inadequate. Addressing the council, the pope urged the bishops to accept it. The bishops, nonetheless, went on to reject the draft and asked that it be revised into a much more expansive treatment. "Paul was mortified."[51] For Yves Congar, the visit symbolized the very issue at stake in the college of bishops/bishop of Rome debate: is the pope separate from and above the college of bishops or part of it as its head? Congar wrote in his journal:

> Today, I twice had the opportunity to say (to Dossetti for Lercaro; to Colombo for Paul VI directly): the next time the Pope comes to a General Congregation *in aula*, he should come in carrying the Gospel! I still have a painful impression of this Friday morning's sitting. Would it not be possible for the Pope to come to participate in a working sitting, in the normal way, as *a member of the council*? Does his being *head* isolate him in such a way, and elevate him to such a degree that he has to stay outside? In fact, the Pope has not *taken part* in the assembly. He has made a "gesture" (he has made many, and some good ones, but while retaining another ideology, and one not so good). He has not fitted in, and it seems that he is not able to. From the time he appeared, and throughout his brief presence, he was like a marshal visiting his troops and taking a spoonful of soup at the field kitchen. The papal theology, worked out *solely* as "*potestas supra*" [power over], throws a deadly shadow over conciliar theology, the theology of communion. It has no insertion into it. But conciliar theology has come to life again, the theology of communion is indefeasible. So the theology of papal *potestas* will have to adapt itself. Ecclesiologically, the Pope's visit to the conciliar assembly struck a note that, to my ears, was disharmonious, and painful to hear.[52]

Another particularly divisive incident that highlighted the tension between council and pope occurred in the middle of the so-called *settimana nera* ("black week"), November 14–21, 1964. This was the last week of the third session, at the end of which *Lumen Gentium* would be officially promulgated.[53] In a final attempt to allay the fears of the agitated minority over

50. O'Malley, *What Happened at Vatican II*, 239.

51. Ibid.

52. Congar, *My Journal of the Council*, 658–59. Original emphasis, which in the original is written in uppercase.

53. Four episodes created the bleak atmosphere in this final week: at the last minute, voting on the document on religious liberty was delayed until the next session; nineteen *modi* were submitted in an attempt to mute the ecumenical fervor of *Unitatis Redintegratio*; the use by

the practical implications of chapter 3, a *Nota Explicativa Praevia* from the Doctrinal Commission (authored by the widely respected *peritus* Philips, and authorized by "a higher authority," presumed to be Paul VI) was distributed to the bishops on November 14, 1964, and formally presented to the assembly by the council's secretary general, Cardinal Pericle Felici, on November 16. The final vote on chapter 3 of *Lumen Gentium* was due to be taken the very next day. The document insisted that the doctrine of collegiality was not meant to erode in any way the jurisdictional primacy of the Roman pontiff. The *Nota* was to be published as an addendum to the text of *Lumen Gentium*, even though it did not originate from the council and the council did not vote on it and promulgate it as its own. "Technically it was an explanation of the criteria to use when voting, but it was announced as if it were an introductory and restrictive interpretation."[54] This *de facto* attempt to control the postconciliar interpretation of *Lumen Gentium*'s doctrine of collegiality in its chapter 3, seemingly according to a preconciliar mentality, caused great consternation among the majority.

Historians will long continue to debate the motives of Paul VI in this puzzling affair: was he simply giving in to curial pressure or perhaps acting out of a genuine desire to hold the council together in order to avoid a walk out by the minority, as had happened at Vatican I? According to Alberto Melloni, the *Nota* regarding interpretation of *Lumen Gentium*'s third chapter "was intended to reassure the minority of the good intentions of the text. In fact, in the weeks before, the pope had been subjected to intense pressure to prevent the chapter being approved. Paul VI did not yield, but he tried to find a way to garner the widest possible consensus on the text."[55] Certainly, as Umberto Betti points out, "[the *Nota*] had the stabilizing effect that the supreme Pontiff was intending: the broadest and most interiorly-convinced consensus among the conciliar assembly."[56] The chapter was approved almost unanimously, with only forty-six against.

Nevertheless, the affair left a nasty taste. It was the last-minute imposition of the *Nota* upon the council, more so than its attempts at juridical clarifi-

---

Paul VI of the ecumenically sensitive title of Mary as Mother of the Church; and the presentation of an explanatory note regarding chapter 3 of *Lumen Gentium*. See Tagle, "The 'Black Week' of Vatican II." Tagle points out that what seemed at the time like setbacks and even reversals in the end would have positive results in the fourth session.

54. Alberto Melloni, "The 'Black Week,'" in *Vatican II: The Complete History*, ed. Alberto Melloni, Federico Ruozzi, and Enrico Galvotti (New York: Paulist Press, 2015), 218–19, at 218.

55. Ibid., 218.

56. Betti, *La dottrina sull'episcopato*, 309.

cation, that caused such anxiety and disappointment among the assembly as it ended its third session, as Joseph Ratzinger remarks:

> [The *Nota Explicativa Praevia*] created no substantially new situation in regard to the Council text itself. The same holds true for the legal aspects of the note. On the one hand it was set up as the correct guideline for interpretation; on the other hand it was not even incorporated into the Council text itself or voted on by the Council; consequently, it was signed neither by the pope nor by the Council fathers but only by General Secretary Felici. Therefore, it must be said that the bitter taste of this note was not really so much in its content (though that was not too balanced either), but in the circumstances under which it appeared.[57]

By the end of *la settimana nera*, "no one doubted that the week had seriously damaged the relationship between the pope and the assembly."[58] With regard to the ongoing significance of the attachment to *Lumen Gentium* chapter 3, Betti maintains, "the Note can never override the promulgated text. Much less can it replace it."[59] Or, as Christopher O'Donnell remarks: "the Note should be interpreted by *Lumen Gentium*, and not the other way round."[60]

Closely related to the debate on the college of bishops/bishop of Rome relationship, and the council/pope relationship, was discussion of the role—within the emerging collegial vision—of the pope's administrative arm, the Roman Curia. In the Catholic imagination, the Curia had become the *de facto* voice of the pope, such that the bishops/pope relationship had been reduced to the bishops/Curia relationship, with the Curia understanding itself and indeed operating effectively as the superior authority. A preparatory schema on the bishops, *De episcoporum ac de diocesium regimine* (On bishops and the rule of dioceses), was sent out to the bishops in April 1963, before the second session (around the time the whole new schema of *De Ecclesia* was being finalized for distribution to the bishops). The text strongly re-affirmed the vision of equating the authority of the Curia with that of the pope: "In the exercise of his supreme and full jurisdictional power over the universal church, the Roman Pontiff makes use of the Congregations of the Roman Curia, which thus in his name and with his authority bring his office to fulfillment for the

57. Ratzinger, *Theological Highlights of Vatican II*, 172.
58. O'Malley, *What Happened at Vatican II*, 246.
59. Betti, *La dottrina sull'episcopato*, 342.
60. O'Donnell, "Bishops, Collegiality," 57.

good of all the churches and in service to the same sacred pastors [the bishops].”[61]

In the final documents of Vatican II, there is only one place where the issue of the Roman Curia is addressed—*Christus Dominus* 9–10: “It is very much the desire of the Fathers of the sacred council that these departments, which have indeed rendered excellent service to the Roman pontiff and to the pastors of the church, should be reorganized in a manner more appropriate to the needs of our time and of different regions and rites” (CD 9). Its soft language belies the assembly's real concern, indeed anger, over the matter. As O'Malley remarks, “The passage gives no hint at the intensity of the bishops' feelings on this topic and is a good example of how deceptive the placid surface of the documents can be. It is not the documents, therefore, that reveal how hot the issue was but the narrative of the battles for control of the council itself.”[62]

The hot issue came to the boiling point most dramatically early in discussion of the preparatory schema on the bishops (November 5–15, 1963); the document resulting from these debates would eventually be promulgated in the fourth session as *Christus Dominus*.[63] Importantly, this debate took place immediately after the crucial month of debate on *Lumen Gentium*. Many of the speakers were critical of the draft and highlighted both its juridical mind-set and general inconsistency with the collegial principles already voted on during the debates on *Lumen Gentium* on October 30, just the week before this debate began.[64] In a word, the implications of episcopal collegiality needed to be embedded structurally. Key issues were the tension between the *de facto* centralization of all power and authority in Rome and the call for greater autonomy to be accorded local bishops in the governing of their dioceses, something that *Lumen Gentium* (and *Sacrosanctum Concilium*) had already authorized.

On November 6, the stark contrast of views in the assembly was symbolized by speeches from curial cardinals, such as Cardinals Ruffini and Brown, and their critics, such as Alfrink and Maximos IV. The same basic tension

---

61. AS II/4, 366. Translation from O'Malley, *What Happened at Vatican II*, 190.

62. Ibid., 304.

63. For a history and analysis of *Christus Dominus*, see Klaus Mörsdorf, “Decree on the Bishop's Pastoral Office in the Church,” in *Commentary on the Documents of Vatican II*, vol. 2, ed. Herbert Vorgrimler (New York: Herder, 1968), 2:165–300; Massimo Faggioli, *Il vescovo e il concilio: Modello episcopale e aggiornamento al Vaticano II* (Bologna: Mulino, 2005); Guido Bausenhart, “Theologischer Kommentar zum Dekret über das Hirtenamt der Bischöfe in der Kirche Christus Dominus,” in *Herders theologischer Kommentar zum Zweiten Vatikanischen Konzil. Band 3*, ed. Peter Hünermann and Bernd Jochen Hilberath (Freiburg: Herder, 2005), 3:225–313.

64. On this debate of the draft schema, see Famerée, “Bishops and Dioceses,” esp. 117–32.

between different visions of the church was again apparent. The *peritus* Congar, who did not attend the debate that day—"I am too exhausted"[65]—recorded his impression from "what people have told me": "We are observing a confrontation between two ecclesiologies. The after-effects of the pontificate of Pius XII are being challenged. And, beyond them, the regime that has prevailed since the Gregorian Reform, on the basis of the identification of the Roman Church with the universal Catholic Church. The Churches are alive, they are there, represented and gathered together in Council, they are asking for an ecclesiology of Church and Churches, and not just of the papal monarchy with the juridical system with which it has provided itself in order to serve its own purposes."[66]

Two days later, Cardinal Josef Frings made a speech that expressed the frustration of many bishops regarding the offices of the Curia.[67] In particular, he directly criticized the Holy Office, its questionable methods, and its false self-perception as the virtual voice-box of the pope and therefore the supreme authority in the church, even presuming to judge the judgements of the ecumenical council then in session. He made specific suggestions: the Curia should be internationalized; members of the Curia should not be consecrated bishops as a reward for service, nor need curial officers necessarily be priests; laypeople should be appointed. He concluded: "This reform of the Curia is necessary. Let us put it into effect."[68] When Frings finished, he received "frenzied" applause.[69] Already scheduled to speak that day, the head of the Holy Office, Cardinal Alfredo Ottaviani, "in a voice shaking with rage and emotion,"[70] passionately defended his curial office and its supreme authority. Ottaviani too received applause, this time mainly from the Italian and curial members of the council. This "clash between the two cardinals . . . dramatized the fundamental issue in the council—*how* the church was to operate in the future: continue its highly centralized mode of operation, with its top-down style of management and apodictic mode of communication, or somehow attenuate them by broader consultation and sharing of responsibility."[71]

---

65. Congar, *My Journal of the Council*, 415.

66. Ibid.

67. AS II/4, 616–18. For discussion of Frings's speech (most likely written by his *peritus*, Joseph Ratzinger) and the response to it by Cardinal Ottaviani, see Famerée, "Bishops and Dioceses," 126–32.

68. Translation from Rynne, *Vatican Council II*, 222.

69. This is the description in the conciliar diary of Bishop Neofito Edelby, as quoted in Famerée, "Bishops and Dioceses," 129.

70. Rynne, *Vatican Council II*, 222.

71. O'Malley, *What Happened at Vatican II*, 193. Original emphasis.

The intervention of Frings and of others later during these ten days of debate in 1963 on the schema on the bishops were defenses of principles already decided on as key for the emerging constitution *Lumen Gentium*. In other words: "The bishops are not branch managers of local offices of the Holy See. Their exercise of power out of authority intrinsic to their office was a corollary to the doctrine of episcopal ordination. That corollary explains in large part why the minority was so fiercely opposed to the doctrine."[72] A fundamental question was: is the Roman Curia only an administrative arm of the Roman Pontiff acting unilaterally, or is it an organ for assisting the Bishop of Rome in his primary role as head of the college of bishops and its principle of unity? For the majority, it was the latter, and they felt it required structural, institutional expression.

> The majority at the council certainly did not press for a statement on collegiality merely to make a theological point. They brought it to the fore, like other *ressourcements*, because it had practical ramifications. The bishops who promoted the doctrine and fought for it so passionately wanted to redress what they saw as the imbalance between the authority exercised especially by the Roman Congregations and their own authority as heads of "local Churches." Collegiality was the supreme instance in the council of the effort to moderate the centralizing tendencies of the ecclesiastical institution, of the effort to give those from the periphery a more authoritative voice not only back home but also in the center.[73]

Nevertheless, in the end, the council was disempowered from making decisions on how such curial reform was to be implemented. Like other popes before him, reform of the Roman Curia was among the issues that Paul VI withdrew from the agenda of the assembled council and reserved to himself.[74] On November 18, 1965, the pope informed the council that he was preparing a *motu proprio* initiating curial reform with a reform of the Supreme Congregation of the Holy Office, including changing its name to the Congregation for the Doctrine of the Faith. Titled *Integrae Servandae*, the *motu proprio* was published in the last days of the council.[75]

72. Ibid., 304.

73. Ibid., 303.

74. See Melloni, "Controversies: Subjects Taken on by the Pope," 232–33. As an example of resistance from popes regarding renewal of the pope's Curia, see throughout O'Malley, *Trent: What Happened at the Council*.

75. AAS 57 (1965): 952–955. See http://w2.vatican.va/content/paul-vi/en/motu_proprio /documents/hf_p-vi_motu-proprio_19651207_integrae-servandae.html. Two years later, Paul VI would further those reforms with the Apostolic Constitution *Regimini Ecclesiae Universae.*

Toward Affective and Effective Collegiality

In addition to reform of the Curia, Vatican II envisaged other ways in which the doctrine of collegiality was to be structurally embedded into the institutional life of the church, for example, national and regional gatherings of bishops and an international synod of bishops. For these, *Christus Dominus* is a key document; as Adrian Hastings observes: "For the renewal of church structures this is the most important document the Council gave us."[76]

One institutional structure called for by the council is that of national and regional gatherings of bishops. Chapter 3 of *Christus Dominus* is titled "Concerning the Cooperation of Bishops for the Common Good of a Number of Churches." Article 36 recalls the ancient practice of synods, provincial councils, and plenary councils. Here bishops from different churches gathered to share their wisdom regarding the regulation of teaching and matters of discipline. "This sacred ecumenical synod expresses its earnest hope that these admirable institutions—synods and councils—may flourish with renewed vigor so that the growth of religion and the maintenance of discipline in the various churches may increasingly be more effectively provided for in accordance with the needs of the times" (CD 36).

Then, in the next two articles, the decree gives special attention to episcopal conferences (CD 37–38). *Lumen Gentium* had earlier addressed the topic briefly. There, article 23 on the church as "a body of churches [*corpus ecclesiarum*]" ends: "This multiplicity of local churches, unified in a common effort, shows all the more resplendently the catholicity of the undivided church. In like fashion, the episcopal conferences at the present time are in a position to contribute in many and fruitful ways to the concrete realization of the collegial spirit [*collegialis affectus*]" (LG 23).[77] And other documents highlight the value and authority of local decision making by episcopal conferences, for example, *Sacrosanctum Concilium* and *Ad Gentes*.[78]

Acknowledging that episcopal conferences were already established in some places throughout the church, *Christus Dominus* 37 goes on to state: "This sacred synod judges that it would be in the highest degree helpful if in all parts of the world the bishops of each country or region would meet regularly, so that by sharing their wisdom and experience and exchanging

76. Hastings, *A Concise Guide to the Documents*, 2:121.

77. Translation corrected. Flannery translates *collegialis affectus* as "the collegiate spirit" (Flannery); Tanner has "the spirit of collegiality."

78. On the authority given to episcopal conferences regarding the liturgy, see *Sacrosanctum Concilium* 22 and 36. On episcopal conferences' responsibility for cultural adaptation of the Gospel within a particular socio-cultural region, see *Ad Gentes* 22.

views they may jointly formulate a program *for the common good of the church*" (CD 37).[79] The notion of "the common good" recurs four times in articles 36–38, as well as in the title of the chapter before the three articles. Article 38 then issues six decrees regarding the establishing of conferences, envisaging not only national conferences but also regional ones where circumstances require it. Moreover, communication between such episcopal conferences is encouraged, as well as communication and common action with prelates of the Eastern churches.

What is not treated is whether any authority is to be accorded these conferences in the teaching of doctrine. As Avery Dulles notes: "Neither in these clauses nor elsewhere in the documents of Vatican II is there any explicit mention of the teaching function of the conferences. . . . In all probability the commissions that drew up these texts did not consider the doctrinal function of the episcopal conference ripe for conciliar decision, and deliberately kept this question open."[80] At the very least, episcopal conferences are structures that facilitate ecclesial communion, as the canonist James Provost proposes: "Not only are conferences an expression of the collegial spirit among bishops; they are also an expression of the communion of the churches the bishops represent. . . . [T]hese two dimensions are intimately connected and thus difficult to distinguish. But it does seem that the conciliar texts themselves reflect an unspoken presumption that conferences do express the communion of churches."[81]

The second institutional structure mandated by the council was an ongoing synod of bishops. There had been several calls by bishops for some permanent "synodal" structure that would realize the dynamic relationship between bishops and pope that the council event itself had at least attempted to embody. The intervention of the Melkite Patriarch Maximos IV Saigh on November 6, 1963, was particularly significant for bringing to bear on the debate an Eastern Catholic *synodal* perspective.[82] Joseph Ratzinger at the time described the possible future structure of a synod of bishops as "a kind

79. Emphasis added.

80. Avery Dulles, "Doctrinal Authority of Episcopal Conferences," in *Episcopal Conferences: Historical, Canonical, and Theological Studies*, ed. Thomas J. Reese (Washington, DC: Georgetown University Press, 1989), 207–31, at 208 and 213.

81. James H. Provost, "Episcopal Conferences as an Expression of the Communion of Churches," in *Episcopal Conferences: Historical, Canonical, and Theological Studies*, ed. Thomas J. Reese (Washington, DC: Georgetown University Press, 1989), 269–89, at 281.

82. See the speech in Maximos IV, "The Supreme Senate of the Catholic Church," in *Council Speeches of Vatican II*, ed. Hans Küng, Yves Congar, and Daniel O'Hanlon (Glen Rock, NJ: Paulist Press, 1964), 133–37. See Famerée, "Bishops and Dioceses," 124–25.

of permanent small council," much in the normal manner of patriarchal synods in the early centuries of the church.[83] As with other issues, however, Paul VI intervened and took it upon himself to determine how such an ongoing episcopal synod would operate rather than allow the assembled ecumenical council of the world bishops the freedom to do so.[84] Accordingly, on September 15, 1965, the pope promulgated a *motu proprio* titled *Apostolica Sollicitudo*, which formally established the synod of bishops.[85]

Many soon expressed their disappointment: the document made no reference at all to collegiality, let alone any explicit reference to *Lumen Gentium*; the proposed synod was to be subordinate to the pope, who alone could convoke it; the pope would control the agenda, decide if the synod's authority would be consultative or deliberative, and, if the later, would need to approve any decisions of the synod. As Ratzinger noted: "This showed a profound difference between the synod, as conceived by the Council, and its papal realization. A collegial organ had been turned into an instrument of the primate to use as he wished."[86] Moreover, the *motu proprio* left a question hanging in the air: what of the relationship between a synod of bishops and the Roman Curia? "Paul VI's decision added a new body to the central government of the Church, but the question of reforming the Curia remained unanswered and would condition the role the synod could have in the future."[87]

Lumen Gentium the year before had made no recommendation for such a body as a way of embedding collegiality structurally into the life of the church. The document on the bishops, *Christus Dominus*—promulgated on October 28, 1965—does, however, call for the establishment of an international synod of bishops: "Since this [synod of bishops] will be representative of the entire catholic episcopate, it will reflect the participation of all the bishops in hierarchical communion in the care of the universal church" (CD 5). Late in the drafting process, a footnote had to be inserted that referred to the *motu proprio*.[88] Contrasting the two documents, Ratzinger observed

83. Ratzinger, *Theological Highlights of Vatican II*, 205.

84. See Melloni, "Controversies: Subjects Taken on by the Pope," 233.

85. AAS 57 (1965): 775–80. For an English translation, see Pope Paul VI, "Synod of Bishops Established," in *The Documents of Vatican II*, ed. Walter M. Abbott (London: Geoffrey Chapman, 1966), 720–24.

86. Ratzinger, *Theological Highlights of Vatican II*, 203.

87. Routhier, "Finishing the Work Begun," 60. Further on the above issues regarding the synod of bishops, see ibid., 55–61.

88. On the *motu proprio*, reactions to it, and the effect on the redrafting of *Christus Dominus* 5, see Faggioli, *Il vescovo e il concilio*, 406–22.

that, whereas *Christus Dominus* had envisaged a collegiality "from below," Paul VI envisaged a collegiality "from above."[89]

In a speech to a public congregation of the council on November 18, 1965, the pope announced that the first Synod of Bishops would be held in 1967. Time would tell if the high hopes of the young Ratzinger would be fulfilled: "If we may say that the synod is a permanent Council in miniature—its composition as well as its name justifies this—then its institution under these circumstances guarantees that the Council will continue after its official end; it will from now on be part of the everyday life of the Church. It will be no mere transitory episode, but will be able to mature what was sown in the often stormy days of the sessions."[90]

Determining Vatican II's vision regarding the relationship between the college of bishops and the Bishop of Rome is a complex task. As Luis Tagle has pointed out: "What has remained as a burning theological, juridical, and structural question for the Church since the Council is the relationship between the bishops and the pope in one episcopal college. The [*Nota Explicativa Praevia*] did not carve out a neat path for popes and bishops to tread. Neither has the constitution *Lumen Gentium* resolved all theological and practical problems. The compromises in *Lumen Gentium* have left the doctrine of collegiality vague enough for it to be acceptable to people of different persuasions. Often conflicting ideas could find their respective justification in the same document."[91] In dispute were conflicting interpretations of the great tradition regarding the nature of ministry in service of the church.

Therefore, on this issue Vatican II calls for a synthesis of its own tortuous efforts to re-receive Vatican I. "Mediation [between conflicting ecclesiologies] was not completely successful. The ecclesiology of *jurisdictio*, or rather that of Vatican I, and the still older and now rediscovered ecclesiology of *communio* are placed side by side but remain unconnected."[92] Nevertheless, although Vatican II is textually faithful in reiterating the teachings of *Pastor Aeternus*, the insertion of those texts into the comprehensive vision of *Lumen Gentium*, and of the Vatican II documents as a whole, brings forth a "surplus of meaning," a new understanding of their significance.[93] As Tillard argues:

89. Ratzinger, *Theological Highlights of Vatican II*, 203.

90. Ibid., 206.

91. Tagle, "The 'Black Week' of Vatican II," 452.

92. Schatz, *Papal Primacy*, 170.

93. On "the surplus of meaning" in the writings of Paul Ricoeur, see, for example, Ricoeur, *Interpretation Theory*.

What *Lumen Gentium* has done is to set this repeat of Vatican I *within a new perspective.* The vision which controls its teaching on the Church is no longer that of the ultramontane majority of 1870, but that of the more balanced and lucid elements in the minority of Vatican I. In other words, the minority of Vatican I has become the majority of Vatican II and vice versa. We may therefore say that at Vatican II *Pastor Aeternus* was "received" in the dogmatic sense by the minority of Vatican I after nearly a century of deepening study and fresh thought. The importance of this new reception in a new climate is too little recognized: Vatican I and Vatican II together form a dialectical unity in which one should be interpreted by the other.[94]

At Vatican II, the Vatican I texts are recontextualized within a new ecclesial framework, one no longer predominantly juridical or papally centred, without, however, ignoring the necessary juridical dimensions or the unitary importance of the pope in the Catholic vision. Accordingly, taking together the three principles *fideles/fidelis*, People of God/hierarchy, college of bishops/bishop of Rome, the order in which the mystery of the church is presented in the council's comprehensive vision strikingly reverses that of preconciliar ecclesiology. The vision no longer begins with the pope and his delegates, the bishops (and their respective jurisdictional powers and authority). Rather, Vatican II's ecclesial vision begins with the *fideles* as the people of God, all those baptized who love God and follow Jesus Christ in faith. It then moves to consideration of local congregations of these *fideles* and the role of their bishop as their center of unity. And finally, it then considers the spiritual interconnection between these local bishops throughout the world, with and under their spiritual head, the Bishop of Rome. The key word here is "spiritual," not "juridical"; the latter dimension should serve to safeguard the former.

In terms of the conciliar rubric *communio*, this approach by the council, as we have already seen, views the church from a particular perspective and ordering—*communio fidelium*, then *communio ecclesiarum*, and only then *communio hierarchica*. In other words, this vision approaches the church first as the *communio fidelium*, the *fideles* who follow Jesus Christ in faith as his disciples. Then second, it approaches the place of the episcopate within the church from the perspective of the church as a *communio ecclesiarum* (a communion of communities of the faithful). Finally, it conceives the bishops of these local churches as a "college" in communion with one another, with and under the pope (*communio hierarchica*). As Pottmeyer states it, in reverse

---

94. Tillard, *The Bishop of Rome*, 35. Emphasis added.

order: "This communion of pope and bishops is an image of the communion of the churches, and the latter, in turn, is an image of the communion of the faithful (*communio fidelium*). The primacy of the pope is a primacy within a communion because he represents and is the concrete embodiment of the universal communion of churches. He needs the catholic witness of the bishops and of the churches and their members, in order to bear witness to, and preserve, the catholicity and unity of the churches."[95] As Pottmeyer states elsewhere: "Not only the pope and the bishops are bearers of *communio,* but the rest of the members of the Church are as well."[96]

As has often been emphasized above, Vatican II presents its receivers with a task of synthesizing the elements of its vision, something that it itself was unable to achieve or was not even intending to do. The historian Klaus Schatz sees a telling parallel between this current postconciliar need for synthesis in the face of Vatican II's lack of systematic integration on the matter of collegiality and primacy and a similar situation in the late Middle Ages.[97] He refers to the theological climate at the time of the reform councils after the Council of Constance.[98] Then, there were two ecclesiologies in tension, what Schatz calls a "papalist ecclesiology" and a "conciliarist ecclesiology."[99] Both of these positions, he believes, were too one-sided: the former saw the pope to be superior to the council; for the latter, the council was superior to the pope. Although the conciliarist theologians were wanting to retrieve elements of a long-forgotten *communio* ecclesiology, Schatz argues their narrow "conciliarist" retrieval of this ancient understanding of the church's nature was as one-sided as their "papalist" opponents. Schatz thus raises a pertinent question for those wanting to synthesize the two unintegrated positions juxtaposed in *Lumen Gentium* and *Christus Dominus* regarding the college of bishops and the Bishop of Rome: "Does this not suggest that if we do not succeed in achieving an integration the results will be similar? Will it not again happen that a purely monarchical ecclesiology will triumph in theory

---

95. Pottmeyer, *Towards a Papacy in Communion*, 118–19.

96. Pottmeyer, "The Episcopacy," 351.

97. See Schatz, *Papal Primacy*, 170.

98. Further on these councils, see Gerald Christianson, Thomas M. Izbicki, and Christopher M. Bellitto, eds., *The Church, the Councils, and Reform: The Legacy of the Fifteenth Century* (Washington, DC: The Catholic University of America Press, 2008).

99. Schatz, *Papal Primacy*, 170.

and practice, and the newly discovered collegial and conciliar aspects will once again be repressed, just as in the fifteenth century?"[100]

Perhaps similar doubts, despite all his work, were already being raised in the mind of the *peritus* Yves Congar as he watched on television the closing ceremony of Vatican II on December 8, 1965, unable to attend that day because of ill health. His journal records:

> First the long, slow procession of the Fathers from the Bronze Door to the precinct of St Peter's. Unfortunately, in silence. Then the trumpets, the music: the Pope. On the *sedia*, wearing a mitre, carrying a pastoral cross in his left hand (yesterday he entered the Council carrying the book of the Gospels—a suggestion I had made to Carlo Colombo). . . . Paul VI has been remarkable. However, from the ecclesiological and ecumenical point of view, I felt some unease in watching the very beautiful ceremony this morning. . . . The Pope got all the attention. He sat enthroned as a sovereign; everything had reference to him. He did not appear to be so much *in* the Church, as above it.[101]

100. Ibid.

101. Congar, *My Journal of the Council*, 874. Original emphasis, which is uppercase in the original.

Principle 21

Magisterium/Theologians

Principle 21: In its service to the people of God of teaching authoritatively, the magisterium necessarily draws on the scholarly expertise of theologians; theologians serve the people of God through their theological enquiry concerning the sources of the faith, past and present, not only by interpreting Scripture and tradition through the lens of present experiences of divine revelation, but also—in a circle of ecclesial understanding—by assisting the magisterium to discern present senses of the faith within the whole people of God through the lens of Scripture and tradition.

"Regarding the relationship between the papal-episcopal magisterium of the Catholic Church and those who do theology, Vatican II signalled the end of one era and the beginning of a transition to another way of relating."[1] The council's actual statements about the discipline of theology, the role of theologians in the church, and the relationship between theologians and the magisterium are—to use John O'Malley's remarks concerning another issue— just one more example "of how deceptive the placid surface of the documents can be. It is not the documents, therefore, that reveal how hot the issue was but the narrative of the battles for control of the council itself."[2] Diversity in theology, differences between theologians and their arguments, and the tensive relationship between theologians and bishops were lively realities in the informal and formal deliberations of the council. Much of the distinctive vision of Vatican II is the result of the council's grappling with these realities. It was such a distinctive feature of the council that this chapter proposes that it constitutes a principle encoded into the vision of Vatican II, what is here called the magisterium/theologians principle.

---

1. Wicks, *Doing Theology*, 105.
2. O'Malley, *What Happened at Vatican II*, 304.

According to Giuseppe Alberigo, "Vatican II was an occasion for testing the ecclesial fruitfulness of the rich and complex activity that had been going on in theology since the 1930s. Once the overwhelming world war had ended in 1918 and the anti-modernist storm had passed, theology, especially in Central Europe, entered a period of extraordinary fruitfulness that found vigorous expression at the Council, where it played a dominant part."[3] The French word *ressourcement* has come to designate the historically conscious approach in Europe from the 1930s through the 1950s regarding both doctrine and liturgical practice within a wide range of theological disciplines researching the early biblical, patristic, and medieval sources of the Christian faith. The result of this *ressourcement* was that the great Christian tradition could no longer be narrowly equated with the monolithic model of Tridentinism that had characterized the Catholic imagination in the centuries leading up to the calling of Vatican II. Significantly, historically conscious scholarship began to challenge the "neothomism" (or "neoscholasticism") that was the intellectual framework for this Tridentinism.[4] Bernard McGinn believes that what had been happening within Thomist studies before Vatican II can be legitimately included in the general category of *ressourcement* studies: "This form of reviving the past also fits those writers who worked toward a more adequate historical understanding of Thomas in the context of his own time and intentions. . . . To introduce historical mindedness into the study of Thomas was seen by some as bringing a Trojan horse into the impregnable Neothomist fortress."[5]

All of the bishops assembled for the council had been educated in the aftermath of the Modernist crisis. The language and arguments of many of the

3. Alberigo, "Transition to a New Age," 602–3.

4. The literature generally uses two terms for naming the theological "school" that dominated Catholic life, theology, and magisterial statements after Leo XIII's *Aeterni Patris*. In this chapter, I follow the usage of Bernard McGinn with the term "neothomism": "Many of the documents, such as the papal encyclical *Aeterni Patris* of 1879, speak of the renewal of 'scholastic philosophy' (*philosophia scholastica*); hence the term 'Neoscholasticism' is often used to describe this movement in modern Catholic thought. In practice, however, Thomas Aquinas was seen as *the* Neoscholastic author. All other scholastics, including such distinctive thinkers as Bonaventure, were reduced to agreeing with Thomas. Hence, the terms 'Neoscholasticism' and 'Neothomism' can be used interchangeably." McGinn, *Thomas Aquinas's Summa Theologiae*, 238n3. For an overview of the distinctive characteristics of this approach, using the term "neoscholasticism," see Francis Schüssler Fiorenza, "Systematic Theology: Task and Methods," in *Systematic Theology: Roman Catholic Perspectives*, ed. Francis Schüssler Fiorenza and John P. Galvin, 2nd and rev. ed. (Minneapolis: Fortress Press, 2011), 1–78, at 20–26.

5. McGinn, *Thomas Aquinas's Summa Theologiae*, 188–89.

preparatory schemas prepared in the two years prior to the council would have been well familiar to them, since these documents were generally couched according to the worldview and categories of the reigning neothomism of the day. As we have seen, basically only the document on the liturgy was judged by the bishops to be worthy of further exploration; most of the others were not received by the council; some would be incorporated as parts of other documents. The rejection of these schemas was, in effect, a remarkable rejection of a theological system that had reigned for hundreds of years and was particularly impressed on Catholic church life by Leo XIII's 1879 encyclical *Aeterni Patris*. An aversion to the theological framework of the then–status quo became more and more apparent as the council progressed.

This phenomenon highlights the dependence of the magisterium on theology and the work of theologians. According to McGinn, at Vatican II the majority of the council fathers fundamentally appropriated the "basic shift in the Catholic theology of the period circa 1935–60, one that turned away from the regnant Neothomist model in three ways: (1) by rigorous historical investigation of what Thomas actually said within the context of the problems of his time; (2) by relativizing Thomas's position in the history of theology, seeing him as a significant figure but not as the ultimate authority on all issues; and (3) by engaging in a serious dialogue with modern forms of philosophy and non-Catholic theology."[6] These three forces in Thomist studies came to a head at the council, such that, as Gerald McCool argues: "The history of the modern Neo-Thomist movement, whose *magna charta* was *Aeterni Patris*, reached its end at the Second Vatican Council."[7]

While the role of the neothomism that had dominated before the council was significantly diminished by the council's end, even one of those calling for a more historical approach to theology in general and to Thomas Aquinas in particular acknowledged Aquinas' continuing importance. The Dominican Yves Congar claims: "It could be shown that St. Thomas, the *Doctor communis*, furnished the writers of the dogmatic texts of Vatican II with the bases

---

6. Ibid., 192. Original numeration. Walter Kasper similarly claims that the crisis within neothomism in the decades before Vatican II was basically due to two issues: a growing historical consciousness regarding human understanding and the shifting place of philosophy in theological method given the diversity within Thomism. Walter Kasper, *The Methods of Dogmatic Theology* (New York: Paulist Press, 1969). For a summary of Kasper on this, see Schüssler Fiorenza, "Systematic Theology: Task and Methods," 25–26.

7. McCool, *From Unity to Pluralism*, 230. More specifically, Komonchak notes: "What ended at Vatican II, at least by the Council's intention, was the ideologically driven reign of one of the many forms of neo-Thomism." Komonchak, "Thomism and the Second Vatican Council," 69.

and the structure their thought."[8] Nevertheless, Joseph Ratzinger, a *peritus* with a more Augustinian bent, would also claim regarding "those forces that actually made Vatican II possible and shaped it": "We are talking about a theology and a piety that developed essentially on the basis of Sacred Scripture, the Fathers of the Church, and the great liturgical heritage of the universal Church. At the Council, the proponents of this theology had been concerned about nourishing the faith, not only on the thinking of the last hundred years, but on the great stream of tradition as a whole, so as to make it richer and livelier but, at the same time, simpler and more accessible."[9] In the latter sessions of the council, the approaches of these two *periti* would come to characterize a further tension that emerged during Vatican II, not only between *ressourcement* theologians, but also between the claims of *ressourcement* and the demands of *aggiornamento*.

Throughout the history of the church, theologians have played some role in the general councils of the church. In the first half of the second millennium, the conciliar participation of theologians waxed and waned between a deliberative role (with voting rights) and a consultative role (with theological advice being given to the council participants).[10] In his study of this period, Nelson Minnich concludes that "theologians continued throughout the period to exercise a major role which was at times masked behind such diminishing formulations as witnesses (*testes*), consultative voice (*vox consultativa*), and minor theologians (*theologi minores*). . . . [T]he expertise of theologians was de facto acknowledged in the procedures used. While bishops insisted on their prerogative to render judgment, the popes and cardinal presidents at all the councils, except perhaps Lateran V, adopted procedures to insure that episcopal judgments were informed by the knowledge of theologians."[11]

8. Yves Congar, "La théologie au Concile: Le 'théologiser' du Concile," in *Situation et tâches présentes de la théologie* (Paris: Éditions du Cerf, 1967), 51–56. Quoted in Komonchak, "Thomism and the Second Vatican Council," 69.

9. Joseph Cardinal Ratzinger, "Ten Years after the Beginning of the Council—Where Do We Stand?," in *Dogma and Preaching: Applying Christian Doctrine to Daily Life* (San Francisco, CA: Ignatius Press, 2011), 377–84, at 382. Komonchak highlights this difference in the interpretations of Congar and Ratzinger. See Komonchak, "Thomism and the Second Vatican Council," 73n31.

10. See the survey in Nelson H. Minnich, "The Voice of Theologians in General Councils from Pisa to Trent," *Theological Studies* 59 (1998): 420–41. See also Yves Congar, "Theologians and the Magisterium in the West: From the Gregorian Reform to the Council of Trent," *Chicago Studies: The Magisterium, the Theologian and the Educator* 17 (1978): 210–24.

11. Minnich, "The Voice of Theologians in General Councils," 440–41.

At the end of this period, when the involvement of theologians had become somewhat diminished compared with earlier councils, theologians at the Council of Trent nevertheless were still playing an influential role. At Trent, a significant procedural feature was the "Congregation of Theologians"; here, theologians would present to the council participants the theological issues at stake in the topic then under debate, and the bishops and other participants would listen without comment. As John O'Malley observes regarding the ecclesial significance of this procedure, "The theologians played . . . an indispensable role at Trent and were fully integrated into the council's functioning. . . . The theologians' deliberations surely raised the level of the discussion in the subsequent General Congregations and made the bishops, as well as the legates, aware of the complexity of the problem [under debate]. Beyond that it is impossible to say what impact they had."[12] Whatever the judgment as to their final contribution, it is certainly clear that, at Trent, "theologians drew up the articles for debate, clarified the issues, helped to draft the decrees, prevented decrees with which they disagreed from being adopted, and consented to those that were passed. . . . [These procedures] clearly indicate that theologians exercised more than a merely consultative voice."[13]

The historian Hubert Jedin sees five models that capture the different ways in which the relationship between theologians and bishops (particularly gathered in council) has functioned across the church's history.[14] The first model is evident in the early church, where most of the bishops were competent theologians in their own right; the second model is exemplified in the early Middle Ages when the typical process of ecclesial judgment was investigation of any contentious issue first by a local synod, then by the synod of Rome, and finally by a universal council; the third model, coming from the fourteenth and fifteenth centuries, envisages university faculties of theology and canon law being considered a teaching authority alongside the pope and bishops, with theologians even having voting rights at some general councils. The procedures used at Trent make up Jedin's fourth model; as we have seen, theologians were officially invited to the council and provided input to the voting bishops on the theological nuances of particular issues under debate.

---

12. O'Malley, *Trent: What Happened at the Council*, 85, 92.

13. Minnich, "The Voice of Theologians in General Councils," 439–40.

14. See Hubert Jedin, "Theologie und Lehramt," in *Lehramt und Theologie im 16. Jahrhundert*, ed. Remigus Bäumer (Münster: Aschendorff, 1976), 7–21. See the summary of Jedin's article in Schüssler Fiorenza, "Systematic Theology: Task and Methods," 62–64.

Jedin's fifth and final model is that adopted at the two councils in the nineteenth and twentieth centuries, the first and the second councils held in the Vatican. "Here no university faculty of theology was corporatively invited as in the medieval period or as at Trent. The bishops were the voting members, and theologians were present primarily as advisers to the bishops."[15] The *peritus* Henri de Lubac, while commenting on the conciliar debate over Scripture and tradition, speaks of the deficiency of this procedure at Vatican II: "Some partisans of the 'two sources' are seeking again to introduce some formulas along that line; it seems to me that they do not understand the question, and that many of those who reject their proposals do not understand it any better. One of the disadvantages of the procedure followed in this council is that when the discussion of a schema is to begin, there is never a broad exposition of the subject by a competent and impartial man, either at a general congregation or in a commission."[16] Nevertheless, at Vatican II, despite their procedurally shadowed presence, the theologians ended up playing an active role. But how is their final contribution to be assessed?

Theology at Vatican II

That theologians would play some role in Vatican II was apparent early in the antepreparatory period, when consultation of the world's bishops began.[17] On June 18, 1959, five months after Pope John XXIII announced his intention to convene a new council, the secretary of state, Cardinal Domenico Tardini, in his capacity also as president of the Antepreparatory Commission, sent a letter to all bishops and superiors of clerical religious orders, requesting suggestions of possible topics the forthcoming council might address. Importantly, he said that they may wish to consult their local expert theologians for advice and perhaps help in formulating their response.[18] The responses to this letter, however, resulted in "scattered signs

---

15. Schüssler Fiorenza, "Systematic Theology: Task and Methods," 63.

16. Henri de Lubac, *Carnets du Concile*, 2 vols. (Paris: Cerf, 2007), entry for October 11, 1965. Quoted in Theobald, "The Church under the Word of God," 319.

17. For an extensive bibliography on the *periti* of Vatican II, see Philippe J. Roy, *Bibliographie du Concile Vatican II* (Città del Vaticano: Libreria Editrice Vaticana, 2012), 131–46.

18. For a translation of Tardini's letter, see Étienne Fouilloux, "The Antepreparatory Phase: The Slow Emergence from Inertia (January, 1959–October, 1962)," in *History of Vatican II*, vol. 1: *Announcing and Preparing Vatican Council II*, ed. Giuseppe Alberigo and Joseph A. Komonchak (Maryknoll, NY: Orbis Books, 1996), 55–166, at 93–94. See also, Wicks, "Theologians at Vatican Council II," 191.

of theologains' input."[19] In a separate consultation sent out on July 18, 1959, Catholic theological faculties throughout the world were also invited to present matters for discussion.[20] In the period from September 1959 to March 1960, the Antepreparatory Commission analyzed all the responses received. They were collated into categories and topics by means of, what Étienne Fouilloux has called, "the two sieves": the neothomist theology of the manuals and canon law.[21] These two "sieves," along with the topics chosen for categorization, would determine the neothomist and juridical shape of many of the documents the commissions prepared for the council.

On June 5, 1960, Pope John formally set up ten preparatory commissions, along with a new Secretariat for Christian Unity, entrusted with the task of drafting these documents. It was envisaged that each of the commissions and the secretariat would eventually include consultant scholars who would be involved in the drafting. Cardinal Tardini urged the heads of these commissions to include among the theologian members and consultants scholars from around the world.[22] Since, as it turned out, the ten preparatory commissions almost mirrored exactly the dicasteries of the Roman Curia, many of those appointed to these preparatory commissions—no doubt partly for practical reasons—ended up being theologians already working within the various offices of the Roman Curia. The Theological Commission paralleled the most powerful of the curial dicasteries, the Holy Office, with its president Cardinal Alfredo Ottaviani being named head of the commission. This body played a dominant and domineering role in the drafting of the preparatory documents, seeing itself as the arbiter of all the other commissions and secretariat. Nonetheless, a few of these bodies were able to act somewhat independently of the Holy Office's control. In particular, the commission for the liturgy, building on the fruits of a half century of liturgical *ressourcement* scholarship, managed to produce a "model draft text,"[23] something that could not be said for the other seventy-five drafts eventually produced. Only the liturgy text would be approved for further discussion by the council and be eventually promulgated; of the remaining schemas, only twenty-one would

19. Wicks, "Theologians at Vatican Council II," 191.

20. For a summary of these responses, see ibid., 195–200.

21. Fouilloux, "The Antepreparatory Phase," 143.

22. For a detailed list of the members and consultants of these preparatory commissions and secretariat, see Alberto Melloni, "The Central Commission and the Preparatory Commissions," in *Vatican II: The Complete History*, ed. Alberto Melloni, Federico Ruozzi, and Enrico Galvotti (New York: Paulist Press, 2015), 58–75.

23. Wicks, "Theologians at Vatican Council II," 202.

end up being more or less incorporated into other documents.[24] The Secretariat for Christian Unity, despite being considered by the Curia something of an anomaly, boldly drafted four schemas, one of which would be eventually presented to the council for consideration. Like the preparatory liturgy commission, its work was firmly grounded in the solid scholarship of decades of *ressourcement* theology, in this case within the ecumenical movement.[25] Further signs of how the council would eventually react negatively to most of the preparatory drafts became evident during the meetings of the Central Preparatory Commission, entrusted with evaluating the preparatory schemas. Here, interventions by cardinals such as Franz König of Vienna and Josef Frings of Cologne raised critical theological issues to which their theological consultants had alerted them. The theologians, respectively, were Karl Rahner and Joseph Ratzinger.[26]

Once the preparatory period ended and the council was about to begin, new *conciliar* commissions were set up. The involvement on these commissions of experts across the theological disciplines was also clearly envisaged. On August 6, 1962, two months before the council opened, Pope John issued a *motu proprio* titled *Appropinquante Concilio*.[27] Setting out the regulations for the forthcoming council, it authorized that individual bishops could be accompanied by their own personal *peritus*, who could advise them on theological issues during the council and help them prepare speeches and written submissions. Furthermore, it stated that the pope would appoint experts (*periti*) from the various theological disciplines as members and consultors of the conciliar commissions, in order to assist the assembly of bishops in their deliberations and drafting of conciliar documents. There were to be restrictions, however, on their participation in the council: the regulations did not envisage that the *periti* could address the assembly in the aula on the subtleties of issues under debate, as had happened at the Council of Trent. Furthermore, these *periti* could not speak during commission meetings, unless invited by the episcopal chairman to do so. (As it would turn out,

24. See Melloni, "The Central Commission and the Preparatory Commissions," 60.

25. For a history of these two movements, see Scheffczyk, "Main Lines of the Development of Theology between the First World War and the Second Vatican Council."

26. See Wicks, "Theologians at Vatican Council II," 206–8.

27. See http://w2.vatican.va/content/john-xxiii/la/motu_proprio/documents/hf_j-xxiii_motu-proprio_19620806_appropinquante-concilio.html. See Klaus Wittstadt, "On the Eve of the Second Vatican Council (July 1–October 10, 1962)," in *History of Vatican II*, vol. 1: *Announcing and Preparing Vatican Council II*, ed. Giuseppe Alberigo and Joseph A. Komonchak (Maryknoll, NY: Orbis Books, 1996), 404–500, at 449–50.

however, many of the commission meetings would see a much freer involve-ment of the *periti*.) The official *periti* would be permitted to come and go throughout the council proceedings in the aula. Once the council finally began, these theologians ended up participating in the council in a variety of other ways, outside the formal proceedings of the commissions. Many of the personal and official *periti* kept journals, which have become an impor-tant source in reconstructing the history of the conciliar drama.[28]

In reviewing the role of theology and of theologians at Vatican II, as well as their relationship with the magisterium meeting in council, apart from these participating *periti*, some consideration should be given to the presence of non-Catholic observers and guests at the council, seated prominently up the front of the aula under the Tribune of St. Longinus, just to the left-hand side of the Presidential Council's table.[29] The observers were the representa-tives officially sent by various denominations that had been invited to send representatives, while the guests were special invitees of the Secretariat for Christian Unity; nevertheless, the literature at times refers to both as "observ-ers." Although these observers and guests were technically not all theologians, they were generally welcomed as a group that was theologically astute and whose views were considered important, given Pope John's ecumenical agenda set for the council. One guest of the Secretariat for Christian Unity, the Prot-estant scholar Oscar Cullmann, remarked: "I am more and more amazed every morning at the way we really form a part of the Council."[30] The observers and guests received all the relevant documents the bishops were working on each day and were able to express their views freely to bishops informally, especially through the regular contact with the officials of the conciliar Sec-retariat for Christian Unity—"even to the point of receiving from them pro-posed emendations of the texts under discussion."[31] The secretariat in effect became the voice-box of the observers and guests: "Through the Secretariat,

---

28. On the importance of memoirs and personal journals of participants in the council, including *periti*, see Alberto Melloni, "Private Journals in the History of Vatican II," in *Vatican II Notebook: A Council Journal, 1962–1963*, ed. Marie-Dominique Chenu (Adelaide, South Australia: ATF Theology, 2015), 1–56, esp. 15–16. See also Leo Kenis, "Diaries: Private Sources for a Study of the Second Vatican Council," in *The Belgian Contribution to the Second Vatican Council*, ed. Doris Donnelly, et al. (Leuven: Peeters, 2008), 29–53.

29. See the plan of the set-up of St. Peter's in Albert Melloni, "Setting Up the Council: St. Peter's Basilica Transforms into a Council Hall," in *Vatican II: The Complete History*, ed. Alberto Melloni, Federico Ruozzi, and Enrico Galvotti (New York: Paulist Press, 2015), 78–81.

30. Quoted in Moorman, "Observers and Guests of the Council," 155.

31. Wicks, *Doing Theology*, 265n4.

the opinions on the drafts of observers from other churches could be heard in the general congregation."[32] As a group, then, the observers and guests of the council "had considerable theological significance at Vatican II."[33]

Also in assessing the interactive role of theology, theologians, and the magisterium at Vatican II, consideration should be given to the invisible presence during council proceedings of the great theologians of church history, from the patristic period to more recent decades. The history of theology and the history of doctrine shows that, while not all theological formulations become official doctrine, all doctrinal formulations necessarily employ the concepts of some theological framework. This axiom remains true at Vatican II, where the voices of figures such as Augustine, Aquinas, Bellarmine, Möhler, or Newman could often be heard echoed in debates in the aula or in commission meetings and, in the final documents, being quoted or cited explicitly, or at least alluded to implicitly. There the theologian quoted most often as *the* authority for Catholic doctrine is Thomas Aquinas, being cited 734 times; Augustine comes in second at 522 times.[34] Nevertheless, a stellar achievement of the council's turn away from the neothomism of recent centuries to a more biblical and patristic notion of the church can be seen in *Lumen Gentium*, where, as Henri de Lubac observes, "we can count in the eight chapters of the Constitution respectively 17, 13, 51, 3, 16, 3, 4 and 27 patristic quotations or references."[35] As de Lubac goes on to note, however, it is not so much the frequency of patristic references in the footnotes but more the content of *Lumen Gentium* that shows its patristic inspiration.[36] The council's own *ressourcement* of patristic thought was later captured in *Dei Verbum*'s affirmation of "living tradition": "The sayings of the church Fathers are a witness to the life-giving presence of this tradition, showing how its riches are poured out in the practice and life of the believing and praying church" (DV 8).

While in the earlier sessions there was a clear divide between classical neothomists and more historically conscious Thomists, Joseph Komonchak

32. Alberto Melloni, "Quoniam Multi: The Commissions," in *Vatican II: The Complete History*, ed. Alberto Melloni, Federico Ruozzi, and Enrico Galavotti (New York: Paulist Press, 2015), 122–23, at 122.

33. Wicks, *Doing Theology*, 274n56.

34. See McGinn, *Thomas Aquinas's Summa Theologiae*, 207.

35. Henri de Lubac, "*Lumen Gentium* and the Fathers," in *Vatican II: An Interfaith Appraisal*, ed. John H. Miller (Notre Dame, IN: University of Notre Dame Press, 1966), 153–75, at 154.

36. Ibid., 154. On the patristic tenor of *Lumen Gentium*, see Daniele Gianotti, *I Padri della Chiesa al Concilio Vaticano II: La teologia patristica nella "Lumen gentium"* (Bologna: Edizioni Dehoniane, 2010).

sees an underlying divide in the latter part of the council between the followers of Augustine and the followers of Aquinas.[37] Much of this debate is the result of a creative tension among the *ressourcement* theologians themselves. Some of the more patristically focused among them, such as de Lubac and Ratzinger, turned toward Augustine and the tradition that followed in his wake, shaped by thinkers such as Bonaventure, and away from the more speculative approaches of the medieval scholastic enterprise. Others, such as Rahner and Congar, took a broader chronological sweep of the tradition in their *ressourcement*, one that included the biblical and patristic period but also sought a more critical yet positive retrieval of Thomas, albeit in the light of an openness to later approaches within a pluralist world of the modern era. Each group had different conceptions of how *ressourcement* and *aggiornamento* should serve as an interpretive lens for the procedure of the other.

As well as these great figures of the church's more distant past, it could be said that other more recent theologians from the past cast their shadow over the debates: Newman, Möhler, Mersch, Adam, Teilhard de Chardin, among many others. To take just one example, some bishops would have already read widely translated books, such as Karl Adam's 1924 work *Das Wesen des Katholizismus*.[38] According to Leo Scheffczyk, "The council was determined by the spirit and content of the theology preceding it. Therefore, in relation to the dogmatic motive, the question 'Who determined the theology of the council?' can be answered by a competent representative of the theology following the First World War [Yves Congar]: 'An intensive work . . . for a good thirty years.' But it may also be added that in dogma the council neither would nor could go beyond the results of this work."[39]

But the most effective role played by theologians in the day-to-day operation of the council came from those *periti* formally appointed by the pope as members of the conciliar commissions. Over the course of the council's four sessions, the number of official *periti* formally appointed by the pope totalled 482.[40] Initially for the first session only 224 were appointed by the

37. Komonchak, "Thomism and the Second Vatican Council"; Komonchak, "Le valutazioni sulla *Gaudium et spes*: Chenu, Dossetti, Ratzinger"; Komonchak, "Augustine, Aquinas or the Gospel *sine glossa*?"

38. Translated as Karl Adam, *The Spirit of Catholicism* (New York: Crossroad, 1997).

39. Scheffczyk, "Main Lines of the Development of Theology between the First World War and the Second Vatican Council," 271. Emphasis added. Scheffczyk is citing Yves Congar, *Situation und Aufgabe der Theologie heute*, 2nd ed. (Paderborn: F. Schöningh, 1971), 31.

40. See the list, showing the various sessions they attended, in "Index Peritorum," in *Acta Synodalia Sacrosancti Concilii Oecumenici Vaticani II: Indices* (Città Vaticana: Typis Polyglot-

pope. As Alberto Melloni has shown, despite a certain breadth in the composition of this mainly European list, "more than half came right from the heart of Catholicism in Rome,"[41] working either in the offices of the Roman Curia or as professors at Roman universities. "Yet," as Melloni goes on to remark, "it was precisely these *periti* who brought to the conciliar documents the influence of the biblical, liturgical, and patristic movements that had emerged and were being established from the beginning of the nineteenth century and had become a key factor in the almost silent renewal of the three decades prior to the council."[42]

According to the perspective of one Australian bishop who attended all four sessions, certain European countries played a dominant role: "At the Second Vatican Council, the French bishops, the Germans and the Belgians were amongst the best organised. However, it was the presence of their theologians rather than their organisation which made their contribution to the council most effective."[43] These three groups can serve here as a framework for selecting only some of the more prominent *periti* of the council.

The Belgian *periti* certainly played a significant role.[44] One outstanding contributor, involved especially in the drafting of *Lumen Gentium*, was Gérard Philips (1899–1972).[45] From 1963, he held the key role of vice secretary for

---

tis Vaticanis, 1999), 937–49. See also the list (totaling only 480) in Alberto Melloni, "The Periti," in *Vatican II: The Complete History*, ed. Alberto Melloni, Federico Ruozzi, and Enrico Galvotti (New York: Paulist Press, 2015), 188–91. Many of the more prominent theologians are included in Michael Quisinsky, Peter Walter, and Clemens Carl, eds., *Personenlexikon zum Zweiten Vatikanischen Konzil* (Freiburg im Breisgau: Herder, 2012).

41. Melloni, "The Periti," 188.

42. Ibid.

43. Rush, "Australian Catholic Theological Association Mass," 142.

44. See Michael A. Fahey, "An Attempt to Synthesize the Conference 'The Contribution of the Belgians to Vatican Council II,'" in *The Belgian Contribution to the Second Vatican Council: International Research Conference at Mechelen, Leuven and Louvain-la-Neuve (September 12–16, 2005)*, ed. Doris Donnelly, et al. (Leuven; Dudley, MA: Peeters, 2008), 685–99.

45. For the journal Philips kept throughout the council, see Karim Schelkens, ed., *Carnets conciliaires de Mgr. Gérard Philips, sécretaire adjoint de la Commission doctrinale: Texte néerlandais avec traduction française et commentaires* (Leuven: Peeters, 2006). See also Leo Declerck, "Brève présentation du 'Journal Conciliaire' de Mgr Gerard Philips," in *Experience, Organisations and Bodies at Vatican II*, ed. Maria Teresa Fattori and Alberto Melloni (Leuven: Bibliotheek van de Faculteit Godgeleerdheid, 1999), 219–31. For assessments of Philips's contribution, see Jan Grootaers, "Gérard Philips: La force dans la faiblesse," in *Actes et acteurs à Vatican II* (Leuven: Leuven University Press and Uitgeverij Peeters, 1998), 382–419; Jan Grootaers, "Diversité des tendances à l'intérieur de la majorité conciliaire: Gérard Philips et Giuseppe Dossetti," in *The Belgian Contribution to the Second Vatican Council: International Research*

the conciliar Doctrinal Commission, where "it was his particular genius to be able to find a way forward amid conflicting views to a consensus which was in no way a compromise."[46] Yves Congar commented on one occasion about Philips's ability to bring to synthesis the diverse perspectives of a drafting committee: "Philips has an astonishing art of integrating everything in a text."[47] Given that skill, and the fact that he was often directly involved in the drafting of texts, his commentary on *Lumen Gentium* became especially authoritative.[48] Other theologians included in the group of Belgian bishops and theologians at Vatican II—who came to be known as *la squadra belga* (the Belgian team)—were Gustave Thils,[49] Lucien Cerfaux,[50] and Charles Moeller.[51]

Among the German-speaking theologians, a few can be selected.[52] According to Klaus Wittstadt, Karl Rahner became "undoubtedly the most influential theologian at the Council";[53] for Alberto Melloni, he was at least "one of the most crucial theological influences on Vatican II."[54] Rahner worked as a *peritus* on various commissions and was involved in the drafting of several texts, some of which touched on favorite themes from his own

Conference at Mechelen, Leuven and Louvain-la-Neuve (September 12–16, 2005), ed. Doris Donnelly, et al. (Leuven; Dudley, MA: Peeters, 2008), 529–62.

46. O'Donnell, "Philips, Gérard (1899–1972)," 362.

47. Congar, *My Journal of the Council*, 315.

48. Philips, *L'Église et son mystère*.

49. See Peter De Mey, "Gustave Thils and Ecumenism at Vatican II," 389–414, and Joseph Famerée, "Gustave Thils et le *De Ecclesia*: Un début d'enquête," 563–84, in *The Belgian Contribution to the Second Vatican Council: International Research Conference at Mechelen, Leuven and Louvain-la-Neuve (September 12–16, 2005)*, ed. Doris Donnelly, et al. (Leuven; Dudley, MA: Peeters, 2008).

50. See Karim Schelkens, "Lucien Cerfaux and the Preparation of the Schema *De fontibus revelationis*," in Donnelly et al., *The Belgian Contribution to the Second Vatican Council*, 415–94.

51. Jared Wicks, "*De Revelatione* under Revision (March–April 1964): Contributions of C. Moeller and Other Belgian Theologians," 461–94, and Claude Soetens, "La contribution de Charles Moeller au Concile Vatican II d'après ses papiers conciliaires," 495–528, in Donnelly et al., *The Belgian Contribution to the Second Vatican Council*.

52. On the contribution of German-speaking theologians from Germany, Austria, and Switzerland, see the various chapters in Hubert Wolf and Claus Arnold, eds., *Die deutschsprachigen Länder und das II. Vatikanum* (Paderborn: Ferdinand Schöningh, 2000). On the contribution of German theology to the council's vision, see Peter Hünermann, "Deutsche Theologie auf dem Zweiten Vatikanum," in *Kirche sein: Nachkonziliare Theologie im Dienst der Kirchenreform: Für Hermann Josef Pottmeyer*, ed. Wilhelm Geerlings and Max Seckler (Freiburg im Breisgau: Herder, 1994), 141–62.

53. Wittstadt, "On the Eve of the Second Vatican Council," 454.

54. Melloni, "The Periti," 188.

writings.[55] Another major contributor was a young professor from Bonn, Joseph Ratzinger. Throughout the council's four sessions, he was the personal *peritus* of the president of the German Episcopal Conference, Cardinal Josef Frings of Cologne, for whom he helped draft documents and conciliar speeches.[56] From the second session on, Ratzinger was appointed to various commissions and subcommissions and helped contribute to the elaboration of important conciliar emphases: "Ratzinger's service as a Vatican II *peritus*, in interaction with the members of the Council, led to remarkable theological accounts of God's revelation, of the human addressee of God's word, of the inspired Scripture, and the mission of the Church amid the human family to which God sent Christ and the Spirit."[57]

Among the French-speaking theologians, Henri de Lubac was among the most well-known at the start of the council. According to Karl-Heinz Neufeld, the influence of de Lubac (like that of others such as Congar and Rahner) went beyond his work on subcommissions; his reputation had gone before him: "At the beginning of the Council, he was often mentioned. However, the other *periti* soon moved much more strongly into the limelight, and his work remained largely hidden, only rarely attracting attention. He influenced

55. See Herbert Vorgrimler, "Karl Rahner: The Theologian's Contribution," in *Vatican II: By Those Who Were There*, ed. Alberic Stacpoole (London: Geoffrey Chapman, 1986), 32–46; Elmar Klinger, "Der Beitrag Karl Rahners zum Zweiten Vatikanum im Licht des Karl-Rahner-Archivs-Elmar-Klinger in Würzburg," in *Experience, Organisations and Bodies at Vatican II*, ed. Maria Teresa Fattori and Alberto Melloni (Leuven: Bibliotheek van de Faculteit Godgeleerdheid, 1999), 261–74; Günther Wassilowsky, "Einblick in die 'Textwerkstatt' einer Gruppe deutscher Theologen auf dem II. Vatikanum," in *Die deutschsprachigen Länder und das II. Vatikanum*, ed. Hubert Wolf and Claus Arnold (Paderborn: Ferdinand Schöningh, 2000), 61–87; Günther Wassilowsky, *Universales Heilssakrament Kirche: Karl Rahners Beitrag zur Ekklesiologie des II. Vatikanums* (Innsbruck; Wien: Tyrolia Verlag, 2001); Andreas R. Batlogg, "Anhang 1: Karl Rahners Mitarbeit an den Konzilstexten," in *Vierzig Jahre II. Vatikanum: Zur Wirkungsgeschichte der Konzilstexte*, ed. Franz Xaver Bischof and Stephan Leimgruber (Würzburg: Echter, 2004), 355–76; Thomas F. O'Meara, "Karl Rahner's 'Remarks on the Schema, 'De Ecclesia in Mundo Hujus Temporis,' in the Draft of May 28, 1965,'" *Philosophy & Theology* 20 (2008): 331–39; Günther Wassilowsky, *Als die Kirche Weltkirche wurde: Karl Rahners Beitrag zum II. Vatikanischen Konzil und seiner Deutung* (München–Freiburg im Breisgau: Univeritätsbibliothek, 2012).

56. See Jared Wicks, "Six Texts by Prof. Joseph Ratzinger as *Peritus* before and during Vatican Council II," *Gregorianum* 89 (2008): 233–311. Ratzinger's own brief account of his council involvement can be found in Joseph Ratzinger, *Milestones: Memoirs, 1927–1977* (San Francisco: Ignatius Press, 1998), 120–39.

57. Wicks, "Six Texts by Prof. Joseph Ratzinger," 253. Further on Ratzinger's contribution to the council, see Pablo Blanco Sarto, "Joseph Ratzinger, perito del Concilio Vaticano II," *Anuario di historia de la Iglesia* 15 (2006): 43–66; Gianni Valente, *Ratzinger al Vaticano II* (Cinisello Balsamo: San Paolo, 2013).

the Council [above all] by his works, which had long since been available in printed form. Many Fathers of the Council had studied books by him, from which they had adopted ideas that, during debates, were repeatedly referred to, positively or negatively."[58] His 1953 work *Méditation sur l'Eglise* was particularly familiar to the bishops.[59] The content of its chapter 4—summed up in the axiom "The church makes the Eucharist, but the Eucharist makes the church"—is echoed in the eucharistic ecclesiology of *Sacrosanctum Concilium*. The title of the first chapter of that same book, "The Church as Mystery," is echoed in the title of the first chapter of *Lumen Gentium*, "The Mystery of the Church," a theme that de Lubac had begun to develop in his earlier works *Catholicisme* and *Corpus Mysticum*.[60] The sixth chapter of *Méditation*, "The Sacrament of Christ," found expression in *Lumen Gentium*'s notion of church as "a kind of sacrament" (LG 1), "the visible sacrament of this saving unity" (LG 9), "the universal sacrament of salvation" (LG 48; GS 45). Despite the council's reception into *Lumen Gentium* of de Lubac's preconciliar work, however, his active role in conciliar commissions later diminished. By October 4, 1965, Yves Congar could note in his journal for that day: "I saw Fr de Lubac briefly, he was very tired, crushed, and down in the dumps: he is not employed in anything, he is not resorted to, he is not given notice of meetings. . . . What can be done? I am going to try to get him invited to the workshop on atheism."[61]

Yves Congar, another Frenchman, was one of the many Dominican *periti*.[62] His exhaustive journal during the council gives insight into not only the personal perspective of one *peritus* but also the day-to-day workings of various commissions.[63] Like de Lubac, Congar's preconciliar writings on church reform, the laity, and ecumenism would have been familiar to many of the council

58. Karl-Heinz Neufeld, "In the Service of the Council: Bishops and Theologians at the Second Vatican Council (for Cardinal Henri de Lubac on His Ninetieth Birthday)," in *Vatican II: Assessment and Perspectives. Twenty-Five Years After (1962–1987)*, ed. René Latourelle (New York: Paulist Press, 1988), 1:74–105, at 90.

59. Published in English as de Lubac, *The Splendor of the Church*.

60. For current English translations, see de Lubac, *Catholicism: Christ and the Common Destiny of Man*; de Lubac, *Corpus Mysticum: The Eucharist and the Church in the Middle Ages; Historical Survey*.

61. Congar, *My Journal of the Council*, 798.

62. See the table of Dominican official and private *periti* in Jorge A. Scampini, "Los Dominicos y el Concilio Vaticano II: Elementos para una visión de conjunto," in *The Dominican Order and the Second Ecumenical Vatican Council*, ed. Paolo Garuti (Rome: Angelicum University Press, 2014), 27–84, at 64–74.

63. See Congar, *My Journal of the Council*.

members.[64] Congar was a member of the historically minded school of Le Saulchoir, whose founding leader, Marie-Dominique Chenu, played a quiet but influential role through the council proceedings.[65] Congar was closely involved in the commissions drafting the four major constitutions of the council, as well as the documents related to priestly ministry, the lay apostolate, the missionary activity of the church, ecumenism, and religious liberty.[66]

For these and *periti* from other language groups, there were different aspects to their daily work on the commissions and assisting individual and groups of bishops. Coping with the analysis and thematizing of the bishops' interventions and submissions was demanding, as Congar records at one point: "The prospect of entering on index cards nine hundred pages of Latin, of discussing this over again, of redoing some texts that will provide further occasions for *modi*, to review all this again . . . this prospect, this enormous process is draining and crushing."[67] Within this work, the obligation on the *peritus* was to be faithful to the council's requests. Congar wrote of his own sense of duty to incorporate into the text only what the council members had wanted, and not his own thoughts. "One can only indicate," he wrote, "*what had been asked for by the Fathers. . . .* All the work of the Commission begins with a study and precise analysis of the interventions made *in aula* or submitted in writing. It is only on this basis that the work planned, that would be very useful in itself, can be done."[68] He then enumerates stages in the normal

64. For example, see Congar, *Divided Christendom*; Congar, *Lay People in the Church*; Yves Congar, *True and False Reform in the Church*, rev. ed. (Collegeville, MN: Liturgical Press, 2011).

65. For Chenu's journal kept during the first two sessions, see Marie-Dominique Chenu, *Vatican II Notebook: A Council Journal, 1962–1963* (Adelaide, South Australia: ATF Theology, 2015). On the contribution of the Le Saulchoir group to Vatican II, see Quisinsky, *Geschichtlicher Glaube in einer geschichtlichen Welt. Der Beitrag von M.-D. Chenu, Y. Congar und H.-M. Féret zum II. Vaticanum*. On Chenu's contribution to *Gaudium et Spes*, see Giovanni Turbanti, "Il ruolo del P. D. Chenu nell'elaborazione della costituzione *Gaudium et Spes*," in *Marie-Dominique Chenu: Moyen-Âge et modernité* (Paris: Le Centre d'études du Saulchoir, 1997), 173–212; Komonchak, "Le valutazioni sulla *Gaudium et spes*: Chenu, Dossetti, Ratzinger."

66. His journal entry for December 7, 1965, the last working day of the council, gives a list of some of the documents he was involved with. See Congar, *My Journal of the Council*, 871. For a comprehensive list of the passages from the journal when Congar discusses particular commission meetings related to his contribution, see the appendix "Chronological Tables Recapitulating Congar's Participation in the Composition of the Various Conciliar Schemas," in ibid., 919–31. A helpful evaluation of this work can be found in Jared Wicks, "Yves Congar's Doctrinal Service of the People of God," *Gregorianum* 84 (2003): 499–550.

67. Congar, *My Journal of the Council*, 788.

68. Ibid. The entry is for September 24, 1965. The italicized text appears in uppercase in the original.

procedure of a commission's work: "It is necessary: (1) seriously to consider comments [from the bishops]; (2) to work out a renovated text, sometimes quite deeply renovated; (3) to submit this to the whole Commission of revision; (4) to discuss the whole thing in the plenary Commission; (5) to write a *relatio*."[69] Within this work, the *periti*'s theological expertise enabled them to select carefully those requests that would improve the text, but without imposing their own opinions. What Jared Wicks describes regarding the necessary elements of judgement and selection in the drafting work for *De Revelatione* would no doubt have applied to the work of any of the commissions and subcommissions: "In some cases the experts had to make selections out of different proposed revisions, to reach a formulation likely to satisfy numerous respondents. At times, when the Fathers expressed their preferences more generally, the expert had to supply a formulation."[70]

The *periti* also served the council in ways beyond their work on commissions. Many bishops were eager to learn more about recent scholarship, so that their deliberations on the council floor would be more informed. To meet this palpable need, throughout the months the council was sitting each year, *periti* would present public lectures around Rome to assist the bishops in a greater appreciation of particular topics under discussion at the time. Many bishops availed themselves of these opportunities. In effect, such informal talks played the role at Vatican II of the formal "Congregations of the Theologians" at the Council of Trent, where theologians laid out the issues for the bishops on the particular topic under discussion. An Australian bishop, Francis Rush, later recalled his regular attendance at these talks by theologians during the sessions of Vatican II:

> Bishops sat at the feet of theologians and were led to serious reflection in preparation for the momentous decisions they had to make. One remembers hearing Rahner at St Peter's College, talking on collegiality; Butler at St Patrick's; Barnabas Ahern, reflecting on the draft of *Dei Verbum*; Courtney Murray, talking on religious liberty after Cardinal Alfrink, introducing him, had made a spirited defence of the Dutch church. One remembers less formal but no less serious discussions over meals with Charles Davis, Helder Camara, Godfrey Diekmann and countless Protestant observers. . . . The relationship of theologians to the *patres concilii* [fathers of the council] is a good illustration of the links that

---

69. Ibid., 818. Original numeration.
70. Wicks, "*De Revelatione* under Revision," 484.

should always exist between bishops and theologians and of the invaluable service that theologians render the *ecclesia docens* [teaching church].[71]

Another Australian bishop, Myles McKeon, could also recall the importance for him, during the council debates on revelation and Scripture, of learning from scholars outside the aula.[72] As Herbert Vorgrimler observes: "A most important effect of the countless gatherings, lectures and conversations which went on *pari passu* with the official sessions was that bishops and theologians learned to know each other."[73]

How, then, should one evaluate the role of theology and theologians at Vatican II, as well as the relationship between the voting members of the council and the *periti*? In at least three places in his council journal, Yves Congar comments on the contribution of the *periti* to the overall result of the council, seemingly giving an inflated role to the theologians. One instance was in response to anxiety expressed at the time by the Roman Curia over the forthcoming publication of a journal to be called *Concilium*, which was to feature mainly *periti* of the council. Congar writes: "They [the Curia] already know that these are the theologians—and not their own!: others . . . —who have made the Council."[74] The following year he recorded: "This Council will have been largely one of theologians who (not all, but a certain number) have contributed an enormous amount of work to it. But they have

71. Rush, "Australian Catholic Theological Association Mass," 142.

72. "At the first session of the Council, I was fortunate to meet a priest who was a professor of Scripture at Notre Dame in the United States. . . . He was one of the scholars with the American bishops. I said to him, 'Look, John, you are just the man I need to give me a complete and clear insight into the whole thing from a modern standpoint.' He was invaluable because I got to understand what we were all talking about and what we should be talking about. There were a lot of things I was out of date with. He told me the books I should read; I got them and studied them, which made the whole thing clearer to me. He was one of the periti, the experts. Many bishops brought their own advisers, theologians or Scripture scholars with them. We used to have regular meetings dealing with different subjects. Along with many others I used to attend the American press conference conducted every afternoon in English. It was good to listen to the various theologians from all over the world, and I got to know quite a few of them." Myles McKeon, "Bishop Myles McKeon: Interviewed by Russell Hardiman," in *Voices from the Council*, ed. Michael R. Prendergast and M. D. Ridge (Portland, OR: Pastoral Press, 2004), 67–80, at 75. The daily briefings to the press that Bishop Myles McKeon refers to can be found published in Floyd Anderson, ed., *Council Daybook, Vatican II: Sessions 1–4*, 3 vols. (Washington, DC: National Catholic Welfare Conference, 1965).

73. Vorgrimler, "Karl Rahner: The Theologian's Contribution," 42.

74. Congar, *My Journal of the Council*, 529. The entry is for May 3, 1964 (which covers the events of several days). The punctuation here is as it appears in the English edition.

not been pampered. We have only the right to get on with the job, but not with any help or favour, or any consideration."[75] A month later, he wrote: "The Council has largely been made by the contribution of theologians. The time after the Council will only preserve the spirit of the Council if it takes up the work of the theologians."[76]

Leonard Swidler and Hans Küng certainly hold to such an inflated interpretation of the *periti*'s significance at Vatican II when they write: "Theologians were the engineers of the massive reforms that were initiated at Vatican II. . . . In essence the theologians wrote the Vatican II documents that the bishops voted on and signed."[77] Congar, however, could not be said to hold that the *periti* "engineered" the council. What Jared Wicks calls Congar's "striking claims"[78] are to be seen in their context at the time and in the context of Congar's general sense of his role as well as some other remarks on the topic. On February 5, 1966, two months after the council's conclusion, Congar takes up his diary again. He is referring to recent appointments of bishops to postconciliar commissions: "But I see above all that the Pope wants to continue the work of the Council with the [bishops] who carried it out. However, these men would not have done what they did without the experts [*periti*]. Now, some experts will be able to be summoned to these post-conciliar Commissions, but none has been made a statutory member of them. I have long seen that one of the major problems of the post-conciliar situation will be to preserve the *organic co-operation*—which alone permitted and brought about the Council—between bishops and theologians."[79] The overall tone, then, of his council journal, despite some overreaching remarks regarding the tireless and indispensable work of the *periti*, portrays the relationship between the conciliar magisterium and its welcomed theologians, clearly in terms of "organic cooperation."

That, certainly, was the sense of the *peritus* Karl Rahner. When asked in an interview whether he was "one of the most significant, internationally renowned key figures of the Second Vatican Council," his reply is telling, as

75. Ibid., 800. The entry is for October 4, 1965.

76. Ibid., 835. The entry is for November 7, 1965.

77. Leonard Swidler and Hans Küng, "The Context: Breaking Reform by Breaking Theologians and Religious," in *The Church in Anguish: Has the Vatican Betrayed Vatican II?*, ed. Hans Küng and Leonard Swidler (San Francisco: Harper & Row, 1987), 189–92, at 189–90. For an assessment of these remarks, see J. F. Kobler, "Were Theologians the Engineers of Vatican II?," *Gregorianum* 70 (1989): 233–50.

78. Wicks, "*De Revelatione* under Revision," 482.

79. Congar, *My Journal of the Council*, 877. Emphasis added.

an indication both of his evaluation of the role of all *periti* at Vatican II and of the scope of his own participation:

> Not really, I think that's an exaggeration. Yes, I was present at the Second Vatican Council. I also had contact with German and Austrian bishops. The Brazilian bishops invited me to speak several times. Once I was with the Polish bishops. I was a member of the theological commission that produced both the decree on the Church and the one on divine revelation, and I was on the commission that wrote the document on the relationship of the Church to the modern world. But by the very nature of things, there were a lot of cooks at the Second Vatican Council, lots of co-workers, theologians, and bishops. If you keep in mind that two thousand bishops suggested hundreds and hundreds of changes for every decree, and that I certainly wasn't the boss of the theological commission or of the theologians, let alone the bishops, then you won't regard me as if I held a key position at the Second Vatican Council. There were a number of different decrees. For the most part, I learned something about most of them only after they had long been completed and approved.[80]

That the bishops were in charge is clear; that they depended on the *periti* is equally clear. The crucial leadership on many levels by the bishops and popes in the conciliar proceedings (especially key figures from Northern Europe) show how the council was far from being "engineered" by the theologians. As Wicks maintains, the contribution of the theologians was certainly indispensable. Nevertheless, as he goes on to note, their work would always have to be ratified by the bishops: "But in all this, the ultimate outcome of the theologians' work was decided by others, that is, by the Council members who were the members of the commissions and who voted in the Aula. The ideas, preferences, and texts drawn up by the theologians were consultative proposals of experts, about which the Council members in different moments decided whether, and in what form, these theological contributions might appear in the schemata placed before the Council and then in the documents approved by the Council."[81]

For Andreas Torres Queiruga, "Vatican II laid foundations and opened doors. The very fact that it took place was a splendid exercise in new possibilities: collaboration between bishops and theologians was not easy to get going but it proved extremely fruitful. Without it the results of the Council

---

80. Karl Rahner, *I Remember: An Autobiographical Interview with Meinold Krauss*, ed. Meinold Krauss (London: SCM Press, 1985), 81–82.

81. Wicks, "Theologians at Vatican Council II," 188.

would have been unthinkable; it was an exercise in Church fellowship, which made it possible to start a new ecclesiology."[82] Wicks' conclusion is that "even without having the authority to make decisions by casting votes on the texts, the theologians serving the Commissions made *essential* contributions to bringing before the Council Fathers the revised documents that in time came to express the results of the Second Vatican Council."[83] Thus, here, with regard to the magisterium/theologians principle as with other matters, the council taught as much by example. The whole conciliar event is a model of bishops and theologians working collaboratively.

Vatican II on Theology

But if that is the spirit of the council, what of the letter? What do the council texts themselves end up saying about the work of theologians, their contribution to the mission of the church, and their relationship with the magisterium in the church? In the order of their promulgation, the following documents highlight various aspects.

Lumen Gentium recognizes that theological scholarship is needed for the ongoing interpretation of doctrine. In discussing the scope of issues to be covered in chapter 8 of *Lumen Gentium* on Our Lady, the council obliquely comments on how the magisterium, here an ecumenical council, does not wish to make judgments on matters that are still openly disputed among theologians: "Therefore this sacred synod . . . does not, however, intend to give a complete doctrine on Mary, nor does it wish to decide those questions which the work of theologians has not yet fully clarified. Those opinions [*sententiae*] therefore may be lawfully retained which are freely propounded in Catholic schools [of theology] concerning her" (LG 54). Later in the chapter, it states: "[The sacred synod] strongly urges theologians and preachers of the word of God to be careful to refrain as much from all false exaggeration as from too summary an attitude in considering the special dignity of the Mother of God. Following the study of sacred scripture, the Fathers, the doctors and the liturgy of the church, and under the guidance of the church's magisterium [*sub ductu magisterii*], let them rightly illustrate the offices and privileges of the Blessed Virgin which always refer to Christ, the source of all truth, sanctity, and devotion" (LG 67).

---

82. Andres Torres Queiruga, "Magisterium and Theology: Principles and Facts," in *Theology and Magisterium. Concilium 2012/2*, ed. Felix Wilfred and Susan A. Ross (London: SCM Press, 2012), 51–63, at 51.

83. Wicks, "*De Revelatione* under Revision," 484. Original emphasis.

Promulgated on the same day as *Lumen Gentium*, the Decree on Ecumenism affirms a necessary freedom for theological enquiry and the legitimacy of diversity in theological approaches to the divine mystery: "While preserving unity in essentials, let all in the church, according to the office entrusted to them, preserve a proper freedom [*debitam libertatem*] in the various forms of spiritual life and discipline, in the variety of liturgical rites, and even in the theological elaborating of revealed truth. In all things let charity prevail. If they are true to this course of action, they will be giving ever richer expression to the authentic *catholicity* and *apostolicity* of the church" (UR 4).[84] Related to maintaining authentic catholicity is the matter of diversity. "What has already been said about legitimate diversity [*legitima diversitate*] we are pleased to apply to differences in theological expression of doctrine [*diversa theologica doctrinarum enuntiatione*]. In the study of revealed truth East and West have used different methods and approaches in understanding and confessing divine things. It is hardly surprising, then, if sometimes one tradition has come nearer to a full appreciation of some aspects of a mystery of revelation than the other, or has expressed them better. In such cases, these various theological formulations are often to be considered *complementary rather than conflicting* [*compleri . . . quam opponi*]" (UR 17).[85]

The Decree thus urges Catholic theologians toward an approach that is historically conscious and ecumenical: "We must become familiar with the outlook of the separated churches and communities. Study is absolutely required for this" (UR 9). "Theology and other branches of knowledge, especially those of a historical nature, must be taught with due regard for the ecumenical point of view, so that they may correspond more exactly with the facts" (UR 9). With such an openness to the sense of the faith of other Christian traditions, Catholic theologians can come to understand "the Catholic faith" even more deeply and come to an ever deeper appreciation of doctrine regarding the revelatory event of God's self-communication in Jesus Christ through the Holy Spirit. Accordingly: "The manner and order in which Catholic belief is expressed should in no way become an obstacle to dialogue with other Christians. . . . When comparing doctrines with one another, [Catholic theologians] should remember that in Catholic doctrine there exists an order or 'hierarchy' of truths, since they vary in their relation to the foundation of the Christian faith. Thus the way will be opened whereby this kind of friendly rivalry [*per fraternam hanc aemulationem*] will incite all to a deeper realization and a

84. Emphasis added.
85. Translation corrected.

clearer expression of *the unfathomable riches of Christ*" (UR 11).[86] This latter phrase is an allusion to *Dei Verbum*'s teaching on revelation as a personal, saving encounter with the living God, in Jesus Christ through the Holy Spirit. In other words, through Catholics' ecumenical dialogue with other Christians, understanding better the doctrines of those other Christian traditions can help Catholics better understand the depths of God's revelatory self-communication in Christ through the Spirit. With statements such as these, Vatican II guides Catholic theologians to balance the propositionalist understanding of revelation expounded at Vatican I with a personalist and more fundamental understanding of revelation.

Two documents on education afforded the council opportunities to highlight further the implications of its vision for theologians and theological scholarship. *Gravissimum Educationis* 11, referring to the "exacting duties of the intellectual apostolate," presents four functions through which Catholic faculties of theology and other related disciplines contribute to the church: "The church anticipates great benefits from the activities of the faculties of the sacred sciences. . . . Their object will be to ensure (1) that an ever more profound understanding [*profundior intellectus*] of sacred revelation be achieved, (2) that the inheritance of Christian wisdom handed down by former generations be more fully opened up [*aperiatur*], (3) that dialogue with our separated brothers and sisters and with non-Christians be promoted, and (4) questions arising from the development of doctrine [*quaestionibus a doctrinarum progressu exortis*] be responded to" (GE 11).[87] These passages articulate the council's faith/history principle and the role of theology in interpreting Scripture and tradition as well as in discerning God's continuing self-communication by interpreting contemporary experiences of revelation.

The council's second document on education is its Decree on the Training of Priests, *Optatam Totius*. Articles 15 and 16, in calling for a revision in the program of studies for seminarians, give indications of the council's vision of theology. Gerald O'Collins's commentary on these articles provides a summary list of eleven aspects of that vision: "It is (1) a sacred science, based on revelation and on (2) the Christ-centred history of salvation. It should be (3) deeply biblical, (4) founded in tradition, (5) guided by the magisterium, (6) ecclesial, (7) liturgical and (8) ecumenical in its concerns, (9) informed

---

86. Emphasis added. The text cites Eph 3:8.
87. Translation corrected. Numeration added.

about and respectful toward other religions, (10) aided in particular by philosophy, and (11) working toward more effective communication."[88]

On the place the philosophy and theology of Thomas Aquinas should play in those studies, the decree's vision is telling. Pope Leo XIII, in his 1879 encyclical *Aeterni Patris*, had set the course of Catholic philosophy, theology, and education through the so-called neothomism movement. The council's preparatory Commission for Studies and Seminaries had presented two schemas for consideration by the council, texts that reaffirmed the centrality of Thomas Aquinas in seminary education.[89] In *Optatam Totius*, the council certainly recommends that seminarians' study of the mysteries of faith should be "guided by St. Thomas" (OT 16). Nevertheless, while they are to be "guided by the philosophical tradition of lasting value . . . at the same time they should take account of modern philosophical developments, particularly those of influence in their own country, as well as recent progress in the sciences, so that with a proper understanding of the present age, they will be equipped for dialogue with people of their time" (OT 15). As John O'Malley remarks on another issue (and, as we have seen, so applicable to other issues), these texts from *Optatam Totius* on the role of St. Thomas in priestly education present further examples "of how deceptive the placid surface of the documents can be. It is not the documents, therefore, that reveal how hot the issue was but the narrative of the battles for control of the council itself."[90] Gerald McCool sees these statements in *Optatam Totius* as historic: "The Church's reliance on the philosophy and theology of St. Thomas as the exclusive speculative system used in the education of her clergy, to which Leo XIII had lent the full weight of the papacy in *Aeterni Patris*, ended definitively with the Second Vatican Council's Decree on Priestly Formation."[91]

Perhaps the council's most authoritative, although understated, affirmation of the ecclesial importance of theological scholarship comes in *Dei Verbum*'s statement that such scholarship constitutes one of the three major means through which the Holy Spirit guides the church in its transmission of the apostolic tradition.

---

88. O'Collins, *Retrieving Fundamental Theology*, 25. Original numeration.

89. On the content and fate of those two preparatory schemas, see Komonchak, "Thomism and the Second Vatican Council," esp. 53–62.

90. O'Malley, *What Happened at Vatican II*, 304.

91. McCool, *From Unity to Pluralism*, 229.

> The tradition that comes from the apostles makes progress in the church, with the help of the Holy Spirit. There is a growth in insight into the realities and words that are being passed on. This comes about through (1) the contemplation and study of believers [*ex contemplatione et studio credentium*] who ponder these things in their heart. It comes from (2) the intimate sense of spiritual realities which they experience. And it comes from (3) the preaching of those who, on succeeding to the office of bishop, have received the sure charism of truth. Thus as the centuries go by, the church is always advancing towards the plenitude of divine truth, until eventually the words of God are fulfilled in it. (DV 8)[92]

As one of the drafters, Umberto Betti, notes in his commentary on this passage, the council was intending here, not so much to give an extensive list, but rather to indicate three general factors in the life of the church by which the living tradition progresses in history through its active reception: "The tradition, infused into the life of the church, causes a reaction in those who come into conscious contact with it. And each reaction becomes, though in a different way, an active factor of its progress. These factors cannot easily be classified into a rigid list, without running the risk of not a few omissions or too approximate estimates. The council has simply limited itself to indicating them through general categories."[93]

That the phrase *ex contemplatione et studio credentium* is a deliberate reference to the work of theologians is clearly evident from the history of the various drafts. After fifteen council fathers called for an explicit reference to theologians, the word *studium* was added after *contemplatio*. The fuller phrase has echoes of Thomas Aquinas's phrase *contemplata tradere* (to pass on the fruits of contemplation);[94] moreover, the Dominican tradition of *studium* would have been presupposed by some bishops (such as the Dominican Cardinal Michael Browne) who had asked for explicit mention of theologians in the passage as well by one of its drafting *periti*, Yves Congar, also a Dominican.[95] As Umberto Betti comments with regard to the means by which

---

92. Numeration added.

93. Betti, *La dottrina del concilio Vaticano II sulla trasmissione della rivelazione*, 256.

94. "Just as it is greater to illuminate something than merely to shine, so it is greater to pass on to others what we have contemplated [*contemplata tradere*] than just to contemplate." *Summa Theologiae* II–II, 188, 6.

95. I am grateful to Jared Wicks and Gerald O'Collins in correspondence for these insights on this passage. In his treatment of Vatican II's statements on the role of theology in the church, O'Collins notes: "*Dei Verbum* draws attention to a reciprocal relationship between theology and tradition. On the one hand, theology relies and draws on tradition (DV 24). On the other hand, theological 'study' is named as one of the factors effecting, under the Holy Spirit, devel-

believers "seek to better understand the inexhaustible riches of the tradition": "In this, the professional theologians have a part of primary importance. With their study and their research, they strive, even at their own risk, to penetrate the divine mysteries, and to open the church to the imperatives, sometimes unsuspected, arising from those mysteries."[96] It was only in the final version of *Dei Verbum* 8 that the third statement on the magisterium was added to the statements on the work of theological scholarship and the *sensus fidelium*.

Article 12 of *Dei Verbum* speaks specifically of the work of biblical scholars. It highlights the need for them to give due attention to the historical context out of which the scriptural texts emerge, in order to attend to "that meaning which the sacred writers, in given situations and granted the circumstances of their time and culture, intended to express and did in fact express, through the medium of a contemporary literary form" (DV 12). It goes on to list some of those contextual conditions: "The customary and characteristic patterns of perception, speech and narrative which prevailed in their time, and to the conventions which people then observed in their dealings with one another." The document then emphasizes, however, that this historical enquiry should be balanced by attention to an ecclesial reading of these texts. Article 11 had already highlighted the inspired nature of the texts, and the activity of the Holy Spirit in guiding the human authors. Now the document emphasizes the concomitant role of the same Holy Spirit in the ongoing interpretation of these scriptural texts within the new contexts of church communities throughout history. It affirms that "sacred scripture must be read and interpreted in the same Spirit in which it was written [*eodem Spiritu quo scripta est*]" (DV 12).[97]

The implication is that the work of Scripture scholars plays an important role in the ecclesial interpretation of Scripture. In that work, scholars must keep in mind three rules (*regulas*): "*the content and unity of the whole of scripture*, taking into account *the living tradition of the entire church* and *the analogy of faith*" (DV 12).[98] It states that "it is the task of exegetes to work, according to these rules, towards a better understanding and explanation of the meaning of sacred scripture *in order that their research may help the*

---

opment in tradition—in the sense of a 'growth in understanding' and progress 'toward the fullness of divine truth' (DV 8)." O'Collins, *Retrieving Fundamental Theology*, 21.

96. Betti, *La dottrina del concilio Vaticano II sulla trasmissione della rivelazione*, 257.

97. Translation corrected. For this translation, see de la Potterie, "Interpretation of Holy Scripture."

98. Emphasis added.

church's judgment to mature [*maturetur*]," a verb that evokes the notion of "living tradition" and the "development" of doctrine alluded to in other parts of the constitution and in other documents. Thus, biblical scholars play a role in forming the judgment of the church regarding the meaning of Scripture. By implication, they are a factor in the living tradition. The phrase "the judgment *of the church*" (*iudicium ecclesiae*) is used twice in the last two sentences of article 12. That this is not to be understood as referring exclusively to the judging role of the magisterium can be inferred from the reference earlier in the article to "the living tradition *of the whole church* [*vivae totius ecclesiae traditionis*]" (DV 12). Certainly, article 10 had earlier affirmed that, ultimately, "the task of *authoritatively* [*authentice*] interpreting the word of God" falls to the episcopal magisterium.[99] Here article 12 ends with the expansive statement: "All that has been said about the manner of interpreting scripture is ultimately subject to the judgment of the church, which exercises the divinely conferred commission and ministry of watching over [*servandi*] and interpreting the word of God" (DV 12). Intratextually: the judgment of the church comes about through the interaction of three ecclesial elements: the work of theologians (including biblical scholars), the *sensus fidelium*, and the magisterium (DV 8).

Later, when addressing the place of Scripture in the life of the church, *Dei Verbum* 23 affirms: "Taught by the Holy Spirit, the spouse of the incarnate Word, which is the church, strives to reach an increasingly more profound understanding of the sacred scriptures, in order to nourish its children with God's words. For this reason also it duly encourages the study of the Fathers, both eastern and western, and of the sacred liturgies. Catholic exegetes and other workers in the field of sacred theology should work diligently together and under the watchful eye of the sacred magisterium [*sub vigilantia sacri magisterii*]" (DV 23). Moreover, it goes on to state, this work should be carried out "in accordance with *the sense of the church* [*secundum sensum ecclesiae*]" (DV 23).[100] This last statement has intratextual echoes with *Dei Verbum* 8 regarding the progress of the apostolic tradition through the Holy Spirit's effecting theological scholarship, the *sensus fidelium*, and the oversight of the magisterium. Moreover, it has intertextual echoes with *Lumen Gentium* 12 on the *sensus fidei totius populi* and the magisterium.

Joseph Ratzinger points out a significant word change in the drafting history of the above passage from *Dei Verbum* 23. It concerns a shift in tone

---

99. Translation corrected.
100. Translation corrected. Emphasis added.

regarding the oversight of the magisterium: "*Vigilantia* was used in Text F to replace the previous term *sub ductu* ['under the guidance'], in order to express the fact that the function of the teaching office is not to lead the way—progress is the concern of scholarship; basically the teaching office has the negative function of describing impenetrable terrain as such."[101] As noted above, *Lumen Gentium* 67 had used the more restrictive term *sub ductu magisterii* regarding theologians' work related to "the special dignity of the mother of God." This passage in *Dei Verbum* 23, therefore, indicates a certain development in the mind of the council regarding the relationship between the magisterium and theologians.

It is also noteworthy that *Dei Verbum*'s discussion of the work of biblical scholars and theologians working under "the watchful eye" of the magisterium (DV 23) comes within discussion of the ministry of the word in the church and the way the Holy Spirit assists that teaching ministry. "Taught [*edocta*] by the Holy Spirit, the spouse of the incarnate Word, which is the church, strives to reach an increasingly more profound understanding of the sacred scriptures, in order to nourish its children with God's words" (DV 23). Both being taught by the same Holy Spirit in respect of their diverse roles, theologians and the magisterium must work "in accordance with the mind of the church [*secundum sensum ecclesiae*]" (DV 23).

Thus *Dei Verbum* 23 and 24 in chapter 6, building on the affirmations made earlier in chapter 2 regarding the personal nature of divine self-revelation, name four ecclesial sources and norms with which the theologian engages: Scripture, the living tradition (including writings of the fathers and revered liturgical practices), the "sense" of the church through the ages, and the magisterium. (Two later documents, *Ad Gentes* and *Gaudium et Spes*, as will be discussed below, will add two further sources the church should access: *culture* and *history*.) Within those sources and norms, the written word of God within the living tradition is a privileged authority: "Sacred theology relies on the written word of God, taken together with sacred tradition, as its permanent foundation. By this word it is powerfully strengthened and constantly rejuvenated, *as it searches out*, under the light of faith [*sub lumine fidei perscrutando*], *all the truth stored up in the mystery of Christ*" (DV 24).[102] Indeed, "the study of the sacred page should be the very soul of sacred theology" (DV 24). The document is here alluding to *Optatam Totius* 16,

101. Ratzinger, "Sacred Scripture in the Life of the Church," 268.
102. Emphasis added.

promulgated three weeks earlier, which states "the study of scripture . . . ought to be the very soul of all theology" (OT 16).[103]

Dei Verbum 24 names the ultimate object of theological enquiry: "all the truth stored up in the mystery of Christ." The phrase "the mystery of Christ" is here equivalent to divine revelation, God's self-communication, as outlined in the first chapter of *Dei Verbum*. Theology interprets this revelation under the light of faith: *sub lumine fidei perscrutando*. This, in turn, echoes the key passage of *Gaudium et Spes* 4, where we find the phrase regarding the church's responsibility "of reading the signs of the times and of interpreting them in the light of the Gospel [*signa temporum perscrutandi et sub evangelii luce interpretandi*]." Thus theology interprets not only the scriptural witness to revelation from the past but also the present saving activity of God in the light of that past witness.

The Decree on the Church's Missionary Activity, *Ad Gentes*, gives particular attention to the role of local theologians in a church that understands itself to be "by its very nature missionary" (AG 2). As already noted, this decree was mainly drafted in the last year of the council and therefore expresses its later thinking. It shows both the council's greater appreciation of culture and its acknowledgment of the indispensable role of local theologians. Two articles in the decree are especially pertinent. Article 22 implies an interdependence between local theologians and the magisterium:

> To achieve this [adaptation to local culture] it is necessary that in each of the great socio-cultural regions, as they are called, theological investigation [*consideratio theologica*] should be encouraged and the facts and words revealed by God, contained in sacred scripture, and explained by the fathers and magisterium of the church, submitted to a new examination [*novae investigationi*] in the light of the tradition of the universal church. In this way it will be more clearly understood by what means the faith can be explained in terms of the philosophy and wisdom of the people, and how their customs, attitude to life and social structures can be reconciled with the standard proposed by divine revelation. Thus a way will be opened for a more profound adaptation in the whole sphere of Christian life. This manner of acting will avoid every appearance of syncretism and false exclusiveness; the Christian life will be adapted [*accommodabitur*] to the mentality and character of each culture, and local traditions together with the special qualities of each national family, illumined

---

103. A footnote cites Leo XIII's *Providentissimus Deus*, 16: "Most desirable is it, and most essential, that the whole teaching of Theology should be pervaded and animated by the use of the divine Word of God."

by the light of the Gospel, will be taken up into a Catholic unity [*unitatem catholicam*]. So new particular churches, each with its own traditions, have their place in the communion of the church [*ecclesiastica communio*], the primacy of Peter which presides over this universal assembly of charity all the while remaining intact. (AG 22)

The next paragraph of the article then refers to the intermediary role of episcopal conferences in this ecclesial process of "adaptation": "And so it is to be hoped, and indeed it would be a very good thing, that episcopal conferences should come together within the boundaries of each great socio-cultural region and by a united and coordinated effort pursue this proposal of adaptation" (AG 22).

Later, article 39 evokes the faith/history principle, with its affirmation that faith's reception of revelation necessarily takes place from within the context of the receiver, as well as the methodological concern in *Gaudium et Spes* to attend to the social, cultural, economic, and political dimensions of the human condition: "University and seminary professors will instruct the young as to *the true condition of the world and the church*, so that the need for a more intense evangelization of non-Christians will be clear to them and feed their zeal. In teaching dogmatic, biblical, moral and historical subjects, they should focus attention on their missionary aspects, so that in this way a missionary awareness will be formed in future priests" (AG 39).[104]

Gaudium et Spes marks a significant acknowledgment by the council of the role of theologians in the mission of the church. Article 44 articulates the magisterium/theologians principle and the common service of both ecclesial groups to the mission of the whole church: "With the help of the Holy Spirit, it is the task of the whole people of God, particularly of its pastors and theologians [*pastorum et theologorum*], to listen to [*auscultare*] and distinguish [*discernere*] the many voices of our times and to interpret them [*interpretari*] in the light of the divine word, in order that the revealed truth may be more deeply penetrated, better understood, and more suitably presented" (GS 44). There are intratextual references here back to the structurally important articles 4 and 11 on the signs of the times; furthermore, the passage has intertextual allusions to the important verbs of *Lumen Gentium* 12 on the *sensus fidelium*: "receives," "adheres," penetrates," and "applies."

In his commentary on *Gaudium et Spes* 44, Yves Congar observes how the article speaks of several "domains" in which the Church receives from

104. Emphasis added.

the world.[105] Two of those domains could be described as "pedagogical" and "epistemological."[106] Epistemological refers to "the opening up of new ways of access to truth."[107] Congar notes how the article focuses on the way "the treasures of cultures" can help the church access truth. Extending Congar's remarks, however, it could be said that "history" itself opens up new ways of access to truth; "history" and "the signs of the times" are sources for the church in its reception of divine revelation, since they are lenses through which Scripture and tradition are to be interpreted; in turn, Scripture and tradition together constitute a lens through which the present revelatory action of God in history (evident in the signs of the times) is to be interpreted. The second domain Congar highlights could be called "pedagogical," i.e., related to the domain of effective communication. Congar states: "The different cultures . . . possess a language which the Church can use to speak to the world and announce the gospel to it."[108] Thus, in these two domains, theologians help the church learn from God whose ongoing activity in human history reveals further depths of God's plan within the changing circumstances of time and place—new, previously unperceived insights into "the truth stored up in the mystery of Christ" (DV 24); also, within those changing circumstances, theologians help the church to preach the Gospel in language that will be understood and relate to the life situations of the receivers of that saving message.

Article 62 of the pastoral constitution constitutes a manifesto for the role of theologians in the church's mission; Gerald O'Collins considers it "one of the richest articles from the council on the role of theologians."[109] Its opening paragraph declares:

> Although the church has contributed largely to the progress of culture, it is a fact of experience that there have been difficulties in the way of harmonizing culture with Christian thought, arising out of contingent factors. These difficulties do not necessarily harm the life of faith, but can rather stimulate a more precise and deeper understanding of that faith. In fact, recent research and discoveries in the sciences, in history and philosophy bring up new questions [*novas quaestiones*]

---

105. Yves Congar, "Part I, Chapter IV: The Role of the Church in the Modern World," in *Commentary on the Documents of Vatican II*, vol. 5, ed. Herbert Vorgrimler (New York: Herder and Herder, 1969), 5:202–23, at 219–21.

106. These are my categories, not Congar's.

107. Congar, "The Role of the Church in the Modern World," 219.

108. Ibid.

109. O'Collins, *Retrieving Fundamental Theology*, 156n10.

which have an important bearing on life itself and demand new scrutiny [*novas investigations*] by theologians. Furthermore, theologians are now being asked, within the methods and limits of theological science, to develop more efficient ways of communicating doctrine to the people of today, for the deposit and the truths of faith are one thing, the manner of expressing them—provided their sense and meaning are retained—is quite another. (GS 62)

This last sentence, of course, alludes to the statement of Pope John XXIII in his opening address to the first session of the council: "The substance of the ancient doctrine of the deposit of faith is one thing, and the way in which it is presented is another."[110]

Later in article 62 of the pastoral constitution, a general statement referring to the *fideles* applies, by implication, to the obligation on theologians. The passage implies that, just as the laity's engagement in the secular world, and the hierarchy's service to the rest of the people of God, are but intensifications of what all the *fideles* are called to, *so too the vocation of the theologian is but an intensification of the intellectual engagement with the lived experiences of the world around them, to which all the* fideles *are called*. Article 62 states: "Therefore, the faithful [*fideles*] ought to work closely with their contemporaries and ought to try to understand their ways of thinking and feeling, as these find expression in current culture. Let the faithful incorporate the findings of new sciences and teachings and the understanding of the most recent discoveries into Christian morality and thought, so that their practice of religion and their moral behaviour may keep abreast of their acquaintance with science and of the relentless progress in technology: in this way they will succeed in evaluating and interpreting everything with an authentically Christian sense [*integro christiano sensu*]" (GS 62). This latter phrase echoes the statements in *Lumen Gentium* on the *sensus fidei* (especially LG 12 and 35).

It is also important to point out that, by implication, these references in *Gaudium et Spes* to the social and natural sciences is an expansion of what should be considered the ancillary disciples for theology, beyond philosophy. With a concern that future priests be imbued with such an open approach to theological enquiry, the pastoral constitution spells out the interdisciplinary implications for theological method, as well as the importance of such enquiry for the very effectiveness of the church's mission:

110. John XXIII, "Pope John's Opening Speech," 715.

Those involved in theological studies in seminaries should be eager to cooperate with people versed in other disciplines by pooling their resources and their points of view. Theological research, while it deepens knowledge of revealed truth, should not lose contact with its own times, so that experts in various fields may be led to a deeper knowledge of the faith. Collaboration of this kind will be beneficial in the formation of sacred ministers; they will be able to present teaching on God, on humanity, and on the world, in a way more suited to our contemporaries, who will then be more ready to accept their word. (GS 62)

This is yet another articulation of what Christoph Theobald calls the council's "pastorality principle": "There can be no proclamation of the gospel without taking account of its recipients [and] 'what' is at stake in the proclamation is already at work in them, in such a way that they can accede to it in all freedom."[111]

Gaudium et Spes 62 is also significant because it shows how the council broke out of a mind-set that envisaged all theologians as ordained ministers of the church. The passage goes on to state: "It is to be hoped that more of the laity [*laici*] will receive adequate theological formation and that some among them will dedicate themselves professionally to these studies and contribute to their advancement" (GS 62). And then, in a strong affirmation of the necessary freedom of theological inquiry, the council states: "For the proper exercise of this role, the faithful, both clerical and lay, should be accorded a lawful freedom of inquiry, of thought, and of expression, tempered by humility and courage in whatever branch of study they have specialized" (GS 62). Significantly, a footnote to this passage refers back to a passage in *Lumen Gentium* 37 the year before that had stated: "The sacred pastors, however, should recognize and promote the dignity and responsibility of the laity in the church. They should willingly use their prudent advice and confidently assign offices to them in the service of the church, leaving them freedom and scope for activity. Indeed, they should encourage them to take on work on their own initiative. They should with paternal love consider attentively in Christ initial moves, suggestions and desires proposed by the laity. Moreover the pastors must respect and recognize the liberty which belongs to all in the earthly city" (LG 37).

---

111. Theobald, "The Theological Options of Vatican II," 94.

In his speech, *Gaudet Mater Ecclesia*, at the opening of the first session, John XXIII had expressed his hope that the council would be "a step forward toward a doctrinal penetration and a formation of consciousness in faithful and perfect conformity to the authentic doctrine, which, however, should be studied and expounded through the methods of research and through the literary forms of modern thought."[112] He then pointed the way toward "a magisterium which is predominantly pastoral in character."[113] In safeguarding authentic doctrine, the church, he said—perhaps ironically— "prefers to make use of the medicine of mercy rather than that of severity. She considers that she meets the needs of the present day by demonstrating the validity of her teaching rather than by condemnations."[114] The council went on to embrace the pope's provocative challenge. In essence, what Vatican II promoted regarding dialogue within the church implies a vision for a new way of relating between the magisterium and theologians: "[The church's mission] requires us first of all to create in the church itself mutual esteem, reverence and harmony, and to acknowledge all legitimate diversity; in this way all who constitute the one people of God will be able to engage in ever more fruitful dialogue, whether they are pastors or other members of the faithful. For the ties which unite the faithful together are stronger than those which separate them: let there be unity in what is necessary, freedom in what is doubtful, and charity in everything" (GS 92).

We have already noted the thesis of Richard Gaillardetz: "that Vatican II consistently transposed oppositional ecclesial relationships into noncompetitive ecclesial relationships, largely by way of its recovery of a theology of the Holy Spirit."[115] This notion of "noncompetitive ecclesial relationships" aptly describes Vatican II's vision of the relationship between the magisterium and theologians, as evident both in the *modus operandi* of the council and in the statements on the theme found throughout its final documents. Just as the council envisaged "a noncompetitive theology of the relationship of the magisterium and the whole Christian faithful,"[116] so too it could be said to have envisaged a noncompetitive relationship between the magisterium and theologians. Of course, signs of a less dialogic way of relating continued to be apparent in the attitudes of several of the bishops until the close of the

112. John XXIII, "Pope John's Opening Speech," 715.
113. Ibid.
114. Ibid., 716.
115. Gaillardetz, *An Unfinished Council*, 92.
116. See ibid., 98–101.

council. Jared Wicks, however, as already noted, sees a fundamental transition taking place: "Regarding the relationship between the papal-episcopal magisterium of the Catholic Church and those who do theology, Vatican II signalled the end of one era and the beginning of a transition to another way of relating."[117]

In this chapter, we have proposed that this new way of relating between the magisterium and theologians, because it was such a distinctive feature of the council's *modus operandi*, which is then captured to some degree in its texts, constitutes a principle in its own right in the vision of Vatican II, what has been here called the magisterium/theologians principle. Set against the background of Vatican II's promotion of dialogue *ad intra* and *ad extra*, Walter Kasper sees implications here for the council's vision of "orthodoxy": "orthodoxy regarded as a process based on dialogue. This approach is based on the conviction that truth in the Church has to emerge from a process of dialogue between all the charisms and tendencies."[118]

It is to Vatican II's vision of dialogue *ad extra* that the final three chapters turn. It will be an encounter in which the council's theologians will once again play an important role.

---

117. Wicks, *Doing Theology*, 105.
118. Kasper, *An Introduction to Christian Faith*, 150.

Principle 22

Catholic/Ecumenical

Principle 22: Despite the ecclesial separations between Eastern and Western Christianity, and within Western Christianity, the "communion" within the whole church of Christ was not completely severed by these separations, even though there are now, consequently, different degrees of communion; while the fullness of communion is to be found between the particular churches of the Catholic Church, the existence of elements of the one church of Christ in other Christian churches and ecclesial communities impels all Christians to strive for full communion among all, a unity that Christ prayed for his disciples.

Regarding the conciliar principles expounded in this and the following chapter, Karl Rahner succinctly articulates the remarkable shift that took place at Vatican II: "The Council represents *a caesura* in the history of the relations of the Catholic Church both with other Christian Churches and communities and with non-Christian world-religions."[1] Likewise, for Avery Dulles, the council's vision on these matters cannot but be interpreted as discontinuous with the church's prior stance: "In all honesty it is not possible to say that Vatican II speaks about the other Churches, the other religions, or religious liberty in the same way as earlier popes and councils had spoken. The ancient doctrine 'Outside the Church, no salvation' has been so drastically reinterpreted by Vatican II that the meaning is almost the opposite of what the words seem to say."[2] Given the radical nature of these shifts, there will be a more extensive examination of the final three principles of Vatican

1. Karl Rahner, "The Abiding Significance of the Second Vatican Council," in *Theological Investigations*, vol. 20 (London: Darton, Longman & Todd, 1981), 20:90–102, at 97. Emphasis added.

2. Avery Dulles, *The Survival of Dogma: Faith, Authority and Dogma in a Changing World* (New York: Crossroad, 1987), 145. For a history of the axiom "*extra ecclesiam nulla salus*," see Sullivan, *Salvation outside the Church?*

II: the Catholic/ecumenical principle, the Christian/religious principle, and the church/world principle.

The axiom *extra ecclesiam nulla salus* (outside the church, no salvation) is particularly associated with Cyprian of Carthage writing in North Africa in the third century and "occurs with frequency and urgency in his writings."[3] A high point in the reception history of Cyprian's axiom is the Bull *Unam Sanctam* of Boniface VIII in 1302.[4] The 1442 Council of Florence's Decree for the Jacobites gives a stark formulation of the axiom's meaning as then understood:

> [The holy Roman church] firmly believes, professes, and preaches that "none of those who are outside of the Catholic Church, not only pagans," but also Jews, heretics, and schismatics, can become sharers of eternal life, but they will go into the eternal fire "that was prepared for the devil and his angels" unless, before the end of their life, they are joined to her. And the unity of the Church's body is of such great importance that the Church's sacraments are beneficial toward salvation only for those who remain within her, and (only for them) do fasts, almsgiving, and other acts of piety and exercises of Christian discipline bring forth eternal rewards. "No one can be saved, no matter how many alms he has given, and even if he sheds his blood for the name of Christ, unless he remains in the bosom and unity of the Catholic Church."[5]

According to this framework, non-Catholic baptized Christians are considered in the same category as nonbaptized adherents of other religions.

Subtle developments over the next five centuries by Catholic theologians attempted to find more inclusive approaches to the axiom.[6] Pius XII's 1943 encyclical *Mystici Corporis* states that, although non-Catholics are not really (*reapse*) members of the Catholic Church, they can be "related" to the Mystical Body of Christ: "by an unconscious desire and longing [*inscio quodam voto ac desiderio*] they have a certain relationship with the Mystical Body of the Redeemer."[7] An important clarification of the encyclical came six years later. A Boston priest, Leonard Feeney, accused the archbishop of Boston of

---

3. Sullivan, *Salvation outside the Church?*, 20.

4. DS 870–75.

5. DS 1351. Denzinger, *Compendium of Creeds, Definitions, and Declarations*, 348–49. Two of the citations are from Fulgentius of Ruspe, and there is a quote from Matt 25:41.

6. See Sullivan, *Salvation outside the Church?*, 69–122.

7. *Mystici Corporis* 103 (http://w2.vatican.va/content/pius-xii/en/encyclicals/documents/hf_p-xii_enc_29061943_mystici-corporis-christi.html).

heresy, claiming he had not adhered to the defined dogma of faith promulgated by the Council of Florence's Decree for the Jacobites. A letter from the Holy Office on August 8, 1949, rebutted Feeney's claims and spoke of the possibility of an implicit desire for salvation, giving a subtler interpretation of the decree.[8]

Nonetheless, despite these attempts at an interpretive development of the axiom, more questions were being raised by the letter than answered, as Francis Sullivan notes: "On one important point the letter of the holy office failed to satisfy ecumenically-minded Catholics as well; as was the case in *Mystici Corporis*, the letter made no distinction between Christians and non-Christians as far as their relation to the mystical body is concerned. In either case, they could be related to it by desire; no reference is made to the fact that by their baptism Christians have a sacramental relationship to the church which non-Christians do not have."[9]

When Vatican II was announced ten years later, this remained an open question, to which the forthcoming council was expected to find an answer. For resources to formulate that answer, the council would draw on decades of ecumenical and interreligious scholarship, especially personal relationships forged between Christians and between Christians and other religious believers.

A Sign of the Times

Like many of the other principles making up the vision of Vatican II, the Catholic/ecumenical principle has its origins in the renewal movements of the decades before the council met.

As early as 1937, in a book titled *Chrétiens Désunis*, Yves Congar could write:

> Ecumenism begins when it is admitted that others, not only individuals but ecclesiastical bodies as well, may also be right though they differ from us; that they too have truth, holiness and gifts of God even though they do not profess our form of Christianity. There is ecumenism, says an active member of this movement, when it is believed that others are Christian not in spite of their particular

---

8. DS 3866–73. Denzinger, *Compendium of Creeds, Definitions, and Declarations,* 795–98. As Francis Sullivan summarizes an important point in the letter: "People who are invincibly ignorant of the fact that God has established the church as a means necessary for their salvation can have a saving relation to the church by a desire which is implicit in their interior dispositions which signify the conformity of their wills to the will of God in their regard." Sullivan, *Salvation outside the Church?,* 139.

9. Sullivan, *Salvation outside the Church?,* 139–40.

confession but in it and by it. Such a conviction governs that complex of ideas which make up the ecumenical attitude—respect for other confessions and the action of the Holy Spirit in them, the sense and the avowal of the past sins, limitations and failures of one's own confession, the desire to know about other confessions and the gifts of God to them and to enter into friendly relations with them, and, pending full unity, as far as possible into effective communion.[10]

Vatican II would go on to endorse much of that vision, but only after a radical reconfiguration of the Catholic imagination regarding the distinction and relationship between "the church of Christ" and "the Catholic Church."

To understand the achievement of Vatican II in addressing the separation of the "churches" (the Eastern Orthodox churches, among others) and "ecclesial communities" (the various bodies resulting from the Protestant Reformation), we need to understand where things stood at the start of the council. What was the impasse through which Vatican II provided a way forward or, at least, provided a new perspective from which a way forward could be envisioned after the council—beyond the event and documents of the council itself?

On the eve of Vatican II, the official position of the magisterium concerning any future unity among Christians was still conceived simply in terms of a model of "return"; that is, ecumenism was officially understood as Catholics urging non-Catholics to become Roman Catholics.[11] Pius XI, in his 1928 encyclical *Mortalium Animos,* captured this vision: "So, Venerable Brethren, it is clear why this Apostolic See has never allowed its subjects to take part in the assemblies of non-Catholics: for the union of Christians can only be promoted by promoting the return to the one true Church of Christ of those who are separated from it, for in the past they have unhappily left it."[12]

Hopes for another way had long been simmering among more ecumenically minded Catholics.[13] Their importance in the history of Catholic involvement in the ecumenical movement was mirrored in the official directives promulgated by the Roman Curia: "In Roman Catholic circles there was a

10. Congar, *Divided Christendom,* 135–36.

11. On "unionism" rather than "ecumenism," see Mauro Velati, *Una difficile transizione: Il Cattolicesimo tra unionismo ed ecumenismo (1952–1964)* (Bologna: Il Mulino, 1996).

12. Article 10. http://w2.vatican.va/content/pius-xi/en/encyclicals/documents/hf_p-xi _enc_19280106_mortalium-animos.html.

13. For a brief history up to the council of the involvement of Catholics within the ecumenical movement, see Erwin Iserloh, "History of the Ecumenical Movement," in *The Church in the Modern Age,* ed. Hubert Jedin, Konrad Repgen, and John Dolan, History of the Church (New York: Crossroad, 1981), 10:458–73, esp. 466–70. See also George H. Tavard, *Two Centuries of Ecumenism* (Notre Dame, IN: Fides Publishers Association, 1960).

deepening interest in the work of the ecumenical movement. The official statements of the Magisterium indirectly demonstrate the vigour of this trend. Warnings were felt to be necessary because the Church's official position was in fact being questioned."[14]

Signs of an official shift began to appear, however, in the decade before the council was called. On December 20, 1949, the Holy Office issued an instruction, *Ecclesia Catholica*, which allowed for a certain involvement by Catholics in ecumenical discussions.[15] That this was a major shift in official Catholic attitudes was noted at the time by the secretary general of the World Council of Churches (WCC), Willem Adolf Visser 't Hooft: "The very fact that such a document was published shows that the Ecumenical Movement has begun to exercise an influence on the ranks of the clergy and among the faithful of the Roman Catholic Church."[16]

Availing themselves of the opportunity that *Ecclesia Catholica* offered, two Dutch priests, Johannes Willebrands and Frans Thijssen, in 1952 brought together a group of ecumenically minded Catholic scholars, which they called the "Catholic Conference for Ecumenical Questions."[17] From then until Vatican II, this varying group of around seventy participants met nine times.[18] At these conferences, the gathered scholars attempted to respond to the various ecumenical issues being discussed at that time by the WCC. In

14. Lukas Vischer, "The Ecumenical Movement and the Roman Catholic Church," in *The Ecumenical Advance: A History of the Ecumenical Movement*, vol. 2: *1948–1968*, ed. Harold E. Fey, 2nd ed. (Geneva: World Council of Churches, 1986), 311–52, at 314.

15. The instruction was officially published a few months later on March 1, 1950, as *Instructio ad locarum ordinarios 'De motione oecumenica'* (*Ecclesia Catholica*), *Acta Apostolicae Sedis* 42 (1950): 12–17. On this as a significant change, see Roger Aubert, "Stages of Catholic Ecumenism from Leo XIII to Vatican II," in *Theology of Renewal*, vol. 2: *Renewal of Religious Structures*, ed. L. K. Shook (New York: Herder and Herder, 1968), 183–203, at 201–2.

16. Quoted in ibid., 202.

17. Hereafter this group will be referred to by the acronym CCEQ. On the history of this group, see Thomas Stransky, "Catholic Conference for Ecumenical Questions," in *Dictionary of the Ecumenical Movement*, ed. Nicolas Lossky et al., 2nd ed. (Geneva: WCC Publications, 2002), 151; Velati, *Una difficile transizione*, 20–174; Peter De Mey, "The Catholic Conference for Ecumenical Questions' Immediate Preparation of the Renewal of Catholic Ecclesiology at Vatican II," in *Toward a History of the Desire for Christian Unity: Preliminary Research Paper*, ed. L. Ferracci (Münster: LIT, 2015), 141–57. On Willebrands's role in the group, see Peter De Mey, "Johannes Willebrands and the Catholic Conference for Ecumenical Questions (1952–1963)," in *The Ecumenical Legacy of Johannes Cardinal Willebrands (1909–2006)*, ed. Adelbert Denaux and Peter De Mey (Leuven; Walpole, MA: Peeters, 2012), 49–77.

18. Fribourg (1952), Utrecht (1953), Mainz (1954), Paris (1955), Chevetogne (1957), Paderborn (1959), Gazzada (1960), Strasbourg (1961), and Gazzada (1963).

between these gatherings, personal contact between Catholic and non-Catholic scholars developed; for example, Willebrands, as CCEQ secretary, forged close ties with his fellow countryman, Visser 't Hooft, secretary general of the WCC. Other ecumenical ventures were afoot. For example, the Benedictine abbey at Chevetogne (earlier located at Amay) had initially sought closer relations with Eastern Orthodox Christians, in order to promote their return to union with the Catholic Church; after the fall of the tsarist regime, discussions with the Russian Orthodox to that end were especially desired. The gradual change in ecumenical approach at Chevetogne was symptomatic, however, of a broader conversion going on within the Catholic Church, from "unionism" to "ecumenism."

These meetings and ecumenical relations had an impact at more official levels. Willebrands would regularly travel to Rome to inform the relevant departments of the Roman Curia of the Conference's activities, lest misunderstandings fester in the Roman Curia. As the historian Roger Aubert observes: "In the absence of all official or unofficial relations, this body, which was in close contact with Roman circles, was to become the link between Catholic ecumenists and the offices of study of the World Council of Churches. Quietly but efficaciously it carried on this delicate work, striving particularly to have Catholic theologians study the themes put on its programs by Geneva and to forward reports, giving the Roman point of view, thus assuring, without being integrated with it officially, the beginning of a dialogue with the World Council."[19]

But distrust could quickly rise to the surface. A significant example is "the Rhodes incident," which captures the delicate climate of the time.[20] In late August 1959 (seven months after the pope's call for a council), the World Council's central committee was meeting on the Greek island of Rhodes, the first time such a meeting had taken place in a country of mainly Orthodox Christians. Catholic representatives were invited. At an informal dinner, discussions were observed taking place between the Catholics and the Orthodox, which were interpreted as the Catholics wanting to enter into a special bilateral relation with the Orthodox. This was seen to be a breach of

---

19. Aubert, "Stages of Catholic Ecumenism," 203.

20. For a brief account of the so-called Rhodes incident, see Fouilloux, "The Antepreparatory Phase," 165–66. See also Karim Schelkens, "L' 'affaire de Rhodes' au jour le jour: La correspondance inédite entre J. Willebrands et C. J. Dumont," *Istina* 54 (2009): 253–77; Joseph A. Komonchak, "The Secretariat for Promoting Christian Unity and the Preparation of Vatican II," *Centro Pro Unione Bulletin* 50 (1996): 11–17, at 11–12.

hospitality during the multilateral meeting. The historian Fouilloux summed up the mood: "Visser 't Hooft was angry"[21] The incident became an important learning moment for Catholic ecumenists, for whom the desire to reengage with the Eastern churches was a long-felt and genuine need.

The CCEQ was to become an important body that would directly shape the way Vatican II addressed the ecumenical agenda set by Pope John. As Thomas Stransky notes: "From this network of scholars came the original staff of Pope John XXIII's Secretariat for Promoting Christian Unity, with Willebrands as the secretary, and most of its first body of consultors. Many CCEQ members were among the key drafters of several Vatican II documents, e.g., Yves Congar, Charles Moeller, Gustave Thils, Jérôme Hamer, Balthasar Fischer, Karl Rahner, Johannes Feiner, Maurice Bévenot, Pierre Duprey and Emmanuel Lanne."[22] Also involved in CCEQ, though not named here by Stransky, was Johannes Witte.[23] Witte would be yet another member of the CCEQ who would figure in the story of the council, later to become involved in the preparatory and conciliar stages. One important person to whom Willebrands was reporting on the activities of the CCEQ was a consultor to the Holy Office, Augustin Bea. Bea was a Scripture scholar who had taught at the Pontifical Biblical Institute and until 1948 had been its rector; for a short time, he was the official confessor to Pope Pius XII. Willebrands believed that Bea would be well placed to help avoid misunderstanding in the Holy Office regarding the CCEQ's activities.[24]

All these ecumenical initiatives and developments would converge once the dynamic of the council was ignited. Indeed, as Gustave Thils observed, the conciliar assembly would itself live through the theological developments

---

21. Fouilloux, "The Antepreparatory Phase," 166.

22. See Stransky, "Catholic Conference for Ecumenical Questions," 151.

23. Witte attended CCEQ meetings in 1952, 1953, 1954, 1955, and 1959. On Witte, see throughout the unpublished thesis of Sandra Arenas Pérez, "Fading Frontiers? An Historical-Theological Investigation into the Notion of the *Elementa Ecclesiae*" (Catholic University of Leuven, Faculty of Theology and Religious Studies, 2013). Also on Witte, see Catherine E. Clifford, "*Elementa Ecclesiae*: A Basis for Vatican II's Recognition of the Ecclesial Character of Non-Catholic Christian Communities," in *La Théologie catholique entre intransigeance et renouveau: La réception des mouvements préconciliaires à Vatican II*, ed. Gilles Routhier et al. (Louvain-La-Neuve; Leuven: Collège Érasme; Universiteitsbibliotheek, 2011), 249–69, at 251n9.

24. For Bea's indirect contact with the CCEQ (up until the seventh meeting in Gazzada, which he attended as president of the Secretariat), see Stjepan Schmidt, *Augustin Bea: The Cardinal of Unity* (New Rochelle, NY: New City Press, 1992), 241–42. For Bea's brief account of his address to the Gazzada meeting, see Augustin Bea, *Ecumenism in Focus* (London: Geoffrey Chapman, 1969), 30.

of these decades: "The history of the years 1943–1960 was repeated, in a shorter lapse of time, at the Second Vatican Council. . . . The conciliar debate, carried out under the banner of ecumenism, quickly made the most of the theological contribution made in ecclesiology since the end of the war of 1940–45, with the result that we now know."[25]

It is significant that Pope John XXIII announced his intention to convene a council (January 25, 1959) during a ceremony to mark the last day of the World Octave of Prayer for the Unity of Christians.[26] Among the reasons for calling the council that the pope gave was "to invite the separated communities to seek again that unity for which so many souls are longing in these days throughout the world."[27] Giuseppe Alberigo remarks: "More than any other aspect, the ecumenical dimension elicited surprise, public interest, and some very lively apprehensions."[28] Five months later, in the pope's first encyclical *Ad Petri Cathedram* published on June 29,1959, his ecumenical fervor was once again evident. There he expressed his hope that the forthcoming council would be "a gentle invitation to seek and find that unity for which Jesus Christ prayed so ardently to His Father in heaven."[29] But the pope's hope here, as it would be initially for many of the council members, was still for a "return" of other Christians to the Catholic Church; this was likewise evident when, formally convoking the council on December 25, 1961, he expressed hope that "the forthcoming Council should provide premises of doctrinal clarity and of mutual charity that will make still more alive in our separated brothers the wish for the hoped-for return to unity."[30] As the official WCC observer at all four sessions of the council, Lukas Vischer, somewhat disappointingly later noted of John XXIII: "The Pope's own under-

25. Gustave Thils, *L'Église et les Églises: Perspectives nouvelles en oecuménisme* (Bruges: Desclée De Brouwer, 1967), 158–59. Quoted in Clifford, "*Elementa Ecclesiae*," 254.

26. What later came to be called "The Week of Prayer for Christian Unity" originated in 1908 within the Anglican Church; it began with the feast of the confession of St. Peter (January 18) and ended on the feast of the conversion of St. Paul (January 25). Abbé Paul Couturier in 1935 proposed a similar worldwide event, formulating as its goal to pray for a unity among Christians "as Christ desires and by whatsoever means he shall choose." See Geoffrey Curtis, *Paul Couturier and Unity in Christ* (London: SCM Press, 1964), 103.

27. Pope John XXIII, "*Questa Festiva*: Announcement of Ecumenical Council and Roman Synod. An Address of Pope John XXIII to the Roman Cardinals (January 25, 1959)," *The Pope Speaks* 5, no. 4 (1958–1959): 398–401, at 401.

28. Alberigo, "Transition to a New Age," 585.

29. http://w2.vatican.va/content/john-xxiii/en/encyclicals/documents/hf_j-xxiii_enc_2906 1959_ad-petri.html

30. John XXIII, "Pope John Convokes the Council: *Humanae Salutis*," 706.

standing of unity did not greatly differ from the traditional view. Like his predecessors he often spoke of return as the only way to unity."[31] His successor, Pope Paul VI, introduced a different tone when, during his opening address for the council's second session, he spoke of "the perfect unity of Christ" (implying that there are grades of unity) and of "the possibility of multiplicity in the unity of the Church." He went on: "It is a council, therefore, of invitation, of expectation, of confidence, looking forward toward a more widespread, more fraternal participation in its authentic ecumenicity."[32]

Throughout its course and in its final documents, the council would come to embrace the ecumenical agenda of Pope John and Pope Paul, albeit, for some bishops, with the limited horizon initially of "return" as the goal. In the opening paragraph of its first document, *Sacrosanctum Concilium* made its own—formally, as an ecumenical council—Pope John's hoped-for agenda. Among the four goals of the council, it lists: "to encourage whatever can promote *the union of all who believe in Christ [ad unionem omnium in Christum credentium]*" (SC 1).[33] This simple description will become important in the council's attempt to focus on what is common between all Christian communities rather than to focus on what divides them. And so, in the following year, the Decree on Ecumenism, *Unitatis Redintegratio*, would begin with the stark statement: "The restoration of unity [*unitatis redintegratio*] among all Christians is one of the principal concerns of the Second Vatican Council" (UR 1). Rather than seeing the restoration of unity as a return of separated Christians to the unity of the one, true "church of Christ" (understood as the Roman Catholic Church), the council would come to envisage the restoration of a full communion that has been disrupted but not destroyed through schism or reformation, a communion in which the separated Christian communities have always continued to participate in some way, albeit not fully since separation.

The council understood itself to be engaging in a discernment process, attentive to the call of God from within the movements of history, by discerning

31. Vischer, "The Ecumenical Movement and the Roman Catholic Church," 323. Vischer then goes on to quote Pope John's 1959 encyclical, *Ad Petri Cathedram* 84: "Note, we beg of you, that when we lovingly invite you to the unity of the Church we are inviting you not to the home of a stranger but to your own, to the Father's house which belongs to all."

32. Paul VI, "Opening Address: Second Session," 147–48. For a summary of this significant address, see "Appendix 2: Opening of the Second Period of Vatican Council II; Pope Paul VI (September 29, 1963)," in Wicks, *Doing Theology*, 152–62.

33. Emphasis added.

the ambiguous "signs of the times."[34] Prior to the council, the ecumenical movement had been discerned as being far from God's designs. For Vatican II, however, the ecumenical movement of the twentieth century was now discerned to be a positive sign of God's will for the church. Already, a year before *Gaudium et Spes* would later highlight the importance of the signs of the times for the church's response to God's urging through the Spirit, the Decree on Ecumenism stated, in an explicit endorsement of the ecumenical movement afoot in the world: "Today, in many parts of the world, under the influence of the grace of the Holy Spirit, many efforts are being made in prayer, word and action to attain that fullness of unity which Jesus Christ desires. This sacred council, therefore, exhorts all the Catholic faithful to recognize the signs of the times and to take an active and intelligent part in the work of ecumenism" (UR 4).

The Secretariat and Drafting the Vision

After the 1959 Rhodes incident, the need became apparent for a special institution for communicating with the other churches and Christian communities. Within a few months, suggestions for such an institution came from Cardinal Lorenz Jaeger of Paderborn and Augustin Bea. Bea asked Fr. Edward Stakemeier from the Johann Adam Möhler Institute in Paderborn to draft a proposal for such a body. Bea presented the proposal to Pope John XXIII. Soon after, on June 5, 1960, the pope issued a *motu proprio* setting up the bodies that were to prepare documents for the council. He created ten preparatory commissions, plus three secretariats, among the latter a *Secretariatus ad Christianorum unitatem fovendam praeparatorius Concilii Vaticani secundi* (i.e., a secretariat for the promotion of the unity of Christians).[35] Cardinal Augustin Bea was to be its president.[36] Father Johannes Willebrands was

34. GS 4.

35. Hereafter, for brevity, this will be referred to as the Secretariat for Christian Unity or the Secretariat. Later, on August 6, 1962, the pope made the Secretariat a permanent body of the council, along with the other ten commissions. For a history of the Secretariat's origins and its contribution to the ecumenical vision of Vatican II, see Thomas Stransky, "The Foundation of the Secretariat for Promoting Christian Unity," in *Vatican II: By Those Who Were There*, ed. Alberic Stacpoole (London: Geoffrey Chapman, 1986), 62–87; Mauro Velati, "'Un indirizzo a Roma': La nascita del Segretariato per l'unità dei cristiani (1959–60)," in *Il Vaticano II fra attese e celebrazione*, ed. Giuseppe Alberigo (Bologna: Il Mulino, 1995), 75–118; Jared Wicks, "Cardinal Bea's Unity Secretariat: Engine of Renewal and Reform at Vatican II," *Ecumenical Trends* 41, no. 11 (2012): 1–5, 15.

36. On Bea and his involvement in the ecumenical movement, see Augustin Bea, *Augustin Cardinal Bea: Spiritual Profile. Notes from the Cardinal's Diary, with a Commentary*, ed. Stjepan

named secretary.[37] That the pope had made this body only a "secretariat" and not an official "commission" was interpreted as an advantage; this would allow the body a certain independence from the ten commissions that were tightly aligned with the ten offices of the Roman Curia.[38]

The *motu proprio* stated that the secretariat's task was to assist other Christians "to follow the work of the council and to find more easily the path by which they may arrive at the unity for which Jesus prayed so ardently."[39] For the Secretariat members themselves, that the council's deliberations on its various topics should all proceed with an ecumenical sensitivity was high on their agenda. Initially the Secretariat created ten subcommissions (this would later be expanded to fifteen). The topics addressed by these subcommissions ranged from the relation to the Roman Catholic Church of nonbaptized Catholics to the issue of conversion and "return" of individuals and of communities to the Roman Catholic Church.[40] The subcommissions produced ecumenically sensitive documents on each of their topics that could be sent to the relevant drafting bodies. Joseph Komonchak observes: "At this early point, then, it does not seem that the SPCU intended to prepare schemata of its own to be proposed to the Council, but rather to prepare texts that would ensure that ecumenical concerns were taken into consideration by the other preparatory commissions. It would only be when this effort seemed to be fruitless that the SPCU began to prepare texts on its own authority."[41]

One important remit for the Secretariat was that it be a point of communication with non-Catholic Christian communities. Included in that remit was the job of inviting these bodies to send official representatives who could observe the proceedings of the council firsthand. In addition, the Secretariat

---

Schmidt (London: Geoffrey Chapman, 1971); Schmidt, *Augustin Bea*; Jerome-Michael Vereb, *"Because He Was a German!" Cardinal Bea and the Origins of Roman Catholic Engagement in the Ecumenical Movement* (Grand Rapids, MI: Eerdmans, 2006).

37. On Willebrands's contribution, including many of his addresses, see the special issue of the bulletin of the Pontifical Council for Promoting Christian Unity, "A Tribute to Johannes Cardinal Willebrands: On the Occasion of His Ninetieth Birthday," *Information Service: The Pontifical Council for Promoting Christian Unity* 101 (1999). See also the various chapters in Adelbert Denaux and Peter De Mey, eds., *The Ecumenical Legacy of Johannes Cardinal Willebrands (1909–2006)* (Leuven; Walpole, MA: Peeters, 2012).

38. See Stransky, "The Foundation of the Secretariat," 66. See also Schmidt, *Augustin Bea*, 348.

39. Quoted in Komonchak, "The Secretariat for Promoting Christian Unity," 12.

40. For a list of the initial ten subcommissions, see Stransky, "The Foundation of the Secretariat," 82.

41. Komonchak, "The Secretariat for Promoting Christian Unity," 13.

was able also to invite particular individuals from those bodies directly, inviting them as "guests" of the Secretariat. Already, on October 30, 1959, just nine months after the pope had made known his intention to call the council, the secretary of state, Cardinal Domenico Tardini, announced at a press conference that the pope intended to invite the separated churches and communities to send official observers to the council.[42] The significance and the effect of the invitation, as well as the eventual presence of these observers and guests in the council aula, cannot be overstated.[43]

When the council began, their very placement within the assembly was highly emblematic. As Alberto Melloni notes: "The non-Catholic observers were accommodated in a position of privilege, and were placed, much to their surprise, on the grandstand of St. Longinus, to the left of the papal throne, from where they were able to follow the work of the council even better than some of the bishops."[44] Their physical presence in such a prominent place in St. Peter's was to become yet another of the symbolic gestures that make up the meaning of the event of the council and give richer context for interpreting the meaning of the texts.[45] Their participation, however, eventually went beyond the mere symbolic. Lukas Vischer, the Reformed theologian who was

42. See the account in Otto Hermann Pesch, *The Ecumenical Potential of the Second Vatican Council* (Milwaukee: Marquette University Press, 2006), 19–20.

43. On the role and significance of the observers and guests at Vatican II, see Mauro Velati, *Separati ma fratelli. Gli osservatori non cattolici al Vaticano II (1962–1965)* (Bologna: Il Mulino, 2014); Yves Congar, "Le rôle des 'Observateurs' dans l'avancée oecuménique," in *Le Concile de Vatican II: Son église, peuple de Dieu et corps du Christ* (Paris: Beauchesne, 1984), 91–98; Thomas Stransky, "Paul VI and the Delegated Observers/Guests to Vatican Council II," in *Paolo VI e l'ecumenismo: Colloquio internazionale di studio (Brescia, 25–27 settembre 1998)* (Brescia: Istituto Paolo VI, 2001), 118–58; Peter De Mey, "The Role of the Observers during the Second Vatican Council," *St Vladimir's Theological Quarterly* 60 (2016): 33–51; Christopher Thomas Washington, *The Participation of Non-Catholic Christian Observers, Guests, and Fraternal Delegates at the Second Vatican Council and the Synods of Bishops: A Theological Analysis* (Rome: Gregorian University Press, 2015). From among many accounts of observers and guests themselves, see Oscar Cullmann, "The Role of the Observers at the Vatican Council," in *Vatican Council II: The New Direction; Essays* (New York: Harper & Row, 1968), 102–6; Moorman, "Observers and Guests of the Council."

44. Alberto Melloni, "The Council Hall and the Placement of the Participants," in *Vatican II: The Complete History*, ed. Alberto Melloni, Federico Ruozzi, and Enrico Galvotti (New York: Paulist Press, 2015), 88–93, at 92.

45. For a plan of the council hall, see Alberto Melloni, "Setting Up the Council: St. Peter's Basilica Transforms into a Council Hall," in *Vatican II: The Complete History*, ed. Alberto Melloni, Federico Ruozzi, and Enrico Galvotti (New York: Paulist Press, 2015), 78–81, at 80–81.

the official observer for the World Council of Churches throughout all four sessions, remarked on their effective, albeit limited, participation:

> The observers had, of course, no possibility of taking any active part in the proceedings. Many of them were instructed by the Churches to exercise the greatest reserve. Yet their very presence had the profound effect of continually pointing to the ecumenical problem. Over and above this, they were able each week to talk informally with members of the Secretariat about the texts being discussed, and many of their comments were passed on to the appropriate commissions. The longer the Council went on, the greater became their freedom of action. Some individual observers produced actual commentaries, and it is possible in some cases to discover traces of these in the conciliar documents. Perhaps even more important were the personal conversations and the meetings in small groups.[46]

Once again, what the historian Jeffrey Murphy remarks regarding another issue is true of the participation of the observers: "Vatican II was not so much a Council as a complex of mini-councils: discussions, dinners, conversations, coffees, Conference meetings, colloquia, canvassing and chats with foreigners."[47]

When the council began, the conciliar assembly conceded to the Secretariat a somewhat exalted role in the achievement of the council ecumenical agenda, with Bea (as Pius XII's personal confessor) accorded great respect whenever he spoke in the aula. The Secretariat played a central role in both assessing the schemas of the preparatory period and ensuring an ecumenical tone be taken in any future drafting. Although most of the schemas that were drafted during the preparatory phase had ecumenical ramifications, only three explicitly concerned the topic of ecumenism: *De Ecclesiae Unitate* (with the incipit *Ut Omnes Unum Sint*) from the preparatory Oriental Commission; chapter 11 of *De Ecclesia* (titled *De Oecumenismo*) from the preparatory Theological Commission; and *De Oecumenismo Catholico (Decretum Pastorale)* drafted by a subcommittee of the Secretariat.[48] The first two were presented

46. Vischer, "The Ecumenical Movement and the Roman Catholic Church," 332.

47. Jeffrey J. Murphy, "The Far Milieu Called Home: Australian Bishops at Vatican II (The Final Session: 1965)," *Australasian Catholic Record* 80, no. 3 (2003): 343–69, at 368.

48. For these three texts in English, see the translations in John Bolger, "The Documents behind the Decree on Ecumenism," *One in Christ* 4 (1967): 472–500. For an analysis of the different theologies apparent in these three documents, see Camillus Hay, "Comparative Ecclesiology of the Documents behind the Decree on Ecumenism," *One in Christ* 4 (1967): 399–416.

to the conciliar assembly and debated at the end of the first session.[49] The schema from the Secretariat was never printed or distributed to the council members; however, many bishops were aware of its existence. In their debates, the bishops expressed dissatisfaction with *Ut Omnes Unum Sint* and chapter 11 of *De Ecclesia*.[50] The decision was implicitly made to excise a specific chapter on ecumenism from future versions of *De Ecclesia* and to have a separate document on ecumenism, which was to draw on the preparatory documents of the Oriental Commission and the Theological Commission as well as the as-yet undistributed but widely known document prepared by the Secretariat. The council entrusted to a mixed commission the task of drawing these three documents into a unified schema on ecumenism.

The drafting of the Decree on Ecumenism was not as complex as some other documents.[51] There were basically two drafts presented to the council. The first draft was debated extensively at the end of the second session (November 18–December 2, 1963).[52] A second revised version was voted on, but

---

49. *Ut Omnes Unum Sint* was debated on November 26, 27, 28, and 30, 1962. Chapter 11 of *De Ecclesia* was debated during December 1, 3, 4, 5, 6, and 7, 1962.

50. Summarizing these responses, Adrian Hastings notes: "Both these drafts, the second especially, gave a rather negative impression. There was a strong stress on the institutional side of the Church but almost no mention of the Holy Spirit in either. . . . Chapter 11 of the Church Constitution was full of warnings about the dangers of 'interconfessionalismus.'" Hastings, *A Concise Guide to the Documents*, 1:171–72.

51. For histories of the drafting of the Decree on Ecumenism, see Velati, *Una difficile transizione*, 319–487; Werner Becker, "History of the Decree on Ecumenism," in *Commentary on the Documents of Vatican II*, vol. 2, ed. Herbert Vorgrimler (New York: Herder, 1968), 2:1–56; Lorenz Jaeger, *A Stand on Ecumenism: The Council's Decree* (London: Geoffrey Chapman, 1965), 3–56; Bernd Jochen Hilberath, "Theologischer Kommentar zum Dekret über den Ökumenismus *Unitatis redintegratio*," in *Herders theologischer Kommentar zum Zweiten Vatikanischen Konzil. Band 3*, ed. Peter Hünermann and Bernd Jochen Hilberath (Freiburg: Herder, 2005), 3:69–223, at 93–103; Claude Soetens, "The Ecumenical Commitment of the Catholic Church," in *History of Vatican II*, vol. 3: *The Mature Council; Second Period and Intersession, September 1963–September 1964*, ed. Giuseppe Alberigo and Joseph A. Komonchak (Maryknoll, NY: Orbis Books, 1998), 3:257–345. For a synoptic presentation of the various drafts, see Francisco Gil Hellín, *Decretum de oecumenismo, Unitatis redintegratio: Concilii Vaticani II synopsis in ordinem redigens schemata cum relationibus necnon patrum orationes atque animadversiones* (Città del Vaticano: Libreria Editrice Vaticana, 2005).

52. During the first intersession, an initial draft was prepared and sent out to the bishops in April 1963. This had three chapters on ecumenism and other Christian churches; a fourth chapter on other religions, especially the Jews, and a fifth on religious liberty were intended to be added later but were not yet ready for distribution. The idea of including these last two chapters was eventually dropped and they became separate documents (*Nostra Aetate* and *Dignitatis Humanae*).

not debated, throughout the third session (October 5–8, 1964), with a chance for further written submissions; the subsequent amendments were then voted on (November 10, 11, 14, 20). At the very last minute, a minority of bishops opposed to certain elements in the decree persuaded Pope Paul VI to propose (on November 19) a number of amendments that the council had no chance of refusing; these changes, however, despite the unrest the papal intervention caused, did not in any way change the fundamental assertions of the document.[53] The decree was promulgated on the last day of the third session, November 21, 1964, along with *Lumen Gentium*. While the latter no longer had a separate ecumenism chapter, three articles in particular did touch on matters highly relevant to the issues being debated in the ecumenism document: articles 8, 14, and 15.

In reconstructing the council's vision regarding what is here called its Catholic/ecumenical principle, certain important hermeneutical points are relevant. First, attending to a hermeneutics of the authors, it is important to bear in mind that *Lumen Gentium* and *Unitatis Redintegratio* were drafted, debated, voted on, and finally promulgated throughout the same time frame—during the second and third sessions, and in the intersessions that preceded them. This meant that the drafting and conciliar decisions regarding one text came to influence the other to some degree. As a result of the decision to have a separate ecumenism document, and not to have a chapter on ecumenism in the document on the church, the full *ecumenical* implications of *Lumen Gentium*'s ecclesiological teachings were deliberately not expanded on in later versions of that document. As Francis Sullivan notes: "The people working on the *schema de Ecclesia* were very much aware of the fact that at the same time a *schema de oecumenismo* was being prepared, and it was their intention to leave the ecumenical aspects of ecclesiology to be handled in that decree."[54] Moreover, from his experience as secretary of the Secretariat's drafting subcommission, Johannes Willebrands recalls the communication going on between the two drafting bodies: "Those who in the Secretariat for Unity prepared the text of the Decree [on Ecumenism] were

53. On the details of this affair, see Tagle, "The 'Black Week' of Vatican II," 406–17. Adrian Hastings downplays the ultimate impact of the intervention on the document's substance: "As a matter of fact not one of the changes which were made could really be said to have major significance. No one doubted the pope's right to intervene, but some people were upset, chiefly at the timing of the intervention—one day before the final approval of the text when any general consideration of the changes had become impossible and rejection was unthinkable." Hastings, *A Concise Guide to the Documents*, 1:173.

54. Sullivan, "The Significance of the Vatican II Declaration," 275.

in regular contact with members of the theological commission [the Doctrinal Commission overseeing the drafting of *Lumen Gentium*] and pressed for the new orientation which offered the prospect of a clear and coherent explanation of the relationship between dis-united Christians and their Churches."[55] Several commentators note the intersecting trajectories of the two drafting processes. After tracing the drafting histories of both documents, Kilian McDonnell concludes: "This means that there is some overlapping, and even repetition of the discussion of the two documents in those areas where there is a common theological concern."[56] Likewise, Sandra Arenas Pérez concludes from her research: "Looking at the chronology, one cannot help but notice that the Doctrinal Commission's debate on *subsistit* coincided with the official council debate on the new *De oecumenismo*, where the very same issue was at stake."[57] Myriam Wijlens emphasizes the impact the drafting of the decree had on the dogmatic constitution: "The development of *Lumen Gentium* and *Unitatis Redintegratio* shows that the drafting of the latter document had a clear influence on the former."[58]

Second, according to a hermeneutics of the final texts, the principles of intratextuality and intertextuality are relevant here for reconstructing the Catholic/ecumenical principle. The sixteen documents need to be read as a corpus, and each in the light of the others. For example, according to the principle of intratextuality, *Lumen Gentium* 8 needs to be read alongside *Lumen Gentium* 15's discussion of other Christians and their communities. And *Lumen Gentium* 15, in turn, needs to be read in the light of *Lumen Gentium* 14, which it presupposes. According to the principle of intertextuality with regard to *Lumen Gentium* 8 and the other documents, Johannes Willebrands argues that "the interpretation of the word '*subsistit in*' cannot be drawn from one phrase or from one paragraph of the Constitution *Lumen*

55. Johannes Willebrands, "The Ecumenical Movement: Its Problems and Driving Force," *One in Christ* 11 (1975): 210–23, at 218. Emphasis added. A historian of the Secretariat's work, Mauro Velati, in his account of the Secretariat's role, notes the deliberate "methodology" of Willebrands and Bea to develop both a bond with the conciliar assembly (through interventions during the council by episcopal members of the Secretariat, such as De Smedt, Volk, and Bea himself), as well as maintaining channels of communication with the relevant commission, either through sending memos on a particular point, or through personal contact. See Velati, *Una difficile transizione*, 333–34.

56. McDonnell, "The Concept of 'Church' in the Documents of Vatican II," 342.

57. Arenas Pérez, "Fading Frontiers? An Historical-Theological Investigation into the Notion of the *Elementa Ecclesiae*," 251.

58. Myriam Wijlens, *Sharing the Eucharist: A Theological Evaluation of the Post Conciliar Legislation* (Lanham, MD: University Press of America, 2000), 192.

Gentium. Other texts must be taken into account, and especially the Decree on Ecumenism, which was able to profit from the new orientation of the Constitution."[59] When promulgating *Lumen Gentium* and *Unitatis Redintegratio* on November 21, 1964, Pope Paul VI emphasized the hermeneutical principle of intertextuality (without naming it as such) when he stated that the doctrine of the church articulated in *Lumen Gentium* is "completed by the declarations contained in the schema On Ecumenism."[60] Francis Sullivan summarizes this statement to mean: "The doctrine on the Church in *Lumen Gentium* was to be interpreted in the light of the further explanations given in the Decree on Ecumenism."[61] That is, the "dogmatic constitution" needs to be interpreted in the light of the lesser-graded "decree." More specifically, as Arenas Pérez states, "*Lumen Gentium* 8 cannot be properly understood without *Unitatis Redintegratio* 3 and vice versa."[62]

Third, according to a hermeneutics of the receivers, appropriation of Vatican II's reconfiguration of the Catholic Church's self-understanding of its relationship to other ecclesial bodies in terms of an inchoate communion ecclesiology has led to a more finely articulated "*communio* ecclesiology" within ecumenical dialogues. Fifty years of reception has brought to clearer light the implications of the council's openings and tentative trajectories. As noted above in the sixth hermeneutical principle, the vision/reception principle, a new question can be put to the conciliar texts that their authors may not have even envisaged or perhaps could not have articulated in a clear, systematic way; but the receiver, from the horizon of a new context, with the benefit of historical research and an intertextual overview of all the council's texts, is able to propose an answer to that new question for that new context.

When attention is given to these three distinct but interrelated levels of hermeneutical enquiry, several issues emerge as central for understanding the council's Catholic/ecumenical principle and its place within the comprehensive vision of Vatican II: the notion of *elementa ecclesiae* as a lens for reconceiving the status of other Christian communities with regard to the church of Christ; the notion of "degrees" of ecclesial communion within an ecumenically oriented *communio* ecclesiology; an appreciation of diversity

---

59. Willebrands, "The Ecumenical Movement," 218.

60. Paul VI, "Closing Address: Third Session," 305.

61. Sullivan, "The Significance of the Vatican II Declaration," 275.

62. Arenas Pérez, "Fading Frontiers? An Historical-Theological Investigation into the Notion of the *Elementa Ecclesiae*," 296.

388   *Ecclesiological Principles*

within a renewed understanding of unity and catholicity; the call to unity as a call to continual ecclesial conversion; the notion of a "hierarchy of truths" as a lens for reconceiving doctrinal differences; the church's commitment to ecumenical dialogue as an implication of the call to greater fidelity to the mission of the church of Christ.

Elementa Ecclesiae and *Subsistit In*

The dominant ecclesiological notion on the eve of the council, that of the church as the Mystical Body of Christ, still remains important in *Lumen Gentium* (art. 7), albeit now reconfigured within a broader, more "trinitarian" ecclesiology. From the second session on, two other notions began to impinge themselves on the conciliar consciousness: that of the church as the people of God and as the temple of the Holy Spirit. Both of these were dear to ecumenical sensibilities, sensibilities the Secretariat continually attempted to bring before the minds of the bishops. For example, the focus of the second chapter of the constitution on "the People of God" was consciously understood by many bishops and *periti* as describing the church in a way that would be especially attractive to Protestants. Joseph Ratzinger recalls that, during the conciliar debates on the church,

> it was asked whether the image of the mystical body was not too narrow a starting-point to be able to define the multitude of different forms of Church membership that now existed thanks to the confusion of human history. For membership the image of the body can only offer the idea of member in the sense of limb: one is either a limb or not, and there are no intermediary stages. But in that case, the question was asked, is not this image's starting-point too narrow, since quite clearly there are intermediary stages? In this way people latched on to the term "the people of God," since in this context it was more capacious and flexible. The Council's constitution on the Church adopted precisely this application when it described the relationship of non-Catholic Christians to the Catholic Church by talking about them being "joined in many ways" and that of non-Christians by talking of them "related," in both cases depending on the idea of the people of God (*Lumen Gentium* 15 and 16). In this way it can be said that the concept of "the people of God" was introduced by the Council as an ecumenical bridge.[63]

---

63. Joseph Ratzinger, "The Ecclesiology of the Second Vatican Council," in *Church, Ecumenism and Politics: New Essays in Ecclesiology* (Slough: St Paul, 1988), 3–28, at 15–16.

Yves Congar likewise remarks on the attractiveness to Protestants of the idea of the people of God.[64]

In reference to the final texts of *Lumen Gentium* and *Unitatis Redintegratio* Thomas Stransky observes: "Both *De Ecclesia* and *De Oecumenismo* shy away from using the words 'member' or 'membership' in the Church, and thus Vatican Council II deliberately avoids a statement that *all* the baptized faithful, non-Catholic as well as Catholic, are members of the Church, though they have different degrees of membership. This nervous avoidance of the *expression* may be owing to the Council's living too closely to the encyclical of Pius XII, *The Mystical Body of Christ.*"[65] The encyclical had spoken of those who are "real" (*reapse*) members of the church, an expression that explicitly excluded non-Catholics who have willfully separated themselves from the Catholic Church.

This notion of *reapse* appears in Philips's 1963 draft of *De Ecclesia* presented to the council assembly during the second session. In an article that was eventually to be redrafted as *Lumen Gentium* 14 (on the ecclesial status of those who are Catholic), the draft schema stated: "Only [*tantum*] they are incorporated into the society of the Church in a real and unqualified way [*reapse et simpliciter loquendo*], who . . ."[66] This exclusive language recalled the language of *Mystici Corporis* 22, a document that uses the word *membrum* eighty-four times: "Actually [*reapse*] only those are to be included as members of the Church who have been baptized and profess the true faith, and who have not been so unfortunate as to separate themselves from the unity of the Body, or been excluded by legitimate authority for grave faults committed."[67] "According to this terminology," remarks Bonaventure Kloppenburg, "a person either is or is not a member of the Church, either belongs to the

64. "The ecumenical interest of the idea of the People of God is obvious, especially in the dialogue with Protestants. . . . What Protestants like about the category of People of God is first, the idea of election and of call, everything depends on God's initiative. Then it is the historicity that it involves in the sense of incompletion and of movement towards eschatology. It suggests less sharply defined frontiers, because it is composed of a multitude assembled by God himself." Congar, "The Church: The People of God," 13.

65. Thomas Stransky, *The Decree on Ecumenism of the Second Vatican Council: A New Translation by the Secretariat for Promoting Christian Unity, with a Commentary by Thomas F. Stransky, C.S.P.* (Glen Rock, NJ: Paulist Press, 1965), 23. Original emphasis.

66. AS II/1, 220. Translation from Kloppenburg, *The Ecclesiology of Vatican II*, 128.

67. http://w2.vatican.va/content/pius-xii/en/encyclicals/documents/hf_p-xii_enc_2906 1943_mystici-corporis-christi.html.

390 Ecclesiological Principles

Church or does not, either is or is not within the unity of the Church. There are no gradations of more or less, of perfect or imperfect."[68]

When the month-long discussion of Philips's new draft of *De Ecclesia* began at the start of the second session, several bishops spoke against the restrictively juridical thinking expressed in the words "only [*tantum*]" and "in a real and unqualified way [*reapse et simpliciter loquendo*]," which were used to describe baptized Catholics and the church. These bishops called for language that was more open and less juridical. A few of their suggestions indicated a new way to move toward some recognition of the ecclesial status of other Christian communities. That way forward involved recognition of the so-called *elementa ecclesiae* ("elements of the church") present in other Christian bodies.

One of those key voices was Bishop Jan van Dodewaard, a member of the Doctrinal Commission. On October 2, 1963, he addressed the council on behalf of the Dutch bishops.[69] Other bishops had proposed similar ideas for revising the schema, but van Dodewaard's speech is significant for the way he brings together those suggestions. First, he proposes that the juridical phrase *reapse et simpliciter loquendo* be deleted and that the schema speak of "those in a bond of perfect union" (implying that there can be other levels of relationship to the church). Second, he suggests a distinction be made between the Roman Catholic Church and the church of Christ. Third, in order to avoid affirming the full identification of the Catholic Church with the church of Christ, he proposes that the exclusive verb *est* in the schema be replaced with the verb *invenitur* ("is found"): the church of Christ as the universal medium of salvation "is found" in the Catholic Church. Fourth, he proposes that the phrase "elements of sanctification" be expanded: "many elements of truth and sanctification may be found [*elementa plura veritatis et sanctificationis inveniri possint*]" outside the Catholic Church.[70] Each of

68. Kloppenburg, *The Ecclesiology of Vatican II*, 128.

69. AS II/1, 433–35. For an analysis of van Dodewaard's speech, see Arenas Pérez, "Fading Frontiers? An Historical-Theological Investigation into the Notion of the *Elementa Ecclesiae*," 247–49.

70. Arenas Pérez observes that "this epistemological widening of the notion of elements" had been proposed by other bishops: "the Dutch bishops Jansen and Moors, who had already brought the notion of the *elementa ecclesiae* into the pre-conciliar arena, and had equated the concept to what they described as *elementa veritatis*. In this regard, van Dodewaard was not the only bishop to intervene. On 30 September 1963 [two days earlier], during the 37th General Congregation, also the German and Scandinavian bishops made suggestions to include '*elementa plura veritatis et sanctificationis.*'" Ibid., 248–49.

these four proposals finds a place, in some form or other, in the final texts of Vatican II. As Myriam Wijlens observes, "Bishop van Dodewaard paved the road toward eliminating *est* and replacing it with *subsistit in*."[71] Van Dodewaard takes a word the draft schema was using to speak of elements of the church of Christ being found outside the Catholic Church and applies it to the church of Christ being found within the Catholic Church. This verb *invenire* was to prove crucial in the history of the change to *subsistit in*, a history that needs to be explored briefly here.

Bishop van Dodewaard was a member of the Doctrinal Commission's subcommission that had overseen the drafting of chapter 1 of *De Ecclesia*, the text that he himself went on to critique when it came to the council floor for discussion. After that debate, this subcommission met again the following month, in November, to incorporate the amendments requested by the bishops, including van Dodewaard's own. When it came to the sentence that used the word *est* to identify strictly the church of Christ with the Catholic Church, van Dodewaard's suggestion of *invenitur* ("is found") was passed over, in order to avoid repetition of the verb *invenire* used later in the sentence (regarding elements of sanctification). The word *adest* ("is present") was used instead, replacing *est*: "This church . . . is present in the Catholic Church." Van Dodewaard himself drafted this new wording.[72] The verbs *invenire* and *adesse* were seen by the subcommission to be "interchangeable."[73] Along with a *Relatio* drafted by Beda Rigaux, which explained that *adest* was to be understood as meaning *concrete inveniri* ("to be found concretely"), the revised chapter 1 was presented to a plenary meeting of the Doctrinal Commission that met November 18–26.[74] On November 26, the *peritus* Heribert Schauf (once a student of Sebastian Tromp, the secretary of the Doctrinal Commission) proposed that *adest* be replaced with the original *est*. From archival material related to that meeting, Alexandra von Teuffenbach has

---

71. Wijlens, *Sharing the Eucharist*, 145–46.

72. On this, see Schelkens, "*Lumen Gentium*'s 'Subsistit in' Revisited," 888.

73. Ibid., 889.

74. For details of this *Relatio*, see ibid., 888–89; Arenas Pérez, "Fading Frontiers? An Historical-Theological Investigation into the Notion of the *Elementa Ecclesiae*," 250. Schelkens mistakenly seems to refer to this report from the subcommission for chapter 1 as a *Relatio* of the plenary Doctrinal Commission. The Doctrinal Commission would subsequently present its own *Relatio* to the council the following year on September 15, 1964, albeit following the line of interpretation of the subcommission's *Relatio*. This was drafted by Gérard Philips, the vice secretary of the Doctrinal Commission.

reconstructed the quick chain of events that started with Schauf's proposal.[75] The secretary Sebastian Tromp suggested a compromise: that the phrase *subsistit in* replace *adest*. There was no objection, and the change was duly recorded by the vice secretary Gérard Philips, the whole episode taking only a few minutes.

Whether Tromp saw his *subsistit in* as equivalent to the exclusive *est* or to the more inclusive *adest* is unimportant in the face of the understanding of the majority on the Doctrinal Commission, which readily accepted the change.[76] Karim Schelkens concludes:

> The continuity in the motivation for the change from *est* to *adest* and then from *adest* to *subsistit*, combined with the importance of van Dodewaard's *invenire*, signifies that all three verbs: *invenire, adesse,* and *subsistere* were used *to elaborate a distinction between the Church of Christ and its concrete realization in the Catholic Church.* The crucial move in this redaction history would be precisely the council's distantiation from a full identification of the Church of Christ with the Roman Catholic Church instigated by van Dodewaard's step from *esse* toward *invenire*. The intermediate changes from *invenire* to *adesse* and from *adesse* to *subsistere* are less important since they all bear the same mark: *an ecumenically motivated awareness of the importance to avoid a description of the relationship between the universal Church of Christ and the Catholic Church in terms of exclusivity.*[77]

That the majority of the Doctrinal Commission was in agreement that *subsistit in* was equivalent to *adest* is confirmed in the *Relatio*, which the vice secretary of the Doctrinal Commission, Philips, provided the following year, giving the reasons for the *subsistit in* change. Before Tromp made his suggestion, Philips had already prepared a draft of this *Relatio* that explained

75. See Alexandra von Teuffenbach, *Die Bedeutung des "subsistit in" (LG 8): Zum Selbstverständnis der katholischen Kirche* (München: Herbert Utz Verlag, 2002), 382–86.

76. For an approach that sees Tromp's understanding of *subsistit in* as equivalent to the exclusive *est* and that proposes *subsistit in* in the final text be interpreted according to how Tromp viewed it, see the work of Alexandra von Teuffenbach and her doctoral supervisor Karl Becker: ibid.; Karl J. Becker, "The Church and Vatican II's 'Subsistit in' Terminology," *Origins* 35, no. 31 (19 January 2006): 514–22. This was originally published in *L'Osservatore Romano* (December 14, 2005). For a contrary view, see Francis A. Sullivan, "A Response to Karl Becker, S.J., on the Meaning of *Subsistit In*," *Theological Studies* 67 (2006): 395–409. On von Teuffenbach's failure to interpret *subsistit in* within the context of the council's overall vision, see Luigi Sartori, "Osservazioni sull'ermeneutica del 'subsistit in' proposta da Alexandra von Teuffenbach," *Rassegna di Teologia* 45 (2004): 279–81.

77. Schelkens, "*Lumen Gentium*'s 'Subsistit in' Revisited," 890–91. Emphasis added.

the theological reason for the change to *adest*, based on the subcommission's earlier *Relatio*. He saw no reason to revise his report when *adest* was substituted with *subsistit in*.[78] The simple reason given in the *Relatio* for explaining why the previous version's *est* had now been replaced by the phrase *subsistit in* was: "so that the expression might better agree with the affirmation about the ecclesial elements which are found elsewhere."[79]

According to a hermeneutics of the authors, which looks to the drafting and debating that led to the final documents, the change to this wording by the Doctrinal Commission (from the word *est* in the previous draft) does indeed appear to have been made *almost incidentally*. And it wasn't even the subject of explicit debate on the council floor; it was only voted on by the council, in the light of an explanatory *Relatio*. But it was a word change that crystallized a major change in the council's mentality, evident in its broader deliberations. Moreover, according to a hermeneutics of the texts—i.e., interrelating an intratextual reading of an individual word, paragraph, chapter within an individual document with an intertextual reading of the whole conciliar corpus of texts—the placement of the verb and preposition *subsistit in* in *Lumen Gentium* 8 assumes paradigmatic importance. The revised wording in that first chapter on the mystery of the church expresses a way of going beyond the impasse of ecumenical division by reconfiguring the Catholic Church's understanding of itself in relation to the universal church of Christ: "This church [of Christ], constituted and organized as a society in the present world, *subsists in* the Catholic Church, which is governed by the successor of Peter and by the bishops in communion with him. Nevertheless, many elements of sanctification and of truth are found outside its visible confines. Since these are gifts belonging to the church of Christ, they are forces impelling towards catholic unity" (LG 8).

In other words, while it marks one of the most significant shifts taken by the Second Vatican Council, the drafting change from *est* to *subsistit in* is

---

78. Regarding Philips's decision to leave his previous draft of the *Relatio* unchanged after the *subsistit in* change, Schelkens asserts: "Philips purposely left his motivation unaltered." Ibid., 890n53. Schelkens is here responding to the contrary view of Karl Becker who believes that this was simply an oversight by Philips. According to Becker, "The text of the *Relatio Generalis* still refers to the first modification (from *est* to *adest*). In all likelihood, therefore, the redactor had not noticed that the last modification introduced by the [Doctrinal] Commission (from *adest* to *subsistit*) should have required a revision of the text of the *Relatio* corresponding to the new terminology." Becker, "The Church and Vatican II's 'Subsistit in' Terminology," 518.

79. AS III/1, 177. Translation taken from Sullivan, "The Significance of the Vatican II Declaration," 274.

not in itself the initiating cause of a paradigm shift but rather a key indicator of a paradigm shift that was already taking place in the mind of the council, away from an exclusive to a more open understanding of "the church and the churches." Therefore, as Arenas Pérez proposes, the phrase "subsists in" needs to be "subordinated" in importance to the notion on which it is based, the notion of *elementa ecclesiae*.[80]

Arenas Pérez's work has explored the theological history of what was originally a Protestant notion.[81] The ecumenical importance for Catholics of *elementa ecclesiae* outside the Catholic Church had been raised in Catholic circles well before its discussion in the council's preparatory stage.[82] For example, already in 1937, Yves Congar—in "the remarkable Chapter Seven of *Chrétiens Désunis*"[83]—employs the term *elementa ecclesiae* and the notion of "varying degrees" of ecclesial relationship, which would become so crucial at Vatican II for finding a way out of the ecumenical impasse (in terms of "degrees of communion").[84] The notion had in fact been mentioned in the preparatory document *De Ecclesia* discussed in the last week of the council's first session (December 1–7). Here, chapter 11 on ecumenism, drafted mainly by the ecumenically minded Johannes Witte, already showed signs of the new directions that would be later taken up in the final document, *Lumen Gentium*.[85]

---

80. Arenas Pérez, "Fading Frontiers? An Historical-Theological Investigation into the Notion of the *Elementa Ecclesiae*," 243.

81. See ibid., 5–205.

82. See throughout Clifford, "*Elementa Ecclesiae*."

83. William Henn, "Yves Congar and *Lumen Gentium*," *Gregorianum* 86, no. 3 (2005): 563–92, at 581. Congar's book was translated as Congar, *Divided Christendom*.

84. Congar writes: "[I]t would seem to the present writer that the various dissident Christian bodies, each in very varying degree, may be regarded in some fashion as *elements* of the Church: elements, that is to say, to the extent in which they have preserved in their very constitution as a religious body elements or principles which pertain to the integral reality of the One Church. The elements or principles are those realities whereby God gathers to Himself from the midst of mankind a People which He destines to be His heirs, and which He incorporates into His Christ." Original emphasis. Congar, *Divided Christendom*, 242.

85. Chapter 11, article 51 states: "It is not only as separate individuals but also as united communities that separated Christians find inducements to come to the Church's unity. For *in these communities there are certain of the elements of the Church* [*elementa quaedam ecclesiae*], especially the Sacred Scriptures and the sacraments, which, as efficacious means and signs of unity, can produce mutual union in Christ and by their very nature, as realities proper to Christ's Church, impel towards unity. Nevertheless, insofar as these communities retain those elements in such a way as to separate them from the fullness of revelation, they in fact constitute one of the causes of the division of Christ's heritage." AS I/4, 82. Translation by Komonchak at https://jakomonchak.files.wordpress.com/2013/07/lg-draft-ch-11-2013.pdf. Emphasis added.

After the sidelining of this preparatory schema at the end of the first session, the responsible committee chose as a basic text one that Gérard Philips had previously prepared in late 1962; the existence of this and other alternative schemas was known to the bishops. But Philips was instructed to include into his own draft ideas from the other alternative schemas, as well as the original *De Ecclesia*. As we have already seen, this new 1963 Philips text (like the original preparatory text) used the verb *est* to identify in an exclusive way the Church of Christ with the Catholic Church.[86] Once again, however, like the preparatory text, it also speaks of "many elements of sanctification [*elementa plura sanctificationis*] which are able to be found [*inveniri possint*] outside the total structure" of the church.[87]

Therefore, as Catherine Clifford identifies, there was already an unresolved tension, or indeed juxtaposition, in Philips's 1963 text presented to the bishops at the start of the second session. The text affirmed both a strict identification of the church of Christ and the Catholic Church, as well as an acknowledgment of *elementa ecclesiae* in other Christian communities: "In a fateful twist, the Philips schema paired sentences from two chapters of the first schema (I and XI), juxtaposing the affirmation of an identity between the one church of Christ—the one, holy, catholic, and apostolic church of the creed—and the Catholic Church, with the recognition of ecclesial realities beyond its borders: 'This church . . . is the catholic Church; nonetheless, some elements of sanctification are still found outside its visible confines.' . . . In the course of the council, it would become necessary to better harmonize these affirmations."[88]

The phrase "elements of the church" refers to, according to Komonchak, "the primary elements that describe the inner life of the Church."[89] The final text of *Lumen Gentium* 8 states that "many elements of sanctification and truth are found outside [the Catholic Church's] visible confines." These elements, it goes on to affirm, are "gifts [*dona*] belonging to the church of Christ." Therefore, the word "church" in the phrase *elementa ecclesiae,* refers to the church of Christ and not to the Catholic Church. No list of these elements or gifts is given in *Lumen Gentium* 8. Several lists, however, can be found elsewhere in the documents: *Lumen Gentium* 14 and 15; and *Unitatis*

---

86. Gil Hellín, ed., *Constitutio dogmatica de ecclesia, Lumen Gentium*, 64.

87. Ibid., 64.

88. Clifford, "*Elementa Ecclesiae*," 253.

89. Joseph A. Komonchak, *Who Are the Church?* (Milwaukee: Marquette University Press, 2008), 71.

Redintegratio 3, 22, and 23. Nowhere in these listings is there any attempt at a systematic arrangement of the elements in order of theological importance.[90] *Lumen Gentium* 14, which looks at "the catholic faithful," mentions faith and baptism, possessing the Spirit of Christ, the means of salvation, ecclesiastical organization, the profession of faith, the sacraments, ecclesiastical government, communion, persevering in charity, and responding to the grace of Christ.[91] In the article that follows, *Lumen Gentium* 15, without actually using the word "elements," which is nevertheless implied, we find a similar but more expansive list: Sacred Scripture, religious zeal, loving faith in God the Father and in Christ, baptism, union with Christ, other sacraments, the episcopate, the Eucharist, devotion to Mary, prayer and spiritual blessings, true union in the Spirit, the Spirit's gifts and graces, and the Spirit's sanctifying power.[92]

Unitatis Redintegratio 3 presents, according to Komonchak, "the strongest statement"[93] of the ecclesial elements: "Some, even very many, of *the most significant* elements and endowments [*insuper ex elementis seu bonis*] which together go to build up and give life to the church itself, can exist outside the visible boundaries of the Catholic Church: the written Word of God; the life of grace; faith, hope and charity, with the other interior gifts of the Holy Spirit, as well as visible elements. All of these, which come from Christ and lead back to Christ, belong to the one Church of Christ" (UR 3). The decree goes on to speak of the diverse liturgical traditions of these communities, which "most certainly can truly engender a life of grace, and one must say, are capable of giving access to that communion which is salvation." Later in the decree, articles 22 and 23 further explore these elements.

As Willebrands points out, this focus on *elementa ecclesiae* was never intended in a reductive sense: "When the Council acknowledges *elementa Ecclesiae*, spiritual and institutional, in other Churches, we should not reproach it with a narrow-minded '*theologia elementorum*,' taking elements only in a quantitative sense and making an addition sum. They indicate spiritual realities like faith, hope and charity, or sacraments, or institutions

---

90. For example, Alois Grillmeier, in commenting on *Lumen Gentium* 15: "The precise determination of the link which binds all Christian Churches or communities with the Catholic Church does not follow a systematic order. Sometimes external factors of Church membership are mentioned, sometimes internal ones. Other factors can be either one or the other." Grillmeier, "Chapter II: The People of God," 178.

91. See the summary table in Komonchak, *Who Are the Church?*, 69.

92. For a summary list, see the table in ibid., 70.

93. Ibid.

which are more than merely human and historical creations. They cover realities which are not quantitatively measurable."[94]

Taking all these lists together, we see that, of fundamental significance are those elements that relate to the spiritual realities explored above in the council's overarching pastoral principle, the revelation/faith principle: an intimate union with the revealing God (loving faith in God and Christ, union with Christ, true union in the Spirit). These all describe faith in its primary sense, faith as believing (*credere*), as a loving relationship with God, what Jesus referred to as the first commandment ("Love the Lord your God with all your heart"), from which is enabled fulfillment of the second commandment.[95] The introductory article of the decree twice refers to Christians as "disciples" who respond to Christ: "all [who] profess to be disciples of the Lord [*discipulos Domini*]"; "all the disciples of Christ [*Christi discipulos*]" (UR 1).[96] As Willebrands notes: "Whoever belongs to Christ belongs to the Church, and hence . . . the limits of the Church are coextensive with those of belonging to Christ. This seems to me the dogmatic reflection behind the transition from *est* to *subsistit in* as it emerges from the Council itself."[97] It is telling that the only occurrence in the Vatican II documents of *communio fidelium* as a description of the church of Christ occurs in *Unitatis Redintegratio* (art. 2). The church of Christ is a communion in the Spirit of those who believe in Jesus Christ as Lord and Savior. As the decree later affirms: "we rejoice that our separated sisters and brothers look to Christ as the source and center of ecclesiastical communion [*communionis ecclesiasticae*]" (UR 20).

Related to this loving faith relationship and the communion it creates is the foundational formulation of the content revealed in that relationship, as articulated by the early church in the canonical Scriptures, along with the creeds and definitions of the early councils. Both the dogmatic constitution and the decree employ the ancient distinction between *fides qua creditur* (faith as a relationship between God and believers) and *fides quae creditur* (faith as an assent to the beliefs of the church), but with the primary emphasis on the former as the source of the latter.[98] The dogmatic constitution speaks

94. Willebrands, "The Ecumenical Movement," 219.
95. Matt 22:37; Luke 10:27. Vatican II refers twice to the first commandment (AA 8; GS 16).
96. Translation corrected.
97. Willebrands, "Vatican II's Ecclesiology of Communion," 183.
98. The distinction goes back to St. Augustine, who states in *De Trinitate* 13.2.5: "But that which is believed is a different thing from the faith by which it is believed [*sed aliud sunt ea quae creduntur, aliud fides qua creduntur*—lit. "one thing are those things which are believed; another thing is the faith by which they are believed"].

of non-Catholic baptized believers as those who "lovingly believe in [*amanter credunt in*] God the Father Almighty and in Christ, the Son of God and the Saviour" (LG 15). The decree speaks of non-Catholic baptized believers by explicitly using the technical term *fides qua creditur*, when referring to "the faith by which they believe in Christ [*fides qua Christo creditur*]" (UR 23). The conciliar lists of *elementa ecclesiae* reveal a common patrimony in terms of *fides quae creditur*, because other Christians too hold on to sacred Scripture and to the ancient rule of faith. Of course, one of the ecclesial elements whereby the churches and ecclesial communities are not fully or perfectly in communion with the Catholic Church is in this area of *fides quae creditur*, the content of their beliefs as formulated in official teaching. *Lumen Gentium* 15 refers to those who "do not profess the faith in its entirety." The doctrinal differences, we shall see, need to be viewed, nevertheless, according to the hierarchy of truths (UR 11) and become the subject of ecumenical dialogue. Overwhelmingly, however, the priority in these passages listing the *elementa ecclesiae* is given to other Christians' *relationship with Christ and the riches which faith and baptism in Christ bestow through the Spirit*. "Other Churches and Ecclesial Communities are not judged in reference to the Catholic Church but in reference to Christ and his mystery."[99] Thus, at work in the conciliar debates regarding the Catholic/ecumenical principle is an evaluation of other Christians and their communities through the lens of the fundamental theo-logical principle noted above: the revelation/faith principle. Other Christians and their communities are acknowledged as likewise enlightened and empowered by the Holy Spirit and as lovingly responding to God's outreach to them in Jesus Christ.

Lumen Gentium 14 lists the couplet "faith and baptism" in reference to Catholics. The ecclesial element of baptism features highly in the council's ecumenical vision. The Catholic Church had long recognized the baptism of non-Catholic Christians.[100] In his 1943 encyclical *Mystici Corporis*, Pius XII includes baptism as the first of three requirements for membership in the church of Christ, alongside orthodoxy and living within the church's juridical unity.[101] Non-Catholics, according to this set of criteria, at least pass

---

99. Wijlens, *Sharing the Eucharist*, 196–97.

100. In reference to UR 3's statement that "all who have been justified by faith in baptism are incorporated into Christ," endnote 19 refers to teachings from the Lateran Council IV, the Council of Lyons II, and the Council of Florence.

101. *Mystici Corporis*, 22: "Actually only those are to be included as members of the Church who have been baptized and profess the true faith, and who have not been so unfortunate as to separate themselves from the unity of the Body, or been excluded by legitimate authority

the first juridical test. Joseph Ratzinger has pointed out that this recognition of the baptism of other Christians is one that the Catholic Church was ironically beholden to, given its juridical view of the church: "According to the Church's legal tradition preserved in [the code of canon law], baptism provided an unlosable form of constitutive membership of the Church. This made it clear that in certain circumstances a legal approach can offer more flexibility and openness than a 'mystical' one."[102]

The theme of baptism had been to the forefront of Augustin Bea's ecumenical theology since he became president of the new Secretariat; it was "a theme he worked out and put before the Church at large as perhaps no one else has."[103] This was evident, not only in the talks he gave throughout Europe on ecumenism, but also in the positions he promoted on preparatory and conciliar commissions, as well as in his interventions on the council floor.[104] Bea's emphasis prevailed. According to *Lumen Gentium* 15's list of the *elementa ecclesiae*, as Grillmeier interprets it, baptism is "the most far-reaching [sacramental] basis of the link between the Catholic Church and non-Catholic Christians."[105] He goes on to state that, in *Lumen Gentium* 15, "it is noteworthy that the union with Christ is stressed."[106] And, as Willebrands highlights: "Where there is grace there is union with Christ; and all union with Christ brings one within the scope of the Church."[107] The Decree on

---

for grave faults committed. 'For in one spirit' says the Apostle, 'were we all baptized into one Body, whether Jews or Gentiles, whether bond or free.' As therefore in the true Christian community there is only one Body, one Spirit, one Lord, and one Baptism, so there can be only one faith. And therefore, if a man refuse to hear the Church, let him be considered—so the Lord commands—as a heathen and a publican. It follows that those who are divided in faith or government cannot be living in the unity of such a Body, nor can they be living the life of its one Divine Spirit." http://w2.vatican.va/content/pius-xii/en/encyclicals/documents/hf_p -xii_enc_29061943_mystici-corporis-christi.html

102. Ratzinger, "The Ecclesiology of the Second Vatican Council," 15.

103. Johannes Willebrands, "Cardinal Augustin Bea: His Contribution to the Ecumenical Movement and to Religious Liberty: Opening Address at the Bea Symposium, 1981," *Information Service. The Pontifical Council for Promoting Christian Unity* 101 (1999): 70–77, at 73.

104. See Emmanuel Lanne, "La contribtion du cardinal Bea à la question du baptême et l'Unité des chrétiens," *Irénikon* 55, no. 4 (1982): 471–99; Johannes Witte, "The Question of Baptism and the Unity of Christians," in *Atti del Simposio Card. Agostino Bea (Roma, 16–19 Dicembre 1981)* (Rome: Libreria Editrice Pontificia Università Lateranense 1983), 223–30. For a summary of Bea's view on baptism and its effects for church membership, see Schmidt, *Augustin Bea*, 402–4.

105. Grillmeier, "Chapter II: The People of God," 178.

106. Ibid., 179.

107. Willebrands, "Vatican II's Ecclesiology of Communion," 181.

Ecumenism eventually goes on to devote articles 22 and 23 to a discussion of the fundamental link that baptism is among those who commit to following Jesus Christ as their Lord and Savior. Consequently, Arenas Pérez can speak of the council's "baptismal ecclesiology": "Both [*Lumen Gentium* and *Unitatis Redintegratio*] agreed in placing the sacrament of baptism at the very heart of ecclesiology, insisting on the importance of conceiving the church as the community of all those who have validly received baptism, and are thereby joined in a real, Christian, ecclesiastical and sacramental unity."[108] The other conciliar documents in several places speak of baptism in terms of entrance into the church.[109] The council does not say, however, that baptism by itself gives *full* incorporation into the Church. Rather, it will go on to speak of degrees of incorporation (*Lumen Gentium*) or degrees of communion (*Unitatis Redintegratio*).[110]

"Churches and Ecclesial Communities"

Affirming that elements of the church of Christ can be found outside the boundaries of the Catholic Church raised two further questions, which the council needed to address. First, do these elements refer just to non-Catholic *individual* Christians, or can they refer also to their *communities* of faith that nourish them? Second, can the communities of faith that emerged from the Protestant Reformations be considered genuinely "ecclesial" communities, or even indeed "churches"?

A historical note is necessary here regarding the distinction the council makes between "churches" and "communities." Since the schism between Eastern and Western Christianity in the eleventh century, the Catholic Church has referred to these separated communities as churches. The preparatory draft of *De Ecclesia* had a reference listing examples of such usages.[111] The Decree on Ecumenism, in a reference to the phrase "separated churches" in article 3, gives a reduced list of some instances.[112] The basis for such ac-

---

108. Arenas Pérez, "Fading Frontiers? An Historical-Theological Investigation into the Notion of the *Elementa Ecclesiae*," 298.

109. LG 7, 11, 14, 21; AA 3; AG 6, 15; PO 5.

110. See the lengthy treatment of baptism in the conciliar texts in Becker, "The Teaching of Vatican II on Baptism."

111. AS I/4, 88–90, endnote 6. This chapter was drafted by the Dutch Jesuit Johannes Witte.

112. Footnote 19. The list follows closely the instances listed by Yves Congar in "Appendix IV: The Terms Used in Official Catholic Documents Concerning Dissidents," in Congar, *Divided Christendom*, 294–95. Drafting of an initial basic text for chapter 1 of the decree was entrusted to Johannes Witte, a member of the Mixed Commission from the Doctrinal Commission, who

knowledgment is that these "churches" continued to possess valid orders and so to celebrate the Eucharist validly. The distinction, therefore, between "churches" and "communities" is grounded on what Francis Sullivan formulates as a principle of "eucharistic ecclesiology": "There is not the full reality of Church where there is less full reality of the Eucharist."[113] Because of this criterion, the various schismatic communities of "Old Catholics" are considered still to be "churches" by the Catholic Church. This is acknowledged in the *Relatio* explaining the title of the section heading in the final text of *Unitatis Redintegratio*, "The Separated Churches and Ecclesial Communities in the West."[114] The question before the council, however, was whether the communities emerging from the various Protestant Reformations possess any *ecclesial* character, even though the Catholic Church may regard their orders and Eucharist to be invalid.

Both *Lumen Gentium* and *Unitatis Redintegratio* address this issue. As seen above, at the end of the first session the council first requested a new document on ecumenism and then a new document on the church. When these two new schemas were debated in the second session, there were calls for both documents to recognize the ecclesial nature of other Christian communities. To recall the timeline of events: debate on the church schema lasted all of October 1963; debate on the first three chapters of the ecumenism schema began on November 18 and lasted until December 2, 1963. It is important to note that, while the latter debate was going on, the Doctrinal Commission was meeting (November 18–26) to consider amendments to the church document after the earlier debate. It was on the last day of that meeting that the insertion of *subsistit in* was made. In tracing these interventions and subsequent redrafting, therefore, we see at work a certain interweaving of the drafting processes of the documents on the church and on ecumenism.

During the debate on the draft article that was to become *Lumen Gentium* 15, many bishops requested that the constitution go beyond a focus on the Catholic Church's relationship with individual baptized non-Catholics and

---

had drafted the original chapter 11 of the preparatory Theological Commission's *De Ecclesia*. On Witte being entrusted with this task, and his incorporation into his draft of the ideas of other *periti*, see Velati, *Una difficile transizione*, 351.

113. Sullivan, "The Significance of the Vatican II Declaration," 282.

114. See AS III/2, 335: "It is to be noted that among the separated communities there are some, namely the Old Catholics, which, like the Orthodox communities, should be called churches, according to sound theological doctrine admitted by all Catholics, in view of the valid sacrament of orders and valid Eucharist which they possess." Translation is taken from Sullivan, *The Church We Believe In*, 53.

that recognition be given to the ecclesial communities within which these elements take their life. Consequently, in the redrafting by the commission after the October debate, a phrase was added to the reference to "other sacraments"; these, it then adds, are recognized and accepted "in their own churches or ecclesiastical communities [*in propriis ecclesiis vel communitatibus ecclesiasticis*]" (LG 15). In presenting this revised text of *Lumen Gentium* to the council fathers the following year (on September 15, 1964), the *Relatio* noted the significance of this seemingly passing addition: "The elements which are mentioned concern not only individuals but their communities as well; *in this fact precisely is located the foundation of the ecumenical movement [in hoc praecise situm est principium motionis oecumenicae]*. Papal documents regularly speak of separated Eastern 'Churches.' For Protestants recent Pontiffs have used the term 'Christian communities.'"[115] The significance of this telling reference to "the foundation [*principium*] of the ecumenical movement" cannot be overstated. The council's recognition of the ecclesiality of other Christian communities, grounded on a theology of *elementa ecclesiae*, provides the key to understanding the council's Catholic/ecumenical principle.

Sandra Arenas Pérez remarks on the significance of this September 15, 1964 *Relatio* for explaining the *subsistit* change as a consequence of the prior debates on the ecclesial status of other churches:

> This explanation is crucial for a correct understanding of the *subsistit* clause, which is often detached from its broader context. Yet, the *Relatio* refers precisely to the necessity of interconnecting the question of the boundaries and the relationship between the Church of Christ and the Catholic Church on the one hand, with the ecumenically motivated use of the notion of the *elementa ecclesiae*. To a certain extent, the "subsistit" clause was subordinated to what follows, thus expressing the intention of the council Fathers to properly safeguard their recognition of the existence of ecclesiality outside the boundaries of the Roman Catholic Church. That said, the "subsistit" clause cannot possibly be taken to signify an exclusivist position, nor can it be understood to describe the relationship between the Roman Catholic Church and the Church of Christ in terms of exclusivity.[116]

---

115. AS III/1, 204. The translation is taken here from Sullivan, "The Significance of the Vatican II Declaration," 281. AS III/1, 208 lists three *periti* from Subcommission II, which drafted the chapter on the People of God (Yves Congar, Emilio Sauras, and Johannes Witte) as the authors of the *Relatio* for this chapter.

116. Arenas Pérez, "Fading Frontiers? An Historical-Theological Investigation into the Notion of the *Elementa Ecclesiae*," 264. Emphasis added.

Following the October 1963 *De Ecclesia* debate (to which the above *Relatio* relates), the debate on *De Oecumenismo* in the latter half of November 1963 also involved interventions and written submissions related to this issue. When debate began on the decree, one of the first to speak was Cardinal Joseph Ritter of St. Louis, Missouri, who proposed that all separated Christian communities (not just the Orthodox and Old Catholics) be referred to in the decree as "churches."[117] This was, likewise, the proposal of Bishop Gabriel Manek, who, in a written submission later in the debate on behalf of some thirty Indonesian bishops, requested:

> The title of "Church" should not only be attributed to the Oriental Churches separated from us, but also to the communities which arose from the Reformation. As communities of baptized Christians they are united among themselves and to us by the bond of faith, hope and charity, through the proclamation and confession of the divine Word and through the worship of God. These communities are in all truth "Churches," even if *in an analogous sense* and *less perfectly* than the Orthodox Churches. They possess visible elements of ecclesial unity. Through holy rites they represent, produce and foster the life of grace, so that we must acknowledge the Holy Spirit present in their midst making use of them as means of salvation. They also receive from that fullness of grace and truth that has been entrusted to the Church.[118]

The council, however, was not to proceed with the language of "church" in regard to the Protestant communities, although Manek's notions of "an analogous sense" and "less perfectly" would come to feature as important elements in a comprehensive understanding of the council's Catholic/ecumenical principle. Also influential in the council's eventual language was the intervention of Cardinal Franz König of Vienna. König proposed that, because the other Christian communities possess "ecclesiastical elements" (*elementa ecclesiastica*), they should be called "ecclesial communities" (*communitates ecclesiales*).[119] This was the term which prevailed, at least in the decree, as Werner Becker comments: "Because the term *ecclesiasticae* seemed to possess an already fixed meaning, it was decided to use the formula

117. AS II/5, 537.
118. AS, II/6, 54–57, at 55. The translation here is taken from Gregory Baum, "The Ecclesial Reality of the Other Churches," *Concilium* 1, no. 4 (1965): 4:34–46, at 35. Emphasis added.
119. AS II/5, 554.

communitates ecclesiales, although the adjective is a neologism in Latin."[120] Thomas Stransky implies that there is a development taking place as the two documents are being drafted: "The Decree is the first church document to use the expression 'ecclesial community.' *Ecclesialis* was coined in preference to a more exact Latin *ecclesiastica* lest the latter, especially in translations, smack too much of a juridical, external label. *De Ecclesia*, however, uses '*communitates ecclesiasticae*' (n. 15)."[121]

Perhaps another reminder of the redaction history of the decree is needed before we proceed. After the discussion in the aula in 1963 on the first version of the decree, the Secretariat's drafting committee during the intersession made changes to the text in the light of the bishops' comments. In the third session, there was no debate on this revised document, only voting, which began with the relevant *Relatio* explaining the rationale of the drafting commission. Then there was the opportunity for more written submissions, from which the drafting commission produced a further revised schema. This was presented to the assembly for voting later in that third session, introduced once again by a *Relatio*. These two *relationes* (September 23 and November 10, 1964) explained why and how the bishops' suggestions had or had not been incorporated into the text. In terms of a hermeneutics of the authors,

---

120. Becker, "History of the Decree on Ecumenism," 34n66. The final documents, somewhat inconsistently, use two Latin adjectives to describe the separate Christian bodies: *ecclesiastica* and *ecclesialis*. As we have seen, *Lumen Gentium* 15 refers to the recognition and acceptance, along with baptism, of other sacraments "in their own churches and ecclesiastical communities [*in propriis ecclesiis vel communitatibus ecclesiasticis*]." *Unitatis Redintegratio*, however, when speaking of "ecclesial communities" does not use the adjective *ecclesiastica* but rather *ecclesialis* in a chapter title as well as in a subsection title. In all the council documents, there are only eight instances of the adjective *ecclesialis*, and they all appear in documents promulgated in the third and fourth sessions. Seven of those instances refer to the phrase "ecclesial communities." The adjective *ecclesiastica*, on the other hand, appears throughout the whole range of the conciliar corpus, from the first (*Sacrosanctum Concilium*) to the last (*Gaudium et Spes*). Strangely, this last promulgated document of the council states: "the Catholic Church deeply appreciates what other Christian churches and ecclesiastical communities [*communitates ecclesiasticae*] have contributed and are contributing cooperatively to the realization of this aim." The previous sentence had described this aim: "that through each of its members and its community as a whole [the church] can help to make the human family and its history still more human" (GS 40). *Unitatis Redintegratio* employs both forms. The form *ecclesialis* appears five times, each in reference to "ecclesial communities" (twice in the title of chapter 3, and the title of subsection 2 of chapter 3) and three times in the main text (twice in UR 19 and once in UR 22). The form *ecclesiastica*, however, appears seven times in the decree, mostly in reference to "ecclesiastical communion [*communio ecclesiastica*]" (UR 3, 4, 6, 13 [twice], 15 and 20).

121. Stransky, *The Decree on Ecumenism of the Second Vatican Council*, 68n31.

these two *relationes* require attention; an affirmative vote for a text meant that the drafting commission's rationale expressed in the *Relatio* implicitly became the council's official position.

The first *Relatio* (September 23, 1964), in presenting the redactions that followed the debate the previous year, stated:

> It must not be overlooked that the communities that have their origin in the separation that took place in the West are not merely a sum or collection of individual Christians, but they are constituted by social ecclesiastical elements [*elementis socialibus ecclesiasticis*] which they have preserved from our common patrimony, and which confer on them *a truly ecclesial character* [*characterem vere ecclesialem*]. In these communities the one sole Church of Christ is present, albeit imperfectly, *in a way that is somewhat like* its presence in particular churches [*quasi tamquam in Ecclesiis particularibus*], and by means of their ecclesiastical elements [*elementis ecclesiasticis*] the Church of Christ is *in some way* [*aliquo modo*] operative in them.[122]

Sullivan underscores the wider implications of this September 23, 1964, *Relatio* on the second draft of the decree: "While the Council did not hesitate to speak of the separated Eastern Churches as 'particular churches' without qualification, it was the mind of the Commission that the western communities that lack the full reality of the Eucharist—without attempting to decide which ones these were—still have a truly ecclesial character, *and are at least analogous to particular churches of the one Church of Christ*."[123]

This notion of being a church in an analogous sense was also implied in the *Relatio* on the third version of the decree later that session (November 10, 1964), after amendments had been made following the previous voting and subsequent written submissions. The *Relatio* listed the reasons why certain requests from the bishops' written submissions had been accepted and why others had not. In response to those bishops who believed it was incompatible, on the one hand, to affirm the oneness of the church and then, on the other, to speak of non-Catholic communities as "churches" and "ecclesial communities," the *Relatio* stated:

> The two-fold expression [in the chapter title] "Churches and ecclesial communities" has been approved by the Council, and is used in a completely

122. AS III/2, 335. The translation here comes from Sullivan, *The Church We Believe In*, 32. Emphasis added. The Latin phrases have been inserted into Sullivan's translation.
123. Sullivan, "The Significance of the Vatican II Declaration," 282–83.

legitimate way. There is indeed only one universal Church, *but there are many local and particular churches.* It is the custom in the Catholic tradition to call the separated eastern communities Churches—local or particular ones to be sure—and in the proper sense of the term. *It is not the business of the council to investigate and decide which of the other communities ought to be called Churches in the theological sense.*[124]

In other words, the council left the issue open and did not decide one way or the other whether "ecclesial communities" are "churches" "*in the theological sense.*" It will be remembered that Bishop Manek, in his 1963 written submission regarding the first version of the decree, when speaking of the communities of the Reformation stated: "These communities are in all truth 'Churches,' even if *in an analogous sense* and less perfectly than the Orthodox Churches." Francis Sullivan concludes that indeed, in the end, while the council did not endorse the language of "church" to speak of the communities of the Reformation, its phrase "ecclesial communities" implies that they were seen by the council as churches in an analogous sense:

> "Subsists in" means that it is in the Catholic Church alone that the Church of Christ continues to exist with all those properties and structural elements that it cannot lose, while at the same time the Council recognized that outside the Catholic Church, there are not merely "elements of Church," but there are "particular Churches," by whose celebration of the Eucharist the Church of God is built up, and there are ecclesial communities that are analogous to particular churches, inasmuch as the one Church of Christ is somehow also present and operative in them for the salvation of their members.[125]

In the final version of the Decree on Ecumenism, approved by vote on November 20 and promulgated the next day, the very first article speaks of other Christians within the context of their communities of faith. It refers to "many Christian communions [*communiones*]" in which "all indeed profess to be disciples of the Lord [*discipulos Domini*]" (UR 1).[126] Similarly, it refers to the ecclesial context of "those who invoke the Triune God and confess Jesus as Lord and Saviour. *They do this not merely as individuals but*

---

124. AS III/7, 35. The translation here is taken from Sullivan, *The Church We Believe In,* 227n36. Emphasis added.
125. Sullivan, "The Significance of the Vatican II Declaration," 272.
126. Translation corrected.

also as members of the corporate groups in which they have heard the Gospel, and which each regards as his or her church, and indeed God's" (UR 1).[127]

Thus the council's final vision focuses, first of all, not on the relationship of the other churches and ecclesial communities to the Catholic Church, but rather on the common relationship both the Catholic Church and the other non-Catholic ecclesial bodies have to the triune God, revealed in Jesus Christ and through the Holy Spirit, who unites them all as the faithful baptized in the one church of Christ. Then, from that perspective, the council focuses on the relationship of the separated churches and communities with the Catholic Church, all as churches (albeit at times analogously so) in the one church of Christ. The theological framework the council uses to address these different aspects of the church's unity and disunity is the theological rubric of *communio*.

Communio Fidelium and Degrees of *Communio Ecclesiarum*

When speaking of the disunity in the "church of God" throughout history,[128] *Unitatis Redintegratio* 3 states: "serious dissensions appeared and large communities became separated [*seiunctae*] from full communion [*plena communione*] with the Catholic Church." Elaboration on three points in this sentence will allow us to explore how acknowledgment of the ecclesial status of other churches and communities opened the council to further nuances in its emerging ecumenical ecclesiology: the Latin word *seiunctae* ("separated"), the notion of "communion," and the notion of "full" communion (and, by implication, less-than-full communion).

The council is quite deliberate in the Latin word it eventually chooses to characterize the divided nature of the Catholic Church's relationship with "the others." The decree throughout uses the adjective *seiunctus* ("estranged") rather than *separatus* ("separated"). It speaks of *seiuncti fratres* (estranged brothers and sisters); it uses *seiunctae* rather than *separatae* to describe the separated status of other churches and ecclesial communities.[129] The suggestion to change the phrase *fratres separati* to *fratres seiuncti* had been made by Archbishop Sebastiano Baggio, who was "well known for his mastery of

127. Emphasis added.

128. The council uses the terms "church of God" and "church of Christ" synonymously when referring to the universal church. For other such terms, see the discussion above in the chapter on the particular/universal principle.

129. The decree uses various cognates of the word twenty-nine times. *Lumen Gentium* twice uses the adjective *seiunctus*, both times in the phrase *fratres seiunctos* (LG 67 and 69); tellingly, it does not use the word *separatus* to describe other Christians and their churches or communities.

the Latin language."[130] According to George Tavard, Baggio argued that "*separati . . .* would imply that there are and can be no relationships between the two sides; *seiuncti,* on the contrary, would assert that something has been cut between them, yet that separation is not complete and need not be definitive."[131] Thus the phrase *fratres seiuncti* is perhaps best translated, according to Tavard, as "'estranged brothers,' rather than 'separated.'"[132] This *style* of language—style of language and style of presence being something John O'Malley considers so indicative of the essence of the conciliar vision—is, therefore, yet another indication of the council's desire for a more generous and expansive understanding of church. As Tavard concludes regarding the historic significance of the use of *seiuncti* and *seiunctae:* "Thus, the Secretariat and the Council worked on the basis that *the result of the Reformation was partial lack of communion, not total separation. . . .* [T]he Reformation did not totally break the communion between the Churches involved."[133]

This notion of continuing "communion" between the Catholic Church and the separated churches and ecclesial communities is presented preeminently in *Unitatis Redintegratio.* The word *communio* occurs thirty-three times in *Lumen Gentium* and thirty-six times in *Unitatis Redintegratio.* When discussing above the *communio/missio* principle, we have already seen how *Lumen Gentium* presents an inchoate *communio* ecclesiology regarding the Catholic Church *ad intra.*[134] *Lumen Gentium,* however, does not approach the ecumenical issue of "the church and the churches" from the perspective of "communion," but rather predominantly from the perspective of the christological image of the church as "a body," with its consequent notion of "incorporation" into that body. *Unitatis Redintegratio,* on the other hand, does approach the ecumenical issue predominantly with the *pneumatological* image of the church as the dwelling place of the Holy Spirit, with its consequent notion of spiritual "communion" among those who dwell there.

---

130. George H. Tavard, "Reassessing the Reformation," *One in Christ* 19 (1983): 355–67, at 360.

131. Ibid., 360. Johannes Feiner likewise notes: "The participle *seiunctae,* which was consciously used instead of *separatae,* also implies an incomplete separation: *seiungere* expresses a less profound separation than *separare.* In English (as in German), however, the nuance is difficult to reproduce." Johannes Feiner, "Commentary on the Decree on Ecumenism," in *Commentary on the Documents of Vatican II,* vol. 2, ed. Herbert Vorgrimler (New York: Herder, 1968), 2:57–164, at 70.

132. Tavard, "Reassessing the Reformation," 360.

133. Ibid. Emphasis added.

134. See Acerbi, *Due ecclesiologie*; Saier, *"Communio" in der Lehre des Zweiten Vatikanischen Konzils.*

Seemingly taking a postconciliar intertextual reading of *Lumen Gentium* and *Unitatis Redintegratio*, Johannes Willebrands believes that "*subsistit in* cannot be authentically understood except in the setting of [an] ecclesiology of communion, and then only if communion is seen not simply horizontally nor merely as between Christians or Christian communities, but also and in the first place as communion with God himself."[135] In other words, it is the *vertical* communion all baptized believers and their communities have with God that brings about the *horizontal* communion among those believers and the communities to which they belong.

Several points of the conciliar vision converge here in the council's attempt to find a way through the ecumenical impasse. To reiterate those points: the call for human beings to share in this divine intimacy was seen above to be the central mystery of the revelation/faith principle; it was seen to be the heart of the council's pastoral agenda; it was also seen to be, earlier in this chapter, *the* fundamental "element of the church," *fides qua creditur*—that loving relationship with God, from which has emerged, in human language, the content of Christian belief, *fides quae creditur*. The decree's first article speaks of "those who invoke the Triune God and confess Jesus as Lord and Saviour."[136] From this loving relationship of the people of God with the God in whom they believe is derived every other aspect that can be said of that people of God in "its doctrine, life and worship" (DV 8). On this vertical communion with God is grounded the horizontal communion among the faithful, those who lovingly respond to God's loving outreach.[137] It is telling that the council's only use of the specific phrase *communio fidelium* occurs in the second article of the decree when it is describing the church of Christ: "It is the Holy Spirit, dwelling in *those who believe [credentes]* and pervading and ruling over *the entire church [totam ecclesiam]*, who brings about that wonderful communion of the faithful *[communionem fidelium]* and joins them together so intimately in Christ that he is the principle of the church's unity" (UR 2).[138] These faithful of the universal church of Christ necessarily gather in local communities that sustain their faith life. *Lumen Gentium* 13

---

135. Willebrands, "Vatican II's Ecclesiology of Communion," 190.

136. This is an allusion to the foundational definition of the World Council of Churches adopted at its inaugural assembly (Amsterdam, 1948): "The World Council of Churches is a fellowship of churches which accept our Lord Jesus Christ as God and Saviour." This allusion is therefore an acknowledgment by the Catholic Church that it is now joining a movement started by others. I am indebted to Peter De Mey for this point.

137. See Kasper, "The Church as Communion."

138. Emphasis added.

and 23 speak of the way the Holy Spirit holds these local communities united among themselves. *Ad Gentes* twice speaks of this union between local churches as a *communio ecclesiarum*.[139] We have seen how Francis Sullivan highlights Vatican II teaching "that outside the Catholic Church, there are not merely 'elements of Church,' but there are 'particular Churches,' by whose celebration of the Eucharist the Church of God is built up, and there are ecclesial communities that are analogous to particular churches, inasmuch as the one Church of Christ is somehow also present and operative in them for the salvation of their members."[140]

Accordingly, just as some passages in *Lumen Gentium* and *Ad Gentes* envisage the Catholic Church as a *communio ecclesiarum*, so too it can be asserted that Vatican II, analogously, approaches the ecumenical question by imagining the universal church of Christ too as a *communio ecclesiarum*. Vatican II's notion of the Catholic Church as a *communio ecclesiarum*, therefore, is expanded by the council, beyond just relationships *within* the Catholic Church to its relationship *with* other Christian churches and indeed, analogously, with ecclesial communities. In other words, whereas *Lumen Gentium moves toward* a communion ecclesiology in its self-understanding of the Catholic Church as a *communio ecclesiarum*, *Unitatis Redintegratio* more explicitly moves toward an *ecumenical* communion ecclesiology, understanding the universal church of Christ likewise as a *communio ecclesiarum*.

Unlike the full communion among local churches within the Catholic Church, however, the *communio* between the Catholic Church and the other "churches" knows different degrees of communion. This too is a new way of conceiving a way through the ecumenical impasse. Since past schisms and reformations did not completely sever communion with the Catholic Church—the resulting churches and communities were *seiunctae*, not *separatae*—the council speaks of their relationship in terms of a continuing communion that nonetheless has different grades. *Unitatis Redintegratio* 3 makes a distinction between "full communion [*communio plena*]" with the Catholic Church, and being "in some, though imperfect, communion with the Catholic Church [*in quadam cum ecclesia catholica communione, etsi non perfecta*]."[141] While this latter phrase refers in the text to non-Catholic individual Christians, the coun-

---

139. On these references in *Ad Gentes* 19 and 38, see the chapter above on the *communio/missio* principle.

140. Sullivan, "The Significance of the Vatican II Declaration," 272.

141. "For those who believe in Christ and have been properly baptized are put in some, though imperfect, communion with the Catholic Church [*in quadam cum ecclesia catholica communione, etsi non perfecta, constituunter*]. Without doubt, the differences that exist in varying degrees [*variis modis*] between them and the Catholic Church—whether in doctrine

cil's emphasis on the ecclesiality of these Christians' communities means the phrase is to be interpreted as applying also to the relationship between those communities and the Catholic Church.[142]

A similar distinction is employed in *Lumen Gentium*, albeit within a different ecclesiological framework, that of the church as the Body of Christ. According to Alois Grillmeier, "the word 'fully' (*plene*) is decisive for the general view of the Constitution as regards the ecclesiastical status of Catholic and non-Catholic Christians."[143] It will be remembered that Bishop van Dodewaard had called for the deletion from the draft of the juridical phrase *reapse et simpliciter loquendo* and proposed a phrase "the bond of *perfect unity*."[144] Three days earlier Pope Paul VI had used this very wording in his opening address for that second session: "[The council's third object] is that which concerns 'the other Christians'—those who believe in Christ but whom we have not the happiness of numbering among ourselves in *the perfect unity* of Christ [*cum vinculo perfectae unitatis Christi coniuncti*], which only the Catholic Church can offer them."[145] Alois Grillmeier comments that the pope's language here "was an implicit acknowledgment that one could be 'imperfectly' or 'incompletely' incorporated into the Church."[146] Cardinal Giacomo Lercaro, in a speech emphasizing the effect of baptism as an incorporation into the church, proposed using the expression "fully and perfectly" to describe the status of Catholics.[147] Bishop Herculanus van der Burgt similarly suggested speaking of "full incorporation."[148] These notions of "fullness" or "perfection" implied the possibility of "less full" or "less perfect" incorporation, without denying some relationship with the church of Christ. The

---

and sometimes in discipline, or concerning the structure of the church—do indeed create many obstacles, sometimes serious ones, to full ecclesiastical communion" (UR 3).

142. In commenting on this sentence in *Unitatis Redintegratio* 3, Francis Sullivan remarks: "What we wish to point out here is that we can rightly speak of a certain though imperfect communion which links these ecclesial communities as such with the Catholic Church. For, as the conciliar commission insisted, they are not a mere sum of individual Christians. If their members are in communion with us by reason of the Christian faith and baptism, it is because their communities have preserved and handed on this faith to them and have initiated them into Christian life by baptism. Everything that justifies speaking of these communities as 'ecclesial' actually constitutes a bond of ecclesial communion linking them to the Catholic Church." Sullivan, *The Church We Believe In*, 61.

143. Grillmeier, "Chapter II: The People of God," 176.

144. AS II/1, 433–35, at 434. Emphasis added.

145. AS II/1, 183–200. The English translation here comes from Paul VI, "Opening Address: Second Session," 147. Emphasis added.

146. Grillmeier, "Chapter II: The People of God," 176.

147. AS II/2, 10. See the discussion of this in Wijlens, *Sharing the Eucharist*, 146–48.

148. AS II/2, 60.

final text of *Lumen Gentium* 14, speaking of "the Catholic faithful," ended up stating: "Fully incorporated [*incorporantur*] into the society of the church are those who, possessing the Spirit of Christ, accept its entire structure and all the means of salvation established within it and who in its visible structure are united [*iunguntur*] with Christ, who rules it through the Supreme Pontiff and the bishops, by the bonds of profession of faith, the sacraments, ecclesiastical government, and communion." Then, the article goes on to acknowledge that there can be a gradation in the degree to which even Catholics realize their baptismal status. For example, they may not "possess the Holy Spirit"; that is, they are not in the state of grace. Consequently, their relationship with the church cannot be described as "full."

This application to individual Catholics of full and less-than-full incorporation in the church opened up possibilities for conceiving non-Catholics' "incorporation" in the church in terms of lesser degrees of incorporation. While the next article (*Lumen Gentium* 15) does not use the image of "incorporation" to describe the relationship between the Catholic Church and other baptized Christians, it does employ the verb *conjungere* and the noun *coniunctio*. It begins by stating that the Catholic Church "is joined to [*coniunctam*] to the baptized who are honoured by the name of Christian." These other Christians, it says, "are sealed by Baptism by which they are joined [*coniunguntur*] to Christ"; there is among them "a true union [*vera coniunctio*] in the Holy Spirit, for by his gifts and graces, his sanctifying power is active in them also." Then, as we explored above, the article proceeds to outline the elements of the church evident in the lives of other Christians and "in their own churches or ecclesiastical communities."

The Decree on Ecumenism too speaks of full and lesser grades of relationship to the church, but not using the image of "incorporation"; rather, it uses the rubric of "communion." While *Lumen Gentium* certainly employs the notion of *communio* in its treatment of the mystery of the Catholic Church, *communio* ecclesiology is not its *explicit* framework for addressing the ecumenical issue. As Myriam Wijlens observes: "Even in its final version, *Lumen Gentium* does not use *communio* in a strict ecumenical sense. . . . The Decree on Ecumenism[, however,] uses *communio* in the ecumenical sense."[149] Therefore, rather than speaking of degrees of incorporation, the decree speaks of degrees of communion.

---

149. Wijlens, *Sharing the Eucharist*, 194–95. Similarly, Stransky notes: "*De Oecumenismo* does not stress the incorporation-imagery, because it prefers 'communion,' a richer and more patristic expression." Stransky, *The Decree on Ecumenism of the Second Vatican Council*, 24.

As Oskar Saier points out, in the decree "the council introduces *the new technical term 'communio* non *plena'* in order to understand the relationship between the Catholic church and non-Catholic Christians."[150] Importantly, "the counter-notion to *'communio,'* namely 'excommunication,' is not used, against all expectation."[151] The decree speaks of "full communion [*plena communio*]" in four different but overlapping ways: "the full communion of the Catholic Church [*plena communio ecclesiae catholicae*]" (UR 3); "full ecclesiastical communion [*plena ecclesiastica communio*]" (UR 3); "perfect ecclesiastical communion [*perfecta communio ecclesiastica*]" (UR 4); and "full catholic communion [*plena communio catholica*]" (UR 4).[152]

Because the church of Christ subsists in the Catholic Church, there is full communion between the particular churches within the Catholic Church; however, because certain churches and communities "became separated from full communion with the Catholic Church," there is "imperfect communion" with the Catholic Church, and "differences . . . of varying degrees" (UR 3).

The goal of the ecumenical movement is "*full* ecclesiastical communion [*plenae ecclesiasticae communioni*]" (UR 3). In the next article, the decree speaks of "*perfect* ecclesiastical communion [*perfectam communionem ecclesiasticam*]" (UR 4). An intertextual reading of the constitution alongside the decree reveals that, while the council's language is not consistent, certain terms are used in an overlapping sense. First, the terms "full" and "perfect" in the phrases "*full* communion" and "*perfect* communion" are to be understood synonymously. Second, the notions of "incorporation" and "communion" in the terms "fully incorporated" and "in full communion" are to be understood synonymously. According to Sullivan, "full incorporation [is] the same as full communion."[153]

Bonaventure Kloppenburg, in an intertextual reading of the various passages in the documents that speak of full and less-than-full incorporation or communion, summarizes the council's vision: "In the light of Vatican II, therefore, we may legitimately speak of a certain communion, imperfect union, less full communion, full communion, full incorporation, full unity, less full unity, imperfect unity, full and perfect unity, growing unity."[154] These

150. Saier, *"Communio" in der Lehre des Zweiten Vatikanischen Konzils,* 22. Emphasis added.
151. Ibid., 22.
152. For a discussion of these four instances, see ibid., 8–10.
153. Sullivan, *The Church We Believe In,* 56.
154. Kloppenburg, *The Ecclesiology of Vatican II,* 129–30. Kloppenburg adds that, in a speech to the Secretariat for Christian Unity on April 28, 1967, Paul VI even said that *"a basic unity*

distinctions enable the council to emphasize the "ecclesiality" of separated churches and ecclesial communities—and therefore their communion "in some way" (*in quadam communione*) with the Catholic Church—while acknowledging that there are varying degrees (*variis modis*) evident in the differences remaining in that relationship.

Francis Sullivan concludes: "If we understand the universal Church as essentially the communion of the particular churches 'in which and from which the universal Church has its existence' (LG 23a), and if one accepts the fact that in the actual state of divided Christianity, both these terms 'communion' and 'churches,' admit greater or less fullness, I believe that one can think of the universal Church as a communion, at various levels of fullness, of bodies that are more or less fully churches."[155] Thus, we can say, when hermeneutically attending to all elements of the council's comprehensive vision: at Vatican II there was first a recognition of "elements of the church of Christ" and, above all, a recognition of the communion other Christian communities experience with the triune God. This amounts to a recognition of their participation in the *communio fidelium* that constitutes the church of Christ. This then leads to a recognition of their participation (albeit analogously, in the case of the "ecclesial communities") in the *communio ecclesiarum,* those local communities in communion with the triune God. The council, therefore, was able to nuance further its notion of *communio ecclesiarum* by distinguishing between being in "full communion [*plena communio*]"—to describe the relationship of churches within the Catholic Church—and being "in some, though imperfect, communion [*in quadam etsi non perfecta communione*]"— to describe the relationship of other Christian churches and ecclesial communities to the Catholic Church, in which the one church of Christ subsists and with whom the "fullness of unity [*plenitudinem unitatis*]" (UR 4) is to be found. Not all communities have all the elements that make up the fullness of the church of Christ. For the communities separated from the Catholic Church, what is particularly lacking, and impelling toward full communion, is participation in the *communio hierarchica.*

In conclusion, the notion of *communio ecclesiarum* enabled the council not only to move toward a new way of conceiving the *ecclesia catholica* in terms of a *communio ecclesiarum* but also to move toward a new way of conceiving the *ecclesia Christi* in terms of a *communio ecclesiarum.* That is,

---

already exists between all baptized Christians by reason of their faith in Christ and the invocation of the Most Holy Trinity." Ibid., 130. Emphasis added.

155. Sullivan, "The Significance of the Vatican II Declaration," 283.

Vatican II moved toward a new way of reimagining the relationship between the Catholic Church (in which the church of Christ subsists) and the "separated churches and ecclesial communities" as a relationship of *communio* (albeit of varying degrees) within the church of Christ. As a way through the ecumenical impasse, this constitutes one of the great discoveries of Vatican II. Through it, the council found a way to imagine the Catholic Church's relationship with "the others," without compromising its own exclusive claim to being the church in which the church of Christ subsists. Heinrich Fries comments on the ecumenical significance of this discovery and the place that the phrase *subsistit in* has within that renewed ecumenical vision:

> Vatican II intended (and proved) to be a council of Church renewal; it intended through this renewal to pave the way for the reunification of divided Christendom. It was therefore decidedly ecumenical and, as such, had to confront the problem of "the Church and the Churches" in a new way. Previous magisterial decisions on the subject had proved unserviceable. They would have conceived of the reunification of divided Christendom as taking only one possible form: a return to the Roman Catholic Church in the form of an unconditional capitulation. For this they were not prepared. In the question of "the Church and the Churches" *Vatican II discovered a principle according to which the Church's identity and continuity were to be preserved not by separating off or denying everything that was not itself but by linking fidelity to itself with openness to others rather than with the denigration of others.*[156]

Along with the recognition of *elementa ecclesiae* in other communities and the consequent change to *subsistit in*, that the church of Christ can be understood, as least analogously, as a *communio ecclesiarum* and that there can be degrees of communion—but communion, nevertheless—between those "churches" became a whole new way of approaching the ecumenical problem. It opened up a new path to what the opening lines of the Decree on Ecumenism calls "the restoration of unity" (*unitatis redintegratio*).

"The Restoration of Unity": Purification, Reform, Dialogue

Gregory Baum observes that, while one may speak of "the 'institutional' perfection of the Catholic Church" in which the church of Christ subsists, "it is, of course, obvious that on her pilgrimage the Catholic Church is not and never will be, simply speaking, the perfect realization of Christ's Church.

---

156. Fries, "Church and Churches," 315–16.

The unfailing perfection of the Catholic Church lies in the authentic heritage of the doctrinal, sacramental and hierarchical gifts that the Holy Spirit preserves in her; in the dynamic possession or assimilation of these gifts, however, the Catholic Church is, according to the Constitution on the Church, in constant need of reform and purification."[157] Alois Grillmeier sees here a remarkable turnaround: "The Council abandoned most decidedly the Catholicism of the militant parade, and set itself constantly against all sorts of 'triumphalism.' Conscious though it is of the indefectibility of the institution founded by Christ, the pilgrim Church is fully aware of its duty of always having to become the Church in ever greater measure."[158]

Recognition of the need for purification, renewal and reform of the Catholic Church emerged at Vatican II not only from an acknowledged need for conversion away from sinfulness in church life. *Lumen Gentium* 15's recognition of the elements of the church in others also implies that the Catholic Church acknowledges the holiness and exemplary fidelity to the Gospel of non-Catholic Christians. Grillmeier states it simply: this article, in effect, reveals how the Catholic Church "is inspired by the example of other Churches and communities."[159] The decree likewise states:

> Catholics must gladly acknowledge and esteem the truly Christian endowments from our common heritage which are to be found among those separated from us. It is right and salutary to recognize the riches of Christ and virtuous works in the lives of others who are bearing witness to Christ. . . . [A]nything wrought by the grace of the Holy Spirit in the hearts of our separated brothers and sisters can contribute to our own edification. Whatever is truly Christian is never contrary to what genuinely belongs to the faith; indeed it can always bring a more perfect realization of the very mystery of Christ and the church (UR 4).

The witness of fidelity of those outside the Catholic Church thus becomes a stimulus to a greater fidelity on the part of Catholics themselves.

One important aspect of the council's humble recognition of the need for conversion to greater fidelity to the Gospel is its appropriation of the biblical notion of the pilgrim people of God, with its sense of incompletion on the way to attainment of perfection only at the end time. This concrete, yet eschatological, notion enabled Vatican II to move beyond, yet without rejecting,

---

157. Baum, "The Ecclesial Reality of the Other Churches," 39.
158. Grillmeier, "Chapter II: The People of God," 181.
159. Ibid., 180.

an ecclesiology focused on a juridical application of the biblical notion of the Body of Christ, as Pius XII's encyclical *Mystici Corporis* tended to do. The notions of the "People of God" and of the spiritual "communion" brought about by the Holy Spirit among that people were considered important from the perspective of the observers and guests sitting in the front rows of the council hall. In the decades before the council, the weaknesses of an over-emphasis on the concept of "the Mystical Body of Christ" had become apparent to Catholic theologians in the light of Protestant critique. Accordingly, as we have seen Joseph Ratzinger remark, "the concept of 'the people of God' was introduced by the Council above all as an ecumenical bridge."[160] What we have yet to explore is how, as Ratzinger goes on to show, the notion of the church as the people of God enabled the council to address the church's sinfulness and the need for ongoing purification and reform: "In this way the idea of reform became a decisive element in the concept of the people of God that could not have been developed in this way from the idea of the body of Christ."[161]

Lumen Gentium 8 affirms that the church of Christ subsists in the Catholic Church. Any temptation to triumphalism from this statement is abruptly corrected later in the article, with an acknowledgment that the Catholic Church is, nevertheless, always in need of purification: "The church . . . clasping sinners to its bosom, at once holy and always in need of purification [*ecclesia . . . semper purificanda*], follows constantly the path of penance and renewal" (LG 8). Then article 15, in reference to Christ's call for unity among Christians, recalls one of the key tasks of the council, that of ecumenical unity, repeating the call to purification: "Mother church never ceases to pray, hope and work that this [unity] may be achieved, and she exhorts her children to purification and renewal [*purificationem et renovationem*] so that the sign of Christ may shine more brightly over the face of the church" (LG 15). As Alois Grillmeier remarks on this passage: "The 'visage' of the Church is its whole visible existence, which, however, must never be taken in disjunction from its inner, invisible and hence impalpable reality. Here, obviously, we are at the heart of the Catholic understanding of the Church, and hence that of the Reformers. . . . [T]he Council understands the words, 'sign of Christ on the visage of the Church,' in the fullest sense of *an inward religious purification and renewal*."[162]

160. Ratzinger, "The Ecclesiology of the Second Vatican Council," 16.
161. Ibid.
162. Grillmeier, "Chapter II: The People of God," 180–81. Emphasis added.

The Decree on Ecumenism goes further, even using the Protestant word *reformatio*: in ecumenical dialogue, "all are led to examine their own faithfulness to Christ's will for the church and, wherever necessary undertake with vigor the task of renewal and reform [*renovationis . . . reformationis*]" (UR 4).[163] For Catholics in particular, it states, this must be a priority: "[Catholics'] primary duty is to make a careful and honest appraisal of whatever needs to be renewed [*renovanda*] and done in the catholic household itself, in order that its life may bear witness more clearly and more faithfully to the teachings and institutions which have been handed down from Christ through the apostles" (UR 4). It goes on: "For although the Catholic church has been endowed with all divinely revealed truth and with all means of grace, yet its members fail to live by them with all the fervor that they should. As a result, the radiance of the church's face shines less brightly in the eyes of our separated sisters and brothers and of the world at large, and the growth of God's kingdom is retarded" (UR 4). As Komonchak succinctly states it: "While 'the fullness of grace and truth' may have been entrusted to the Catholic Church, the degree to which they are received and lived can vary greatly. . . . The gifts of God account for the holiness of the Church; the failure to realize them fully accounts for her constant need of purification."[164]

Lumen Gentium devotes its fifth chapter to the universal call to holiness. With its notion of "spiritual ecumenism" (UR 8), *Unitatis Redintegratio* applies that call to the ecumenical movement, particularly to the Catholic Church's own commitment to "the restoration of unity." The notion of spiritual ecumenism captures the heart of the ecumenical movement as a call to conversion addressed to all churches and ecclesial communities. "Every renewal of the church essentially consists in an increase of fidelity to her own calling" (UR 6). Full ecclesial unity between separated churches and ecclesial communities will be realized only through a constantly renewed reception in faith by all Christians of God's foundational self-revelation in Christ through the Spirit. The decree states it starkly: "There can be no ecumenism worthy of the name without interior conversion. For it is from *newness of attitudes of mind* [*ex novitate mentis*], from self-denial and unstinted love, that desires of unity take their rise and develop in a mature way" (UR 7).[165] The text cites in a footnote Ephesians 4:23: "be renewed in the spirit of your

---

163. On these two terms, see Peter De Mey, "Church Renewal and Reform in the Documents of Vatican II: History, Theology, Terminology," *The Jurist* 71 (2011): 360–400.

164. Komonchak, *Who Are the Church?*, 74–75.

165. Tanner translates *novitas mentis* as "the renewal of our minds."

minds."[166] The next article (UR 8) parallels the notion of a new attitude of mind with the notion of a "*change of heart* [*cordis conversio*]." Both notions echo the gospel invocation of Jesus: *metanoiete*, "turn around your mind and heart" (Mark 1:15).[167] The decree immediately goes on to speak of this ecumenical application of the revelation/faith principle in terms of "spiritual ecumenism": "This change of heart and holiness of life, along with public and private prayer for the unity of Christians, should be regarded as the soul [*anima*] of the whole ecumenical movement, and merits the name, 'spiritual ecumenism'" (UR 8). We have seen how the conciliar revelation/faith principle encapsulates the council's pastoral desire to respond anew as a church to God's revelatory and saving outreach in Christ through the Spirit. In the decree, this faith response is simply stated as the desire "to live holier lives according to the Gospel": "The faithful should remember that they promote union among Christians better, that indeed they live it better, when they try to live holier lives according to the Gospel. For the closer their union with the Father, the Word, and the Spirit, the more deeply and easily will they be able to grow in mutual love" (UR 7).

Spiritual ecumenism relates, therefore, to what was above called *fides qua creditur*. That fundamental notion of loving relationship with God is related to the notion of *fides quae creditur*, human articulation of the content revealed in revelation. Having acknowledged an equality with other Christians on the level of intimacy with God in Christ through possessing the grace of the Holy Spirit, the decree acknowledges: "Without doubt, the differences that exist in varying degrees [*variis modis*] between them and the Catholic Church—whether in doctrine and sometimes in discipline, or concerning the structure of the church—do indeed create many obstacles, sometimes serious ones, to full ecclesiastical communion. The ecumenical movement is striving to overcome these obstacles" (UR 3).

In committing the Catholic Church to the ecumenical movement, Vatican II makes a commitment to one of the important means through which the differences between Christians can best be addressed: ecumenical dialogue. When the drafting of both *Lumen Gentium* and *Unitatis Redintegratio* was well advanced, Paul VI issued his encyclical *Ecclesiam Suam,* before the start

166. NRSV translation.

167. This text, however, is not cited or quoted in the Decree on Ecumenism, only alluded to. For the two instances where the council does cite Mark 1:15, see *Lumen Gentium* 5 and *Ad Gentes* 8.

of the third session (August 6, 1964).[168] Dialogue was its central leitmotif, eventually becoming a central leitmotif of the council itself. Throughout *Ecclesiam Suam*, the Latin word for "dialogue," used seventy-seven times, is *colloquium* and its cognates (the word *dialogus* does not appear at all).[169] In the final documents of Vatican II, however, there are two words used to refer to dialogue or conversation: *dialogus* and *colloquium*. The work of Ann Nolan shows that, with one exception, the documents refer to formal ecumenical dialogue between churches as *dialogus*.[170]

Ecumenical dialogue is both the result of and the stimulus for greater fidelity to the Gospel: "[In dialogue] all are led to examine their own faithfulness to Christ's will for the church and, wherever necessary, undertake with vigor the task of renewal and reform" (UR 4). Dialogue becomes a challenge to a newness of mind (*novitas mentis*) and a conversion of the heart (*conversio cordis*), the keys to "spiritual ecumenism." Both may require an openness to the possibility that the Holy Spirit has been the one who has brought forth in the other church or community this different doctrine, liturgical practice, or discipline: "Nor should we forget that anything wrought by the grace of the Holy Spirit in the hearts of our separated brothers and sisters can contribute to our own edification. Whatever is truly Christian is never contrary to what genuinely belongs to the faith; indeed it can always bring a more perfect realization of the very mystery of Christ and the church" (UR 4). Dialogue, therefore, should be open to the divine origin of difference and diversity in the other: "While preserving unity in essentials, let all in the church, according to the office entrusted to them, preserve a proper freedom in the various forms of spiritual life and discipline, in the variety [*diversitate*] of liturgical rites, and even in the theological elaborating of revealed truth. In all things let charity prevail. If they are true to this course of action, they will be giving ever richer expression to *the authentic catholicity and apostolicity of the church*" (UR 4).[171] The council here approaches the ecumenical question of "unity" also in terms of its related notion of "catholicity"—the catholicity of the church is diminished because of the lack of unity. Moreover, with regard to apostolicity, dialogue can be a challenge to self-examination with regard to one's own tradition's authentic apostolicity and fidelity to Scripture and tradition. In

168. For the English translation, see Pope Paul VI, *Ecclesiam Suam*.
169. For the Latin text, see http://w2.vatican.va/content/paul-vi/la/encyclicals/documents/hf_p-vi_enc_06081964_ecclesiam.html.
170. Nolan, *A Privileged Moment*, 177–223.
171. Emphasis added.

fact, Vatican II's ecumenical vision is a self-examination on the part of the Catholic Church with regard to all four marks of the church cited in the creed: unity, holiness, catholicity, and apostolicity.

With regard to the issue of difference and diversity, the mark of "catholicity" is especially relevant to ecumenical dialogue, since it is a counterbalance to a possible overemphasis on unity, in the form of "uniformity." The Vatican II documents use the word "catholicity" (*catholicitas*) eight times across only three documents, most times in the Decree on Ecumenism: *Lumen Gentium* (13, 23), *Unitatis Redintegratio* (4 [three times], 17), and *Ad Gentes* (1, 4). A classic text here is *Lumen Gentium* 13, which treats of the interrelationship between unity and catholicity, speaking of "legitimate differences [*legitimas varietates*]." As explored above in the unity/diversity principle, there was here a development in the mind of the council toward this greater recognition of catholicity as diversity, and not as uniformity.[172] The effects of this development are evident in the notion of catholicity in the Decree on Ecumenism. Reading the three instances of the word "catholicity" in *Unitatis Redintegratio* 4 intertextually, i.e., in relationship with the other instances of the word throughout the corpus, reveals a trajectory indicating an openness to explore, through ecumenical dialogue, whether the differences between the churches and ecclesial communities might well lead to a recognition among the broader *communio ecclesiarum* of "legitimate diversity" in doctrine, liturgy, and governance. Just as *Gaudium et Spes* 92 speaks of "legitimate diversity" within the Catholic Church, *Unitatis Redintegratio* 17 speaks of "legitimate diversity" outside the Catholic Church.

The Catholic ecumenist George Tavard, a *peritus* for the Secretariat during the council, certainly believed this to be the case. He raises the question:

> Among the positions that could be adopted by Catholic theology, is there one that would regard the Reformation, not only as a providential movement that somehow went awry, but as the proposal of a valid alternative? Can Anglican theology in the main lines of the Elizabethan settlement, Lutheran theology as Luther proposed it or as embodied in the *Confession Augustana* [*sic*], Calvinist theology as Calvin expounded it in his major works, be considered valid

172. The 1963 draft of this article had presented catholicity in terms exclusively of universality. An intervention from the White Father missionary Archbishop Antoine Grauls of Gitega, Burundi, called for a greater recognition in the text of the diverse contexts within which the Gospel must be proclaimed. This was incorporated into the next revision of this part of the article. The *peritus* Yves Congar was given responsibility for the revision. For Grauls's speech, see AS II/2, 69–70.

ways of formulating the mystery of Christ? Can the reforms of doctrine, liturgy, and Church structure operated under the impact of the main Reformers be recognized in the Catholic Church as legitimate applications of the principle of Christian freedom in pursuit of a better understanding and practice of the gospel?[173]

Certainly, the council teaches, in the text quoted above: "While preserving unity in essentials . . . preserve a proper freedom . . . even in the theological elaborating of revealed truth" (UR 4). Here one of the council's groundbreaking statements—on the " 'hierarchy' of truths"—presents the challenge: "in ecumenical dialogue, Catholic theologians, standing fast by the teaching of the church yet searching together with separated brothers and sisters in the divine mysteries, should do so with love for the truth, with charity, and with humility. When comparing doctrines with one another there exists an order or 'hierarchy' of truths, since they vary in their relation to *the foundation of the Christian faith*. Thus the way will be opened whereby this kind of friendly rivalry [*fraternam aemulationem*] will incite all to a realization and clearer expression of *the unfathomable riches of Christ*" (UR 11).[174]

The "foundation of the Christian faith" is nowhere defined in the documents, but from the comprehensive vision of the council it can be found expressed in four interrelated doctrines of Christian belief: Incarnation, Trinity, Salvation, Grace. The church is called to be a sacrament mediating the divine encounter with humanity encapsulated in these foundational truths. The notion of a hierarchy of truths, rather than appealing to a relativism in Christian truth, is a demand to ground all affirmations of belief and practice on this foundation of Christian truth: the reality of the eternal God reaching

---

173. Tavard, "Reassessing the Reformation," 366.

174. Emphasis added. On the council's debates and final teaching regarding the hierarchy of truths, see Ulrich Valeske, *Hierarchia Veritatum: Theologiegeschichtliche Hintergründe und mögliche Konsequenzen eines Hinweises im Ökumenismusdekret des II. Vatikanischen Konzils zum zwischenkirchlichen Gespräch* (München: Claudius Verlag, 1968); Yves Congar, "On the Hierarchia Veritatum," in *The Heritage of the Early Church*, ed. David Neiman and Margaret Schatken (Rome: Pont. Institutum Orientalium, 1973), 409–20; William Henn, *The Hierarchy of Truths according to Yves Congar, O.P.* (Roma: Editrice Pontificia Università Gregoriana, 1987); Karl Rahner, "A Hierarchy of Truths," in *Theological Investigations*, vol. 21 (London: Darton, Longman & Todd, 1988), 21:162–67; George H. Tavard, " 'Hierarchia Veritatum': A Preliminary Investigation," *Theological Studies* 32 (1971): 278–89; Beinert, "Hierarchy of Truths." On the notion of "truth" presented throughout the conciliar corpus, see Mathijs Lamberigts and Karim Schelkens, "Some Remarks on the Notion of Truth in the Documents of Vatican II," in *Orthodoxy, Process and Product*, ed. Mathijs Lamberigts, Lieven Boeve, and Terrence Merrigan (Walpole, MA: Peeters, 2009), 205–28.

out to humanity in history in Jesus Christ through the Holy Spirit. In other words, the notion of the hierarchy of truths is but another formulation of the primary revelation/faith principle, which ultimately guided the council's pastoral agenda. Here, as an element of the Catholic/ecumenical principle, it is a call to Catholic theologians, and to the Catholic Church as a whole, to see other Christians and their beliefs in the light of this primary principle.

The Decree on Ecumenism is something more than just a conciliar "text"; it is a "deed," a performative action. Yves Congar believed that the Decree on Ecumenism "has bearings comparable to the great historical decisions that have decided the course of events for centuries afterwards."[175] Its historical meaning is broken open by symbolic gestures, such as the presence of the observers and guests in the council hall, the meeting of Paul VI and Athenagoras in Jerusalem, and, on the last working day of the council, the mutual withdrawal of excommunications between Rome and Constantinople.

Paul VI, in his opening address at the second session, had spoken of the unknown future and of trust that God will lead Christians to find a way through the difficulties that ecumenical engagement brings: "And should historical reality tend to weaken our hopes, we shall try to recall the comforting words of Christ: 'Things that are impossible with men are possible with God' (Luke 18:27)."[176] As Otto Hermann Pesch observes: "The Second Vatican Council did not point out any concrete path to unity of the Church; it did not even open up more territory in which to look for a path."[177] What it did point out, however, was the need to be open to the promptings of the Holy Spirit and to trust that a way would be found for fulfilling Christ's will that all should be one, in the way Christ would will it. In its final article, the decree displays this open-ended trust: "Now . . . we confidently look to the future. . . . This holy council firmly hopes that the initiatives of the sons and daughters of the Catholic Church, joined with those of their separated brothers and sisters, will go forward, *without obstructing the ways of divine*

175. *Concile oecuménique Vatican II: Constitutions, décrets, déclarations, messages, texte français et latin, tables biblique et analytiques et index des sources* (Paris: Centurion, 1967), 189–90. The translation here is taken from Maurice Villain, "The Debate about the Decree on Ecumenism," *Concilium* 4, no. 2 (April 1966): 59–69, at 61.

176. Paul VI, "Opening Address: Second Session," 148.

177. Pesch, *The Second Vatican Council*, 195.

Providence, and *without prejudicing the future inspirations of the Holy Spirit*" (UR 24).[178] Pesch remarks on the council's confidence that the way of ecumenical dialogue especially will enable the future inspirations of the Holy Spirit to emerge: "The Council trusts that ways to unity will evince themselves in this dialogue, under the guidance of the Holy Spirit, ways that now we might at best just be able to glimpse. The very devotion to the doctrine of the Church is entrusted, even delivered over to, the work of the Spirit in this dialogue."[179]

178. Emphasis added.
179. Pesch, *The Second Vatican Council*, 208.

Principle 23

Christian/Religious

Principle 23: Eschewing past ways of relating to adherents of Judaism and non-Christian religions that lead to enmity and division among human beings, the church of Christ best witnesses faithfully to Jesus Christ not only in word but in deed, by seeking unity despite differences in belief; acknowledging God's revelatory and saving presence in the lives of other believers, and engaging with them in love and in dialogue, the church commits itself to a new way of acting and relating that sacramentally makes present the God of Jesus Christ, who seeks the salvation of all and respects the religious freedom of all.

Soon after Pope John announced in 1959 that he would be convoking an ecumenical council, Yves Congar wrote of a new awareness that he sensed characterized the times in which the council would meet: "This new awareness of the existence of 'Others,' this need to take an interest in them, is one of the most characteristic traits of the present generation of Christians."[1] If the Catholic/ecumenical principle had its origins in shifts that were taking place before Vatican II convened, the council's Christian/religious principle emerged initially from Pope John and then from within the council and the Secretariat for Promoting Christian Unity. The specific document the council would end up promulgating on the theme, *Nostra Aetate*, is the shortest of all, a mere five articles, yet its drafting generated some of the most intense debates and background intrigue of all the council. Other conciliar documents touch on and develop the principle. But the tortuous history of *Nostra Aetate*'s birth reveals the neuralgic nature of the topic the council was dealing

---

1. Yves Congar, "Le Concile, l'Eglise et . . . 'les Autres,' " *Lumière et Vie* 45 (November–December 1959): 69–92, at 74. Translation from Mauro Velati, " 'The Others': Ecumenism and Religions," in *Vatican II: A Forgotten Future? Concilium 2005/4*, ed. Alberto Melloni and Christoph Theobald (London: SCM Press, 2005), 35–47, at 35.

with and the dramatic shift in sensibility and perspective that its final Christian/religious principle encapsulates.

The previous chapter has already outlined the long history of the axiom *extra ecclesiam nulla salus*. In a blanket exclusion from salvation of all "outside" the Roman Catholic Church, the axiom groups together Christian schismatics and heretics, Jews, adherents of other religions, and nonbelievers. There was no distinction here between other baptized Christians and the nonbaptized; nor was there a distinction between Jews and believers of other religions, whether monotheistic or otherwise. Just as the Catholic/ecumenical principle articulated a Catholic discovery of genuine Christian otherness and of God's saving activity within all the baptized of the church of Christ, so too the Christian/religious principle would come to articulate a Catholic discovery of genuine religious otherness and of God's saving activity outside the church of Christ. The initial catalyst for that discovery would be a conversion to a new way of seeing the relationship between the church of Christ and the religion out of which it had grown and with whom it continues to be closely related, as witnessed in its "Old Testament"—the religion of Judaism. This conversion would also require Catholic Christians to confront the question whether Christian anti-Judaism had contributed to the antisemitism that ended in the evils of the Shoah.

"The Jewish Question" on the Eve of the Council

The bishops who gathered for the Second Vatican Council were only too aware of the dark history of Christian-Jewish relations and of the evils perpetrated against Jews during the Second World War, which had ended only seventeen years before the start of the council. The Nuremberg trials had been held between November 20, 1945, and October 1, 1946. Strangely, however, such revelations of the horrors of the Shoah did not immediately shake Christians into taking a new perspective on their relationship to the Jewish people and to Judaism. As John Connelly observes of those immediate years after the war:

> For the time being, anti-Judaism remained intact, and Christians saw no reason to examine Christianity for its support of antisemitism. For one thing, Nazi violence went beyond the Jews, and even if the Nazis used Christian arguments for measures taken against Jews, that could not explain the killing of millions of other human beings, for example the Gypsies. For another thing, the Nazis had sought to destroy Christianity, and from the moment the European churches emerged from the war, they portrayed themselves as victims, even

in Germany. Like the Jews, they suffered the violence of the pagan juggernaut and sacrificed priests and pastors in the Nazi camps.[2]

The evils of the Shoah slowly, however, began to impinge on Christian minds. Yves Congar, in his council diary for March 16, 1963, after meeting the Jewish community of Strasbourg, recorded the view they expressed to him: "The first Council to be held after Auschwitz cannot say nothing about these things."[3]

Out of this history emerged at least five fundamental questions that were live issues on the eve of the council. (1) Can the Jewish people be accused of "deicide" because of the death of Jesus Christ? (2) With the coming of the church of Christ, were the Jewish people thereby rejected as God's chosen people and the Jewish religion thereby "superseded" by the Christian religion? (3) Does the Christian faith continue to be related in some way with the Jewish faith out of which it grew and whose scriptures it continues to venerate and use every day? (4) Is it legitimate for Christians to undertake a "mission to the Jews," seeking their conversion to Christianity? (5) Has anti-Judaism contributed to antisemitism on the part of Christians throughout history? These five questions had long plagued the relationship between the Jewish people and Judaism and the Christian church. And they were being asked with greater urgency throughout the twentieth century, by both Christians and Jews.

The story of a shift among many Christians to a new perspective on these matters includes prophetic voices among Catholics in the first half of the twentieth century. For example, Karl Thieme was a Protestant who, in the early 1930s, was outspoken about Nazi policies against the Jews as well as the capitulation of Protestant churches to those policies. In 1934, Thieme and a group of his friends converted to Catholicism. Threatened in Germany, he moved to Switzerland, where he lived until the end of the war, waging his own war against antisemitism. He "became the most influential Catholic writer on the Jewish question in the twentieth century."[4]

Thieme soon came in contact with another prophetic figure at the time, an Austrian Jew, who had converted to Catholicism and became a priest. Johannes (later "John") Oesterreicher was on a similar quest to combat

2. John Connelly, *From Enemy to Brother: The Revolution in Catholic Teaching on the Jews, 1933–1965* (Cambridge, MA: Harvard University Press, 2012), 175.

3. Congar, *My Journal of the Council*, 283.

4. Connelly, *From Enemy to Brother*, 121.

428 *Ecclesiological Principles*

antisemitism within Catholicism, as exemplified by the ambiguous views of the Jesuit provincial in Austria in the 1930s, Georg Bichlmair.[5] Thieme and Oesterreicher were also united in their conviction "that the church's relation to the Jews should be ecumenical, not missionary."[6] After moving to the United States, Oesterreicher was involved in founding the Institute of Judeo-Christian Studies in Seton Hall University, and would eventually work within the Secretariat for the Promotion of the Unity of Christians, participating in the drafting of *Nostra Aetate*.

Each in their own way, and together through their interaction, Thieme and Oesterreicher set out "to undo the anti-Judaism on which antisemitism thrived."[7] Mary Boys sees in them trailblazers within the Catholic world: "Catholics like Thieme and Oesterreicher who were interested in relations with Jews in the 1950's were, as Michael Phayer writes, like 'sixteenth-century scientists who suspected the sun did not revolve around the earth but could not explain heliocentrism.' Yet they and others with whom they collaborated had begun articulating the basic elements of an ecclesiastical heliocentrism, that is, the theological groundwork for *Nostra Aetate* no. 4."[8] In other words, they began approaching the mystery of Judaism and Christianity from a theology of God, rather than from a narrow theology of the church. Now, God is made center.

Another important factor in this shift in perspective in the decades before the council was a shift in biblical scholarship regarding St. Paul's letter to the Romans, especially chapters 9–11, which speak of the mystery of Israel. Here the influence on Catholic exegetes of the Swiss Reformed scholar, Karl Barth, is crucial. Barth's interpretation of Romans 11:29 in the *Church Dogmatics* shifted over the decades to emphasizing its relevance to God's past, present, and future love for the Jewish chosen people.[9] Barth's exegesis would have an impact on the *periti* of Vatican II: "Certainly [John Oesterreicher] and other members of the committee that drafted *Nostra Aetate* were familiar with Barth's *Church Dogmatics* even before [the council]."[10]

---

5. See ibid., 5–6, 22–27.

6. Ibid., 126.

7. Ibid., 7.

8. Mary C. Boys, "What *Nostra Aetate* Inaugurated: A Conversion to the 'Providential Mystery of Otherness,'" *Theological Studies* 74 (2013): 73–104, at 84.

9. See Joseph Sievers, "How Irrevocable? Interpreting Romans 11:29 from the Church Fathers to the Second Vatican Council," *Gregorianum* 87, no. 4 (2006): 748–61, at 754–57.

10. Ibid., 757.

Despite these positive voices, however, it cannot be said that, on the eve of Vatican II, there was a groundswell calling for change in the church's official attitude to the Jews and Judaism, or to non-Christian believers and their religions. Michael Fitzgerald observes: "There were, it is true, some pioneers who were advocating a more open attitude towards the followers of other religions, and the churches in the Middle East and in Asia were accustomed to living out their Christian faith in a milieu marked by other religions. Yet, there was in the church at large no strong movement promoting interfaith dialogue (comparable to the biblical, liturgical, and ecumenical movements), which could have provided a stimulus for treating this theme."[11] The dynamics generated by Vatican II itself would become that stimulus.

Before the council met, there had already been various statements made on "the Jewish question" by significant religious groups. For example, a group calling itself the "International Council of Christians and Jews" came together, in direct reaction to the horror of the Holocaust (or Shoah); among this group was a French secular Jew, Jules Isaac, who would come to play a pivotal role in challenging the Second Vatican Council to address the question of the Jews and the Catholic Church. At its second conference in the Swiss town of Seelisberg in 1947, the group produced a list of proposals for Christian teaching in the future, which, if heeded, would avoid a repetition of the Holocaust. The statement became known as "The Ten Points of Seelisberg."[12] It is difficult to choose just one example from among the ten statements. Perhaps the tenth is the most compelling: "Avoid speaking of the Jews as if the first members of the Church had not been Jews."

Another significant statement came from the first assembly of the World Council of Churches meeting in Amsterdam in 1948. It resolved: "We call upon all the Churches we represent to denounce anti-Semitism, no matter what its origin, as absolutely irreconcilable with the profession and practice of the Christian faith. Anti-Semitism is a sin against God and man. Only as we give convincing evidence to our Jewish neighbors that we seek for them the common rights and dignities which God wills for his children, can we come to such a meeting with them as would make it possible to share with them the

11. Michael L. Fitzgerald, "Vatican II and Interfaith Dialogue," in *Interfaith Dialogue: Global Perspectives*, ed. Edmund Kee-Fook Chia (New York: Palgrave Macmillan, 2016), 3–15.

12. From multiple sources for this document, one could access http://www.ccjr.us/dialogika-resources/documents-and-statements/roman-catholic/second-vatican-council/naprecursors/1231-seelisberg-1. Other statements that could be cited are the "Schwalbach Theses" and the "Theses for Evanston," which Karl Thieme wrote, from the same website.

best which God has given us in Christ."[13] At its third assembly in New Delhi in 1961, the World Council of Churches repeated its earlier statement, adding: "The Assembly urges its member Churches to do all in their power to resist every form of anti-Semitism. In Christian teaching the historic events which led to the Crucifixion should not be so presented as to fasten upon the Jewish people of today responsibilities which belong to our corporate humanity, not to one race or community. Jews were the first to accept Jesus, and Jews are not the only ones who do not yet recognize him."[14] But would there be some similar statement from the forthcoming Second Vatican Council?

Undoubtedly "the decisive impulse" for a statement by the council on the Jews was the resolve of Pope John XXIII.[15] When the future pope was apostolic nuncio in Bulgaria and Turkey during World War II, he had been instrumental in protecting Jews; moreover, once elected pope, he removed the words *perfidus* and *perfidia iudaica* from the Good Friday liturgy. Even so, when he called the Second Vatican Council, he had not envisioned that it should produce a statement on Catholics and Jews.

It seems that the pivotal change in that regard came after an encounter the pope had on June 13, 1960. Jules Isaac had come to Rome, requesting an audience with the pope. He had references from the local Catholic bishop in the town where he lived. Isaac's wife, daughter, and son-in-law had died in Auschwitz.[16] He had written on the Christian roots of antisemitism, what he called "the theology of contempt."[17]

An audience was granted. When Isaac met the pope, he presented him with a dossier of his writings, as well as the Ten Points of Seelisberg which

---

13. Quoted in John M. Oesterreicher, "Declaration on the Relationship of the Church to Non-Christian Religions: Introduction and Commentary," in *Commentary on the Documents of Vatican II*, vol. 3, ed. Herbert Vorgrimler (New York: Herder, 1969), 1–136, at 43–44.

14. Quoted in ibid., 44. Other statements from Christian churches included the theses proposed at a meeting at Bad Schwalbach in 1950 and the statement of the Lutheran World Federation, meeting at Løgumkloster, Denmark, in 1964.

15. Reinhard Neudecker, "The Catholic Church and the Jewish People," in *Vatican II: Assessment and Perspectives. Twenty-five Years After (1962–1987)*, ed. René Latourelle (New York: Paulist Press, 1989), 3:282–323, at 283.

16. See the account in Jules Isaac, "Note on a Week in Rome," *SIDIC: Service International de Documentation Judéo-Chrétienne* 1, no. 3 (1968): 11–13. See also Oesterreicher, "Declaration on the Relationship of the Church to Non-Christian Religions," 2–4; Marco Morselli, "Jules Isaac and the Origins of *Nostra Aetate*," in *Nostra Aetate: Origins, Promulgation, Impact on Jewish-Catholic Relations*, ed. Neville Lamdan and Alberto Melloni (Berlin: LIT Verlag, 2007), 21–28.

17. See the English translation of Jules Isaac, *The Teaching of Contempt: Christian Roots of Anti-Semitism* (New York: Holt, Rinehart and Winston, 1964).

he had played a part in drafting. Isaac's journal, recorded shortly after the meeting, captures some of the content of his pitch to the pope, the specific request that Isaac made, and the promise that the pope, in return, also made:

> Today there exists a purifying counter-current which grows stronger every day. However, recent inquiries have shown that "the teaching of contempt" still remains. Between these two contrary tendencies Catholic opinion is divided, remains floating. This is why it is indispensable that there be raised a voice from the highest possible level, from the "summit"—the voice of the head of the Church—to point out the right direction to everyone, and solemnly condemn "the teaching of contempt" in its anti-Christian essence. . . . Then I present my *Note conclusive* and the suggestion to create a sub-committee to study the question. The pope immediately responds, "Since the beginning of our conversation I've thought of that." Several times during my brief talk he had shown his understanding and sympathy. . . . But it's the end. . . . In telling him of all my gratitude for his welcome, I ask if I can carry away a bit of hope. He cries, "You have a right to more than hope!" Smiling, he adds, "I'm the chief, but I must also consult, have the offices study the questions raised. It isn't an absolute monarchy here." And we say good-bye, again simply shaking hands.[18]

According to Stjepan Schmidt, "prior to Jules Isaac's audience [Pope John] had never thought that the Council should address this subject."[19] The journey to *Nostra Aetate* had begun; Jewish-Catholic relations would soon be on the council's agenda. Both Jules Isaac and John XXIII would die three years later, however, after the first year of the council's deliberations. The progress through the coming council of a document on the Jews would be significantly dependent on a third person, Augustin Bea.

Toward the end of Isaac's conversation with John XXIII, in order to ensure that his assurances not be lost, the pope asked Isaac to set up a meeting with Cardinal Bea on the matters raised in the dossier Isaac had presented. That meeting took place within two days. Three months later, Bea requested a meeting with Pope John. As the cardinal recalls it: "Pope John XXIII received me in audience on 18 September, 1960 and charged the Secretariat for Christian Unity with the task of preparing a Declaration dealing with the Jewish

---

18. Isaac, "Note on a Week in Rome," 12–13. On Isaac's request to set up "a papal committee to study 'The Jewish Question,'" see Thomas Stransky, "The Genesis of *Nostra Aetate*: An Insider's Story," in *Nostra Aetate: Origins, Promulgation, Impact on Jewish-Catholic Relations*, ed. Neville Lamdan and Alberto Melloni (Berlin: LIT Verlag, 2007), 29–53, at 31.

19. Schmidt, *Augustin Bea*, 332n91. Schmidt is drawing on the comment in the memoirs of Pope John's personal secretary, Loris Capovilla.

people."[20] According to Thomas Stransky, it was in fact Bea who had proposed the idea that the Secretariat prepare a document on the Jews for consideration by the forthcoming council. As Stransky emphatically records it: "Upon *Bea's initiative and recommendation*, John XXIII mandated that the SPCU facilitate 'the Jewish Question' during the Council preparations."[21]

Bea began seeking formal relations with the secular and religious Jewish communities.[22] Jesuit colleagues in Rome suggested he start with "the Jewish Pope," Nahum Goldmann, who was a central figure in the major international Jewish organizations.[23] Despite the difference between secular and religious Jewish perspectives, and the diversity among Judaism (Orthodox, Conservative, Reform), a relationship began building through the medium of the Secretariat. "After so many centuries, Jews finally had a friendly address and official listening post in the Vatican."[24]

In this preparatory period, some theological institutions and groups of Jews and Christians around the world sent in requests for the council to address the relationship between the Catholic Church and Jews. Three examples can be selected.[25] Nineteen Jesuit priests teaching at the Pontifical Biblical Institute in Rome submitted a petition that the council address the issue and provided clarification on biblical texts that had often been misused regarding the Jews and Judaism. Thirteen priests teaching at the Institute of Judaeo-Christian Studies of Seton Hall University, including John Oesterreicher, sent a statement of essential points the group felt the council should address, all related to working toward better relations and understanding between Catholics and Jews. Perhaps the most substantial of the submissions came from an international study group of priests and laypeople who had been meeting regularly in the Dutch town of Apeldoorn. Each member of

20. Augustin Bea, *The Church and the Jewish People: A Commentary on the Second Vatican Council's Declaration on the Relation of the Church to Non-Christian Religions* (London: Geoffrey Chapman, 1966), 22.

21. Stransky, "The Genesis of *Nostra Aetate*," 32. Original emphasis.

22. See Michael Attridge, "The Struggle for *Nostra Aetate*: The 'Quaestione Ebraica' from 1960–62: Issues and Influences," in *La Théologie catholique entre intransigeance et renouveau: La réception des mouvements préconciliaires à Vatican II*, ed. Gilles Routhier et al. (Louvain-La-Neuve; Leuven: Collège Érasme; Universiteitsbibliotheek, 2011), 213–30.

23. Stransky, "The Genesis of *Nostra Aetate*," 51. Goldmann was president of the World Jewish Congress and co-chairman of the World Conference of Jewish Organizations.

24. Ibid., 39.

25. On these three submissions, see Oesterreicher, "Declaration on the Relationship of the Church to Non-Christian Religions," 8–17. The texts of the following three documents (and others) can be found at http://www.ccjr.us/dialogika-resources/documents-and-statements /roman-catholic/second-vatican-council/naprecursors.

the so-called Apeldoorn group represented a publication or group founded for the purpose of promoting reconciliation between Christians and Jews. John Oesterreicher and Karl Thieme were members of this group. All three of these, and other submissions, were important resources for the Secretariat as it began preparing a document for consideration by the council.

The Drafting History of *Nostra Aetate*

In the council's antepreparatory stage, a letter had been sent out to the world's bishops seeking their suggestions for the council's agenda. In the replies that came in, the issue of the church's relationship with the Jews did not feature significantly, nor did the issue of the church's relationship with non-Christians religions. By the time the council met, the composition of the conciliar assembly showed diverse perspectives on the issue of the Jews. Cardinal Edward Cassidy summarizes the differing starting points on the issue among the council members:

> For the council fathers coming from Europe and North America, relations with the Jewish people were of particular interest, especially as a consequence of their treatment by the Germans during the Second World War. Bishops from other parts of the world at first found it difficult to understand what the fuss was all about, since many of them had very few Jews in their countries and only a vague knowledge of the horrors of the *Shoah*. On the other hand, relations with other world religions were of particular concern to bishops from Asia and Africa, but far less to those from Europe and the Americas.[26]

Opposition to a positive statement on the Jews and Judaism would come mainly from two distinct groups. First, Eastern Catholic bishops in predominantly Muslim countries of the Middle East and Egypt feared their Catholic communities would suffer because of a perceived official approval by the Vatican for the political state of Israel. Their pastoral fears were real, and their opposition to *Nostra Aetate* over the next three years would be constantly voiced for this reason, as well as for the fact that their liturgical rites had texts that openly blamed the Jews for the death of Jesus. Second, there was a deeper, and more sinister, opposition at work, one that would be working alongside the opposition of the Arab bishops but using the differing motives of others for their own ends. This was the dark shadow cast across the council's proceedings of a "Catholic antisemitism" that motivated a small

---

26. Edward Idris Cassidy, *Ecumenism and Interreligious Dialogue: Unitatis Redintegratio, Nostra Aetate* (New York: Paulist Press, 2005), 128.

minority of the bishops in the council hall. They would not, in the end, prevail, but their machinations would succeed somewhat in depleting *Nostra Aetate* of its more pungent points.

According to John O'Malley: "Few issues ignited such bitter controversy both inside and outside the council as the relationship of the church to the Jews, and then to other religions. Few of the documents, that is to say, bumped along on such a rough road as *Nostra Aetate*."[27] It is a story of how a statement on "the Jews" became a statement on "the other religions," including Judaism.[28] There would eventually be seven versions of a text.[29]

27. O'Malley, *What Happened at Vatican II*, 6–7. For the history of the debates and drama, see Soetens, "The Ecumenical Commitment of the Catholic Church," 275–88; Vilanova, "The Intersession (1963–1964)," 380, 430–31; Giovanni Miccoli, "Two Sensitive Issues: Religious Freedom and the Jews," in *History of Vatican II*, vol. 4: *The Church as Communion; Third Period and Third Intersession, September 1964–September 1965*, ed. Giuseppe Alberigo and Joseph A. Komonchak (Maryknoll, NY: Orbis Books, 2004), 4:95–193, at 135–93; Riccardo Burigana and Giovanni Turbanti, "The Intersession: Preparing the Conclusion of the Council," in *History of Vatican II*, vol. 4: *The Church as Communion; Third Period and Third Intersession, September 1964–September 1965*, ed. Giuseppe Alberigo and Joseph A. Komonchak (Maryknoll, NY: Orbis Books, 2004), 453–615, at 546–59; Mauro Velati, "Completing the Conciliar Agenda," in *History of Vatican II*, vol. 5: *The Council and the Transition; The Fourth Period and the End of the Council, September 1965–December 1965*, ed. Giuseppe Alberigo and Joseph A. Komonchak (Maryknoll, NY: Orbis Books, 2006), 5:185–273, at 211–21.

28. Specifically on the drafting history, see Oesterreicher, "Declaration on the Relationship of the Church to Non-Christian Religions"; Georges Cottier, "L'historique de la Déclaration," in *Les relations de l'Eglise avec les religions non chrétiennes: Déclaration "Nostra aetate." Texte latin et traduction française*, ed. Antonin-Marcel Henry (Paris: Editions du Cerf, 1966), 37–78; Roman A. Siebenrock, "Theologischer Kommentar zur Erklärung über die Haltung der Kirche zu den nichtchristlichen Religionen, *Nostra Aetate*," in *Herders theologischer Kommentar zum Zweiten Vatikanischen Konzil. Band 3*, ed. Peter Hünermann and Bernd Jochen Hilberath (Freiburg: Herder, 2005), 3:591–693, at 633–43. Another translation of Oesterreicher's original German commentary can be found in John M. Oesterreicher, *The New Encounter between Christians and Jews* (New York: Philosophical Library, 1986), 103–295. For briefer histories, see Mathijs Lamberigts and Leo Declerck, "Vatican II on the Jews: A Historical Survey," in *Never Revoked: Nostra Aetate as Ongoing Challenge for Jewish-Christian Dialogue*, ed. Marianne Moyaert and Didier Pollefeyt (Grand Rapids: Eerdmans, 2010), 13–56; Mathijs Lamberigts, "Nostra Aetate 2, Vatican II on Hinduism and Buddhism: A Historical Survey," in *The Living Legacy of Vatican II: Studies from an Indian Perspective*, ed. Paul Pulikkan (Bengaluru, India: ATC Publishers, 2017), 159–85; John Borelli, "*Nostra Aetate*: Origin, History, and Vatican II Context," in *The Future of Interreligious Dialogue: A Multi-Religious Conversation on Nostra Aetate*, ed. Charles L. Cohen, Paul F. Knitter, and Ulrich E. Rosenhagen (Maryknoll, NY: Orbis Books, 2017), 23–43.

29. For a synopsis of only the four major versions, see Francisco Gil Hellín, ed., *Declaratio de Ecclesiae habitudine ad religionis non-christianas, Nostra aetate: Concilii Vaticani II synopsis in ordinem redigens schemata cum relationibus necnon patrum orationes atque animadversiones* (Roma: Pontificia Universitas Sanctae Crucis, 2013). For English translations of these drafts,

Parallel to this drama would be another, concerning the closely related issue of religious freedom and the dignity of conscience. Just as in the drafting histories of *Nostra Aetate* and *Dignitatis Humanae*—when the conversation on one text was being "overheard" in the conversation on the other—so too these two texts in their final form remain in "intertextual" conversation.[30]

After Pope John had authorized Cardinal Bea on September 18, 1960, to prepare a statement for the council on the Jews, Bea then entrusted the task to Father John Oesterreicher, the same Oesterreicher who had been in debate with fellow German Karl Thieme. Oesterreicher initially gathered an international group of four scholars: himself, Gregory Baum, Leo Rudloff, and George Tavard. Meeting several times in New Jersey, the group drafted for the Secretariat a study document they titled "Questions Concerning the Jews" (*Questiones de Iudaeis*).[31] The Secretariat soon set up a subcommittee to prepare a document for eventual inclusion on the council's agenda. With Oesterreicher playing a key role, the subcommittee prepared a draft titled "Decree on the Jews" (*Decretum de Iudaeis*). A warmth pervades this document that will be lost in later versions; it states that the church "acknowledges with a heart full of gratitude" the church's origins in the faith from the Jewish

---

see the website Dialogika of St Joseph's University's Institute for Jewish-Catholic Relations: http://www.ccjr.us/dialogika-resources/documents-and-statements/roman-catholic/second -vatican-council/na-drafts. They are also available at the website of Boston College's Center for Jewish-Christian Learning: https://www.bc.edu/content/dam/files/research_sites/cjl/texts /cjrelations/resources/education/NA_draft_history.htm. For just the section on the Jews and Judaism in these seven versions in English, see Maria Brutti, "Drafts Leading to the Conciliar Declaration Nostra Aetate," *in The Catholic Church and the Jewish People: Recent Reflections from Rome*, ed. Philip A. Cunningham, Norbert J. Hofmann, and Joseph Sievers (New York: Fordham University Press, 2007), 191–200.

30. The next chapter will trace the redaction history of *Dignitatis Humanae*. For more on that history, see Silvia Scatena, *La fatica della libertà: L'elaborazione della dichiarazione "Dignitatis humanae" sulla libertà religiosa del Vaticano II* (Bologna: Il Mulino, 2003); Pietro Pavan, "Declaration on Religious Freedom," in *Commentary on the Documents of Vatican II*, vol. 4, ed. Herbert Vorgrimler (New York: Herder, 1969), 4:49–86, at 49–62; Roman A. Siebenrock, "Theologischer Kommentar zur Erklärung über die religiöse Freiheit," in *Herders theologischer Kommentar zum Zweiten Vatikanischen Konzil*, ed. Peter Hünermann and Bernd Jochen Hilberath (Freiburg: Herder, 2005), 4:125–218, at 152–65; Nicholas J. Healy, "The Drafting of *Dignitatis Humanae*," in *Freedom, Truth, and Human Dignity: The Second Vatican Council's Declaration on Religious Freedom; A New Translation, Redaction History, and Interpretation of Dignitatis Humanae*, ed. David L. Schindler and Nicholas J. Healy (Grand Rapids, MI: Eerdmans, 2015), 211–42.

31. For the text of this document, see "Questions Concerning the Jews: Proposals from the Secretariat for Christian Unity, November 1961," in *Jews and Catholics Together: Celebrating the Legacy of Nostra Aetate*, ed. Michael Attridge (Ottawa: Novalis, 2007), 166–76.

faith. Indeed: "The Church loves this people." Citing St. Paul in Romans 11:28, it states that it would be "an injustice to call this people accursed" because they are beloved of God. The church "condemns most severely" injustices and wrongs done to the Jews. "Whoever despises or persecutes this people does injury to the Catholic Church."[32]

In June 1962, however, when this draft was presented to the Central Preparatory Commission for approval, for political reasons the commission decided to withdraw the draft from the list of schemas to be considered by the council. As Bea recalls: "Unfortunately, at this precise moment, news came through that certain Jewish organisations were to be represented at Rome in connection with the Ecumenical Council and this produced some vociferous protests on the part of the Arab nations. It was, therefore, considered prudent to allay anxiety by removing the schema on the Jews from the agenda of the Council."[33] The immediate problem was the so-called Wardi affair. Dr. Chaim Wardi was an official working in religious affairs for the newly founded State of Israel. Involved in this affair was the World Jewish Congress, an umbrella organization that had been founded before the Second World War for the diplomatic support of Jewish communities and organizations. On June 12, 1962, without any consultation with Jewish groups or with the Vatican, its president, Nahum Goldmann, announced that he was sending Wardi to Rome as the Congress's representative, presumably to the forthcoming ecumenical council. Suspicions were raised that the State of Israel through this move was wanting to procure Vatican approval for the State of Israel. Accordingly, there was much negative reaction to the announcement, especially from Arab governments and Catholic bishops in those Arab countries. The immediate upshot was that the Central Preparatory Commission removed the *Decretum de Iudaeis* from the agenda of the council and the first session proceeded without any discussion of the Jewish question, except for the intervention of one bishop, Méndez Arceo from Cuernavaca, Mexico, who, on November 27, complained: "where are the Jews on the agenda?"[34]

Bea was determined not to let the matter die. Pope John, he knew, had first initiated the idea of a statement on the Jews, but Bea needed a reaffirmation of that commitment. In December 1962, he wrote directly to Pope John requesting his renewed support for continuing to develop a statement on the

32. These passages are taken from the English translation of this text in Brutti, "Drafts Leading to the Conciliar Declaration *Nostra Aetate*," 191–92.

33. Bea, *The Church and the Jewish People*, 23.

34. Quoted in Stransky, "The Genesis of *Nostra Aetate*," 42.

Jews. Such a statement, he said, should emphasize "the bond of brotherhood between Christians and Jews" and the need for "purification of spirit and conscience" after "the incredible and appalling crimes of National Socialism against six million Jews."[35] He also noted that such a statement needed to address the accusation of deicide and depiction of the Jews as rejected and forever accursed by God. In a brief note in reply—but addressed directly to the council itself—the pope expressed his full support for the cardinal's approach and for the further development of a statement on the Jews.[36]

The Secretariat went to work and produced a revised and expanded version of its earlier decree on the Jews; it reiterated that document's explicit rejection of the Jews as "a deicidal people" and repeated that the church "deplores and condemns" hatred and persecution of the Jews. With the decision having been made that the statement would now become the fourth chapter of the Decree on Ecumenism, however, the text begins by recontextualizing the document: "Having dealt with the basic principle of Catholic Ecumenism, we do not wish to pass over in silence the fact that these principles are also to be applied, with due regard to the given situation, to dialogues and acts of cooperation with people who are not Christians, but adore God or, at least, animated by God's will, try to keep the moral law implanted in human nature following their conscience."[37] The rationale here for including a chapter on the Jews within an ecumenism document followed a certain logic: "If ecumenism is meant to end schisms between Christians, the new people of God, cannot it be concerned also with the Christian-Jewish division, the first schism of all within God's people?"[38]

This draft was due to be presented to the council in the second session along with the rest of the chapters of the Decree on Ecumenism, *De Oecumenismo*. Only the first three chapters on Christian ecumenism, however, had been sent out to the bishops before the 1963 session started; the fourth chapter on the Jews and the fifth chapter on religious freedom were not yet ready. These were eventually distributed to the bishops after the opening of the second session, but before the debate began; chapter 4 was distributed

35. See Oesterreicher, "Declaration on the Relationship of the Church to Non-Christian Religions," 43.

36. See Velati, *Una difficile transizione*, 380–81.

37. Translation from "Draft B" in Brutti, "Drafts Leading to the Conciliar Declaration *Nostra Aetate*," 192.

38. Hastings, *A Concise Guide to the Documents*, 1:196.

on November 8 and chapter 5 on November 16. Chapter 4 was titled "On the Relations of Catholics to Non-Christians, especially Jews."[39]

The debate on *De Oecumenismo* lasted from November 18 until December 2, 1963. In turn with the reporters on the other chapters, Bea presented his *Relatio* on chapter 4. But discussion over the next two weeks would focus mainly on the first three chapters, which concerned ecumenism between Christian churches and ecclesial communities. Nevertheless, when the debate opened, bishops were first able to give general reactions to all chapters of the document. Immediately, "the leaders of the Eastern Churches rose up in a solid phalanx against Chapter IV."[40] Those calling for a rejection of any positive statement on the Jews makes an impressive list: the patriarch of the Syriac church at Antioch, Cardinal Ignace Tappouni; the Coptic patriarch of Alexandria, Stefanos I; the Melkite patriarch of Antioch, Maximos IV; the Latin patriarch of Jerusalem, Alberto Gori; the Armenian patriarch of Cilicia, Peter XVI. Central to their *pastoral concerns* was the harm that any positive statement on the Jews would have for Christian minorities in Arabic and Muslim countries such as theirs. But also, as one commentator at the time interpreted what was happening, "politics held theology in chains."[41]

But there was another group in the aula that was opposed to the statement. As the commentator René Laurentin describes it, "an anti-Semitic opposition was stirring under cover."[42] Around this time a pamphlet rejecting the statement on the Jews had been distributed to all the bishops. Written in Italian by a pseudonymous author called "Bernardus," the pamphlet claimed that "the Jews are a deicide people, accursed and harmful, against whom the Church must defend herself, today as in the past. . . . [T]hese claims, together with the repression of the Jews through the centuries, belong to the

---

39. AS II/5, 431–32. This version constitutes the first column (I), with the heading *"Caput IV: De Catholicorum habitudine ad non Christianos et maxime ad iudaeos,"* in Francisco Gil Hellín, "Nostra Aetate: Synopsis," in *Declaratio de Ecclesiae habitudine ad religionis non-christianas, Nostra aetate: Concilii Vaticani II synopsis in ordinem redigens schemata cum relationibus necnon patrum orationes atque animadversiones,* ed. Francisco Gil Hellín (Roma: Pontificia Universitas Sanctae Crucis, 2013), 2–45. For an English translation of the relevant section on the Jews, see "Draft B" in Brutti, "Drafts Leading to the Conciliar Declaration *Nostra Aetate,*" 192–93.

40. Oesterreicher, "Declaration on the Relationship of the Church to Non-Christian Religions," 48.

41. Quoting Antoine Wenger. See ibid., 49.

42. René Laurentin, "The Jewish Question at Vatican II," in *The Declaration on the Relation of the Church to Non-Christian Religions,* ed. René Laurentin and Josef Neuner (Glen Rock, NJ: Paulist Press, 1966), 17–77, at 24.

normative tradition of the Church." The pamphlet went on to cite the 1751 edict of the Holy Inquisition for the Jews.

It was precisely this mentality that Bea had directly addressed in his *Relatio* when he said: "The aim of this very brief decree is to call to the attention of Christ's faithful these truths concerning the Jews which are affirmed by the apostle [Paul] and contained in the deposit of faith."[43] Bea went on: "But why is it so necessary precisely today to recall these things? The reason is this: Some decades ago anti-Semitism, as it is called, was prevalent in various regions and in a particularly violent and criminal form, especially in Germany under the rule of National Socialism, which through hatred for the Jews committed frightful crimes, extirpating several million of Jewish people. . . . Moreover, accompanying and assisting this whole activity was a most powerful and effective 'propaganda,' as it is called, against the Jews."[44] And, no doubt having in mind the mentality of some in the conciliar hall who agreed with the pamphlet of "Bernardus," the cardinal continued: "Now, it would have been almost impossible that some of the claims of that propaganda did not have an unfortunate effect even on the faithful Catholics, the more so since the arguments advanced by that propaganda often enough bore an appearance of truth, especially when they were drawn from the New Testament and from the history of the Church."[45]

Despite the two groups in opposition, "a far more than expected barrage of positive support came from the cardinals, archbishops and bishops."[46] The council members were able to send in written submissions regarding suggestions for further changes. Over the next two sessions, those opposed to the document would continue to make an impact on the drama, debates, and voting. But, for the moment, while the three chapters on relations with other Christians and their communities were basically approved, the fate of the fourth and fifth chapters was still left up in the air by the end of the second (1963) session.

A month later, in early 1964 (January 4–6), Pope Paul VI set off on pilgrimage to the Holy Land. He would meet Muslims and Jews. Given the uncertain state of the document on the Jews, the venture was fraught with political

---

43. Augustin Bea, "Addresses to the Council," in *The Church and the Jewish People: A Commentary on the Second Vatican Council's Declaration on the Relation of the Church to Non-Christian Religions* (London: Geoffrey Chapman, 1966), 154–72, at 156.

44. Ibid., 157.

45. Ibid.

46. Stransky, "The Genesis of *Nostra Aetate*," 44.

dangers. The pope began by visiting the kingdom of Jordan and ended up in the State of Israel, thereby wanting to show respect to both Muslims and Jews alike.[47] The Israelis were lukewarm, because the pope would not explicitly recognize the State of Israel. "On the other hand, Israeli and Jordanian Muslims and Christians were spontaneously jubilant, and this surprisingly positive reception, genuinely displayed by King Hussein, would influence in particular the Middle East bishops when, at the third session, *Nostra Aetate* was extended beyond Judaism to include Islam."[48] Historical actions can have consequences not perceived at the time: "The Pope could not foresee that his sensitive conduct and the most positive reception by King Hussein and other Muslim Jordanians would influence the Middle East Patres when the separate schema *Nostra Aetate* extends beyond Judaism to include also Islam."[49]

Meanwhile, the Secretariat's drafting committee revised their text in the light of the comments of the previous year's debate, with familiar phrases still appearing: "with a heart full of gratitude" (regarding the beginnings of the church's faith); "deplores and condemns hatred and persecution of the Jews, whether it arose in the past or in our own times"; "never present the Jewish people as one rejected, cursed, or guilty of deicide nor do or teach anything that could give rise to hatred or contempt of the Jews in the hearts of Christians."[50] As Giovanni Miccoli observes: "In substance, the text . . . retained the fundamental lines and ideas of the preceding draft."[51] This was presented to the plenary session of the Secretariat when it met from February 24 to March 7, 1964.[52] For reasons that remain unclear, it was not in fact a

---

47. For a detailed account, with references to other relevant literature, see Thomas Stransky, "Paul VI's Religious Pilgrimage to the Holy Land," in *I viaggi apostolici di Paolo VI*, ed. Rodolfo Rossi (Brescia: Istituto Paolo VI, 2004), 341–73. Stransky observes from his research the generally positive reception the pope received: "Wherever they could, Christians and Muslims in Jordan, and Christians, Muslims and Jews in Israel, enthusiastically welcomed Paul VI—a 'Pope-fever.' No banners of protest, no jeers, no folded arms or solemn faces. Nowhere in the Arab and Israeli newspapers could I find negative judgments on the persona of Giovanni Battista Montini. All respected him as a humble, gentle 'man of God,' who was responsibly carrying the burdens of the leader of the largest worldwide Church as 'the Pope of peace.' . . . The different opposing opinions and judgements focused on the intentional or inadvertent ways *a)* the religious Pilgrim was handling unavoidable political facts; and *b)* the Jordanian and Israeli governments were respecting the 'eminentemente religioso' motive of the Pilgrim." Ibid., 371–72.

48. Stransky, "The Genesis of *Nostra Aetate*," 45.

49. Stransky, "Paul VI's Religious Pilgrimage to the Holy Land," 373.

50. Translation from "Draft C" in Brutti, "Drafts Leading to the Conciliar Declaration *Nostra Aetate*," 193–94.

51. Miccoli, "Two Sensitive Issues," 142.

52. This version does not appear in Héllin's synopsis.

proper "plenary" meeting; some of the members who were not bishops, as well as some of the nonmember *periti*, were not invited. At this stage, there was still no mention in the text of other religions, only Judaism.

When this draft was sent to the Coordinating Commission for approval at its next meeting (April 16–17, 1964), the members were unhappy with it. The text, they said, should be placed in a wider context of the world's monotheistic religions and a general treatment of the solidarity of the human family and the avoidance of hatred and persecution. It seems the commission was also wanting to be sensitive to the objections of Arab nations and the fears of the Eastern Catholic churches, as well as wanting to acknowledge the difficulty seen by some in going against the church's practice of accusing the Jews of deicide. In addition, the president of the commission, Cardinal Amleto Cicognani, felt that an explicit mention of Islam would be diplomatically helpful.[53] In a letter to Bea, Cicognani listed the major changes that were requested. Giovanni Miccoli summarizes the letter: "Mention must be made of 'the connection between the Jewish people and the Holy Catholic Church, while avoiding in the whole text any reference to deicide.' Then 'the other non-Christian peoples' were to be mentioned 'as children of God.' The sentences that followed 'were to affirm the principle of universal brotherhood and of condemnation of any kind of oppression of peoples and races.'"[54] Moreover, Cicognani stated that the document was to be separated from the ecumenism decree and should be a free-standing *appendix* to the ecumenism decree, as a declaration with the title "On the Jews and Non-Christians." In other words, the document would no longer be presented as chapter 4 of *De Oecumenismo* but simply as an appendix to that document. According to the regulations of the council, the text was the Secretariat's responsibility. "Obviously, however, the letter represented an authoritative intervention that, by removing any specific reference to persecutions of the Jews and to accusations connected with the passion of Christ, would radically change the balance and scope of the discourse by emptying it of all its original motivations."[55] In effect, it was no longer really the Secretariat's text; it had become "the Co-ordinating Commission's text,"[56] with the Secretariat required to produce the document.

---

53. On these reasons, see Lamberigts and Declerck, "Vatican II on the Jews," 26.

54. Miccoli, "Two Sensitive Issues," 143–44.

55. Ibid., 144.

56. Oesterreicher, "Declaration on the Relationship of the Church to Non-Christian Religions," 70.

The next week, Johannes Willebrands set up a meeting on April 25 with the two *periti* Yves Congar and Charles Moeller and entrusted them with writing a draft. In fact, Congar came to the meeting with a plan for the document already prepared.[57] The task was completed within two days, with Congar confident that, although the word "deicide" had been removed, the substance of the Secretariat's statement on the Jews was intact.[58] The draft was sent to Cardinal Felici of the General Secretariat, who then sent it on to Pope Paul (with a note indicating that he felt the draft didn't fully implement the Coordinating Commission's requests). Pope Paul made his own suggestions, seemingly influenced by the pressure from conservative cardinals such as Luigi Ciappi and Michael Browne.[59] "That he accepted in substance the proposals of Ciappi and Browne does not necessarily mean that he shared their reasons for suggesting them. . . . Clearly, however, in accepting the suggestions of Ciappi and Browne, Paul VI showed himself, once again, to be open to arguments that appealed to respect for tradition and to the duty to avoid formulations that could in any way sound like an explicit denial of that tradition."[60]

After a round of further editing in May and June, in which Bea was involved, the text was finally approved by the Coordinating Committee on June 26, 1964, and sent to the council members in July, as an appendix to the ecumenism decree, to be discussed in the third session due to start on September 14.[61] The text had three parts, as instructed: (1) the common patrimony in the faith shared by Jews and Christians; (2) the common origin of all human beings in the one God the Father; and (3) condemnation of all forms of discrimination. There were three notable innovations in this version. First, there was an explicit reference to monotheistic Islam and a general reference to other religions; in these religions is manifest, it stated, "the ray

57. See Congar's entry for April 25, 1964, in Congar, *My Journal of the Council,* 521–22. Congar records his reaction to the Coordinating Commission's reduction of the statement on the Jews: "Really, it is quite scandalous and unacceptable that the Church, in order to please some Arab governments that obey no other reason than just an instinct that is simplistic and all-inclusive, should have to refrain from saying what should be said on a question which comes within its province, and on which it has a duty to speak. I believe that the *whole* of the Secretariat's text should be retained, while removing only the *word* 'deicide', and expressing the idea in some other way." Ibid., 522.

58. See Congar's journal entry for April 27, in ibid.

59. On the influence of Ciappi and Browne on Paul VI, see Miccoli, "Two Sensitive Issues," 149–52.

60. Ibid., 152.

61. This version constitutes the second column in Héllin's synopsis.

of that truth which gives light to every person born into this world." Second, the problematic word "deicide" was removed, leaving a whiff of the old accusation of guilt for Jesus' death heaped on the Jews past and present. Third, it seemed to imply that a mission to converting the Jews was justified.

This draft—in effect, that envisaged by the Coordinating Commission—had taken a significant shift away from the Secretariat's singular focus on the Jews. But this wasn't just a whim on the part of the Coordinating Commission. A desire among the conciliar assembly for having a more expansive text, beyond one just on the Jews but on all non-Christian religions, had been bubbling for some time. Importantly, the draft for *Lumen Gentium* 16 was already speaking of the believers of non-Christian religions, explicitly mentioning the Jews and Muslims. Moreover, some in the conciliar assembly would have been well aware of how, in the decades leading up to the council, a "smaller and less organized group of scholars, missionaries, and church leaders was at work seeking to present a positive assessment of Muslims and the Islamic faith. You would find them among Missionaries of Africa (Pères Blancs, or White Fathers), Dominicans, and Jesuits active in the Middle East, Africa, and India."[62] Some from these orders would be co-opted to work in Roman departments, for example, Josef Cuoq, a Missionary of Africa and a specialist in Islam, and Georges Anawati, an Egyptian Dominican and likewise a specialist in Islam. Also important for the story of *Nostra Aetate*, was the fact that Cardinal Giovanni Battista Montini, before becoming Pope Paul VI, had been influenced by the thought of the scholar Louis Massignon, whose writings on Islam were well known.[63] Paul VI's openness also to the other non-Christian religions had become more apparent when, in his first year as pope, on September 12, 1963, he announced that "a secretariat will also be founded in due time for those who are members of non-Christian religions."[64] The idea for such a secretariat had not emerged out of the council itself but on its peripheries, and the idea was then eventually suggested to Paul VI.[65] As John Borelli remarks: "This expression of commitment to interreligious relations in broad terms by the newly elected Pope Paul was

62. Borelli, "*Nostra Aetate*," 26.

63. On the friendship and correspondence between Massignon and Montini, see Christian S. Krokus, "Louis Massignon's Influence on the Teaching of Vatican II on Muslims and Islam," *Islam and Christian–Muslim Relations* 23, no. 3 (2012): 329–45, at 334–36.

64. Quoted in Ralph M. Wiltgen, *The Rhine Flows into the Tiber: A History of Vatican II* (Devon: Augustine Publishing Co., 1978), 78.

65. On the history of the idea, and the personal involvement of the Divine Word priest, Ralph Wiltgen, see ibid., 73–78.

extraordinary when we consider that no draft on the topic had yet been presented to the council fathers and that few of them were aware of any developments in that direction."[66] The "Secretariat for Non-Christians" was eventually established on Pentecost Sunday the following year, May 19, 1964.

But most important of all, calls for reference in the declaration to religions other than Judaism had been heard in the November debate the previous year. For example, Bishop Fortunato Da Viega Coutinho from India, on November 22, spoke "most emphatically":[67] "Judaism had to be treated in the universal context of relation with other religions of Asia and Africa, for, whatever be the precautions, the present text would be used for political ends."[68] Others made similar pleas, such as Cardinal Bueno y Monreal of Spain and Cardinal Peter Doi of Japan. Thus, as John O'Malley observes, "it became clear by the fall of 1963 that the council could not treat the Jews without treating other non-Christian religions, especially Islam, which like Christianity and Judaism descended from the patriarch Abraham. Bishops from the 'new churches' of Asia wanted Buddhism and Hinduism included."[69] Now, as the debate in the third session was about to begin, the council would hear further calls for an enlargement of the declaration.

Fortuitously for the fate and direction of the declaration, about six weeks before the debate was to begin, Pope Paul released his encyclical *Ecclesiam Suam*. It was to become a further catalyst for an extended treatment of other religions.[70] The leitmotif of the encyclical was "dialogue." God is in dialogue with humanity and the church must model that dialogic attitude: "The Church must enter into dialogue with the world in which it lives. It has something to say, a message to give, a communication to make."[71] The pope

---

66. Borelli, "*Nostra Aetate*," 27.

67. Oesterreicher, "Declaration on the Relationship of the Church to Non-Christian Religions," 86.

68. AS II/5, 744–45. This paraphrase of Coutinho's speech comes from Paul Pulikkan, *Indian Church at Vatican II: A Historico-Theological Study of the Indian Participation in the Second Vatican Council* (Trichur [Kerala-India]: Marymatha Major Seminary, 2001), 316. Accordingly, Coutinho called for the proposed Secretariat for non-Christian Religions (which the pope had already announced) to prepare a new expanded text in collaboration with the Secretariat for Christian Unity.

69. O'Malley, *What Happened at Vatican II*, 221.

70. On the general impact of the encyclical on the council, see Vilanova, "The Intersession (1963–1964)," 448–57. Regarding its influence on *Nostra Aetate*, see Fitzgerald, "Vatican II and Interfaith Dialogue," 5–9.

71. *Ecclesiam Suam* 65. See http://w2.vatican.va/content/paul-vi/en/encyclicals/documents /hf_p-vi_enc_06081964_ecclesiam.html.

explicitly mentions the non-Christian religions. In speaking of the church's desire to enter into different circles of dialogue with the world, the encyclical states: "We do not wish to turn a blind eye to the spiritual and moral values of the various non-Christian religions, for we desire to join with them in promoting and defending common ideals in the spheres of religious liberty, human brotherhood, education, culture, social welfare, and civic order. Dialogue is possible in all these great projects, which are our concern as much as theirs, and we will not fail to offer opportunities for discussion in the event of such an offer being favorably received in genuine, mutual respect."[72] The encyclical set a tone for the conciliar debate to come.

The following month, discussion on the new draft of the declaration took place over two days, September 28–29, 1964. John Oesterreicher calls it "the great debate."[73] Some of the speeches "represent a climax in the history of the Declaration."[74] Cardinal Bea was received appreciatively when he stood to present his *Relatio* a few days earlier on September 25, 1964: "The thunderous applause that greeted Bea as soon as he appeared at the microphone would be repeated at the end of his address; it was homage to the man himself but probably also a sign that the audience was aware of the many difficulties the schema had had to overcome before it could be discussed in the hall."[75] Bea was hardly enthusiastic about the text he was introducing to the council but emphatic about its positive points. Sardonically, he remarked: "The Coordinating Commission of the Council knows that it has had to spend a great deal of time on this short document."[76] In effect, he urged the council to strengthen a text the Coordinating Commission had weakened.

The speeches began. From among the thirty speakers, a few can be chosen as examples of, first, a concern to improve the statement on the Jews and, second, a concern to expand the document to give greater attention to other religions.[77]

---

72. *Ecclesiam Suam* 108.

73. Oesterreicher, "Declaration on the Relationship of the Church to Non-Christian Religions," 67–80.

74. Ibid., 67.

75. Miccoli, "Two Sensitive Issues," 135. For Bea's *Relatio*, see AS III/2, 558–64.

76. Translation from Bea, "Addresses to the Council," 160.

77. For English translations of the speeches quoted below, see the resources website *Dialogika* of St Joseph's University's Institute for Jewish-Catholic Relations: http://www.ccjr.us/dialogika -resources/documents-and-statements/roman-catholic/second-vatican-council/na-debate. References to the official Latin text for each speech will be given in the footnotes below.

When Cardinal Richard Cushing (Boston) got to the microphone, "in his booming voice," he implicitly criticized the weak text before him:[78] "In this declaration we must with clear and plain words deny that the Jews are guilty of our Savior's death, except inasmuch as humanity sinned and therefore crucified Him, and indeed still crucify Him. We must especially censure those who attempt to justify injustice, hatred or even persecution of the Jews as if they were Christian actions. We have all seen the evil fruit of this kind of reasoning. In this sacred gathering, in this solemn moment we should cry out: there is no Christian reason—either theological or historical—for injustice, hatred or persecution towards our Jewish brothers." He pleaded, in conclusion: "I ask you, Venerable Brothers, whether or not we should humbly confess before the world that Christians quite frequently did not reveal themselves as true Christians, faithful followers of Christ, toward our Jewish brothers? In this our age, how many have suffered! How many have died because of the indifference of Christians, because of their silence? There is no need to enumerate those crimes that have been committed in our times. If not many Christian voices cried out in recent years against great injustices, let our voices, nonetheless, humbly cry out now!"[79]

Cardinal Joseph Ritter (St. Louis), was no less forthright:

> I am speaking not of a need to avoid political or racial pressure or to conciliate, nor of a need to pursue human approval, but simply of a need to make reparation for the injustice of centuries. Even we Christians, for many centuries already, have been guilty of a mistake and injustice towards the Jews. We, as in rather many instances, used to take it for granted that God had abandoned this people. Christians, even ecclesiastical documents, used to accuse the Jewish people of the passion and death of Christ. In prayers, the people used to be called "the perfidious nation," the "nation of deicides that at one time called down the blood of the Savior upon itself." We have the opportunity today, as we gather in Ecumenical Council, to get rid of, and to make amends for such mistakes and injustices.[80]

He then subtly called for a stronger document: "The draft presents a declaration that furnishes a good beginning for this purpose. But the declaration can be better still, and, I think, needs some improvements."[81]

78. O'Malley, *What Happened at Vatican II*, 217.
79. AS III/2, 593–94.
80. AS III/2, 599–600.
81. AS III/2, 599–600.

Cardinal John Heenan (Westminster) queried the dramatic change from the previous text: "It is natural to ask why these changes were made. It is impossible that one would not notice how this version differs in tenor and spirit. For, the present declaration is less kind, less gracious, less friendly. The document prepared by the Secretariat for Unity—after the observations of the Council Fathers have been carefully considered—is not in all its words the document that you have in your hands."[82] He said the changed text had been produced by "inexperienced experts" (*periti imperiti*). Heenan was implicitly blaming an unnamed source for watering down the Secretariat's text. Heenan was the Secretariat's co–vice president, and his target, as it later was revealed, was the president of the Coordinating Committee, Cardinal Amleto Cicognani.[83]

Several speakers called for an even more expanded treatment of all the major world religions. Cardinal Franz König (Vienna), who had a long interest in non-Christian religions, remarked: "I am happy that the Muslims received special mention. They adore one personal God who is merciful, i.e., Allah. If, however, brevity and space do not stand in the way, mention could be made of those who are close to monotheism in the religions of venerable antiquity, i.e., in Asia and Africa."[84] Cardinal Ernesto Ruffini, a curial official from the conservative minority, felt that the document, in addition to mentioning Muslims, should also treat "the followers of the remaining religions, especially among the Buddhists and Hindus, who are no less in number than the Muslims and are not, in my estimation, more distant or remote from the Christian religion than the disciples of Mohammed. Consequently I ask that those who are concerned with the final composition of the declaration consider whether it is better to reckon all non-Christian religions, especially those that are the most widespread in the world, or would it be enough to mention them together, in general terms."[85]

Bishop Yves Plumey (Cameroon), after acknowledging that the Jews "are closer to us" than believers of other religions, went on to speak of his own experience of the closeness of Muslims to Christianity: "The Muslims, more than all other non-Christians, understand Christ. Heirs of Abraham, they completely recognize Jesus as first in holiness among the prophets. . . . They piously visit the sanctuaries of Mary, they join in processions in her honor,

82. AS III/3, 37–39.
83. On Heenan's speech, see Stransky, "The Genesis of *Nostra Aetate*," 48.
84. AS III/2, 594–96.
85. AS III/2, 585–87.

they devoutly honor her images." Referring to the spirit of dialogue called for by Pope Paul, he hoped that, "filled with this evangelical spirit, those Christians who live with Muslims will very opportunely behave in an utterly fraternal way with them." In such a spirit, "the friendship of very many priests and laity, who have attempted for years to take the lead and slowly spread wider the way of love among Christians, Jews, and Muslims, i.e. among the children of Abraham, will be extended so that the way may be open to a greater knowledge 'of God's ways' among people of good will."[86]

Speaking on behalf of the bishops of Japan, Bishop Lawrence Satoshi Nagae approved of the way the document spoke in terms of a ray of the truth enlightening every person. Therefore, he said, terms such as "pagans" and "paganism" are to be "happily rejected." Alongside the explicit mention of Muslims, however, "a similar mention, at least in a general way, should be made of the other significant religions."[87] The Vietnamese bishop, Simon Hoa Nguyen van Hien, noted: "More than half of the whole world's population are neither Christians nor Jews. The Council does well in saying something about them."[88] The Maronite Archbishop Pietro Sfair reminded his fellow bishops that St. John Damascene did not consider the Muslims infidels but rather *Christian* heretics.[89] The Indian archbishop, Joseph Parecattil, highlighted the need for the church to better understand the ancient religions of India and China: "The Catholicity of the Church demands that she enter into dialogue with these religions that, by learning their way of thinking and of conceiving, she may in a fuller and more intelligible way propose the divine, ineffable mystery to human beings." Moreover, he said, "by calling together interreligious groups for study and prayer, by letting even non-Christians pray in our Churches, and finally by active cooperation with them in social, political, cultural and moral affairs we can in some way now incipiently express this unity until all the servants of God are gathered together in his one Church."[90] And other bishops spoke in similar terms; the need to witness to the love of Jesus Christ when relating to other believers was a regular theme.

Several speakers, however, were against promulgating a statement at all on the topic of the Jews, for theological, not pastoral, reasons. At times cloaking their real views behind the reasons of others (such as the Eastern bishops),

---

86. AS III/3, 15–17.
87. AS III/3, 20–21.
88. AS III/3, 23–25.
89. AS III/3, 41–43.
90. AS III/3, 43–45.

their speeches present, in the words of Alberto Melloni, "a gallery of opinions that is shocking because of the resonance they have with a tradition of Christian antisemitisms of different forms and degrees of danger that go back for thousands of years."[91] It is thus difficult to avoid the historical conclusion that there were indeed bishops among the conciliar assembly whose views were tainted with the anti-Judaism, leading to antisemitism, that Jules Isaac had called "the theology of contempt." But their deeper reasons were most often disguised, as Miccoli observes: "The fathers who were opposed to the schema in order to safeguard and defend the traditional teaching preferred in public discussion to conceal the substantive reasons for their opposition behind the widely varying arguments of others."[92]

The overall outcome of the debate was positive: "Of the more than thirty interventions made in the course of the two general congregations [daily sittings] the majority were in favor of the schema, although with different emphases and justifications."[93] Most approved the new expanded format; many were critical of the way the statement on the Jews had been toned down; many called for a return to the previous document of the Secretariat, with its explicit denunciation of "deicide," and of the Jews as a people rejected and cursed by God. And many called for greater attention to the religions that the majority of humanity follow.[94]

But the Jewish question had been the original issue and was still an urgent one. In 1966, Rabbi Marc H. Tanenbaum of the American Jewish Committee captured the positive aspects of "the great debate," in particular with regard to the Jews:

> The moment of truth, as those of us who were privileged to be in Rome were able to observe, occurred on those two days when thirty-five cardinals and bishops from twenty-two countries arose on the floor of St. Peter's, and one after another, in terms more powerful and committed than had ever been heard before, called upon the Catholic Church to condemn anti-Semitism as

91. Alberto Melloni, "*Nostra Aetate* and the Discovery of the Sacrament of Otherness," in *The Catholic Church and the Jewish People: Recent Reflections from Rome*, ed. Philip A. Cunningham, Norbert J. Hofmann, and Joseph Sievers (New York: Fordham University Press, 2007), 129–51, at 140.

92. Miccoli, "Two Sensitive Issues," 163–64.

93. Ibid., 159.

94. For a list of the twelve areas where emendations were requested by the speakers and written submissions, see Oesterreicher, "Declaration on the Relationship of the Church to Non-Christian Religions," 95.

a sin against the conscience of the church. Thirty-one of the cardinals and bishops from every major continent of the world took positions regarding Catholic attitudes in relation to the Jewish people, Judaism, the role of Israel in salvation history, the synagogue and its continued relevance, conversion, anti-Semitism—positions that have never been heard before in 1,900 years of Catholic-Jewish history, positions articulated with such friendship, indeed, fraternal love, as to make clear that a profound turning point had taken place in our lifetime.[95]

Therefore, despite the opposition of a small minority, the debate on the declaration produced an overall positive outcome for the document: "Not only had the overall discussion shown the schema to be widely favored, but . . . with regard to the amputations and diminutions introduced during the intersession, the fathers asked that the text be clarified and strengthened."[96] Hopes were high that a revised version of the declaration could be produced and be accepted when it would come up for voting later in the session. By the end of the debate, it was evident that there had been "a new awakening to the mystery of Israel in the hearts of many bishops."[97]

But threats to the document had still not been eliminated. Nine days after the September 28–29 debate, the continuing machinations of the minority opposition behind the scenes soon emerged. The Secretariat, emboldened by the positive tone of so many of the speeches in the debate, had quickly got to work preparing the next draft. During its plenary meeting on October 9, however, Bea read out two letters he had just received from the council's general secretary, Cardinal Pericle Felici. The letters related to two documents for which the Secretariat had responsibility. The first letter related to another threatened document, the one on religious freedom; this, the letter stated, was now to be rewritten by a mixed subcommission consisting, not only of Secretariat members, but also of well-known conservatives such as Cardinal Michael Browne and Archbishop Marcel Lefebvre, both of whom were antagonistic to the whole notion of religious freedom. The second letter related to the Declaration on the Jews and non-Christian religions. This text, the letter stated, was now to be a brief addition to chapter 2 of *Lumen Gentium* on the people of God, and,

95. Marc H. Tanenbaum, "Vatican II: An Interfaith Appraisal; A Jewish Viewpoint," in *A Prophet for Our Time: An Anthology of the Writings of Rabbi Marc H. Tanenbaum*, ed. Judith Hershcopf Banki and Eugene J. Fisher (New York: Fordham University Press, 2002), 75–98, at 85.

96. Miccoli, "Two Sensitive Issues," 166.

97. Oesterreicher, "Declaration on the Relationship of the Church to Non-Christian Religions," 81.

like the text on religious freedom, was to be reworked by a mixed subcommission. In other words, the role of the Secretariat was being diminished. The crisis that erupted hit the media. The pope was certainly involved in the affair, albeit under pressure from the conservatives. Bea wrote to, and then met with, the pope; a group of the leading cardinals of the council also wrote to the pope, "with great distress."[98] A positive outcome ensued. Within a few days, the situation had been returned to what it was before Felici's machinations. The ploy had failed, for the moment. "No one apologized, and no one explicitly disowned anything that had been written. The incident suddenly seemed almost like a bad dream that was now past and had no power to harm. In fact, however, opponents of the two schemas had not laid down their arms."[99] There would be further battles in the next session.

The Secretariat returned to its task of revising the declaration according to the wishes of the bishops, revealed in the great debate, and the later written submissions. At this stage, the content of the statement debated by the bishops was mainly focused on the church's special relation with the Jews and with Judaism, with a small addition on Islam and good will to all. Islam was here considered to hold a special place, because it was, like Judaism and Christianity, a monotheistic religion, that saw itself as an "Abrahamic" religion. But now, with the September calls from the council floor to expand the document to the church's relations with all the other major religions of the world, particularly Hinduism and Buddhism, as well as other religious traditions, the Secretariat was being asked to broaden its scope. As Mathijs Lamberigts observes: "For a long time, the [Secretariat] had not been willing to enlarge the declaration on the Jews, either because they were of the opinion that they lacked expertise, or because they thought this was not part of their job. After the September debate and the loud and clear voices of many fathers about other religions, it was finally decided to create special temporary commissions."[100]

The cardinal archbishop of Vienna, Franz König, had a particular interest in the document. Not only had he made an intervention during "the great debate" calling for the document to include a treatment of the religions of Asia and Africa, he had also published books in the 1950s on the topic of Christianity and other religions.[101] Soon after the Felici affair, he decided to

98. On these days, see O'Malley, *What Happened at Vatican II*, 224–26.

99. Ibid., 226.

100. Lamberigts, "*Nostra Aetate* 2, Vatican II on Hinduism and Buddhism," 173.

101. Franz König, *Christus und die Religionen der Erde: Handbuch der Religionsgeschichte* (Wien: Herder, 1951); Franz König, *Religionswissenschaftliches Wörterbuch: Die Grundbegriffe* (Freiburg: Herder, 1956).

intervene further in the drama. Through the mediation of a priest working at the Secretariat, Thomas Stransky, he arranged to meet four council *periti* on October 20, 1964, in the sacristy of St. Peter's Basilica. Two were *periti* on the Doctrinal Commission, Yves Congar and Charles Moeller, both of whom had been directly involved earlier in the year in drafting the previous version. The third was a Jesuit, Paul Pfister, who was a *peritus* for the Japanese bishops. The fourth was another Jesuit, Josef Neuner, likewise a *peritus*, in his case for the bishops of India; he was also a *peritus* helping draft the document on the church's missionary activity. As König expressed it after the meeting: "Their help was needed because the text on the Jews had to be expanded if it were to survive."[102] On the next day, October 21, 1964, "a meeting was held at the [Secretariat]. There it was decided to enlarge the text: it should start with a short introduction. Nr. 2 should deal with the unity of the human race and should speak about some major religions, giving both Islam (nr. 3) and Judaism (nr. 4) their own paragraph."[103] In choosing that order, it was decided to reverse the order in which *Lumen Gentium* 16 (to be officially promulgated a month later) would briefly treat the same groups: Jews, Muslims, other believers, and nonbelievers of good will.

The following day, two days after the meeting in the sacristy of St. Peter's, Stransky called the group of four *periti* together once again. He presented them with the outline the Secretariat had come up with the day before. Two elements in the plan for a larger document had already been drafted. First, a statement on the Jews was in hand. Second, a longer statement on Islam had also been drafted by scholars of Islam recently recruited into the Secretariat; on October 9, 1964 (the very day Felici's letter would be sent to Bea), these four consultors of the Secretariat—Georges Anawati, Josef Cuoq, Robert Caspar, and Jean Corbon—had drafted a paragraph on Islam, that "essentially became section 3 of the next draft."[104] Retrospectively, what was mainly missing at this stage were the passages that would become articles 1 and 2 of *Nostra Aetate*.

102. Quoted in Borelli, "*Nostra Aetate*," 38.

103. Lamberigts, "*Nostra Aetate* 2, Vatican II on Hinduism and Buddhism," 173.

104. As Borelli records: "A separate working group on Islam has come into existence within the SPCU, with Georges Anawati (already a consultor), Josef Cuoq (now undersecretary of the Secretariat for Non-Christians), and his fellow Missionary of Africa, Robert Caspar, now appointed a SPCU consultor to help with passages on Islam. Jean Corbon, a diocesan priest from Lebanon, joined them as a fourth consultor. They met on October 9, 1964, convened by John Long, SJ, an SPCU staff member. They wrote what essentially became section 3 of the next draft, which would be devoted entirely to relations with Muslims." Borelli, "*Nostra Aetate*," 37.

Four days after Stransky's meeting with the four *periti*, on October 25, 1964, Willebrands presided over a meeting of the four drafters of the extra text. Each *peritus* had been asked to bring proposals for a possible text on the "other" non-Christian religions, other than Islam and Judaism. At the meeting, the proposal of each *peritus* was considered. Congar had worked all that day on his draft to present to the meeting. He later recorded in his journal, with some disappointment but with begrudging acknowledgment: "I worked all morning and until 4.00pm on a text on non-Christian religions. It was a waste of time, because, at our working meeting at 4.30pm, with Mgr Willebrands, Moeller, Neuner and Pfister, my text was of no use. A combination was made out of those of Neuner and Pfister, that did compel recognition, it must be said."[105] Thus the texts of Neuner and Pfister were combined. Given their respective expertise, the passage on Hinduism came from Neuner, and that on Buddhism from Pfister. The questions referring to the longings of the human heart were later added, drafted by Charles Moeller, who had been included in the drafting committee.[106]

The fourth draft was, therefore, the combination of work mainly by three different drafting committees, working in different time frames. First, the statement on the Jews, the original focus of the document, had been several times reworked but was still to meet further resistance in the council. Second, a paragraph on Muslims had already been drafted by Anawati and Cuoq. Third, König's group of four *periti*, gathered by Stransky and overseen by Willebrands, quickly drafted the first two articles. All that was needed was to knit the pieces together: "The SPCU staff, with the help of some of these consultors, combined the sections into a single text under the direction of Willebrands."[107] By October 30, 1964, the fourth draft was complete; it would end up being fairly close to the final form of *Nostra Aetate*. The Secretariat sent the text to the Doctrinal Commission, which approved it on November 12. "The precise, clear and brief [fourth draft of] *Nostra Aetate* impressed the coordinating authorities and the Pope. They saw no need to burden the third session with another open debate, so they scheduled only Cardinal Bea's presentation [*Relatio*] and voting on specific questions for November 20."[108]

With echoes of the still-to-be-completed *Gaudium et Spes*, this fourth draft now had the compelling incipit "*Nostra aetate*" ("In our times"). Its

105. Congar, *My Journal of the Council*, 643.
106. On Thomas Stransky's recollection of this, see Borelli, "*Nostra Aetate*," 39n57.
107. Ibid., 39.
108. Stransky, "The Genesis of *Nostra Aetate*," 50.

formal title no longer had the words "on the Jews" but simply: "Declaration on the Church's Relation to Non-Christian Religions" (*Declaratio de ecclesiae habitudine ad religiones non-Christianas*).[109] No longer treating just the Jews, the document had five articles, with the long fought-over statement on the Jews comprising the fourth article. It opened with a vision of humanity's common origin and end in God; this origin and destiny was implanted in humanity's religious impulse, raising questions constantly in the human heart. Accordingly, the draft then presented the nonmonotheistic religions of Hinduism and Buddhism in a positive way. A longer section followed on the monotheistic religion of Islam. Then followed the section on the Jews and the monotheistic religion of Judaism, with a condemnation of the accusation of deicide reintroduced into the text. A conclusion reiterated the common origins of all in God, the common identity of all people as children of God, and the consequent responsibility to love and respect all human beings as fellow children of God. Any discrimination and persecution among the children of God must be deplored and condemned.

On the last working day of the third session, November 20, 1964, Cardinal Bea introduced to the council the expanded schema, amazingly completed a mere two months after "the great debate" at the beginning of this third session.[110] The bishops had received copies of the schema just two days before Bea's *Relatio*; hence, there was little time to study the document, so different from the previous draft. But Bea presented a persuasive account of its major features, assuring the bishops that the elements that had been introduced were all in response to suggestions emerging out of the previous debate and subsequent written submissions: "Our Secretariat has taken pains to consider all suggestions honestly and sincerely in order to produce a document which would be, as far as possible, worthy of the discussion which led to it, and worthy of the Council. It will be for you to judge whether and to what extent it has succeeded."[111] The voting immediately to follow would decide that. He reminded the bishops of the historic nature of the document's focus on non-Christian religions: "No Council in the history of the Church, unless I am mistaken, has ever set out so solemnly the principles concerning them. This consideration must be given full weight. . . . On the Church lies the grave duty of initiating dialogue with them by every means she can find which will

---

109. AS III/8, 637–43. This schema constitutes the third column in Hellín's synopsis.

110. For Bea's *Relatio*, see AS III/8, 649–51. Translation from Bea, "Addresses to the Council," 166–69.

111. Translation from ibid., 166.

help her to do so. . . . As the Declaration points out, this can be done by our acknowledgement of the spiritual and moral values which are present in each religion, and by our sincere respect for those who belong to them."[112] It had also been decided, Bea told the bishops, that the Declaration would not be an appendix to the Decree of Ecumenism but rather an appendix to the finalized text of *Lumen Gentium*.[113]

When voting took place that day (with no debate), the vast majority considered that the Secretariat had indeed succeeded in its mandate. There were three votes taken. The first related to articles 1–3 (on other religions, and Hinduism, Buddhism, and Islam in particular); of the total of 1,996 who voted that day, only 136 voted negatively. The second related to articles 4 and 5 (on the Jews and a condemnation of discrimination and persecution; only 185 voted negatively). The last vote was a judgment on the document as a whole; only ninety-nine negative votes were recorded. In that final vote, however, the bishops were given the opportunity to vote "yes, with reservations," with an opportunity to submit suggestions for modification. A further 242 bishops voted this way. The drafting committee, therefore, still had some work to do. But clearly, the trend in the voting indicated a successful result for the document. Because it was the last working day, and because the rules of the council required two votes on the final version of a document, further fine-tuning of the declaration would have to be left until the intersession before the fourth session the following year, when the final voting would take place.

Still further challenges to the document were on the horizon, however. Indeed, it was as if a "holy war" was now being declared against it.[114] The

---

112. Ibid., 168.

113. Bea explained to the bishops: "The Presidents of the Council, the Co-ordinating Commission and the Moderators think that the Declaration should be made part of the Constitution on the Church as the title of the present Declaration suggests, speaking as it does of the relation of the *Church* to non-Christian Religions. In order not to interrupt the flow of the argument of the Constitution, and so delay an early vote and promulgation, it now seems best to attach this new Declaration at the end of the Constitution on the Church as an Appendix. To attach it to the Constitution has the further advantage that its purely religious character would be emphasised, and any political interpretation would be thereby excluded. At the same time, the weight and impact of the Declaration would be all the greater if it is added to a dogmatic Constitution, even though the aim of the Declaration is pastoral rather than dogmatic." Ibid., 167. Various other options had been considered: for example, to insert the section on the Jews into the body of *Lumen Gentium* and to disperse the remaining sections throughout other conciliar documents such as *Gaudium et Spes* and *Ad Gentes*.

114. See the section "The 'Holy War' against the Declaration" in Oesterreicher, "Declaration on the Relationship of the Church to Non-Christian Religions," 101–5.

main target of this continuing attack was the section on the Jews, with major resistance from outside the council still coming from both Muslims and Christians in the Middle East. For the Muslims, the issue was the ongoing political one—suspicion that positive statements about the Jews in *Nostra Aetate* was simply an underhand recognition by the Vatican of the status of the State of Israel. For example, on November 25, 1964 (five days after the vote on the fourth draft), Radio Cairo read out a manifesto of the "Constituent Council of the Islamic World," "in which the Catholic Church was reminded that its hostile policy would produce enmity between the Islamic and the Christian worlds."[115] For the Arab Christians, it was that potential enmity that alarmed them; their negativity arose out of a fear of future persecutions of Catholic Christians, given their minority status in Muslim countries. But also they resisted *Nostra Aetate*'s attempt to absolve the Jews, past and present, of the guilt for Jesus' death. Sometimes their attacks against the council itself bordered on the vitriolic. And the pushback from Christians came not only from Arab Eastern Catholics; other Christian churches in the region joined in the chorus of criticism. "The months between spring and autumn 1965, that is the time before the fourth session of the Council, were particularly depressing. One piece of bad news followed the other."[116]

Given this environment, and even though the success of *Nostra Aetate* seemed assured after the voting of November 20, 1964, the Secretariat in 1965 sought to assuage the fears of at least one group opposed to it, the Eastern Catholic bishops. It was considered futile to attempt to win over another opposing group among the council members, that small band of conservative bishops collectively known in the council as the *Coetus Internationalis Patrum* (International Group of Fathers). But the Secretariat, and indeed Pope Paul, felt it important to win support for the declaration from the former group.[117] To that end, Bea sent two members of the Secretariat, Johannes Willebrands and Pierre Duprey, on two trips to the Middle East in March and April 1965, first to Syria and Lebanon, and then to Jerusalem and

---

115. Ibid., 105.

116. Ibid., 113.

117. As Gregory Baum remarks: "Technically they were a qualified minority and their opposition had to be taken seriously. The Council is not a parliament in which a majority may simply overrule the minority by votes; the attempt is always made, within fidelity to truth, to adapt the drafts in such a way that the minority may be gained, at least in part." Gregory Baum, "The Conciliar Statement on the Jews," in *Ecumenical Theology, No. 2*, ed. Gregory Baum (New York: Paulist, 1967), 262–72, at 268.

Cairo. The trips were not a success; the delegates still met a wall of resistance from the Near Eastern bishops.

This failure contributed to the pessimistic cloud that hung over the next plenary meeting of the Secretariat convened for May 1965, "probably their most difficult and stormy meeting on *Nostra Aetate*."[118] That the text should be dropped altogether was still being proposed. This move was effectively counted by a strong intervention by Bishop Josef Stangl, the bishop of Würzburg. He urged the meeting that it would be a lack of moral leadership not to promulgate the document. Pleading as a voice from the church in Germany, a stronger text was needed, he said, given the Nazi's persecution of the Jews. Stangl won the day, with no more talk of withdrawing the declaration from the council agenda.

Another reason for the pessimism regarding the success of the Secretariat's hard work on the statement on the Jews was an intervention Pope Paul had made regarding the fourth draft. First, he called for removal of the term "deicide" (the Secretariat had long fought for a deliberate use of the word, in order to name, and then reject, an ancient Christian accusation). Second, he called for removal of the verb *damnat* ("condemns") regarding antisemitism and discrimination. These had been two changes demanded by the Arab bishops of the Catholic Eastern churches of the Middle East. But, for the Secretariat from the beginning, both words encapsulated fundamental values it wanted enshrined in the declaration. Given the difficult debates, however, they were realists. Eventually compromise formulations were arrived at that avoided the problematic terms. In answer to objections that certain biblical texts were being ignored, additions were made to the text noting that some Jews at the time did not receive Jesus positively and that some had called for his death.

In the end, as a member of the Secretariat records, "the majority [of the plenary meeting] had become convinced that an obstinate clinging to the text would endanger all ecumenical efforts in the Middle East and would destroy all hope of a reunion of the Churches of East and West or at least of closing the wounds of centuries (the dream of Paul VI)."[119] Oesterreicher goes on to emphasize that accepting the changes demanded by the minority of Eastern bishops had not damaged the substance of the text: "If after the vote somebody had told the bishops: 'Now you have capitulated to the Arabs after all! More, you have done violence to your own conscience,' one of those who

118. Borelli, "*Nostra Aetate*," 41.

119. Oesterreicher, "Declaration on the Relationship of the Church to Non-Christian Religions," 113.

had voted for removing the words 'guilty of deicide' would certainly have answered: 'Not at all! We have made a *verbal* compromise for the sake of a higher good; we have removed four words without touching the sense for the sake of the well-being of our Christian brethren in the Middle East, but above all for the sake of the unity of the Church.'"[120] Likewise, another a member of the Secretariat, Gregory Baum, remarked:

> Measured by what the minority ultimately desired—namely the total suppression of the Declaration—the few changes were very minor concessions. They were disappointing, nonetheless. If there had been no previous version for comparison, the final text would not have produced the same reactions. This is the price one has to pay for the conciliar process involving more than 2,000 bishops; since so many viewpoints from all parts of the world have to be respected, some issues cannot be solved as neatly as we desire. But the conciliar process, with its parliamentary forms, has so many advantages that one ought to pay this price gladly.[121]

The Secretariat also decided that yet another delegation was worthwhile before the final voting, to plead with the resistant Eastern Orthodox bishops. Accordingly, a group was sent to Beirut, Jerusalem, and Cairo to meet the Eastern Catholic bishops there between July 18–24. Pope Paul agreed to send letters to the bishops endorsing the visits. The strategy worked. The Eastern bishops, now feeling that their voice had been heard, bowed to the wishes of the pope and the majority of the council and agreed to vote favorably on the final text when presented to the council.

The revised text was sent out to the council participants in August 1965, now as a discrete declaration in its own right, unattached to any other document.[122] On October 14, 1965, Bea delivered his *Relatio* to the council assembly just before they were to cast their final vote on the declaration.[123] In accordance with the purpose of any *Relatio*, Bea explained to the assembly how the changes made by the Secretariat's drafting commission accorded with the bishops' suggested amendments after the November 20, 1964, vote; he explained why some suggestions had not been heeded and why others had been incorporated. He gave particular attention to the omission of the word "deicide," which the Secretariat had earlier protected so strongly. In the end, Bea reported, the fact that the Secretariat had accepted the objections of some

120. Ibid., 111.
121. Baum, "The Conciliar Statement on the Jews," 271.
122. AS IV/4, 690–725. This constitutes the fourth column in Héllin's synopsis.
123. AS IV/4, 722–25. See also Héllin, 183–85.

bishops (the Eastern bishops) did not mean that the substance of what the Secretariat was trying to protect had been undermined. He proposed that the new wording in fact succeeded in protecting that substance:

> It is obvious to anyone who reads the text, just now read and explained, that the *substance* of what we wished in the earlier text to express by this word is found exactly and completely expressed in the next text. I well know that some give great psychological, as the current term has it, importance to this word. Nevertheless, I say: if this word is misunderstood in so many regions, and if the same idea can be expressed by other more apt words, then does not pastoral prudence and Christian charity forbid us to use the word, does it not require that we explain the matter in other words? I say that this is required by the same "religious, evangelical love" which impelled John XXIII to order that this Declaration be prepared and which last year inspired you to approve it. Our Secretariat judged this emendation to be of great importance, in order that the Declaration itself be everywhere rightly understood and accepted, in spite of the various difficulties. Thus, I strongly urge you to consider this emendation in the light of pastoral prudence and evangelical charity.[124]

There was no debate scheduled. It is important to remember, however, that approval (or otherwise) of the rationale behind a drafting committee's *Relatio* was implied in the voting on the text. There were nine votes over two days, October 14 and 15, 1965, with four of the votes specifically related to the problematic issues related to the Jewish question. The last vote was a judgment on the whole document.[125] Approximately the same pattern of negative votes as the previous year's votes was evident. When, on October 28, the required second vote was taken on whether the whole text should be promulgated, only eighty-eight bishops voted negatively (two weeks earlier 250 voted against it)—a remarkable result for a document with such a tortuous history: "Whoever had witnessed all the crises and vicissitudes of the Declaration on the Jews from close by could only regard the triumph of that day as a miracle."[126]

Interpreting *Nostra Aetate*

Whereas *Lumen Gentium* 16 "goes from the centre to the periphery, from those who are closest to those who are most distant,"[127] *Nostra Aetate* proceeds

---

124. Translation from Bea, "Addresses to the Council," 171.

125. For a list of the nine topics for voting, see Oesterreicher, "Declaration on the Relationship of the Church to Non-Christian Religions," 128.

126. Ibid., 129.

127. Grillmeier, "Chapter II: The People of God," 182.

from the periphery, with those who are most distant. The Jews are no longer treated first. Starting with those who are most distant from the church enables the declaration, through the very structure of its argument, to begin by highlighting what John Oesterreicher calls "the omnipresence of grace."[128] It is important to keep in mind that, as the *expensio modorum* on the final version explained: "The aim of the Declaration is not an exhaustive presentation of the religions and their faults and weaknesses, it is rather to point to the connections between peoples and their religions which serve as a basis for dialogue and co-operation. Hence it takes more notice of that which unites (Christians and non-Christians) to one another."[129]

In its opening article, the declaration states that it wants to focus, not on differences between religions, but rather on "what people have in common and what tends to bring them together."[130] It then reiterates elements of the council's protological/eschatological principle regarding God's plan for humanity and divine providence over human affairs: "Humanity forms but one community," since all come from God the creator. Moreover, "all share a common destiny, namely God. His providence, evident goodness, and saving designs extend to all humankind, against the day when the elect are gathered together in the holy city which is illumined by the glory of God, and in whose splendor all peoples will walk." Along the human journey, people turn to different religions for answers to the questions that arise in the hearts of all, concerning the meaning of being human and the meaning of the ultimate mystery that pervades human existence.

Article 2 then goes on to explore "the deep religious sense" (*intimo sensu religioso*) evident in the followers of the religions of the world. There is "a certain awareness of a hidden power, which lies behind the course of nature and the events of human life." Some religions acknowledge a supreme being; some even speak of God as Father. This brings forth a whole way of life and even precise concepts for formulating answers to those questions arising in human hearts. Then, three sentences (in the Latin text) follow, giving brief descriptions of the beliefs and practices of Hinduism, Buddhism, and other religious traditions in general.

128. See Oesterreicher, "Declaration on the Relationship of the Church to Non-Christian Religions," 90–93.

129. *Expensio modorum*, ad I, 2, p. 13. Quoted in ibid., 94.

130. For a summary and analysis of the final text of *Nostra Aetate*, see Gerald O'Collins, *The Second Vatican Council on Other Religions* (Oxford: Oxford University Press, 2013), 84–108.

Then follows the core statement and hermeneutical key of articles 1–2 (and article 3 that follows): "The Catholic Church rejects nothing of what is *true and holy* in these religions. It has a high regard for the manner of life and conduct, the precepts and doctrine which, although differing in many ways from its own teaching, nevertheless often reflect a ray of that truth which enlightens all men and women" (NA 2). The pair "true and holy" evokes parallels with another pair in *Lumen Gentium* 16, "of good or of truth," both alluding to the pair "grace and truth" found in John's gospel.[131]

Immediately following, however, in accordance with the hermeneutical proclamation/dialogue principle, there is an affirmation of Christian belief: "Yet [the Catholic Church] proclaims and is in duty bound to proclaim without fail, Christ who is the way, the truth and the life. In him, in whom God reconciled all things to himself, people find the fullness of their religious life" (NA 2). (But, as article 5 will go on to proclaim, the fundamental way in which witness is given to Christ is through fulfillment of Christ's injunction to love, "for all are created in God's image" [NA 5].) And then, as a dialogic balance to that proclamation, we find "the gentle, but clear and commanding exhortation"[132] that concludes article 2: "The church, therefore, urges its sons and daughters to enter with prudence and charity into dialogue and collaboration [*per colloquia et collaborationem*] with members of other religions. Let Christians, while witnessing to their own faith and way of life, acknowledge, preserve and encourage the spiritual and moral truths found among non-Christians, together with their social life and culture" (NA 2).[133] Paul Knitter sees great significance in these injunctions: "*Nostra Aetate*, I think we can say, made dialogue with persons of other religions *an ethical responsibility*, even an obligation. This call to dialogue, I am suggesting, did much more to transform the Catholic Church, and eventually other Christian

---

131. John 1:14, 17. Gerald O'Collins observes: "'True and holy', as well as 'good or truth', echo the Johannine language about the Word being 'full of grace and truth' and about 'grace and truth' coming through Jesus Christ (John 1:14, 17). The two conciliar statements and the prologue all speak of 'truth.' What is 'holy' (NA 2) or 'good' (LG 16) overlaps with 'grace' (John), without their being strict equivalents. *Ad Gentes* 9 maintains the Johannine pair unchanged when referring to the elements of 'truth and grace' found among various peoples." Ibid., 15–16.

132. Paul F. Knitter, "*Nostra Aetate*: A Milestone in the History of Religions? From Competition to Cooperation," in *The Future of Interreligious Dialogue: A Multi-Religious Conversation on Nostra Aetate*, ed. Charles L. Cohen, Paul F. Knitter, and Ulrich E. Rosenhagen (Maryknoll, NY: Orbis Books, 2017), 45–58, at 46.

133. Translation corrected.

churches as well, than the positive doctrinal teachings about 'the elements of truth and good' in other faiths."[134]

Article 3 is devoted entirely to Islam. In a longer treatment than that given to Hinduism, Buddhism, and other religions, the article highlights the monotheistic aspects of Islam, aspects that make it one of the Abrahamic religions, along with Judaism and Christianity. "The Council stresses our common father in faith, Abraham. This is where Louis Massignon, one of the great pioneers in Moslem dialogue, told us to begin."[135] The differences from Christianity are noted but so are the similarities, such as venerating Jesus as a prophet and honoring his mother, the Virgin Mary. That there have long been "quarrels and dissensions" between Christians and Muslims is acknowledged. But, emphasizing the council's desire to focus on what is common and what leads to unity among humanity, the council makes a decisive shift from the church's attitude in the past: "The sacred council now pleads with all to forget the past, and urges that a sincere effort be made to achieve mutual understanding; for the benefit of all, let them together preserve and promote peace, liberty, social justice and moral values." This marks the end of the first structural part of the declaration (articles 1–3). Article 4, for so long the singular focus of the debating period, constitutes, structurally, the second part of the declaration, the council's statement on the Jews.

Article 4 makes five major affirmations, each of which marks a renewal in the attitude of the Catholic Church to Jews and to Judaism. First, the council affirms the special bond Christians have with Jews and with Judaism. The introductory sentence places the whole article at the very heart of the council's agenda—to reflect on the mystery of the church for the purpose of renewing it: "Sounding [*perscrutans*] the depths of the mystery which is the church, this sacred council remembers [*meminit*] the spiritual ties which link the people of the new covenant to the stock of Abraham." In other words, the council recognizes that any renewal of the church demands a reconnection with its origins. The Latin text emphasizes "the links which spiritually join" Christians and Jews (*vincoli, quo populus novi testamenti cum stirpe Abrahae spiritualiter coniunctus est*).[136] Already here we have the first remark-

---

134. Knitter, "*Nostra Aetate*: A Milestone in the History of Religions?," 46. Emphasis added.

135. Hastings, *A Concise Guide to the Documents*, 1:201.

136. There are expressions of "remembering" (*meminit*), "not forgetting" (*nequit ecclesia oblivisci*), "keeping constantly before its eyes" (*semper prae oculis habet*). Despite these intents of renewal in attitude, however, a long history of forgetting is being masked here, as Marco Morselli comments: "It cannot forget: but for centuries and millennia the Church did forget.

able aspect of this historic statement from Vatican II: "From the time of Christian antiquity up to that of Vatican II, there had been hardly any development of the Church's teaching on the mystery of Jewish existence. . . . The problem [of the relationship of Church and Synagogue] was really the Cinderella of theology."[137] As the article acknowledges, "all Christ's faithful . . . as people of faith are daughters and sons of Abraham." The patriarchs, prophets, Jesus, and his mother Mary were Jews. Referring to an image St. Paul uses in Romans 11:17-24, it states: the church "draws nourishment from that good olive tree onto which the wild olive branches of the Gentiles have been grafted."

Second, the council rejects a theology of supersessionism, because God has not cancelled the ancient covenant. The Jewish religion has enduring value in God's eyes. "It clearly lays to rest the doctrine of supersessionism which considered the role of Israel entirely superseded by that of the church."[138] The appeal to St. Paul here is key. Referring to his conclusion to chapters 9–11 of Romans, and after acknowledging that many Jews had not accepted Jesus, the declaration states: "Even so [*nihilominus*], the apostle Paul maintains that the Jews remain very dear to God [*carissimi*], for the sake of the patriarchs, since God does not take back the gifts he bestowed or the choice he made" (NA 4). The conciliar text is here paraphrasing Romans 11:28-29, which states: "As regards the gospel they are enemies of God for your sake; but as regards election they are beloved, for the sake of their ancestors; for the gifts and the calling of God are irrevocable."[139] This key Pauline text is quoted or cited in two conciliar documents: *Nostra Aetate* 4 refers to verse 28 once, and then elsewhere to verses 28-29; *Lumen Gentium* 16 refers to 28-29 once. Later in article 4, a similar rejection of former Catholic teaching is implied: "It is true that the church is the new people of God, yet the Jews should not be spoken of as rejected or accursed as if this followed from holy scripture." With this rereading of Scripture, *Nostra Aetate* 4 "placed inspiration from [St. Paul's letter to the] Romans at the center of Catholic understanding of the Jewish people."[140]

With *Nostra Aetate* . . . it is as if the Church is reawakening from a long sleep. It remembers." Morselli, "Jules Isaac and the Origins of *Nostra Aetate*," 27.

137. Oesterreicher, "Declaration on the Relationship of the Church to Non-Christian Religions," 39.

138. Sievers, "How Irrevocable? Interpreting Romans 11:29," 758.

139. NRSV translation.

140. Connelly, *From Enemy to Brother*, 190.

Third, the council promotes mutual understanding between Christians and Jews. This is to be fostered by biblical and theological studies, as well as through "friendly dialogue [*fraternis colloquiis*]." Later in the article, it continues this theme by urging attention in other areas: "all must take care, lest in catechizing or in preaching the word of God, they teach anything which is not in accord with the truth of the Gospel message or the spirit of Christ."

Fourth, the council says no to accusing the Jews of "deicide" (although that word is no longer used in the final text). The Jews, then and now, are not corporately guilty of the death of Christ: "Even though the Jewish authorities and those who followed their lead pressed for the death of Christ, neither all Jews indiscriminately at that time, nor Jews today, can be charged with the crimes committed during his passion." The last sentence of the article affirms that Christ died "because of the sins of all, so that all might attain salvation."

Fifth, the council says no to antisemitism, using the two verbs *reprobat* ("reproves") and *deplorat* ("deplores"); the stronger verb *damnat* ("condemns") had been removed. Here we find the one use of the word "antisemitism" (*antisemitismus*) in all the documents of Vatican II. The text only alludes to the painful history of the church's relationship with the Jews and the evils perpetrated against them: "Indeed, the church reproves [*reprobat*] every form of persecution against whomsoever it may be directed. Remembering [*memor*], then, its common heritage with the Jews and moved not by any political consideration, but solely by the religious motivation of Christian charity, it deplores [*deplorat*] all hatreds, persecutions, displays of antisemitism [*antisemitisimi*] levelled at any time or from any source against the Jews."[141] Article 5 repeats the verb *reprobat* regarding "any discrimination against people or any harassment of them on the basis of their race, color, condition in life or religion." The theological basis of the church's doctrine is the common origin of all human beings in God the Father, with its ethical demand to treat all other human beings as our sisters and brothers.

141. Alberto Melloni notes that the council was here attempting to address, primarily, *theological* antisemitism within the church itself: "A struggle, therefore, was underway around critical points of theological antisemitism; it was not the antisemitism of Arab Christians that caused concern—an antisemitism that was partly dissimulated and partly disguised as a pan-Arabic solidarity, and which even the great Patriarch Maximos IV had largely shared. Even the antisemitism of the Nazi and the Fascist type that was echoed in a few voices was only a secondary factor. The problem was *theological* antisemitism, with the political implication that the whole *respublica christiana* ['Christian society'] in general, and the state of the Church in particular, had inspired this in centuries of history and of culture." Melloni, "*Nostra Aetate* and the Discovery of the Sacrament of Otherness," 139.

How should one assess the final version of article 4 of *Nostra Aetate*? Certainly, as Reinhard Neudecker notes, "the agitated history of the Declaration . . . has left its traces in the document."[142] Cardinal Bea, the document's persistent advocate, conceded: "In fact we do not think in any way that this document is absolutely perfect—something in any case humanly impossible—and that therefore it must be defended at all costs as a whole and in every detail. . . . It is hardly surprising that there should be difficulties enough in a document which deals with a problem two thousand years old in scarcely five hundred words."[143] In the end, article 4 does not explicitly mention the Shoah, or the dark history of Catholic antisemitism, or the anti-Judaism of the theology of supersessionism, or the word "deicide." Moreover, throughout the drafting, the text had lost much of its warmth when speaking of the Jews; certainly, that striking sentence in the Secretariat's original draft from the preparatory period was long gone: "The Church loves this people." Nevertheless, this concise text, reduced though it was, *opened a door*, and led the Catholic Church across a threshold that would lead to wider vistas throughout the document's postconciliar reception.[144] That it was brief and to the point had its advantages. While lamenting that article 4 does not fulfill "Abraham Heschel's request for reference to 'the permanent preciousness' of Jews as Jews,"[145] John Connelly observes, regarding the article's terseness:

> Yet there was something providential to keeping the statement focused. It took away impediments to deeper understanding, and given the mentality of the time, *saying more harbored risks*. In October 1965, many bishops raised their hand in ethical assent while unthinkingly keeping to their anti-Judaic views. Even Cardinal Bea, who tirelessly defended the statement in the darkest moments, had not fully absorbed its implications. In November 1965 Bea wrote

142. Neudecker, "The Catholic Church and the Jewish People," 284.

143. Bea, *The Church and the Jewish People*, 12.

144. Acknowledging the text's weaknesses, René Laurentin nevertheless sees *Nostra Aetate*'s statement on the Jews in article 4 as a text that has opened a door that has been long held shut and indeed locked: "It is a step within the possible, but it is not negligible. Like the *Constitution on the Church* in its chapter on collegiality, like the *Constitution on the Sacred Liturgy*, like the *Decree on the Ministry and Life of Priests*, and like many other Council documents, the text on the Jews opens locks that have been jammed for centuries. Not without difficulty, or grinding, or pressure in the opposite direction, a door has been opened. The movement of dialogue and friendship between the Catholic Church and Israel, which has been in preparation for a long time, will be able to develop on healthy grounds." Laurentin, "The Jewish Question at Vatican II," 54.

145. Connelly, *From Enemy to Brother*, 267–68.

that Jerusalem had once been destroyed because of the "guilt" of its inhabitants, "since they directly witnessed the preaching, the miracles, the solemn entrance of Jesus." Furthermore, he wrote, the Jewish people was "no longer the people of God in the sense of being the instrument of salvation for humanity."[146]

And how should *Nostra Aetate* as *a whole text* be interpreted? Reid Locklin has offered a cogent proposal, by interrelating a hermeneutics of the authors with a hermeneutics of the texts.[147] From one perspective—attending to the tortuous drafting process during which the issue of the Jews was to the forefront of concern from the very start—*Nostra Aetate* 4 can indeed be seen as "the core of the Declaration," as one of the drafters, Gregory Baum, puts it.[148] From another perspective—attending to the final form of the text—the fourth article would seem to assume a less central position within the progressive argument of the whole document. "Certainly, if one reads the declaration as one would read most other texts, one would look for its interpretative key closer to the beginning of the text than to its middle. If the history of interpretation of *Nostra Aetate* privileges *Nostra Aetate* 4, we might say, its literary structure tends to privilege *Nostra Aetate* 1–2."[149]

Thus, according to Locklin's interpretation, there are two separate parts to the final text of the declaration, which developed throughout the drafting process in "relative autonomy" from one another.[150] Each part reads as "a coherent whole, with its own interpretative trajectory,"[151] "each with its own distinctive approach, emphases, and subsequent reception,"[152] each "arising as they did from different origins, proceeding from different principles, and thus generating different controversies."[153] The first part, Locklin proposes, advances what he calls a "universalist" perspective, which moves from the universal to the particular, while the second part advances a "particularist" perspective,

146. Ibid., 268. Emphasis added.

147. See Reid Locklin, "One Text, Two Declarations: Theological Trajectories from *Nostra Aetate*," *Theological Studies* 78, no. 1 (2017): 49–71. Locklin refers, for this hermeneutical framework, to Rush, *Still Interpreting Vatican II*. See Locklin, "One Text, Two Declarations," 53n12.

148. Baum, "The Conciliar Statement on the Jews," 262.

149. Locklin, "One Text, Two Declarations," 52.

150. Ibid., 55.

151. Ibid., 56.

152. Ibid., 52.

153. Ibid., 56.

which moves from the particular to the universal.[154] These stand in "intratextual tension" with each other within the text when read as a whole.[155]

One could add that this tension within the declaration itself stands in *inter*textual tension with *Lumen Gentium* 16, which structures its discussion in the reverse order, beginning its treatment of "the religious others" with the Jewish people.[156] The interpreter is required to relate these intratextual and intertextual tensive positions by locating them, not only in relation with each other, but also within the council's comprehensive vision of God's plan for humanity and the church's mission in the world.

Within *Nostra Aetate*, both of the positions Locklin distinguishes employ their own hermeneutical key. For those taking a particularist perspective, the issue of "the Jews" remains, hermeneutically, a controlling element of the whole document. For those seeing a universalist perspective, there is affirmation of divine light and grace in the other religions, what Oesterreicher calls "the omnipresence of grace." This perspective too remains, hermeneutically, a controlling element of the whole document.

Certainly, the council might have highlighted more strikingly the church's ongoing intimate relationship with the Jewish religion if the statement on the Jews had been located in any one of the earlier placements being considered; options that were considered were as a chapter or appendix of *Unitatis Redintegratio* or as an addition to *Lumen Gentium*. After the expanded fourth draft was produced, the question was naturally raised: had the section on the Jews, originally the sole focus of the document, now been reduced in importance? Not necessarily so, according to John Oesterreicher, referring to the fourth draft: "The Declaration on the Jews remained the centre of the whole document, though the other parts were not reduced to secondary importance."[157] Both parts have their own independent integrity, with each protecting each other's affirmations—but with the historic statements on the Jews acting as a catalyst for the historic statement on the other religions. And it would remain so until the final version was promulgated. Referring to the final version of the text, and the possibilities that had been considered about simply inserting the statement on the Jews in other documents, a member

---

154. Ibid., 52.

155. Ibid., 53.

156. O'Collins uses the phrase "the religious others" throughout O'Collins, *The Second Vatican Council on Other Religions.*

157. Oesterreicher, "Declaration on the Relationship of the Church to Non-Christian Religions," 97.

of the staff at the Secretariat, Thomas Stransky, observes: "I remain convinced also that the enlargement of *Nostra Aetate* through inclusion of other religions protected the Jewish theme intact, and both its opponents and its supporters knew it. The gem could not be removed from its larger setting, and its fragments scattered about in other texts."[158] König had been right when gathering the four *periti* in the sacristy of St. Peter's: "The text on the Jews had to be expanded if it were to survive."

René Laurentin sees in the broadening of the declaration's scope something providential: "The difficulties met by the text on the Jews had obliged the Church, in a positive way, to open herself to extremely new horizons."[159] He then notes a parallel between the fate of the historical Jews and the fate of the earlier conciliar draft statement on the Jews, now recontextualized: "'Their failure means riches for the Gentiles,' wrote St Paul (Rom 11:12). Everything happened as though that principle had found an unexpected application here, by the progressive enlarging of the decree *On the Jews* to the *Declaration on Non-Christian Religions* taken all together."[160] Bea implied this when presenting the fourth draft in his *Relatio* of November 20, 1964. He began by saying: "This Declaration might well be compared to the biblical grain of mustard seed. Originally it was my intention to make a short and simple statement on the relation between the Church and the Jewish people. But in the course of time, and particularly in the course of the discussions in this Assembly, this seed, thanks to you, has almost grown into a tree, in which all the birds of the air are nesting."[161]

The remarkable aspect of this drafting history, then, is the way the debate had opened up the need for a similarly broader and more open statement on the major world religions, first the other major monotheist religion, Islam, then the other major religions of Hinduism and Buddhism, as well as the other religious traditions. Half a century later, John Connelly remarks on the interrelationship between the two parts of *Nostra Aetate*:

> In recognizing that special blessings rested upon the Jews, the universal church spoke in terms of one people's particular identity, but five decades later we see that recognizing the particular also led to a new appreciation for the universal. Without its need to speak about the Jews after the Holocaust, the church may not have spoken about other non-Christian faiths. But having spoken about

158. Stransky, "The Genesis of *Nostra Aetate*," 52.
159. Laurentin, "The Jewish Question at Vatican II," 35.
160. Ibid.
161. AS III/8, 649. Translation from Bea, "Addresses to the Council," 166.

the Jews, it could not remain silent on the others. . . . By answering the question "Who are the Jews?" the Catholic Church had found its way across previously insurmountable boundaries to tolerance, to recognizing that God extends grace to all human beings.[162]

Similarly, Alberto Melloni sees in the history of the text, despite its difficulties, a final result that is groundbreaking:

> Was *De Judaeis* watered down or sold out to the opportunities of the moment? From the point of view of the redaction, this might appear to be the case, but in substance, the opposite is true. In the text and in life, in experience and in history, Judaism has become the paradigm not only of interreligious dialogue, but also *the paradigm of every difference, the sacrament of all otherness*, the *locus theologicus* where the Christians can show that every "other" alludes in its very alterity to the One who is totally other and yet is totally close to every woman and to every man. It is this mystery of salvation that marks "our age." In the documents of the Second Vatican Council, it is affirmed that our time can respond to the challenge that this mystery represents.[163]

In conclusion, as Paul Knitter observes, "what makes *Nostra Aetate* so revolutionary is to be found not primarily in what it, and other Vatican II documents, say *about* other religions, but, rather, in what it says about how Christians should *act* toward other religious believers. *Nostra Aetate* opens up whole new directions—not, primarily, in its *doctrine* about the meaning of the other religions, but rather in its *ethics* about how Christians should interact and relate to followers of other religions."[164] That ethical injunction resounds starkly from the declaration's final article 5: "We cannot truly pray to God the Father of all if we treat any people as other than sisters and brothers, for all are created in God's image. People's relation to God the Father and their relation to other women and men are so dependent on each other that the Scripture says 'they who do not love, do not know God' (1 Jn 4: 8)" (NA 5). For one historian of Vatican II, *Nostra Aetate* "provided the Catholic Church with a new mission, with a new role in the world—a mission of mediation in a divided world."[165]

162. Connelly, *From Enemy to Brother*, 299.
163. Melloni, "*Nostra Aetate* and the Discovery of the Sacrament of Otherness," 151. Emphasis added.
164. Knitter, "*Nostra Aetate*: A Milestone in the History of Religions?," 45. Original emphasis.
165. John W. O'Malley, "Dialogue and the Identity of Vatican II," *Origins* 42, no. 25 (November 22, 2012): 398–403, at 403.

Other Conciliar Texts

While *Nostra Aetate* consumed most of the council's discussion of the Jews and of other religions, it was not the only document to address the matter. Two other documents before its promulgation (*Sacrosanctum Concilium* and *Lumen Gentium*) had said things about the issue, and two documents after its promulgation (*Ad Gentes* and *Gaudium et Spes*) would, in some way, address the theme, even adding important nuances to the council's teaching.

Therefore, *Nostra Aetate* needs to be interpreted in the light of other statements throughout the conciliar corpus. These too are significant in reconstructing the vision of Vatican II's Christian/religious principle. Here, the hermeneutical notion of *intertextuality* comes into play. For example, *Nostra Aetate* opens with a general treatment of the world with its diversity of cultures and religions and the need to recognize the right of all to live in freedom. The declaration therefore assumes all that is said on that topic in *Dignitatis Humanae*, the Decree on Religious Freedom. John Borelli is right to interpret *Nostra Aetate* within the whole conciliar event and the rest of its final documents: "In understanding why the text of *Nostra Aetate* is the way that it is, one should look at the whole of Vatican II and not isolate any text or other official act, paragraph, or sentence from the whole. . . . The first context of *Nostra Aetate* is the council itself and the variety of streams and developments flowing into it and through its complicated proceedings."[166]

Taking an intertextual reading across the conciliar corpus raises a series of further related questions. If God desires the salvation of all, what is the extent of God's saving activity in the world? If the church is understood as "the universal sacrament of salvation," is God's saving activity restricted to divine activity within the Catholic Church? Within the Christian churches? Or within other religions with adherents who believe in God but not Christ? What of the adherents of the nontheistic religions, such as Buddhism? What of those who do not believe and are, indeed, hostile to religion and/or to Christianity?

Before *Nostra Aetate* was promulgated on October 28, 1965, two other conciliar documents had explicitly touched on the theme of the church and

---

166. Borelli, "*Nostra Aetate*," 42. Likewise, Michael Fitzgerald remarks: "*Nostra Aetate* is not to be taken in isolation, but rather must be read in conjunction with the other documents of Vatican II. It cannot be isolated from *Ad Gentes*, which deals with the mission of the church in a world marked by religious plurality. It is obviously related to *Gaudium et Spes*, which outlines how the church relates to the modern world. Above all, it finds its theological foundation in *Lumen Gentium*, the Dogmatic Constitution on the Church." Fitzgerald, "Vatican II and Interfaith Dialogue," 4.

other Christian religions. Brief mention should be made of the council's first document promulgated. Just as it did with regard to the leitmotif of "participation" (and other themes), so too the Constitution on the Sacred Liturgy, *Sacrosanctum Concilium*, leads the way with regard to an openness to non-Christian religions, at least implicitly. Gerald O'Collins speaks of the constitution exhibiting "a worldwide mindset" right from the start, with its vision of the church as orientated "to those who are outside" (SC 2).[167] The opening sentence of its first chapter on general principles quotes the classic text regarding God's universal salvific will (1 Tim 2:4; SC 5). And in calling for the restoration of the prayer of the faithful, the constitution mandates the universal concern the prayer should always have: "By this prayer in which the people are to take part, intercession will be made for the church, for the civil authorities, for those oppressed by various needs, for all humankind, and for the salvation of the entire world" (SC 53).

The other relevant document promulgated before *Nostra Aetate* was *Lumen Gentium*. It devotes one article to the church and other religions.[168] Here in the dogmatic constitution we see seeds of what will grow into the declaration a year later. Among the final documents, what each says on the church and other religions stands in intertextual tension because of their different starting and end points: the constitution begins its reflection on the mystery of religious otherness by a discussion on the specialness of the Jews, and the declaration leads up to the Jews as its end point.

Article 16, situated toward the end of *Lumen Gentium*'s second chapter on the people of God, begins with the affirmation that "those who have not yet accepted the Gospel are related to the People of God in various ways" (LG 16). Earlier in the chapter we find the presupposition of that statement, in a passage that opens article 13: "All women and men are called to belong to the new people of God. This people, therefore, whilst remaining one and unique, is to be spread throughout the whole world and to all ages in order that the plan of God's will may be fulfilled: he made human nature one in the beginning and has decreed that all his children who were scattered should be finally gathered together as one. It was for this purpose that God sent his Son" (LG 13). That same article ends with the statement: "All are called to this catholic unity of the People of God which prefigures and promotes universal peace. And to it belong, or are related in different ways: the Catholic

---

167. O'Collins, *The Second Vatican Council on Other Religions*, 63.

168. On the drafting history specifically of *Lumen Gentium* 16, see Gavin D'Costa, *Vatican II: Catholic Doctrines on Jews and Muslims* (Oxford: Oxford University Press, 2014), 144–53.

faithful, others who believe in Christ, and finally all of humankind, called by God's grace to salvation" (LG 13).

Article 16 goes on to speak of four groups of people "who have not yet accepted the Gospel." These, however, are treated in an order that later *Nostra Aetate* will reverse: Jews, Muslims, believers of other religions, and nonbelievers of good will. The theological framework overarching the article's statements on these groups is "the plan of salvation," "divine providence," and the universal salvific will of God (citing the classic text 1 Tim 2:4: "God our Savior, who desires everyone to be saved and to come to the knowledge of the truth"). The tone of the article is eirenic, emphasizing what is positive in these others without failing to proclaim firmly the church's christological beliefs in Christ as the universal Savior.

Beginning with those closest in relationship to Christians, the Jewish people, it recalls the ancient covenant and retrieves a long-forgotten affirmation of St. Paul, that the Jewish people are always beloved of God and God has never revoked his gifts from them (Rom 11:28-29). The text then turns to Muslims, who are acknowledged as monotheists like Jews and Christians, worshiping the one Creator God; they too are encompassed in "the plan of salvation." This one sentence on Islam is historic: "For the first time since the Arab prophet Muhammad (d. 632) founded Islam, an ecumenical council of the Catholic Church offered some explicit teaching on Muslims."[169] While the article leaves open many of the issues raised, "it is hard to escape the conclusion," says Gerald O'Collins, "that the constitution recognizes some revealing and saving efficacy in Islam. In some way the Muslim religion enjoys a specific role in mediating the knowledge of God and grace of God."[170]

The third group close to God are "those who in shadows and images seek the unknown God, since he gives to everyone life and breath and all things." This alludes to St. Paul's speech on the Areopagus in Athens (the text cites Acts 17:25-28). Although they are unaware of the Gospel, these are people "who nevertheless seek God with a sincere heart, and, moved by grace, try in their actions to do his will as they know it through the dictates of their conscience—these too may attain eternal salvation."[171] But the text fails to speak of the relevance of these people's adherence to a particular religion,

169. O'Collins, *The Second Vatican Council on Other Religions*, 73.
170. Ibid., 74.
171. On this last point, the text, in a footnote, refers to the famous case of Father Feeney from Boston, and the letter of the Holy Office to the archbishop of Boston. DS 3866–73. Denzinger, *Compendium of Creeds, Definitions, and Declarations*, 795–98.

something that gives shape to their religious life (something that the other conciliar documents will do).

Finally, there are those people of good will who, without any fault of theirs, have no explicit knowledge of God. Here we find a list of divine realities and dispositions that present a positive statement of their status before God: they are caught up in the mystery of "divine providence"; they are provided "the assistance necessary for salvation"; they can experience "grace"; their lives exhibit "whatever of good or truth." This is all "a preparation for the Gospel" (citing Eusebius of Caesarea); moreover, unbeknown to them, it is Christ who is at work, "enlightening" them (a reference to revelation) that he may lead them to "life" (a reference to salvation).[172] This last point evokes the prologue of John's gospel: "The true light, which enlightens everyone, was coming into the world" (John 1:9). (These are all themes that other conciliar documents will apply more broadly to the other groups.) The article also speaks of those who willfully resist such divine overtures. As a segue into the following article, article 16 ends with a statement of the need for the church to be ever committed to bringing the Christian Gospel to all these groups.

Article 17, then, expands on this mission of the church to evangelize. Emphatically it states that Christ is "the source of salvation for the whole world." The church's missionary task is "to proclaim the truth which saves . . . to the very ends of the earth." Importantly, the article alludes to Justin Martyr's notion of "the seeds of the Word" being sown everywhere: "The effect of [the church's evangelizing] activity is that whatever good is found sown in people's hearts and minds, or in the rites and customs of peoples, is not only saved from destruction, but is purified, raised up, and perfected for the glory of God, the confusion of the devil, and the happiness of humanity."[173] The article ends with eschatological hope, that all will be drawn into the people of God, the Body of Christ, and the temple of the Holy Spirit.

Having sown its own seeds of newness in giving such a positive vision throughout the article, it does not, however, set out to provide a complete theological synthesis. "How actual justification (in faith and love) finally

---

172. On the significance and word order of the double notions of "good or truth" and "enlightenment and life" in this passage, Gerald O'Collins observes: "When reflecting on the religious condition of 'others' in terms of 'whatever good and truth is found' among them, the Council suggested two distinguishable but inseparable dimensions of the divine self-communication that has blessed them: salvation ('good') and revelation ('truth'). Johannine language of revelation and salvation (in that order) followed at once when our passage introduced 'enlightening' and 'life.'" O'Collins, *The Second Vatican Council on Other Religions*, 77.

173. See Justin Martyr, *Second Apology*, 8, 10, 13.

comes about is not said in the Constitution, which is only concerned to show that all relationships to God are at once orientated to the acceptance of the God of salvation, and hence are an ordination towards the people of God. This is what is common to the people of God and to those who seek God."[174] *Nostra Aetate* goes into these matters more deeply, as does the Decree on the Church's Missionary Activity.

The other two conciliar documents that treat matters related to the Christian/religious principle are *Ad Gentes* and *Gaudium et Spes*, both promulgated at the end of the council. The Decree on the Church's Missionary Activity repeats, but adds to, several points already made in particularly *Lumen Gentium* and *Nostra Aetate*. On one point, it introduces further teaching beyond the other documents.[175]

First, *Ad Gentes* repeats, but enhances, the trinitarian vision of *Lumen Gentium*. The first chapter (AG 2–9) outlines the doctrinal principles that should guide missionary activity. Whereas *Nostra Aetate* had not mentioned the Holy Spirit at all, *Ad Gentes* presents a trinitarian vision of God's saving activity in the world, with articles 2, 3, and 4 devoted to God the Father, Jesus Christ, and the Holy Spirit, respectively. Article 4 highlights the role of the Spirit in the economy of salvation, with a striking passage that has implications for the activity of the Holy Spirit in non-Christian religions: "Without doubt, the Holy Spirit was at work in the world before Christ was glorified."

The missionary decree also repeats from *Lumen Gentium* 17 the language of Justin Martyr regarding the seed of goodness sown in the hearts, rites, and cultures of peoples. Article 9 speaks of how "whatever is found sown [*seminatum*] in people's minds and hearts, or in the particular customs and cultures of peoples, far from being lost is purified, raised to a higher level and reaches its perfection." Article 11 urges missionaries to "respect those seeds of the word which lie hidden" among the national and religious traditions of the people with whom they live. Article 15 repeats the imagery and highlights the agency of the Holy Spirit in the reception of Christ: "the Holy Spirit, who calls all women and men to Christ and arouses in their hearts the submission of faith by the seed of the word and the preaching of the gospel." Article 18 likewise speaks of "traditions of asceticism and contemplation, whose seeds have been sown by God in certain ancient cultures before the preaching of the gospel."

---

174. Grillmeier, "Chapter II: The People of God," 183.

175. For what follows, I am drawing on O'Collins, *The Second Vatican Council on Other Religions*, 109–27.

There are three further ways in which the missionary decree repeats points made in other documents. First, employing the Johannine pair "truth and grace" we saw used in *Lumen Gentium* and *Nostra Aetate*, it speaks of "those elements of truth and grace, which are found among peoples, and which are, as it were, a secret presence of God" (AG 9). Second, Eusebius of Caesarea's notions of divine pedagogy and "preparation for the Gospel" can be found repeated in article 3: "in the loving providence of God [religious yearnings and practices] may be a pedagogy leading to God [*paedagogia ad Deum*] and be a preparation for the gospel [*praeparatione evangelica*]." Finally, the decree repeats the calls for dialogue and cooperation with non-Christians: "Just as Christ penetrated to people's hearts and by a truly human dialogue led them to the divine light, so too his disciples, profoundly pervaded by the Spirit of Christ, should know and converse with those among whom they live, that through sincere and patient dialogue they themselves might learn of the riches which a generous God has distributed among the nations" (AG 11). The theme is repeated elsewhere, in articles 12, 16, 34, and 41.

However: "On one key theme, the universality of revelation and faith, *Ad Gentes* broke new ground."[176] Article 7 emphasizes the universal salvific will of God (repeating the classic text, 1 Tim 2:4-5). Because salvation can be found in no other name than that of Jesus (Acts 4:12), the church "has the obligation and also the sacred right to evangelize." Nevertheless, concerning those in invincible ignorance of the Gospel and the necessity of the church for salvation, the decree states: "in ways known to himself God can lead those who, through no fault of their own are ignorant of the gospel, to that faith without which it is impossible to please him (Heb 11:6)" (AG 7). Gerald O'Collins interprets this passage as referring to "saving faith":[177] "Recognizing explicitly that the divine activity of revelation and the human response of faith also take place among those who follow other religions or none at all occurs briefly in *Ad Gentes* [7]. But the decree stands apart in being the first text from the twenty-one ecumenical councils of Catholic Christianity to acknowledge expressly (a) that God's self-revelation reaches all people, and (b) that human beings, no matter who they are and where they are, can and should respond with faith."[178]

Whereas the council's agenda at its opening in 1962 envisaged some statement regarding the Catholic Church and the Jews (which became *Nostra Aetate* 4), *Gaudium et Spes* emerged out of the dynamic of the council only

176. O'Collins, "Vatican II on Other Living Faiths," 121.
177. O'Collins, *The Second Vatican Council on Other Religions*, 120.
178. Ibid., 118.

once it started. The drafting of both documents reveals the council's developing universalist vision regarding God's revelatory and saving activity in the world, albeit within its proclamation/dialogue principle. The two documents are to be read in tandem. As Adrian Hastings remarks: "When reading *Nostra Aetate* 1, it is well to turn to *Gaudium et Spes* 11–12 and 24–26. Indeed the Church's whole new positive attitude to non-Christian religions must be understood within the context of her attitude to the modern world and the growing world society in which we have all to participate."[179]

The pastoral constitution repeats some of the themes we have seen in the other documents. That all human beings are created in God's image and likeness and therefore have a common origin and destiny in God and that God's plan envisages unity among all human beings is a vision that pervades the constitution. "God, who has a parent's care for all of us, desired that all men and women should form one family and deal with each other as brothers and sisters. All, in fact, are destined to the very same end, namely God himself, since they have been created in the likeness of God" (GS 24; see also GS 12, 22, 29, 34, 41, 52, 68). From the dignity of all comes the right of all to religious freedom (GS 26). Moreover, because of the equal dignity of all, discrimination is to be rejected: "All women and men are endowed with a rational soul and are created in God's image; they have the same nature and origin and, being redeemed by Christ, they enjoy the same divine calling and destiny; there is here a basic equality between all. . . . [A]ny kind of social or cultural discrimination in basic personal rights on the grounds of sex, race, color, social conditions, language or religion, must be curbed and eradicated as incompatible with God's design" (GS 29).

The constitution's christological benchmark is clear; it does not recoil from the fundamental proclamation of the Christian faith. Jesus Christ is the "most perfect embodiment" of humanity, he who is the "image of the invisible God" (Col 1:15; GS 22). He reveals "the mystery of humanity" and, through the power of the Holy Spirit, enables human beings "to fulfil the new law of love" (GS 22). This central article goes on: "All this holds true not only for Christians but also for all people of good will in whose hearts grace is active invisibly. For since Christ died for everyone, and since all are in fact called to one and the same destiny, which is divine, we must hold that the Holy Spirit offers to all the possibility of being made partners, in a way known to God, in the paschal mystery" (GS 22).

---

179. Hastings, *A Concise Guide to the Documents*, 1:200.

The constitution also reprises themes from the other documents regarding the hidden presence and activity of God in the lives and practices of non-Christian believers: allusions to the "seeds of the word" motif (GS 3, 18); the motif of "preparation for the Gospel" (GS 40, 57); the Johannine doublet of "true and good" (GS 15, 28), with variations of "true, good and just" (GS 42) and "true, good and beautiful" (GS 57, 76).[180]

Perhaps the greatest contribution *Gaudium et Spes* makes to the issue of the church's relations with non-Christian believers is the pastoral constitution's extended treatment of the themes of dialogue and collaboration. Its doctrine on the relation of the church and non-Christian religions is to be interpreted through the lens of its advocacy of a new way of relating to non-Christian religions and their adherents (a dynamic that enables a renewed interpretation of the doctrine). The opening preface articulates the very purpose of the constitution as seeking dialogue with the whole human family (GS 3). This theme recurs throughout the document (GS 28, 40, 84). The conclusion of the constitution proposes for the church a dialogic engagement with the world, envisaging four concentric circles of dialogue. Regarding the Christian/religious principle, it states: "Our thoughts also go out to all who acknowledge God and who preserve precious religious and human elements in their traditions; it is our hope that frank dialogue will spur us all on to receive the impulses of the Spirit with fidelity and act upon them with alacrity" (GS 92).

For Francis Sullivan, the council's teaching regarding the salvific value of other religions constitutes a "development of doctrine."[181] Gerald O'Collins similarly asserts: "The accumulation of evidence establishes decisively that, by its teaching on 'non-Christian religions,' the Council brought a dramatic change in doctrine . . . a massive shift in the official doctrine and practice of the Catholic Church. If this is not a case of considerable discontinuity and, when we remember the Council of Florence, a case of reversal, some odd

180. For a fuller treatment of these points, see O'Collins, *The Second Vatican Council on Other Religions*, 128–42.

181. Francis A. Sullivan, "Vatican II and the Postconciliar Magisterium on the Salvation of the Adherents of Other Religions," in *After Vatican II: Trajectories and Hermeneutics*, ed. James Heft (Grand Rapids, MI: Eerdmans, 2012), 68–95, at 68, 95.

criteria must be operating for those who want to see only continuity."[182] With its acknowledgment in *Lumen Gentium* 8 of the church's need for purification because of the sinfulness of the church, in *Nostra Aetate* the Catholic Church finally faces Catholic racism and Catholics' sinful past with regard to the Jews, albeit in muted tones. For Paul Knitter, the broader teaching on other religions is unprecedented:

> The council stands as a milestone in the history of what the Christian church has said about other faiths and about itself in relation to them. Never before had a church, in its official pronouncements, dealt so extensively with other religions, never before had it said such positive things about them; never before had it called upon all Christians to take these religions seriously and dialogue with them. Compared to the "Outside the church, no salvation" view that held sway from the fifth to the sixteenth centuries, Vatican II is not just a milestone, but a fork in the road.[183]

But even more so, "the importance of *Nostra Aetate* consists not only in what it affirms but above all in the consequences it has had."[184] The council moves away from an exclusive focus on defending "truth" (in terms of its doctrinal heritage) and embraces an approach that combines *a defense of truth through goodness*. What is "right" is best manifested through a display of what is "good." What Cardinal Bea remarked on November 20, 1964, concerning the action plan that *Nostra Aetate* set forth is true of all that the council states, throughout the corpus of its documents, regarding the Christian/religious principle: "The Declaration ought to lead to effective action. Its principles and spirit should inspire the lives of all Christians and all men, so that the dialogue explained by the Pope in the encyclical *Ecclesiam Suam* may be begun. It is here, in the fruits which this Declaration should and will have after the Council, that its main importance lies."[185]

As the hermeneutical proclamation/dialogue principle proposes, any interpretation of what the council is teaching should presume that it is attempting to hold on to the fundamental beliefs of Christianity (and of the Catholic Church), *and yet* do so in a way that does not perpetuate an ideo-

182. O'Collins, *The Second Vatican Council on Other Religions*, 204.

183. Paul F. Knitter, *Introducing Theologies of Religions* (Maryknoll, NY: Orbis Books, 2002), 75.

184. Sievers, "How Irrevocable? Interpreting Romans 11:29," 757.

185. Quoted in Oesterreicher, "Declaration on the Relationship of the Church to Non-Christian Religions," 130.

logical drumbeat, particularly that of the second millennium, an approach that had produced such disastrous results across the centuries in interreligious relations. The council wanted a new way. That way was the way of *rapprochement* and dialogue along with *an ethical commitment* to a new way of acting and relating. But such commitments to a new way, for the council, did not mean foregoing proclamation of fundamental beliefs; it did, however, presuppose that authentic witness would do more to persuade than ideological warfare. What Heinrich Fries has said of Vatican II's Catholic/ecumenical principle might well capture, in an equally striking way, the essence of the council's Christian/religious principle: "In the question of 'the Church [and other religions]' Vatican II discovered a principle according to which the Church's identity and continuity were to be preserved not by separating off or denying everything that was not itself but by linking fidelity to itself with openness to others rather than with the denigration of others."[186]

186. Fries, "Church and Churches," 316.

Principle 24
Church/World

Principle 24: God calls the church to serve all humanity and to promote the dignity, common good, and unity of all peoples; rather than simply reproaching the world for its failings, the church must reach out to all human beings in practical solidarity and open dialogue within the ever-shifting conditions of human history, manifesting the genuine face of God and helping transform the world according to God's plan.

Vatican II wanted the church to present a new face to the world. The council's church/world principle encapsulates that conciliar vision in two interrelated ways. First, the council called the church to be present in the world like a sacrament, manifesting and actualizing God's compassionate and saving love, by promoting human dignity, the common good, and the unity of all peoples. Second, since "God so loved the world that he gave his only Son" (John 3:16), the council desired that the church, while proclaiming the living Gospel boldly, should do so in a way that is genuinely open in dialogue to the wisdom and sincerity of other voices in the world (through whom God might very well be also speaking), without, however, being blind to the errors and evils that impede God's plan.

The first aspect of the church/world principle had always been at the fore in the church's pastoral presence in society throughout the centuries. Vatican II, for the first time in a conciliar statement, sought to rejuvenate that mission of solidarity and offer an agenda for an increasingly complex world. On the council's second-to-last day, December 7, 1965, after having just promulgated *Gaudium et Spes*, Pope Paul VI spoke of this impulse almost as a rediscovery on the part of the council: "The old story of the Good Samaritan has been the model of the spirituality of the council. A feeling of boundless sympathy has permeated the whole of it. The attention of our council has been absorbed by the discovery of human needs."[1] He then went on to emphasize that the council saw service to humanity as the proper mode of the church's presence in the world: "All this rich teaching is channeled in one direction, the service of mankind, of every condition, in every weakness and need. The Church has, so to say, declared herself the servant of humanity, at the very time when her teaching role and her pastoral government have, by reason of the council's solemnity, assumed greater splendor and vigor: *the idea of service has been central.*"[2]

Regarding the second aspect, the desire for a church that both proclaims boldly and listens humbly, the council made what can only be described as a dramatic about-face in the Catholic Church's official position. Along the way, however, the council struggled at times to articulate theologically this dialogic relationship with the world. Consequently, the tortuous history of the conciliar debate on the topic itself becomes a tensive element embedded in the church/world principle. The very difficulty of coming to a final articulation becomes an object lesson in the diverse approaches to good Catholic theology, since the bishops and *periti* could not always agree on the proper methodological approach and theological framework for capturing the desired vision of a church that relates dialogically with the world in the ever-shifting conditions of human history. As the hermeneutical proclamation/dialogue principle notes, Vatican II was wanting to be faithful in proclaiming the truth of Christian revelation but to do so in a way that engaged with the shifting conditions of modern life.

These two aspects, the church as a Good Samaritan and the church as a willing dialogue partner, are both closely related to the vision of a church that is "pastoral" and make up the two intertwined elements of the final conciliar principle, the church/world principle.

From Syllabus to Counter-Syllabus

One major reason for the difficulty the council had in articulating a more open stance to the world was the church's long entrenched position of negativity to so many features of the "modern" world against which it identified itself. In the church's more recent history, particularly since the Enlightenment and the French Revolution, as well as the changing political landscape in Europe during the nineteenth century, the church had adopted a strident, indeed

---

1. Paul VI, "Closing Address: Fourth Session," 360.
2. Ibid., 361. Translation corrected. Emphasis added.

antagonistic, attitude to "the world."[3] It felt the world was turned against it. "If the Age of Reason had threatened the authority of the church in various intellectual spheres, the Age of Revolution threatened its very existence."[4]

Perhaps nothing symbolizes better the siege mentality adopted by nineteenth-century popes than the 1864 document called the *Syllabus of Errors*.[5] Appended to the encyclical *Quanta Cura* of Pope Pius IX, it was a collection of eighty perceived errors in contemporary society that the pope had previously condemned, ranging from religious freedom to political liberalism and the separation of church and state. The *Syllabus* characterized a refusal by the Catholic Church to engage with contemporary thought and the socio-political shifts going on throughout Europe. Its answer to these contemporary errors lay in emphasizing the spiritual authority of the papacy. Among many Catholics the *Syllabus* helped promote the cause of an even more entrenched "ultramontanism."[6] While this reached its greatest formulation at the First Vatican Council five years later, the *Syllabus of Errors* remained emblematic over the next century for a particularly antagonistic self-understanding of the Catholic Church in relationship with the world beleaguering it.

In his opening address at Vatican II's second session, soon after becoming pope, Paul VI spoke of "the main objectives of the council."[7] In describing the fourth and final objective (*"the dialogue of the church with the contemporary world"*), the pope used the image of a bridge: "The council will build a bridge toward the contemporary world."[8] The metaphor implicitly evoked the image of a divide or gulf that had opened up historically between the

---

3. On the impact of these social and political forces on the Catholic Church, see Nicholas Atkin and Frank Tallett, *Priests, Prelates, and People: A History of European Catholicism since 1750* (London: I. B. Taurus, 2003); Christopher M. Clark and Wolfram Kaiser, eds., *Culture Wars: Secular-Catholic Conflict in Nineteenth-Century Europe* (New York: Cambridge University Press, 2003); Stephen Schloesser, "Reproach vs. *Rapprochement*: Historical Preconditions of a Paradigm Shift in the Reform of Vatican II," in *50 Years On: Probing the Riches of Vatican II*, ed. David G. Schultenover (Collegeville, MN: Liturgical Press, 2015), xi–xlix; John A. Dick, Karim Schelkens, and Jürgen Mettepenningen, *Aggiornamento? Catholicism from Gregory XVI to Benedict XVI* (Leiden: Brill, 2013), 28–44.

4. T. Howland Sanks, *Salt, Leaven, and Light: The Community Called Church* (New York: Crossroad, 1992), 99. Quoted in Richard R. Gaillardetz and Catherine E. Clifford, *Keys to the Council: Unlocking the Teaching of Vatican II* (Collegeville, MN: Liturgical Press, 2012), 88.

5. DS 2901–80. See Denzinger, *Compendium of Creeds, Definitions, and Declarations*, 590–98.

6. On the "ultramontane" view of the church, see O'Malley, *Vatican I*, 1–107.

7. Paul VI, "Opening Address: Second Session," 146–50. The pope summarized these four objectives: "the knowledge, or—if you prefer—the awareness of the Church; its reform; the bringing together of all Christians in unity; the dialogue of the Church with the contemporary world." Ibid., 146.

8. Ibid., 148.

church and wider society, particularly during the Pian era of the previous 150 years.[9] One of those Pian popes, Pius IX, in the eightieth and last of his *Syllabus of Errors*, had condemned the following belief: "The Roman pontiff can and should reconcile and adapt himself to progress, liberalism, and the modern culture."[10] Ninety-nine years later, in 1963, another Roman pontiff, Paul VI, now speaks to an ecumenical council of a bridge of reconciliation that the council intended to build, for the sake of a more effective mission in the world: "Let the world know this: The Church looks at the world with profound understanding, with sincere admiration and with the sincere intention not of conquering it, but of serving it; not of despising it, but of appreciating it; not of condemning it, but of strengthening and saving it."[11] The historian John O'Malley captures the vast difference between the stance symbolized by the *Syllabus of Errors* and that symbolized by Vatican II: "A stance of reconciliation replaced a stance of alienation."[12]

Writing ten years after the close of the council, Joseph Ratzinger, also using the language of "reconciliation," provides an insight into what Vatican II was doing: "If it is desirable to offer a diagnosis of the text [of *Gaudium et Spes*] as a whole, we might say that (in conjunction with the texts on religious liberty and world religions) it is *a revision of the Syllabus of Pius IX*, a kind of *countersyllabus*."[13] For Ratzinger, the 1864 *Syllabus of Errors* of Pius IX was marked by "one-sidedness . . . in response to the situation created by the new phase of history inaugurated by the French Revolution."[14] The three texts of *Gaudium et Spes*, *Dignitatis Humanae*, and *Nostra Aetate* constitute a "counter-syllabus," he said, because they are "an attempt at an official reconciliation with the new era inaugurated in 1789."[15]

For Jared Wicks, Ratzinger's notion of a "counter-syllabus" strikingly captures the historic nature of the council's shift in attitude to the contemporary world, when seen in contrast to the previous 150 years.[16] Wicks

9. On the Pian era, from Pope Pius VI (1775–1799) to Pope Pius XII (1939–1958), see O'Malley, *What Happened at Vatican II*, 53–92. The pontificates of Pius VI and Pius XII bracket the period from the eve of the French Revolution to the eve of the Second Vatican Council.

10. DS 2980. See Denzinger, *Compendium of Creeds, Definitions, and Declarations*, 598.

11. Paul VI, "Opening Address: Second Session," 149.

12. O'Malley, "Vatican II Revisited as Reconciliation," 7.

13. Ratzinger, "Church and World," 381. Emphasis added.

14. Ibid., 381.

15. Ibid., 382.

16. See Jared Wicks, *Investigating Vatican II: Its Theologians, Ecumenical Turn, and Biblical Commitment* (Washington, DC: The Catholic University of America Press, 2018), 7, 30n55, 109–13, and 230–31.

proposes that Ratzinger's list of key documents be expanded and applies the notion of "counter-syllabus" also to *Unitatis Redintegratio*, for it too, he asserts, has "a 'counter' and 'corrective' character."[17] Thus, for Wicks, these four documents form a cumulative whole—and indeed a subversive subset—within the conciliar corpus, a whole that is greater than the contribution of each of the four documents on their own. Wicks notes that the dramatic difference from the past constituted by these four documents is simply illustrated by the fierce opposition to all four of these texts by the minority of around "10 to 15 per cent" of the conciliar assembly, especially the *Coetus Internationalis Patrum*.[18] They opposed it because, if accepted, it would mean *a change in church teaching*, something the *Syllabus* couldn't envisage. But, with the historical consciousness that the faith/history principle has explored, the notion of change was something the council was beginning to see in a new light.

This chapter proposes that one major characteristic of Vatican II's counter-syllabus can be formulated as a final principle, the church/world principle. We have already explored in detail the drafting history of two documents making up the council's counter-syllabus (taking Wicks's expanded list): *Unitatis Redintegratio* and *Nostra Aetate*. Discussion above regarding the Catholic/ecumenical principle has examined the former, and the Christian/religious principle, the latter. It is now necessary to explore the issues at stake in the drafting of the remaining two documents: *Dignitatis Humanae* and *Gaudium et Spes*, both promulgated on December 7, 1965. Some of the themes treated in these two documents have been examined previously: the chapter on the revelation/faith principle has discussed faith and religious freedom; the chapter on the protological/eschatological principle has discussed the tensions experienced within the council in articulating a theological anthropology; and the chapter on the *fideles/fidelis* principle has explored the inviolability of an individual's conscience and the intertextual meaning of *Dignitatis Humanae* 3 (on the individual believer's discovery of

17. Ibid., 113.

18. O'Malley, *What Happened at Vatican II*, 8. On the history and impact of the *Coetus*, and its appeal to the *Syllabus*, see Philippe J. Roy, "La préhistoire du *Coetus internationalis Patrum*: Une formation romaine, antilibéral et contre-révolutionnaire," in *La Théologie catholique entre intransigeance et renouveau: La réception des mouvements préconciliaires à Vatican II*, ed. Gilles Routhier, et al. (Louvain-La-Neuve; Leuven: Collège Érasme; Universiteitsbibliotheek, 2011), 321–54; Philippe Roy-Lysencourt, "Histoire du *Coetus Internationalis Patrum* au concile Vatican II," *Laval Théologique et Philosophique* 69 (2013): 261–79.

truth) for understanding the council's vision of the role the *sensus fidelium* should play in the teaching office of the church.

The next section will look closely at the church/world issue that emerged during drafting of the much longer pastoral constitution. The history of the shorter Declaration on Religious Liberty is certainly tortuous but can be summarized here more briefly.[19] The 1864 *Syllabus of Errors* clearly condemned any talk of religious freedom.[20] Therefore, when raised on the council agenda, the discussion was destined to be stormy. "Probably, taken all in all, this was the most bitterly disputed question which the Council tackled."[21]

Key figures in the history of the schema include Cardinal Augustin Bea (a promoter of the schema from the beginning), Bishop Émile de Smedt (who presented the *relationes* to the council), along with John Courtney Murray (the American *peritus* who had written much on the topic).[22] Another key "protagonist" was a collective of ultraconservative bishops, made up of several like-minded groups: the *Coetus Internationalis Patrum*;[23] most of the Spanish hierarchy; and certain cardinals of the Roman Curia, such as Alfredo Ottaviani, Michael Browne, and Giuseppe Siri. If there was any collective in the council hall that would appeal to the authority of Pius IX's *Syllabus of Errors*, it was this group. As a voting bloc, they had over two hundred signatures. They stridently opposed any attempt to change the church's long-held teaching; as O'Malley summarizes it: "The basic premise of the teaching was that only truth has a right to freedom, or, put negatively

---

19. On the drafting of *Dignitatis Humanae*, see Scatena, *La fatica della libertà*; Pavan, "Declaration on Religious Freedom," 49–62; Siebenrock, "Theologischer Kommentar zur Erklärung über die religiöse Freiheit," 152–65; Healy, "The Drafting of *Dignitatis Humanae*."

20. A few examples can be selected. The fifteenth error condemned is the belief: "Everyone is free to embrace and profess the religion that by the light of reason he judges to be true." DS 2915. Denzinger, *Compendium of Creeds, Definitions, and Declarations*, 592. The seventy-ninth error states: "It is in fact false that civil freedom of worship and the full right granted to all to express openly and publicly any opinions and views lead to an easier corruption of morality and of the minds of people and help to propagate the plague of indifferentism." DS 2979. Ibid., 598.

21. Hastings, *A Concise Guide to the Documents*, 2:76.

22. Murray began to be officially involved in the drafting of the schema with Pietro Pavan only after the first conciliar debate on the schema in September 1964. On the importance of Murray's contribution, see Dominique Gonnet, *La liberté religieuse à Vatican II la contribution de John Courtney Murray, SJ* (Paris: Cerf, 1994); Dominique Gonnet, "L'apport de John Courtney Murray au schéma sur la liberté religieuse," in *Les commissions conciliaires à Vatican II*, ed. Matthijs Lamberigts, Claude Soetens, and Jan Grootaers (Leuven: Bibliotheek van de Faculteit Godgeleerdheid, 1996), 205–15.

23. On the historical background of this group's mentality, see Roy, "La préhistoire du *Coetus internationalis Patrum*."

as it often is, 'error has no rights.' "[24] Many of the bishops opposing any promotion of religious freedom came from Catholic-majority countries like Spain and Italy, which, after the revolutionary changes to society in the nineteenth century, had been able to negotiate special concordats to safeguard the religious freedom of Catholics but not necessarily of others. There was an inherent hypocrisy in the church's position that the council would come to correct. The special treatment the church expected, ever since the ancient Constantinian edict, was finally undone. In this sense, as Peter Hünermann and others have remarked, Vatican II here marks a break with the Constantinian era.[25]

As the previous two chapters on the Catholic/ecumenical and Christian/religious principles have already noted, the council's statement on religious freedom was originally part of the Decree on Ecumenism (drafted by the Secretariat for Promoting Christian Unity), first as its fifth chapter, and then, in the next draft, as an appendix to the document. Linking the topic with that of ecumenism followed the rationale that ecumenical openness implied a recognition of religious freedom. By 1964, the statement had become a separate document. It was seen to be a topic with much wider ramifications than simply an issue related to ecumenism. It related to the church/world issue. The ambiguity of the church's previous position on religious freedom and the dignity of conscience, therefore, needed to be reexamined within a much vaster landscape. But affirming religious freedom for all would be a dramatic change from previous church teaching. Indeed, it would have implications for reconceiving how the mystery and mission of the church was to be understood.

All of these issues came up during debate on the third draft of the schema during the third session (September 23–25 and 28, 1964). The draft emphasized the necessary freedom of the act of faith for all believers, no matter what their religion; no government or religious body has the right to coerce people in the matter of faith; individuals have the sacred right to follow responsibly the dictates of their own informed consciences; governments must protect individuals and their religious organizations from any impediments to the free practice of religion. In bringing together notions such as *imago Dei*, an informed conscience, human dignity, the common good, and a reconfigured relationship between church and state, the draft was drawing on a *ressourcement* of the Catholic tradition that marked a shift away from

24. O'Malley, *What Happened at Vatican II*, 212.
25. See, for example, Hünermann, "Kriterien für die Rezeption des II. Vatikanischen Konzils."

preconciliar papal teaching up to Pius XII.[26] It was clear that, if this new vision was accepted by the council, it would directly impact on the way the Roman Catholic Church deals with civil governments throughout the world. Cardinal Bea, in 1961, had remarked on the newness of these ideas: "This is not traditional teaching, but life today is not traditional."[27]

There were forty-four speeches over four days.[28] Despite widespread support for the schema, there was also fierce opposition. Those opposed were quick to point out the contrast with traditional teaching and with the current practice of concordats between church and state. The Australian Cardinal Norman Gilroy joined the usual spokespersons for the minority (Ruffini, Ottaviani, Browne, Siri), with advocacy of the "error has no rights" approach: "Is it really possible for an ecumenical council to say that any heretic has the right to draw the faithful away from Christ, the Supreme Pastor, and to lead them to pasture in their poisoned fields?"[29] But strong support came from the American cardinals and from bishops in communist countries. Nevertheless, even those in favor knew that the schema needed improvement. When the debate ended, the drafting commission set to work on revising the text, in order for it to be sent back to the council for voting before the session ended.

During the last week of this third session, the so-called *settimana nera* (black week), the fate of the declaration was, however, caught up in a storm of other conciliar affairs, as has been discussed above. One element of the drama was the decision by the council authorities (Paul VI, at the urging of the conservative collective) to postpone a vote on the now revised religious liberty schema. As with the other issues related to this "black week," this apparent ploy to scuttle the schema caused deep consternation even outside the council hall; it was a text for which the secular press, and indeed many throughout the non-Catholic world, had such high hopes. While a vote on the text was delayed until the fourth session, Paul VI promised that this issue would be the first matter of discussion when the next session opened. So, despite the angst, the delay resulted in a much better result. During the

26. On the break with previous teaching that these ideas constituted, see Bernard Lucien, *Études sur la liberté religieuse dans la doctrine catholique: Grégoire XVI, Pie IX et Vatican II* (Tours: Éditions Forts dans la foi, 1990).

27. Quoted in Miccoli, "Two Sensitive Issues," 100.

28. For English translations of six key speeches in this debate, see "Religious Liberty," in *Third Session Council Speeches of Vatican II*, ed. William K. Leahy and Anthony T. Massimini (Glen Rock, NJ: Paulist Press, 1966), 41–62.

29. AS III/2, 611–12. Quoted in O'Malley, *What Happened at Vatican II*, 218.

intersession, after considering suggestions submitted by bishops after the third session ended, the Secretariat for Christian Unity came up with a much richer text. The *peritus* Pietro Pavan summarizes this new draft: "The structure of the fourth schema is basically the same as that of the third, the essential elements of which are taken over. They are, however, presented in a shorter, clearer and more orderly form, the sequence of thought being less complicated and more evident. Hence not a few fathers considered it providential that the third schema had been neither discussed nor voted on in the aula, though of course not as regards the motives nor the manner in which the final decision had been arrived at."[30]

When the fourth session began, as the pope had promised, the schema on religious freedom was the first item on the agenda. The debate over five days (September 15–17, 20–21, 1965) "was perhaps the most violent ever to have taken place in the aula."[31] The council seemed to be divided into three groups: those who were happy with the draft; those who were generally happy but wanted further changes; and those who were against it, either not wanting a schema at all or requiring it to be totally rewritten from the ground up. Although many voices in support were heard, the opponents were vociferous. The fate of the schema seemed so uncertain. A vote on whether the bishops wanted this text as a basis for further discussion, however, soon clarified the uncertainty. In favor were 1,997; against were 224. The vote revealed "that the opponents were a much, much smaller number than the interventions in St Peter's suggested."[32] After the Secretariat had incorporated the bishops' spoken and written requests (despite more obstructionist attempts by the conservatives, especially by appealing directly to the pope), the final vote was taken. Still, there were 249 negative votes, "one of the largest negative votes at this stage of its process for any document of the council."[33] Nevertheless, it was clear: on several "errors" of Pius IX's *Syllabus of Errors*, the Catholic Church had taken an about-face.

Some of the central affirmations of the declaration have already been discussed in relation to other conciliar principles: the dignity and social nature of the human person; the necessary freedom of the act of faith; the inviolability of conscience, along with the corresponding responsibility of all to work for the common good of all. Some further salient points can be

---

30. Pavan, "Declaration on Religious Freedom," 56.
31. Ibid., 57.
32. O'Malley, *What Happened at Vatican II*, 257.
33. Ibid., 358.

summarized here. Rather than working from abstract principles, such as "error has no rights," the declaration begins with the dignity and rights of the human person: "the right to religious freedom is based on the very dignity of the human person as known through the revealed word of God and by reason itself" (DH 2). It defends the right of all peoples to be free from co-ercion by others, either state or church, in matters of religious belief and practice. The sacred act of faith must be a free act: a free act of loving submis-sion to God and an act free from human coercion. If there is any force in-volved, it is the power of truth: "Truth can impose itself on the human mind by the force of its own truth, which wins over the mind with both gentleness and power" (DH 1).

Since she herself had used coercion in her own history, this all meant for the Catholic Church that a new disposition and modality in its proclamation of the Christian truth was required in the church's relationship with the world. Perhaps the most compelling reason given by the council for conver-sion to a new model is a biblical warrant: *the way Jesus himself proclaimed divine truth* (see DH 11). As many of the bishops and *periti* pointed out, there is no specific Scripture passage that can be called upon to justify the principle of religious freedom. For such a scriptural grounding, the council turned first to the overall witness of Scripture and then more specifically to the wit-ness of Jesus' own words and behavior: "God has regard for the dignity of the human person which he himself created; human persons are to be guided by their own judgment and to enjoy freedom. This fact received its fullest manifestation in Christ Jesus in whom God perfectly revealed himself and his ways" (DH 11). Then the rest of article 11 goes on to highlight aspects of Jesus' ministry—not only his words, but also his mode of speaking, of relat-ing, and of behaving. A selection of passages illustrates the declaration's appeal to Jesus' content and manner of teaching, as well as manner of relating and acting. Jesus, who was "meek and humble of heart, acted patiently in attracting and inviting his disciples." He set out "to invite the faith of his hearers and give them assurance, but not to coerce them." He taught that God lets weeds grow among the wheat until harvest time. "He did not wish to be a political Messiah who would dominate by force but preferred to call himself the Son of Man who came to serve." He saw himself as "the Servant of God who 'will not break a bruised reed or quench a smouldering wick.'" He "bore witness to the truth but refused to use force to impose it on those who spoke out against it. His kingdom does not establish its claims by force, but is established by bearing witness to and hearing the truth." This truth "grows by the love with which Christ, lifted up on the cross, draws people to himself." In sum, Jesus' ministry was characterized by meekness, humility, patience, attraction, invitation, assurance—not condemnation or coercion—along with a desire not to crush those who fail but to allow the power of God's grace to work among "the weeds" to a successful end. The declaration then goes on to show how the early church imitated this way of Jesus: "The disciples of Christ strove to persuade people to confess Christ as Lord, not however, by applying coercion or with the use of techniques unworthy of the Gospel but, above all, by the power of the word of God."

After such a remarkable appeal to the praxis of Jesus, the following article 12, with a certain defensiveness, contrasts this ideal with the facts and the church's attitudes and actions in the past: "Although in the life of the People of God in its pilgrimage, through the vicissitudes of human history, there have at times appeared patterns of behaviour which were not in keeping with the spirit of the Gospel and were even opposed to it, *it has always remained the teaching of the church that no one is to be coerced into believing*" (DH 12).[34] It then immediately goes on to intimate that this teaching on religious liberty is, however, indeed a development in the church's doctrine: "Thus the leaven of the Gospel has long been at work in people's minds and has contributed greatly to a wider recognition by them in the course of time of their dignity as persons. It has contributed too to the growth of the conviction that in religious matters the human person should be kept free from all manner of coercion in civil society" (DH 12).

As the famous statement of John Courtney Murray notes: development of doctrine was "*the* issue under the issues" at Vatican II—and it remains embedded in its comprehensive vision.[35] In his introduction to the Abbott translation of *Dignitatis Humanae*, John Courtney Murray remarks:

> It can hardly be maintained that the Declaration [on Religious Liberty] is a milestone in human history—moral, political, or intellectual. The principle of religious freedom has long been recognized in constitutional law, to the point where even Marxist-Leninist political ideology is obliged to pay lip-service to it. In all honesty it must be admitted that the Church is late in acknowledging the validity of the principle. In any event, the document is a significant event in the history of the Church. It was, of course, the most controversial document of the whole Council, largely because it raised with sharp emphasis the issue that lay continually below the surface of all the conciliar debates—the

34. Translation corrected. Emphasis added.
35. Murray, "This Matter of Religious Freedom," 43.

issue of the development of doctrine. The notion of development, not the notion of religious freedom, was the real sticking-point for many of those who opposed the Declaration even to the end. The course of the development between the *Syllabus of Errors* (1864) and *Dignitatis Humanae Personae* (1965) still remains to be explained by theologians. But the Council formally sanctioned the validity of the development itself; and this was a doctrinal event of high importance for theological thought in many other areas.[36]

The Travails of a "Pastoral" Constitution

We have seen how, according to Adrian Hastings, *Dignitatis Humanae* addressed what was probably "the most bitterly disputed question which the Council tackled."[37] Also we have seen how *Unitatis Redintegratio* and *Nostra Aetate* likewise faced strong opposition from the small conciliar minority of around "10 to 15 per cent."[38] We now come to the fourth document of the counter-syllabus, *Gaudium et Spes*. It too had its problems, notes Jan Grootaers: "None of the sixteen texts promulgated by Vatican II went through as slow, as long, and as complex a development as the schema that, last on the list on the Coordinating Commission's agenda in January 1963, was therefore called schema XVII."[39]

36. Murray, "Religious Freedom," 673.
37. Hastings, *A Concise Guide to the Documents*, 2:76.
38. O'Malley, *What Happened at Vatican II*, 8.
39. Grootaers, "The Drama Continues between the Acts: The 'Second Preparation' and Its Opponents," 412. For a synoptic presentation of the four major drafts, along with the various *relationes* ("reports") to the council assembly by the drafting commissions, see Gil Hellín, ed., *Constitutionis pastoralis de ecclesia in mundo huius temporis Gaudium et spes*. The most extensive history of this process can be found in Turbanti, *Un Concilio per il Mondo Moderno*. In what follows, a further important source will be the relevant sections throughout Giuseppe Alberigo and Joseph A. Komonchak, eds., *History of Vatican II*, 5 vols. (Maryknoll, NY: Orbis Books, 1996–2004). See also Charles Moeller, "Pastoral Constitution on the Church in the Modern World: History of the Constitution," in *Commentary on the Documents of Vatican II*, vol. 5, ed. Herbert Vorgrimler (New York: Herder and Herder, 1969), 5:1–76; Hans-Joachim Sander, "Theologischer Kommentar zur Pastoralkonstitution über die Kirche in der Welt von heute, Gaudium et Spes," in *Herders theologischer Kommentar zum Zweiten Vatikanischen Konzil*, ed. Peter Hünermann and Bernd Jochen Hilberath (Freiburg: Herder, 2005), 4:581–886, at 616–91. For briefer overviews of the drafting history, see Mark G. McGrath, "The Constitution on the Church in the Modern World," in *Vatican II: An Interfaith Appraisal*, ed. John H. Miller (Notre Dame, IN: University of Notre Dame, 1966), 397–412; Henri de Riedmatten, "History of the Pastoral Constitution," in *The Church Today: Commentaries on the Pastoral Constitution on the Church in the Modern World*, ed. Group 2000 (New York: Newman Press, 1967), 1–40; Norman P. Tanner, *The Church and the World: Gaudium et Spes, Inter Mirifica* (Mahwah, NJ: Paulist Press, 2005), 3–37; Lawler, Salzman, and Burke-Sullivan, *The Church in the Modern World*, 13–40.

It is necessary for us now to trace through in some detail that slow, long, and complex drafting history, because, as Otto Hermann Pesch remarks, "this history is almost more important than the end product itself. The opening of the Church to the world was completed *in the process of the work* on a text about the opening of the Church to the world."[40] Examining the detailed history is necessary because, first, it will enable us to see more clearly the profound *methodological, theological,* and indeed *ecclesiastical-political* difficulties the council experienced in articulating this final element of its desired "counter-syllabus." Second, it will highlight a recurring problem: one of the major reasons why the bishops kept sending the schema back for redrafting was that *the right tone of address* had not yet been found. The council wanted to speak in a new way, because it had come to understand itself, the speaker, in a new kind of relationship with those to whom it was speaking—"the world."

When Pope John XXIII formally convoked the council on December 25, 1961, with his apostolic constitution *Humanae Salutis,* he spoke of the earthly dimension of the church's mission: "Though not having direct earthly ends, [the church] cannot, however, in its mission fail to interest itself in the problems and worries of here below. It knows how beneficial to the good of the souls are those means that are apt to make the life of those individual men who must be saved more human. It knows that by vivifying the temporal order with the light of Christ it reveals men to themselves; it leads them, therefore to discover in themselves their very nature, their own dignity, their own end."[41] The pope goes on to list some aspects of human affairs that make up that concern for the "more human": "Hence, the living presence of the Church extends, by right and by faction, to the international organizations, and to the working out of its social doctrine regarding the family, education, civil society, and all related problems. . . . In this way, the beneficial influence of the Council deliberations must, as we sincerely hope, succeed to the extent of imbuing with Christian light and penetrating with fervent spiritual energy not only the intimacy of the soul but the whole collection of human activities."[42]

Nevertheless, despite this directive, among the more than seventy documents drafted in the preparatory stage, there was no document focusing directly on this fundamental issue. *Gaudium et Spes* would turn out to be such a document. It was a text that emerged out of the dynamic of the council

---

40. Pesch, *The Second Vatican Council,* 307. Emphasis added.
41. John XXIII, "Pope John Convokes the Council: *Humanae Salutis,*" 707.
42. Ibid., 707.

itself—"out of the very heart of Vatican Council II."[43] Among the preparatory schemas, there were certainly a few that treated some of the themes that the pastoral constitution would go on to address.[44] But their tone was generally antipathetic toward "the world."

In the first session, Pope John XXIII in his opening address, *Gaudet Mater Ecclesia*, lamented how the pessimism of the church's traditional stance toward the world was still prevalent:

> In the daily exercise of our pastoral office, we sometimes have to listen, much to our regret, to voices of persons who, though burning with zeal, are not endowed with too much sense of discretion or measure. In these modern times they can see nothing but prevarication and ruin. They say that our era, in comparison with past eras, is getting worse, and they behave as though they had learned nothing from history, which is, none the less, the teacher of life. They behave as though at the time of former Councils everything was a full triumph for the Christian idea and life and for proper religious liberty. We feel we must disagree with those prophets of gloom, who are always forecasting disaster, as though the end of the world were at hand. In the present order of things, Divine Providence is leading us to a new order of human relations which, by men's own efforts and even beyond their very expectations, are directed toward the fulfillment of God's superior and inscrutable designs. And everything, even human differences, leads to the greater good of the Church. It is easy to discern this reality if we consider attentively the world of today.[45]

On October 20, 1962, nine days after Vatican II began, the council released its first document, a message addressed to all humanity.[46] The final text was a revised version of an initial draft penned mainly by Chenu, with contributions from Congar and others.[47] It was the first time in the history of ecumenical councils that a council sought to speak, not just to the church's own

43. McGrath, "The Constitution on the Church in the Modern World," 398.

44. See the list in ibid., 398n1. Of these preparatory schemas, four groups of documents in particular touched on topics that *Gaudium et Spes* would later treat: *De Ordine Morali* (On the moral order), *De Castitate, Matrimonio et Familia, Virginitate* (On chastity, marriage and the family, and virginity), *De Ordine Sociali* (On the social order), and *De Communitate Gentium* (On the Community of Nations).

45. John XXIII, "Pope John's Opening Speech," 712–13.

46. AS I/1, 230–32. For an English translation, see "Message to Humanity," in *The Documents of Vatican II*, ed. Walter M. Abbott (London: Geoffrey Chapman, 1966), 3–7.

47. On the origins of the idea for such a message and the theological critiques made of Chenu's original text by other *periti* and bishops, see Turbanti, *Un Concilio per il Mondo Moderno*, 119–35.

members, but to the whole world.[48] Pope John endorsed the message and indeed "desired that it should be the first official act of the Council."[49] In its message, the council promises to turn its attention to the needs of the whole world, not just the Catholic Church:

> Coming together in unity from every nation under the sun, we carry in our hearts the hardships, the bodily and mental distress, the sorrows, longings and hopes of all the peoples entrusted to us. We urgently turn our thoughts to all the anxieties by which modern humanity is afflicted. Hence, let our concern swiftly focus first of all on those who are especially lowly, poor, and weak. Like Christ, we would have pity on the multitude weighed down with hunger, misery, and lack of knowledge. We want to fix a steady gaze on those who still lack the opportune help to achieve a way of life worthy of human beings.[50]

It would take the whole duration of the council for it to formulate such a vision, with *Gaudium et Spes* being approved on the very last voting day.

After the message was released, there were further indications that the council wanted to broaden its focus, beyond just intramural concerns, to that of the world in which it exists. Discussion of the *ad intra/ad extra* principle has already noted how this distinction arose, both as a practical aid to dividing up the council's agenda and as a way of focusing the council on Pope John's earlier concern for a positive view of the church's relationship with the world. After the first session and the adoption by the conciliar assembly of the *ad intra/ad extra* framework, Pope John set up a Coordinating Commission and asked it to come up with a reduced agenda. On January 27, 1963, the commission produced a list of seventeen possible documents. The first was the document on the church (*De Ecclesia*); the last on the list was a document called "On the active presence of the church in the world" (*De presentia activa Ecclesiae in mundo*). As the last of seventeen, it was thus, initially, referred to as Schema XVII. The Coordinating Commission decided that this document be written by a "mixed commission," with representatives from the Doctrinal (sometimes referred to as "Theological") Commission and the Commission on the Lay Apostolate.[51] The two cardinals chairing

48. See Walter Abbott's footnote added to "Message to Humanity," 3n2.
49. See the introductory commentary by Walter M. Abbott, "Opening Message," in *The Documents of Vatican II*, ed. Walter M. Abbott (London: Geoffrey Chapman, 1966), 1–2, at 1.
50. "Message to Humanity," 5.
51. See Giovanni Turbanti, "La commissione mista per lo schema XVII–XIII," in *Les commissions conciliaires à Vatican II*, ed. Matthijs Lamberigts, Claude Soetens, and Jan Grootaers (Leuven: Bibliotheek van de Faculteit Godgeleerdheid, 1996), 217–50.

those two commissions, Alfredo Ottaviani and Fernando Cento, would also co-chair the Mixed Commission. Cardinal Suenens, in his capacity also as a member of the Coordinating Commission, was charged with reporting back to that commission on the progress of the schema. The Mixed Commission's brief was to prepare a document of six chapters: on the Christian vocation; the human person and human rights; marriage and the family; culture; the social and economic spheres; the worldwide community of nations and global peace.

Throughout the history of its drafting, there would be multiple versions of the document.[52] These, however, can be grouped under four major drafts, named according to the place where their drafting meetings first took place: the Rome, Malines, Zürich, and Ariccia schemas. Each makes important contributions to the forging of a final document. The Roman and Malines schemas were drafted throughout 1963, but each would be rejected as an inadequate base text for conciliar debate. The Zürich schema, after being further revised, would be the first version to come before the council, in the third session of 1964 (October 10–November 5; November 9–10). The Ariccia schema, also after further revision, would be discussed in the fourth session of 1965 (September 21–October 7). Apart from strong differences over topics such as the ends of marriage, communism, atheism, and the use of nuclear weapons, much of the heat in the drafting and debate would relate to the diversity in the methodological and theological models being proposed by bishops and *periti* for conceiving a positive relationship between "church" and "world," the subject of the schema's first part. This drafting history below reveals a tense conciliar dynamic that becomes embedded, between the lines, as it were, of the final text of *Gaudium et Spes*, and becomes an important teaching from Vatican II about theological method and theological diversity.

From February until May 1963, the Mixed Commission, comprising of around sixty members, drafted a succession of five versions of a text, resulting in the Roman schema.[53] The *periti* on the drafting subcommittees for the proposed sections included Yves Congar, Jean Daniélou, Pietro Pavan, Bernhard Häring, Johannes Hirschmann, Philippe Delhaye, Pierre Haubtmann, Charles Moeller, and Roberto Tucci. Daniélou played a prominent role in drafting the text. Laypeople were also involved in these meetings: "Despite the more than reserved attitude of several bishops of the Theological [Doctrinal] Commission,

52. See Vilanova, "The Intersession (1963–1964)," 402.
53. See Turbanti, *Un Concilio per il Mondo Moderno*, 181–262.

23 laymen were invited, 14 of whom were able to attend; three more were invited as observers, one of them a woman, Miss R. Goldie."[54]

Importantly, during this period of drafting, on April 11, 1963, Pope John XXIII promulgated his encyclical *Pacem in Terris*, addressed to all people of good will.[55] It spoke of the positive signs of the times and envisioned a world of peace among the peoples of the earth. The encyclical in a sense presented a problem for the drafters of the Roman schema, according the *peritus* Henri de Riedmatten: "It put the editors of the conciliar text in a somewhat embarrassing position. It seemed to them that *Pacem in terris* had covered much of the material that they were supposed to be working on."[56] While it did not have a direct influence on the Roman schema, *Pacem in Terris* would end up providing firmer direction for future drafters of the document's first part: they should attend to the movements of history and integrate that analysis with the schema's later attention to particular pastoral issues.

Eventually after further revisions, the Roman schema was ready for consideration by the Mixed Commission in May 1963. The sickness of Pope John XXIII, however, and his eventual death on June 3 added uncertainty to all activities related to the council. The new pope, Paul VI, had been, as cardinal of Milan, one of those supporting a division of the council's agenda into *ad intra* and *ad extra* documents. At his inauguration on June 30, he spoke of how he intended to make the success of the council a central aspect of his pontificate.[57]

The fate of the Roman schema was still to be decided. When the Coordinating Commission met on July 3–4, 1963, to discuss the schema, the report of Cardinal Suenens was not favorable: the notion of *imago Dei*, while important, was not integrated enough throughout the text; there was a similar lack of integration between natural law and the Christian Gospel, and between theological principles and concrete applications. Moreover, the cardinal lamented, the treatment of specific pastoral issues lacked deep analysis and the whole text was too European, without consideration of other cultures in the world. The Coordinating Commission concurred and eventually rejected the Roman schema for many of the same reasons. Nevertheless, despite these negative

54. Moeller, "Pastoral Constitution: History," 15. For Rosemary Goldie's account of her involvement in the council, see Goldie, *From a Roman Window*, 64–87.

55. John XXIII, *Pacem in Terris*.

56. de Riedmatten, "History of the Pastoral Constitution," 19.

57. https://w2.vatican.va/content/paul-vi/it/homilies/1963/documents/hf_p-vi_hom_1963 0630_incoronazione-paolo-vi.html. The pope would again use the image of a "bridge" in his opening address for the second session of the council.

assessments, in retrospect it is evident that the Roman schema marked an important first step in the development toward an acceptable text. For example, one aspect that endured until the final version was its division into two parts: one theoretical, looking to theological principles, and the other pastoral, looking to specific issues. Furthermore, this early text employed the biblical notion of *imago Dei* as the biblical ground for its notion of the human person, once again a feature that would endure throughout all versions, as would the text's anthropological approach to the church/world relationship.

With the rejection of the Roman schema, the task of bringing a new schema into being was now entrusted by the Coordinating Commission directly to the person who had promoted the notion of having a text on the church *ad extra*, Cardinal Suenens of Malines. Suenens began by informally inviting a group of experts to meet at his residence in Malines, Belgium. It met for three days of drafting, September 6–8, 1963, concentrating on composition of a new text for the first part of the document.[58] The group was made up of some of the council's major theological minds: Lucien Cerfaux, Gérard Philips, Albert Prignon, Gustave Thils, Albert Dondeyne, Philippe Delhaye, Charles Moeller, Roberto Tucci, Karl Rahner, Beda Rigaux, and Yves Congar.[59] According to Dries Bosschaert, these eleven constituted "a unique group of theologians, highly respected for their work on Christian anthropology in the preconciliar years."[60] Congar records: "We were very relaxed and could work well."[61]

Themes emerged at Malines that would remain elements of future drafts along the way to *Gaudium et Spes*, for example, the church having a "mission" in the world; the church as a "servant." Congar, in particular, stressed the need for this focus on service.[62] Moeller summarizes his point: "A type of presence of the Church in the world must be achieved which is not one of power and domination but of service. And this kind of presence should also guarantee the principle of free access to the gospel without compulsion of

58. For accounts of the meeting, see Grootaers, "The Drama Continues between the Acts: The 'Second Preparation' and Its Opponents," 422–29; Turbanti, *Un Concilio per il Mondo Moderno*, 276–88.

59. See the list in Congar, *My Journal of the Council*, 313.

60. Dries Bosschaert, "Understanding the Shift in *Gaudium et Spes*: From Theology of History to Christian Anthropology," *Theological Studies* 78 (2017): 634–58, at 636.

61. Congar, *My Journal of the Council*, 313.

62. That year, Congar had published a book in French calling for a servant church (*Pour une église servante et pauvre*), translated as Yves Congar, *Power and Poverty in the Church* (Baltimore: Helicon, 1964).

any kind."[63] In the debates and text of the Malines meeting, the positive and ambiguous elements of the world were accented, along with the reality of change in the world, the need for redemption, and eschatological hope. As one who participated in the discussions, Moeller remarks: "In this way a double tension was discovered, between the Church as a heavenly structure founded on the word of God, on the one hand, and the world which is developing, growing together and seeking true justice on the other. There is also a tension within the world itself, between positive and negative aspects of its own evolution."[64] Throughout the meeting, Rahner and Congar differed in their approaches to this tension.[65] The text's article on "the ambiguity of earthy goods" illustrates the schema's attempt at bridging optimism and pessimism with Christian hope (as summarized here by Moeller): "Unity but also divisions and wars; mastery over nature but also the enslavement of millions of men in the technological machine; freedom, but actual inability of the masses concretely to achieve this freedom. All this leads to a simple conclusion: the radical impossibility of eradicating all roots of disorder from the world; the need to seek salvation."[66]

After the meeting, Philips took on the task of weaving the insights of the group into a coherent text. This text was then reviewed and further revised at a second meeting in Malines a few weeks later, on September 17, when a smaller group assembled, this time with Suenens himself. The *periti* present were Philips, Prignon, Cerfaux, Moeller, Delhaye, Rigaux, Tucci, and Congar. Philips once again had the task of making the final changes. According to Bosschaert, "The Malines text presented an anthropology with elements of

63. Moeller, "Pastoral Constitution: History," 22. The Faith and Order meeting of the World Council of Churches in July 1963, just a few months earlier, had framed its discussion of the church/world relationship in terms of a trilogy: communion, service, witness. Echoes of these themes resound throughout the Malines text. On a letter the observer Lukas Vischer had earlier written to Archbishop Guano of the mixed commission urging that an ecumenical view to be reflected in the schema, see ibid., 19–21.

64. Ibid., 22.

65. "Congar, who was probably the best prepared of any for a debate on the presence and action of the Church in the world, since he had published several books on the topic, argued that, to be heard by non-Christians, the schema needed to be presented as a theology of history. Rahner argued to the contrary that such an approach risked undervaluing some important theological problems, particularly those of the relationship between nature and grace and the presence of sin in the world, on which he had written extensively. It would not do, he urged, to present an overly optimistic picture of 'the world.'" Lawler, Salzman, and Burke-Sullivan, *The Church in the Modern World*, 23.

66. Moeller, "Pastoral Constitution: History," 24.

both clusters [transcendence/eschatology and immanence/incarnation]. On the one hand, it focused on divine transcendence with human beings described in an eschatological framework. On the other hand, it offered an anthropology that started from a theology of creation with a positive view of reality and its completion. In short, the redactors developed a single text on the mission of the church in the world, with anthropology as one of its main threads, showing marks of both tendencies in the 'theology of history' current of thought."[67]

When the mixed commission met two months later on November 29, 1963, it rejected the Malines text as inadequate. Moeller records:

> Considerable objections were raised to the Malines schema. It was regarded as a good contribution but its purely theological perspective was criticized. Many wanted to follow the style of *Mater et Magistra* and *Pacem in Terris*, so as to gain a hearing from modern humanity. Furthermore it was thought that the Malines text would lose its impact if it did not speak in concrete terms of concrete things. At the same time at least a few members acknowledged that from the theological point of view this text represented an advance on the old Chapter 1 of Text 2 [the Roman schema]; instead of a very definite but rather one-sided view of man as the image of God, they now had a more open approach to the relations between Church and world.[68]

The experiences of the Roman and Malines drafting teams had brought to the surface of debate the complexity of the issues. So similarly, at this meeting of the Mixed Commission, there was lively debate between proponents of two points of view regarding method and theology. On one side, there were "those who contended that a truly Conciliar approach to social questions must be theological in the proper sense of proceeding from data of revelation to doctrinal conclusion."[69] From a different perspective, there was "the other school, arguing ardently from the profound impact caused in the world by the two great social encyclicals of Pope John XXIII (*Mater et Magistra* and *Pacem in Terris*) that any document meant to speak to the modern world

---

67. Bosschaert, "Understanding the Shift in *Gaudium et Spes*," 645. Bosschaert is referring to the different approaches to a theology of history among Catholic scholars in the decades leading up to Vatican II. For a survey of that debate, see Gianluigi Pasquale, *La Teologia della Storia della Salvezza nel Secolo XX* (Bologna: Edizioni Dehoniane, 2001).

68. Moeller, "Pastoral Constitution: History," 25–26.

69. McGrath, "The Constitution on the Church in the Modern World," 401.

must begin from a consideration of the world's problems and speak to men in language and with arguments that they can understand and accept."[70]

The commission decided to create a new "central sub-commission," entrusting it with the task of composing a text with a more pastoral style. "From the beginning the idea of the central sub-commission was not to correct the Roman text or that of Malines, but to draft a completely new text";[71] however, the new text should still appropriate elements from the earlier versions. Bishop Emilio Guano (Livorno, Italy) was appointed president, and the moral theologian Bernhard Häring was appointed secretary general, to be assisted by the *peritus* Pierre Haubtmann. Häring's presence was significant; his approach to moral theology would come to shape much of the style and content of the Zürich draft.[72] But he was regarded with suspicion by one of the cochairs of the Mixed Commission, Cardinal Alfredo Ottaviani. Häring nevertheless found support from the other co-chair, Cardinal Fernando Cento.[73]

At this stage, it was envisaged that the material on specific pastoral issues would constitute *adnexa* (appendices), with separate subcommissions set up to examine each issue. For the first "doctrinal section," the commission chose a new group of experts. Only Tucci, Moeller, Philips, and Congar from the Malines group were retained (Rahner was not included). Häring, Hirschmann, Daniélou, and Pavan who worked on the original Roman schema were now brought back. Raymond Sigmond and Henri de Riedmatten were new additions. In effect, the decision was to begin all over again. Moeller, who had been involved in the earlier two schemas' discussion of the epistemological, methodological, and theological issues, later reflected with a certain chagrin: "It may be wondered, however, whether much time was not lost by this decision [to begin again] and whether what had been achieved in the earlier texts was not in practice forgotten."[74]

---

70. Ibid.

71. Turbanti, *Un Concilio per il Mondo Moderno*, 305.

72. On Häring's role contribution to *Gaudium et Spes*, the council's approach to moral theology, and the council's broader pastoral vision, see James Keenan, "Vatican II and Theological Ethics," *Theological Studies* 74 (2013): 162–90, at 169–74.

73. In his autobiography, Häring records: "My main contribution to the Council—at least when it comes to the amount of time and energy I put in—was in the pastoral constitution *Gaudium et Spes*. Cardinal Fernando Cento, the copresident of the mixed commission, to which this task was entrusted, publicly called me the 'quasi-father of *Gaudium et Spes*.' Of course, I consider this statement much exaggerated. On the other hand, I have to say that the constant support of this good-humoured cardinal greatly encouraged me and my work." Bernhard Häring, *Free and Faithful: My Life in the Catholic Church. An Autobiography* (Liguori, MO: Liguori/Triumph, 1998), 94.

74. Moeller, "Pastoral Constitution: History," 27.

On December 30, 1963, a small group of bishops and *periti* from the new central subcommission met to consider the several suggestions that had already been submitted by bishops, some of whom were members of the central subcommission, who had arranged meetings during the intersession with their own *periti*.[75] From these suggestions, and the original mandate of the central subcommission, the group decided on the overall approach the new text should take: it should be *anthropological*, they decided, rather than take the overly theological perspective of the Malines text. It also decided on the themes that the schema should incorporate. Prominent among these were dialogue (Paul VI had stressed the theme when opening the second session earlier in September); the signs of the times (an expression used by John XXIII in *Pacem in Terris* earlier in April; Dom Helder Câmara was among the bishops promoting this); the church as the people of God (a key theme that had emerged earlier in October during the debate on *Lumen Gentium*). Other themes selected were the need for the church to respect the autonomy of earthly realities; the recognition of a now pluralist society, as the context of the faithful having to live their faith today; the importance of human dignity and religious freedom.[76] Throughout the following January, on the basis of these guidelines, the sociologist Raymond Sigmond (who also co-opted the sociologist Louis Dingemans), along with Bernhard Häring, drafted a preliminary text in French.[77]

To review this text, the central subcommission gathered at the Jesuit residence in Zürich between February 1–3, 1964.[78] The group consisted of seven bishops from the central commission and six *periti*, as well as two lay auditors.[79] The text that resulted from the Zürich meeting had four chapters: an anthropological depiction of the state of the world; theological principles on the church/world relationship; the activity of Christians in the world; pressing issues in the world of today. The whole document began: "The joys and sorrows, the hopes and anxieties of the people of today, especially of the poor

75. Vilanova, "The Intersession (1963–1964)," 403–6.

76. See Moeller, "Pastoral Constitution: History," 57–58.

77. On reconstructing the authorship of this initial text, see Turbanti, *Un Concilio per il Mondo Moderno*, 326.

78. For accounts of the Zürich meeting, its text, and the further revision made, see Moeller, "Pastoral Constitution: History," 27–41; Turbanti, *Un Concilio per il Mondo Moderno*, 334–98; Vilanova, "The Intersession (1963–1964)," 408–15.

79. The bishops were Guano (president), Hengsbach, Ménager, Ancel, McGrath, Schröffer, Wright, and Glorieux. The *periti* were Häring (secretary), Tucci, Hirschmann, Sigmond, de Riedmatten, and Moeller. Two lay auditors were also invited: Mieczyslaw de Habicht (Poland) and Ramon Sugranyes de Franch (Spain).

and those who suffer, are also the joys and sorrows, the hopes and anxieties of this synod." The Latin *incipit* (the opening line) of the Zürich text was thus "*Gaudium et luctus*" (The joys and sorrows). The new official title had become "Constitution on the Church in the Modern World."

"The striking thing about the new draft was the warmth of its tone and the clearly scriptural and Christian perspective in which it broached the problems."[80] The text emphasized the solidarity of Christians with the peoples of the world and their sense of responsibility to dialogue with them, since humanity is one people created by the one God, and given a common task: "We live on the earth that God has entrusted to our care and cultivation."[81] In describing the state of the contemporary world, the document highlighted its ambivalent aspects. From the perspective of Henri de Riedmatten, one of the drafting *periti*, the text was balanced in its theological assessments: "There was joy for its positive aspects and worried concern over the anxiety of contemporary man, whose newfound power hurls him into worrisome events and anxious doubts. The text clearly traced the problem back to its root cause—sin—and it did not cover over man's transcendent supernatural vocation. But the Christian is not excused from contributing to the progress of this world, and hence he must come to know and understand it."[82] But the Zürich group was only too aware of the text's remaining weaknesses, especially in getting the balance right on issues such as the rightful autonomy of the temporal order, the eschatological dimension of human existence, and the transitory nature of this world.[83] To address these remaining issues, a smaller group of *periti* was given the task of later refining the text: Bernhard Häring, Raymond Sigmond, Roberto Tucci, and Henri de Riedmatten.

---

80. de Riedmatten, "History of the Pastoral Consitution," 23.

81. Quoted in ibid.

82. Ibid. Lawler and Salzman likewise highlight the authors' attempt at balance: "The Zürich text sought a *via media* between the two extremes of hyper-naturalism and hyper-supernaturalism. The first was rampant in the world of the 1960s, especially in its extreme form of atheism which enclosed men within the material world and taught that there was nothing beyond that world. The second had led over the years to contempt of the world, an attitude that held that any positive valuation of human worldly realities was a betrayal of the human's eternal vocation. . . . [Instead, the text proposed] a double vocation for humankind. Women and men are called to the kingdom of God, but they are called also to be concerned with worldly affairs in which there are many values open to the kingdom of God: values such as solidarity, justice, love, marriage and family, culture, arts and sciences." Lawler, Salzman, and Burke-Sullivan, *The Church in the Modern World*, 25.

83. See de Riedmatten, "History of the Pastoral Consitution," 23–24.

The revised schema was reviewed at a series of meetings of the Mixed Commission (March 4, 9, 12). Difficulties relating to translating the French text into Latin in the meantime had to be overcome. At further meetings of the Mixed Commission, a few accused the text of "Häringism," a reference to the theological approach of the editor-in-chief Bernhard Häring.[84] Nevertheless, the schema was accepted by the Coordinating Commission on June 26, 1964, as suitable for now being debated in the council. It was at this meeting that the numbering of the schema on the conciliar agenda was changed from Schema XVII to Schema XIII. In July it was sent out to the bishops, for consideration at the third session, due to begin on September 14, 1964. However, just as John XXIII's encyclical *Pacem in Terris* had injected a new element for consideration by the drafters of the Roman schema in April of the previous year, so now on August 6, 1964, Pope Paul VI released his encyclical on "dialogue," *Ecclesiam Suam*, with its impact on the now-numbered Schema XIII yet to be determined.

The Zürich schema was taken up by the council more than a month after the start of the session.[85] Debate took place over twelve general congregations (October 20–November 5 and November 9–10, 1964).[86] There would be over 150 speeches. The co-chair of the Mixed Commission, Cardinal Fernando Cento, began with a *relatio* that gave a general introduction to the schema.[87] He wasted no time in referring to the pope's recent encyclical on dialogue and highlighting the schema's implicit dialogic model for depicting the church/world relationship. Then Bishop Emilio Guano presented his *relatio* summarizing the document.[88] He said the schema understood the term "world" as "the universe and the family of man in its unity and diversity." Quoting John 3:16, he gave a positive sense to the term: "It must be remembered that the Church loves the world, even as does the Father who 'so loved the world that he gave his only begotten Son.'"[89]

---

84. The main critics in this regard were Cardinal Ottaviani and Sebastian Tromp. See Turbanti, *Un Concilio per il Mondo Moderno*, 362–63.

85. For the Latin text, see AS III/5, 116–42, 147–201. By this stage, the text had an introduction and four short chapters: the human vocation; the church's service to humanity; Christians' activity in the world; some selected topics related to Christian responsibilities in the world. Attached to this were five *adnexa* (appendices): the human person in society; marriage and family; culture; economic and social life; human solidarity, justice, and peace.

86. An extensive account of the debate, with summaries of the major interventions, can be found in Turbanti, *Un Concilio per il Mondo Moderno*, 399–458.

87. AS III/5, 201–3.

88. AS III/5, 203–14.

89. Quoted in de Riedmatten, "History of the Pastoral Constitution," 26.

The points raised in the subsequent debate ranged from the theoretical to the practical, with a variety of perspectives on world poverty, atheism, communism, racism, war, and the use of nuclear warheads. The topics of marriage and the "ends" of marriage (procreation and conjugal love) were among the more explosive topics. Three times the bishops were reminded that the matter of birth control had been taken off the council agenda and was being examined by a papal commission. That did not stop interventions from bishops, however, such as Patriarch Maximos Saigh and Cardinal Suenens, who called for change in the church's teaching. "We must avoid another 'Galileo case.' One is enough for the church," pleaded Suenens.[90] For Henri de Riedmatten, "it was one of the most dramatic moments of the council."[91] Also striking among the interventions were those from bishops calling for the church to support and promote the role of women in society—for example, Bishop Gérard Coderre, of Saint-Jean de Québec (who spoke on behalf of forty other bishops) and Bishop Augustin Frotz, auxiliary bishop of Cologne.[92] Some felt the text was too Western, without proper acknowledgment of the diversity of cultures throughout the world. A common request from the bishops was that the appendices be incorporated into the main text, so that they would then have conciliar authority. The question of the addressees of the schema was also raised: to whom are we speaking?

But the umbrella issue across the whole debate was still the question of the most appropriate theoretical framework for shaping the church/world debate from a theological perspective. In particular, the conciliar discussion of the schema's chapter 3, on Christians living in the world, saw an issue raised that would remain neuralgic until the final voting on the schema. Cardinal Frings (whose personal *peritus* was Joseph Ratzinger) made a criticism of the theological imbalance in the draft text: it overemphasized a theology of the incarnation and gave little attention to a theology of the cross. Others said the same thing, and yet others praised the text for its balance. John O'Malley captures the tension: "At stake here were two broad theological traditions. The so-called Augustinian (or eschatological) tradition, which

90. Quoted in O'Malley, *What Happened at Vatican II*, 238.
91. de Riedmatten, "History of the Pastoral Constitution," 27.
92. For Coderre's speech, see AS III/5, 728–30. Translated in Gérard Coderre, "Woman's Role in the Divine Plan," in *Third Session Council Speeches of Vatican II*, ed. William K. Leahy and Anthony T. Massimini (Glen Rock, NJ: Paulist Press, 1966), 205–8. For Frotz's speech, see AS III/6, 42–44. Translation in Augustin Frotz, "Women's Increasing Dignity and Influence," in *Third Session Council Speeches of Vatican II*, ed. William K. Leahy and Anthony T. Massimini (Glen Rock, NJ: Paulist Press, 1966), 208–11. See O'Malley, *What Happened at Vatican II*, 235.

the Germans wanted to make sure was given its due, was more negative on human capabilities and on the possibility of reconciliation between 'nature and grace'. . . . The other tradition was more dependent on the theology of the Eastern Fathers of the church and took its Western form most notably in Aquinas. In it the Incarnation was the key mystery, through which all creation was reconciled and raised to a higher dignity than before."[93] This tension related also to the issue of whether the schema was overly optimistic in its assessment of the world, giving too much credit to what human beings can achieve, and too little regard to evil, the power of sin, and the transitory nature of this present world. The very words "world" and "church" needed greater clarity in the text, said many bishops.

Within a week after the close of the third session on November 16, 1964, the Mixed Commission met for the first of three meetings to begin its task of revising the text in the light of the bishops' requests. It was decided that, if the bishops' demands were to be met, a thorough revision of the Zürich schema would be needed and, to do that, a whole new drafting commission needed to be formed. In this new arrangement, Häring was no longer to be the editor-in-chief. His relationship with the Roman Curia was becoming problematic, and, moreover, some bishops in their speeches had criticized him, if not by name.[94] Nevertheless, he was to continue to play an influential role.[95] Fr. Pierre Haubtmann was appointed the new editor-in-chief.

It was decided that a plenary meeting of the Mixed Commission, along with all the subcommissions, should take place in the town of Ariccia outside of Rome between January 31 and February 6, 1965.[96] It was a large gathering.

---

93. O'Malley, *What Happened at Vatican II*, 235.

94. "Häring had proved too intransigent in his dealings with both the subcommission and Cardinal Ottaviani's Doctrinal Commission." Lawler, Salzman, and Burke-Sullivan, *The Church in the Modern World*, 27. Häring's account of this in his memoirs disguises these problems: "Around that time, there was a reorganization in the editorial commission that relieved me of some of the burden of my work. I remained the nominal editorial secretary, but Canon Hauptmann now took over the crucial work for the main part of the text. It did the cause good. On the subcommission for the chapter on marriage and the family in *Gaudium et Spes*, I was replaced by Father Edward Schillebeeckx, without being excluded from further collaboration. This reassignment, too, was a fortunate stroke of fate." Häring, *Free and Faithful: My Life in the Catholic Church*, 99. On the possible reasons for replacing Häring with Hauptmann, see Turbanti, *Un Concilio per il Mondo Moderno*, 478–81.

95. According to James Keenan, the theology of marriage and of conscience are the "two particular dimensions of *Gaudium et Spes* [that] bear the indelible traits of Häring." Keenan, "Vatican II and Theological Ethics," 173.

96. On the Ariccia meeting, see Turbanti, *Un Concilio per il Mondo Moderno*, 471–613.

And, over a longer time than previous meetings. There were thirty bishops, thirty-five official *periti*, and seventeen laypeople. Including secretaries, a total of eighty-seven people made up the meeting. Included among the lay auditors were Rosemary Goldie and Sr. Mary Luke Tobin. The invited *periti* included, among others, Karl Rahner, Alois Grillmeier, Otto Semmelroth, Joseph Ratzinger, Yves Congar, Jean Daniélou, Edward Schillebeeckx, Charles Moeller, Pierre Haubtmann, Bernhard Häring, Roberto Tucci, and Pietro Pavan. Unfortunately, neither Rahner nor Ratzinger could be present, due to other commitments.[97] Concerning Rahner, Turbanti remarks: "Among the theologians, Rahner's absence was significant; later, too, he would remain on the periphery of the work on the schema and even strongly oppose the results achieved."[98]

After his appointment as chief editor, Haubtmann had drawn up a preliminary draft all by himself and brought it to the Ariccia meeting. Certainly his fellow Frenchman, Congar, was happy with it, writing in his journal on the second day at Ariccia: "I have read the new text of the [first part]. It is by Haubtmann, following the *ideas* of the old schema, the comments of the Fathers, the consultation with thirty-five international organisations and comments received from here and there. . . . In my view this text is clearly better than the Zürich-Häring one. *It has found the right tone*, and that is half the battle. It is a text that the people will be able to read; it brings in doctrine (perhaps not enough, and not sufficiently) *within the context* of human realities."[99] But others also arrived with their own ideas. Archbishop Karol Wojtyla came with a text to present in the name of the Polish bishops. The Germans came without a text of their own but ended up mostly criticizing everyone else's.

The schema still was to have two interrelated parts: a "doctrinal" part and a second part, which would incorporate the material from the earlier chapter 4 into each of the later five appendices. Much of this work required a complete reworking of the Zürich text. The meeting's work was well structured, with the chapters being allocated to subcommittees that met separately. The subcommittee on "the signs of the times" played an important role, having been given the task of writing the opening section and an introduction to the whole document. Bishop Mark McGrath was given oversight. There was only one plenary meeting, on the last day, when each subcommittee gave a report.

97. See ibid., 503.
98. Burigana and Turbanti, "The Intersession: Preparing the Conclusion," 524.
99. Congar, *My Journal of the Council*, 710. Original emphasis.

Once again, the working language of the schema was French. The meeting "agreed unanimously that the style of the document under examination was at last just what was needed. It was indubitably characterized by solid, vigorous and clear language with texts and quotations in support, bearing the evident stamp of a French style. Later some asked for it to be modified a little in the direction of greater sobriety. An effort was made, however, to maintain the same concrete style throughout, at least in Part I. It did in fact stimulate interest and was aimed both at head and heart."[100]

As soon as the meeting concluded on February 6, an editing committee met in Rome to further refine the Ariccia text. Gérard Philips was seconded to bring his editing and synthesizing skills to bear on the lengthy document. The text was then presented at a plenary meeting of the Mixed Commission (March 29–April 6, 1965), which criticized imprecisions in the doctrinal section and proceeded to further revise the text. On May 11, the Coordinating Commission gave its approval, and finally, on May 28 the pope gave his approval for the schema to be distributed to the council's participants. It now had the incipit "*Gaudium et Spes*," and was now titled a "Pastoral Constitution."[101] The bishops and their *periti* now had over three months to evaluate the text before the fourth session began on September 14, 1965.

Two German *periti*, Karl Rahner and Joseph Ratzinger, very soon published articles of the text, proposing positions which would influence the German bishops' response.[102] At the end of August, a few weeks before the council was due to open, the German bishops gathered in the town of Fulda for their annual assembly.[103] But it was also an opportunity to prepare themselves for the

100. Moeller, "Pastoral Constitution: History," 50–51.

101. Moeller in his commentary refers to the revised Ariccia schema as "Text 5." It appears as the second column in Francisco Gil Hellín, "*Gaudium et Spes* Synopsis," in *Constitutionis pastoralis de ecclesia in mundo huius temporis Gaudium et spes: Concilii Vaticani II synopsis in ordinem redigens schemata cum relationibus necnon patrum orationes atque animadversiones* (Città del Vaticano: Libreria Editrice Vaticana, 2003), 1–751.

102. For Rahner's article, see Karl Rahner, "Über den Dialog in der pluralistischen Gesellschaft," *Stimmen der Zeit* 176 (August 1965): 321–30. For Ratzinger's, see Joseph Ratzinger, "Angesichts der Welt von heute: Überlegungen zur Konfrontation mit der Kirche in Schema XIII," *Wort und Wahrheit* 20 (1965): 493–504. This was later published in English as Ratzinger, "The Christian and the Modern World."

103. The Scandinavian bishops also took part. For an account of the meeting, see Turbanti, *Un Concilio per il Mondo Moderno*, 620–26; Giovanni Turbanti, "Toward the Fourth Period," in *History of Vatican II*, vol. 5: *The Council and the Transition; The Fourth Period and the End of the Council, September 1965–December 1965*, ed. Giuseppe Alberigo and Joseph A. Komonchak (Maryknoll, NY: Orbis Books, 2006), 5:1–47, at 18–19.

forthcoming final session of the council. Cardinal Julius Döpfner had asked his personal *peritus* for the council, Karl Rahner, to prepare a response to Schema XIII. Döpfner then send Rahner's assessment to Franz Hengsbach, the bishop of Essen, who would be presenting a report at the Fulda meeting on Schema XIII. Importantly, Hengsbach was a member of the central subcommission for Schema XIII.

Like his previous article, Rahner's position paper was critical of the schema.[104] He had five major objections.[105] First, the document's sociological approach did not adequately explain its theological methodology; in its analysis of the contemporary world, the way a faith perspective did or did not come to bear on that analysis was not made clear. Second, the classic distinction between "the order of creation" and "the order of redemption" was poorly addressed; in particular, the depiction of the meaning of Christians' activity in the world needed clarification, as did the meaning of the very term "world." Third, the document lacked a theology of sin and a proper Christian pessimism regarding the church/world relationship; instead, it presumed the world could be improved simply by Christians working harder and that human progress was inevitable. Fourth, and consequently, the document's theology of history failed to emphasize the history of salvation and that the battle against the power of evil is never ending until the eschaton. Fifth, the text's Christian anthropology was muddled, with key notions such as *imago Dei* and human dignity being poorly presented and needing to be conceived around a theology of the cross. Rahner concluded by proposing to the bishops that the council had two options: either leave the document to be completed by a special commission after the council or simply call the document a "letter" from the council.

There was heated debate. Hengsbach acknowledged Rahner's criticisms, but, as a member of the drafting subcommission, he reminded the bishops of the document's positive aspects and assured them that the forthcoming conciliar debate could address any negative aspects. Hengsbach won the day. A reasonably positive document of *animadversiones* (suggested changes),

104. This unpublished text is titled "Anmerkungen zum Schema *De ecclesia in mundo huius temporis* (in der Fassung vom 28.5.65)." See an analysis in O'Meara, "Karl Rahner's 'Remarks on the Schema, "*De Ecclesia in Mundo Hujus Temporis*," in the Draft of May 28, 1965.'"

105. For a summary of Rahner's points, see Komonchak, "Le valutazioni sulla *Gaudium et spes*: Chenu, Dossetti, Ratzinger," 118–19. See also Komonchak, "Augustine, Aquinas or the Gospel *sine glossa*?," 104–5.

with an attachment listing most of Rahner's negative points, was submitted to the drafting commission.[106]

But the Germans' negativity to the Ariccia schema was balanced by the positivity of other, equally respectable, theological voices. For example, a week after the fourth session began, one of the key figures in the *ressourcement* theology of the decades before Vatican II, the Dominican Marie-Dominique Chenu, gave a public lecture in Rome on September 22. He basically rejected all of Rahner's criticisms as unfounded and gave his full backing to the schema. As Komonchak notes: "Chenu's defence of the basic method and orientation of *Gaudium et Spes* did not derive, or did not simply derive, from his congenital optimism; it had theological grounds."[107] Ratzinger observed, with an element of understatement, that at this stage "a certain conflict between German and French theology began to be visible."[108] And yet, both sides seemed to be grounded on equally solid theological principles; the greatest minds in the Catholic Church couldn't seem to come up with an agreed-upon synthesis.

In a genuine attempt to iron out the differences between the two groups before the debate on the council floor began, the French bishop Léon-Arthur Elchinger organized a group of French, Belgian, Dutch, and German bishops and *periti* to meet on September 17, three days after the start of the fourth session and four days before the debate on Schema XIII was due to begin.[109] Congar calls it a "'conciliar strategy' meeting."[110] It turned out to be "decisive for subsequent work on Schema 13."[111] Elchinger began by presenting the

106. AS V/3, 28–33, 902–10. "Animadversiones propositae nominee Conferentiae Episcoporum linguae Germaniae et Scandiae ad Schema Constitutionis Pastoralis 'De ecclesia in mundo huius temporis (forma a die 28.5.65).'"

107. Komonchak, "Augustine, Aquinas or the Gospel *sine glossa*?," 109. Surprisingly, Chenu had been given little role in the council's commissions. On his contribution to *Gaudium et Spes*, especially on the "signs of the times" subcommission, see Turbanti, *Un Concilio per il Mondo Moderno*, 643–51. See also Quisinsky, *Geschichtlicher Glaube in einer geschichtlichen Welt. Der Beitrag von M.-D. Chenu, Y. Congar und H.-M. Féret zum II. Vaticanum.* For his journal for the first two years of the council, see Chenu, *Vatican II Notebook: A Council Journal, 1962–1963.*

108. Ratzinger, *Theological Highlights of Vatican II*, 218.

109. The German bishops were Volk, Reuss, Hengsbach, and Gnädinger. The other bishops were Elchinger, Garrone, Ancel, Marty (Congar also mentions "a Dutch bishop"). The *periti* included Haubtmann, Schillebeeckx, Daniélou, Rahner, Ratzinger, Semmelroth, Moeller, Hirschmann, Philips, and Neuner.

110. Congar, *My Journal of the Council*, 779.

111. Moeller, "Pastoral Constitution: History," 60.

purpose of the gathering; as Congar recalls, he said "the point [of the meeting] was to come to an agreement (the German bishops on one side and the French on the other should decide on their common attitude by Monday). Schema XIII should not be rejected or demolished, because that would play into the hands of the conservatives, but it should be improved."[112] The *peritus* Johannes Hirschmann reported on the Fulda meeting, presenting the assessment of the Germans.[113] Rahner raised his point about theological gnoseology; Ratzinger raised many criticisms, above all regarding the text's excessive optimism and lack of attention to the reality of sin. The concerns of the Dutch *peritus* Schillebeeckx paralleled somewhat those of Rahner and Ratzinger. Congar voiced his own concerns: "The lack of synthesis in the area of anthropology and christology. The major question is the union between anthropology and theology."[114] The French *peritus* Pierre Haubtmann, the editor-in-chief of the document, whose preliminary draft had become the base text for discussion at Ariccia, defended the text's approach as being faithful to the wishes of the council fathers; as Moeller recalls, Haubtmann reminded the meeting that "seven-tenths of the fathers had wished the starting-point to be truths common to all, not the natural order—a term which for that reason had been avoided in the text—but the biblical presentation of those truths common to all, so that gradually they could move forward to the more profoundly Christian truths, that is, to the crucified and risen Christ."[115]

112. Congar, *My Journal of the Council*, 779.

113. Moeller summarizes the German position presented by Hirschmann: "They contended that the doctrine on man and the world needed supplementing. Attention should be directed more to man's temporal and historical character; the point of view of the text was too static. The doctrine of sin was inadequate, so was the *theologia crucis* and the *theologia eschatologica*. They also reproached the text with naturalism, optimism and oversimplification of some problems. It was not made clear what was contributed by faith, what was the task of the Church through its hierarchy and through the faithful. Insufficient distinction was drawn between principles and practical prescriptions. Insufficient account was taken of the ecumenical point of view in the way the problems were stated. As regards, style, too, much more account should have been taken of the mentality of unbelievers, and it ought to have been stated that the text itself was incomplete on many points. Finally, they expressed grave doubts whether it was opportune to call the whole document a 'Pastoral Constitution.' What was needed as, for example, K. Rahner, said, was a theological gnoseology to make it clear what the Church was enunciating as propositions and what it was recommending as directives." Moeller, "Pastoral Constitution: History," 59.

114. Congar, *My Journal of the Council*, 779.

115. Moeller, "Pastoral Constitution: History," 60. Haubtmann had been particularly inspired by the writings of Henri de Lubac. In an interview on September 30, Haubtmann neatly summarized his positive assessment of the schema: "The schema does not start off with the natural

The result of the meeting was a reluctant agreement from the Germans not to reject the text outright in the forthcoming final conciliar debate, but rather to work for its improvement. To that end, it was agreed that key theologians who had criticized the text should be added to each of the ten drafting committees. Among those would be Rahner, Ratzinger, Alois Grillmeier, Otto Semmelroth, and Johannes Hirschmann. Their presence on these committees would eventually lead to changes that make for greater balance in the text.[116] As Moeller remarks, this September 17 meeting, and its consensus agreement between the major disputing groups before the conciliar debate began, turned out to be critical for the successful passage of the schema through the council: "It meant that all revisions during the last two stages were made on the general lines that *a balance must be struck between the opposing tendencies of the two ways of envisaging the problem.*[117]

Conciliar debate on the schema began on September 21, 1965, and ended on October 8, with thirteen general congregations devoted to the schema and over 160 speeches delivered.[118] When presenting the final version to the council for their approval, the *relator*, Archbishop Garrone, proposed to the bishops that the pastoral constitution "is at the very heart of the council." Importantly, he went on to link this *Pastoral* Constitution on the Church,

---

order and then proceed to the supernatural order, as if the human person had two separate vocations laid one atop the other. It starts off with truths which, though they belong to the order of faith, are commonly held also by non-Christians; then it moves on to the deepest truths of faith that are summed up in Christ the Lord. This is something entirely different. This approach has been used because last year many Council fathers demanded that the schema deal with the most commonly held truths. That is the rationale behind the arrangement of the first three chapters; it is a response to this demand." DC LXII (1965), col. 1489. Quoted in de Riedmatten, "History of the Pastoral Constitution," 31.

116. "These changes reflected Germanophone-led criticisms, namely, that the document was excessively optimistic and gave insufficient attention to sin, that it had 'naturalistic' tendencies (collapsing everything to the 'natural' order), and that it relied too heavily on the incarnation and not enough on the cross." Brandon Peterson, "Critical Voices: The Reactions of Rahner and Ratzinger to 'Schema XIII' (*Gaudium et Spes*)," *Modern Theology* 31 (2015): 1–26, at 8–9. For a list of the people working on ten subcommissions for the final drafting, see Moeller, "Pastoral Constitution: History," 63n88.

117. Moeller, "Pastoral Constitution: History," 61. Emphasis added.

118. On the debate, see Turbanti, *Un Concilio per il Mondo Moderno*, 651–86. Turbanti's comment is telling, regarding his reasons for the relative brevity of his thirty-five-page account: "Considering that in this second debate themes and topics already enunciated in the previous year were proposed again, and that the privileged place of confrontation was now that of the Mixed Commission, we can follow the succession of this series of interventions more rapidly." Ibid., 651n69.

Gaudium et Spes, with the council's earlier *Dogmatic* Constitution on the Church, *Lumen Gentium*: "It is the prolongation of the Constitution on the Church, and it represents an endeavor to place the Church in dialogue with the world, truthfully and realistically. In *Lumen Gentium* the Church readied herself so that she could talk to the world. It will become increasingly obvious that between *Lumen Gentium* and this Constitution there is a passage from *preparing for action* to *the action itself.*"[119]

The debate first focused on the whole schema and then on each of the two parts with their separate chapters. Discussion of the first part related to its methodology and underlying theological framework, as well as the issue of whether communism and atheism should be explicitly condemned. In discussion of the second part of the schema, issues such as the ends of marriage and the use of nuclear weapons took up much of the council's attention. It was no surprise that certain conservative bishops were highly critical of the whole text and many of these particular issues. The Germans raised their usual concerns, but, faithful to the September 17 accord, they were "more moderate by far."[120] Among the German speaking bishops, it was only Paulus Rusch, the Austrian bishop of Innsbruck-Feldkirch, who "really attacked the schema."[121] Another critical voice was, surprisingly, that of the archbishop of Bologna, Giacomo Lercaro. His personal *peritus*, Father Giuseppe Dossetti, had drafted his speech. Lercaro took a "more radical and evangelical" approach to analyzing the schema.[122] Support for the text, along with certain criticisms, came not only from the French-speaking bishops. Melkite Patriarch Maximos Saigh of Antioch praised the schema's Christology, as requested by the bishops in the previous year's debate: "Many voices in the council called for a text properly centered on Christ and manifesting a Spirit of love to the world. This is essential, and the current schema, on our view, has satisfied."[123]

When debate ended on October 8, 1965, the ten subcommissions not only had the task of assessing the requests made during the council speech, but also twenty thousand requests in the written submissions. They had two months before the final voting was to take place. On December 7, *Gaudium*

---

119. AS IV/1, 553–58. Quoted in McGrath, "The Constitution on the Church in the Modern World," 397–98. Emphasis added.

120. O'Malley, *What Happened at Vatican II*, 259.

121. Routhier, "Finishing the Work Begun," 134n343.

122. Komonchak, "Augustine, Aquinas or the Gospel *sine glossa*?," 107.

123. AS IV/2, 451–53. Translation from Peterson, "Critical Voices," 9n47.

et Spes was finally approved, with 2,309 votes in favor, seventy-five against, and seven invalid.

Creative Tensions and Legitimate Diversity

Charles Moeller, who was intimately involved in the drafting of *Gaudium et Spes*, highlights both the hard work and the theological integrity of both "sides" in the seeming impasse of articulating a church/world principle: "The version put to the vote by the fathers before its promulgation *represented the consensus of the two main tendencies which had stood confronted since the beginning of work on Schema 13*: one a concrete outlook marked by a certain fundamental optimism, the other a dialectical, paradoxical attitude insisting on the polyvalency of the world in which the Church lives."[124] Both outlooks needed articulation in the council's vision.

Therefore, as Peter Hünermann observes: "An overall assessment of *Gaudium et Spes* is not a simple task."[125] It was clear what the intention was: to move away from the church/world relationship envisaged in the *Syllabus of Errors* to a vision counter to that. But in achieving that goal, "a document had to be drafted for which there was no prior model. . . . The wearisome labors of the various commissions attested to the difficulties of grasping this new vision of the Church in the world."[126] According to Hünermann, it was obvious to many that *Gaudium et Spes* "was only a first attempt."[127] Nonetheless, its achievements far outweigh any weaknesses:

> The significance of the pastoral constitution and the fundamental importance of the positions taken in this document are not cancelled out by the limitations of the individual chapters and the problems still remaining. That is not surprising after an almost four-hundred-year history of alienation. The objection was rightly raised, later on, that insufficient attention was given to the theology of the cross, the world's challenge to faith, and the breakdown and fragility of all human works. All that must be admitted. Even more serious are the theological objections that the Council did not keep to the line taken in *Lumen Gentium*, but over lengthy stretches fell back into thinking based on natural law. These limitations,

124. Moeller, "Pastoral Constitution: History," 60. Emphasis added.
125. Peter Hünermann, "The Final Weeks of the Council," in *History of Vatican II*, vol. 5: *The Council and the Transition; The Fourth Period and the End of the Council, September 1965–December 1965*, ed. Giuseppe Alberigo and Joseph A. Komonchak (Maryknoll, NY: Orbis Books, 2006), 5:363–483, at 422.
126. Ibid., 422–23.
127. Ibid., 423.

too, must be admitted. Nevertheless, the vision set down in this document and the overall direction it gave the Church seem more important.[128]

These "limitations" directly relate to the various tensions in the drafting process, as different approaches of the bishops and theological *periti* vied for recognition, tensions that can still be felt in the final text. First, there was tension between a *sociological* and a *theological,* approach to addressing the issues as well as to structuring the document, if it was, as it purported, to address in a pastoral way the men and women of the time, believers and unbelievers. Generally, it was the French-Belgian group of bishops and theologians who promoted the sociological approach, while the German bishops and theologians promoted a more theological approach.

Second, parallel to this debate was the tension regarding the appropriate method, *deductive* or *inductive.* The former started from Christian beliefs and sought to apply them to contemporary life; the latter began with an analysis of the contemporary conditions within which human beings must live out their Christian values and then went on to give the results of that analysis a theological interpretation. Yves Congar has noted the distinctiveness of the methodology that eventually predominates, but not exclusively, in *Gaudium et Spes*:

> In dogmatic matters and, for the most part, in ethical and social matters as well, our theology [before the council] normally proceeded by deduction. We applied established principles with our attention fixed upon a firm doctrinal datum. But, when Vatican II set out to speak of the Church in today's world, it realized that the starting point should be a set of facts. Hence an investigative, descriptive, and inductive method was indicated. . . . The world indeed does give something to the very datum on which theology lives. And the same may be said about man's experience on the one hand, and the life of the people of God on the other.[129]

Third, and parallel to this debate, was the issue of whether to start from *anthropology* and move to *Christology,* or the other way around. How does the church speak most effectively of Jesus Christ as the exemplar of the fully alive human being in a way that speaks to the historical particularity and diversity of human experience today? Although the methodological approach

128. Ibid., 426.
129. Yves M.-J. Congar, "Theology's Tasks after Vatican II," in *Theology of Renewal*, vol. 1: *Renewal of Religious Thought*, ed. L. K. Shook (New York: Herder and Herder, 1968), 1:47–65, at 57.

taken was an inductive one (starting with the conditions of being human into today's world), the exemplar proposed was a dogmatic one, Jesus Christ, the true human being. As we have seen, the late insertion of the christological article 10 (penned initially by Ratzinger) was intended to first set up a christological affirmation before the four chapters of part 1 present their inductive analyses, at the end of which come the four capstone affirmations of Jesus Christ regarding the four themes (GS 22, 32, 38–39, 45).

Fourth, the "tension" between a *Christocentric* and a *Pneumatocentric* approach was a tension that affected all of the council's developing work, with Eastern Orthodox theologians seeing the default Western "christomonism" evident in the emerging documents. It was a tension that marked the developing theological anthropology of *Gaudium et Spes*. Nevertheless, the final document shows evidence of the council's shift toward a greater sensitivity to the role of the Holy Spirit, albeit undeveloped.[130] Ratzinger, for example, sees in the final text "a strong pneumatological emphasis in the context of a Trinitarian outline of history."[131] Furthermore, according to Ratzinger, "The meaning of the conciliar text as a whole may be taken to be that, as opposed to a one-sided, purely Christological and 'chronological' outlook, it brings to the fore the pneumatological and 'kairological' aspect, and as it were finds the point at which this is anchored."[132] Nevertheless, despite the christological-pneumatological balance in these sections, it is not consistently applied throughout the pastoral constitution, which remains lacking in any *sustained emphasis* on the Spirit's role in alerting the church to God's providential activity within the shifting horizons of human history, provoking newness in human perception of God's ongoing revelation in Jesus Christ through the Holy Spirit. The final judgment must be that a much more pneumatological version could have been possible, and the final text is a much-watered down version; the changing conditions of human historicity and *how* the Holy Spirit enables humanity to discern new directions are themes little treated.

Fifth, throughout the council's four years of work (once the majority had decided to move on from a neoscholastic approach) there emerged a tension between proponents of a newly retrieved *Thomist* vision (e.g., Chenu, Congar)

130. See above the chapter on the christological/pneumatological principle.
131. Joseph Ratzinger, "Introductory Article and Chapter 1: The Dignity of the Human Person," in *Commentary on the Documents of Vatican II*, vol. 5, ed. Herbert Vorgrimler (New York: Herder and Herder, 1969), 5:115–63, at 115.
132. Ibid., 116.

and an *Augustinian* vision of human being (Daniélou, de Lubac, Ratzinger), all under the long shadows of Plato and Aristotle.[133] Both visions are apparent at different points in *Gaudium et Spes*.

Sixth, there remains a cluster of related tensions: between a more *optimistic* and a more *dialectical* vision of humanity and its possibilities and/or temptations; between an *incarnational* and an *eschatological* perspective; between an emphasis on the *incarnation* and on the *cross*; and between *sin* and *salvation*. An optimistic approach speaks of human beings and their future history with a confidence in "progress" and the power of science and technology to solve the problems of the world, bringing forth a brand-new day for humanity. While it may have tended to reflect, in some way, the optimistic mood of the 1960s, this tendency in the council was also wanting to give expression to the eschatological hope of the Christian vision: that it was in *this* world that God was incarnate and within which God was calling human beings to collaborate in building the kingdom of God, albeit not to be fully realized in human time. This vision tended to be promoted by followers of the Thomist approach. On the other hand, the more dialectical approach wanted to highlight the propensity of human beings to evil, emphasizing the human being as sinner rather than as creative co-operator in history with the Creator God; this vision highlighted the horrors of history and the realism of the doctrine of original sin. Those of an Augustinian bent were promoting this reminder that the earthly city was far from being the city of God. One approach emphasized the doctrines of creation and the incarnation (as sanctifying the created order as graced); the other approach emphasized the doctrine of redemption, the need for a Savior, and the cross as a "complement" to the doctrine of the incarnation.

As we have seen, *periti* such as Rahner and Ratzinger were co-opted on to drafting subcommissions late in the fourth session precisely in order to bring greater theological balance to the text in these areas. According to Avery Dulles, it was successful: "*Gaudium et Spes* has often been characterized as too optimistic. But in reading it I am struck by the number of times it speaks of original sin, of diabolical influences in the world, of anxiety, suffering, and death, and of the ruinous effects of personal sin. It gives considerable attention to the problems of our day, including the decline of reli-

---

133. Komonchak, "Augustine, Aquinas or the Gospel *sine glossa*?"; Joseph A. Komonchak, "La Redazione della Gaudium et Spes," *Il Regno* 44 (1999): 446–55; Komonchak, "Le valutazioni sulla *Gaudium et spes*: Chenu, Dossetti, Ratzinger"; Komonchak, "Thomism and the Second Vatican Council."

gious practice, the growth of atheism, and the current clash of ideologies."[134] Dulles goes on to cite, as an example, article 37 of the pastoral constitution: "The whole of human history has been the story of dour combat with the powers of evil, stretching, as our Lord tells us, from the very dawn of history until the last day. Finding themselves in the battlefield, men and women have to struggle to do what is right, and it is at great cost to themselves, and aided by God's grace, that they succeed in achieving their own inner integrity" (GS 37). Tellingly, however, the last paragraph of article 37 provides an important balance to the picture of human sinfulness and failure, with its declaration of the intrinsic goodness of God's created world and the ultimate power of God's grace within that world: "Redeemed by Christ and made a new creature by the Holy Spirit, a person can, and indeed must, love the things which God has created: it is from God that they have been received, and it is as coming from God's hand that they are seen and revered" (GS 37).

Seventh, there was the tension between an *ahistorical* notion of human being and a *historical* one. The classicist ahistorical notion conceived of the human being as constituted by an immutable human nature. Reflecting the council's shift toward greater historical consciousness in retrieving the Christian tradition, expressed in its two leitmotifs of *ressourcement* and *aggiornamento*, the historical understanding of being human shifted toward a greater recognition of particularity in human experience. While static notions of human "nature" are still to be found, there is a trajectory toward giving greater acknowledgment of more dynamic and personalist notions of the human "condition."

Eighth, there was the tension between an *extrinsic* model of God's relation to creation and humanity and an *intrinsic* model of God's action. This is related to models of God's action and the workings of divine grace and the tension between *God's freedom* and *human freedom* under divine grace. These themes had been vigorously debated by *ressourcement* philosophers and theologians before the council, and they are not quite resolved in the final text of *Gaudium et Spes*.[135] But the intrinsic model of God's action

134. Avery Dulles, "The Mission of the Church in *Gaudium et spes*," in *The Church and Human Freedom: Forty Years after Gaudium et Spes*, ed. Darlene Fozard Weaver (Villanova, PA: Villanova University Press, 2006), 26–37, at 31–32.

135. On the rejection of extrinicist models in the work of *ressourcement* theologians such as Henri de Lubac and Chenu, see Henri de Lubac, *The Mystery of the Supernatural* (London: Geoffrey Chapman, 1967); Quisinsky, *Geschichtlicher Glaube in einer geschichtlichen Welt. Der Beitrag von M.-D. Chenu, Y. Congar und H.-M. Féret zum II. Vaticanum*; Turbanti, "Il ruolo del P. D. Chenu nell'elaborazione della costituzione *Gaudium et Spes*."

predominates in the themes of history and the need for all the faithful, pastors and laity, to cooperate with one another and with God in discerning God's will for human beings within the new conditions of history.

Elements of each pole in the above eight tensions can be still found juxtaposed in the final document. Resolving each of these tensions turned out to be unrealizable; the best theological minds in the Catholic world couldn't agree. The approved text of *Gaudium et Spes*, however, sets out the final judgment of the council regarding each of the above. In the final vote on whether the document should be promulgated, the negative vote had reduced to seventy-five, with 2,309 bishops in favor. As we have seen on other issues at the council, this consensus vote was achieved because the council had found a way to juxtapose statements presupposing different theological frameworks, or by using open-ended language that covered different approaches, while still indicating a trajectory toward a possible synthesis. In this way, a consensus of the vast majority of bishops could be arrived at.

The unresolved "battle" between the French and German bishops and their *periti* is instructive. It is a case of theological diversity strikingly reminiscent of another seemingly intractable debate in the history of the church, that of the so-called *De Auxiliis* controversy, regarding the relation between divine grace and human free will.[136] In much the same way as the indefinite "resolution" of the *De Auxiliis* controversy, the voting on *Gaudium et Spes* could be said to have ended with a similar decision by the conciliar assembly regarding the various theological issues related to the relationship between the church and the world that had so plagued the drafting process from the very start. While other typologies could be found, Komonchak's depiction

---

136. Lasting from 1582 until 1611, it turned out being not only a theological dispute regarding the doctrine of grace but also a battle between the differing theological approaches of two major religious orders in the Catholic Church. Two of the major protagonists were the Dominican Domingo Báñez and the Jesuit Luis de Molina. After years of scholarly investigations into the respective strengths and weaknesses of the two theological positions, the dispute was finally ended, or rather paused, when Pope Paul V declared that both sides could continue to hold their different positions, but were not to attack the other position as unorthodox. The papal declaration reads: "In the affair concerning the aids (of grace), the supreme pontiff has granted to both the disputants and their consultants permission to return to their countries or houses. . . . [I]t is most strictly forbidden by the same Most Holy Lord that, in treating this subject, anyone should judge or censure in any way his opposing party. . . . Rather, he wishes that (both sides) mutually abstain from harsh words expressing bitterness of spirit." DS 1997, in Denzinger, *Compendium of Creeds, Definitions, and Declarations*, 453. For a concise overview of the *de auxiliis* controversy and its "resolution," see T. Ryan, "Congregatio De Auxiliis," in *New Catholic Encyclopedia* (Detroit: Gale, 2003), 4:110–13.

of the two "sides" of the conciliar debate as "neo-Augustinian" and "neo-Thomist" can be heuristically useful, because it captures echoes in the conciliar debate of two major approaches to the Christian mystery throughout the church's history. Both perspectives provide insights into the mystery, with each having its particular strengths and weaknesses. That Vatican II found a way to incorporate both perspectives—although in a way that perhaps either side was not necessarily happy with—is a fundamental learning that the council passes on to the church regarding legitimate theological diversity for the sake of ecclesial unity. Hence, before it felt it could go on to call for unity through dialogue with three groups of "outsiders" in *Gaudium et Spes* 92, Vatican II calls for unity through dialogue within the Catholic Church, emphasizing not only the importance of diversity but also a Christian quality and tone in debate: "Such a mission requires first of all to create in the church itself mutual esteem, reverence and harmony, and to acknowledge all legitimate diversity. . . . [L]et there be unity in what is necessary, freedom in what is doubtful, and charity in everything" (GS 92).

But, within the theological diversity evident in the drafting of *Gaudium et Spes*, and still embedded in the final text, the council is clearly indicating a trajectory toward a new Catholic synthesis, given its own *ressourcement* and critique of the two millennia of Christian tradition regarding the church/world relationship. According to John O'Malley, the thrust of that trajectory is "more incarnational than eschatological, closer to Thomas Aquinas than to Karl Barth, more reminiscent of the Fathers of the Eastern Church than of Augustine—more inclined to reconciliation with human culture than to alienation from it, more inclined to see goodness than sin, more inclined to speaking words of friendship and encouragement than of indictment."[137] Certainly Paul VI, in his closing address on December 7, believed the council was showing a deliberate direction:

> [The council] dwelt upon humanity's ever twofold facet, namely, man's wretchedness and his greatness, his profound weakness—which is undeniable and cannot be cured by himself—and the good that survives in him which is ever marked by a hidden beauty and an invincible serenity. But one must realize that this council, which exposed itself to human judgment, insisted very much more upon this pleasant side of man, rather than on his unpleasant one. Its attitude was very much and deliberately optimistic. A wave of affection and admiration flowed from the council over the modern world of humanity.

137. O'Malley, *What Happened at Vatican II*, 310–11.

Errors were condemned, indeed, because charity demanded this no less than did truth, but for the persons themselves there was only warning, respect and love. Instead of depressing diagnoses, encouraging remedies; instead of direful prognostics, messages of trust issued from the council to the present-day world. The modern world's values were not only respected but honoured, its efforts approved, its aspirations purified and blessed.[138]

What O'Malley concludes regarding the overall vision of Vatican II is particularly true of *Gaudium et Spes* and the other three documents of the counter-syllabus: "The result was a message that was traditional while at the same time radical, prophetic while at the same time soft-spoken. In a world increasing wracked with discord, hatred, war, and threats of war, the result was a message that was counter-cultural while at the same time responsive to the deepest human yearnings. Peace on earth. Good will to men."[139]

A Church Loving the World for God's Sake

The church/world principle synthesizes Vatican II's vision regarding this new relationship with the world, particularly as articulated in its four documents of the counter-syllabus. O'Malley gives a pithy summary of the council's reconfiguration of this relationship: "The church, it made clear, is *in* the modern world—not above it, not below it, not for it, not against it. Therefore, like everybody else *in* the world, the church must assume its share of responsibility for the well-being of the world, not simply denounce what it finds wrong."[140] For Adrian Hastings:

> *Gaudium et Spes* shows the Church's deep concern for the whole spectrum of human life in a way that no other ecclesiastical document has ever done. To be the Church in a full and living sense the people of God must be thoroughly worldly—that is to say, fully involved in all sides of the life of this world. The Church's mission is a mission in this world, affecting the condition of human society and being affected by it in every possible way. Personal problems and social problems, family problems, cultural problems, economic problems, political problems, international problems—these constitute the very stuff of the life of the people of God, just as they constitute the stuff of the world's life.[141]

---

138. Paul VI, "Closing Address: Fourth Session," 360–61.
139. O'Malley, *What Happened at Vatican II*, 311.
140. Ibid., 297. Original emphasis.
141. Hastings, *A Concise Guide to the Documents*, 2:67.

The context in which God's plan unfolds is "the world" (*mundus*). The council uses the word *mundus* 271 times (albeit in varying senses). In Scripture and throughout the tradition, the term has a wide range of meanings, from the positive to the negative. Therefore, during the drafting process of *Gaudium et Spes*, there was much debate over the need to clarify the particular sense in which the council was using the term in each case.[142] Accordingly, after first introducing the document's ecclesiological intent—to address "the presence and function of the church in the *mundus* of today" (GS 2)—*Gaudium et Spes* goes on to explain how it understands the different but overlapping aspects of "the world":

> The world which the council has in mind is the world of women and men, the entire human family seen in its total environment [*cum universitate rerum inter quas vivit*]. It is the world as the theatre of human history, bearing the marks of its travail, its triumphs and failures. It is the world which Christians believe has been created and is sustained by the love of its maker, has fallen into the slavery of sin but has been freed by Christ, who was crucified and rose again in order to break the stranglehold of the evil one, so that it might be fashioned anew according to God's plan [*propositum*] and brought to fulfillment. (GS 2)[143]

The document later gives a further, specifically negative, sense of "the world": "The church of Christ, trusting in the design [*consilio*] of the creator and accepting that progress can contribute to humanity's true happiness, still feels called upon to echo the words of the apostle: 'Do not be conformed to this world' (Rom 12:2). 'World' here means a spirit of vanity and malice whereby human activity, from being ordered to the service of God and humanity, is reduced to being an instrument of sin" (GS 37). As we have seen, Bishop Emilio Guano, in his *relatio* presenting the Zürich text to the conciliar body in the third session, reminded the assembly of the positive countenance with which God looks upon "the world," quoting John 3:16: "God so loved the world that he gave his only Son, so that everyone who believes in him may not perish but may have eternal life."[144]

---

142. For an examination of the range of meanings the word has in the Bible and in the tradition, as well as the various interventions during the council calling for emphasis on particular aspects across this range of meanings, see Antony Nirappel, "Towards the Definition of the Term 'World' in *Gaudium et Spes*," *Ephemerides Theologicae Lovanienses* 48 (1972): 89–126.

143. Translation corrected.

144. AS III/5, 203–14.

Joseph Komonchak notes the dynamic sense in which *Gaudium et Spes* 2 uses the word: "*World* is what human beings have made, are making and will make by the use of their freedom; perhaps it is less the world as 'the theater of human history' (GS 2) than the world as the drama of human history."[145] He goes on to note: "Underlying this is an expanded anthropology which goes beyond a merely psychological consideration, which is content to relate Gospel and grace to the drama of the individual's self-responsibility, to a fuller view which relates God's gifts and the church as their embodiment to the larger drama of the collective and historical self-responsibility of mankind, *a drama in which the church participates* in all its joy and hope, its grief and anguish, its greatness and its misery."[146] Therefore, explicit in the church/world principle, is the theological vision that God's plan envisages the active involvement of free yet responsible human beings, albeit within the realm of divine grace.

Significantly, therefore, the word "history" appears in the council's account of its understanding of "world." The noun *historia* and the adjective *historicus* appear a total of thirty-eight times in the Latin text of *Gaudium et Spes*. From the very first paragraph, it speaks positively of the solidarity the disciples of Christ have with humanity and its history: "Nothing that is genuinely human fails to find an echo in their hearts. . . . [They are] bearers of a message of salvation for all of humanity. That is why they cherish a feeling of deep solidarity [*revera intime coniunctam*] with the human race and its history" (GS 1).

The church turning toward the world with such a look of compassionate understanding is expressed in the metaphor of the "face." The church's face—the council, in effect, says—should radiate benevolence rather than a scolding glare. The council desired to shift from renouncing and reproaching the world to seeking a more empathetic *rapprochement* with the world. It wanted to shift away from centuries of disaffection and to show affection, since God so loves the world that he sent his only Son. How much the church should still be suspicious of the world remained a point of contention to the end of the council. But that the church's face to the world should be different from that of previous centuries was the clear intention of the vast majority of the bishops.

The metaphor of the "face" appears in several passages throughout the council documents. *Lumen Gentium* in its very first paragraph boldly proclaims: "the light of Christ . . . is resplendent on the face of the church [*super faciem ecclesiae*]." That this is not quite the case in the church's history the document acknowledges a little later in article 8: "The church . . . clasping

---

145. Komonchak, "The Ecclesiology of Vatican II," 766.
146. Ibid., 766. Emphasis added.

sinners to its bosom, at once holy and always in need of purification [*sancta simul et semper purificanda*], follows constantly the path of penance and renewal [*poenitentiam et renovationem*]." Further on, article 15 states: "Mother church . . . exhorts her children to purification and renewal [*purificationem et renovationem*] so that the sign of Christ may shine more brightly over the face [*super faciem*] of the church." In this call for ecclesial conversion, the council is clearly calling for an "about-face" on the part of the Catholic Church. *Gaudium et Spes,* using the Latin word *vultus* (countenance, face, look, expression), develops this call for conversion and acknowledges that the way Christians speak, behave, and relate can impede the mission of the church: "Believers can thus have more than a little to do with the rise of atheism. To the extent that they are careless about their instruction in the faith, or present its teaching falsely, or even fail in their religious, moral or social life, they must be said to conceal rather than to reveal the genuine face of God and religion [*Dei et religionis genuinum vultum*]" (GS 19).

And so, the pastoral constitution reminds ministers of their responsibility: "Let all pastors of souls bear in mind that by their daily behaviour and concerns *they are presenting the face of the church to the world* [*mundo faciem ecclesiae*] and that people judge from that the power and truth of the Christian message" (GS 43). The text here in a footnote cites *Lumen Gentium* 28, which states: "[Priests] should be mindful that by their daily conduct and solicitude they should show the face of a truly priestly and pastoral ministry to believers and unbelievers alike, to Catholics and non-Catholics" (LG 28). Then the same article 43 closes by quoting *Lumen Gentium* 15: "Guided by the Holy Spirit the church ceaseless exhorts her children 'to purification and renewal so that the sign of Christ may shine more brightly over the face of the church'" (GS 43). The acknowledgment that the face of the church is not always resplendent with the light of Christ constitutes a fundamental concern in the overall pastoral and reform agenda of Vatican II: that the face of the church should faithfully mirror the genuine face of the God whom she proclaims.[147] This goes to the very core of the church/world principle. The counter-syllabus is a call by the council for ecclesial purification and renewal in its relationship to the world around it.

While the whole of the pastoral constitution, and indeed all documents making up the council's counter-syllabus, seek to lay out the reconfigured church/world principle, the fourth chapter of the pastoral constitution is

---

147. See Rush, "Ecclesial Conversion after Vatican II."

particularly devoted to this theme (GS 40–45). The chapter is titled "The Task of the Church in the World of Today." Adrian Hastings believes it to be one of the gems of the whole conciliar corpus: "Undoubtedly this chapter constitutes one of the very high points in the Council documents. Though it is quite short it draws together many of the greatest conciliar themes: the lordship of Christ, the unifying action of the Holy Spirit, the servant Church, the significance of history, the tension between the present and the eschatological, the 'autonomy' of the laity, the meaning and urgency of true unity, freedom, humanization. This chapter probably represents the most mature piece of writing the Council anywhere produced."[148] It affirms that the church is to be immersed in the world, not apart from it: "it is to be a leaven and, as it were, the soul of human society in its renewal by Christ and transformation into the family of God" (GS 40). While Christians' great gift to the world is Jesus Christ, the council acknowledges that the world does in fact offer service to the church: "the people of God, and the human race of which it forms part, are of service to each other" (GS 11). Article 44 provides an extended reflection on that striking acknowledgment, so counter to the previous condemnations of the 1864 *Syllabus*: "The church is not unaware how much it has profited from the history and development of humankind. It profits from the experience of past ages, from the progress of the sciences, and from the riches hidden in various cultures, through which great light is thrown on human nature and new avenues to truth are opened up" (GS 44). Accordingly, the church must listen to the guidance of the Holy Spirit coming from the world: "With the help of the Holy Spirit, it is the task of the whole People of God, particularly of its pastors and theologians, to listen and distinguish the many voices of our times and to interpret them in the light of the divine word, in order that the revealed truth may be more deeply penetrated, better understood, and suitably presented" (GS 44).

It is within this fourth chapter that we find two references to the metaphor of the church's face (GS 43). Significantly, the metaphor appears alongside the notion of the church as a visible and tangible sacrament of God in the world. In describing what the church offers society, the pastoral constitution highlights the church's potential as a unifier of peoples, using the notion of sacrament: "The encouragement of unity is in harmony with the deepest nature of the church's mission, for it is 'a sacrament—a sign and instrument, that is, of communion with God and of the unity of the whole human race.' . . . The

---

148. Hastings, *A Concise Guide to the Documents*, 2:68.

impact which the church can have on modern society is due to *an effective living of faith and love,* not to any external power exercised by purely human means" (GS 42). The passage is here quoting the opening paragraph of *Lumen Gentium.* And then a few articles later—at a structurally significant point in the pastoral constitution, the closing article of part 1—it once again quotes *Lumen Gentium*: "Every benefit the People of God can confer on humanity during its earthly pilgrimage is rooted in the church's being 'the universal sacrament of salvation,' at once manifesting and actualizing the mystery of God's love for humanity" (GS 45, quoting LG 48). The face of the church, therefore, should first bestow the countenance of God's love for humanity, so that its credibility may allow God's grace to make it an effective instrument actualizing God's saving grace.

But who is "church" in the council's understanding of the church/world principle? The council speaks at different times of three aspects of the church's presence in the world: individual believers, the collective of believers, the official institution. Each of these three aspects assumes importance in the church/world principle. The second part of the pastoral constitution explores five areas of the church's life in the world: the family, the cultural sphere, economic and social life, political life, and relationships among nations.

The pastoral constitution speaks twice of "the whole People of God," with the phrase "People of God" recurring a total of seven times. The references to "laypeople" are confined to article 43 (four times, regarding what the church offers to humanity) and to article 62 (two times, regarding the participation of laypeople in theological scholarship). The word "hierarchy" does not appear at all in the pastoral constitution, with the word "bishops" used four times, "priests" six times, and "deacons" not mentioned at all. Therefore, in speaking of the church in the world, the pastoral constitution envisages all of the faithful playing an active role in society according to their particular charism and ministry. The "faithful" are referred to twenty-six times, "believers" eleven times, and "disciples" of Christ four times. Thus, as the *fideles/fidelis* principle emphasizes, the council does not isolate the role of the ordained to the sphere of "church" nor the laity to that of "world." The church (all of the faithful) lives *in* the world, not outside it. While the ordained "in a special way" attend to the inner life of the church, they too are active "in the world," just as the laity are active in the world, but also called to participate fully in the inner life of the church, through participation in the "inner" aspects of the three offices of Christ. Nonetheless, 99.99 percent of the "church" is not ordained and virtually constitutes the daily reality of what the council means by "the church in the world."

As the quote from *Lumen Gentium* 1 shows, the council's depiction of the church as a sacrament draws on the scholastic notion of "sign and instrument": the "sign" of the church is its face to the world; the "instrument" that the church can be refers to its role as a mediator of God's grace. Since grace builds on nature, the effectiveness of the instrument, however, is conditioned by the credibility of the sign, albeit under the aegis of divine grace. In this regard, the council emphasizes the importance of Christian "witness." The notion of "witness" appears regularly throughout the conciliar corpus; the Latin words are *testimonium* (used eighty-seven times), *testis* (twenty-eight times), *testificari* (seven times). The decree *Ad Gentes* has twenty-one references to "witness" and its cognates. There are twenty instances throughout *Lumen Gentium*, applying to all the faithful in the first instance and then to the hierarchy and laity. *Christus Dominus* uses the word four times in reference to the ministry of bishops. *Apostolicam Actuositatem* uses it twelve times in reference to laypeople, and *Perfectae Caritatis* twice in reference to religious. In the four documents making up the council's counter-syllabus, there are six cognates of the word "witness" in *Unitatis Redintegratio*, two in *Nostra Aetate*, four in *Dignitatis Humanae*, and fourteen in *Gaudium et Spes*.

Whether the term "church" is used to refer to baptized individuals, the collective group of Christians, or the church as a public institution, the notion of witness is central for conceiving the mission of the church in the world. As the pastoral constitution puts it so starkly: "It is the function of the church to render God the Father and his incarnate Son present and as it were visible, while ceaselessly renewing and purifying itself under the guidance of the Holy Spirit. This is brought about chiefly by *the witness of a living and mature faith*" (GS 21). We have already seen above, in the passage on the church as a sacrament: "The impact which the church can have on modern society is due to *an effective living of faith and love*" (GS 42). This notion of witness, even if the word itself is not always used, pervades the council's depiction of Christians' responsibility in family life, culture, economic and social life, political life, and international relations.

Lumen Gentium had already linked the theme of witness with the presence of laypeople in the world. "All lay people, through the gifts which they have received, are at once the witnesses and the living instruments of the mission of the church itself 'according to the measure of Christ's gift'" (LG 33).[149] "Christ is the great prophet who proclaimed the kingdom of the Father both

---

149. The passage is quoting Eph 4:7.

by the testimony of his life and by the power of his word. Until the full manifestation of his glory, he fulfils this prophetic office, not only through the hierarchy who teach in his name and by his power, but also through the laity. He accordingly both establishes them as witnesses and provides them with a sense of the faith [*sensus fidei*] and an attractiveness of speech so that the power of the Gospel may shine out in daily family and social life" (LG 35).[150] This passage links back to the affirmation earlier in *Lumen Gentium* 12 of the participation by all the *fideles* (lay and ordained) in the prophetic office of Christ through their witness; within this living of faith through witness comes a "sense of the faith."

In *Gaudium et Spes*, the laity are called "citizens of the world" (GS 43). Here too the theme of witness recurs. "The laity are called to participate actively in the entire life of the church; not only are they to animate the world with the spirit of Christianity, they are to be witnesses to Christ in all circumstances and at the very heart of the human community" (GS 43). In the second-to-last paragraph of *Gaudium et Spes*'s concluding article, we find what can well constitute a summary of the church/world principle:

> It is the Father's will that we should recognize Christ our brother in the persons of all men and women and should love them with an active love, in word and deed, thus *bearing witness to the truth*; and it is his will that we should share with others the mystery of his heavenly love. In this way people all over the world will awaken to a lively hope, the gift of the Holy Spirit, that they will one day be admitted to the haven of peace and utter happiness in their homeland radiant with the glory of the Lord. (GS 93)[151]

The discussion above of the *communio/missio* principle has highlighted the council's theology of mission as one of ecclesial presence. It noted how the words *praesens* and *presentia* are peppered throughout *Ad Gentes*. Moreover, the discussion above on *Dignitatis Humanae* noted how the council's vision of ecclesial presence through dialogue is grounded on the praxis of dialogue that characterized the spirit of Christ's own mission and its marks of meekness, humility, patience, attraction, invitation, assurance: "Just as Christ penetrated to people's hearts and by a truly human dialogue [*colloquio*] led them to the divine light, so too his disciples, profoundly pervaded by the Spirit of Christ, should know and converse with those among whom they live,

150. Translation corrected.
151. Translation corrected. Emphasis added.

that through sincere and patient dialogue [*dialogo*] they themselves might learn of the riches which a generous God has distributed among the nations. They must at the same time endeavour to illuminate these riches with the light of the gospel, set them free, and bring them once more under the dominion of God the saviour" (AG 11). *Dignitatis Humanae* ends its overview of Jesus' mode of speaking and praxis, as well as that of the early church, by using the recurring theme of "witness to the truth": "For he bore witness to the truth but refused to use force to impose it on those who spoke out against it. His kingdom does not establish its claims by force, but is established by bearing witness to and hearing the truth and it grows by the love with which Christ, lifted up on the cross, draws people to himself" (DH 11).

Paul VI, in his closing address to the council, spoke of this new tone that the council sought to adopt: "[The council] has spoken with the accommodating friendly voice of pastoral charity; its desire has been to be heard and understood by everyone; it has not merely concentrated on intellectual understanding but has also sought to express itself in simple, up-to-date, conversational style, derived from actual experience and a cordial approach which make it more vital, attractive and persuasive; it has spoken to modern man as he is."[152] The positive attitude comes from Vatican II's desire to concentrate on "what people have in common and what tends to bring them together" (NA 1) rather than on what divides.

The conciliar focus on "witness" is captured in Paul Knitter's observation regarding the Christian/religious principle that we have noted above. It applies equally to the church/world principle, and more specifically to the notion of witness: "What makes [*Gaudium et Spes*] so revolutionary is to be found not primarily in what it, and other Vatican II documents, say *about* [the world], but, rather, in what it says about how Christians should *act* toward [the world]. [*Gaudium et Spes*] opens up whole new directions—not, primarily, in its *doctrine* about the meaning of the [world], but rather in its *ethics* about how Christians should interact and relate to [other human beings]."[153]

The council's "ethics" is evident, among other themes, in the theme of service. "One of the most striking and generally acceptable consequences of Vatican II has been that the Catholic Church has become more conscious of the fact that God intended Christ's Church to serve the whole of mankind,

152. Paul VI, "Closing Address: Fourth Session," 361.
153. Knitter, "*Nostra Aetate*: A Milestone in the History of Religions?," 45. Original emphasis.

and so the whole world."[154] The word "serve" appears eighteen times in the pastoral constitution alone, and the word "service" (with overlapping meanings) thirty times. The preface of *Gaudium et Spes* ends with the sentence: "The church is not motivated by earthly ambition but is interested in one thing only—to carry on the work of Christ under the guidance of the Holy Spirit, who came into the world to bear witness to the truth, to save and not to judge, to serve [*ut ministraret*] and not be served" (GS 3). And then, in the final concluding article of the pastoral constitution, service is once again highlighted in the summary statement: "Mindful of the words of the Lord: 'By this all will know that you are my disciples, if you have love for one another' (Jn 13:35), Christians can yearn for nothing more ardently than to serve [*inserviant*] the people of this age successfully with increasing generosity" (GS 93).

This service is intended to be practical. We have already noted how, for Paul VI, the model of the Good Samaritan came to characterize the spirituality of the council. *Gaudium et Spes* 27 urges: "Today, there is an inescapable duty to make ourselves the neighbour of every individual, without exception, and to take positive steps to help a neighbour whom we encounter, whether that neighbour be an elderly person abandoned by everyone, a foreign worker who suffers the injustice of being despised, a refugee, an illegitimate child wrongly suffering for a sin of which the child is innocent, or a starving human being who awakens our conscience by calling to mind the words of Christ: 'As you did it to one of the least of these my brothers or sisters, you did it to me'" (GS 27).[155]

The chapter in the pastoral constitution on the economy speaks of economic inequality: "Luxury and misery exist side by side" (GS 63). The church is being challenged by Christ himself to be active in the world: "It is all the more urgent, now that the greater part of the world is in such poverty: it is as if Christ himself were appealing to the charity of his followers through the mouths of these poor people" (GS 88). The responsibility to serve, by concretely responding to this situation, is incumbent upon all: "It is the duty of the entire People of God, following the teaching and example of bishops, to alleviate the hardships of our times within the limits of its means, giving generously, as was the ancient custom of the church, not merely out of what is superfluous but also out of necessities" (GS 88).

154. Jan Groot, "The Church as Sacrament of the World," *Concilium* 1, no. 4 (January 1968): 27–34, at 27.

155. The passage is quoting Matt 25:40.

530   *Ecclesiological Principles*

Several times throughout this book we have had occasion to highlight the centrality of the leitmotif "dialogue" in the council's vision. Along with other themes such as "face," "presence," and "witness," the notion of "dialogue" characterizes the council's reconfiguration of the church/world relationship. Certainly this is true also of the council's whole vision: "No single word, with the possible exception of *aggiornamento*, would be more often invoked to indicate what the council was all about."[156] The word occurs twelve times throughout the pastoral constitution. In its concluding image of four concentric circles of dialogue, the last circle is dialogue with the world:

> For our part, our eagerness for such dialogue, conducted with appropriate discretion and leading to truth by way of love alone, excludes nobody; we would like to include those who respect outstanding human values without realizing who the author of those values is, as well as those who oppose the church and persecute it in various ways. Since God the Father is the beginning and the end of all things, we are all called to be brothers and sisters; we ought to work together without violence and without deceit to build up the world in a spirit of genuine peace. (GS 92)

It is particularly chapter 4 of the pastoral constitution's first part (40–45) that expands explicitly on the dialogic relationship envisaged between church and world. It begins: "All we have said up to now . . . provides a basis for discussing the relationship between the church and the world and the dialogue between them [*mutui dialogi*]" (GS 40). Regarding the responsibility of bishops and priests, it states: "Let them prepare themselves by careful study to meet to enter into dialogue [*dialogo*] with the world and with people of all shades of opinion" (GS 43). Not all bishops over the years of debate thought that the dialogic principle should be consistently applied. For example, one of the bishops wanting a condemnation of communism was Archbishop Karol Wojtyla from Krakow in Poland. His position can be contrasted with that of Cardinal Šeper, archbishop of Zagreb in Yugoslavia. Both bishops lived under communist regimes. Šeper, however, argued that communism should not be condemned because he believed dialogue was the more productive way forward.[157] Šeper's view prevailed.

All of these themes—face, presence, witness, dialogue—can be neatly summarized in John O'Malley's basic interpretation of Vatican II, that it was

---

156. O'Malley, *What Happened at Vatican II*, 80.
157. AS IV/2, 435–37.

fundamentally all about "style." In its relationship with the world, Vatican II wanted to change the style of relating to the world, "from exclusion to inclusion, from hostility to friendship, from rivalry to partnership, from suspicion to trust."[158] The very way of speaking in the conciliar documents are part of the message, as we have seen Paul VI noting. While O'Malley's thesis applies to the council's vision regarding life within the church, it also called for, in its relationship with the world "outside" the church, "a conversion to a new style of thinking, speaking, and behaving, a change from a more authoritarian and unidirectional style to a more reciprocal and responsive model . . . a model largely based on *persuasion* and *invitation*."[159] As noted above, these are the very words used in *Dignitatis Humanae* 11 of Jesus' style of ministry—persuasion and invitation.

Much of this empathy toward the world and to humanity was explicitly inspired by the Christian humanism characterizing Catholic thought in the decades leading up to the council.[160] The word "humanism" appears three times in *Gaudium et Spes* (7, 55, 56), sometimes in the negative sense of the word, referring to secular humanism, a philosophy that sees no place for God in its vision. In article 55, however, the council embraces a positive sense of the term: "All over the world the sense of autonomy and responsibility increases with effects of the greatest importance for the spiritual and moral maturity of humankind. This will become clearer to us if we advert to the unification of the world and the duty imposed on us to build up a better world in truth and justice. We are witnessing the birth of a new humanism, where people are defined before all else by their responsibility to their sisters and brothers and at the court of history" (GS 55). In his closing address of December 7, 1965, Paul VI, himself very much influenced by the humanist philosopher Jacques Maritain, directly addressed secular humanists, inviting them to recognize the common ground the council's Christian humanism shares with them: "We call upon those who term themselves modern humanists, and who have renounced the transcendent value of the highest realities, to give the council credit at least for one quality and to recognize our own new type of humanism: we, too, in fact, we more than any others, honour mankind."[161]

158. O'Malley, *What Happened at Vatican II*, 307.

159. Ibid., 11. Emphasis added.

160. Angelo Bianchi and Giancarlo Andenna, eds., *Il Concilio Vaticano II, crocevia dell'umanesimo contemporaneo* (Milano: Vita e Pensiero, 2015).

161. Paul VI, "Closing Address: Fourth Session," 360.

In conclusion, with its counter-syllabus, Vatican II deliberately set out to move on from the negative attitude to the contemporary world, so starkly formulated in the *Syllabus of Errors*. In turning rather to the model of Jesus' own mode of relating in his ministry, Vatican II sought to adopt a new stance in relationship to the world. And in so doing, the council saw itself, not so much to be rejecting the past, as finding its true Christian identity within an often hostile world. What we have seen in discussing the previous two principles regarding the insight of Heinrich Fries indeed applies also here to the church/world principle: "In the question of 'the Church [and the world]' Vatican II discovered a principle according to which the Church's identity and continuity were to be preserved not by separating off or denying everything that was not itself but by linking *fidelity to itself* with *openness to others* rather than with the denigration of others."[162] Or, in the words of John O'Malley: "The fathers chose to praise the positive aspects of Catholicism and establish the church's identity on that basis, rather than by making Catholicism look good by making others look bad."[163]

162. Fries, "Church and Churches," 316. Emphasis added.
163. O'Malley, *What Happened at Vatican II*, 305.

Epilogue

Receiving the Vision

In his work on the development of doctrine, John Henry Newman highlighted a particular class of development, which he called "historical development." Such development, he said, is "the gradual formation of opinion concerning persons, facts, and events. Judgments, which were at one time confined to a few, at length spread through a community, and attain general reception by the accumulation and concurrence of testimony. Thus some authoritative accounts die away; others gain a footing, and are ultimately received as truths."[1] Vatican II was just such an event of accelerated and concentrated "historical development" over four years, when the council appropriated much of the *ressourcement* scholarship and pastoral experience of the previous three decades. Using a more critical hermeneutical model than the organic one of "development," Vatican II was an event of ecclesial conversion to a new style of being church *ad intra* and *ad extra* and a conversion of the Catholic imagination regarding faith and history.

The principles articulated throughout this book reconstruct the essential elements of the vision of Vatican II. They have been distilled from an examination of the council's deliberations, along with an examination of the texts resulting from those deliberations. Just as the council's sixteen documents "implicitly cross-reference one another . . . are coherent with one another and play off one another,"[2] so too do these twenty-four principles. Just as the two terms within a principle stand in positive tension with each other, so too all principles stand in positive tension with one another. Their reciprocal relationship means that each necessarily implies yet qualifies the others, each from a different perspective of the mystery of God's presence and activity in history and of the church's mystery as a sacrament of that divine presence and activity. Therefore, in synthesizing the comprehensive vision of Vatican

---

1. John Henry Newman, *An Essay on the Development of Christian Doctrine*, 6th ed. (Notre Dame, IN: University of Notre Dame Press, 1989), 46–47.
2. O'Malley, *What Happened at Vatican II*, 310.

II, these principles are to be held in a tensive equilibrium as mutually inter-pretive and mutually corrective, while keeping in mind the primacy of the theo-logical principles over the ecclesiological.

When Vatican II ended on December 8, 1965, it entered into "history," the condition of human existence marked by time and place, culture and circumstance, certainty and uncertainty. And within those historical condi-tions, the council would itself have "a history." A council can have no "effect" without "reception"; for it to be effective, its vision must be received. Both as an historic event in the life of the church and as an authoritative collection of texts, "Vatican II" has now undergone a history of reception for more than half a century. To varying degrees and in diverse ways, the council has been received, or not received, across the globe, in multiple geographical and cultural areas of the church. If, as Karl Rahner perceived, Vatican II imagined a truly world church, then the global diversity that has marked the council's reception is precisely what the council itself envisaged, albeit inchoately, with regards to its own history.[3]

In evaluating the global reception of Vatican II, the twenty-four principles articulated above might well function as criteria for assessing faithful or in-adequate reception of the conciliar vision at the local, national, regional, continental, and universal levels. On the one hand, applying those twenty-four criteria would show the many ways in which the conciliar vision has been appropriated to some degree into Catholic life. On the other hand, it also would show that a full reception of these principles is far from being realized. More than fifty years after Vatican II, the church still struggles to inculcate many of the shifts of the council into the rhythm of its daily life. As Karl Rahner observes: "It will certainly be a long time before the Church which has been given the Second Vatican Council will be the Church of the Second Vatican Council."[4]

As Joseph Komonchak asserts: "Just as there is no church apart from the churches, so how the council was received by the church can only be studied by how the council was received by the churches, that is, as the lived history, or histories, of Vatican II."[5] Comprehensive research into those histories of the

3. On Rahner's interpretation of Vatican II as a shift toward a genuinely world church, see Rahner, "Basic Theological Interpretation."

4. Rahner, "The Council: A New Beginning," 28.

5. Joseph A. Komonchak, "Afterword: The Church and the Churches," in *Catholics in the Vatican II Era: Local Histories of a Global Event*, ed. Kathleen Sprows Cummings, Timothy Matovina, and Robert A. Orsi (New York: Cambridge University Press, 2018), 275–90, at 288.

global reception of Vatican II by local churches is only just beginning.[6] In the meantime, there have been various overall evaluations of the council's reception. Writing twenty years after the council's close, Hermann Pottmeyer saw already two phases in that reception: an initial phase of "excitement" and a second phase (depending on one's point of view) either of "disillusionment" or of "truth and realism."[7] Henri de Lubac certainly saw an almost-immediate phase of "decomposition" and "crisis."[8] Not insignificant in this history of reception is the fact that the half-century since Vatican II has been stamped by the twenty-six-year pontificate of Pope John Paul II (1978–2005) and the eight-year pontificate of Benedict XVI (2005–2013), both participants at Vatican II as bishop and as *peritus*, respectively.[9] Massimo Faggioli portrays the narrative of the council's reception in these years in terms of a "battle."[10] According to Richard Lennan, one reason for this problematic reception has been the four-hundred-year dominance of an unchanging, monolithic Catholicism: "Contributing to this mixed character of the Council's reception was the fact that the church's history . . . left Catholics unskilled in discerning and negotiating possibilities for change. More specifically, there was no lived memory of how the dynamics of the *sensus fidei* might operate as the Council had advocated. Since descending models of authority had been so prominent, there was little awareness of either the theory or practice needed to nurture a communion of faith, including dealing with differences."[11]

6. For example, see the results of a global consultation in Mathijs Lamberigts, Gilles Routhier, Pedro Rubens Ferreira Oliveira, Christoph Theobald, and Dries Bosschaert, eds., *50 Years after the Vatican II Council: Theologians from All over the World Deliberate* (Paris: Federatio Internationalis Universitatem Catholicarum, 2015). Important in this regard is the international project coordinated by the German theologian Peter Hünermann for a thorough revision of the *Herders theologischer Kommentar*. This five-year project will result in a multi-volume commentary on the documents of Vatican II that will take into account the reception of each of the sixteen conciliar documents across the various continents. For the original commentary, see Peter Hünermann, Bernd Jochen Hilberath, and Guido Bausenhart, eds., *Herders theologischer Kommentar zum Zweiten Vatikanischen Konzil*, 5 vols. (Freiburg: Herder, 2004–2006).

7. Pottmeyer, "A New Phase in the Reception of Vatican II," 33–34. For a similar assessment, see Kasper, "The Continuing Challenge of the Second Vatican Council," 166–67.

8. See Henri de Lubac, "The Church in Crisis," *Theology Digest* 17 (1969): 312–25.

9. For one assessment regarding the relationship of these pontificates to Vatican II, see Dick, Schelkens, and Mettepenningen, *Aggiornamento?*, 183–213.

10. See Faggioli, *Vatican II*. See also Massimo Faggioli, "Vatican II: The History and the Narratives," in *50 Years On: Probing the Riches of Vatican II*, ed. David G. Schultenover (Collegeville, MN: Liturgical Press, 2015), 61–81.

11. Richard Lennan, "Roman Catholic Ecclesiology," in *The Routledge Companion to the Christian Church*, ed. Gerard Mannion and Lewis S. Mudge (New York: Routledge, 2008), 234–50, at 243.

Twenty years after the council's close, John Paul II convoked a special sitting of the Synod of Bishops to consider the reception of Vatican II over that time. Its Final Report proposed a key for interpreting the council's documents: "The ecclesiology of communion is the central and fundamental idea of the Council's documents."[12] Despite this choice of a single hermeneutical key, however, the synod was not singular in its composition and theology. Avery Dulles saw among the attending bishops, and within the Synod's Final Report, three "schools" of theology at work: a neo-Augustinian school with an eschatological and other-worldly viewpoint; a communitarian school, with an incarnational and this-worldly viewpoint; and a liberationist school, with a socio-economic-political albeit biblical viewpoint.[13] The first was concerned to give priority to the transcendent and sacral emphases of the Augustinian stream of the Catholic tradition evident in the conciliar documents; the second, to the immanent and secular emphases of the Thomist and humanist streams; the third, to the social engagement and critical impulse of the biblical-prophetic stream. Since the 1985 Synod of Bishops, the same typology could well be used heuristically to characterize the diversity and tensions within the global reception of Vatican II, constituting, as it were, three models of church in the contemporary Roman Catholic imagination.

It would seem that the election of the Argentinian Jorge Bergoglio as Pope Francis in March 2013 has introduced a further phase in the reception of Vatican II, bringing together in a new form the phases of "excitement" and "disappointment"/"realism." Here, however, while the disappointment also centers on the fact that the vision of the council is still unrealized, the "realism" centers also on the plight of the poor and the tenderness of God's mercy for moral failures. This new phase also seems to be marking a shift in balance in church life by giving a different weighting to the various streams of the Catholic tradition. If the neo-Augustinian school's emphasis on divine transcendence and suspicion of the world characterized the pontificates of John Paul II and Benedict XVI, then the incarnational and social justice emphases of the neo-Thomist and prophetic traditions are now being given greater emphasis by Francis, without downplaying the suspicion of the Augustinian vision. He speaks of the dangers of over-intellectualizing the faith and of the church being too self-referential, i.e., focusing too much on itself, rather than

12. Extraordinary Synod of Bishops 1986: C.1.
13. See Avery Dulles, "The Reception of Vatican II at the Extraordinary Synod of 1985," in *The Reception of Vatican II*, ed. Giuseppe Alberigo, Jean Pierre Jossua, and Joseph A. Komonchak (Washington, DC: The Catholic University of America Press, 1987), 349–63.

being missionary and outward-looking. While still focusing on *ad intra* and *communio* concerns, Francis is equally *ad extra* and *missio* oriented, with a particular priority given to those who are physically and spiritually poor, marginalized, and suffering. He has a strong focus on the pneumatological dimensions of the church and on a baptism ecclesiology: the church, he says, is "the Temple of the Holy Spirit, the Temple in which God works, the Temple in which, with the gift of Baptism, each one of us is a living stone. This tells us that no one in the Church is useless. . . . [W]e are all necessary for building this Temple! No one is secondary. No one is the most important person in the Church, we are all equal in God's eyes. Some of you might say 'Listen, Mr Pope, you are not our equal.' Yes, I am like each one of you, we are all equal, we are brothers and sisters!"[14]

Vatican II is clearly Pope Francis's "compass."[15] He has made the theme of divine mercy a prominent one in his pontificate, referring to Pope John XXIII's phrase "the medicine of mercy" in the opening speech at the council.[16] In his bull *Misericordiae Vultus* calling for the celebration of the Extraordinary Jubilee Year of Mercy, Pope Francis stresses that he deliberately chose December 8, 2015, as the starting date, since it was the fiftieth anniversary of the close of the Second Vatican Council:

14. The Wednesday audience catechesis on *Lumen Gentium* 4, in Pope Francis, "Where We Are All Equal and No One Is Useless," *L'Osservatore Romano* (July 3, 2013): 3.

15. This was the image used by John Paul II in *Novo Millennio Ineunte*, 57: "What a treasure there is, dear brothers and sisters, in the guidelines offered to us by the Second Vatican Council! For this reason I asked the Church, as a way of preparing for the Great Jubilee, to *examine herself on the reception given to the Council.* Has this been done? . . . With the passing of the years, *the Council documents have lost nothing of their value or brilliance.* They need to be read correctly, to be widely known and taken to heart as important and normative texts of the Magisterium, within the Church's Tradition. Now that the Jubilee has ended, I feel more than ever in duty bound to point to the Council as *the great grace bestowed on the Church in the twentieth century:* there we find a sure compass by which to take our bearings in the century now beginning." http://w2.vatican.va/content/john-paul-ii/en/apost_letters/2001/documents/hf_jp-ii_apl_20010106_novo-millennio-ineunte.html. Original emphasis.

16. *Misericordiae Vultus* 4: "We recall the poignant words of Saint John XXIII when, opening the Council, he indicated the path to follow: 'Now the Bride of Christ wishes to use the medicine of mercy rather than taking up arms of severity. . . . The Catholic Church, as she holds high the torch of Catholic truth at this Ecumenical Council, wants to show herself a loving mother to all; patient, kind, moved by compassion and goodness toward her separated children.'" https://w2.vatican.va/content/francesco/en/apost_letters/documents/papa-francesco_bolla_20150411_misericordiae-vultus.html. For John XXIII's opening speech, see John XXIII, "Pope John's Opening Speech," 716.

I have chosen the date of 8 December because of its rich meaning in the recent history of the Church. In fact, I will open the Holy Door on the fiftieth anniversary of the closing of the Second Vatican Ecumenical Council. The Church feels a great need to keep this event alive. With the Council, the Church entered a new phase of her history. The Council Fathers strongly perceived, as a true breath of the Holy Spirit, a need to talk about God to men and women of their time in a more accessible way. The walls which for too long had made the Church a kind of fortress were torn down and the time had come to proclaim the Gospel in a new way. It was a new phase of the same evangelization that had existed from the beginning. It was a fresh undertaking for all Christians to bear witness to their faith with greater enthusiasm and conviction. The Church sensed a responsibility to be a living sign of the Father's love in the world.[17]

And then again, on the occasion of his opening the Holy Door to start the Year of Mercy, he repeated the reference to Vatican II:

Today, here in Rome and in all the dioceses of the world, as we pass through the Holy Door, we also want to remember another door, which fifty years ago the Fathers of the Second Vatican Council opened to the world. This anniversary cannot be remembered only for the legacy of the Council's documents, which testify to a great advance in faith. Before all else, the Council was an encounter. A genuine *encounter between the Church and the men and women of our time*. An encounter marked by the power of the Spirit, who impelled the Church to emerge from the shoals which for years had kept her self-enclosed so as to set out once again, with enthusiasm, on her missionary journey. It was the resumption of a journey of encountering people where they live: in their cities and homes, in their workplaces. Wherever there are people, the Church is called to reach out to them and to bring the joy of the Gospel, and the mercy and forgiveness of God. After these decades, we again take up this missionary drive with the same power and enthusiasm. The Jubilee challenges us to this openness, and demands that we not neglect *the spirit which emerged from Vatican II, the spirit of the Samaritan*, as Blessed Paul VI expressed it at the conclusion of the Council.[18]

---

17. *Misericordiae Vultus* 4.

18. Pope Francis, Homily for the Mass and opening of the Holy Door, Saint Peter's Square, Tuesday, December 8, 2015, Immaculate Conception of the Blessed Virgin Mary. http://w2 .vatican.va/content/francesco/en/homilies/2015/documents/papa-francesco_20151208 _giubileo-omelia-apertura.html. Original emphasis.

Here Pope Francis, as he did when proclaiming the year of mercy, embraces the image that Paul VI had offered to the world as best capturing what he called "the spirituality of the council," the image of the Good Samaritan.[19]

But the reception and implementation of the council by popes is not the only dimension by which Vatican II's reception is to be evaluated. The hermeneutical vision/reception principle has already noted how Alois Grillmeier's three elements of reception of the early councils can be adapted to the reception of Vatican II. A brief sketch of these dimensions can only be outlined here. A fuller account of the global reception of Vatican II in these three dimensions would need to apply more specifically the criteria provided by the twenty-four principles enunciated above.

First, the *official reception* of Vatican II refers to the interpretation, promulgation, and implementation of the conciliar vision by popes and local bishops once the council ends.[20] This dimension not only includes the institutional and structural reforms initiated during the pontificates of Paul VI, John Paul I, John Paul II, Benedict XVI, and Francis, but also the style of their governance in promoting and implementing these reforms. There are already varying assessments of these pontificates in regard to their fidelity or otherwise to both the spirit and letter of Vatican II. The first three of these popes participated in the council as bishops and the fourth as a young *peritus*. Pope Francis was ordained a priest four years after the council's end, but much of his seminary training was affected by the council and its documents.[21] But conciliar reception also demands commitment from bishops. At the local level, once the council ended, each of the participating bishops was charged with bringing the council home. Here too further research is needed on a global history of how local bishops, over the last half century, have personally embraced the conciliar vision and implemented it (or otherwise). Nevertheless, as Gilles Routhier emphasizes, this official dimension of reception is still "just a little part of the story."[22]

---

19. See Paul VI, "Closing Address: Fourth Session," 360–61.

20. Grillmeier calls this dimension "kerygmatic reception." Gilles Routhier defines "kerygmatic reception" as "the totality of the efforts of the pastors in view of proclaiming, promoting and putting in practice the teaching of the Council." Gilles Routhier, "Reception of Vatican II and Elements for Further Studies," in *The Living Legacy of Vatican II: Studies from an Indian Perspective*, ed. Paul Pulikkan (Bengaluru, India: ATC Publishers, 2017), 90–109, at 94.

21. See Massimo Borghesi, *The Mind of Pope Francis: The Intellectual Journey of Jorge Mario Bergoglio* (Collegeville, MN: Liturgical Press, 2018).

22. Routhier, "Reception of Vatican II and Elements for Further Studies," 95.

Second, *theological reception* refers to the work of academic theologians attempting to bring to synthesis the vision of the conciliar decisions and documents, whether as a whole or with regard to particular teachings.[23] This reception has taken place from multiple perspectives: geography; culture; race; gender; power relationships; social, ecological, economic, and political conditions. Since the council, theologians have a keener awareness of the call to aid their local communities to listen to, discern, and determine the *sensus fidelium*, and to offer local theologies as articulations of the lived faith of their communities.[24] These theologies exemplify the legitimate theological diversity across local churches, as outlined in the unity/diversity principle. Moreover, as the faith/history principle highlights, Vatican II moved toward a greater appreciation of the historicity of the human condition and the contexts out of which the faithful receives God's ongoing revelatory and saving presence in history. Over the decades since the council ended, the "historical conscious-ness" that the council embraced has had its own history and turned critically toward itself.[25] It has become more reflexive, more aware of distortions in the tradition, and more acutely aware of the distorting lenses through which present-day receivers of the council can view the past—and the present.[26] So many examples could be given of diverse contextual theologies that have emerged over the last fifty years, faithful to the emerging model of reform embedded in the conciliar vision when taken as a whole. In the light of this more critical historical consciousness, ongoing ecclesial conversion to the vision of Vatican II also necessarily includes attention to possible distorting elements in the conciliar vision itself, so that any retrieval in the present does not perpetuate any distortions of the past. For example, to state the obvious, Vatican II was an all-male affair, except for the women on some subcommis-

23. See the fine survey and typology of postconciliar theologies in Dick, Schelkens, and Mettepenningen, *Aggiornamento?*, 198–209.

24. For one early expression of this attention to local context after the council, see Robert J. Schreiter, *Constructing Local Theologies* (Maryknoll, NY: Orbis Books, 1985); Robert J. Schreiter, "Mediating the Global and the Local in Conversation: Challenges to the Church in the Twenty-First Century," in *Theology and Conversation: Towards a Relational Theology*, ed. Jacques Haers and P. De Mey (Leuven; Dudley, MA: Peeters, 2003), 439–55; Robert J. Schreiter, *The New Catholicity: Theology between the Global and the Local* (Maryknoll, NY: Orbis Books, 1997).

25. For example, see the comments of Mark Day, *The Philosophy of History* (New York: Continuum, 2008), 156.

26. On this, the literature is vast. For one example, here on the importance of Michael Foucault for theology, see Vincent J. Miller, "History or Geography? Gadamer, Foucault, and Theologies of Tradition," in *Theology and the New Histories*, ed. Gary Macy (Maryknoll, NY: Orbis Books, 1999), 56–85.

sions and the women auditors in the third and fourth sessions.[27] Theological
reception of Vatican II continues to address such issues.

Third, the *spiritual reception* of Vatican II refers to appropriation of the
council's call for a deeper faith response to God's saving revelation within
the daily life and practice of all the faithful. The council refers to this call as
"the universal call to holiness." If official reception refers to "top-down reception," then spiritual reception refers to what could be called the "bottom-up
reception" of the council. This was the pastoral goal of the council, which
was intended to underpin its shifts in theological teaching and reforms of
ecclesial institutions and structures. It is to this dimension of spiritual reception that Karl Rahner refers when he remarks:

> The grace of God has given us these achievements of the Council, and now
> the post-conciliar reforms have been left in our hands as commissions which
> can be realistically fulfilled. When the government of the bishops is service,
> humble, humbler than before; when the priests more selflessly and purely,
> whether with results or not, administer the word of God and the grace of the
> sacraments; when the laymen criticize less and cooperate more eagerly; when
> all take up the cross of their existence and carry it after Christ more patiently,
> and see the light of God in the darkness with brighter eyes of faith; when
> everyone recognizes himself as a sinner and yet redeemed by the grace of God;
> when everyone begins to love God more; when everyone tries a little bit more
> each day to replace the egotistic hardness of his heart with a little more active
> love of neighbour; when there are Christians who are influenced neither by
> the brutal bellowing uproar nor by the cowardly whispering of nationalistic
> or militaristic egotism; when a few Christian men and women in the openness
> of their living more clearly demand and more clearly say what is right and not
> what is merely expedient, then the Council will have achieved its goal, will
> have fulfilled its meaning. This goal disappears into the silent mystery of God,
> who alone knows our hearts and deeds. But the Church must have the courage
> to face the inevitability of her mission. Otherwise she would not be what she
> is and must daily become.[28]

Thus, the overarching principle against which the reception of Vatican II is
to be judged is the theo-logical revelation/faith principle, since this principle

27. See Heyder and Muschiol, eds., *Katholikinnen und das Zweite Vatikanische Konzil*;
Valerio, *Madri del Concilio*; McEnroy, *Guests in Their Own House*.
28. Rahner, "The Council: A New Beginning," 31–32.

captures the council's pastoral aim. The council desired of the church greater fidelity to the Gospel of Jesus Christ. Although the council set about reform of the church, its ecclesiological vision of that reform was grounded on a renewed vision of God's way of working with humanity within history and of humanity's response in history to God. Thus, appropriating this renewed teaching on the nature of divine revelation and the nature of human faith is key to understanding both Vatican II's whole vision and its deepest spiritual reception. In the end, it is the spiritual reception of Vatican II that is the ultimate test: whether it has enlivened the faith of Catholics, leading them to both a more intense living of the Gospel and a keener "sense of the faith"—"the intimate sense of spiritual realities which [believers] experience" (DV 8).

Leonardo Boff is referring to this dimension of reception when he speaks of the "spiritual meaning" of Vatican II's vision and the need for creativity in its reception in local churches, in his case in Latin America:

> The ultimate justification for creative reception in ecclesiology lies in a sane epistemology of the act of faith. . . . According to an intelligent epistemology, the meaning of a text (setting forth, for example, a rule or some other determination) emerges not only from the minds of the authors of the text (from the *mens patrum*, in the case of a conciliar text)—but also from the addressees, who are coauthors of the text, inasmuch as it is they who insert the message of the text into the vital contexts in which they find themselves. The addressees, too, place accents, and perceive the relevancy and pertinence of aspects of the text in question that illuminate or denounce historical situations. The original meaning of the text—the meaning contained in the "letter"—stirs new echoes when that text is heard in determinate circumstances. The spiritual meaning becomes revealed. To read, then, is always, to *re*read. Whenever we understand, we interpret; this is how our spirit is structured. The original message does not remain a cistern of stagnant water. It becomes a font of living water, ready to generate new meanings, by prolonging and concretizing the original meaning. The latter functions as a generator of new life through the new significations it awakens.[29]

In terms of what Boff calls "a sane epistemology of the act of faith," and from the perspective of what *Lumen Gentium* 12 calls the "prophetic office" of the whole body of the faithful, Grillmeier's three dimensions of official, theological, and spiritual reception correspond to the three factors by which, as *Dei Verbum* 8 teaches, the Holy Spirit guides the church to be faithful to the apostolic tradition throughout history: the *sensus fidelium* (spiritual

---

29. Boff, "Creative Acceptance of Vatican II," 18. Original emphasis.

reception), theology (theological reception), and the magisterium (official reception). The reception—or nonreception—of Vatican II's vision occurs in all three dimensions—spiritual, theological, and official. It is here also, through the interaction of the *sensus fidelium*, theology, and the magisterium, that a proper assessment can be made of how faithfully the Catholic Church— "the whole body of the faithful" (LG 12)—has *de facto* received and applied the vision of Vatican II in the decades that have passed since its close. If spiritual reception is the pastoral goal of the council, and if it is through the *sensus fidelium* that such spiritual reception can be found to be best articulated, then attention to the *sensus fidelium* by theologians and the magisterium is vital for accessing the lived application of Vatican II's vision within new contexts, decades later. The fundamental condition for such ecclesial listening, however, has yet to be effectively implemented: provision of participatory structures for enabling genuine interaction between the *sensus fidelium*, theologians, and the magisterium.

It is here that Pope Francis's reconfiguration of the notion of "synodality" is inviting the church into a new phase in the reception of Vatican II. On October 17, 2015, halfway through the second synod of bishops on marriage and the family, there was a commemoration of the fiftieth anniversary of Pope Paul VI's creation during Vatican II of the synod of bishops, a new ecclesial structure called for by the council. Pope Francis, in a carefully crafted speech, spoke of "synodality" and of his desire for "a synodal church." He uses, as a contrast image, one that was familiar in theology and catechesis before the council, that of the pyramid, with the pope at the apex, and a descending order of ecclesial importance.[30] "Synodality is a constitutive element of the Church. . . . In this Church, as in an inverted pyramid, the top is located beneath the base. . . . A synodal Church is a Church which listens, which realizes that listening 'is more than simply hearing.' It is a mutual listening in which everyone has something to learn. The faithful people, the college of bishops, the Bishop of Rome: all listening to each other, and all listening to the Holy Spirit, the 'Spirit of truth,' in order to know what [the Spirit] 'says to the Churches.'"[31] Here Francis is foregrounding conciliar

30. Address at the Ceremony Commemorating the Fiftieth Anniversary of the Institution of the Synod of Bishops, October 17, 2015 (hereafter cited in footnotes as "October 17, 2015, Address"), http://w2.vatican.va/content/francesco/en/speeches/2015/october/documents/papa-francesco_20151017_50-anniversario-sinodo.html.
31. Ibid. The pope is quoting here his own document *Evangelii Gaudium* 171, along with John 14:17; Rev 2:7. For *Evangelii Gaudium*, see http://w2.vatican.va/content/francesco/en/apost_exhortations/documents/papa-francesco_esortazione-ap_20131124_evangelii-gaudium.html.

motifs such as participation, the Holy Spirit, *sensus fidelium*, and dialogue and bringing the conciliar vision to a new synthesis, one that is faithful to all the principles that the council expounded.

Pope Francis, as we know, did not participate in the Second Vatican Council. But Vatican II is a backdrop to all he says. He wants to take *the whole* of the council's vision, and, for him, the whole is more than the sum of the parts.[32] The various emphases of his pontificate—a church that is poor, a merciful church, a missionary church, etc.—are attempts to name vital aspects of what he interprets as the comprehensive vision of the council. "A synodal church" is one such aspect, but one that, like the others, the council itself didn't quite bring to neat formulation. "Synodality" is his catch-all phrase for how he believes the Second Vatican Council is envisioning the church *ad intra*—in its inner workings—without wanting to separate the church's inner life with the effectiveness of its outward (*ad extra*) mission in the world.

The Vatican II documents never once use the word "synodality." Nor the adjective, "synodal." The noun "synod" is found 136 times. In many of those instances, the council is referring to itself as a "sacred synod," seeing "council" and "synod" as synonyms that are just Greek (*synodos*) and Latin (*concilium*) transliterations. So, by implication, "synodality" here means simply "conciliarity": all bishops meeting with the Bishop of Rome to govern and teach the church. Then, when the documents speak of smaller episcopal "synods" at the national, regional and international levels, these synods are still intended as instruments of episcopal and papal governance and teaching, i.e., expressions of episcopal collegiality.[33] Here "synodality" equates to "collegiality" (between bishops and pope) exercised in a more collaborative way.[34] Even diocesan synods and diocesan and pastoral councils at the local level appear to be extensions of episcopal collegiality exercised in a "downward" direction. There is little room in these texts for self-generating impulses in the other direction. In other words, strictly speaking, for Vatican II—when one looks at the explicit statements of the final texts—synodality is much more an ele-

---

32. See *Evangelii Gaudium* 234–37.

33. For an examination of the conciliar texts on synods, see Massimo Faggioli, "Vatican II and the Agenda for Collegiality and Synodality in the Twenty-First Century," in *A Council for the Global Church: Receiving Vatican II in History* (Minneapolis: Fortress Press, 2015), 229–53.

34. For studies on synodality as a form of a more collaborative collegiality, see Winfried Aymans, *Das synodale Element in der Kirchenverfassung*, Münchener theologische Studien III, Kanonistische Abteilung (München: Max Hueber Verlag, 1970); Alberto Melloni and Silvia Scatena, eds., *Synod and Synodality: Theology, History, Canon Law and Ecumenism in New Contact. International Colloquium Bruges 2003* (Münster: Lit Verlag, 2005).

ment of its intention to balance papal primacy with episcopal collegiality (by calling for more dialogical and collaborative structures between the pope and the episcopal college) than it is a promotion of an "upward" direction in the teaching, sanctifying and governing aspects of the Catholic Church.

For Pope Francis, "synodality" is something much richer, more encompassing, and more radical. It is more than just an element of a primacy and collegiality exercised more collaboratively; he speaks of "episcopal collegiality within an entirely synodal church." And to emphasize the difference, he immediately repeats his distinction between the "two different phrases: 'episcopal collegiality' and an 'entirely synodal church.'"[35] As one synod participant captured it, after listening to that October 17 speech: synodality now means "not some of the bishops some of the time but all of the Church all of the time."[36] Since the pope is using "synodality" as a neat catch-all phrase for how Vatican II envisioned the church *ad intra* (with significant implications for how it envisioned the church *ad extra*), and in a way that goes beyond what the council explicitly stated regarding synods, a new theology of "synodality" within the Catholic Church needs to be more fully developed.[37] Although the council never uses the exact term "synodality," and although its references to synods is more about a specific notion of conciliarity and collegiality, such a new theology of synodality, as Pope Francis is now conceiving it, can nevertheless be shown to be grounded in the comprehensive ecclesiology of Vatican II, when all principles of its vision are taken together as a whole.

The notion of "a listening church, a synodal church" is an attempt to bring to greater realization the council's vision of a more participatory and dialogic style of ecclesial engagement, *ad intra* and *ad extra*. The concentric circles of dialogue outlined in *Gaudium et Spes* 92 begins with dialogue within the church. Lest his concern for a synodal church *ad intra* be misunderstood as too "self-referential," in his 2015 synodality address Pope Francis remarks on why synodality *ad intra* is necessary for its mission *ad extra*: "Our gaze also extends to humanity as a whole. *A synodal Church is like a standard lifted up among the nations* in a world which—while calling for participation, solidarity and transparency in public administration—often consigns the fate of entire peoples to the grasp of small but powerful groups." A church that

35. October 17, 2015, Address.

36. Archbishop Mark Coleridge, "From Wandering to Journeying: Thoughts on a Synodal Church," *Australasian Catholic Record* 93, no. 3 (July 2016): 340–50, at 348.

37. In March 2018, the International Theological Commission published their document "Synodality in the Life and Mission of the Church," which lays the foundations of such a theology. See http://www.vatican.va/roman_curia/congregations/cfaith/cti_documents/rc_cti_20180302_sinodalita_en.html.

is dialogic in its own life is more effective when it seeks to reach out to others in dialogue, for the sake of a more dialogic and less confrontative world. In reading the signs of the times, and interpreting them through wide dialogue, the church may very well encounter new things that God wishes to reveal, in Christ through the Spirit. Pope Francis alluded to this on October 11, 2017, when he urged: "It is not enough to find a new language in which to articulate our perennial faith; it is also urgent, in the light of the new challenges and prospects facing humanity, that the Church be able to express *the 'new things' of Christ's Gospel, that, albeit present in the word of God, have not yet come to light.* This is the treasury of 'things old and new' of which Jesus spoke when he invited his disciples to teach the newness that he had brought, without forsaking the old (cf. Mt 13:52)."[38]

More than fifty years after the council, new questions continue to be posed to the tradition regarding the church's nature, mission, structures, and ministries, questions that Vatican II did not address, and could not even have envisaged at that time. Nevertheless, receivers may indeed find answers to those new questions, from a comprehensive interpretation of the council and all its documents, as they imagine the whole conciliar vision and its principles realized in their new context. In an interview soon after the close of Vatican II, Yves Congar stated: "The danger now is that we shall cease to search and simply go on drawing on the inexhaustible reserves of Vatican II. . . . It would be a betrayal of the *aggiornamento* if this were regarded as permanently fixed in the texts of Vatican II."[39] The same spirit of *ressourcement* and *aggiornamento* that the bishops embraced at Vatican II continues to challenge the church to address these new questions with similar fidelity and creativity. To that end, the very last words of the very last document promulgated by Vatican II, *Gaudium et Spes* 93, are a doxology to continue inspiring us with confidence: "Glory be to him whose power, working in us, can do infinitely more than we can ask or imagine; glory be to him from generation to generation in the Church and in Christ Jesus forever and ever. Amen."[40]

38. https://w2.vatican.va/content/francesco/en/speeches/2017/october/documents/papa-francesco_20171011_convegno-nuova-evangelizzazione.html.

39. Quoted in Mark Schoof, *A Survey of Catholic Theology 1800–1970* (New York: Paulist Press, 1970), 265.

40. Eph 3:20-21. The New Jerusalem Bible translation.

Bibliography

Abbott, Walter M. "Opening Message." In *The Documents of Vatican II*, edited by Walter M. Abbott, 1–2. London: Geoffrey Chapman, 1966.

Acerbi, Antonio. *Due ecclesiologie: Ecclesiologia giuridica ed ecclesiologia di comunione nella "Lumen Gentium."* Bologna: Edizioni Dehoniane, 1975.

Adam, Karl. *The Spirit of Catholicism*. New York: Crossroad, 1997.

Ahern, Barnabas. "The Eschatological Dimensions of the Church." In *Vatican II: An Interfaith Appraisal*, edited by John H. Miller, 293–300. Notre Dame: University of Notre Dame, 1966.

Alberigo, Giuseppe. "The Announcement of the Council: From the Security of the Fortress to the Lure of the Quest." In *History of Vatican II, Vol. 1: Announcing and Preparing Vatican Council II*, edited by Giuseppe Alberigo and Joseph A. Komonchak, 1:1–54. Maryknoll, NY: Orbis Books, 1996.

———. "The Christian Situation after Vatican II." In *The Reception of Vatican II*, edited by Giuseppe Alberigo, Jean Pierre Jossua, and Joseph A. Komonchak, 1–24. Washington, DC: Catholic University of America Press, 1987.

———. "Cristianesimo e storia nel Vaticano II." *Cristianesimo nella Storia* 5 (1984): 577–92.

———. "Dalla uniformità liturgica del concilio di Trento al pluralismo del Vaticano II." *Rivista Liturgica* 69 no. 5 (1982): 604–19.

———. "Luci e ombre nel rapporto tra dinamica assembleare e conclusioni conciliari." In *L'evento e le decisioni: Studi sulle dinamiche del Concilio Vaticano II*, edited by Maria Teresa Fattori and Alberto Melloni, 501–22. Bologna: Il Mulino, 1997.

———. "Major Results, Shadows of Uncertainty." In *History of Vatican II, Vol. 4: The Church as Communion. Third Period and Third Intersession, September 1964–September 1965*, edited by Giuseppe Alberigo and Joseph A. Komonchak, 4:617–40. Maryknoll, NY: Orbis Books, 2004.

———. "Transition to a New Age." In *History of Vatican II, Vol. 5: The Council and the Transition. The Fourth Period and the End of the Council, September 1965–December 1965*, edited by Giuseppe Alberigo and Joseph A. Komonchak, 5:573–644. Maryknoll, NY: Orbis Books, 2006.

Alberigo, Giuseppe, and Joseph A. Komonchak, eds. *History of Vatican II*. 5 vols. Maryknoll, NY: Orbis Books, 1996–2004.

Alberigo, Giuseppe, and Franca Magistretti. *Constitutionis Dogmaticae Lumen Gentium: Synopsis Historica*. Bologna: Istituto per le Scienze Religiose, 1975.

———. "Introduction." In *Constitutionis Dogmaticae Lumen Gentium: Synopsis Historica*, xvii–xxii. Bologna: Istituto per le Scienze Religiose, 1975.

Anderson, Floyd, ed. *Council Daybook, Vatican II: Sessions 1–4*. 3 vols. Washington, DC: National Catholic Welfare Conference, 1965.

Antón, Angel. "Local Church/Regional Church: Systematic Reflections." *The Jurist* 52 (1992): 553–76.

Aparicio Valls, María del Carmen. *La plenitud del ser humano en Cristo: La revelación en la Gaudium et spes.* Roma: Pontificia Università Gregoriana, 1997.

Arenas Pérez, Sandra "Fading Frontiers?: An Historical-Theological Investigation into the Notion of the *Elementa Ecclesiae*." Catholic University of Leuven, Faculty of Theology and Religious Studies, 2013.

Atkin, Nicholas, and Frank Tallett. *Priests, Prelates, and People: A History of European Catholicism since 1750.* London: I.B.Taurus, 2003.

Attridge, Michael. "The Struggle for *Nostra Aetate*: The '*Quaestione Ebraica*' from 1960–62: Issues and Influences." In *La Théologie catholique entre intransigeance et renouveau: La réception des mouvements préconciliaires à Vatican II*, edited by Gilles Routhier, Philippe J. Roy, Karim Schelkens, and Philippe Roy-Lysencourt, 213–30. Louvain-La-Neuve; Leuven: Collège Érasme; Universiteitsbibliotheek, 2011.

Aubert, Roger. "Stages of Catholic Ecumenism from Leo XIII to Vatican II." In *Theology of Renewal. Vol. 2: Renewal of Religious Structures*, edited by L. K. Shook, 183–203. New York: Herder and Herder, 1968.

Aymans, Winfried. *Das synodale Element in der Kirchenverfassung*, Münchener theologische Studien III, Kanonistische Abteilung. München: Max Hueber Verlag, 1970.

———. "Die Communio Ecclesiarum als Gestaltgesetz der einen Kirche." *Archiv für katholisches Kirchenrecht* 39 (1970): 70–75.

Azevedo, Marcello de C. "Inculturation: I. The Problem." In *Dictionary of Fundamental Theology*, edited by René Latourelle and Rino Fisichella, 500–10. Middlegreen, Slough, UK: St Paul, 1994.

Batlogg, Andreas R. "Anhang 1: Karl Rahners Mitarbeit an den Konzilstexten." In *Vierzig Jahre II. Vatikanum: Zur Wirkungsgeschichte der Konzilstexte*, edited by Franz Xaver Bischof and Stephan Leimgruber, 355–76. Würzburg: Echter, 2004.

Baum, Gregory. "The Conciliar Statement on the Jews." In *Ecumenical Theology, No. 2*, edited by Gregory Baum, 262–72. New York: Paulist, 1967.

———. "The Ecclesial Reality of the Other Churches." *Concilium* 1 no. 4 (1965): 4:34–46.

———. *Man Becoming: God in Secular Language.* New York: Herder and Herder, 1970.

Bausenhart, Guido. "Theologischer Kommentar zum Dekret über das Hirtenamt der Bischöfe in der Kirche Christus Dominus." In *Herders theologischer Kommentar zum Zweiten Vatikanischen Konzil. Band 3*, edited by Peter Hünermann and Bernd Jochen Hilberath, 3:225–313. Freiburg: Herder, 2005.

Bea, Augustin. "Addresses to the Council." In *The Church and the Jewish People: A Commentary on the Second Vatican Council's Declaration on the Relation of the Church to Non-Christian Religions*, 154–72. London: Geoffrey Chapman, 1966.

———. *Augustin Cardinal Bea: Spiritual Profile. Notes from the Cardinal's Diary, with a Commentary.* Edited by Stjepan Schmidt. London: Geoffrey Chapman, 1971.

———. *The Church and the Jewish People: A Commentary on the Second Vatican Council's Declaration on the Relation of the Church to Non-Christian Religions.* London: Geoffrey Chapman, 1966.

———. *Ecumenism in Focus.* London: Geoffrey Chapman, 1969.

Becker, Karl J. "The Church and Vatican II's 'Subsistit in' Terminology." *Origins* 35 no. 31 (19 January 2006): 514–22.

———. "The Teaching of Vatican II on Baptism: A Stimulus for Theology." In *Vatican II Assessment and Perspectives: Twenty-Five Years After (1962–1987). Volume 2*, edited by René Latourelle, 2:47–99. New York: Paulist Press, 1989.

Becker, Werner. "History of the Decree on Ecumenism." In *Commentary on the Documents of Vatican II. Volume 2*, edited by Herbert Vorgrimler, 2:1–56. New York: Herder, 1968.

Beinert, Wolfgang. "Die Una Catholica und die Partikularkirchen." *Theologie und Philosophie* 42 (1967): 8–10.

———. "Hierarchy of Truths." In *Handbook of Catholic Theology*, edited by Wolfgang Beinert and Francis Schüssler Fiorenza, 334–36. New York: Crossroad, 1995.

Benedict XVI. "Interpreting Vatican II." *Origins* 35 no. 32 (January 26, 2006): 534–39.

Berríos, Fernando, Jorge Costadoat, and Diego García, eds. *Signos de estos tiempos. Interpretación teológica de nuestra época*. Santiago de Chile: Ediciones Universidad Alberto Hurtado, 2008.

Betti, Umberto. *La dottrina del concilio Vaticano II sulla trasmissione della rivelazione: Il capitolo II della costituzione dommatica Dei Verbum*. Roma: Spicilegium Pontificii Athenaei Antoniani, 1985.

———. *La dottrina sull'episcopato del Concilio Vaticano II: Il capitolo III della Costituzione dommatica Lumen Gentium*. Roma: Spicilegium Pontificii Athenaei Antoniani, 1984.

Bevans, Stephen B. "Decree on the Church's Missionary Activity." In *Evangelization and Religious Freedom: Ad Gentes, Dignitatis Humanae*, edited by Stephen B. Bevans and Jeffrey Gros, 3–148. New York: Paulist Press, 2009.

———. "Revisiting Mission at Vatican II: Theology and Practice for Today's Missionary Church." *Theological Studies* 74 (2013): 261–83.

Bianchi, Angelo, and Giancarlo Andenna, eds. *Il Concilio Vaticano II, crocevia dell'umanesimo contemporaneo*. Milano: Vita e Pensiero, 2015.

Billot, Louis. *Tractatus de ecclesia Christi: Sive continuatio theologiae de verbo incarnato*. Ed. quinta 2 vols. Roma: Universitatis Gregorianae, 1927.

Blanco Sarto, Pablo. "Joseph Ratzinger, perito del Concilio Vaticano II." *Anuario di historia de la Iglesia* 15 (2006): 43–66.

Bluett, J. J. "The Mystical Body of Christ: 1890–1940." *Theological Studies* 3 (1942): 261–89.

Boersma, Hans. *Nouvelle Théologie and Sacramental Ontology: A Return to Mystery*. New York: Oxford University Press, 2009.

Boff, Leonardo. *Die Kirche als Sakrament im Horizont der Welterfahrung: Versuch einer Legitimation und einer struktur-funktionalistischen Grundlegung der Kirche im Anschluss an das II. Vatikanische Konzil*. Paderborn: Verlag Bonifacius-Druckerei, 1972.

———. "Theology of Liberation: Creative Acceptance of Vatican II from the Viewpoint of the Poor." In *When Theology Listens to the Poor*, 1–31. San Francisco: Harper & Row, 1988.

Bolger, John. "The Documents behind the Decree on Ecumenism." *One in Christ* 4 (1967): 472–500.

Bonnet, Piero Antonio. "The *Christifidelis* Restored to His Role as Human Protagonist in the Church." In *Vatican II Assessment and Perspectives: Twenty-Five Years After (1962–1987). Volume 1*, edited by René Latourelle, 1:540–67. New York: Paulist Press, 1988.

Borelli, John. "*Nostra Aetate*: Origin, History, and Vatican II Context." In *The Future of Interreligious Dialogue: A Multi-Religious Conversation on Nostra Aetate*, edited by Charles L. Cohen, Paul F. Knitter, and Ulrich E. Rosenhagen, 23–43. Maryknoll, NY: Orbis Books, 2017.

Borghesi, Massimo. *The Mind of Pope Francis: The Intellectual Journey of Jorge Mario Bergoglio.* Collegeville, MN: Liturgical Press, 2018.

Bosschaert, Dries. "Understanding the Shift in *Gaudium et Spes*: From Theology of History to Christian Anthropology." *Theological Studies* 78 (2017): 634–58.

Boulding, Mary Cecily. "The Doctrine of the Holy Spirit in the Documents of Vatican II." *Irish Theological Quarterly* 51 (1985): 253–67.

Bouyer, Louis. *The Paschal Mystery: Meditations on the Last Three Days of Holy Week.* Chicago: Regnery, 1950; French original 1945.

Boyle, Nicholas. "On Earth, As In Heaven." *The Tablet*, 9 July 2005, 12–15.

Boys, Mary C. "What *Nostra Aetate* Inaugurated: A Conversion to the 'Providential Mystery of Otherness.'" *Theological Studies* 74 (2013): 73–104.

Brechter, Suso. "Decree on the Church's Missionary Activity." In *Commentary on the Documents of Vatican II. Volume 4*, edited by Herbert Vorgrimler, 4:87–181. New York: Herder and Herder, 1969.

Bredeck, Michael. *Das Zweite Vatikanum als Konzil des Aggiornamento: Zur hermeneutischen Grundlegung einer theologischen Konzilsinterpretation.* Paderborn: Schöningh, 2007.

Brutti, Maria. "Drafts Leading to the Conciliar Declaration *Nostra Aetate*." In *The Catholic Church and the Jewish People: Recent Reflections from Rome*, edited by Philip A. Cunningham, Norbert J. Hofmann, and Joseph Sievers, 191–200. New York: Fordham University Press, 2007.

Bugnini, Annibale. *The Reform of the Liturgy, 1948–1975.* Collegeville, MN: Liturgical Press, 1990.

Burigana, Riccardo. *La Bibbia nel concilio: La redazione della costituzione "Dei verbum" del Vaticano II.* Bologna: Il Mulino, 1998.

Burigana, Riccardo, and Giovanni Turbanti. "The Intersession: Preparing the Conclusion of the Council." In *History of Vatican II, Vol. 4: The Church as Communion. Third Period and Third Intersession, September 1964–September 1965*, edited by Giuseppe Alberigo and Joseph A. Komonchak, 453–615. Maryknoll, NY: Orbis Books, 2004.

Burke, Thomas, ed. *Catholic Missions: Four Great Missionary Encyclicals.* New York: Fordham University Press, 1957.

Butler, Christopher. *The Theology of Vatican II.* London: Darton Longman & Todd, 1967.

Casel, Odo. *The Mystery of Christian Worship, and Other Writings.* Edited by Burkhard Neunheuser. Westminster, MD: Newman Press, 1962.

Cassidy, Edward Idris. *Ecumenism and Interreligious Dialogue: Unitatis Redintegratio, Nostra Aetate*, Rediscovering Vatican II. New York: Paulist Press, 2005.

Cazelles, Henri. "Le Saint-Esprit dans les textes de Vatican II." In *Le Mystère de l'Esprit Saint*, edited by Henri Cazelles, Georges Lefebvre, Albert Greiner and Pàvel Nikolàjevic Evdokímov, 161–86. Tours: Mame, 1968.

Cerfaux, Lucien. *The Church in the Theology of St Paul.* 2nd ed. Edinburgh: Thomas Nelson, 1959.

Chantraine, Georges. "L'Enseignement du Vatican II concernant l'Esprit Saint." In *Credo in Spiritum Sanctum: Atti del Congresso Teologico Internazionale di Pneumatologia*, 2:993–1010. Città del Vaticano: Libreria Editrice Vaticana, 1983.

Charue, André Marie. "Le Saint-Esprit dans *Lumen Gentium*." *Ephemerides Theologicae Lovanienses* 45 (1969): 359–79.

Chenu, Marie Dominique. "The History of Salvation and the Historicity of Man in the Renewal of Theology." In *Theology of Renewal. Vol. 1: Renewal of Religious Thought*, edited by L. K. Shook, 153–66. New York: Herder and Herder, 1968.

————. "The Signs of the Times." In *The Church Today: Commentaries on the Pastoral Constitution on the Church in the Modern World*, edited by Group 2000, 43–59. New York: Newman Press, 1967.

Chenu, Marie-Dominique. *Vatican II Notebook: A Council Journal, 1962–1963*. Adelaide, South Australia: ATF Theology, 2015.

Christianson, Gerald, Thomas M. Izbicki, and Christopher M. Bellitto, eds. *The Church, the Councils, and Reform: The Legacy of the Fifteenth Century*. Washington, DC: Catholic University of America Press, 2008.

Clark, Christopher M., and Wolfram Kaiser, eds. *Culture Wars: Secular-Catholic Conflict in Nineteenth-Century Europe*. New York: Cambridge University Press, 2003.

Clifford, Catherine E. "*Elementa Ecclesiae*: A Basis for Vatican II's Recognition of the Ecclesial Character of Non-Catholic Christian Communities." In *La Théologie catholique entre intransigeance et renouveau: La réception des mouvements préconciliaires à Vatican II*, edited by Gilles Routhier, Philippe J. Roy, Karim Schelkens, and Philippe Roy-Lysencourt, 249–69. Louvain-La-Neuve; Leuven: Collège Érasme; Universiteitsbibliotheek, 2011.

Coderre, Gérard. "Woman's Role in the Divine Plan." In *Third Session Council Speeches of Vatican II*, edited by William K. Leahy and Anthony T. Massimini, 205–08. Glen Rock, NJ: Paulist Press, 1966.

Coleridge, Archbishop Mark. "From Wandering to Journeying: Thoughts on a Synodal Church." *Australasian Catholic Record* 93 no. 3 (July 2016): 340–50.

Concile oecuménique Vatican II: Constitutions, décrets, déclarations, messages, texte français et latin, tables biblique et analytiques et index des sources. Paris: Centurion, 1967.

Congar, Yves. "Bloc-Notes sur le Concile." *Information Catholique Internationale* (15 November 1964): 14–16.

————. "The Church: Seed of Unity and Hope for the Whole Human Race." *Chicago Studies* 5 (1966): 25–39.

————. "The Church: The People of God." *Concilium* 1 no. 1 (1965): 7–19.

————. "Die christologischen und pneumatologischen Implikationen der Ekklesiologie des II. Vatikanums." In *Kirche im Wandel: Eine kritische Zwischenbilanz nach dem Zweiten Vatikanum*, edited by Giuseppe Alberigo, Hermann J. Pottmeyer and Yves Congar, 111–23. Düsseldorf: Patmos, 1982.

————. *Diversity and Communion*. London: SCM Press, 1984.

————. *Divided Christendom: A Catholic Study of the Problem of Reunion*. London: Geoffrey Bles, 1939.

————. "The Hierarchy as Service: Scriptural Sources and Historical Development." In *Power and Poverty in the Church*, 15–100. Baltimore: Helicon, 1964.

————. "La théologie au Concile: Le 'théologiser' du Concile." In *Situation et tâches présentes de la théologie*, 51–56. Paris: Éditions du Cerf, 1967.

————. "A Last Look at the Council." In *Vatican II: By Those Who Were There*, edited by Alberic Stacpoole, 337–58. London: Geoffrey Chapman, 1986.

————. *Lay People in the Church: A Study for a Theology of Laity*. Translated by Donald Attwater. 2d rev. ed. Westminster, MD: Newman Press, 1965.

————. "Le Concile, l'Eglise et . . . 'les Autres'." *Lumière et Vie* 45 (November–December, 1959): 69–92.

————. "Le rôle des 'Observateurs' dans l'avancée oecuménique." In *Le Concile de Vatican II: Son église, peuple de Dieu et corps du Christ*, 91–98. Paris: Beauchesne, 1984.

———. *My Journal of the Council*. Collegeville, MN: Liturgical Press, 2012.

———. "On the Hierarchia Veritatum." In *The Heritage of the Early Church*, edited by David Neiman and Margaret Schatken, 409–20. Rome: Pont. Institutum Orientalium, 1973.

———. "Part I, Chapter IV: The Role of the Church in the Modern World." In *Commentary on the Documents of Vatican II. Volume 5*, edited by Herbert Vorgrimler, 5:202–23. New York: Herder and Herder, 1969.

———. "The People of God." In *Vatican II: An Interfaith Appraisal*, edited by John H. Miller, 197–207. Notre Dame: University of Notre Dame, 1966.

———. "The Pneumatology of Vatican II." In *I Believe in the Holy Spirit. Volume I. The Holy Spirit in the "Economy": Revelation and Experience of the Spirit*, 167–73. New York: Crossroad, 1997.

———. *Power and Poverty in the Church*. Baltimore: Helicon, 1964.

———. "Reception as an Ecclesiological Reality." *Concilium* 77 (1972): 43–68.

———. "Renewal of the Spirit and Reform of the Institution." In *Readings in Church Authority: Gifts and Challenges for Contemporary Catholicism*, edited by Gerard Mannion, Richard Gaillardetz, Jan Kerkhofs, and Kenneth Wilson, 512–17. Burlington, VT: Ashgate, 2003.

———. "Renewed Actuality of the Holy Spirit." *Lumen Vitae: International Review of Religious Education* 28 no. 1 (1973): 13–30.

———. *Situation und Aufgabe der Theologie heute*. 2. Aufl ed. Paderborn: F. Schöningh, 1971.

———. "Theologians and the Magisterium in the West: From the Gregorian Reform to the Council of Trent." *Chicago Studies. The Magisterium, the Theologian and the Educator* 17 (1978): 210–24.

———. "Theology's Tasks after Vatican II." In *Theology of Renewal. Vol. 1: Renewal of Religious Thought*, edited by L. K. Shook, 1:47–65. New York: Herder and Herder, 1968.

———. "Titles and Honours in the Church: A Short Historical Study." In *Power and Poverty in the Church*, 101–31. Baltimore: Helicon, 1964.

———. *Tradition and Traditions: An Historical and a Theological Essay*. London: Burns & Oates, 1966.

———. *True and False Reform in the Church*. rev. ed. Collegeville, MN: Liturgical Press, 2011.

———. "Unité, diversité et divisions." In *Sainte Église: Études et approches ecclésiologiques*, 105–30. Paris: Cerf, 1963.

Connelly, John. *From Enemy to Brother: The Revolution in Catholic Teaching on the Jews, 1933–1965*. Cambridge, MA: Harvard University Press, 2012.

Connolly, James M. *The Voices of France*. New York: Macmillan, 1961.

Cooke, Bernard J. *Ministry to Word and Sacraments: History and Theology*. Philadelphia: Fortress Press, 1976.

Corecco, Eugenio. "Aspects of the Reception of Vatican II in the Code of Canon Law." In *The Reception of Vatican II*, edited by Giuseppe Alberigo, Jean Pierre Jossua, and Joseph A. Komonchak, 249–96. Washington, DC: Catholic University of America Press, 1987.

Cottier, Georges. "L'historique de la Déclaration." In *Les relations de l'Eglise avec les religions non chrétiennes: Déclaration "Nostra aetate." Texte latin et traduction française*, edited by Antonin-Marcel Henry, 37–78. Paris: Editions du Cerf, 1966.

"Council Statistics." In *Council Daybook: Vatican II, Session 4*, edited by Floyd Anderson, 366. Washington, DC: National Catholic Welfare Conference, 1966.

Crollius, Roest. "What Is So New about Inculturation?" *Gregorianum* 59 (1978): 721–38.

Cullmann, Oscar. *Christ and Time: The Primitive Christian Conception of Time and History.* Rev. ed. Philadelphia: Westminster Press, 1964.

———. "The Role of the Observers at the Vatican Council." In *Vatican Council II: The New Direction. Essays*, 102–06. New York: Harper & Row, 1968.

Curnow, Rohan. "Stirrings of the Preferential Option for the Poor at Vatican II: The Work of the 'Group of the Church of the Poor.'" *The Australasian Catholic Record* 89 (2012): 420–32.

———. *The Preferential Option for the Poor: A Short History and a Reading Based on the Thought of Bernard Lonergan.* Milwaukee, WI: Marquette University Press, 2012.

Curran, Charles E. "Strand Three: Natural Law." In *The Development of Moral Theology: Five Strands*, 73–147. Washington, DC: Georgetown University Press, 2013.

Curtis, Geoffrey. *Paul Couturier and Unity in Christ.* London: SCM Press, 1964.

Cuva, Armando. "La participation des fidèles à la liturgie selon la constitution *Sacrosanctum Concilium*." *La Maison-Dieu* 241 (2005): 137–49.

D'Costa, Gavin. *Vatican II: Catholic Doctrines on Jews and Muslims.* Oxford: Oxford University Press, 2014.

Daley, Brian E. "Knowing God in History and in the Church: *Dei Verbum* and 'Nouvelle Théologie.'" In *Ressourcement: A Movement for Renewal in Twentieth-Century Catholic Theology*, edited by Gabriel Flynn and Paul D. Murray, 333–51. Oxford: Oxford University Press, 2011.

Dalmais, Irénée Henri. "Theology of the Liturgical Celebration." In *The Church at Prayer: An Introduction to the Liturgy. Volume 1: Principles of the Liturgy*, edited by Aimé Georges Martimort, 227–80. Collegeville, MN: Liturgical Press, 1985.

Daly, Gabriel. *Creation and Redemption.* Wilmington, DE: M. Glazier, 1989.

———. *Transcendence and Immanence: A Study in Catholic Modernism and Integralism.* Oxford: Oxford University Press, 1980.

Day, Mark. *The Philosophy of History.* New York: Continuum, 2008.

De Clerck, Paul. "La Participation Active: Perspectives Historico-Liturgiques, de Pie X à Vatican II." In *The Active Participation Revisited: La Participation Active 100 ans après Pie X et 40 ans après Vatican II*, 13–31, 2004.

de la Potterie, Ignace. "Interpretation of Holy Scripture in the Spirit in Which It Was Written (*Dei Verbum* 12c)." In *Vatican II: Assessment and Perspectives. Twenty-Five Years After (1962–1987). Volume 1*, edited by René Latourelle, 1:220–66. New York: Paulist Press, 1988.

de Lubac, Henri. "Apologetics and Theology." In *Theological Fragments*, 91–104. San Francisco: Ignatius Press, 1989.

———. *Carnets du Concile.* 2 vols. Paris: Cerf, 2007.

———. *Catholicism: Christ and the Common Destiny of Man.* San Francisco: Ignatius Press, 1988.

———. "The Church in Crisis." *Theology Digest* 17 (1969): 312–25.

———. *Corpus Mysticum: The Eucharist and the Church in the Middle Ages. Historical Survey.* Edited by Laurence Paul Hemming and Susan Frank Parsons. London: SCM, 2006.

———. "*Lumen Gentium* and the Fathers." In *Vatican II: An Interfaith Appraisal*, edited by John H. Miller, 153–75. Notre Dame: University of Notre Dame Press, 1966.

———. *The Mystery of the Supernatural.* London: Geoffrey Chapman, 1967.

———. *The Splendor of the Church.* San Francisco: Ignatius Press, 1999.

De Maio, Romeo. *The Book of the Gospels at the Oecumenical Councils*. Rome: Biblioteca Apostolica Vaticana, 1963.

de Margerie, Bertrand. "The Trinitarian Doctrine of Vatican II." In *The Christian Trinity in History*, 223–45. Still River, MA: St. Bede's Publications, 1982.

De Mey, Peter. "Authority in the Church: The Appeal to Lk 22:21–34 in Roman Catholic Ecclesiology and in the Ecumenical Movement." In *Luke and His Readers: Festschrift A. Denaux*, edited by R. Bieringer, Gilbert van Belle and Jozef Verheyden, 307–23. Dudley, MA: Leuven University Press, 2005.

———. "The Bishop's Participation in the Threefold *Munera*: Comparing the Appeal to the Pattern of the *Tria Munera* at Vatican II and in the Ecumenical Dialogues." *The Jurist* 69 (2009): 31–58.

———. "The Catholic Conference for Ecumenical Questions' Immediate Preparation of the Renewal of Catholic Ecclesiology at Vatican II." In *Toward a History of the Desire for Christian Unity: Preliminary Research Paper*, edited by L. Ferracci, 141–57. Münster: LIT, 2015.

———. "Church as Sacrament: A Conciliar Concept and Its Reception in Contemporary Theology." In *The Presence of Transcendence: Thinking "Sacrament" in a Postmodern Age*, edited by Boeve L. and Ries J., 181–96. Leuven: Peeters, 2001.

———. "Church Renewal and Reform in the Documents of Vatican II: History, Theology, Terminology." *The Jurist* 71 (2011): 360–400.

———. "The Daily Eucharist at the Council as Stimulus and Test Case for Liturgical Reform." *Questions Liturgiques/Studies in Liturgy* 95 (2014): 28–51.

———. "Gustave Thils and Ecumenism at Vatican II." In *The Belgian Contribution to the Second Vatican Council: International Research Conference at Mechelen, Leuven and Louvain-la-Neuve (September 12–16, 2005)*, edited by Doris Donnelly, Joseph Famerée, Mathijs Lamberigts, and Karim Schelkens, 389–414. Leuven; Dudley, MA: Peeters, 2008.

———. "Johannes Willebrands and the Catholic Conference for Ecumenical Questions (1952–1963)." In *The Ecumenical Legacy of Johannes Cardinal Willebrands (1909–2006)*, edited by Adelbert Denaux and Peter De Mey, 49–77. Leuven; Walpole, MA: Peeters, 2012.

———. "Recent Views of *Lumen Gentium*, Fifty Years after Vatican II." *Horizons* 39 no. 2 (2012): 252–81.

———. "The Role of the Observers during the Second Vatican Council." *St Vladimir's Theological Quarterly* 60 (2016): 33–51.

de Riedmatten, Henri. "History of the Pastoral Constitution." In *The Church Today: Commentaries on the Pastoral Constitution on the Church in the Modern World*, edited by Group 2000, 1–40. New York: Newman Press, 1967.

de Smedt, Émile-Joseph. "Il sacerdozio dei fedeli." In *La Chiesa del Vaticano II: Studi e commenti intorno alla Costituzione dommatica 'Lumen Gentium'*, edited by Guilherme Baraúna, 453–64. Firenze: Vallecchi Editore, 1965.

———. *The Priesthood of the Faithful*. New York: Paulist Press, 1962.

Declerck, Leo. "Brève présentation du 'Journal Conciliaire' de Mgr Gerard Philips." In *Experience, Organisations and Bodies at Vatican II*, edited by Maria Teresa Fattori and Alberto Melloni, 219–31. Leuven: Bibliotheek van de Faculteit Godgeleerdheid, 1999.

Delhaye, Philippe, Michel Guéret, and Paul Tombeur. *Concilium Vaticanum II: Concordance, index, listes de fréquence, tables comparatives*. Louvain: Publications du CETÉDOC, 1974.

Denaux, Adelbert, and Peter De Mey, eds. *The Ecumenical Legacy of Johannes Cardinal Willebrands (1909–2006)*. Leuven; Walpole, MA: Peeters, 2012.

Denzinger, Heinrich. *Compendium of Creeds, Definitions, and Declarations on Matters of Faith and Morals.* Edited by Peter Hünermann, Helmut Hoping, Robert L. Fastiggi, and Anne Englund Nash. 43rd, rev. and enl. ed. San Francisco: Ignatius Press, 2012.

Dick, John A., Karim Schelkens, and Jürgen Mettepenningen. *Aggiornamento?: Catholicism from Gregory XVI to Benedict XVI.* Leiden: Brill, 2013.

"Dogmatic Constitution on Divine Revelation." In *Commentary on the Documents of Vatican II. Volume 3,* edited by Herbert Vorgrimler, 155–272. New York: Herder, 1969.

Doré, Joseph. "Vatican II Today." In *Vatican II: A Forgotten Future?,* edited by Alberto Melloni and Christoph Theobald, 137–47. London: SCM Press, 2005.

Doyle, Dennis M. *Communion Ecclesiology: Vision and Versions.* Maryknoll, NY: Orbis Books, 2000.

———. "Otto Semmelroth, SJ, and the Ecclesiology of the 'Church as Sacrament' at Vatican II." In *The Legacy of Vatican II,* edited by Massimo Faggioli and Andrea Vicini, 203–25. New York: Paulist Press, 2015.

Drilling, Peter J. "Common and Ministerial Priesthood: *Lumen Gentium,* Article Ten." *Irish Theological Quarterly* 53 (1987): 81–99.

Driscoll, Jeremy. "Reviewing and Recovering *Sacrosanctum Concilium*'s Theological Vision." *Origins* 43 no. 29 (19 December, 2013): 479–87.

Dulles, Avery. "The Church Always in Need of Reform: *Ecclesia Semper Reformanda.*" In *The Church Inside and Out,* 37–50. Washington, DC: United States Catholic Conference, 1974.

———. "The Church and the Kingdom." In *A Church for All Peoples: Missionary Issues in a World Church,* edited by Eugene LaVerdiere, 13–30. Collegeville, MN: Liturgical Press, 1993.

———. "Doctrinal Authority of Episcopal Conferences." In *Episcopal Conferences: Historical, Canonical, and Theological Studies,* edited by Thomas J. Reese, 207–31. Washington, DC: Georgetown University Press, 1989.

———. "The Mission of the Church in *Gaudium et spes.*" In *The Church and Human Freedom: Forty Years after Gaudium et spes,* edited by Darlene Fozard Weaver, 26–37. Villanova, PA: Villanova University Press, 2006.

———. *Models of the Church.* Expanded ed. New York: Image Books Doubleday, 2002.

———. "The Reception of Vatican II at the Extraordinary Synod of 1985." In *The Reception of Vatican II,* edited by Giuseppe Alberigo, Jean Pierre Jossua, and Joseph A. Komonchak, 349–63. Washington, DC: Catholic University of America Press, 1987.

———. *Revelation Theology: A History.* New York: Seabury Press, 1969.

———. *The Survival of Dogma: Faith, Authority and Dogma in a Changing World.* New York: Crossroad, 1987.

———. "Vatican II and the Church's Purpose." *Theology Digest* 32 (1985): 341–52.

———. "Vatican II Reform: The Basic Principles." In *The Catholic Faith: A Reader,* edited by Lawrence Cunningham, 47–63. New York: Paulist Press, 1988.

Dupuis, Jacques. "The Christocentrism of Vatican II." In *Jesus Christ and His Spirit: Theological Approaches,* 33–58. Bangalore: Theological Publications in India, 1977.

———. "Unity of Faith and Dogmatic Pluralism." In *Jesus Christ and His Spirit: Theological Approaches,* 59–82. Bangalore: Theological Publications in India, 1977.

———. "Western Christocentrism and Eastern Pneumatology." In *Jesus Christ and His Spirit: Theological Approaches,* 21–31. Bangalore: Theological Publications in India, 1977.

Durrwell, François-Xavier. *The Resurrection: A Biblical Study.* New York: Sheed and Ward, 1960; French original 1954.

Eger, J. *Salus gentium*. University of Munich: Unpublished dissertation, 1947.

Eisenbach, Franziskus. *Die Gegenwart Jesu Christi im Gottesdienst: Systematische Studien zur Liturgiekonstitution des II. Vatikanischen Konzils*. Mainz: Matthias-Grünewald-Verlag, 1982.

Elich, Tom. "Full, Conscious and Active Participation." In *Vatican Council II: Reforming Liturgy*, edited by Carmel Pilcher, David Orr and Elizabeth Harrington, 25–42. Hindmarsh, SA: ATF Theology, 2013.

Epis, Massimo. "Introduzione all costituzione dogmatica *Dei Verbum*." In *Dei Verbum: Commentario ai documenti del Vaticano II, Vol. 5*, edited by Serena Noceti and Roberto Repole, 13–89. Bologna: Edizioni Dehoniane, 2017.

Erhueh, Anthony O. *Vatican II: Image of God in Man. An Inquiry into the Theological Foundations and Significance of Human Dignity in the Pastoral Constitution on the Church in the Modern World, "Gaudium et spes."* Rome: Urbaniana University Press, 1987.

Extraordinary Synod of Bishops. "Final Report." In *Documents of the Extraordinary Synod of Bishops November 28–December 8, 1985*, 17–51. Homebush, Australia: St Paul Publications, 1986.

Faggioli, Massimo. *Il vescovo e il concilio: Modello episcopale e aggiornamento al Vaticano II*. Bologna: Mulino, 2005.

———. "*Sacrosanctum Concilium* and the Meaning of Vatican II." *Theological Studies* 71 (2010): 437–52.

———. *True Reform: Liturgy and Ecclesiology in Sacrosanctum Concilium*. Collegeville, MN: Liturgical Press, 2012.

———. "Vatican II and the Agenda for Collegiality and Synodality in the Twenty-First Century." In *A Council for the Global Church: Receiving Vatican II in History*, 229–53. Minneapolis: Fortress Press, 2015.

———. *Vatican II: The Battle for Meaning*. New York: Paulist Press, 2012.

———. "Vatican II: The History and the Narratives." In *50 Years On: Probing the Riches of Vatican II*, edited by David G. Schultenover, 61–81. Collegeville, MN: Liturgical Press, 2015.

Fahey, Michael A. "An Attempt to Synthesize the Conference 'The Contribution of the Belgians to Vatican Council II." In *The Belgian Contribution to the Second Vatican Council: International Research Conference at Mechelen, Leuven and Louvain-la-Neuve (September 12–16, 2005)*, edited by Doris Donnelly, Joseph Famerée, Mathijs Lamberigts, and Karim Schelkens, 685–99. Leuven; Dudley, MA: Peeters, 2008.

Famerée, Joseph. "Bishops and Dioceses and the Communications Media (November 5–25, 1963)." In *History of Vatican II, Vol. 3: The Mature Council. Second Period and Intersession, September 1963–September 1964*, edited by Giuseppe Alberigo and Joseph A. Komonchak, 3:117–88. Maryknoll, NY: Orbis Books, 1998.

———. "Gustave Thils et le *De Ecclesia*: Un début d'enquête." In *The Belgian Contribution to the Second Vatican Council: International Research Conference at Mechelen, Leuven and Louvain-la-Neuve (September 12–16, 2005)*, edited by Doris Donnelly, Joseph Famerée, Mathijs Lamberigts, and Karim Schelkens, 563–84. Leuven; Dudley, MA: Peeters, 2008.

Fattori, Maria Teresa, and Alberto Melloni, eds. *L'Evento e le decisioni: Studi sulle dinamiche del Concilio vaticano II*. Bologna: Il Mulino, 1997.

Faulk, Edward. *101 Questions and Answers on Eastern Catholic Churches*. Mahwah, NJ: Paulist Press, 2007.

Feiner, Johannes. "Commentary on the Decree on Ecumenism." In *Commentary on the Documents of Vatican II. Volume 2*, edited by Herbert Vorgrimler, 2:57–164. New York: Herder, 1968.

Ferrone, Rita. *Liturgy: Sacrosanctum Concilium*, Rediscovering Vatican II. New York: Paulist Press, 2007.

Fitzgerald, Michael L. "Vatican II and Interfaith Dialogue." In *Interfaith Dialogue: Global Gerspectives*, edited by Edmund Kee-Fook Chia, 3–15. New York: Palgrave Macmillan, 2016.

Flynn, Gabriel, and Paul D. Murray, eds. *Ressourcement: A Movement for Renewal in Twentieth-Century Catholic Theology*. Oxford: Oxford University Press, 2011.

Forte, Bruno. *The Church: Icon of the Trinity. A Brief Study*. Boston, MA: St Paul Books and Media, 1991.

———. "Le prospettive della ricerca teologica." In *Il Concilio Vaticano II: Recezione e attualità alla luce del Giubileo*, edited by Rino Fisichella, 419–29. Milan: San Paolo, 2000.

Fouilloux, Étienne. "The Antepreparatory Phase: The Slow Emergence from Inertia (January, 1959–October, 1962)." In *History of Vatican II, Vol. 1: Announcing and Preparing Vatican Council II*, edited by Giuseppe Alberigo and Joseph A. Komonchak, 55–166. Maryknoll, NY: Orbis Books, 1996.

Fries, Heinrich. "Church and Churches." In *Problems and Perspectives of Fundamental Theology*, edited by René Latourelle and Gerald O'Collins, 309–26. New York: Paulist Press, 1982.

Francis, Pope. "Where We Are All Equal and No One Is Useless." *L'Osservatore Romano* (3 July 2013): 3.

Frotz, Augustin. "Women's Increasing Dignity and Influence." In *Third Session Council Speeches of Vatican II*, edited by William K. Leahy and Anthony T. Massimini, 208–11. Glen Rock, NJ: Paulist Press, 1966.

Fuchs, Josef. "Natural Law." In *The New Dictionary of Catholic Social Thought*, edited by Judith A. Dwyer and Elizabeth L. Montgomery, 669–75. Collegeville, MN: Liturgical Press, 1994.

Fuellenbach, John. *Church: Community for the Kingdom*. Maryknoll, NY: Orbis Books, 2002.

Gabrielli, Timothy R. *One in Christ: Virgil Michel, Louis-Marie Chauvet, and Mystical Body Theology*. Collegeville, MN: Liturgical Press, 2017.

Gadamer, Hans-Georg. "The Problem of Historical Consciousness." *Graduate Faculty Philosophy Journal* 5 no. 1. "H.-G. Gadamer," Special Issue (1975): 8–52.

———. *Truth and Method*. 2nd rev. ed. New York: Crossroad, 1989.

Gaillardetz, Richard R. *The Church in the Making: Lumen Gentium, Christus Dominus, Orientalium Ecclesiarum*, Rediscovering Vatican II. New York: Paulist Press, 2006.

———. *Ecclesiology for a Global Church: A People Called and Sent*. Maryknoll, NY: Orbis Books, 2008.

———. *Teaching with Authority: A Theology of the Magisterium in the Church*. Collegeville, MN: Liturgical Press, 1997.

———. *An Unfinished Council: Vatican II, Pope Francis, and the Renewal of Catholicism*. Collegeville, MN: Liturgical Press, 2015.

Gaillardetz, Richard R., and Catherine E. Clifford. *Keys to the Council: Unlocking the Teaching of Vatican II*. Collegeville, MN: Liturgical Press, 2012.

Galot, Jean. "Maria, tipo and modello della Chiesa." In *La Chiesa del Vaticano II: Studi e commenti intorno alla Costituzione dommatica 'Lumen Gentium'*, edited by Guilherme Baraúna, 1156–71. Firenze: Vallecchi Editore, 1965.

Gasser, Vinzenz. *The Gift of Infallibility: The Official Relatio on Infallibility of Bishop Vincent Gasser at Vatican Council I.* Edited by James T. O'Connor. 2nd updated ed. San Francisco: Ignatius Press, 2008.

Gerrish, Brian A. "Theology and the Historical Consciousness." In *Revisioning the Past: Prospects in Historical Theology,* edited by Mary Potter Engel and Walter E. Wyman, 281–97. Minneapolis: Fortress Press, 1992.

Gertler, Thomas. *Jesus Christus: Die Antwort der Kirche auf die Frage nach dem Menschsein. Eine Untersuchung zu Funktion und Inhalt der Christologie im ersten Teil der Pastoralkonstitution "Gaudium et Spes" des Zweiten Vatikanischen Konzils.* Leipzig: St. Benno, 1986.

Ghirlanda, Gianfranco. *"Hierarchica communio": Significato della formula nella "Lumen Gentium".* Roma: Università Gregoriana Editrice, 1980.

———. "Universal Church, Particular Church, and Local Church at the Second Vatican Council and in the New Code of Canon Law." In *Vatican II Assessment and Perspectives: Twenty-Five Years After (1962–1987). Volume 2,* edited by René Latourelle, 2:233–71. New York: Paulist Press, 1989.

Gianotti, Daniele. *I Padri della Chiesa al Concilio Vaticano II: La teologia patristica nella "Lumen gentium".* Bologna: Edizioni Dehoniane, 2010.

Gil Hellín, Francisco, ed. *Constitutio dogmatica de divina revelatione, Dei verbum: Concilii Vaticani II synopsis in ordinem redigens schemata cum relationibus necnon patrum orationes atque animadversiones.* Città del Vaticano: Libreria Editrice Vaticana, 1993.

———, ed. *Constitutio dogmatica de ecclesia, Lumen Gentium: Concilii Vaticani II synopsis in ordinem redigens schemata cum relationibus necnon patrum orationes atque animadversiones.* Città del Vaticano: Libreria Editrice Vaticana, 1995.

———, ed. *Constitutionis pastoralis de ecclesia in mundo huius temporis Gaudium et spes: Concilii Vaticani II synopsis in ordinem redigens schemata cum relationibus necnon patrum orationes atque animadversiones.* Città del Vaticano: Libreria Editrice Vaticana, 2003.

———, ed. *Declaratio de Ecclesiae habitudine ad religionis non-christianas, Nostra aetate: Concilii Vaticani II synopsis in ordinem redigens schemata cum relationibus necnon patrum orationes atque animadversiones.* Roma: Pontificia Universitas Sanctae Crucis, 2013.

———. *Decretum de oecumenismo, Unitatis redintegratio: Concilii Vaticani II synopsis in ordinem redigens schemata cum relationibus necnon patrum orationes atque animadversiones.* Città del Vaticano: Libreria Editrice Vaticana, 2005.

———. *"Gaudium et Spes* Synopsis." In *Constitutionis pastoralis de ecclesia in mundo huius temporis Gaudium et spes: Concilii Vaticani II synopsis in ordinem redigens schemata cum relationibus necnon patrum orationes atque animadversiones,* 1–751. Città del Vaticano: Libreria Editrice Vaticana, 2003.

———. "Nostra Aetate: Synopsis." In *Declaratio de Ecclesiae habitudine ad religionis non-christianas, Nostra aetate: Concilii Vaticani II synopsis in ordinem redigens schemata cum relationibus necnon patrum orationes atque animadversiones,* edited by Francisco Gil Hellín, 2–45. Roma: Pontificia Universitas Sanctae Crucis, 2013.

Gile, Joseph M. "*Dei Verbum:* Theological Critiques from within Vatican II, 1964–1965. A Retrieval and Analysis of the Unaccepted Theological Critiques Raised in Response to the Schema on Revelation during the Third and Fourth Periods of the Second Vatican Council." Unpublished Dissertation, Gregorian University, 2004.

Goldie, Rosemary. *From a Roman Window: Five Decades: The World, the Church and the Catholic Laity.* Blackburn, Vic.: HarperCollinsReligious, 1998.

Gonnet, Dominique. "L'apport de John Courtney Murray au schéma sur la liberté religieuse." In *Les commissions conciliaires à Vatican II*, edited by Matthijs Lamberigts, Claude Soetens and Jan Grootaers, 205–15. Leuven: Bibliotheek van de Faculteit Godgeleerdheid, 1996.

———. *La liberté religieuse à Vatican II la contribution de John Courtney Murray, SJ.* Paris: Cerf, 1994.

Granfield, Patrick. "The Church as *Societas Perfecta* in the Schemata of Vatican I." *Church History* 48 (1979): 431–46.

———. "The Church Local and Universal: Realization of Communion." *The Jurist* 49 (1989): 449–71.

———. *The Limits of the Papacy: Authority and Autonomy in the Church.* London: Darton, Longman and Todd, 1987.

———. "The Priority-Debate: Universal or Local Church?" In *Ecclesia Tertii Millennii Advenientis: Omaggio al P. Angel Antón*, edited by Fernando Chica Arellano, Sandro Panizzolo, and Harald Wagner, 152–61. Casale Monferrato: Piemme, 1997.

———. "The Rise and Fall of *Societas Perfecta*." *Concilium* 157 (1982): 3–8.

Grillmeier, Alois. "Chapter I: The Mystery of the Church." In *Commentary on the Documents of Vatican II. Volume 1*, edited by Herbert Vorgrimler, 1:138–52. London: Burns & Oates, 1967.

———. "Chapter II: The People of God." In *Commentary on the Documents of Vatican II. Volume 1*, edited by Herbert Vorgrimler, 1:153–85. London: Burns & Oates, 1967.

———. *Christ in Christian Tradition. Volume Two: From the Council of Chalcedon (451) to Gregory the Great (590–604). Part One: Reception and Contradiction: The Development of the Discussion about Chalcedon from 451 to the Beginning of the Reign of Justinian.* Atlanta: John Knox Press, 1987.

———. "Dogmatic Constitution on Divine Revelation: Chapter III." In *Commentary on the Documents of Vatican II. Volume 3*, edited by H. Vorgrimler, 3:199–246. New York: Herder, 1969.

———. "The Reception of Chalcedon in the Roman Catholic Church." *Ecumenical Review* 22 (1970): 383–411.

Groot, Jan. "The Church as Sacrament of the World." *Concilium* 1 no. 4 (January 1968): 27–34.

Grootaers, Jan. "Diversité des tendances à l'intérieur de la majorité conciliaire: Gérard Philips et Giuseppe Dossetti." In *The Belgian Contribution to the Second Vatican Council: International Research Conference at Mechelen, Leuven and Louvain-la-Neuve (September 12–16, 2005)*, edited by Doris Donnelly, Joseph Famerée, Mathijs Lamberigts, and Karim Schelkens, 529–62. Leuven; Dudley, MA: Peeters, 2008.

———. "The Drama Continues between the Acts: The 'Second Preparation' and Its Opponents." In *History of Vatican II, Vol. 2: The Formation of the Council's Identity. First Period and Intercession, October 1962–September 1963*, edited by Giuseppe Alberigo and Joseph A. Komonchak, 2:359–514. Maryknoll, NY: Orbis Books, 1997.

———. "Gérard Philips: La force dans la faiblesse." In *Actes et acteurs à Vatican II*, 382–419. Leuven: Leuven University Press and Uitgeverij Peeters, 1998.

Grosche, Robert. *Pilgernde Kirche.* Freiburg im Breisgau: Herder, 1938.

Gutiérrez, Gustavo. *A Theology of Liberation: History, Politics, and Salvation.* Rev. ed. Maryknoll, NY: Orbis Books, 1988.

Hamer, Jérôme. *The Church is a Communion.* London: Geoffrey Chapman, 1964.

Hardon, John A. "Robert Bellarmine's Concept of the Church." In *Studies in Medieval Culture*, edited by John R. Sommerfeldt, 2:120–27. Kalamazoo, MI: Western Michigan University, 1966.

Häring, Bernhard. *Free and Faithful: My Life in the Catholic Church. An Autobiography*. Liguori, MO: Liguori/Triumph, 1998.

Hastings, Adrian. *A Concise Guide to the Documents of the Second Vatican Council*. 2 vols. London: Darton Longman & Todd, 1968–1969.

———. *A Concise Guide to the Documents of the Second Vatican Council. Volume 1*. London: Darton Longman & Todd, 1968.

———. *A Concise Guide to the Documents of the Second Vatican Council. Volume 2*. London: Darton Longman & Todd, 1969.

———. "The Key Texts." In *Modern Catholicism: Vatican II and After*, edited by Adrian Hastings, 56–67. London: SPCK, 1991.

Haughey, John C. "Charisms: An Ecclesiological Exploration." In *Retrieving Charisms for the Twenty-first Century*, edited by Doris Donnelly, 1–16. Collegeville, MN: Liturgical Press, 1999.

Häussling, Angelus A. "Pascha-Mysterium. Kritisches zu einem Beitrag in der dritten Auflage des Lexicon für Thelogie und Kirche." *Archiv für Liturgiewissenschaft* 41 (1999): 157–65.

Hay, Camillus. "Comparative Ecclesiology of the Documents behind the Decree on Ecumenism." *One in Christ* 4 (1967): 399–416.

Hayes, Zachary. *Visions of a Future: A Study of Christian Eschatology*. Collegeville, MN: Liturgical Press, 1990.

Healy, Nicholas J. "The Drafting of *Dignitatis Humanae*." In *Freedom, Truth, and Human Dignity: The Second Vatican Council's Declaration on Religious Freedom. A New Translation, Redaction History, and Interpretation of Dignitatis Humanae*, edited by David L. Schindler and Nicholas J. Healy, 211–42. Grand Rapids, MI: Eerdmans, 2015.

Hellwig, Monika. "Eschatology." In *Systematic Theology: Roman Catholic Perspectives*, edited by Francis Schüssler Fiorenza and John P. Galvin, 2:349–72. Minneapolis: Fortress Press, 1991.

Henn, William. *The Hierarchy of Truths according to Yves Congar, O.P.* Roma: Editrice Pontificia Università Gregoriana, 1987.

———. *The Honor of My Brothers: A Short History of the Relation between the Pope and the Bishops*. New York: Crossroad, 2000.

———. "Yves Congar and *Lumen Gentium*." *Gregorianum* 86 no. 3 (2005): 563–92.

Herberg, Will. "Five Meanings of the Word 'Historical.'" *The Christian Scholar* 47 no. 4 (1964): 327–30.

Hertling, Ludwig. *Communio: Church and Papacy in Early Christianity*. Chicago: Loyola University Press, 1972.

Heyder, Regina, and Gisela Muschiol, eds. *Katholikinnen und das Zweite Vatikanische Konzil: Petitionen–Berichte–Fotografien*. Münster: Aschendorff, 2018.

Hilberath, Bernd Jochen. "Theologischer Kommentar zum Dekret über den Ökumenismus *Unitatis redintegratio*." In *Herders theologischer Kommentar zum Zweiten Vatikanischen Konzil. Band 3*, edited by Peter Hünermann and Bernd Jochen Hilberath, 3:69–223. Freiburg: Herder, 2005.

Hogan, Linda. *Confronting the Truth: Conscience in the Catholic Tradition*. New York: Paulist Press, 2000.

———. "Conscience in the Documents of Vatican II." In *Conscience*, edited by Charles E. Curran, 82–88. New York: Paulist Press, 2004.

Hoping, Helmut. "Theologischer Kommentar zur Dogmatischen Konstitution über die göttliche Offenbarung." In *Herders theologischer Kommentar zum Zweiten Vatikanischen Konzil. Band 3*, edited by Peter Hünermann and Bernd Jochen Hilberath, 3:695–831. Freiburg: Herder, 2005.

Hünermann, Peter, ed. *Das Zweite Vatikanische Konzil und die Zeichen der Zeit heute.* Freiburg im Breisgau: Verlag Herder, 2006.

———. "Deutsche Theologie auf dem Zweiten Vatikanum." In *Kirche sein: Nachkonziliare Theologie im Dienst der Kirchenreform: Für Hermann Josef Pottmeyer*, edited by Wilhelm Geerlings and Max Seckler, 141–62. Freiburg im Breisgau: Herder, 1994.

———. "The Final Weeks of the Council." In *History of Vatican II, Vol. 5: The Council and the Transition. The Fourth Period and the End of the Council, September 1965–December 1965*, edited by Giuseppe Alberigo and Joseph A. Komonchak, 5:363–483. Maryknoll, NY: Orbis Books, 2006.

———. "The Ignored 'Text': On the Hermeneutics of the Second Vatican Council." In *Vatican II: A Forgotten Future?*, edited by Alberto Melloni and Christoph Theobald, 118–36. London: SCM Press, 2005.

———. "Kriterien für die Rezeption des II. Vatikanischen Konzils." *Theologische Quartalschrift* 191 (2011): 126–47.

———. "Reign of God." In *Sacramentum Mundi: An Encyclopedia of Theology*, edited by Karl Rahner, 5:233–40. New York: Herder and Herder, 1970.

———. "Theologischer Kommentar zum Dekret über die Missionstätigkeit der Kirche: *Ad gentes*." In *Herders theologischer Kommentar zum Zweiten Vatikanischen Konzil. Band 4*, edited by Peter Hünermann and Bernd Jochen Hilberath, 4:219–336. Freiburg: Herder, 2005.

Hünermann, Peter, and Bernd Jochen Hilberath. "Verzeichnis der Bibelstellen." In *Herders theologischer Kommentar zum Zweiten Vatikanischen Konzil. Band 1. Die Documente des Zweiten Vatikanishen Konzils: Konstitutionen, Dekrete, Erklärungen*, 751–60. Freiburg: Herder, 2004.

Hünermann, Peter, Bernd Jochen Hilberath, and Guido Bausenhart, eds. *Herders theologischer Kommentar zum Zweiten Vatikanischen Konzil.* 5 vols. Freiburg: Herder, 2004–2006.

Hunt, Anne. "The Trinitarian Depths of Vatican II." *Theological Studies* 74 (2013): 3–19.

"Index Peritorum." In *Acta Synodalia Sacrosancti Concilii Oecumenici Vaticani II: Indices*, 937–49. Cittá Vaticana: Typis Polyglottis Vaticanis, 1999.

Innocenti, Ennio. "Le citazioni pontifiche nei documenti conciliari." *Concretezza* 12 (16 July 1966): 6–10.

Isaac, Jules. "Note on a Week in Rome." *SIDIC: Service International de Documentation Judéo-Chrétienne* 1 no. 3 (1968): 11–13.

———. *The Teaching of Contempt: Christian Roots of Anti-Semitism.* New York: Holt, Rinehart and Winston, 1964.

Iserloh, Erwin. "History of the Ecumenical Movement." In *The Church in the Modern Age*, edited by Hubert Jedin, Konrad Repgen, and John Dolan, 10:458–73. New York: Crossroad, 1981.

Jaeger, Lorenz. *A Stand on Ecumenism: The Council's Decree.* London: Geoffrey Chapman, 1965.

Jauss, Hans Robert. "Antiqui/moderni (Querelle des Anciens et des Modernes)." In *Historisches Wörterbuch der Philosophie*, edited by Joachim Ritter, 1:410–14. Basel/Stuttgart: Schwabe & Co., 1971.

——. "Horizon Structure and Dialogicity." In *Question and Answer: Forms of Dialogic Understanding*, 197–231. Minneapolis: University of Minnesota Press, 1989.

——. "Ursprung und Bedeutung der Fortschrittsidee in der 'Querelle des Anciens et des Modernes.'" In *Die Philosophie und die Frage nach dem Fortschritt*, edited by H. Kuhn and R. Wiedmann, 51–72. München, 1964.

Jedin, Hubert. "Theologie und Lehramt." In *Lehramt und Theologie im 16. Jahrhundert*, edited by Remigus Bäumer, 7–21. Münster: Aschendorff, 1976.

Jenny, Henri. *Le mystère pascal dans l'année chrétienne*. 4e éd. revue et augm. ed. Paris: Equipes enseignantes, 1958.

——. *The Paschal Mystery in the Christian Year*. Translated by Allan Stehling and John Lundberg. Notre Dame, IN: Fides Publishers, 1962.

John XXIII, Pope. "Ad Petri Cathedram." In *The Papal Encyclicals. Volume 5: 1958–1981*, edited by Claudia Carlen, 5–20. Wilmington, NC: McGrath Publishing Company, 1981.

——. "Pacem in Terris." In *The Papal Encyclicals. Volume 5: 1958–1981*, edited by Claudia Carlen, 107–29. Wilmington, NC: McGrath Publishing Company, 1981.

——. "Pope John Convokes the Council: *Humanae Salutis*." In *The Documents of Vatican II*, edited by Walter M. Abbott, 703–09. London: Geoffrey Chapman, 1966.

——. "Pope John's Opening Speech to the Council." In *The Documents of Vatican II*, edited by Walter M. Abbott, 710–19. London: Geoffrey Chapman, 1966.

——. "*Questa Festiva*: Announcement of Ecumenical Council and Roman Synod. An Address of Pope John XXIII to the Roman Cardinals (January 25, 1959)." *The Pope Speaks* 5 no. 4 (1958–59): 398–401.

——. "Radio Message of September 11 1962." In *Discorsi Messagi Colloqui del S. Padre Giovanni XXIII*, 4:524. Vatican City: Editrice Vaticana, 1960–1967.

Jungmann, Josef Andreas. "Constitution on the Sacred Liturgy." In *Commentary on the Documents of Vatican II. Volume 1*, edited by Herbert Vorgrimler, 1:1–87. London: Burns & Oates, 1967.

Kaczynski, Reiner. "Theologischer Kommentar zur Konstitution über die heilige Liturgie *Sacrosanctum Concilium*." In *Herders theologischer Kommentar zum Zweiten Vatikanischen Konzil*, edited by Peter Hünermann and Bernd Jochen Hilberath, 2:1–227. Freiburg: Herder, 2004.

Kähler, Martin. *The So-Called Historical Jesus and the Historic Biblical Christ*. Philadelphia: Fortress Press, 1988.

Karakunnel, George. *The Christian Vision of Man: A Study of the Theological Anthropology in "Gaudium et Spes" of Vatican II*. Bangalore: Asian Trading Corp., 1984.

Kasper, Walter. *The Catholic Church: Nature, Reality and Mission*. London: Bloomsbury, 2014.

——. "The Church as a Universal Sacrament of Salvation." In *Theology and Church*, 111–28. New York: Crossroad, 1989.

——. "The Church as Communion: Reflections on the Guiding Ecclesiological Idea of the Second Vatican Council." In *Theology and Church*, 148–65. New York: Crossroad, 1989.

——. "The Continuing Challenge of the Second Vatican Council: The Hermeneutics of the Conciliar Statements." In *Theology and Church*, 166–76. New York: Crossroad, 1989.

——. *Die Lehre von der Tradition in der römischen Schule: Giovanni Perrone, Carlo Passaglia, Clemens Schrader*. Freiburg: Herder, 1962.

———. *An Introduction to Christian Faith*. London: Burns & Oates, 1980.

———. *The Methods of Dogmatic Theology*. New York: Paulist Press, 1969.

———. "On the Church: A Friendly Reply to Cardinal Ratzinger." *America* 184 (April 23–30, 2001): 8–14.

———. "The Renewal of Pneumatology in Contemporary Catholic Life and Theology: Towards a Rapprochement between East and West." In *That They May All Be One: The Call to Unity*, 96–121. New York: Burns & Oates, 2004.

———. "The Theological Anthropology of *Gaudium et Spes*." *Communio* 23 (1996): 129–40.

Keenan, James. "Vatican II and Theological Ethics." *Theological Studies* 74 (2013): 162–90.

Kemper, Jeffrey M. "Liturgy Notes." *Liturgical Ministry* 8 (Winter 1999): 46–51.

Kenis, Leo. "Diaries: Private Sources for a Study of the Second Vatican Council." In *The Belgian Contribution to the Second Vatican Council*, edited by Doris Donnelly, Joseph Famerée, Mathijs Lamberigts, and Karim Schelkens, 29–53. Leuven: Peeters, 2008.

Kerr, Fergus. *After Aquinas: Versions of Thomism*. Malden, MA: Blackwell Publishers, 2002.

Klinger, Elmar. "Der Beitrag Karl Rahners zum Zweiten Vatikanum im Licht des Karl-Rahner-Archivs-Elmar-Klinger in Würzburg." In *Experience, Organisations and Bodies at Vatican II*, edited by Maria Teresa Fattori and Alberto Melloni, 261–74. Leuven: Bibliotheek van de Faculteit Godgeleerdheid, 1999.

Kloppenburg, Bonaventure. *The Ecclesiology of Vatican II*. Chicago: Franciscan Herald Press, 1974.

Knitter, Paul F. *Introducing Theologies of Religions*. Maryknoll, NY: Orbis Books, 2002.

———. "*Nostra Aetate*: A Milestone in the History of Religions? From Competition to Cooperation." In *The Future of Interreligious Dialogue: A Multi-Religious Conversation on Nostra Aetate*, edited by Charles L. Cohen, Paul F. Knitter, and Ulrich E. Rosenhagen, 45–58. Maryknoll, NY: Orbis Books, 2017.

Kobler, J. F. "Were Theologians the Engineers of Vatican II?" *Gregorianum* 70 (1989): 233–50.

Koernke, Theresa F. "Mystery Theology." In *The New Dictionary of Sacramental Worship*, edited by Peter E. Fink, 883–91. Collegeville, MN: Liturgical Press, 1990.

Komonchak, Joseph A. "Afterword: The Church and the Churches." In *Catholics in the Vatican II Era: Local Histories of a Global Event*, edited by Kathleen Sprows Cummings, Timothy Matovina, and Robert A. Orsi, 275–90. New York: Cambridge University Press, 2018.

———. "Augustine, Aquinas or the Gospel *sine glossa*? Divisions over *Gaudium et spes*." In *Unfinished Journey: The Church 40 Years after Vatican II. Essays for John Wilkins*, edited by Austen Ivereigh, 102–18. London: Continuum, 2003.

———. "Benedict XVI and the Interpretation of Vatican II." In *The Crisis of Authority in Catholic Modernity*, edited by Michael James Lacey and Francis Oakley, 93–110. New York: Oxford University Press, 2011.

———. "Concepts of Communion: Past and Present." *Cristianesimo nella Storia* 16 (1995): 321–40.

———. "The Council of Trent at the Second Vatican Council." In *From Trent to Vatican II: Historical and Theological Investigations*, edited by Raymond F. Bulman and Frederick J. Parrella, 61–80. New York: Oxford University Press, 2006.

———. "The Ecclesiology of Vatican II." *Origins* 28 (April 22, 1999): 763–68.

———. "The Enlightenment and the Construction of Roman Catholicism." *Annual of the Catholic Commission on Intellectual and Cultural Affairs* (1985): 31–59.

————. "*Humani Generis* and *Nouvelle Théologie*." In *Ressourcement: A Movement for Renewal in Twentieth-Century Catholic Theology*, edited by Gabriel Flynn and Paul D. Murray, 138–56. Oxford: Oxford University Press, 2011.

————. "Is Christ Divided? Dealing with Diversity and Disagreement." *Origins* 33 (17 July 2003): 140–47.

————. "La Redazione della Gaudium et Spes." *Il Regno* 44 (1999): 446–55.

————. "Le valutazioni sulla *Gaudium et spes*: Chenu, Dossetti, Ratzinger." In *Volti di fine Concilio: Studi di storia e teologia sulla conclusione del Vaticano II*, edited by Joseph Doré and Alberto Melloni, 115–53. Bologna: Il Mulino, 2000.

————. "The Local Church." *Chicago Studies* (1989): 320–34.

————. "The Local Church and the Church Catholic: The Contemporary Theological Problematic." *The Jurist* 52 (1992): 416–47.

————. "Modernity and the Construction of Roman Catholicism." *Cristianesimo nella Storia* 18 (1997): 353–85.

————. "Returning from Exile: Catholic Theology in the 1930s." In *The Twentieth Century: A Theological Overview*, edited by Gregory Baum, 35–48. Maryknoll, NY: Orbis Books, 1999.

————. "The Secretariat for Promoting Christian Unity and the Preparation of Vatican II." *Centro Pro Unione Bulletin* 50 (1996): 11–17.

————. "The Significance of Vatican Council II for Ecclesiology." In *The Gift of the Church: A Textbook on Ecclesiology in Honor of Patrick Granfield, O.S.B*, edited by Peter C. Phan, 69–92. Collegeville, MN: Liturgical Press, 2000.

————. "The Struggle for the Council during the Preparation of Vatican II (1960–1962)." In *History of Vatican II, Vol. 1: Announcing and Preparing Vatican Council II*, edited by Giuseppe Alberigo and Joseph A. Komonchak, 167–356. Maryknoll, NY: Orbis Books, 1996.

————. "Theology and Culture at Mid-Century: The Example of Henri de Lubac." *Theological Studies* 51 (1990): 579–602.

————. "Thomism and the Second Vatican Council." In *Continuity and Plurality in Catholic Theology: Essays in Honor of Gerald A. McCool*, edited by Anthony J. Cernera, 53–73. Fairfield, CT: Sacred Heart University Press, 1998.

————. "Toward an Ecclesiology of Communion." In *History of Vatican II, Vol. 4: The Church as Communion. Third Period and Third Intersession, September 1964–September 1965*, edited by Giuseppe Alberigo and Joseph A. Komonchak, 1–93. Maryknoll, NY: Orbis Books, 2004.

————. "Vatican II and the Encounter between Catholicism and Liberalism." In *Catholicism and Liberalism: Contributions to American Public Philosophy*, edited by R. Bruce Douglass and David Hollenbach, 76–99. Cambridge: Cambridge University Press, 1994.

————. "Vatican II as an 'Event.'" In *Vatican II: Did Anything Happen?*, edited by David G. Schultenover, 24–51. New York: Continuum, 2007.

————. *Who Are the Church?* Milwaukee, WI: Marquette University Press, 2008.

König, Franz. *Christus und die Religionen der Erde: Handbuch der Religionsgeschichte*. Wien: Herder, 1951.

————. *Religionswissenschaftliches Wörterbuch: Die Grundbegriffe*. Freiburg: Herder, 1956.

Koselleck, Reinhart. *Futures Past: On the Semantics of Historical Time*. Cambridge, MA: MIT Press, 1985.

Koster, Mannes Dominikus. *Ekklesiologie im Werden*. Paderborn: Bonifacius–Druckerei, 1940.

Krokus, Christian S. "Louis Massignon's Influence on the Teaching of Vatican II on Muslims and Islam." *Islam and Christian–Muslim Relations* 23 no. 3 (2012): 329–45.

Küng, Hans. "The Charismatic Structure of the Church." *Concilium* 4 (1965): 23–33.

Lafont, Ghislain. *Imagining the Catholic Church: Structured Communion in the Spirit*. Collegeville, MN: Liturgical Press, 2000.

Lamberigts, Mathijs. "Nostra Aetate 2, Vatican II on Hinduism and Buddhism: A Historical Survey." In *The Living Legacy of Vatican II: Studies from an Indian Perspective*, edited by Paul Pulikkan, 159–85. Bengaluru, India: ATC Publishers, 2017.

Lamberigts, Mathijs, and Leo Declerck. "The Role of Cardinal Léon-Joseph Suenens at Vatican II." In *The Belgian Contribution to the Second Vatican Council*, edited by Doris Donnelly, Joseph Famerée, Mathijs Lamberigts, and Karim Schelkens, 61–217. Leuven: Peeters, 2008.

———. "Vatican II on the Jews: A Historical Survey." In *Never Revoked: Nostra Aetate as Ongoing Challenge for Jewish-Christian Dialogue*, edited by Marianne Moyaert and Didier Pollefeyt, 13–56. Grand Rapids: Eerdmans, 2010.

Lamberigts, Mathijs, Gilles Routhier, Pedro Rubens Ferreira Oliveira, Christoph Theobald, and Dries Bosschaert, eds. *50 Years after the Vatican II Council: Theologians from All over the World Deliberate*. Paris: Federatio Internationalis Universitatem Catholicarum, 2015.

Lamberigts, Mathijs, and Karim Schelkens. "Some Remarks on the Notion of Truth in the Documents of Vatican II." In *Orthodoxy, Process and Product*, edited by Mathijs Lamberigts, Lieven Boeve, and Terrence Merrigan, 205–28. Walpole, MA: Peeters, 2009.

Lambert, Bernard. *De Rome à Jérusalem: Itinéraire spirituel de Vatican II*. Paris: Editions du Centurion, 1964.

Lamberts, Jozef. "L'évolution de la notion de 'participation active' dans le mouvement liturgique du vingtième siècle." *La Maison-Dieu* 241 (2005): 77–120.

Laminski, Adolf. "Die Entdeckung der pneumatologischen Dimension der Kirche durch das Konzil und ihre Bedeutung." In *Sapienter ordinare: Festgabe für Erich Kleineidam*, edited by Fritz Hoffmann, Konrad Feiereis, and Leo Scheffczyk, 392–405. Leipzig: St. Benno, 1969.

Langan, John. "Christian Doctrine in a Historically Conscious World." In *Faithful Witness: Foundations of Theology for Today's Church*, edited by Leo J. O'Donovan and T. Howland Sanks, 132–50. New York: Crossroad, 1989.

Lanne, Emmanuel. "La contribtion du cardinal Bea à la question du baptême et l'Unité des chrétiens." *Irénikon* 55 no. 4 (1982): 471–99.

Latourelle, René. "Dei Verbum: II. Commentary." In *Dictionary of Fundamental Theology*, edited by René Latourelle and Rino Fisichella, 218–24. Middlegreen, Slough, UK: St Paul, 1994.

———. *Theology of Revelation*. Staten Island, NY: Alba House, 1966.

Laurentin, René. "The Jewish Question at Vatican II." In *The Declaration on the Relation of the Church to Non-Christian Religions*, edited by René Laurentin and Josef Neuner, 17–77. Glen Rock, NJ: Paulist Press, 1966.

Lawler, Michael G., Todd A. Salzman, and Eileen Burke-Sullivan. *The Church in the Modern World: Gaudium et Spes Then and Now*. Collegeville, MN: Liturgical Press, 2014.

le Guillou, Marie-Joseph. "Church: II. Ecclesiology." In *Sacramentum Mundi: An Encyclopedia of Theology*, edited by Karl Rahner, 1:317–27. New York: Herder and Herder, 1968.

Lécuyer, Joseph. "Il triplice ufficio del Vescovo." In *La Chiesa del Vaticano II: Studi e commenti intorno alla Costituzione dommatica 'Lumen Gentium'*, edited by Guilherme Baraúna, 851–71. Firenze: Vallecchi Editore, 1965.

Lefebvre, Solange. "Conflicting Interpretations of the Council: The Ratzinger–Kasper Debate." In *The New Pontificate: A Time for Change? Concilium 2006/1*, edited by Erik Borgmann, Maureen Junker-Kenny, and Janet Martin Soskice, 95–105. London: SCM, 2006.

Legrand, Hervé. "Collégialité des évêques et communion des églises dans la réception de Vatican II." *Revue des Sciences Philosophiques et Théologiques* 75 (1991): 545–68.

———. "Forty Years Later: What Has Become of the Ecclesiological Reforms Envisaged by Vatican II?" In *Vatican II: A Forgotten Future?*, edited by Alberto Melloni and Christoph Theobald, 57–72. London: SCM Press, 2005.

———. "Les évêques, les églises locales et l'église entière: Évolutions institutionnelles depuis Vatican II et chantiers actuels de recherche." *Revue des Sciences Philosophiques et Théologiques* 85 no. 1 (2001): 461–509.

Lennan, Richard. "Communion Ecclesiology: Foundations, Critiques, and Affirmations." *Pacifica* 20 (2007): 24–39.

———. " 'Narcissistic Aestheticism'?: An Assessment of Karl Rahner's Sacramental Ecclesiology." *Philosophy and Theology* 25 (2013): 249–70.

———. "Roman Catholic Ecclesiology." In *The Routledge Companion to the Christian Church*, edited by Gerard Mannion and Lewis S. Mudge, 234–50. New York: Routledge, 2008.

———. "The Theology of Karl Rahner: An Alternative to the *Ressourcement*?" In *Ressourcement: A Movement for Renewal in Twentieth-Century Catholic Theology*, edited by Gabriel Flynn and Paul D. Murray, 405–22. Oxford: Oxford University Press, 2011.

Leo XIII, Pope. "Aeterni Patris." In *The Papal Encyclicals. Volume 2: 1878–1903*, edited by Claudia Carlen, 17–27. Wilmington, NC: McGrath Publishing Company, 1981.

Lewis, Charlton T., and Charles Short. *A Latin Dictionary: Founded on Andrews' Edition of Freund's Latin Dictionary*. Rev., enl., and in great part rewritten ed. Oxford: Clarendon Press, 1951.

Locklin, Reid. "One Text, Two Declarations: Theological Trajectories from *Nostra Aetate*." *Theological Studies* 78 no. 1 (2017): 49–71.

Löhrer, Magnus. "La gerarchia al servizio del populo christiano." In *La Chiesa del Vaticano II: Studi e commenti intorno alla Costituzione dommatica 'Lumen Gentium'*, edited by Guilherme Baraúna, 699–712. Firenze: Vallecchi Editore, 1965.

Lonergan, Bernard J. F. "The Transition from a Classicist Worldview to Historical-Mindedness." In *A Second Collection*, edited by William F. J. Ryan and Bernard J. Tyrrell, 1–9. London: Darton, Longman and Todd, 1974.

Löser, Werner. "People of God." In *Handbook of Catholic Theology*, edited by Wolfgang Beinert and Francis Schüssler Fiorenza, 527. New York: Crossroad, 1995.

Lucien, Bernard. *Études sur la liberté religieuse dans la doctrine catholique: Grégoire XVI, Pie IX et Vatican II*. Tours: Éditions Forts dans la foi, 1990.

Mackey, James P. *The Modern Theology of Tradition*. New York: Herder and Herder, 1963.

Magnani, Giovanni. "Does the So-Called Theology of the Laity Possess a Theological Status?" In *Vatican II Assessment and Perspectives: Twenty-Five Years After (1962–1987). Volume 1*, edited by René Latourelle, 1:568–633. New York: Paulist Press, 1988.

Mansi, Giovanni Domenico. *Sacrorum conciliorum, nova et amplissima collectio*. 54 vols. Graz: Akademische Druck-u. Verlagsanstalt, 1960.

Marini, Piero. *Serving the People of God: Remembering Sacrosanctum Concilium.* Ottawa: Novalis, 2006.

Markey, John J. *Creating Communion: The Theology of the Constitutions of the Church.* Hyde Park, NY: New City Press, 2003.

Martina, Giacomo. "The Historical Context in Which the Idea of a New Ecumenical Council Was Born." In *Vatican II Assessment and Perspectives: Twenty-Five Years After (1962–1987),* edited by René Latourelle, 1:3–73. New York: Paulist Press, 1988.

Maximos IV, Patriarch. "Servant of the Servants of God." In *Council Speeches of Vatican II,* edited by Hans Küng, Yves Congar, and Daniel O'Hanlon, 72–75. Glen Rock, NJ: Paulist Press, 1964.

———. "The Supreme Senate of the Catholic Church." In *Council Speeches of Vatican II,* edited by Hans Küng, Yves Congar and Daniel O'Hanlon, 133–37. Glen Rock, NJ: Paulist Press, 1964.

McBrien, Richard P. *The Church: The Evolution of Catholicism.* New York: HarperOne, 2008.

———. "People of God." In *The HarperCollins Encyclopedia of Catholicism,* edited by Richard P. McBrien, 984–85. New York: HarperCollins, 1995.

McCann, Dennis P. "Signs of the Times." In *The New Dictionary of Catholic Social Thought,* edited by Judith A. Dwyer and Elizabeth L. Montgomery, 881–83. Collegeville, MN: Liturgical Press, 1994.

McConville, William. "Mission." In *The New Dictionary of Theology,* edited by Joseph A. Komonchak, Mary Collins, and Dermot A. Lane, 664–68. Dublin: Gill and Macmillan, 1987.

McCool, Gerald A. *From Unity to Pluralism: The Internal Evolution of Thomism.* New York: Fordham University Press, 1989.

McDonnell, Kilian. "The Concept of 'Church' in the Documents of Vatican II as Applied to Protestant Denominations." *Worship* 44 (1970): 332–49.

———. "The Ratzinger/Kasper Debate: The Universal Church and Local Churches." *Theological Studies* 63 (2002): 227–50.

McEnroy, Carmel Elizabeth. *Guests in Their Own House: The Women of Vatican II.* New York: Crossroad, 1996.

McEvoy, James Gerard. "Church and World at the Second Vatican Council: The Significance of *Gaudium et Spes.*" *Pacifica* 19 (2006): 37–57.

———. *Leaving Christendom for Good: Church-World Dialogue in a Secular Age.* Lanham: Lexington Books, 2014.

———. "Proclamation As Dialogue: Transition in the Church-World Relationship." *Theological Studies* 70 (2009): 875–903.

McGinn, Bernard. *Thomas Aquinas's Summa Theologiae: A Biography.* Princeton, NJ: Princeton University Press, 2014.

McGrath, Mark G. "The Constitution on the Church in the Modern World." In *Vatican II: An Interfaith Appraisal,* edited by John H. Miller, 397–412. Notre Dame: University of Notre Dame, 1966.

McKeon, Myles. "Bishop Myles McKeon: Interviewed by Russell Hardiman." In *Voices from the Council,* edited by Michael R. Prendergast and M. D. Ridge, 67–80. Portland, OR: Pastoral Press, 2004.

Melloni, Alberto. "The Beginning of the Second Period: The Great Debate on the Church." In *History of Vatican II, Vol. 3: The Mature Council. Second Period and Intersession, September 1963–September 1964,* edited by Giuseppe Alberigo and Joseph A. Komonchak, 3:1–115. Maryknoll, NY: Orbis Books, 1998.

———. "The Periti." In *Vatican II: The Complete History*, edited by Alberto Melloni, Federico Ruozzi, and Enrico Galvotti, 188–91. New York: Paulist Press, 2015.

———. "The 'Black Week.'" In *Vatican II: The Complete History*, edited by Alberto Melloni, Federico Ruozzi, and Enrico Galvotti, 218–19. New York: Paulist Press, 2015.

———. "Quoniam Multi: The Commissions." In *Vatican II: The Complete History*, edited by Alberto Melloni, Federico Ruozzi, and Enrico Galavotti, 122–23. New York: Paulist Press, 2015.

———. "Setting Up the Council: St. Peter's Basilica Transforms into a Council Hall." In *Vatican II: The Complete History*, edited by Alberto Melloni, Federico Ruozzi, and Enrico Galvotti, 78–81. New York: Paulist Press, 2015.

———. "Calendar of the Congregations." In *Vatican II: The Complete History*, edited by Alberto Melloni, Federico Ruozzi, and Enrico Galvotti, 240–57. New York: Paulist Press, 2015.

———. "The Central Commission and the Preparatory Commissions." In *Vatican II: The Complete History*, edited by Alberto Melloni, Federico Ruozzi, and Enrico Galvotti, 58–75. New York: Paulist Press, 2015.

———. "Controversies: Subjects Taken on by the Pope." In *Vatican II: The Complete History*, edited by Alberto Melloni, Federico Ruozzi, and Enrico Galvotti, 232–35. New York: Paulist Press, 2015.

———. "The Council Hall and the Placement of the Participants." In *Vatican II: The Complete History*, edited by Alberto Melloni, Federico Ruozzi, and Enrico Galvotti, 88–93. New York: Paulist Press, 2015.

———. "Eastern Rite Catholics." In *Vatican II: The Complete History*, edited by Alberto Melloni, Federico Ruozzi, and Enrico Galvotti, 186–87. New York: Paulist Press, 2015.

———. "*Nostra Aetate* and the Discovery of the Sacrament of Otherness." In *The Catholic Church and the Jewish People: Recent Reflections from Rome*, edited by Philip A. Cunningham, Norbert J. Hofmann, and Joseph Sievers, 129–51. New York: Fordham University Press, 2007.

———. "Observers and Guests." In *Vatican II: The Complete History*, edited by Alberto Melloni, Federico Ruozzi, and Enrico Galvotti, 192–99. New York: Paulist Press, 2015.

———. "Private Journals in the History of Vatican II." In *Vatican II Notebook: A Council Journal, 1962-1963*, edited by Marie-Dominique Chenu, 1–56. Adelaide, South Australia: ATF Theology, 2015.

Melloni, Alberto, and Silvia Scatena, eds. *Synod and Synodality: Theology, History, Canon Law and Ecumenism in New Contact. International Colloquium Bruges 2003.* Münster: LIT Verlag, 2005.

Mersch, Émile. *The Whole Christ: The Historical Development of the Doctrine of the Mystical Body in Scripture and Tradition.* Translated by John R. Kelly. Milwaukee: The Bruce Publishing Company, 1938.

"Message to Humanity." In *The Documents of Vatican II*, edited by Walter M. Abbott, 3–7. London: Geoffrey Chapman, 1966.

Mettepenningen, Jürgen. *Nouvelle Théologie—New Theology: Inheritor of Modernism, Precursor of Vatican II.* London: T & T Clark, 2010.

Meyer, Jan H. F., and Ray Land. "Threshold Concepts and Troublesome Knowledge: Linkages to Ways of Thinking and Practising within the Disciplines." In *Improving Student Learning: Theory and Practice, 10 Years on*, edited by Chris Rust, 412–24. Oxford: Oxford Centre for Staff & Learning Development, 2003.

Miccoli, Giovanni. "Two Sensitive Issues: Religious Freedom and the Jews." In *History of Vatican II, Vol. 4: The Church as Communion. Third Period and Third Intersession, September 1964–September 1965,* edited by Giuseppe Alberigo and Joseph A. Komonchak, 4:95–193. Maryknoll, NY: Orbis Books, 2004.

Michalski, Melvin. *The Relationship between the Universal Priesthood of the Baptized and the Ministerial Priesthood of the Ordained in Vatican II and in Subsequent Theology: Understanding "essentia et non gradu tantum," Lumen gentium no. 10.* Lewiston, NY: Mellen University Press, 1996.

Miller, Charles Henry. *"As It is Written": The Use of Old Testament References in the Documents of Vatican Council II.* St. Louis: Marianist Communications Center, 1973.

Miller, Vincent J. "History or Geography? Gadamer, Foucault, and Theologies of Tradition." In *Theology and the New Histories,* edited by Gary Macy, 56–85. Maryknoll, NY: Orbis Books, 1999.

Minnich, Nelson H. "The Voice of Theologians in General Councils from Pisa to Trent." *Theological Studies* 59 (1998): 420–41.

Moeller, Charles. "Église dans le Monde d'aujourd'hui." *Documentation Catholique* 63 (September 1966): 1485–507.

———. "History of *Lumen Gentium*'s Structure and Ideas." In *Vatican II: An Interfaith Appraisal,* edited by John H. Miller, 123–52. Notre Dame: University of Notre Dame Press, 1966.

———. "Il fermento delle idee nella elaborazione della Costituzione." In *La Chiesa del Vaticano II: Studi e commenti intorno alla Costituzione dommatica 'Lumen Gentium',* edited by Guilherme Baraúna, 155–89. Firenze: Vallecchi Editore, 1965.

———. "Pastoral Constitution on the Church in the Modern World: History of the Constitution." In *Commentary on the Documents of Vatican II. Volume 5,* edited by Herbert Vorgrimler, 5:1–76. New York: Herder and Herder, 1969.

Molinari, Paolo. "L'indole escatologica della Chiesa peregrinante and i suoi rapporti con la Chiesa celeste." In *La Chiesa del Vaticano II: Studi e commenti intorno alla Costituzione dommatica 'Lumen Gentium',* edited by Guilherme Baraúna, 1113–33. Firenze: Vallecchi Editore, 1965.

Montcheuil, Yves de. *Aspects de l'Église,* Unam Sanctam, 18. Paris: Les Éditions du Cerf, 1949.

Moorman, John R. H. "Observers and Guests of the Council." In *Vatican II: By Those Who Were There,* edited by Alberic Stacpoole, 155–69. London: Geoffrey Chapman, 1986.

Mörsdorf, Klaus. "Decree on the Bishop's Pastoral Office in the Church." In *Commentary on the Documents of Vatican II. Volume 2,* edited by Herbert Vorgrimler, 2:165–300. New York: Herder, 1968.

Morselli, Marco. "Jules Isaac and the Origins of *Nostra Aetate*." In *Nostra Aetate: Origins, Promulgation, Impact on Jewish-Catholic Relations,* edited by Neville Lamdan and Alberto Melloni, 21–28. Berlin: LIT Verlag, 2007.

Müller, Christof. *Die Eschatologie des Zweiten Vatikanischen Konzils: Die Kirche als Zeichen und Werkzeug der Vollendung,* Würzburger Studien zur Fundamentaltheologie, Bd. 28. Frankfurt am Main: Peter Lang, 2002.

Murphy, Jeffrey J. "The Far Milieu Called Home: Australian Bishops at Vatican II (The Final Session: 1965)." *Australasian Catholic Record* 80 no. 3 (2003): 343–69.

Murray, John Courtney. "Is It Basket Weaving?: The Question of Christianity and Human Values." In *We Hold These Truths: Catholic Reflections on the American Proposition,* 175–96. New York: Sheed and Ward, 1960.

────. "Religious Freedom." In *The Documents of Vatican II*, edited by Walter M. Abbott, 672–74. London: Geoffrey Chapman, 1966.

────. "This Matter of Religious Freedom." *America* 112 (January 9, 1965): 40–43.

Neudecker, Reinhard. "The Catholic Church and the Jewish People." In *Vatican II: Assessment and Perspectives. Twenty-five Years After (1962–1987)*, edited by René Latourelle, 3:282–323. New York: Paulist Press, 1989.

Neufeld, Karl-Heinz. "In the Service of the Council: Bishops and Theologians at the Second Vatican Council (for Cardinal Henri de Lubac on His Ninetieth Birthday)." In *Vatican II: Assessment and Perspectives. Twenty-Five Years After (1962–1987)*, edited by René Latourelle, 1:74–105. New York: Paulist Press, 1988.

Neunheuser, Burkhard. "Odo Casel in Retrospect and Prospect." *Worship* 50 (1976): 489–503.

Newman, John Henry. *An Essay on the Development of Christian Doctrine*. 6th ed. Notre Dame, IN: University of Notre Dame Press, 1989.

────. *On Consulting the Faithful in Matters of Doctrine*. New York,: Sheed and Ward, 1962.

Nicolussi, G. "La sacramentalità dell'episcopato nella 'Lumen Gentium,' Cap. III: Brevi cenni sulla penetrazione dell'idea nel testo conciliare." *Ephemerides Theologicae Lovanienses* 47 (1971): 7–63.

Nirappel, Antony. "Towards the Definition of the Term 'World' in *Gaudium et Spes*." *Ephemerides Theologicae Lovanienses* 48 (1972): 89–126.

Nitsche, Bernhard. "Geistvergessenheit und die Wiederentdeckung des Heiligen Geistes im Zweiten Vatikanischen Konzil." In *Atem des sprechenden Gottes: Einführung in die Lehre vom Heiligen Geist*, edited by Bernhard Nitsche, 102–44. Regensburg: Pustet, 2003.

Noceti, Serena, and Roberto Repole, eds. *Dei Verbum: Commentario ai documenti del Vaticano II, Vol. 5*. Bologna: Edizioni Dehoniane, 2017.

Nolan, Ann Michele. *A Privileged Moment: Dialogue in the Language of the Second Vatican Council, 1962–1965*. New York: Peter Lang, 2006.

O'Collins, Gerald. *Christology: A Biblical, Historical, and Systematic Study of Jesus*. Oxford: Oxford University Press, 1995.

────. "*Ressourcement* and Vatican II." In *Ressourcement: A Movement for Renewal in Twentieth-Century Catholic Theology*, edited by Gabriel Flynn and Paul D. Murray, 372–91. Oxford: Oxford University Press, 2011.

────. *Rethinking Fundamental Theology*. Oxford: Oxford University Press, 2011.

────. *Retrieving Fundamental Theology: The Three Styles of Contemporary Theology*. New York: Paulist Press, 1993.

────. "Revelation Past and Present." In *Vatican II: Assessment and Perspectives. Twenty-Five Years After (1962–1987). Volume 1*, edited by René Latourelle, 1:125–37. New York: Paulist Press, 1988.

────. *Revelation: Towards a Christian Interpretation of God's Self-Revelation in Jesus Christ*. Oxford: Oxford University Press, 2016.

────. *The Second Vatican Council on Other Religions*. Oxford: Oxford University Press, 2013.

────. "Vatican II on Other Living Faiths." In *The Second Vatican Council: Message and Meaning*, 105–23. Collegeville, MN: Liturgical Press, 2014.

────. "Vatican II on the Liturgical Presence of Christ." In *The Second Vatican Council: Message and Meaning*, 89–104. Collegeville, MN: Liturgical Press, 2014.

────. "Vatican II's Constitution on Divine Revelation: *Dei Verbum*." *Pastoral Review* 9 no. 2 (2013): 12–18.

———. "Was the Teaching of Vatican II Nourished and Ruled by the Word of God?" In *The Second Vatican Council: Message and Meaning*, 177–205. Collegeville, MN: Liturgical Press, 2014.

O'Collins, Gerald, and Edward G. Farrugia. *A Concise Dictionary of Theology*. 3rd ed. New York: Paulist Press, 2013.

O'Connell, Marvin R. *Critics on Trial: An Introduction to the Catholic Modernist Crisis*. Washington, DC: Catholic University of America Press, 1994.

O'Donnell, Christopher. "Bishops, Collegiality." In *Ecclesia: A Theological Encyclopedia of the Church*, 57–59. Collegeville, MN: Liturgical Press, 1996.

———. *Ecclesia: A Theological Encyclopedia of the Church*. Collegeville, MN: Liturgical Press, 1996.

———. "Inculturation." In *Ecclesia: A Theological Encyclopedia of the Church*, 210–11. Collegeville, MN: Liturgical Press, 1996.

———. "Philips, Gérard (1899–1972)." In *Ecclesia: A Theological Encylopedia of the Church*, 362. Collegeville, MN: Liturgical Press, 1996.

O'Donnell, John. "Historie/Geschichte." In *Dictionary of Fundamental Theology*, edited by René Latourelle and Rino Fisichella, 432–33. Middlegreen, Slough, UK: St. Paul, 1994.

O'Gara, Margaret. "Three Successive Steps toward Understanding Papal Primacy in Vatican I." *The Jurist* 64 no. 1 (2004): 208–23.

O'Malley, John W. "Dialogue and the Identity of Vatican II." *Origins* 42 no. 25 (November 22, 2012): 398–403.

———. *Four Cultures of the West*. Cambridge, MA: Belknap Press of Harvard University Press, 2004.

———. "'The Hermeneutic of Reform': A Historical Analysis." *Theological Studies* 73 (2012): 517–46.

———. "The Millennium and the Papalization of Catholicism." In *Catholic History for Today's Church: How Our Past Illuminates Our Present*, 7–13. Lanham, MD: Rowman & Littlefield, 2015.

———. "Reform, Historical Consciousness, and Vatican II's *Aggiornamento*." In *Tradition and Transition: Historical Perspectives on Vatican II*, 44–81. Wilmington, DE: Michael Glazier, 1989.

———. *Trent: What Happened at the Council*. Cambridge, MA: Belknap Press of Harvard University Press, 2013.

———. *Vatican I: The Council and the Making of the Ultramontane Church*. Cambridge, MA: Belknap Press of Harvard University Press, 2018.

———. "Vatican II: Did Anything Happen?" In *Vatican II: Did Anything Happen?*, edited by David G. Schultenover, 52–91. New York: Continuum, 2007.

———. "Vatican II Revisited as Reconciliation: The Francis Factor." In *The Legacy of Vatican II*, edited by Massimo Faggioli and Andrea Vicini, 3–25. New York: Paulist Press, 2015.

———. *What Happened at Vatican II*. Cambridge, MA: Belknap Press of Harvard University Press, 2008.

O'Meara, Thomas F. "Karl Rahner's 'Remarks on the Schema, "De Ecclesia in Mundo Hujus Temporis," in the Draft of May 28, 1965." *Philosophy & Theology* 20 (2008): 331–39.

Oesterreicher, John M. "Declaration on the Relationship of the Church to Non-Christian Religions: Introduction and Commentary." In *Commentary on the Documents of Vatican II. Volume 3*, edited by Herbert Vorgrimler, 1–136. New York: Herder, 1969.

————. *The New Encounter between Christians and Jews*. New York: Philosophical Library, 1986.

Örsy, Ladislas. *The Church Learning and Teaching*. Dublin: Dominican Publications, 1987.

————. "Episcopal Conferences: *Communio* among the Bishops." In *Receiving the Council: Theological and Canonical Insights and Debates*, 16–34. Collegeville, MN: Liturgical Press, 2009.

Osborne, Kenan B. *Ministry: Lay Ministry in the Roman Catholic Church, Its History and Theology*. New York: Paulist Press, 1993.

————. *Priesthood: A History of Ordained Ministry in the Roman Catholic Church*. New York: Paulist Press, 1989.

Pasquale, Gianluigi. *La Teologia della Storia della Salvezza nel Secolo XX*. Bologna: Edizioni Dehoniane, 2001.

Paul VI, Pope. "Closing Address: Fourth Session." In *Council Daybook: Vatican II, Session 4*, edited by Floyd Anderson, 359–62. Washington, DC: National Catholic Welfare Conference, 1966.

————. "Closing Address: Second Session." In *Council Daybook: Vatican II, Sessions 1 and 2*, edited by Floyd Anderson, 331–35. Washington, DC: National Catholic Welfare Conference, 1965.

————. "Closing Address: Third Session." In *Council Daybook, Vatican II: Session 3*, edited by Floyd Anderson, 303–07. Washington, DC: National Catholic Welfare Conference, 1965.

————. "Ecclesiam Suam." In *The Papal Encyclicals. Volume 5: 1958–1981*, edited by Claudia Carlen, 135–60. Wilmington, NC: McGrath Publishing Company, 1981.

————. "Opening Address: Fourth Session." In *Council Daybook: Vatican II, Session 4*, edited by Floyd Anderson, 4–7. Washington, DC: National Catholic Welfare Conference, 1966.

————. "Opening Address: Second Session." In *Council Daybook: Vatican II, Sessions 1 and 2*, edited by Floyd Anderson, 143–50. Washington, DC: National Catholic Welfare Conference, 1965.

————. "Opening Address: Third Session." In *Council Daybook, Vatican II: Session 3*, edited by Floyd Anderson, 6–10. Washington, DC: National Catholic Welfare Conference, 1965.

————. "Synod of Bishops Established." In *The Documents of Vatican II*, edited by Walter M. Abbott, 720–24. London: Geoffrey Chapman, 1966.

Pavan, Pietro. "Declaration on Religious Freedom." In *Commentary on the Documents of Vatican II. Volume 4*, edited by Herbert Vorgrimler, 4:49–86. New York: Herder, 1969.

Pesch, Otto Hermann. *The Ecumenical Potential of the Second Vatican Council*. Milwaukee, WI: Marquette University Press, 2006.

————. *The Second Vatican Council: Prehistory—Event—Results—Posthistory*. Milwaukee, WI: Marquette University Press, 2014.

Peterson, Brandon. "Critical Voices: The Reactions of Rahner and Ratzinger to 'Schema XIII' (*Gaudium et Spes*)." *Modern Theology* 31 (2015): 1–26.

Philipon, Michel. "La Santissima Trinità e la Chiesa." In *La Chiesa del Vaticano II: Studi e commenti intorno alla Costituzione dommatica 'Lumen Gentium'*, edited by Guilherme Baraúna, 329–50. Firenze: Vallecchi Editore, 1965.

Philips, Gérard. "The Church: Mystery and Sacrament." In *Vatican II: An Interfaith Appraisal*, edited by John H. Miller, 187–96. Notre Dame: University of Notre Dame, 1966.

————. "Dogmatic Constitution on the Church: History of the Constitution." In *Commentary on the Documents of Vatican II. Volume 1*, edited by Herbert Vorgrimler, 105–37. London: Burns & Oates, 1967.

——. *L'Église et son mystère au II Concile du Vatican: Histoire, texte et commentaire de la Constitution Lumen Gentium.* Paris: Desclée, 1967.

——. "L'Église, sacrement et mystère." *Ephemerides Theologicae Lovanienses* 42 (1968): 405–14.

Pius X, Pope. "Pascendi Dominici Gregis." In *The Papal Encyclicals. Volume 3: 1903–1939,* edited by Claudia Carlen, 71–98. Wilmington, NC: McGrath Publishing Company, 1981.

Pius XII, Pope. "Divino Afflante Spiritu." In *The Papal Encyclicals. Volume 4: 1939–1958,* edited by Claudia Carlen, 65–79. Wilmington, NC: McGrath Publishing Company, 1981.

——. "Humani Generis." In *The Papal Encyclicals. Volume 4: 1939–1958,* edited by Claudia Carlen, 175–84. Wilmington, NC: McGrath Publishing Company, 1981.

——. "Mystici Corporis Christi." In *The Papal Encyclicals. Volume 4: 1939–1958,* edited by Claudia Carlen, 37–63. Wilmington, NC: McGrath Publishing Company, 1981.

Pottmeyer, Hermann J. "Die Mitsprache der Gläubigen in Glaubenssachen. Eine alte Praxis und ihre Wiederentdeckung." *Internationale katholische Zeitschrift "Communio"* 25 (1996): 135–47.

——. "The Episcopacy." In *The Gift of the Church: A Textbook on Ecclesiology in Honor of Patrick Granfield, O.S.B,* edited by Peter C. Phan, 337–53. Collegeville, MN: Liturgical Press, 2000.

——. "A New Phase in the Reception of Vatican II: Twenty Years of Interpretation of the Council." In *The Reception of Vatican II,* edited by Giuseppe Alberigo, Jean Pierre Jossua, and Joseph A. Komonchak, 27–43. Washington, DC: Catholic University of America Press, 1987.

——. "Reception and Submission." *The Jurist* 51 (1991): 269–92.

——. *Towards a Papacy in Communion: Perspectives from Vatican Councils I & II.* New York: Crossroad, 1998.

——. "Tradition." In *Dictionary of Fundamental Theology,* edited by René Latourelle and Rino Fisichella, 1119–26. Middlegreen, Slough, UK: St Paul, 1994.

——. *Unfehlbarkeit und Souveränität: Die päpstliche Unfehlbarkeit im System der ultramontanen Ekklesiologie des 19. Jahrhunderts.* Mainz: Matthias-Grünewald-Verlag, 1975.

Potworowski, Christophe F. *Contemplation and Incarnation: The Theology of Marie-Dominique Chenu.* Montreal: McGill-Queen's University Press, 2001.

Prodi, Paolo. *Il paradigma tridentino: Un'epoca della storia della Chiesa.* Brescia: Morcelliana, 2010.

Provost, James H. "Episcopal Conferences as an Expression of the Communion of Churches." In *Episcopal Conferences: Historical, Canonical, and Theological Studies,* edited by Thomas J. Reese, 269–89. Washington, DC: Georgetown University Press, 1989.

Prusak, Bernard P. *The Church Unfinished: Ecclesiology through the Centuries.* New York: Paulist Press, 2004.

Puglisi, James F. "Presider as *Alter Christus,* Head of the Body?" *Liturgical Ministry* 10 (Summer 2001): 153–58.

Pulikkan, Paul. *Indian Church at Vatican II: A Historico-Theological Study of the Indian Participation in the Second Vatican Council.* Trichur (Kerala-India): Marymatha Major Seminary, 2001.

Queiruga, Andres Torres. "Magisterium and Theology: Principles and Facts." In *Theology and Magisterium. Concilium 2012/2,* edited by Felix Wilfred and Susan A. Ross, 51–63. London: SCM Press, 2012.

"Questions Concerning the Jews: Proposals from the Secretariat for Christian Unity, November 1961." In *Jews and Catholics Together: Celebrating the Legacy of Nostra Aetate*, edited by Michael Attridge, 166–76. Ottawa: Novalis, 2007.

Quisinsky, Michael. *Geschichtlicher Glaube in einer geschichtlichen Welt. Der Beitrag von M.-D. Chenu, Y. Congar und H.-M. Féret zum II. Vaticanum.* Berlin: LIT Verlag, 2007.

Quisinsky, Michael, Peter Walter, and Clemens Carl, eds. *Personenlexikon zum Zweiten Vatikanischen Konzil.* Freiburg im Breisgau: Herder, 2012.

Raguer, Hilari. "An Initial Profile of the Assembly." In *History of Vatican II, Vol. 2: The Formation of the Council's Identity. First Period and Intercession, October 1962–September 1963*, edited by Giuseppe Alberigo and Joseph A. Komonchak, 2:167–232. Maryknoll, NY: Orbis Books, 1997.

Rahner, Karl. "The Abiding Significance of the Second Vatican Council." In *Theological Investigations. Volume 20*, 20:90–102. London: Darton, Longman & Todd, 1981.

———. "Basic Theological Interpretation of the Second Vatican Council." In *Theological Investigations, Volume 20*, 20:77–89. London: Darton, Longman & Todd, 1981.

———. *The Church after the Council.* New York: Herder and Herder, 1966.

———. *The Church and the Sacraments.* Freiburg: Herder, 1963.

———. "Church and World." In *Sacramentum Mundi: An Encyclopedia of Theology*, edited by Karl Rahner, 1:346–57. New York: Herder and Herder, 1968.

———. "The Church: A New Image." In *The Church after the Council*, 35–73. New York: Herder and Herder, 1966.

———. "The Council: A New Beginning." In *The Church after the Council*, 9–33. New York: Herder and Herder, 1966.

———. "The Hierarchical Structure of the Church, with Special Reference to the Episcopate. Articles 18–27." In *Commentary on the Documents of Vatican II. Volume 1*, edited by Herbert Vorgrimler, 186–218. London: Burns & Oates, 1967.

———. "A Hierarchy of Truths." In *Theological Investigations. Volume 21*, 21:162–67. London: Darton, Longman & Todd, 1988.

———. *I Remember: An Autobiographical Interview with Meinold Krauss.* Edited by Meinold Krauss. London: SCM Press, 1985.

———. "On the Divine Right of the Episcopate." In *The Episcopate and the Primacy*, edited by Karl Rahner and Joseph Ratzinger, 64–135. London: Burns & Oates, 1962.

———. "Priestly Existence." In *Theological Investigations. The Theology of the Spiritual Life*, 3:239–62. London: Darton, Longman and Todd, 1967.

———. "The Teaching Office of the Church in the Present-Day Crisis of Authority." In *Theological Investigations. Volume 12*, 12:3–30. London: Darton, Longman & Todd, 1974.

———. "The Theology of the Symbol." In *Theological Investigations. Volume 4*, 4:221–52. London: Darton, Longman & Todd, 1966.

———. *The Trinity.* New York: Herder and Herder, 1970.

———. "Über den Dialog in der pluralistischen Gesellschaft." *Stimmen der Zeit* 176 (August 1965): 321–30.

Ratzinger, Joseph. "Angesichts der Welt von heute: Überlegungen zur Konfrontation mit der Kirche in Schema XIII." *Wort und Wahrheit* 20 (1965): 493–504.

———. "Chapter I: Revelation Itself." In *Commentary on the Documents of Vatican II. Volume 3*, edited by Herbert Vorgrimler, 170–80. New York: Herder, 1969.

————. "Chapter II: The Transmission of Divine Revelation." In *Commentary on the Documents of Vatican II. Volume 3*, edited by Herbert Vorgrimler, 181–98. New York: Herder, 1969.

————. "Chapter VI: Sacred Scripture in the Life of the Church." In *Commentary on the Documents of Vatican II. Volume 3*, edited by H. Vorgrimler, 3:262–72. New York: Herder, 1969.

————. "The Christian and the Modern World." In *Dogma and Preaching: Applying Christian Doctrine to Daily Life*, 162–80. San Francisco: Ignatius Press, 2011.

————. "Church and World: An Inquiry into the Reception of Vatican Council II." In *Principles of Catholic Theology: Building Stones for a Fundamental Theology*, 378–93. San Francisco: Ignatius Press, 1987.

————. "Dogmatic Constitution on Divine Revelation: Origin and Background." In *Commentary on the Documents of Vatican II. Volume 3*, edited by Herbert Vorgrimler, 155–66. New York: Herder, 1969.

————. "The Ecclesiology of the Second Vatican Council." In *Church, Ecumenism and Politics: New Essays in Ecclesiology*, 3–28. Slough: St Paul, 1988.

————. "Introductory Article and Chapter 1: The Dignity of the Human Person." In *Commentary on the Documents of Vatican II. Volume 5*, edited by Herbert Vorgrimler, 5:115–63. New York: Herder and Herder, 1969.

————. "La collegialità episcopale: Spiegazione teologica del testo conciliare." In *La Chiesa del Vaticano II: Studi e commenti intorno alla Costituzione dommatica 'Lumen Gentium'*, edited by Guilherme Baraúna, 733–60. Firenze: Vallecchi Editore, 1965.

————. "La mission d'après les autres textes conciliaires." In *L'activité missionnaire de l'Eglise: Décret "Ad gentes,"* edited by Louis-Marie Dewailly, Giocondo Maria Grotti, Saverio Paventi and Johannes Schütte, 121–47. Paris: Cerf, 1967.

————. "The Local Church and the Universal Church: A Response to Walter Kasper." *America* 185 (November 19, 2001): 7–11.

————. *Milestones: Memoirs, 1927–1977*. San Francisco: Ignatius Press, 1998.

————. "On the Interpretation of the Tridentine Decree on Tradition." In *Revelation and Tradition*, edited by Karl Rahner and Joseph Ratzinger, 50–66. New York: Herder and Herder, 1966.

————. "Review of the Postconciliar Era—Failures, Tasks, Hopes." In *Principles of Catholic Theology: Building Stones for a Fundamental Theology*, 367–78. San Francisco: Ignatius Press, 1987.

————. "Ten Years after the Beginning of the Council—Where Do We Stand?" In *Dogma and Preaching: Applying Christian Doctrine to Daily Life*, 377–84. San Francisco: Ignatius Press, 2011.

————. *Theological Highlights of Vatican II*. New York: Paulist Press, 2009.

"Religious Liberty." In *Third Session Council Speeches of Vatican II*, edited by William K. Leahy and Anthony T. Massimini, 41–62. Glen Rock, NJ: Paulist Press, 1966.

Ricoeur, Paul. "The Hermeneutical Function of Distanciation." In *From Text to Action: Essays in Hermeneutics, II*, 75–88. Northwestern University Press, 1991.

————. *Interpretation Theory: Discourse and the Surplus of Meaning*. Fort Worth, TX: Texas Christian University Press, 1976.

Rikhof, Herwi. *The Concept of Church: A Methodological Inquiry into the Use of Metaphors in Ecclesiology*. London: Sheed and Ward, 1981.

Roberson, Ronald. *The Eastern Christian Churches: A Brief Survey*. 6th rev. ed. Roma: Orientalia Christiana, 1999.

Rouquette, Robert. "Bilan du concile." *Études* (January 1963): 94–111.

Routhier, Gilles. "Finishing the Work Begun: The Trying Experience of the Fourth Period." In *History of Vatican II, Vol. 5: The Council and the Transition. The Fourth Period and the End of the Council, September 1965–December 1965*, edited by Giuseppe Alberigo and Joseph A. Komonchak, 5:49–184. Maryknoll, NY: Orbis Books, 2006.

———. "Reception of Vatican II and Elements for Further Studies." In *The Living Legacy of Vatican II: Studies from an Indian Perspective*, edited by Paul Pulikkan, 90–109. Bengaluru, India: ATC Publishers, 2017.

Roy, Philippe J. *Bibliographie du Concile Vatican II*. Città del Vaticano: Libreria Editrice Vaticana, 2012.

———. "La préhistoire du *Coetus internationalis Patrum*: Une formation romaine, antilibéral et contre-révolutionaire." In *La Théologie catholique entre intransigeance et renouveau: La réception des mouvements préconciliaires à Vatican II*, edited by Gilles Routhier, Philippe J. Roy, K. Schelkens, and Philippe Roy-Lysencourt, 321–54. Louvain-La-Neuve; Leuven: Collège Érasme; Universiteitsbibliotheek, 2011.

Roy-Lysencourt, Philippe. "Histoire du *Coetus Internationalis Patrum* au concile Vatican II." *Laval Théologique et Philosophique* 69 (2013): 261–79.

Ruddy, Christopher. " 'In my end is my beginning': *Lumen Gentium* and the Priority of Doxology." *Irish Theological Quarterly* 79 (2014): 144–64.

Ruggieri, Giuseppe. "Beyond an Ecclesiology of Polemics: The Debate on the Church." In *History of Vatican II, Vol. 2: The Formation of the Council's Identity. First Period and Intercession, October 1962–September 1963*, edited by Giuseppe Alberigo and Joseph A. Komonchak, 2:281–357. Maryknoll, NY: Orbis Books, 1997.

———. "Esiste una teologia di papa Giovanni?" In *Un cristiano sul trono di Pietro: Studi storici su Giovanni XXIII*, edited by Enzo Bianchi, 253–74. Gorle, Bologna: Servitium, 2003.

———. "Faith and History." In *The Reception of Vatican II*, edited by Giuseppe Alberigo, Jean Pierre Jossua, and Joseph A. Komonchak, 91–114. Washington, DC: Catholic University of America Press, 1987.

———. "The First Doctrinal Clash." In *History of Vatican II, Vol. 2: The Formation of the Council's Identity. First Period and Intercession, October 1962–September 1963*, edited by Giuseppe Alberigo and Joseph A. Komonchak, 2:233–66. Maryknoll, NY: Orbis Books, 1997.

———. "Towards a Hermeneutic of Vatican II." *Concilium* 1 (1999): 1–13.

Rush, Francis. "Australian Catholic Theological Association Mass, Banyo Seminary, 6 July 1989." In *Life to Me Is Christ: Selected Talks and Homilies of Archbishop Francis Rush*, edited by Ormond Rush and Mary Coman, 141–43. Strathfield, NSW: St Pauls Publications, 2010.

———. "Speech at the 1985 Extraordinary Synod of Bishops, Rome, 27 November 1985." In *Life to Me Is Christ: Selected Talks and Homilies of Archbishop Francis Rush*, edited by Ormond Rush and Mary Coman, 92–94. Strathfield, NSW: St Pauls Publications, 2010.

Rush, Ormond. "The Australian Bishops of Vatican II: Participation and Reception." In *Vatican II: The Reception and Implementation in the Australian Church*, edited by Neil Ormerod, Ormond Rush, et al., 4–19. Melbourne: John Garrett, 2012.

———. "Ecclesial Conversion after Vatican II: Renewing 'the Face of the Church' to Reflect 'the Genuine Face of God.' " In *50 Years On: Probing the Riches of Vatican II*, edited by David G. Schultenover, 155–74. Collegeville, MN: Liturgical Press, 2015.

———. *The Eyes of Faith: The Sense of the Faithful and the Church's Reception of Revelation*. Washington, DC: Catholic University of America Press, 2009.

———. "The Offices of Christ, *Lumen Gentium* and the People's Sense of the Faith." *Pacifica* 16 (2003): 137–52.

———. "Roman Catholic Ecclesiology from the Council of Trent to Vatican II and Beyond." In *The Oxford Handbook of Ecclesiology*, edited by Paul Avis, 263–92. Oxford: Oxford University Press, 2018.

———. *Still Interpreting Vatican II: Some Hermeneutical Principles*. New York: Paulist Press, 2004.

Ryan, T. "Congregatio De Auxiliis." In *New Catholic Encyclopedia*, 4:110–13. Detroit: Gale, 2003.

Rynne, Xavier. *Vatican Council II*. Maryknoll, NY: Orbis Books, 2002.

Saier, Oskar. *"Communio" in der Lehre des Zweiten Vatikanischen Konzils: Eine rechtsbegriffliche Untersuchung*. Munich: EOS Verlag, 1973.

Sander, Hans-Joachim. "Das singulare Geschichtshandeln Gottes: Eine Frage der pluralen Topologie der Zeichen der Zeit." In *Herders theologischer Kommentar zum Zweiten Vatikanischen Konzil. Band 5. Die Documente des Zweiten Vatikanishen Konzils: Theologische Zusammenschau und Perspektiven*, edited by Peter Hünermann and Bernd Jochen Hilberath, 5:134–47. Freiburg: Herder, 2006.

———. "Theologischer Kommentar zur Pastoralkonstitution über die Kirche in der Welt von heute, Gaudium et Spes." In *Herders theologischer Kommentar zum Zweiten Vatikanischen Konzil*, edited by Peter Hünermann and Bernd Jochen Hilberath, 4:581–886. Freiburg: Herder, 2005.

Sanks, T. Howland. *Salt, Leaven, and Light: The Community Called Church*. New York: Crossroad, 1992.

Sartori, Luigi. "Osservazioni sull'ermeneutica del 'subsistit in' proposta da Alexandra von Teuffenbach." *Rassegna di Teologia* 45 (2004): 279–81.

Sauer, Hanjo. "The Doctrinal and the Pastoral: The Text on Divine Revelation." In *History of Vatican II, Vol. 4: The Church as Communion. Third Period and Third Intersession, September 1964–September 1965*, edited by Giuseppe Alberigo and Joseph A. Komonchak, 4:196–231. Maryknoll, NY: Orbis Books, 2004.

———. *Erfahrung und Glaube: Die Begründung des pastoralen Prinzips durch die Offenbarungskonstitution des II. Vatikanischen Konzils*. Frankfurt am Main: P. Lang, 1993.

Scampini, Jorge A. "Los Dominicos y el Concilio Vaticano II: Elementos para una visión de conjunto." In *The Dominican Order and the Second Ecumenical Vatican Council*, edited by Paolo Garuti, 27–84. Rome: Angelicum University Press, 2014.

Scatena, Silvia. *La fatica della libertà: L'elaborazione della dichiarazione "Dignitatis humanae" sulla libertà religiosa del Vaticano II*. Bologna: Il Mulino, 2003.

Schatz, Klaus. "The Gregorian Reform and the Beginning of a Universal Ecclesiology." In *Reception and Communion Among Churches*, edited by Hervé Legrand, Julio Manzanares, and Antonio García y García, 123–36. Washington, DC: Catholic University of America Press, 1997.

———. *Papal Primacy: From Its Origins to the Present*. Collegeville, MN. Liturgical Press, 1996.

Schaut, A. "Die Kirche als Volk Gottes: Selbstaussagen der Kirche im römischen Messbuch." *Benediktinische Monatsschrift* 25 (1949): 187–95.

Scheffczyk, Leo. "Main Lines of the Development of Theology between the First World War and the Second Vatican Council." In *The Church in the Modern Age*, edited by Hubert Jedin, Konrad Repgen, and John Dolan, 10:260–98. New York: Crossroad, 1981.

Schelkens, Karim, ed. *Carnets conciliaires de Mgr. Gérard Philips, sécretaire adjoint de la Commission doctrinale: Texte néerlandais avec traduction française et commentaires.* Leuven: Peeters, 2006.

———. *Catholic Theology of Revelation on the Eve of Vatican II: A Redaction History of the Schema De fontibus revelationis (1960–1962).* Boston: Brill, 2010.

———. "L' 'affaire de Rhodes' au jour le jour: La correspondance inédite entre J. Willebrands et C.J.Dumont." *Istina* 54 (2009): 253–77.

———. "Lucien Cerfaux and the Preparation of the Schema *De fontibus revelationis.*" In *The Belgian Contribution to the Second Vatican Council,* edited by Doris Donnelly, Joseph Famerée, Mathijs Lamberigts, and Karim Schelkens, 415–94. Leuven: Peeters, 2008.

———. "*Lumen Gentium*'s 'Subsistit in' Revisited: The Catholic Church and Christian Unity after Vatican II." *Theological Studies* 69 (2008): 875–93.

Schillebeeckx, Edward. *Christ, the Sacrament of Encounter with God.* London: Sheed and Ward, 1963.

———. "Preface." In *The Concept of Church: A Methodological Inquiry into the Use of Metaphors in Ecclesiology,* edited by Herwi Rikhof, xi–xiii. London: Sheed and Ward, 1981.

Schloesser, Stephen. "Against Forgetting: Memory, History, Vatican II." In *Vatican II: Did Anything Happen?,* edited by David G. Schultenover, 92–152. New York: Continuum, 2007.

———. "Reproach vs. *Rapprochement:* Historical Preconditions of a Paradigm Shift in the Reform of Vatican II." In *50 Years On: Probing the Riches of Vatican II,* edited by David G. Schultenover, xi–xlix. Collegeville, MN: Liturgical Press, 2015.

Schmidt, Stjepan. *Augustin Bea: The Cardinal of Unity.* New Rochelle, NY: New City Press, 1992.

Schnackenburg, Rudolf. *God's Rule and Kingdom.* New York: Herder and Herder, 1963.

Schoof, Mark. *A Survey of Catholic Theology 1800–1970.* New York: Paulist Press, 1970.

Schreiter, Robert J. *Constructing Local Theologies.* Maryknoll, NY: Orbis Books, 1985.

———. "Mediating the Global and the Local in Conversation: Challenges to the Church in the Twenty-First Century." In *Theology and Conversation: Towards a Relational Theology,* edited by Jacques Haers and P. De Mey, 439–55. Leuven; Dudley, MA: Peeters, 2003.

———. *The New Catholicity: Theology between the Global and the Local.* Maryknoll, NY: Orbis Books, 1997.

Schüssler Fiorenza, Francis. "Church, Social Mission of." In *The New Dictionary of Catholic Social Thought,* edited by Judith A. Dwyer and Elizabeth L. Montgomery, 151–71. Collegeville, MN: Liturgical Press, 1994.

———. "Systematic Theology: Task and Methods." In *Systematic Theology: Roman Catholic Perspectives,* edited by Francis Schüssler Fiorenza and John P. Galvin, 1–78. Minneapolis: Fortress Press, 2011.

———. "Vatican II." In *The Routledge Companion to Modern Christian Thought,* edited by Chad Meister and James Beilby, 364–75. New York: Routledge, 2013.

Schützeichel, Heribert. "Die unbegrenzte Wirkkraft des Heiligen Geistes in der Sicht des II. Vatikanischen Konzils." *Theologische Zeitschrift* 108 no. 2 (1999): 108–22.

———. "The Holy Spirit according to Vatican II." *Theology Digest* 48 no. 2 (2001): 140–42.

Segreteria Generale del Concilio. "Tavole Riassuntive." In *I Padri Presenti al Concilio Ecumenico Vaticano II.* Roma: Segreteria Generale del Concilio, 1966.

Semmelroth, Otto. *Die Kirche als Ursakrament.* Frankfurt a.M.: Knecht, 1953.

————. "The Eschatological Nature of the Pilgrim Church and Her Union with the Heavenly Church." In *Commentary on the Documents of Vatican II. Volume 1*, edited by Herbert Vorgrimler, 280–84. London: Burns & Oates, 1967.

————. "La Chiesa, nuovo populo di Dio." In *La Chiesa del Vaticano II: Studi e commenti intorno alla Costituzione dommatica 'Lumen Gentium'*, edited by Guilherme Baraúna, 439–52. Firenze: Vallecchi Editore, 1965.

Siebenrock, Roman A. "Theologischer Kommentar zur Erklärung über die Haltung der Kirche zu den nichtchristlichen Religionen, *Nostra Aetate*." In *Herders theologischer Kommentar zum Zweiten Vatikanischen Konzil. Band 3*, edited by Peter Hünermann and Bernd Jochen Hilberath, 3:591–693. Freiburg: Herder, 2005.

————. "Theologischer Kommentar zur Erklärung über die religiöse Freiheit." In *Herders theologischer Kommentar zum Zweiten Vatikanischen Konzil*, edited by Peter Hünermann and Bernd Jochen Hilberath, 4:125–218. Freiburg: Herder, 2005.

Sievers, Joseph. "How Irrevocable? Interpreting Romans 11:29 from the Church Fathers to the Second Vatican Council." *Gregorianum* 87 no. 4 (2006): 748–61.

Silanes, Nereo. "El Espiritu Santo y la Iglesia en el Concilio Vaticano II." In *Credo in Spiritum Sanctum: Atti del Congresso Teologico Internazionale di Pneumatologia*, 2:1011–24. Città del Vaticano: Libreria Editrice Vaticana, 1983.

————. "Panorámica Trinitaria del Concilio." *Estudios Trinitarios* 1 (1967): 7–44.

————. "Trinidad y Revelación en la Constitución Dei Verbum." *Estudios Trinitarios* 17 (1983): 143–214.

Smulders, Peter. "La Chiesa sacramento della salvezza." In *La Chiesa del Vaticano II: Studi e commenti intorno alla Costituzione dommatica 'Lumen Gentium'*, edited by Guilherme Baraúna, 363–86. Firenze: Vallecchi Editore, 1965.

Snyder, Howard A. *Models of the Kingdom*. Nashville: Abingdon Press, 1991.

Soetens, Claude. "The Ecumenical Commitment of the Catholic Church." In *History of Vatican II, Vol. 3: The Mature Council. Second Period and Intersession, September 1963–September 1964*, edited by Giuseppe Alberigo and Joseph A. Komonchak, 3:257–345. Maryknoll, NY: Orbis Books, 1998.

————. "La contribution de Charles Moeller au Concile Vatican II d'après ses papiers conciliaires." In *The Belgian Contribution to the Second Vatican Council*, edited by Doris Donnelly, Joseph Famerée, Mathijs Lamberigts, and Karim Schelkens, 495–528. Leuven: Peeters, 2008.

Southerwood, W. T. *The Wisdom of Guilford Young*. George Town, Tas.: Stella Maris Books, 1989.

Stransky, Thomas. "Catholic Conference for Ecumenical Questions." In *Dictionary of the Ecumenical Movement*, edited by Nicolas Lossky et al., 151. Geneva: WCC Publications, 2002.

————. *The Decree on Ecumenism of the Second Vatican Council: A New Translation by the Secretariat for Promoting Christian Unity, with a Commentary by Thomas F. Stransky, C.S.P.* Glen Rock, NJ: Paulist Press, 1965.

————. "The Foundation of the Secretariat for Promoting Christian Unity." In *Vatican II: By Those Who Were There*, edited by Alberic Stacpoole, 62–87. London: Geoffrey Chapman, 1986.

————. "The Genesis of *Nostra Aetate*: An Insider's Story." In *Nostra Aetate: Origins, Promulgation, Impact on Jewish-Catholic Relations*, edited by Neville Lamdan and Alberto Melloni, 29–53. Berlin: LIT Verlag, 2007.

————. "Paul VI and the Delegated Observers/Guests to Vatican Council II." In *Paolo VI e l'ecumenismo: Colloquio internazionale di studio (Brescia, 25–27 settembre 1998)*, 118–58. Brescia: Istituto Paolo VI, 2001.

———. "Paul VI's Religious Pilgrimage to the Holy Land." In *I viaggi apostolici di Paolo VI*, edited by Rodolfo Rossi, 341–73. Brescia: Istituto Paolo VI, 2004.

Strotmann, Théodore. "La Chiesa come mistero." In *La Chiesa del Vaticano II: Studi e commenti intorno alla Costituzione dommatica 'Lumen Gentium'*, edited by Guilherme Baraúna, 314–28. Firenze: Vallecchi Editore, 1965.

Suenens, Léon-Joseph Cardinal. "The Charismatic Dimension of the Church." In *Council Speeches of Vatican II*, edited by Hans Küng, Yves Congar, and Daniel O'Hanlon, 25–34. Glen Rock, NJ: Paulist Press, 1964.

———. "A Plan for the Whole Council." In *Vatican II: By Those Who Were There*, edited by Alberic Stacpoole, 88–105. London: Geoffrey Chapman, 1986.

Sullivan, Francis A. *The Church We Believe In: One, Holy, Catholic, and Apostolic*. New York: Paulist Press, 1988.

———. *Magisterium: Teaching Authority in the Catholic Church*. New York: Paulist Press, 1983.

———. "A Response to Karl Becker, S.J., on the Meaning of *Subsistit In*." *Theological Studies* 67 (2006): 395–409.

———. *Salvation outside the Church?: Tracing the History of the Catholic Response*. New York: Paulist Press, 1992.

———. "The Significance of the Vatican II Declaration That the Church of Christ 'Subsists In' the Roman Catholic Church." In *Vatican II Assessment and Perspectives: Twenty-Five Years After (1962-1987). Volume 2*, edited by René Latourelle, 2:272–87. New York: Paulist Press, 1989.

———. "Vatican II and the Postconciliar Magisterium on the Salvation of the Adherents of Other Religions." In *After Vatican II: Trajectories and Hermeneutics*, edited by James Heft, 68–95. Grand Rapids, MI: Eerdmans, 2012.

Swidler, Leonard, and Hans Küng. "The Context: Breaking Reform by Breaking Theologians and Religious." In *The Church in Anguish: Has the Vatican Betrayed Vatican II?*, edited by Hans Küng and Leonard Swidler, 189–92. San Francisco: Harper & Row, 1987.

Tagle, Luis Antonio. "The 'Black Week' of Vatican II (November 14–21 1964)." In *History of Vatican II, Vol. 4: The Church as Communion. Third Period and Third Intersession, September 1964–September 1965*, edited by Giuseppe Alberigo and Joseph A. Komonchak, 4:387–452. Maryknoll, NY: Orbis Books, 2004.

Tanenbaum, Marc H. "Vatican II: An Interfaith Appraisal. A Jewish Viewpoint." In *A Prophet for Our Time: An Anthology of the Writings of Rabbi Marc H. Tanenbaum*, edited by Judith Hershcopf Banki and Eugene J. Fisher, 75–98. New York: Fordham University Press, 2002.

Tanner, Norman P. *The Church and the World: Gaudium et Spes, Inter Mirifica*, Rediscovering Vatican II. Mahwah, NJ: Paulist Press, 2005.

———. "The Church in the World (*Ecclesia ad Extra*)." In *History of Vatican II, Vol. 4: The Church as Communion. Third Period and Third Intersession, September 1964–September 1965*, edited by Giuseppe Alberigo and Joseph A. Komonchak, 4:269–386. Maryknoll, NY: Orbis Books, 2004.

———. *Decrees of the Ecumenical Councils*. 2 vols. Washington, DC: Georgetown University Press, 1990.

Tavard, George H. *The Church, Community of Salvation: An Ecumenical Ecclesiology*. Collegeville, MN: Liturgical Press, 1992.

———. *De Divina Revelatione: The Dogmatic Constitution on Divine Revelation of Vatican Council II. Commentary and Translation.* Glen Rock, NJ: Paulist Press, 1966.

———. "'Hierarchia Veritatum': A Preliminary Investigation." *Theological Studies* 32 (1971): 278–89.

———. *The Pilgrim Church.* New York: Herder and Herder, 1967.

———. "Reassessing the Reformation." *One in Christ* 19 (1983): 355–67.

———. *Two Centuries of Ecumenism.* Notre Dame, IN: Fides Publishers Association, 1960.

Teuffenbach, Alexandra von. *Die Bedeutung des "subsistit in" (LG 8): Zum Selbstverständnis der katholischen Kirche.* München: Herbert Utz Verlag, 2002.

Theobald, Christoph. "The Church under the Word of God." In *History of Vatican II, Vol. 5: The Council and the Transition. The Fourth Period and the End of the Council, September 1965–December 1965,* edited by Giuseppe Alberigo and Joseph A. Komonchak, 5:275–362. Maryknoll, NY: Orbis Books, 2006.

———. *La réception du concile Vatican II: I. Accéder à la source.* Paris: Cerf, 2009.

———. "The Theological Options of Vatican II: Seeking an 'Internal' Principle of Interpretation." In *Vatican II: A Forgotten Future? Concilium 2005/4,* edited by Alberto Melloni and Christoph Theobald, 87–107. London: SCM Press, 2005.

Thils, Gustave. ". . . en pleine fidélité au Concile du Vatican II." *La foi et le temps* 10 (1980): 274–309.

———. *L'Église et les Églises: Perspectives nouvelles en oecuménisme.* Bruges: Desclée De Brouwer, 1967.

Tillard, Jean-Marie. *The Bishop of Rome.* Wilmington, DE: Michael Glazier, 1983.

———. *L'église locale: Ecclésiologie de communion et catholicité.* Paris: Cerf, 1995.

Torrell, Jean-Pierre. *A Priestly People: Baptismal Priesthood and Priestly Ministry.* Mahwah, NJ: Paulist Press, 2013.

"A Tribute to Johannes Cardinal Willebrands: On the Occasion of His Ninetieth Birthday." *Information Service. The Pontifical Council for Promoting Christian Unity* 101 (1999).

Turbanti, Giovanni. "Il ruolo del P. D. Chenu nell'elaborazione della costituzione *Gaudium et Spes.*" In *Marie-Dominique Chenu: Moyen-Âge et modernité,* 173–212. Paris: Le Centre d'études du Saulchoir, 1997.

———. "La commissione mista per lo schema XVII-XIII." In *Les commissions conciliaires à Vatican II,* edited by Matthijs Lamberigts, Claude Soetens, and Jan Grootaers, 217–50. Leuven: Bibliotheek van de Faculteit Godgeleerdheid, 1996.

———. "Toward the Fourth Period." In *History of Vatican II, Vol. 5: The Council and the Transition. The Fourth Period and the End of the Council, September 1965–December 1965,* edited by Giuseppe Alberigo and Joseph A. Komonchak, 5:1–47. Maryknoll, NY: Orbis Books, 2006.

———. *Un Concilio per il Mondo Moderno: La Redazione della Costituzione Pastorale "Gaudium et Spes" del Vaticano II.* Bologna: Il Mulino, 2000.

Valente, Gianni. *Ratzinger al Vaticano II.* Cinisello Balsamo (MI): San Paolo, 2013.

Valerio, Adriana. *Madri del Concilio: Ventitré donne al Vaticano II.* Rome: Carocci, 2012.

Valeske, Ulrich. *Hierarchia Veritatum: Theologiegeschichtliche Hintergründe und mögliche Konsequenzen eines Hinweises im Ökumenismusdekret des II. Vatikanischen Konzils zum zwischenkirchlichen Gespräch.* München: Claudius Verlag, 1968.

Vance-Trembath, Sally. *The Pneumatology of Vatican II: With Particular Reference to Lumen Gentium and Gaudium et Spes*. Saarbrücken: Lambert Academic Publishing, 2010.

Vanhoye, Albert. "The Biblical Question of 'Charisms' After Vatican II." In *Vatican II Assessment and Perspectives: Twenty-Five Years After (1962–1987)*. Volume 1, edited by René Latourelle, 1:439–68. New York: Paulist Press, 1988.

Velati, Mauro. "Completing the Conciliar Agenda." In *History of Vatican II, Vol. 5: The Council and the Transition. The Fourth Period and the End of the Council, September 1965–December 1965*, edited by Giuseppe Alberigo and Joseph A. Komonchak, 5:185–273. Maryknoll, NY: Orbis Books, 2006.

———. " 'The Others': Ecumenism and Religions." In *Vatican II: A Forgotten Future? Concilium 2005/4*, edited by Alberto Melloni and Christoph Theobald, 35–47. London: SCM Press, 2005.

———. *Separati ma fratelli. Gli osservatori non cattolici al Vaticano II (1962–1965)*. Bologna: Il Mulino, 2014.

———. " 'Un indirizzo a Roma': La nascita del Segretariato per l'unità dei cristiani (1959–60)." In *Il Vaticano II fra attese e celebrazione*, edited by Giuseppe Alberigo, 75–118. Bologna: Il Mulino, 1995.

———. *Una difficile transizione: Il Cattolicesimo tra unionismo ed ecumenismo (1952–1964)*. Bologna: Il Mulino, 1996.

Vereb, Jerome-Michael. *"Because He Was a German!": Cardinal Bea and the Origins of Roman Catholic Engagement in the Ecumenical Movement*. Grand Rapids, MI: Eerdmans, 2006.

Verstraeten, J., ed. *Scrutinizing the Signs of the Times in the Light of the Gospel*, Proceedings of the Expert Seminar Leuven-Louvain-la-Neuve, 9–11 September 2004. Leuven: Peeters Press, 2007.

Vilanova, Evangelista. "The Intersession (1963–1964)." In *History of Vatican II, Vol. 3: The Mature Council. Second Period and Intersession, September 1963–September 1964*, edited by Giuseppe Alberigo and Joseph A. Komonchak, 3:347–490. Maryknoll, NY: Orbis Books, 1998.

Villain, Maurice. "The Debate about the Decree on Ecumenism." *Concilium* 4 no. 2 (April 1966): 59–69.

Vischer, Lukas. "The Ecumenical Movement and the Roman Catholic Church." In *The Ecumenical Advance: A History of the Ecumenical Movement. Volume 2: 1948–1968*, edited by Harold E. Fey, 311–52. Geneva: World Council of Churches, 1986.

Vodola, Max. "John XXIII, Vatican II, and the Genesis of *Aggiornamento*: A Contextual Analysis of Angelo Roncalli's Works on San Carlo Borromeo in Relation to Late Twentieth Century Church Reform." PhD Thesis, School of Philosophical, Historical and International Studies, Monash University, Melbourne, 2010.

Vonier, Anscar. *The People of God*. London: Burns, Oates & Washburn, 1937.

Vorgrimler, Herbert. "Karl Rahner: The Theologian's Contribution." In *Vatican II: By Those Who Were There*, edited by Alberic Stacpoole, 32–46. London: Geoffrey Chapman, 1986.

Washington, Christopher Thomas. *The Participation of Non-Catholic Christian Observers, Guests, and Fraternal Delegates at the Second Vatican Council and the Synods of Bishops: A Theological Analysis*. Rome: Gregorian University Press, 2015.

Wassilowsky, Günther. *Als die Kirche Weltkirche wurde: Karl Rahners Beitrag zum II. Vatikanischen Konzil und seiner Deutung*. München–Freiburg im Breisgau: Univeritätsbibliothek, 2012.

———. "Einblick in die 'Textwerkstatt' einer Gruppe deutscher Theologen auf dem II. Vatikanum." In *Die deutschsprachigen Länder und das II. Vatikanum*, edited by Hubert Wolf and Claus Arnold, 61–87. Paderborn: Ferdinand Schöningh, 2000.

———. *Universales Heilssakrament Kirche: Karl Rahners Beitrag zur Ekklesiologie des II. Vatikanums*. Innsbruck; Wien: Tyrolia Verlag, 2001.

Wicks, Jared. "Cardinal Bea's Unity Secretariat: Engine of Renewal and Reform at Vatican II." *Ecumenical Trends* 41 no. 11 (2012): 1–5, 15.

———. "*De Revelatione* under Revision (March–April 1964): Contributions of C. Moeller and Other Belgian Theologians." In *The Belgian Contribution to the Second Vatican Council: International Research Conference at Mechelen, Leuven and Louvain-la-Neuve (September 12–16, 2005)*, edited by Doris Donnelly, Joseph Famerée, Mathijs Lamberigts, and Karim Schelkens, 461–94. Leuven; Dudley, MA: Peeters, 2008.

———. *Doing Theology*. New York: Paulist Press, 2009.

———. *Investigating Vatican II: Its Theologians, Ecumenical Turn, and Biblical Commitment*. Washington, DC: Catholic University of America Press, 2018.

———. "Six Texts by Prof. Joseph Ratzinger as *Peritus* before and during Vatican Council II." *Gregorianum* 89 (2008): 233–311.

———. "Theologians at Vatican Council II." In *Doing Theology*, 187–223. New York: Paulist Press, 2009.

———. "Vatican II on Revelation—From behind the Scenes." *Theological Studies* 71 (2010): 637–50.

———. "Yves Congar's Doctrinal Service of the People of God." *Gregorianum* 84 (2003): 499–550.

Wijlens, Myriam. "The Doctrine of the People of God and Hierarchical Authority as Service in Latin Church Legislation on the Local Church." *The Jurist* 68 (2008): 328–49.

———. *Sharing the Eucharist: A Theological Evaluation of the Post Conciliar Legislation*. Lanham, MD: University Press of America, 2000.

Willebrands, Johannes. "Cardinal Augustin Bea: His Contribution to the Ecumenical Movement and to Religious Liberty: Opening Address at the Bea Symposium, 1981." *Information Service. The Pontifical Council for Promoting Christian Unity* 101 (1999): 70–77.

———. "The Ecumenical Movement: Its Problems and Driving Force." *One in Christ* 11 (1975): 210–23.

———. "Vatican II's Ecclesiology of Communion." *One in Christ* 23 (1987): 179–91.

Willis, Wendell, ed. *The Kingdom of God in 20th-Century Interpretation*. Peabody, MA: Hendrickson Publishers, 1987.

Wiltgen, Ralph M. *The Rhine Flows into the Tiber: A History of Vatican II*. Devon: Augustine Publishing Co., 1978.

Witczak, Michael G. "The Manifold Presence of Christ in the Liturgy." *Theological Studies* 59 (1998): 680–702.

Witherup, Ronald D. *Scripture: Dei Verbum*, Rediscovering Vatican II. Mahwah, NJ: Paulist Press, 2006.

Witte, Johannes. "The Question of Baptism and the Unity of Christians." In *Atti del Simposio Card. Agostino Bea (Roma, 16–19 Dicembre 1981)*, 223–30. Rome: Libreria Editrice Pontificia Università Lateranense, 1983.

Wittstadt, Klaus. "On the Eve of the Second Vatican Council (July 1–October 10, 1962)." In *History of Vatican II, Vol. 1: Announcing and Preparing Vatican Council II*, edited by

Giuseppe Alberigo and Joseph A. Komonchak, 404–500. Maryknoll, NY: Orbis Books, 1996.

Wolf, Hubert, and Claus Arnold, eds. *Die deutschsprachigen Länder und das II. Vatikanum.* Paderborn: Ferdinand Schöningh, 2000.

Wood, Susan. "Continuity and Development in Roman Catholic Ecclesiology." *Ecclesiology* 7 no. 2 (2011): 147–72.

———. "The Sacramentality of Episcopal Consecration." *Theological Studies* 51 (1990): 479–96.

Zizioulas, John. "The Theological Problem of 'Reception.'" *Centro Pro Unione Bulletin* 26 (1984): 3–6.

Zoghby, Elias. "Unità e diversità della Chiesa." In *La Chiesa del Vaticano II: Studi e commenti intorno alla Costituzione dommatica 'Lumen Gentium'*, edited by Guilherme Baraúna, 522–40. Firenze: Vallecchi Editore, 1965.

Index of Names

Index of Subjects

Ad Gentes: on dialogue, 255; on
   drafting of, 322–323; on
   evangelization, 181, 215–229, 474–
   475, 526–528; on Jesus Christ, 69;
   on salvation, 100, 102, 111; on the
   church, 57, 96, 98, 209–210, 213,
   215–229, 243, 270–271, 309, 364–
   365, 410; on the Holy Spirit, 49–50;
   on the Trinity, 55
Ad Petri Cathedram, 245, 255, 378,
   379n31
Aeterni Patris, 173, 338, 359
Aeternus Unigeniti Pater, 312
aggiornamento, 17–21, 22, 92, 141, 168,
   185, 339, 346, 517, 546
anthropology, theological. *See* person,
   human
antisemitism, 426–442, 446, 449, 450,
   457, 464, 465, 478
Apeldoorn group, the, 432–433
Apostolicam Actuositatem: on mission,
   218, 236, 279–280, 282, 526; on
   salvation, 102; on the church, 213,
   236; on the laity, 267, 270, 526
Appropinquante Concilio, 343
Augustinianism, 20, 504–505, 516, 519,
   536
authorial intention, 4, 8

baptism, 263–265, 398–400, 412
birth control, 322, 504
bishops: college of, 206, 207, 210, 228–
   229, 247, 248, 267, 309–335, 544–
   545; mission of, 104; role of, 191,
   194, 211, 291–295, 300–305;

sacramental consecration of, 316–
   318. *See also* episcopal conferences;
   Synod of Bishops
Buddhism, 444, 447, 451, 453, 454, 460

Catholic Conference for Ecumenical
   Questions, 375–377
charism, 275–283
christocentrism, 10n25, 62, 63, 64–65
Christology, 28, 62–64, 79, 114, 115–
   118, 121, 123, 124, 510, 514
christomonism, 62, 63, 64–65, 78, 279,
   515
Christus Dominus, 69, 189, 192, 194,
   294, 296, 309, 326, 329, 331, 526
church: and Holy Spirit, 78, 97, 212, 236,
   515; and Jesus Christ, 58, 89, 94–98,
   529; and kingdom, 133–137; and
   revelation, 158–159; and salvation,
   102, 111, 307; and the poor, 90–91,
   92n43; and Trinity, 56–57, 87, 178;
   and world, 251–258, 489, 492, 493–
   494, 499–505, 508, 513–519 passim,
   520–531; as analogy of the
   incarnation, 88–89, 93, 243; as
   communion, 6n12, 52, 189, 193,
   200–215, 227–229, 285, 308, 334,
   387, 400–407, 409, 536; as juridical
   structure, 86, 87, 88, 285, 287, 289,
   291, 295–296, 308; as mystery, 81,
   83–92, 111, 114; as (mystical) body
   of Christ, 83, 87, 93, 209, 236, 239,
   281, 287, 288, 372, 388, 417; as
   People of God, 178, 260–267, 284,
   287–289, 299, 302, 303–308, 309,

591

Index of References to Council Documents

The first number of each row is the article number, which is followed by the page numbers on which references to the article are found.